D0947273

The Postmodern Bible

The Postmodern Bible

The Bible and Culture Collective:
George Aichele
Fred W. Burnett
Elizabeth A. Castelli, editor
Robert M. Fowler
David Jobling
Stephen D. Moore, editor
Gary A. Phillips, editor
Tina Pippin
Regina M. Schwartz, editor
Wilhelm Wuellner

Yale
University
Press
New Haven
and
London

Designed by Nancy Ovedovitz. Set in Sabon type by Tseng Information
Systems, Inc. Printed in the United States of America by Vail-Ballou
Press, Binghamton, New York.

Library of Congress Cataloging-in-Publication Data

The postmodern Bible / the Bible and Culture Collective ; George
Aichele . . . [et al.].
        p.   cm.
    Includes bibliographical references and index.
    ISBN 0-300-06090-4 (cloth)
        0-300-06818-2 (pbk.)
    1. Bible—Hermeneutics.   2. Postmodernism.   3. Bible—Criticism,
interpretation, etc.—History—20th century.   I. Aichele, George.
II. Bible and Culture Collective.
BS476.P67   1995
220.6′01—dc20   94-29748
                              CIP

A catalogue record for this book is available from the British Library.

10   9   8   7   6   5   4   3   2

Nine of us wish to dedicate our collaborative effort in this volume to the tenth member of our collective, Wilhelm Wuellner, on the occasion of his retirement from a long and productive career of teaching and scholarship. We have benefited enormously from his careful critique and personal integrity. Wilhelm's ready humor, willingness to risk, and commitment to collaborative process inspires us and gives us hope.

Contents

▌Acknowledgments

The collective process that gave rise to our book was sustained in many ways. For financial support we wish to thank the Annenberg Research Institute, Baldwin-Wallace College, the College of the Holy Cross, the College of Wooster, the Faculty Development Committee of Anderson University, and Wichita State University. Our work was supported by two generous American Academy of Religion Collaborative Research Grants (1990–92).

For support of the public presentation of our work we wish to thank Eugene Lovering (Society of Biblical Literature), Ronald Schliefer (Group for Early Modern Culture), and the Modern Language Association Religion and Literature Group. Our collaborative meetings succeeded because of the help we received from the Sisters of Adelynrood, the staff of the Venice Beach House, and Robert Funk and the Westar Institute, where the idea of collective work was initially conceived and met its first challenge.

Collaboration extended well beyond the group of ten to include many persons who read and commented on draft material and ideas that became an extension of the process which is this volume. We especially single out members of the Beatrice M. Bain Research Group on Women and Gender at the University of California at Berkeley and students in the Holy Cross First-Year Program Religious Studies seminar. We were aided by the advice and critique of many women and men: Wes Bergen, Christina Crosby, Linda Day, Robert Detweiler, William Scott Green, Randy Litchfield, Lois Ann Lorentzen, Catherine Rose, Hal Taussig, Jenifer Ward, and Elizabeth Weed.

Finally, we especially acknowledge the strong support and encouragement we have received from colleagues at Yale University Press, in particular Charles Grench, who appreciated our vision of a different mode and manner of biblical scholarship, and Eliza Childs, whose keen copyediting eyes and ears enabled us to retain in these pages our different voices and at the same time to speak collectively with one.

Contributors

GEORGE AICHELE teaches in the Department of Philosophy and Religion at Adrian College. He is the author of *Theology as Comedy: Critical and Theoretical Implications* and *The Limits of Story* and is co-editor with Tina Pippin of *Fantasy and the Bible*. He has also published articles on Mark, translation theory, science fiction, and postmodernism. He is currently editing a volume on intertextuality and the Bible with Gary Phillips.

FRED W. BURNETT teaches in the Department of Religious Studies at Anderson University. He is the author of *The Testament of Jesus-Sophia: A Redaction-Critical Study of the Eschatological Discourse in Matthew*. He has also published articles on poststructuralist, postmodernist, and ideological biblical criticism. He is currently working on a book on the narrative representation of Jewish characters in Matthew.

ELIZABETH A. CASTELLI teaches in the Religion Department at Barnard College. She is the author of *Imitating Paul: A Discourse of Power*. She has also written on gender and religion, feminist biblical translation, and early Christian asceticism. She is currently working on a book on the body in early Christianity.

ROBERT M. FOWLER teaches in the Department of Religion at Baldwin-Wallace College. He has written *Loaves and Fishes: The Function of the Feeding Stories in the Gospel of Mark* and *Let the Reader Understand: Reader-Response Criticism and the Gospel of Mark*. He is currently researching the convergence of electronic technology, poststructuralist critical theory, and collaborative learning.

DAVID JOBLING teaches at St. Andrew's College. He is a past president of the Canadian Society of Biblical Studies. He is the author of a two-volume work, *The Sense of Biblical Narrative,* and is co-editor with Stephen Moore of *Poststructuralism as Exegesis* and with Tina Pippin of *Ideological Criticism of Biblical Texts*. He is also co-chair with Pippin of the Ideological Criticism Group of the Society of Biblical Literature.

STEPHEN D. MOORE teaches in the Department of Religion at Wichita State University. He has written *Literary Criticism and the Gospels: The Theoretical Challenge, Mark and Luke in Poststructuralist Perspectives: Jesus Begins to Write,* and *Poststructuralism and the New Testament: Derrida and Foucault at the Foot of the Cross*. He has also co-edited *Mark and Method: New Approaches in Biblical Studies* and *Poststructuralism as Exegesis.*

GARY A. PHILLIPS teaches in the Department of Religious Studies at the College of the Holy Cross. He has edited *Poststructural Criticism and the Bible: Text/History/Discourse* and has written extensively on postmodernism, poststructuralism, ideological criticism, and semiotics. He is chair of the Semiotics and Exegesis Section of the Society of Biblical Literature. He is currently completing a book on deconstruction and the ethics of reading, editing a volume on intertextuality and the Bible with George Aichele, and co-authoring a book with Daniel Patte on pedagogy and teaching the New Testament.

TINA PIPPIN teaches in the Department of Bible and Religion and the Women's Studies Program at Agnes Scott College. She is the author of *Death and Desire: The Rhetoric of Gender in the Apocalypse of John* and is co-editor with George Aichele of *Fantasy and the Bible* and with David Jobling of *Ideological Criticism of Biblical Texts*. She is also co-chair with Jobling of the Ideological Criticism Group of the Society of Biblical Literature. Her other academic interests include the study and enactment of liberatory pedagogy.

REGINA M. SCHWARTZ teaches in the English Department at Northwestern University. She is the author of *Remembering and Repeating: Milton's Theology and Poetics* and editor of *The Book and the Text: The Bible and Literary Theory* and *Desire in the Renaissance: Literature and Psychoanalysis*. She is currently completing a book on monotheism, violence, and identity.

WILHELM WUELLNER taught at the Pacific School of Religion and in the Graduate Theological Union. His publications include *The Meaning of "Fishers of Men," The Surprising Gospel: Intriguing Psychological Insights from the New Testament* (with Robert C. Leslie), and *Hermeneutics and Rhetorics: From "Truth and Method" to Truth and Power*. He has also written numerous articles on rhetorical criticism.

The Postmodern Bible

Introduction

In the humanities, collective formulations are almost invariably trivial (what worthwhile book after the Pentateuch has been written by
a committee?).
—George Steiner (1988: 36)

TOWARD TRANSFORMING READINGS OF THE BIBLE

We begin with a truism: the Bible has exerted more cultural influence on
the West than any other single document. Understanding that influence in
late twentieth-century Western culture presents a major challenge to biblical scholarship. Yet the dominant methodologies of historical criticism have
been both the very foundation of modern biblical interpretation and the
major obstacle to making sense of the Bible's ongoing formative influence
over culture and society. Historical criticism brackets out the contemporary
milieu and excludes any examination of the ongoing formative effects of the
Bible. By embracing scientific method as the key in the search for historical
truth, modern biblical scholarship has kept faith with the Enlightenment's
desire to do away with ambivalence and uncertainty once and for all by
effectively isolating the text and its criticism from the reader's cultural con-

1

text, values, and interests. The pervasive modern emphasis on the objective recovery of the ancient context in which biblical texts were produced has had the double effect of obscuring the significance of the Bible in contemporary Western culture and of turning the Bible into an historical relic, an antiquarian artifact. It has also produced a modern biblical scholarship that, for many, has become a curatorial science in which the text is fetishized, its readings routinized, its readers bureaucratized. Moreover, historical criticism has implicitly veiled the historical character of biblical scholarship's entanglements with modernity and has therefore left unexamined its own critical and theoretical assumptions as well as the cultural conditions that produced, sustained, and validated them.

In reaction, we are arguing for a *transformed* biblical criticism, one that would recognize that our cultural context is marked by aesthetics, epistemologies, and politics quite different from those reigning in eighteenth- and nineteenth-century Europe where traditional biblical scholarship is so thoroughly rooted. We are also arguing for a *transforming* biblical criticism, one that undertakes to understand the ongoing impact of the Bible on culture and one that, therefore, benefits from the rich resources of contemporary thought on language, epistemology, method, rhetoric, power, reading, as well as the pressing and often contentious political questions of "difference"—gender, race, class, sexuality and, indeed, religion—which have come to occupy center stage in discourses both public and academic. In short, we hope in this volume to contribute to the process of bringing biblical scholarship into meaningful and ongoing engagement with the political, cultural, and epistemological critiques that have emerged "in modernity's wake" (Phillipson) and that have proved so fruitful in other literary studies and cultural criticism.

We have named our collective argument *The Postmodern Bible*. What is at stake in such a naming? What does it mean to describe the Bible as postmodern? Why does postmodernism matter to biblical scholarship? The various critical stances brought together here under the sign "postmodernism," for all their differences, share a suspicion of the claim to mastery that characterizes traditional readings of texts, including modern biblical scholarship. This suspicion is at once epistemological and political. That is, by sweeping away secure notions of meaning, by radically calling into question the apparently stable foundations of meaning on which traditional interpretation is situated, by raising doubts about the capacity to achieve ultimate clarity about the meaning of a text, postmodern readings lay bare the contingent and constructed character of meaning itself. Moreover, by challenging traditional interpretations that claim universality, completeness, and supremacy over other interpretations, postmodern readings demonstrate that traditional interpretations are themselves enactments of domination or, in simpler terms, power plays.

The suspicion of mastery that characterizes postmodernism does not insist upon the rejection of modernity but exacts a thorough self-consciousness from it and inspires a desire for change. As Zygmunt Bauman articulates it:

> Postmodernity is no more (but no less either) than the modern mind taking a long, attentive and sober look at itself, at its conditions and its past works, not fully liking what it sees and sensing the urge to change. Postmodernity is modernity coming of age: modernity looking at itself at a distance rather than from inside, making a full inventory of its gains and losses, psychoanalysing itself, discovering the intentions it never before spelled out, finding them mutually canceling and incongruous. Postmodernity is modernity coming to terms with its own impossibility; a self-monitoring modernity, one that consciously discards what it was once unconsciously doing. (1991:272)

Neither the aim nor the impact of this postmodern process of destabilization is political or moral relativism. Rather, postmodern readings function as political and ethical responses to other readings which claim that their own foundations exist outside of a field of power. For, "To establish a set of norms that are beyond power or force is itself a powerful and forceful conceptual practice that sublimates, disguises and extends its own power play through recourse to tropes of normative universality. And the point is not to do away with foundations, or even to champion a position that goes under the name of antifoundationalism. . . . Rather, the task is to interrogate what the theoretical move that establishes foundations *authorizes,* and what precisely it excludes and forecloses" (Butler, 1992:7).

We do not believe that this kind of theoretical engagement of texts is coterminous with political struggle as it is commonly understood in society and culture, but we do believe that the strategies of reading we are promoting in this book are part of the broader political activity to call reigning structures of power and meaning into question and thereby to contribute to and enable change (cf. Meaghan Morris, 5–6).

The politics of reading is therefore an obvious focus for our book, and clearly we are arguing that this politics is present not only explicitly in the chapters on feminist/womanist and ideological criticisms, but also implicitly in the other chapters that take up critiques of traditional epistemologies and theories of discourse. Hence our decision, for example, to include chapters on such topics as poststructuralism, psychoanalytic criticism, and rhetorical criticism—a decision that reflects our wish to keep epistemological questions (and their political implications) firmly in the foreground. We also decided to examine two methods—structuralist and reader-response criticisms—whose importance has waned in neighboring fields, but which have played (and continue to play) a crucial role in opening up biblical scholarship to literary and cultural critical theory. We have included them in order to critique them. In short, each of our seven chapters takes up a strategy of reading that either is well established in nonbiblical critical theory or constitutes a force to be reckoned with in current biblical studies. Overall, our chapters amount to discussions of what you can know and how you can know it (structuralism and poststructuralism); how you as a subject of knowledge are shaped (reader-response, rhetorical, and psychoanalytic criticisms); and who benefits ultimately from what you claim to know (ideological and feminist/womanist criticisms). At the same time, our chapters have in common a shared concern for a set of issues and problems that exceed any one theory or strategy of reading but are endemic to the multidisciplinary debates on postmodernism.

Several of these reading strategies differ explicitly from modern historical-critical approaches. These strategies focus critical attention on the power the Bible currently wields in culture and society and show that historical critics have in any case been implicated in these power relations, generally without recognizing or acknowledging it. Even on those rare occasions when historical criticism acknowledges its complicity in the establishment and maintenance of the Bible's cultural power, it stops short of taking the necessary next step: the radical recasting of the premises and practices of biblical interpretation. No reading, our own included, can escape these intricate matrices of power. For us, there is no innocent reading of the Bible, no reading that is not already ideological. But to read the Bible in the traditional scholarly manner has all too often meant reading it, whether deliberately or not, in ways that reify and ratify the status quo—providing warrant for the subjugation of women (whether in the church, the academy, or society at large), justifying colonialism and enslavement, rationalizing homophobia, or otherwise legitimizing the power of hegemonic classes of people. There would be no reason to bother with another volume on biblical studies and critical theory if we did not believe that scholarship goes beyond the legislative act of "objective description" toward transformation of critical understandings and practices in the field, the culture, and especially ourselves. We do not assume that in order to be "informed" one must adopt any or all of the theoretical positions engaged here and therefore read as a feminist or as a deconstructionist or as a psychoanalyst or as a rhetorical critic. But we do think it is important to acknowledge that every reader reads theoretically in some way or other— as Terry Eagleton has put it, "hostility to theory . . . means an opposition to other people's theories and an oblivion of one's own" (1983:viii)—that self-reflexive understandings are no longer a luxury but a necessity. Or, as Althusser put it: "As there is no such thing as an innocent reading, we must say what reading we are guilty of" (1970:14).

Within our group, we have had serious and substantive debates about the nature of our own ideological interests and arguments about "what reading we are guilty of." Engaging in self-reflexive reading has meant a heightened sense of our various social locations and speaker-positions, which cannot be reduced to a facile litany of gender, race, class, and institutional locations. Indeed, we have come to recognize that, as Rajeswari Sunder Rajan has observed, "location . . . is not simply an address. One's affiliations are multiple, contingent, and frequently contradictory" (8). We have experienced with real resonance the profundity of Rajan's formulation as we have struggled to understand the ways in which we have all been constituted as speaking subjects in this book, caught up in the tension of both privilege and marginalization. For example, we all share an unmerited racial privilege attendant to being white in late twentieth-century United States culture and, as academics, we also possess some kind of professional privilege vis-à-vis many other kinds of work in our society; moreover, some of us inherit the gender privilege that remains largely entrenched in our society and in the institutions in which we work. At the same time, our institutional locations are by no means monolithic, either in terms of the expectations placed upon each of us in our daily work or in terms of the rewards bestowed upon (or withheld from!) each of us by our particular institutions. Our own theoretical and political investments and commitments emerge from this "multiple, contingent, . . . frequently contradictory" and hybrid set of locations, from the double recognition of the privilege and power that are embedded in critical practice *and* the social and cultural constraints within which we do our work.

In this volume we do not pretend for a moment that we are pioneers on this path, with no precursors or fellow travelers. In recent years, engaging the Bible in explicitly theoretical ways has generated much fruitful activity, producing new seminars at the professional meetings, new journals and monograph series devoted to innovative ways of reading the Bible, and more books than we could begin to list. To date much of this activity has been concentrated in North America. Many of the seminars devoted to such topics as feminism, poststructuralism, and ideological criticism and the Bible have been hosted by the Society of Biblical Literature, although other professional societies outside North America are beginning to take up these issues as well. Moreover, there have been significant conferences on the Bible and theory at the University of Colorado, Georgetown University, and the University of California at Riverside, as well as a number of NEH seminars addressing these matters. In terms of journals, the best-known forum for such approaches has been *Semeia: An Experimental Journal for Biblical Criticism* (Scholars Press, 1974–), which is an American publication. Recently, however, the European publisher E. J. Brill has launched a similar journal, *Biblical Interpretation: A Journal of Contemporary Approaches,* which has a companion monograph series, as does *Semeia.* New series have appeared such as Westminster/John Knox Press's "Literary Currents in Biblical Interpretation," or Sheffield Academic Press's "Readings: A New Biblical Commentary," to name only two examples. Much of this fertile work has been conducted by scholars who are not located strictly within the guild of biblical studies, by literary and cultural critics with such vastly different perspectives as Robert Alter, Mieke Bal, Roland Barthes, Cornel West, Harold Bloom, Jacques Derrida, Northrop Frye, René Girard, Geoffrey Hartman, Luce Irigaray, Frank Kermode, Julia Kristeva, Jacques Lacan, Louis Marin, Meir Sternberg, and others. And, indeed, some of the most compelling postmodern interventions into biblical texts may ultimately emerge from outside of the academic framework altogether, producing challenging and creative disciplinary *and* professional border crossings.

An example of this kind of work can be found in filmmaker and screenwriter Paul Hallam's provocative volume, *The Book of Sodom* (1993). Hallam's project, "to explore some of the metaphorical uses to which the city has been put, to tease out the essential Sodom, and rescue, or at least reinvestigate Sodom's reputation" (2), is implicitly a postmodern endeavor and, moreover, a stunning work. The book opens with an extended quotation from Genesis 18–19, followed by an "outwork" guidebook and autobiographical essay, "Sodom: A Circuit-Walk," itself a pastiche of reflections on Bibles, commentaries, pulp fiction, cinematic representations, and coming of age as a gay man in Britain under the shadow of elusive biblical Sodom. An anthology of a range of high and low culture representations of Sodom is framed by this opening essay and a shorter concluding "outwork," "Sodom: Looking Back." The opening to "Sodom: A Circuit-Walk" demonstrates its critical orientation: "There is no Sodom, there are only Sodom texts. Stories of Sodom, commentaries, footnotes, elaborations and annotations upon Sodom" (15). Part way through a moving self-reflection, Hallam remarks insightfully: "I was worried, writing this. Too much autobiography? But the more I read the commentaries, the more they all seem like autobiographies, albeit disguised. Everyone so certain they've been there, seen Sodom" (84). The Circuit-Walk closes with a confession with which many a postmodern reader of the Bible and its commentaries will feel a familiar, synecdochal resonance: "I soon felt trapped by the commentaries. . . . I remembered that for me the Sodom story was never really the Bible's at all. It was all of these stories. . . . For years, I would wrap myself in its convolutions, its grand melancholy. Climb in . . ." (96).

Unquestionably, all "literary approaches" to the Bible should not be lumped together. We would want to distinguish our own collaborative volume, both in the mode of its production and in its content, from Alter and Kermode's *Literary Guide to the Bible,* for example, which quite conspicuously and deliberately excludes feminist, ideological, psychoanalytic, deconstructive, or Marxist approaches, as its editors frankly inform us (4). This conscious exclusion seems to underwrite a broader project of protecting a certain form of canonical literary criticism without acknowledging its own ideological character. Either they are unwilling or—less likely—they are unable to address the institutionalizing and normative effects their own theoretical choices have upon the texts they read and the readers they reach, all the while giving the impression that they define and speak authoritatively for a monolithic literary approach. What they remain silent about, we feel compelled in our volume to disclose. What they have dispatched to the margins, we find to be central and energizing. We are convinced that the critical practices explicitly excluded from Alter and Kermode's account will be increasingly vital to a biblical scholarship responsive to a postmodern culture.

Throughout this volume, our hope is to clarify rather than to obscure difficult discourses, to diminish their often intimidating character, and to encourage our colleagues and students to enter into this compelling, challenging, if sometimes confounding theoretical discussion about the Bible and postmodernity. Toward this end, we have adopted the strategy in each chapter of illustrating the approach in question with brief but emblematic examples. After engaging the principal theoretical underpinnings of the approach, we describe ways in which the particular interpretive strategy has taken root and is blossoming in the field and then conclude with some reflection upon what may lie ahead for biblical critics who undertake to read this way. At the end of each chapter we suggest further readings. For both practical and theoretical reasons, we have not said everything that might be said about any of the approaches in question.

Throughout, we have imagined ourselves writing for our students, for a literate public, and for colleagues in the academy—both those who know much about traditional biblical scholarship but little about contemporary critical theory and those who are conversant in literary and cultural criticisms but to whom biblical interpretation remains largely unexplored territory. We have also imagined an audience not limited by the boundaries of the academy, but encompassing a broader range of people interested in the compelling and contentious effects of the Bible on culture, including those who read the Bible in specific religious contexts. Despite the attendant difficulties of attempting to locate such an intellectual middle ground, we have tried to keep foremost in our minds the question: what might an engaged reader need to know in order to make sense of the Bible in relation to contemporary culture? We have tried to be sparing in our use of technical terminology. Unavoidably, however, to do justice to contemporary critical theory, we have made use of some technical language, striving to clarify these terms as we use them—including the key defining term of the volume, *postmodernism*.

POSTMODERNISM

In discussions of contemporary culture, few terms are used or abused more than *postmodernism* (Hutcheon, 1989:1). Indeed, the range of meanings for the term is incredibly broad. Depending on whom one is reading or talking to, it can mean incredulity toward the legitimizing "metanarratives" that we have inherited from the Enlightenment (Lyotard, 1984); the "crisis of legitimation" over the principles and values that govern late twentieth-century life (Habermas, 1976); an anti-aesthetic impulse that is intensely self-reflexive and whose characteristic vehicle of expression is the "pastiche" (cf. Foster, 1983); or a global cultural phenomenon encountered in mass media, mass culture, information technology, and multinational capitalism

(Jameson, 1991). If we try to define the postmodern in reference to the modern, the definitions continue to proliferate, for "one critic's postmodernism is another critic's modernism" (Huyssen, 59). Like many concepts turned into commodities for consumer culture, this fashionably ambiguous term has even taken up residence in the fashion industry as a ready-to-hand marketing tag for the latest in designer clothing (cf. Handy, 69).

However variously it may be defined, most critics would concur that "we are within the culture of postmodernism to the point where its facile repudiation is as impossible as an equally facile celebration of it is complacent and corrupt. Ideological judgment on postmodernism today necessarily implies, one would think, a judgment on ourselves as well as on the artifacts in question" (Hutcheon, 1988a:63).

Rather than unthinking repudiations or mindless approbations of postmodernism, what is necessary is a critical engagement with its substance—its debates, its theories, and its practices in all of their aesthetic, social, and political aspects. As we see it, the postmodern does not signify a simple, homogeneous answer to the past or present nor a unified critical position with respect to the future. The postmodern has to do with transformation in the local ways we understand ourselves in relation to modernity and to contemporary culture and history, the social and personal dimensions of that awareness, and the ethical and political responses that it generates. The postmodern as unruly, nebulous, elusive, decentered, and decentering (cf. Wakefield, 1) needs to be engaged creatively and critically rather than summarily dismissed or fetishized as the latest intellectual fashion.

Among the many critics attempting to make sense of the postmodern condition, Jean-François Lyotard has helped us to shape and refine our own understanding of the postmodern and its implications for biblical studies. For Lyotard, the "postmodern condition" can be identified in terms of three principal transformational trajectories within culture. The first is the *aesthetic*, the realm of the arts, along with architecture, where the focus has been on the constructed nature of the work, the play of surfaces, the obliteration of the traditional distinction between high and mass culture, and—particularly in the visual and literary arts—a preoccupation with the ineffable, the inexpressible, the "unsayable" (see Tyler). This preoccupation with the unsayable has been a pervasive one for a number of French poststructuralist thinkers such as Jacques Derrida, Jacques Lacan, and Julia Kristeva (see chap. 3 and chap. 5 below).

The second trajectory Lyotard singles out is the *epistemological*, which he characterizes as the "incredulity toward metanarratives." The term *modern*, for Lyotard, designates "any science that legitimates itself with reference to a metadiscourse ... making an explicit appeal to some grand narrative, such as the dialectics of the Spirit, the hermeneutics of meaning, the emancipation of the rational or working subject, or the creation of wealth" (1984:xxiii).

To such totalizing gestures Lyotard opposes the postmodern preference for "many language games—a heterogeneity of elements," which "only give rise to institutions in patches—local determinism" (xxiv). The postmodern critique of the Enlightenment legacy seeks to make us more sensitive to differences, better able to think about incommensurability and change, and aware of the socially constructed character of knowledge and the various means of its production (see below, esp. chaps. 2 and 3). It also attempts to engage indeterminacy, chaos, and ambiguity—not as the failures of modernity but as its inevitable other side.

Inextricably bound up with the epistemological critique is Lyotard's third trajectory, the *political*. Since postmodernism signals a crisis of legitimation at the heart of scientific knowledge itself, it has important social, political, and ecological consequences. In particular, it engenders the suspicion that the desire for consensus so characteristic of the scientific worldview is a phallocratic and universalizing one (our terms, not his), a desire to suppress heterogeneity. (See esp. chap. 6 and chap. 7.) Moreover, postmodern critique contributes to an emerging critique of technology's ever-increasing hegemony in the West, particularly when that hegemony is inexorably and, perhaps, inevitably linked to an ideology of mastery and hence to practices of violence (Bauman, 1992). The euphoric embrace of technological prowess and the concomitant marginalization of dissent in the Persian Gulf war are but one recent example of the deadly merger of technological and political mastery under the sign of scientific progress. Here postmodernism's epistemological challenge to the universalist and objectivist claims of the scientific worldview has clear ethical, political, and ecological consequences. It remains to be seen whether technology in its postmodern applications may not also contribute to its own destabilization and ultimately to positive political (that is to say, radically democratic) ends, as some postmodern theorists of technology have argued (Bolter; Landow; Lanham; J. Hillis Miller, 1991).

It is therefore ironic that one of the common complaints brought against postmodernist, or more particularly poststructuralist, reading strategies—especially deconstruction and other so-called nihilistic ways of reading—is that they are politically or ethically neutral. Not only is this a strong mis-reading of Derrida (although it is true of some deconstructive criticism), it also reflects a strategy to block a certain kind of thinking about ethics and politics. As the argument is usually formulated, ethics and politics are only possible when certain philosophical foundations are in place (see Caputo); to call these foundations into question is to fall outside of the realms of both ethics and politics, hence to be both amoral and apolitical. In response to the claim that postmodernity is devoid of ethical or moral dimensions while modernity is steeped in ethical concerns, Bauman has argued forcefully to the contrary: "On the whole, modernity contributed little, if anything, to the enrichment of moral problematics. Its role boiled down to the substitution of legal for moral regulations and the exemption of a wide and growing sector of human actions from moral evaluation" (1992:201).

With Bauman, we strongly believe that postmodern sensibilities are by no means removed from social engagement or political action (see also Butler and Scott; Flax, 1987; and Siebers). Indeed, part of what is at stake in our project is giving expression to what has been variously called "a political form of postmodernism" (Jameson), "a postmodernism of resistance" (Foster), or "a postmodern politics" (Hutcheon). As Bauman has argued:

> Postmodernity may be interpreted as fully developed modernity taking a full measure of the anticipated consequences of its historical work; as modernity that acknowledged the effects it was producing throughout its history, yet produced inadvertently, rarely conscious of its own responsibility, by default rather than design, as by-products often perceived as waste. Postmodernity may be conceived of as modernity conscious of its true nature—*modernity for itself.* . . . The postmodern condition can therefore be described, on the one hand, as modernity emancipated from false consciousness; on the other, as a new type of social condition marked by the overt institutionalization of the characteristics which modernity—in its designs and managerial practices—set about to eliminate and, failing that, tried to conceal. (1992:187–88)

Taking seriously the implications of this rendering of postmodernism for our work entails heeding the continuing importance of traditional forms of biblical criticism while at the same time acknowledging the various systems of power (disciplinary, epistemological, cultural) that have kept these strategies—and not others—in place. We want to introduce our readers to the rich critical possibilities that emerge from a postmodern look at the Bible, a perspective that underscores self-reflexivity, heterogeneity, contingency, and difference, while remaining engaged in specific, concrete ways with the Bible, with one another, and with a world that is changing even as we write.

POSTMODERNISM AND BIBLICAL STUDIES

In recent years a diverse host of literary and cultural criticisms have migrated into the land of modern biblical studies. That landscape today reflects dramatic changes when compared to the situation just a generation ago. Then redaction criticism represented the cutting-edge critical approach, and French structuralism was hailed by many as the *nouvelle critique* destined to change the face of traditional biblical scholarship. Indeed, in the millenarian mind-set of some critics in the 1970s, historical criticism seemed all but eclipsed. The generative power of post-historical methods, especially those funneled through the aperture of literary theory, offered the promise of new critical life in the wake of what was taken to be historical criticism's intellectual and moral bankruptcy (see esp. Wink, 1–18; Maier). But while the terrain has changed significantly, historical criticism has not ended nor has traditional biblical scholarship been widely discredited, displaced, or taken up into a new synthesis. Instead, certain uncomfortable questions have come back with insistence: Whose history does historical criticism relate? How does that history get told? Who is empowered to do the telling? What changes in the social fabric does biblical studies effect—or fail to effect? What is biblical scholarship's role in the effort to achieve social justice?

Like its near neighbor literary studies, biblical studies has become home to a throng of theoretical discourses and critical methods that have crisscrossed the borders traditionally separating disciplines in the humanities and social sciences. They have found the Bible fertile soil and they are thriving. In the eyes of some, this immigration looks more like an invasion. But to treat the changes taking place in contemporary biblical studies as something that is being imposed upon biblical studies from without, rather than as a consequence of the very impulses that are constitutive of modern critical study of the Bible, is not to appreciate the ongoing potency and vitality of modernity. Paradoxically, it is modernity that has helped create the condition for the transformations under way today, even in their strange poststructuralist and postmodernist permutations. Lyotard states it forcefully: the " 'postmodern' signifies not the end of modernism, but another relation to modernism" (1989b:277). One way to understand this relationship would be to see that postmodernism foregrounds, heightens, and problematizes modernity's enabling assumptions about reference, representation, method, and subjectivity. In this sense, the crisis of legitimation confronting biblical criticism today—whose reading counts? how are different readings adjudicated?—is a direct consequence of the intensification of those very aspects of critical self-consciousness that were prominent in the birth of modern scientific study of the Bible (Frei, 1–16) and in the development of what Timothy Reiss calls the dominant "analytico-referential discourse" of the Enlightenment (cf. Hayden White, 1978:51–80). Both the postmodern and the modern share common cause in reaction to the grip of an uncritical premodern tradition.

To the extent that biblical scholars have engaged the postmodernism debate directly, they have tended to view it from such perspectives as reader-oriented criticism (Fowler, 1991; McKnight, 1988), textuality and language (Aichele, 1989; Moore, 1989b, 1992, 1994; Schwartz, 1990a), or institutional and social structures (Burnett, 1990b; Castelli, 1991a; Jobling, 1991a; Phillips, 1990a; 1990b; 1994a; Schwartz, 1991)—although these distinctions are somewhat leaky at best. Reader-response criticism, in particular, has served as a primary gateway for biblical critics leaving historical criticism and entering postmodern territory. As Fred Burnett has put it, "reader-response has become the last 'decompression chamber' for many redaction critics before they surface into [post]modern criticism" (1990b:54). At the same time, however, reader-response criticism has also covertly functioned as a safe-house for biblical critics who prefer to stay within the secure confines of traditional biblical scholarship and not plunge into the defamiliarized world of the postmodern (see chap. 1).

One aspect of this defamiliarization poses a particular challenge for biblical studies. Given the progressive view of history that we have inherited from the Scientific Revolution and the Enlightenment, the temptation is great to think of the relation between modern and postmodern in simple, unitary, chronological terms. As Andreas Huyssen puts it, "rather than being bound to a one-way history of modernism which interprets it as a logical unfolding toward some imaginary goal . . . we are beginning to explore its contradictions and contingencies, its tensions and internal resistances to its own 'forward' movement" (217).

Such explorations are especially significant for biblical scholarship, which has frequently been marked by a consuming missionary desire for a one-way history. The unfolding drama of salvation history has tended to merge imperceptibly in the minds of biblical scholars with a secular methodological drama, one in which the progressive refinement of historical methods promises to lead to ever more certain knowledge about not only the original contexts and meanings of the biblical texts but their theological truth. Stephen Moore frames the issue this way: "Does the modernist project in biblical studies—broadly speaking, the attempt to retrieve the original meanings of the biblical texts (authorial intentions objectified in textual features)—ever admit of completion? What, at minimum, should be necessary in order that it might be completed? An objective biblical text whose fixed, innate properties admit of cumulative retrieval? A sleeping text that awaits our kiss?" (1989b:174).

Notwithstanding the loud protestations to the contrary of critics like Habermas and Steiner, biblical critics attuned to these postmodern discussions wonder whether not only the modern critical apparatus but the entire Enlightenment project itself may be illusory. Robert Fowler, relying upon Hassan, cites as a "grand index" of the postmodern "an increasing recognition that reading and interpretation is always interested, never disinterested; always significantly subjective, never completely objective; always committed and therefore always political, never uncommitted and apolitical; always historically-bound, never ahistorical. The modernist dream of disinterested, objective, distanced, abstract truth is fading rapidly" (1989a:21).

Biblical scholars have been slow to awaken from the dream in which positivist science occupies a space apart from interests and values, to awaken to the realization that our representations of and discourse about what the text meant and how it means are inseparable from what we *want* it to mean, from how we *will* it to mean. Such desire and gratification, repression and occlusion have made psychoanalytic theory an important resource for postmodern biblical criticism as it takes up its modern inheritance and works through it. A call has gone out for psychoanalytic readers, many of them also feminist and deconstructive interpreters—Freud, Lacan, Kristeva, Irigaray, Barthes, Derrida and others—to aid in re-reading biblical texts, as well as the writing pads of modern biblical criticism (see chap. 5).

Throughout, the preoccupation with representation has become to an unprecedented degree a political concern, a concern to expose the systems of power that authorize certain representational strategies while prohibiting or invalidating others. Insistent feminist and womanist questioning of patriarchal structures challenges the master narratives of modernity (which themselves deeply inform modern biblical scholarship), as well as the biblical narratives themselves, exposing them as narratives of male mastery. In her 1987 presidential address to the Society of Biblical Literature, Elisabeth Schüssler Fiorenza claimed: "If scriptural texts have served not only noble causes but also to legitimate war, to nurture anti-Judaism and misogynism, to justify the exploitation of slavery, and to promote colonial dehumanization . . . then the responsibility of the biblical scholar cannot be restricted to giving the readers of our time clear access to the original intentions of the biblical writers. It must also include the elucidation of the ethical consequences and political functions of biblical texts in their historical as well as in their contemporary sociopolitical contexts" (1988:15).

Although Schüssler Fiorenza remains deeply suspicious of the contribution poststructuralist and other postmodernist discourses can make toward changing present social structures, we are more confident (see chap. 6). With Schüssler Fiorenza, we are certain that the future of biblical criticism hinges squarely on its ability and willingness to make gender, race, ideology, and institutional power substantive concerns—which means a change in institutional structures, discourses, and practices. Going beyond Schüssler Fiorenza, we think that postmodern critique extends to those very notions of liberation and sociality that derive from modernist frameworks. But so far, with few exceptions, the vast majority of biblical critics have been slow to read against the grain of the biblical texts and the institution of traditional biblical scholarship, and they have been generally content to re-enact the ideologies inscribed in their respective narratives and metanarratives (see esp. chap. 7).

In reaction to this situation, we have written *The Postmodern Bible*. We wrote out of concern about systems of power—institutional, ecclesiastical, cultural—that authorize or block what can be said or written about the Bible. We wrote out of concern about the politics of inclusion and exclusion that determine whose reading of the Bible counts, whose does not, and why. We wrote eager to see explicit acknowledgments of ethical stances, ideological positionings, self-critical and self-reflexive consciousness, and affirmations of the positive values of difference and multiplicity. Most important, we wrote out of a concern to make sense of the Bible in a cultural context for which there can be no detailed, comprehensive, or fully accurate road map.

THE BIBLE AND CULTURE COLLECTIVE

That this book is a work of collective authorship is by no means incidental or ancillary to our purpose. Our commitment to the collective process—

generating ideas as a group, writing each chapter in small working groups, making revisions and editing as a group, hammering out consensus on every aspect of the volume—is itself part of our implicit critique of prevailing understandings of authorship and our effort to transform disciplinary practices (see Woodmansee and Jaszi; Canadian Feminist Ethics Theory Group; Childers and hooks). To varying extents and in various ways, each of us has experienced the frustrations of writing as an individual modern self, an authorial ego replete with will, intention, and the desire to possess the text and to control the process. This collective process became our means to contest an epistemology and a set of disciplinary practices that privilege the autonomous self, an ideology that values private ownership, and a professional discursive practice that legitimates the production and dissemination of knowledge in one form at the expense of another.

Along the way, each of us experienced the mutual support, the friendship, and the fun of participating in something larger than any one of us, as well as the frustrations and the challenges of working together in a group that is anything but monolithic. Yet a collective work on the Bible seemed like an especially apt forum for such an effort since its composition too was collective, its chapters never signed, its cultural milieu predating the advent of the modern authorial self and copyright law. We have struggled with problems of identity and purpose, and we have learned how to read and write corporately, differently, in a way that is appropriate for our time and place. We have come out of this process with a different name and identity to show for our efforts: The Bible and Culture Collective. As our volume took shape, a communal sense of its significance took precedence over the promotion of individual wills and agendas. "I didn't like the collective idea at first," confessed one of our members in a letter to the group. "Standard academic authorship is depersonalizing enough, I thought (all those footnotes serving as proof that I have ingested the thoughts of the authorities). But then I came to believe in the Book." Out of our frustrations with institutionalized forms of isolation and out of our desire to imagine and enact an alternative to them, we entered into a collaborative experiment to find a better way to think and write about the Bible. The practical challenges of this experiment were significant: getting all ten of us together on eight occasions in different cities across Canada and the United States, reproducing and mailing drafts and critiques and revisions, staying in near-constant conversation on the telephone and the Internet, writing the grants to support our collective activities, spending our own money when institutional support was insufficient. Indeed, there are numerous practical impediments to this sort of collaborative work, which we soon realized. At the same time, the commitment to the collective character of our work—and the responsibility we felt toward one another—grew over time and encouraged us to continue writing together over four and a half years, in spite of such material and logistical obstacles.

It is important to say, nevertheless, that the "we" used throughout this volume is problematic. As a corporate identity, if poststructuralist theorists are correct, it is a highly unstable construct—and, indeed, "we" have struggled over the creative and difficult consequences of our construction of this collective self. Moreover, the corporate project has its real hazards. Chief among them is the danger that our distinctive voices would become homogenized by cooptation and compromise, that our individual critical concerns would become dulled in the effort to achieve consensus, that the nuances of our personal positions might lose their subtlety in the group voice. "We" have different expertises, different interests, different critical perspectives, different reading styles, different working situations. "We" take our leads from different thinkers, focus on different texts (both biblical and theoretical), have different institutional roles, embrace different religious and secular traditions. "We" were frequently caught up in heated arguments about what was best to say and do. In reflecting upon this variegated and, on occasion, contentious "we," many of us came face to face with the instability and composite nature of our individual identities.

Another one of our group expressed the following reservation: "By the time I turned in my activist credentials for academic ones, I had emerged with a highly developed cynicism about the possibility of working collectively . . . that undoubtedly explains what might periodically come across as my bad attitude toward collectivity, consensus, and the dissolution of dissent that can be part of both processes. That said, I also feel ultimately that my contribution is being swept up in an exciting process whereby the sum is truly greater (and radically different) than its parts." Aware of the pitfalls of collectivity, nonetheless, we have tried to retain the flavor of our differences, even at the risk of a certain unevenness of style. We have laughed to imagine some industrious source critic someday trying to disentangle our respective voices: the D source (David), E (Elizabeth), F (Fred), the G source (is that Gary, George, or Gina?), R (Robert), S (Stephen), T (Tina), and W (Wilhelm).

Scholarship can be a lonely business. But we managed to break through its isolations for discrete moments, staring at the computer screens together, scratching notes on drafts in groups, generating marginal glosses that, like our drafts, immediately ceased to be the property of one individual. Questions of ownership, responsibility, and privilege never completely disappeared but were struggled with in the context of a largely unprecedented opportunity to work together. We engaged in conflicts over what to call this book, what name we would take as its authors, how to acknowledge different levels of effort and responsibility in the writing and production process, and indeed how to represent our collaborative process publicly. We tolerated relentless ribbing from one another about our foibles—which we came to know only too well—and in general yanked, poked, prodded, and teased each other to move out of the habits of thought, the parameters of discourse, the hallowed assumptions each had brought to the project.

Collaborative scholarship is not free of professional and personal risks and costs. Still, we remain committed to the importance of working collectively. For many of us, the humanistic models of scholarship that we accepted unquestioningly as graduate students now seem wooden and stultifying by comparison. All of us would concur with the assessments of two of our members: "The group process has been better for me than the isolationist model of scholarly work. Ideological biases, which I otherwise would not have noticed, have been exposed, and insecurities like 'I really don't know much about that' could be admitted after a certain level of trust had been reached. Infighting could occur without being taken as a personal affront. Deep friendships have formed." "Somehow the process of production (which the reader will never experience, nor perhaps understand), embodies the hopes of humanistic and postmodern scholarship alike: that a useful piece of scholarship could be produced because real differences were maintained and affirmed."

In short, we think Steiner has it wrong in the epigraph to this Introduction. Collective formulations need not be trivial; ours has made a profound difference to each of us. We believe such collaborative efforts are important strategies of resistance, revitalization, and transformation, promising new ways of producing knowledge in a discipline that has relied much too heavily on individualistic models of scholarship.

Finally, as we talked about the uncertain postmodern future of biblical studies, we always imagined our primary audience to be our students, and, as we wrote, we consciously addressed ourselves to the next generation of readers and scholars. "Criticism," Roland Barthes has argued, "is not an 'homage' to the truth of the past or to the truth of 'others'—it is a construction of the intelligibility of our own time" (1972b:260). We look forward to a time when the next generation makes *its* collective statements, constructs the intelligibility of its own time, and makes our own attempts at such collective critique old hat.

1 | Reader-Response Criticism

READING THE FEEDING STORIES IN MARK

Readers of the Gospel of Mark have long puzzled over two very similar episodes, the feeding of the five thousand in Mark 6:30–44 and the feeding of the four thousand in Mark 8:1–10. In both episodes Jesus feeds a large crowd with just a few loaves and fishes. In both episodes the disciples collect baskets full of leftover pieces of bread and fish. Perhaps most perplexing of all, in both episodes the disciples seem utterly unaware of what Jesus is capable of doing to feed the crowd. Granted, they might not have understood what Jesus was doing the first time he feeds a crowd, but is it reasonable that they would be just as obtuse the second time around?

Such questions have long driven the historical-critical discussion of the feeding stories in Mark (Fowler, 1981:5–42; Neirynck, 18–19). From the mid-nineteenth century to the present, many have claimed that the best explanation of the two feeding stories in Mark is that they are variants of a single traditional story, and thus the solution to this puzzle lies in the existence of multiple oral or written sources predating the Gospel. This and other apparent redundancies in Mark have played a key role in source theories about the relationship between the canonical Gospels and in redactional theories aimed at peeling redactional embellishments away from pre-Gospel traditions. Defenders of the Two-Source Hypothesis have asked, Does repetition originate with Mark, and do Matthew and Luke edit out Mark's redundancies, each in his own way? Defenders of the Griesbach Hypothesis have asked, Could Mark be creating redundancies from similar material he is receiving from Matthew on the one hand and Luke on the other? Redaction critics have asked, Does repetition in Mark reflect the preservation of variants of the same tradition? Or does repetition represent the evangelist's own redactional constructions in imitation of received tradition?

With the publication in 1972 of Frans Neirynck's *Duality in Mark*, an encyclopedic survey of "pleonasms, redundancies, and repetitions in Mark" (Neirynck, 71), a new stage emerged in these source-critical and redaction-critical discussions. Neirynck's exhaustive survey demonstrates conclusively that repetitious constructions are present throughout Mark, from the level of phrases, clauses, and sentences, up to entire episodes. The repetitions in Mark reflect the pervasive, consistent writing style of the author, not the occasional, accidental preservation of tradition variants. Furthermore, Neirynck demonstrates that these repetitious constructions are not in fact redundant, and therefore again not so easily chalked up to tradition variants. Rather, they are usually "two-step progressions" (cf. Rhoads and Michie, 47–48): the second half of these dual constructions typically takes the reader a step beyond the first half. In light of Neirynck's work, any source- or redaction-critical operation that takes as its central move the dismantling of dual constructions in Mark faces the formidable challenge of having to decide how far to go. Once one starts, there is no obvious place to stop. Neirynck insinuates that the magnitude of Markan duality overwhelms the capacity of the source- and redaction-critical machinery to dismantle it (see also Kelber, 1976:42; 1983:67–68).

To date Neirynck has catalogued the textual evidence for duality in Mark but has drawn few conclusions about its function in Mark's narrative, so he has severely problematized source-critical and redaction-critical treatments of duality in Mark without offering an alternative approach. Since source criticism and redaction criticism are classic philological-historical methodologies, which in the twentieth century have commonly been succeeded by formalist approaches focusing on the internal structures of the text, it is not surprising that Neirynck's work has been taken up in the new formalist interpretations of Mark. Such work often marches under the banner of the *narrative criticism*[1] of the Gospels, of which Rhoads and Michie's *Mark as Story* is exemplary.

In spite of Rhoads and Michie's predominant formalist orientation, their tendency to comment constantly on the reader and the reading experience suggests another critical approach, one that pushes beyond formalist modes: reader-response criticism. The feeding stories in Mark have enjoyed a long, rich history of reading, which offers an attractive opportunity for the exercise of reader-response criticism. After all, the source critic and the redaction critic propose their hypotheses in response to their own experience of reading the Gospel. Sometimes they report their reading experience in explicit terms, but usually it is disguised as claims for the discovery of putative sources and redactions. A standard move for a reader-response critic is to translate such disguised (and usually unconscious) responses to reading into an explicit, self-conscious vocabulary concerned with readers and reading. Frequently reader-response critics argue that major interpretive cruxes, such as the problem of the two feeding stories in Mark, are not problems in the text per se, but problems in our own experience of reading the text. Whereas philological-historical criticism seeks out the "world behind the text"—the history of the text's production—its practitioners have often overlooked their own participation in the "world in front of the text"—the history of the text's reception.[2] One of the richest resources for reader-response criticism of the Bible are the disguised reading reports in the philological-historical commentaries that fill the shelves of our libraries.

Readers of Mark have repeatedly stumbled over 8:4, the peevish question uttered by the disciples in the midst of the second feeding story—"How can one feed these people with bread here in the desert?" Gould puts it most

---

[1] The label *narrative criticism* received impetus from Rhoads; the best handbooks describing the practice of narrative criticism of the Gospels are Rhoads and Michie and Powell (1990a); the best critical survey of the development of narrative criticism is Moore (1989b:1–68); see also chap. 2 below.

[2] On the worlds "behind" and "in front of" texts, see Ricoeur, 1981a; Edgar McKnight (1985:xviii). Also relevant here is Gadamer's notion of *Wirkungsgeschichte* (effective-history) and the Constance School's concern for *Rezeptionsgeschichte* (history of reception) (Gadamer, 267–74; Jauss, 1970; 1982a; Robert Fowler, 1991:228–60). "History," in these views, is not a once-upon-a-time, long ago and far away event but the ongoing encounter with a text in which we ourselves are enmeshed and to which we contribute. For a different view, see the discussion of Derrida and Foucault in chap. 3 below.

sharply when he declares that it is "psychologically impossible" that the disciples should be so obtuse, since they have already witnessed and participated in the earlier feeding incident (142). The step usually taken next is crucial. If the question in 8:4 is impossible, then it must be rejected. But how then shall we explain its presence in Mark? Taylor (1966:630), Branscomb (136), Gould, and many others agree: the two feeding stories are variants of the same story, and the Gospel writer's (careless?) repetition of both versions, both of which include the disciples' lack of insight into Jesus' power, accidentally makes the disciples look stupid. Thus we can safely discount the disciples' question in 8:4. It is not to be taken seriously.

From the vantage point of the reader-response critic, here are readers acknowledging a reading experience but then repudiating it. As a result, their reading experience is not explained, but rather explained away. Taylor, Branscomb, Gould, and company have forfeited an opportunity to consider not what is happening in the text, but what is happening in themselves as they read the text.

Ideological critiques of the historical-critical yearning for objective, impartial, impersonal knowledge are common these days and could easily be aimed here at Taylor, Branscomb, Gould, and company. Before rolling out the heavy ideological artillery, however, reader-response criticism can provide an important first step toward consciousness-raising about our own reading experiences. One early effort to begin to come to terms with what biblical scholars have experienced in reading Mark 8:4 employed Wayne Booth's (1974) discussion of the rhetoric of irony (Fowler, 1981:91–99; 1991:11–14, 167–75).

Reading Mark 8:4 is a classic experience of dramatic irony. The stupidity of the disciples in Mark 8:4 is indeed remarkable, precisely because it contrasts with the insight and understanding possessed by the reader of the Gospel. As one of the slogans of reader-response criticism declares, "reading this passage is the experience of learning how to read this passage," so if we can face up to the dramatic irony in 8:4, we may be better equipped to deal with still more dramatic irony elsewhere in Mark. That generations of readers have found Mark's Gospel to be full of messianic secrecy and mysterious revelation suggests that the experience of reading this Gospel is an extended encounter with a strong rhetoric of indirection that ranges far beyond even irony (Fowler, 1991).

The critical literature on Mark is full of observations of the obtuseness of the disciples in the story, but seldom is the question asked, If the characters in the story do not understand, who does? That the characters in the story do not "see" or "hear" properly—this is regularly observed. That the audience of the story does "see" and "hear"—this is seldom observed. In this regard, a comment by Robert Guelich about the first of the two feeding stories in Mark is noteworthy. Although the feeding of the five thousand is classified as a miracle story, and although miracle stories usually involve someone witnessing and acclaiming the miracle, it is remarkable in the feeding of the five thousand that absolutely no one in the story shows any sign of grasping what has happened. Guelich observes this lack of observation: "one of the most spectacular of Jesus' miracles takes place essentially un-noticed" (Guelich, 343). What Guelich does not notice is that he himself *has* noticed the miracle.

Philological-historical critics try to look behind the text, while formalist critics try to look inside it. Their eyes are focused to miss what is happening in front of the text—their own encounter with the text in the act of reading. Since biblical critics have lacked the vocabulary necessary to talk about their own reading experience (that is, the biblical-critical guild has not promoted the use of such language), such talk as there is among biblical critics about readers and reading is fortuitous and unreflective. Reader-response criticism promotes self-reflective reading and gives us words with which to talk about what we have always experienced, but unawares, and always talked about, but haphazardly. It challenges the biblical-critical guild to face up to its approved (and disapproved) reading practices.

Wayne Booth is helpful by encouraging us to attend to our experience of reading irony, but he does not help us much to expose the ideology or psychology that has led generations of biblical scholars to suppress their responses to their own reading experience. Nor does our reader-oriented discussion of the feeding stories in Mark fully disclose its own ideological agenda. It is but a first step toward a self-conscious, self-reflexive critical praxis.

MAPPING READER-RESPONSE CRITICISM

Paradoxically, the point most commonly agreed on by reader-response critics is that reader-response criticism is too varied to be defined adequately. Susan Rubin Suleiman's disclaimer is typical: "Audience-oriented criticism is not one field but many, not a single widely trodden path but a multiplicity of crisscrossing, often divergent tracks that cover a vast area of the critical landscape in a pattern whose complexity dismays the brave and confounds the faint of heart" (Suleiman and Crosman, 6; see also Tompkins, 1980:ix; Mailloux, 1982:19; Freund, 6; Rabinowitz, 1989:82; Holub, 1984:xii–xiii). Such standard disclaimers should be taken with a grain of salt, however, because the critic offering it usually proceeds to offer her best attempt at a definition. For example, after the comment above, Suleiman's very next line reads: "I intend to map here, however tentatively, the principal tracks in the landscape." Discussions of reader-response criticism regularly employ this double gesture: "reader-response criticism is impossible to define, but I shall define it for you." Reader-response criticism may not be precisely definable, but it is at least an identifiable cluster of theories and critical practices.

A simple but powerful story is often told about the evolution of reader-response criticism. It runs something like this: Once upon a time there was the New Criticism. The New Critics legislated against readers and their subjective responses to reading by proclaiming something they called the "Affective Fallacy": "The Affective Fallacy is a confusion between the poem and its results. . . . It begins by trying to derive the standard of criticism from the psychological effects of a poem and ends in impressionism and relativism" (Wimsatt, 21). Now in these latter days (so the story goes), reader-response critics have moved beyond the formalism of the New Criticism. They reject the validity of the Affective Fallacy; they deny that texts make meaning; rather, they affirm that readers make meaning; what counts now is readers and the experience of reading (Tompkins, 1980:ix, 209; Freund, 5–6; Flynn and Schweickart, ix; Mailloux, 1982:20, 66, 209).[3]

Jane Tompkins's version of the story of reader-response criticism is more sweeping than most, not only rehearsing its past and present, but also daring to predict its future. Her anthology tells a story that ranges, as her subtitle suggests, from formalism to poststructuralism (Tompkins, 1980). The "coherent progression" of her version of the story points ahead to new understandings of worldview, the literary text, and discourse ("language as a form of power") that are portended but not yet fully realized in reader-response criticism (ix–x, 226).

---

[3] This story is distinctly Anglo-American. The story of the rise of German reception theory would be quite different, featuring prominently European traditions of phenomenology and hermeneutics (for that story, see Holub, 1984). One sure sign of the wide currency of the story of reader-response criticism is that it has given rise to satire; see Eagleton's story of the "reader's liberation movement" (1982).

Almost in the same breath as the denial that reader-response criticism can be defined, the reader-response critic often declares that some common concern unites reader-response critics. Tompkins's statement is typical: "Reader-response criticism is not a conceptually unified position, but a term that has come to be associated with work of critics who use the words *reader, the reading process,* and *response* to mark out an area for investigation" (1980:ix; cf. 201; Mailloux, 1982:19–20; Rabinowitz, 1989:82; Richter, 1158). One of the more audacious claims for common concern is the frequent observation that all criticism has entered "the era of the reader" (Leitch, 1988:211; see also Eagleton, 1983:74) or "the Age of Reading" (Abrams, 1979:566). The scope of the standard anthologies of reader-response criticism is instructive in this regard. The essays in the Tompkins anthology are said to "represent a variety of theoretical orientations: New Criticism, structuralism, phenomenology, psychoanalysis, and deconstruction" (1980:ix). The essays in the Suleiman and Crosman volume represent "six varieties (or approaches to) audience-oriented criticism: rhetorical; semiotic and structuralist; phenomenological; subjective and psychoanalytic; sociological and historical; and hermeneutic" (6–7). In their hermeneutic category are included deconstructionists such as Derrida, de Man, and Miller. Consequently, within the schema of both of these major anthologies just about everyone in the world of literary criticism is given a niche, which is only fitting if indeed we are all living in the Age of Reading. Were we to follow the lead of Tompkins, Suleiman, and Crosman, we might argue that virtually every theoretical approach addressed in this volume is a version of reader-response criticism. However, for the purposes of this book we have cordoned off supposedly separate spaces for a handful of theoretical perspectives, only one of which we are calling "reader-response criticism."[4]

As we get more comprehensive in our description of reader-response criticism, the biases and exclusions of this chapter should become more evident. For instance, the taxonomy below, adapted from that of Steven Mailloux

---

[4] The "Name Our Age" game is played many ways today. The "Age of Reading" also goes by the name of "postmodernism" or "poststructuralism." A more materialist, technologically oriented label might acknowledge that we have moved out of the "Age of Gutenberg" into the "Electronic Age of Secondary Orality" (Ong, 1982). That is, perhaps all the theoretical orientations of this printed book (or any other) are too narrowly focused for a world in which the predominant forms of communication are no longer typographic, but electronic (cf. Boomershine).

(1982:19–65; cf. 1989:29–36; 1990), while helpful within certain limits, is predominantly American, white, male, and academic. Later in the chapter we will indicate how reader-response criticism might connect with readers and reading practices not adequately represented by this taxonomy.

Psychological or Subjective	Interactive or Phenomenological	Social or Structural Models
Norman Holland	(early) Stanley Fish	(later) Stanley Fish
David Bleich	Wolfgang Iser	Jonathan Culler
	Wayne Booth	Gerald Prince
		Seymour Chatman
		Hans Robert Jauss
		Judith Fetterley

Lurking within this taxonomy are at least three major theoretical questions: (1) Is reading primarily an individual or social experience? (2) Which dominates the reading experience, the text or the reader? (3) Is "the reader" an expert reader or an ordinary reader? The *psychological or subjective cluster* takes question 1 as paramount and answers resoundingly in favor of the individual. Their answer to question 2 is that the reader dominates, and their answer to question 3 is typically that "the reader" is an ordinary reader, indeed, often a beginning student. The *interactive or phenomenological cluster* takes question 2 as pivotal, for this cluster is concerned primarily to hold the reader and text together in a balanced and reciprocal relationship.[5] In answer to question 3, sometimes this cluster's reader is expert (Fish; Iser) and sometimes ordinary (Booth). Question 1 is of least concern to this cluster, but the assumption usually seems to be that reading is more of an individual than social activity. The *social or structural cluster,* like the psychological/subjective cluster, regards question 1 as pivotal but answers strongly in favor of the social location and conventions for reading. If question 2 is answered at all in this cluster, responses may vary widely, oddly enough, but since the social aspects of reading are assumed to predominate, question 2 may be ignored. Regarding question 3, some social/structural theorists (Fish; Culler; Jauss) seem to presuppose an expert reader, while others seem to favor an ordinary reader (Fetterley). We will begin our discussion of this taxonomy with crit-

[5] We shall observe later how reader-response criticism in biblical studies has gravitated toward the interactive/phenomenological cluster, resulting in a neglect of both the psychological/subjective and the social/structural perspectives.

ics who concern themselves primarily with the psychological or subjective reading experiences of individual readers.

Probably more than any other critic, Norman Holland has long pursued a psychological approach to the interpretation of the reading experience. Employing insights derived from ego psychology, Holland and his students first establish each person's *identity theme*. An identity theme is an "invariant," "unchanging essence," a "central, unifying pattern" that defines a person's "personality" or "character" (Holland, 1975b:121). Central to Holland's enterprise is his claim that an interpretation of a text is shaped by the identity theme of the reader: "all of us, as we read, use the literary work to symbolize and finally to replicate ourselves." In interpretation, "identity re-creates itself" (Holland, 1975b:124). Holland refines this re-creative process into four modalities, summarized by the acronym DEFT: defenses, expectations, fantasies, and transformation (Holland, 1975b:124–27; 1976b:342). We approach texts with expectations characteristic of our particular identity theme. We employ characteristic defense mechanisms to try to gratify desires and avoid anxiety. We project our fantasies upon the text. Finally, we transform our fantasizing into a meaningful whole. The result of reading is thus a unity, not found ready-made in the text but constructed in the mind of the reader in conformity with the reader's identity theme. Holland lays aside traditional critical concern for the unity of texts and replaces it with a psychological theory of the unity of the self: "*Identity* is the *unity* I find in a *self* if I look at it as though it were a *text*" (Holland, 1975b:121).

Holland has refined his theory over the years in a dialogue with David Bleich (Holland, 1976a; Bleich, 1976a; 1976b; Holland and Bleich). Bleich practices what he calls *subjective criticism* and is more interested in pedagogy than in psychological theory per se (Bleich, 1975b; 1978). The site of reading for him is typically the college classroom. In blatant violation of the Affective Fallacy, Bleich is more concerned with eliciting students' emotions and feelings than their abstract concepts; for him interpretation is grounded in personal, emotional response to reading: perceptions, affects, and associations. Bleich invites his students to articulate their subjective emotional response to reading in "response statements," which are then shared and discussed in the classroom, leading to a communal interpretation and shared knowledge. Bleich's personal and subjective approach to reading thus ends with a social result, but his *interpretive community* is one created in the process of negotiating a communal interpretation. Unlike Stanley Fish's interpretive community, Bleich's community does not exist prior to and therefore cannot control the interpretive process.[6]

Critiques of Holland's work often begin with the question, Why ego psychology? Why use this psychological theory instead of some other? From the perspective of other psychological theories, Holland's claim that identity themes are constant and unchangeable is arguable, to say the least. Seeking the unity of the self is just as problematic as seeking the unity of the text (see chap. 5 below). Holland merely shifts the locus of one of today's major problematics of interpretation from the text to the self.

Bleich's critics note that he goes about as far as one can in stressing the subjectivity of the individual's reading experience. What is hard to see, however, is if reading is so fundamentally personal and subjective, how is it even possible for readers to agree to relinquish their personal perspectives for the purpose of creating a communal interpretation (Mailloux, 1982:33)? How is it possible to escape solipsism?

To remedy the deficiencies in their theoretical constructs, both Holland (1992) and Bleich (1988) are expanding the scope of their theories to incorporate concerns more typical of the social or structural end of the reader-response critical spectrum. They speak now of intersubjectivity and no longer of simply subjectivity, they discuss how the norms and conventions for reading are constrained by communities, and they address ethical and political issues in reading, such as gender, race, and class.[7] It remains to be seen how successful these expansions will be. It is also unclear whether the theorists at the social end of the spectrum above will reciprocate by incorporating more insights from psychology into their predominantly social models.

When we move on to the interactive or phenomenological model, the predominant question becomes whether the text or the reader dominates the reading experience. While both psychological/subjective and social/structural reader-response critics tend to stress the preeminence of the reader over

---

[6] Also, Bleich does not pursue the temporal experience of reading as do Booth, (the early) Fish, and Iser (see further below).

[7] For example, see Bleich's (1988) discussion of the gender basis for epistemology in masculine versus feminine identity formations and thought styles. Bleich's critical praxis of aiding ordinary readers to negotiate their respective subjective experiences in a communal setting is similar to much feminist critical praxis; see "Critiquing the Critic as Reader" and "The Future of Reading," below and chap. 6.

the text, in interactive or phenomenological models a dialectical relationship between the text and reader is posited. At times it may even appear that the text dominates the reader, which in a supposedly reader-oriented critical theory requires some explanation.

In his early work, such as *Surprised by Sin* (1971) and *Self-Consuming Artifacts* (1972), Stanley Fish practiced "affective stylistics" (Fish, 1970), a painstaking analysis of the word-by-word experience of reading. Although Fish supposedly shifts the focus of critical attention to the reader and the reading experience, it is clear nevertheless that the text still dominates the reader. For example, in *Self-Consuming Artifacts* Fish discusses texts that he claims initiate readers into insights or understandings, only to withdraw or unravel them later. Such reading experiences are understood by Fish to be scripted in minute detail by the text, and the reader has little choice but to play along.

In his later work, collected in *Is There a Text in This Class?* (1980), Fish exposes the domineering text and the duped reader of his earlier work as a critical fiction, a useful rhetorical strategy for appealing to an audience of formalist critics that already assumes the dominance of texts over readers. In fact, Fish now confesses, texts never dictate to readers—readers always dictate to texts. Even the identification of what might seem the most objective, incontrovertible characteristics of a text is always already an interpretation by a reader. Texts are construed (as whatever they are deemed to be) always and only by readers in the act of reading.

This seems simply to replace a dominance of the text with a dominance of the reader, but Fish outflanks the text versus reader debate that typifies interactive/phenomenological models of reading by introducing his notion of the interpretive community. Readers are not free to read texts in a willful, unconstrained manner, he says, because critical readers are trained, licensed, and regulated by the communities in which they read.[8]

Thus, Fish's early interactive/phenomenological model of reading mutates into a social/structural model. Since the publication of *Is There a Text in This Class?* Fish has continued to explore the politics and rhetorics of interpretive communities (see esp. Fish, 1989; 1990). The theoretical resources undergirding these new developments are becoming more sharply defined as

[8] Note that for Fish, as for most of the reader critics represented in Mailloux's taxonomy, the reader tends to be a critical reader, an "informed reader," a member of a professional guild of critics. Such a reader is far from Holland's or Bleich's average, unlicensed reader.

Fish is increasingly associated with the resurgence of the neo-pragmatism of philosophers such as Richard Rorty.[9]

Wolfgang Iser is virtually unique as a central player in both American reader-response criticism and German reception theory. His major books (e.g., *The Implied Reader* and *The Act of Reading*) have appeared both in German and English. Iser is arguably the best-known and most influential theorist of reader-response criticism in the United States; he is by far the most influential figure in the appropriation of reader-response criticism by biblical critics. As with the other major theorists of reader-response criticism, we will only sketch the broad contours of Iser's theory here; later, however, we will offer a more extensive critique of Iser's work and its wide appropriation in biblical studies.

The major theoretical influence on Iser is the phenomenology of Roman Ingarden (Iser, 1978:98–99, 170–82; Holub, 1984:22–29, 83–96). Consequently, central in Iser's account of the reader's aesthetic encounter with the text is a phenomenological description of the reader's act of "concretizing" or "realizing" the text as a "literary work." Key here is his famous concept of the implied reader. Inspired by Wayne Booth's term, the *implied author*, which for Booth is a cluster of values, perceptions, and standards of judgments embedded in the text, Iser's implied reader is neither exactly in the text nor outside it. Iser's implied reader is a product of the encounter *between* the text and the reader, a realization of potentialities *in* the text but produced *by* a real reader: "The term [implied reader] incorporates both the prestructuring of the potential meaning by the text, and the reader's actualization of this potential through the reading process" (Iser, 1974:xii).

Iser's account of the phenomenology of the reading experience accentuates the temporal experience of reading. As the reader reads, he encounters in the text a "wandering viewpoint" that "travels along *inside*" the text object (Iser, 1978:108–9). The wandering viewpoint moves through the text, participating in a "dialectic of protension and retention" (1978:112) or "anticipation and retrospection" (1974:280)—the reader constantly anticipates what lies ahead in the reading experience and reviews and reevaluates what has passed: "We look forward, we look back, we decide, we change our decisions, we form expectations, we are shocked by their nonfulfillment, we question, we muse, we accept, we reject; this is the dynamic process of recreation" (1978:288).

---

[9] Cf. the similar pragmatic rhetorical turn of Steven Mailloux (1989; 1990).

Reading, for Iser, is the education of the reader. He uses a variety of images to describe the mutation of the reader's perceptions of the elements of the text in the course of reading: In the temporal flow of reading certain elements of the text come into the "foreground" of our purview, pushing other elements into the "background"; using Gestalt theory, Iser can speak of "figure and ground"; borrowing from Alfred Schütz, he can speak of "theme and horizon" (1978:92–103). "Thus every moment of reading is a dialectic of protension and retention, conveying a future horizon yet to be occupied, along with a past (and continually fading) horizon already filled; the wandering viewpoint carves its passage through both at the same time and leaves them to merge together in its wake" (1978:112). As the reading experience is enacted, and as horizons appear and disappear, the reader strives to create "coherence" out of the disparate, mutating, fleeting moments of reading. As the reader exchanges one gestalt for another, he must always be practicing "consistency building" (1978:122–30, 183–85). One of the chief challenges to the reader's psychological need to build consistency are the "blanks," "gaps," and "spots of indeterminacy" that every text possesses. Iser's extensive discussions of how the reader fills the text's *Leerstellen* (blanks or gaps) and concretizes the *Unbestimmtheitsstellen* (spots of indeterminacy) in the act of reading is a central, classic theoretical resource of reader-response criticism (1974:passim; 1978:passim), especially in biblical studies. But it is also flawed in certain key respects, as we shall see later.

The inclusion of Wayne Booth in a discussion of reader-response criticism needs some explanation, since Booth himself would not claim to be a reader-response critic. Nevertheless, Booth's brand of rhetorical criticism has strong affinities with other theories that emphasize the interplay of reader and text. It is therefore fitting that Tompkins includes Booth's influential *The Rhetoric of Fiction* in the bibliography of her anthology, and that Suleiman and Crosman consider Booth "an exemplary representative" (8) of their rhetorical category of audience-oriented criticism.

Booth has always been interested in readers and reading, his focus having been the rhetorical strategies woven into the text, presumably by the text's author. But Booth is too shrewd to claim that he can lay his hands on the flesh-and-blood author via the text. Rather, his inquiry is into the points of view, norms, and standards of judgment espoused by the implied author of a text. Iser's term, *implied reader,* was coined by analogy to Booth's notion of the implied author, but in fact both concepts are already present in Booth: "the author creates, in short, an image of himself and another image of his reader; he makes his reader, as he makes his second self, and the most successful reading is one in which the created selves, author and reader, can find complete agreement" (Booth, 1983:138).[10] As the title of his best-known work testifies, Booth is interested in the rhetoric of fiction: the ways an author "tries, consciously or unconsciously, to impose his fictional world upon the reader"; that is, "the author's means of controlling his reader" (Booth, 1983:xiii).[11]

Booth pursued these interests long before the current wave of critical engagement with questions of rhetoric and ethics. Booth's practice of a sophisticated version of rhetorical criticism is a critical precursor to the explosion of interest in rhetoric within literary theory as well as biblical studies (Tompkins, 1980:201–32; Eagleton, 1983:205–7; Mailloux, 1989; Fish, 1990; see further chap. 4.). Likewise, Booth's long pursuit of questions of ethics in relation to both texts and readers prefigures the now-regular appearance of titles on the ethics of reading and the ethics of interpretation (Miller, 1987a; Booth, 1988; Schüssler Fiorenza, 1988; Siebers). Long before recent debates on the recovery of pedagogy in research universities, Booth was well known as a committed teacher (Booth, 1988). It is with justification that Frank Kermode calls Booth the "rejected father" of much contemporary reader-oriented criticism (Kermode, 1975).

Furthermore, Booth's work has been widely influential in the narrative criticism of the Gospels and in biblical reader-response criticism. Booth's orthodox, traditional respect for texts, his adroit practice of close reading, and his steadfast conviction that somehow in reading there can be a meeting of the minds of the author and reader, all plays very well with biblical scholars. As a result, he is often embraced as an eminently safe and sane resource for the biblical scholar who would be a literary critic. In Gospel studies, Booth's *The Rhetoric of Fiction* has become a standard resource, and *A Rhetoric of Irony* has inspired studies of irony and rhetorics of indirection in the Gospels (Culpepper; Dawsey; Duke; Fowler, 1981; 1991; Staley; see the opening section above).

The third cluster in our taxonomy of reader-response theories is the social or structural cluster. Theorists in this cluster consider reading as a fundamentally communal enterprise; they hold that the reading experience is

[10] To be sure, there are important differences between Booth's and Iser's understandings of the implied reader; see the discussion of Iser above.

[11] Booth practices unabashedly a text-oriented version of reader criticism, and reader critics who are more reader-oriented than he will fault him for that. However, the truth may be that most reader critics continue to reify the text—some, like Booth, admit it, whereas many do not. For example, a prominent critique of Iser is that he remains text-oriented but does not admit it.

shaped primarily by socially defined conventions for reading. Perhaps the best known example of this position is Stanley Fish and his theory of interpretive communities (Fish, 1980), which was discussed briefly above. Fish first made a name for himself by operating within the interactive/phenomenological cluster (Fish, 1970; 1971; 1972). He has since tried to abandon that cluster and its pivotal text versus reader dilemma by moving over to the social/structural cluster. Fish now tries to sidestep the text versus reader debate by declaring repeatedly that both the text and the reader are always defined by the interpretive community in which the reader reads the text.

However, when he sings the new theme song of "It's All Social," Fish merely exchanges one set of problems for another. These days Fish sticks to sweeping theoretical pronouncements and does much less practical criticism than he did in the days of *Surprised by Sin* or *Self-Consuming Artifacts*. Fish can avoid the text versus reader debate in which he used to revel only as long as he talks about criticism without actually doing it. As Jonathan Culler shrewdly observes, to do reader-response criticism is to tell stories about reading, and such stories require the participation of both a reader and a text (Culler, 1982:74). Were he to resume practical criticism, Fish would almost certainly have to start talking again about the text or reader.

A far more serious critique takes aim at Fish's notion of the interpretive community. Many have charged that Fish's interpretive communities are static, homogeneous, hypothetical abstractions. They lack the concrete political and ethical complexities of actual communities of flesh-and-blood readers (Burnett, 1990b:62–63; Fowler, 1991:35–36; Leitch, 1988:219; Pratt, 1986:50–52).

Fish's interest in the social constraints upon reading is akin to Jonathan Culler's project of *structuralist poetics,* which has mutated into a poststructuralist, deconstructionist project (Culler, 1975b; 1981; 1982). Like a number of the representatives of the social/structural cluster, Culler is more interested in critical theory than in the interpretation of individual texts per se. Culler asks, What constitutes "literary competence" (1975b:113–30), the knowledge of the "procedures and conventions of reading" (1981:125) that makes possible the reader's understanding of a text? Culler is interested in the socially defined codes and conventions, shared by texts and readers, that define the conditions of the (un)readability or the (un)intelligibility of texts.[12]

[12] The "convention" business is booming in reader-response criticism; on the conventions of narrative and interpretation, see especially Mailloux (1982) and Peter Rabinowitz (1987).

Besides contributing structuralist and poststructuralist discussions of reading conventions, another major contribution of structuralism to reader-response criticism derives from structuralist narratology. We have already alluded to the crucial notion of the implied reader (Iser; Booth). Add to that the *narratee*, a term coined by Gerald Prince (1971; 1980), and we are well on our way to the communication model of the text that has become indispensable in the narrative criticism of the Gospels and biblical reader-response criticism.[13] Seymour Chatman's *Story and Discourse* has achieved almost canonical status as the predominant source through which the communication model and narratological theory generally have been introduced into Gospel criticism.[14]

Another social/structural model of reader-response criticism is exemplified by Wolfgang Iser's colleague at the University of Constance, Hans Robert Jauss. Jauss's theoretical impulse derives from European traditions of phenomenology and hermeneutics, and his chief concern is *Rezeptionsgeschichte* and *Rezeptionsästhetik*—the history and aesthetics of a text's reception by its various historical audiences (Jauss, 1982a; 1982c). In an important programmatic lecture delivered in 1967, Jauss urged the reformulation of traditional literary history as the history and aesthetics of the reception of literary texts (Jauss, 1970). Jauss's reception history explores the sociohistorical context of the reception of literary genres and texts. What are the cultural, ethical, literary expectations of readers in a particular historical moment? What is the *Erwartungshorizont*—"horizon of expectation"—for a generation of readers?[15] Jauss's aesthetics of reception examines how different texts fit or do not fit within the expectations of the historical moment. This allows evaluation of the text by gauging its "aesthetic distance" from

[13] To date most biblical reader-response criticism can be characterized as the search for the implied reader or narratee of biblical texts. The blindspot of this endeavor is the neglect of the flesh-and-blood reader who claims to be able to find the implied reader or narratee suspended in the amber of the text. Most biblical reader-response criticism remains resolutely formalist—what counts is supposed to be already there in the text—and neither the psychological/subjective nor the social/structural dimensions of the reader-response critic's own agenda is given consideration. That is, much literary criticism of the Bible is comfortable with formalist-structuralist criticism but has yet to face up to the challenges posed by poststructuralism and the broad postmodern debate.

[14] Another major narratological resource for biblical scholars is Genette; less often invoked are Eco and Riffaterre.

[15] Implied here are crucial notions derived from the hermeneutical tradition, such as "prejudice" and "fore-understanding" (Gadamer).

the prevailing *Erwartungshorizont*. The more the literary work pushes and strains against the prevailing horizon of expectation, the more artistic it may be judged. Inferior literary works merely presume and confirm the horizon, without challenging it, and are consequently all too easily assimilated by their readers. Frequently works that challenge their contemporary horizon are only appreciated generations later.

A common critique of Jauss's program of reception studies is that it is easier to describe in the abstract than to carry out in the concrete. For example, Susan Suleiman charges that his horizons are too homogeneous—sociohistorical contexts for reading are far more diverse and conflicting than Jauss lets on (Suleiman and Crosman, 37). Also, Jauss and his colleagues at Constance have been criticized by colleagues in the former German Democratic Republic, who have charged that the notion of reception theory prevailing at the Constance School is too privatistic, bourgeois, and apolitical (Holub, 1984:121–34).

In spite of these critiques, nevertheless, Jauss's program of reception studies has pointed in a direction that many seem eager to travel. Without his grand theoretical sweep (and often with only passing acknowledgment of Jauss), one of the major recent developments in the social/structural cluster of reader-response criticism is a decisive move toward the writing of histories of the reception of specific texts in specific sociohistorical settings (Machor). Note Steven Mailloux's reception histories of *Red Badge of Courage* (1982:160–65,178–91), *Moby Dick* (1982:170–78), and *Huckleberry Finn* (1988:100–29); Jane Tompkins's work on the reception of *Uncle Tom's Cabin* (1985:122–46); Janice Radway's study of the readers of contemporary romance novels. While Jauss's challenge to reformulate literary history as reception history is being heeded (whether Jauss himself has been the inspiration is another matter), biblical studies has not yet begun to attend seriously to the reception history of biblical texts.[16] As long as biblical reader-response critics concentrate on the implied reader and narratee *in* the biblical texts, they will continue to neglect the reception *of* biblical texts by flesh-and-blood readers.

The last social/structural model we will examine is the feminist reader-response criticism of Judith Fetterley, as exemplified by Fetterley's influential

---

[16] One exception is Robert Fowler (1991:228–60). If the cherished history of exegesis in biblical studies were ever to become self-conscious, self-reflexive, and self-critical praxis, it could be transformed into a rich and exciting history of reception.

book *The Resisting Reader*. Fetterley's central thesis is that the canon of American fiction is relentlessly androcentric and misogynist, as is the educational establishment in which the canon is taught. Women and men alike are indoctrinated "to identify as male" (1978:xii) as they read and interpret literature, a process that she labels *immasculation* (xx). An insidious result is that even women are led to internalize misogyny and to identify against themselves.

Consequently, Fetterley urges her students not to give automatic, unthinking assent to the classic works of American fiction, or to its masculine-identified defenders, but instead to become "resisting readers" (xxii), self-consciously reading against the grain of the literature and the literary establishment. "The first act of the feminist critic must be to become a resisting rather than assenting reader and, by this refusal to assent, to begin the process of exorcising the male mind that has been implanted in us. The consequence of this exorcism is the capacity for what Adrienne Rich describes as re-vision—the act of looking back, of seeing with fresh eyes, of entering an old text from a new critical direction" (xxii). Fetterley offers her work "as a self-defense survival manual for the woman reader lost in the masculine wilderness of the American novel" (viii).

Several points are worth noting regarding Fetterley's model of reader-response criticism. One is that, unlike the vague, abstract interpretive communities of some of the other representatives of the social/structural cluster, Fetterley's interpretive community consists of flesh-and-blood, politically engaged, feminist readers. In fact, reader-response criticism has commonly revealed its sharpest political, ethical, and ideological edge when wielded by feminist critics (Kennard, 1981a; 1981b; Kolodny; Flynn, 1983; 1986; 1991; Schweickart, 1985; 1986; Flynn and Schweickart).

Related to this point is a second, namely, that like many feminist critics, Fetterley is deeply concerned with issues of pedagogy and of the empowerment of real readers. In this regard Fetterley has much in common with Holland, Bleich, and others of the psychological/subjective cluster, whereas most of the theorists of the interactive/phenomenological and the social/structural clusters seem to assume that the reader is a hypothetical expert reader.[17]

---

[17] This is a reminder that, although this taxonomy accentuates the differences between theorists, common concerns and points of agreement cut across the different clusters. For example, recall that Holland and Bleich are currently incorporating social/structural features into

Third, oddly enough, in this concretely social and explicitly political version of reader-response criticism, the interaction of reader and text that is characteristic of the phenomenological/interactive cluster returns to center stage. To argue that the canon of American fiction is at its core androcentric and misogynist presumes there is a determinant core already there in these texts. To read against the grain of these texts is to operate on the assumption that there is a grain against which to read. It is not simply that women should repudiate the social conventions of androcentrism and misogyny perpetuated by generations of masculine-identified critics. Fetterley takes pains to demonstrate that androcentrism and misogyny are in the texts themselves. Paradoxically, Fetterley's comparatively radical social/structural version of reader-response criticism depends upon a comparatively conservative belief in a stable and determinant text. To be sure, in Culler's language Fetterley is telling a story of reading, and in order for her feminist practice of reading to be strong, she needs a strong misogynist text to resist. In short, her theory of the text is a rhetorical strategy necessitated by the kind of story of reading she wishes to tell and the political project she intends to promote. Is it ever otherwise for anyone?

CRITIQUING THE CRITIC AS READER

For some in other academic disciplines reader-response criticism is (wrongly perhaps) considered passé (Holland, 1992; Freund, 10); for many in biblical studies, however, it is still regarded as cutting edge. Among the latter, some see reader-response criticism, along with literary criticism generally, as a potential threat to the traditional historical-critical methods (e.g., Scot McKnight, 121–37; Hagner, 85), while others see it as one of the most promising of the new developments (e.g., Keegan, 73, 90, 153; cf. Morgan and Barton, 258–59; Vander Weele, 145–46).

Most of the application of reader-response criticism to the Bible being carried out in North America by New Testament scholars focuses upon the canonical Gospels. Their work has tended to cluster in the experimental jour-

---

their psychological/subjective theories. However, none of the exemplars of the social/structural cluster we have examined has displayed any inclination to reciprocate, but one can find social/structural theorists who have done this; see, for example, the feminist, psychoanalytic reader-response criticism of Temma Berg.

nal *Semeia* (31 [1985]; 48 [1989]).[18] Other than dissertations (Cassel; Darr, 1987; Fowler, 1981; Howell; Moore, 1986; Staley), few monographs have appeared that attempt to apply reader-response criticism single-mindedly to biblical narratives (Fowler, 1991, is the most ambitious example to date, followed, perhaps, by Darr, 1992). Other monographs have enlisted the concept of "the reader," but it has been used as part of an eclectic methodology called *narrative criticism* (e.g., Culpepper; Edwards; Keegan; Kingsbury, 1988a; Rhoads and Michie; Sternberg, 1985; Tannehill, 1986; 1990).[19]

The works of reader-response criticism that biblical scholars have produced surely must appear strange to secular literary critics because of the predominance of historical concerns. As Stanley E. Porter rightly points out: "Reader-response criticism privileges the present reader, not the past. If the historical question as traditionally posed in Biblical studies is not bracketed, if only temporarily, reader-response criticism will never have a genuine opportunity to contribute to New Testament studies, but will be reader-response criticism virtually in name only" (285). The most important point to be made about reader-response criticism in biblical studies, then, is that it has so far stayed within the theoretical boundaries of a philologically oriented historical criticism.

Since reader-response criticism was an offshoot of the union between redaction criticism and narrative criticism (see chap. 2), it is not surprising that it has remained a complement of historical criticism. North American biblical scholars, in particular, have developed their own brand of reader-response criticism, so that one can rightly speak of a "peculiarly American style of New Testament scholarship" in this respect (Moore, 1989b:xv). Unquestionably, Wolfgang Iser's reader-response theory has been appropriated in such scholarship more than anyone else's. In what follows we will be concerned particularly with those elements in Iser's theory that have been amenable to appropriation by historical critics. We will show how the appropriation of Iser's theory has left unaltered the fundamental concepts of historical criticism, especially the notion of a stable text with determinate meanings. Our overriding concern for the remainder of this chapter, however, will be the appropriation of reader-response criticism that has taken

---

[18] *Semeia* 48 was the product of an ongoing seminar of the Studiorum Novi Testamenti Societas, "The Role of the Reader in the Interpretation of the New Testament."

[19] For more on narrative criticism, see chap. 2 below.

place in biblical studies without a corresponding ideological self-reflection. It will be argued that the unreflective grafting of readerly terminology onto historical-critical scholarship has produced an ideological mutation that is blind to both the oppressive and liberating power of its critical discourses (cf. Eagleton, 1983:194–217). We will suggest how reader-response theories can be utilized more fully as opposed to being truncated by the ideology of historical criticism. We will contend that as biblical reader-response critics become more self-reflective, their work will be enhanced by many other reading strategies already at work within biblical studies, such as poststructuralist, deconstructionist, feminist, womanist, and liberationist strategies.

A first tenet that biblical reader-response critics share with historical-critics is that the text is an object, a "thing-in-itself," which controls the reading process. Richard Edwards typifies most biblical reader-response critics in this respect: "when I speak about the reader I am not attempting to describe a real person (of the first, third, tenth, or twentieth century) but the person posited *by the text* as the reader" (10). Many biblical critics who employ formalist models of reading have found Iser's view of the text attractive at some point in their work (even if some of them later abandoned it) because it supports their view of the text as an object.[20]

For Iser the text exists with a certain potentiality of meaning before any interpretive activity begins. In one sense Iser's implied reader *is* the meaning potential that preexists its actualization by real readers as they fill in the textual gaps and blanks (1974:32). As Iser puts it, the implied reader "embodies all those predispositions necessary for a literary work to exercise its effect—*predispositions laid down, not by an empirical outside reality, but by the text itself. Consequently, the implied reader as a concept has his roots firmly planted in the structure of the text;* he is a construct and in no way to be identified with any real reader" (1978:34, emphasis ours). In this sense Iser clearly gives an objective status to the text, which is appealing to any formalist model of reading (cf. Mailloux, 1982:56; Poland, chaps. 1–3). Iser's view "of the text as stable but schematic is one of the more innovative and attractive aspects of his theory" for biblical critics (Darr, 1992:20).

Iser, however, does not focus all of his attention upon the textual object.

---

[20] See, e.g., Janice Capel Anderson, 1985a:71–72; Burnett, 1985:92; Darr, 1992:20; Heil, 1991; 1992:272; Keegan, 96; Lategan, 70; Petersen, 1984:40–43; Powell, 1990a:18, cf. 16; Rhoads and Michie, 1; Staley; Tannehill, 1986:3–4; Lategan and Vorster, 95–112.

One of the strongest reasons for Iser's appeal to North American scholars has been his determination to hold in tension the twin poles of the textual object and the real reader's subjectivity, so that one is not effaced by the other. In a pungent critique, Stanley Fish accuses Iser of equivocation in the interminable subject-object debate about whether the reader or the text controls the production of meaning. Fish contends that Iser wants to have it both ways: he wants an autonomous text with meaning potential, but he also wants an equally autonomous reader who is led by textual clues to a proper realization of that text's potential meaning. As we have seen, however, Fish shows that there is neither an autonomous text nor an autonomous reader in the way that Iser (and biblical critics) would like to believe. Meaning is made possible only through the communal reading strategies that are used to actualize a text; as such, meaning precedes both text and reader (1981:3).

In his reply to Fish, Iser tries to distinguish between the text-as-object and the text-as-interpretation: *"the 'something' which is to be mediated exists prior to interpretation, acts as a constraint on interpretation,* has repercussions on the anticipations operative in interpretation, and thus contributes to a hermeneutical process, the result of which is both a mediated given and a reshuffling of the initial assumptions. Professor Fish, however, creates a new hermeneutics by fusing interpretation and that which is to be interpreted into an indistinguishable whole, thus replacing the given by interpretation itself" (1981:84, emphasis ours; cf. 83).

In defending his theory, Iser gives an objective status to the text. Iser also attributes an authority to the text by contending that patterns in the textual object control the subjectivity of the reader's interpretation (1978:9). Iser's emphasis upon the power of the objective text has a strong appeal to biblical reader-response critics who believe that the text controls the latitude of the real reader's responses, even as it simultaneously reveals its implied (original) reader(s).

Although biblical critics have never practiced historical criticism in a monolithic way, its prescriptive goal always has been to discover "the objective meaning of the text" (Kaiser and Kümmel, 49; cf. Hoy, 42). Whether the critic takes the position that there is only one determinate meaning or an acceptable range of meanings for the text, undergirding both views is "the epistemological conviction that the text has a determinate meaning, that the text is a transparent window to an extra-textual referent, and that the referent can be discussed with some degree of accuracy" (Burnett, 1990b:53). A meaning, or an acceptable range of meanings, is then determined by a consensus among the various congregations of historical-critical readers (Funk, 1976:7).

From the perspective of most historical critics, then, virtually every form of reader-response criticism should pose a radical challenge since its emphasis upon meaning as an "event" undermines or is counter to the prescriptive goal of historical criticism. Reader-response criticism directly "challenges the critical assumption that a disinterested reader can approach a text objectively and obtain verifiable knowledge by applying certain scientific strategies" (E. McKnight, 1988:15; cf. Keegan, 76–81, 162). Some forms of reader-response criticism go so far as to undercut altogether the sociohistorical referent of the text for which historians are searching (e.g., Bleich, 1978:10–37; Holland, 1973:2–3, 84–85; 1968:xv–xvii; cf. Vander Weele, 132–35, 142). Since the reader and the text are interdependent for reader-response critics, the text as a privileged autonomous object is displaced in favor of the reader's experience (Fowler, 1991:25; Freund, 2; Leitch, 1988:214–15). Meaning is not in the past (when the text was produced) or in the text as an object, but meaning is produced in the reader's present when the text is read (Murfin, 142). For reader-response critics meaning is not a content in the text which the historian simply discovers; meaning is an experience which occurs during the reading process.

Biblical critics, however, have traditionally engaged in a kind of close reading that has presupposed the efficacy of the biblical text to guide them to historically verifiable knowledge (cf. Kelber, 1983:32–34). Blinded by this presupposition, biblical reader-response critics continue to believe that *somehow* there must be a connection between the reader-in-the-text, the original audience, and the biblical critic (Keegan, 112–13; Darr, 1992:26; cf. Moore, 1989b:76–77). The historical concern for the original audience of a biblical text has driven biblical narrative critics to attempt to recreate the original reading experiences of the earliest Christians or Jews, and their endeavors have influenced biblical reader-response critics. Mark Powell, for example, avows that "the goal of narrative criticism is to read the text as the implied reader" (1990a:20; cf. Beavis, 1987; 1989). He tries to clarify what he means by changing "implied reader" to "ideal reader" in another study: "The goal of narrative criticism is to interpret every text the way that its ideal reader would interpret it" (1990b:72). By *ideal reader* Powell means that reader who "*is described and defined entirely by the text*, while an implied reader (in the sense that secular literary critics use the term) is defined through the dialectical tension of a real reader's encounter with the text" (76 n.33, emphasis ours). The notion of the implied (original) reader, though, may become so generalized that biblical critics can claim that what is really at issue in the term are the historical competencies, or the general "cultural literacy," which an author assumed for his or her audience (Darr, 1992:26, 176 n.9).

What is not so clearly evident in the historical quest for the implied (original) reader, however, is the theological agenda that is usually operating in biblical narrative criticism. For example, since the implied (original) reader of the biblical text was a "believer," one could say that in order to assume the role of that reader one "must regard himself or herself as a member of the believing community," which the document presupposes (Keegan, 129; cf. Kelber, 1979:92–96; Powell, 1990a:88–89; Rhoads and Michie, 2). In other words, reader-response criticism can have a positive exegetical and hermeneutical role if it "sees the believing community as the proper reader of the Bible" (Keegan, 146). It is only a short hermeneutical step from this to say that reader-response criticism "offers scholars a means of restoring the ancient relationship between Bible and Church, of viewing the Bible as the Church's book" (146). Once this claim is made, then it can be said candidly that "one who does not participate in the faith community that is presupposed of the implied reader of a given text simply cannot read that text" (147; cf. 98).

The reason that a nonbeliever cannot read and understand the biblical text is that "in the case of inspired literature what a real author creates is influenced by the Holy Spirit. The implied author that one discerns in a biblical book is, therefore, the inspired author. In a similar way the implied reader of a biblical book is the inspired reader" (155). That is to say, the value systems and the concerns of the Church "are defined by the text as the necessary precondition for reading the text. *These pre-conditions are in the text* because they are put there by the implied author (inspired author) *and are required of the implied reader* (the Church, the inspired reader)" (155, emphasis ours). In this example historical and theological concerns merge to produce a normative reader-response criticism which leads to a correct (and infallible?) knowledge if the reader follows the textual indicators.

Biblical narrative criticism, then, implicitly carries a theological agenda that has been inherited from historical criticism. As Robert Funk so eloquently put it: "so-called scientific biblical scholarship, by and large, took up arms against traditionalism in the castle of Sacred Scripture and ended by occupying the castle itself, *while denying that it had done so*. These anomalies make the Society of Biblical Literature a fraternity of scientifically trained scholars with the soul of a church" (1976:7, emphasis ours). The biblical reader-response criticism being created in the laboratories of the Society of Biblical Literature is an ideological mutant of historical criticism and biblical narrative criticism. Although to most biblical critics it appears to be a normal scion, it would astound the villagers if it ever stumbled down the mountain to fraternize with secular reader-response critics (cf. Funk, 1976:7).

Any concerns, then, about a radical reader-response criticism invading biblical studies are entirely overblown (cf. Powell, 1990a:20; Darr, 1992:13, 173 n.4). At this time, the reader in biblical reader-response criticism is clearly an emotionally retarded one that has been created according to the indispensable formula of historical criticism, namely, "dispassionate objectivity and psychological distance" (Moore, 1989b:97; cf. Mailloux, 1982:39). Since any knowledge that is produced by biblical reader-response critics must be empirically verified and adjudicated by the guild, biblical reader-response criticism will be confined to the laboratory for some time to come (Tuckett, 180; cf. Robert Fowler, 1985:5–6). The guild, which consists of several constituencies acting more or less in concert with one another (churches, synagogues, colleges, universities, theological schools, and professional societies), finally acts as the master reader who regulates the proliferation of aberrant readings (cf. Burnett, 1990b:66–72). The ideological barricades that historical critics have placed around the biblical texts are firmly in place for biblical reader-response critics, and the villagers who have not vowed allegiance to traditional historical-critical values will not be able to storm the castle's laboratory in the foreseeable future.

A further tenet of biblical reader-response critics that dovetails with Iser's theory involves their view of "meaning." Their goal of understanding the implied (original) reader of the biblical text, or of somehow uniting with it, is almost identical with Iser's view of meaning. "Meaning" has two inter-related aspects for Iser, and both of them appeal strongly to biblical critics. The two aspects are meaning as reference and meaning as event. Iser summarizes his view of meaning this way: "Meaning is the referential totality which is implied by the aspects contained in the text and which must be assembled in the course of reading. Significance is the reader's absorption of the meaning into his own existence. Only the two together can guarantee the effectiveness of an experience which entails the reader constituting himself by constituting a reality hitherto unfamiliar to himself" (1978:151; cf.

Petersen, 1984:42). Meaning occurs, then, when real readers actualize the roles proffered by the text-as-object *and* experience a new subjectivity (Iser, 1989:26–27).

Iser's notion of meaning as reference enables the biblical reader-response critic to assemble aspects of the textual object as he or she has been trained to do by the guild of professional readers. Thus the referential part of the critic's reading experience tends to replicate what other historical critics have already assembled. Biblical reader-response critics who are still operating within the meaning-as-reference framework of historical criticism believe that their readings correspond to a real sociohistorical referent. In spite of their belief, biblical reader-response discourse is self-referential. It is discourse about historical discourse, not about some alleged object in the world, such as the Matthean community, especially since "the Matthean community" is a linguistic and imaginative construct of historical critics (Burnett, 1990:64; Culler, 1982:130; Derrida, 1976:102–3; Phillips, 1985:111–16; Wuellner, 1989c:43–44). Biblical reader-response critics, then, tend to replicate the results of historical critics. Moore puts it as follows:

> Like the conventional exegete (the redaction critic, for example), the reader-oriented exegete feels an understandable need to excise incoherent, trivial, oversubjective, or otherwise inappropriate elements from his or her responses so as to assume a readerly alter ego that meets the profession's standards of accreditation. On this view, the readings that reader-oriented Gospel critics produce are not qualitatively different from those of other critics. Indeed, one of their valuable features . . . is precisely that of making the implicit features of our critical reading explicit by narrativizing our standard moves and reflecting them back to us as in a mirror. (1989b:106)

This mirroring of historical-critical results—and the consequent inability to be self-reflexive about their own discourse—explains why biblical reader-response critics can be accused (as Moore's statement implies) of being simply camouflaged redaction critics (cf. Scot McKnight, 137). The strong appeal of Iser's approach to biblical critics, then, is that the assured results of historical criticism appear to have been validated by yet another methodology.

Iser's second connotation of meaning-as-significance appeals to biblical critics, because for them, as for Iser, reading leads to the reader's personal transformation. The reader becomes "a reality hitherto unfamiliar to himself" because the expectations that he or she formulates during the reading process are undercut (1978:151). The reader is then caught in a dilemma, usually a moral one, so that he or she has to envisage a solution. The text educates the reader by forcing the reader to undergo a process of self-evaluation and self-criticism so that the upshot of the reading process is a new self-understanding (1974:36–47). This transformation of the reader's self is the "event" character of meaning for Iser. The reader's new subjectivity, however, occurs within the framework of the referential connections which were made by overcoming the indeterminacies involved in reading the textual object. The framework for the reader's transformation, then, is the reading protocol of the professional guild that guides how referential connections should be made in order to surmount the difficulties (e.g., the indeterminacies) that are posed by the text. Since Iser contends that professional reading strategies guide the referential connections a critic makes, he can make the professional critic's engagement with the textual object the authority for judging any particular reading. In this way aberrant reading experiences can be tightly controlled by professional critics (cf. Leitch, 1988:235). One cannot understand a text and experience a personal transformation until one becomes "a slave of the text" and shares an ideology about *how* to read it (Keegan, 97). The appeal of these constraints to biblical critics is that a transformation of readers is allowed, but the boundaries for that experience are already well marked by historical or theological agendas (cf. Darr, 1992:32, 179 n.5; Powell, 1990a:90–91).

The engagement of the biblical reader-response critic with the text, then, occurs on more than just the cognitive level; it operates on an affective level as well. More than just cognitive knowledge about the past is gained from reading biblical texts. Biblical reader-response critics who share Iser's view of the real reader's personal transformation emphasize the new subjectivity that the reader stands to gain. Operating within a referential set of unacknowledged theological and historical reading strategies, the reader-critic experiences the fullness of the hope of the resurrection by playing the narrative role of the first Christians themselves. Moore observes: "In the stories of reading . . . told by reader-oriented gospel critics, the reader emerges as the hero or heroine whose actions and progress are central. Jesus generally plays the supporting role, as the one whose enigmatic words and deeds provide the complicating factors that fuel the plot of the story of reading" (1989b:83). The personal transformation is achieved as the reader-critic overcomes the text's inconsistencies, gaps, indeterminacies, and arrives, through a process of consistency-building, at a coherent meaning. The critic's success at negotiating the obstacles posed by the text, however, is possible only because he or she willingly becomes a slave to the guiding power of the textual object and to historical-critical principles for interpreting it.

It is not difficult, then, to fathom why Iser's views about the text and the reader's transformation have appealed to biblical critics. For many biblical scholars, reading has long been understood as an event in which the language of the text leads to a new self-understanding. In theological terms, Iser's model of the reader's transformation has enticed biblical scholars to retrieve the disregarded principles of the New Hermeneutic. The latter's emphasis upon the transformation of the reader's self-understanding has been recovered in such a way that it almost goes unnoticed in its new literary-critical disguise. Gerhard Ebeling and Ernst Fuchs in particular were concerned about language's effect upon the reader and the reader's response of faith. In general for both Ebeling and Fuchs the language of the text calls forth "faith," or a new understanding of existence, by acting upon the reader. In their view, language, through the textual medium, is given priority over the reader's existential response since it is language that "makes being into an event," that is, language enables the "word of God" to "speak" (Fuchs, 207; cf. Ebeling, 305–22). "With this startling insight," as Robert Funk says, "the direction of the flow between interpreter and text that has dominated modern biblical criticism from its inception is reversed, and hermeneutics in its traditional sense becomes hermeneutic, now understood as the effort to allow God to address man through the medium of the text" (1966:11).

By emphasizing submission to the transcendent and transforming Word, the New Hermeneutic allowed the reader only a submissive role in the reading process. In this regard it is not altogether amenable to biblical reader-response criticism. The New Hermeneutic also emphasized, however, both the transforming power of the text's language and the reader as the sole authority who could attest to the truth of his or her transformation. These two concerns have persisted in biblical reader-response criticism. The new hermeneuts' goal of experiencing a new understanding of existence called forth by the text is homologous to the goal of biblical reader-response critics who seek personal transformation by recreating the implied (original) reader's experience. Iser's theory is ideally suited to allow biblical critics to retrieve the New Hermeneutic's principle of submission to the biblical text's authority as a means to the reader's personal transformation.

However, for Iser and for biblical critics alike, to emphasize the reader's personal transformation does not imply a solipsistic view of reading in which anything goes. As we have seen, the referential aspect of meaning partly controls the process by referring any individual's reading to the proper range of responses as determined by the scholarly guild (Darr, 1992:36). Thus the individual reader is free to have a transforming experience, but only within acceptable limits. Iser's view of the interaction between the text and the reader enforces a limited pluralism. A final reason for Iser's appeal to biblical critics, therefore, is that his theory allows for the traditional pluralism of historical criticism to continue.

Generally speaking, historical criticism in biblical studies shares the tenets of democratic pluralism held by other first world academicians. On the one hand, democratic pluralists hold that a text has a determinate core of meaning, but they oppose the idea that it can have only one correct meaning (e.g., Alter, 1989:213; Wayne C. Booth, 1977:407–9; 1979:1–36). If it is true that the text has a determinate range of meanings without mandating only one correct meaning, then it follows that all readers stand in an egalitarian relation to the text and to its potential to effect their transformation. It means, in short, that there is an unchanging textual object upon which readers simply have different perspectives because of their different reading models (Alter, 1989:216; cf. Darr, 1992:20). On the other hand, traditional pluralists also emphasize that there must be limits to readers' perspectives. Although there is no way to predict how individual readers actually will handle the many elements of the text, there certainly cannot be as many *correct* readings as there are individual readers. To imply the latter would mean that the textual object is not stable enough to exercise control over readers *and* provide adjudicators with the necessary criteria to decide whether any particular reading has conformed to the information in the text itself (Alter, 1989:215, 220–21, 227–28; Darr, 1992:20).

For traditional pluralists, then, the appropriate range of readings and what counts as a transforming experience are decided by commonly accepted reading strategies. Egalitarian pluralists believe that the readings that are selected as better than others within professional societies are done so solely on the basis of their scholarly merits. By scholarly merits they mean that these readings have dealt better than other readings have with the facts of the text itself, have successfully overcome textual obstacles, and have succeeded in disclosing the text's internal consistency and coherence (Alter, 1989:221).

The tenets of democratic pluralism are also accepted within the academic field of historiography, so that the assured results of historians constitute the criteria for adjudicating the acceptable range of interpretations. The concept of history itself is usually not questioned as much as the reading strategies that historians think will bring them ever closer to knowing what really happened. Their focus upon refining reading methods, however, has been "purchased at the cost of ignoring or repressing their knowledge of contemporary historical theory and practice" (Hayden White, 1986:484). What they have felt obliged to ignore or repress is the unsettling possibility that "the historical milieux," which really "exist" for historians, are themselves products of their own "fictive capability" (White, 1978:89; cf. Schüssler Fiorenza, 1988:13–14).

As good democratic pluralists, biblical historians also will not say that their historical proofs and evidence are already inscribed within their reading strategies. Nor have they been willing to admit—even with all of their talk about the "hermeneutical circle"—that the only way one could know if one has arrived at what really happened is by reference to one's own reading strategies, strategies that had defined the relevant data and predetermined how they should be interpreted in the first place (Burnett, 1990b:57–58; cf. Darr, 1992:27, 177 n.15). Like other historians, biblical critics have traditionally tried to elevate explanation over interpretation. Biblical critics explain what happened, and their explanations are then passed off as objective. Interpretation is then seen as trying "to fill in the textual gaps" in order to produce a coherent work, but the essential story ("the text") is objective and stays the same for all historians (Hayden White, 1978:51–55; cf. Darr, 1992:17–23).

Iser's theory has helped biblical reader-response critics keep their positivistic and pluralistic reading strategies in place, and it has not undermined traditional pluralism for several reasons (Fish, 1981:3–4). First, Iser's brand of reader-response criticism puts critics themselves in the position of adjudicating the acceptable range of readings without forcing them to admit that their readings only have referential and epistemological value in relation to the reading practices of their guild. Second, and most important, Iser's theory leaves the traditional canon intact *as well as the way that it has been traditionally understood* by the consensus of the guild (cf. Peter Rabinowitz, 1987:231). Not only are the readings of nonspecialists excluded, but the voices of dissenting scholars within the guild remain marginalized until they gravitate toward the discursive center by adopting both the generally accepted reading strategies and conclusions. Only then will they be given a serious hearing. The critiques of accepted readings by both nonspecialists and marginalized specialists, therefore, are excluded a priori by the preexisting historical-critical consensus. That same consensus is now being validated anew by biblical reader-response critics. Because of the homogenizing tendencies within its ideology of egalitarian pluralism, Iser's form of reader-response criticism as it has been used in biblical scholarship certainly presents no danger of "decentering" the prevailing discursive practices (cf. Schüssler Fiorenza, 1988:10–11). Iser's view of reading not only supports an egalitarian ideology of reading but, as we will show below, it masks the role played by power and politics in the adjudication of readings (see Bal, 1987:12–15; Burnett, 1990b:58–72; Hassan, 1986; Rooney).

The curious thing is that some reader-response critics do call the basic tenets of liberal pluralism into question (Leitch, 1988:235). Both Bleich and Holland, for example, have opened the door to the possibilities that each reading has its own idiosyncratic validity, and that such readings are arbitrary since they cannot be predicted with any degree of probability. Iser himself has some poststructuralist "seeds" within his theory for a forceful critique of pluralism (1989:215–35), but neither he nor biblical critics have allowed them to grow. For example, Iser recognizes that "any meaning, any interpretation, *automatically carries with it the seeds of its own invalidity,* for it must exclude everything that runs counter to it" (1989:150; cf. 175, emphasis ours). He also acknowledges that meanings that any readers produce—even historians—are "nothing but a substitute for reality" (179; cf. 175, 187, 219). Iser does not necessarily mean, of course, that nothing happened in the past; he only means that one's access to what happened is through language and through narrative constructs written by historians themselves.[21] The crux of Iser's point for biblical critics is that *writing about historical events is like writing a fictional account.* Iser himself makes this point: "Thus in philosophical discourse—particularly that of the empiricists—at one moment fiction is being unmasked as an invention, and the next it is being elevated to the status of a necessity. Small wonder that it turned into a burden for epistemology, which could not come to grips with the dual nature of the fact that make-believe is indispensable for organizing that which appears to be given. . . . What distinguishes fiction in philosophical discourse from fiction in literary discourse is the fact that in the former it remains veiled whereas in the latter it discloses its own fictional nature" (1989:240–41). The implication of Iser's statement for biblical critics is

---

[21] Cf. Beardslee, 1989:185; Burnett, 1990b:64; Kozicki and Canary; Cook; Danto; Edelson; Margolis; Spence; Wallace; Hayden White, 1973, 1978; Young, 1981:1–11.

surely that they cannot know the past on its own terms but only through their narrative constructs (cf. Joan W. Scott, 1988; 1992b).

If one were to take Iser seriously on this point, then even the referent of the term *history* would be recognized to be indeterminate. That recognition, in turn, could lead to many different ways of doing historiography (cf. Hayden White, 1986:482). The crux of the epistemological question, then, which is raised by the poststructuralist elements within Iser's own theory is: what can biblical historians claim that they know or understand? As long as biblical reader-response critics continue a partial appropriation of Iser's theory as a complement to the ideology of historical criticism, the predetermined answer to this question will be: "we know the historical situation and experience of the (original) implied readers of biblical texts." This answer is unsatisfying because it shows a lack of critical self-reflection and, as we will suggest in the next section, it evades the crucial questions of power and the politics of interpretation which are at work in any critical discourse.

THE FUTURE OF READING

In this section we will first discuss the implications of poststructuralist and postmodern literary theory for reader-response criticism. It will be argued that if biblical critics attend to the poststructuralist trajectory in Iser's theory itself, not to mention in literary theories generally, then a shift in consciousness would be required concerning their critical practices. It will be suggested that the subject-object dichotomy of text versus reader has collapsed *theoretically* with the advent of poststructuralist and postmodernist literary theories, and that it is thus no longer a viable *practical* model for biblical critics to use. It will be shown that the theoretical collapse of the subject-object dichotomy reveals that both the text and the critic are constituted by interpretive conventions. Since interpretive conventions constitute both text and reader, "meaning" must be seen as a hermeneutical relation to the reading practices of one's own discipline. Furthermore, since hermeneutical relations entail political power, it will be argued that an ideological analysis should be a integral part of any critical reading strategy. One of the purposes of an ideological analysis would be to scrutinize the sociopolitical location of critics together with their proposed sociohistorical locations for the origins of biblical texts. Our purpose in offering a poststructuralist critique of reader-response criticism, then, is to offer one scenario of how reader-response criticism might be enhanced by the disparate reading agendas that are currently at work in the profession. It will be argued that a poststructuralist approach to reader-response criticism would help critics see more clearly that critics within the same reading community do not have egalitarian sociopolitical relationships to the text. If this is acknowledged, then there is a chance that readings from every sociopolitical location could play a role in how the assured results of biblical criticism are adjudicated.

While it is certainly true that all criticism is predicated upon reading it does not follow that critics necessarily reflect upon *how* they read. Many reader-response critics themselves are guilty of this lack of self-reflectiveness, so much so that Mailloux can say that "most reader-response critics and theorists fail to examine the status of their own discourse on reading" (1982:192). The great irony here is that reader-response critics are claiming "to make the implicit features of 'reading' explicit" (Freund, 6).

Since Mailloux made his observation, the subject-object dichotomy (reader versus text), which buttressed much of early reader-response criticism, has collapsed under the weight of poststructuralist and postmodernist literary theory, especially deconstruction (see chap. 3 below). With the demise of the subject-object dichotomy, reader-response theorists are faced with a number of serious questions. Temma Berg has summarized some of them:

> Postmodern literary theory has become, almost more than anything else, the problematics of reading, for to examine the process of reading is to raise a host of difficult, though fascinating, questions. Above all, we want to know, How do we read? Can we construct a model of reading which will indicate how reading may occur without, as is usually the case, insisting on how we believe reading should occur? How do text and reader affect one another? (Indeed, is there a text?) What purpose does reading serve? How do we assimilate, appropriate, and use what we have read? How does our reading change us? Ultimately, questions about reading lead us to questions about self and its relationship to the world it encounters. (248; cf. Everman:111–27)

With few exceptions biblical scholars have not yet acquiesced to the collapse of the text-reader dichotomy. Biblical scholars continue to affirm that the "text-as-such" and the "reader-as-such" exist apart from interpretive conventions, and they still use the text-reader dichotomy as the key to critical reading (e.g., Darr, 1992:17). Biblical reader-response critics still focus their attention on the text and the control it exercises over the reader. What they have not given serious thought to is the most fundamental tenet of reader-response criticism, namely, that "reader-response criticism refers to a group of critics who explicitly study, not a text, but readers reading a text" (Holland, 1990:55). Biblical critics have always used a great deal of terminology about the reader's experience, but the focus of their attention always turns back to interpreting the text (cf. Fowler, 1991:14–24).

Biblical reader-response criticism, then, is almost an oxymoron because biblical scholars are still in what Tompkins refers to as the beginning stage in the theoretical development of reader-response criticism: a fixation upon the text as an object (1980:ix). In Tompkins's view the status of the text has been a quintessential issue in the entire development of reader-response criticism. Ironically, biblical reader-response critics routinely list Tompkins's anthology in their bibliographies without acknowledging its governing premise, namely, that "the objectivity of the text is the concept that these essays, whether they intended it or not, eventually destroy" (x; cf. Freund, 5).

If biblical reader-response critics did take seriously the collapse of their dichotomous text-reader model, then critical attention could shift from the textual object to *how* readers make meaning within a set of particular reading conventions (Adam, 180–81). Furthermore, once reading practices are viewed as the site of the construction of reality and are questioned self-reflexively, then this could open up the question of the ethics and politics of reading that has surfaced so forcefully in other guilds (Mailloux, 1989:141–49). The call for a "second stage" of reflection is already explicit in Tompkins' anthology: "As emphasis on the reader tends first to erode and then to destroy the objective text, there is an increasing effort on the part of reader-oriented critics to redefine the aims and methods of literary study. *The change in theoretical assumptions forces a change in the kinds of moral claims critics can make for what they do*" (x, emphasis ours). The potential for such reflection is already at work within the discursive practices of biblical scholarship;[22] it just has not been appropriated. It remains to be seen whether or not biblical scholars will move in the direction of acute self-reflexiveness about the text-reader dichotomy, much less to a second-level reflection about the politics and morality of reading. Such self-reflexivity is clearly the most difficult kind of theorizing for theorists of reading to do (cf. Freund, 136).

[22] See, e.g., Aichele, 1989; Burnett, 1990b; Schüssler Fiorenza, 1988; D. H. Fisher; Fowler, 1989, 1991; Jobling, 1990; Moore, 1989b, 1989c; Phillips, 1990a, 1990b.

To admit that "subject and object are indivisibly bound" (Freund, 5) is extremely risky because it entails the corollary that " 'the reader', like 'the text', is constituted by the descriptive discourse of which it is a part" (Mailloux, 1982:202). When most reader-response critics recognize that the text's objective status has been called into question, they turn away from that issue and "assert the priority of 'the reader' " (202). Mailloux has pointed out the problem: "The mistake here is to assume that ideal readers are interpretive constructs while actual readers are not critical constructions at all and that the reading experiences of ideal readers are critical fictions while those of actual readers are 'really there' independent of any reader-response critic's interpretive framework" (204).

Biblical critics—whether they are exponents of historical, sociological, or literary schools—tend to believe that the *historical* (original) readers that they have constructed are the ones who were really there because real, competent readers have reconstructed them or because these readers are implied in the text. If "all readers are hypothetical and all reading experiences critically constructed," then "in reader-response criticism, the description of reading is always an interpretive construct based on assumptions about who a reader is and what he or she does while reading" (Mailloux, 1982:202). In other words, the implied reader and the real reader-critic do not enjoy an independent objective status apart from the critical discourses that are used to speak about the text.

The step that biblical critics have not yet taken is to admit that the implied reader for whom they are reading is themselves, and that the implied readers whom they construct are reading strategies by which to verify their own readings (cf. Robert Fowler, 1991:26–31). What they learn from the text is usually what they already know, and the hypostatized ideal reader is actually none other than the super-biblical critic him- or herself (cf. Moore, 1989b:97). Perhaps it is time for biblical critics to speak of the "implied interpreter" instead of the implied reader (Stern, 1991:86–87). The charge that Suleiman levels at Wayne Booth certainly applies to biblical reader-response critics as well: "The usefulness of these notions [of the implied reader and the implied author] becomes especially clear if one considers a fact that Booth is aware of but whose implications he is perhaps unwilling to pursue: namely, that the implied author and the implied reader are *interpretive constructs* and, as such, participate in the circularity of all interpretation. I construct the images of the implied author and implied reader gradually as I read a work, and then use the images I have constructed to validate my reading" (Suleiman and Crosman, 1980:11; cf. Belsey, 1980:29–36; Jefferson and Robey, 89; Mailloux, 1979:95). To confess this, however, would be to admit that one's relationship to the knowledge which has been gained from reading would not be that of a subject to an objective text but a *hermeneutical* relation to the discursive practices of one's own discipline (Aronowitz, 1990:14; Freund, 5; Iser, 1989:209; Mailloux, 1989:171).

The implications of admitting a hermeneutical relation to the knowledge gained from critical reading are staggering for historians. Probably one reason why biblical critics have avoided serious engagement with Fish's theory of reader-response is that it would compel critics to reflect upon their interpretive conventions, which Fish contends write their texts (cf. Burnett, 1990b:54–60; Porter, 1990:289). If reading conventions write texts, this means that adjudicators of different readings could not appeal in a facile way to "the text" since that is the very "object" in dispute (Fish, 1980:340; cf. Burnett, 1990b:57–60). The focus of dispute would be instead upon the different implied readers, or different interpreters, however they may be defined theoretically. Accepting Fish's view of things means that the notions of the autonomous text and independent reader are interpretive constructs: "The surprising but necessary outcome of this [Fish's] attack on the independence of textual meaning is to undermine not only the formalist position but also the grounds for reader-response criticism as an alternative project. . . . Indeed, the opposition of subject and object ceases to be relevant when reader and text are made to disappear into discursive systems of intelligibility, systems which are not a reflection of reality, but are that which is responsible for the 'reality' of readers and texts. And *without a subject/object opposition, reader-response criticism also disappears at a stroke.* . . . The reader's self is itself a sign—another text" (Freund, 108, emphasis ours). The slide from autonomous text and reader to interpretive conventions cannot be halted by appeal to an "autonomous interpretive community" either, as Fish himself attempts. Not only is the reader's self constituted by the reading conventions of his or her interpretive community, but those reading conventions themselves become another construct, another text, another sign to be read. At this point, the world of textuality threatens to devour the positivistic historian since the notion of history itself, which is a product of an interpretive community, intersects with other discursive communities, and those with still other communities, and so on indefinitely (Burnett, 1990b:59–63).

In the face of this iconoclastic understanding of text, reader, and reading conventions, the partial appropriation by biblical critics of Iser's view of the implied reader rescues them from the world of textuality. If the goal of biblical reader-response critics is to read *as* the original implied reader of any given text, then it would be a heavy blow to admit that the implied reader is not identical with any real reader either in the past or in the present. Iser himself makes this point, though he does not completely pursue it. For Iser the text does indeed contain a *Weltanschauung*, or a social reality, from the time of its production, but "in its reproduction . . . its component parts have been altered, its frame of reference has changed, its validity has, to a degree, been negated" (1974:34). It is this altered "repertoire of the familiar" that impels the real reader to actualize the potential of the text and to signal the difference between any real reader and the implied reader (34–35).

In Iser's view the "recodification of social and historical norms" by a text is just as true for the readers who were contemporaneous with the production of that text as it is for later readers. For the former the text enables them "to see what they cannot normally see in the ordinary process of day-to-day living," while later real readers are enabled "to grasp a reality that was never their own" (1978:74). Once the text's potential is actualized in the reader's conscious experience (1978:211), ancient literature is able to function as Enlightenment literature in Iser's view, that is, it functions didactically to call familiar norms into question and lead to new insights (1978:94, 210–12; cf. Darr, 1992:32, 170). This disorienting or defamiliarizing function of the text for *all* readers is too frequently overlooked when Iser's view is appropriated. Fish has pointed out one important implication of Iser's view for historians: "Iser avoids the hard choice, also implicit in Hirsch's distinction, between historical and ahistorical interpretation. The readers contemporary to an author are in no more a privileged position than the readers of later generations; for both sets of readers are provoked to an act of construction rather than an act of retrieval; and since the blueprint for construction is significantly incomplete—it displays gaps and blanks and indeterminacies— no instance of construction is more accurate, in the sense of being truer to an historically embodied meaning, than any other" (1981:4). For example, when biblical scholars try to enter the textual world of Matthew, the only way they can do so is to become an implied reader through their own constructs of what the Matthean world was like (Malina, 266; cf. Berg, 260; Kingsbury, 1988b). The real confession that historical critics need to make is that the relation of text to context is not a physical or material relation. It is a figurative one, that is, "a sign to sign relation," which makes problematic how the context is "in" the text or how the text re-presents the context (Jacques-Alain Miller, 1990:33). The borders of text and context can only be separated theoretically, or ideologically if the nature of the context's reconstruction is erased from critical discussion, and the delimitation of "the context" can only be an arbitrary move since there is no outer limit on any context (e.g., where does "the world of Matthew" begin and end?). The point is: if the implications of reader-response theory in general, or of Fish and Iser in particular, were carried to their logical conclusion by biblical critics, then they would be led into the poststructuralist world of textuality as regards both the text and the reader-critic, a world where questions of the indeterminacy of meaning, ideology, and the politics of reading are already being engaged (Bové; cf. Hogan, 1990a).

The admission that reading and the reader's imagination are communally constrained is as far as Fish is prepared to go with the concept of meaning. The text and its reading refer only to one's own interpretive community. Any reference beyond this reading community is considered by Fish to be fallacious. His argument rules out of bounds a priori, then, any discussion of conflict between different interpretive communities (cf. Pratt, 1986:30). The *reading community* is a reified and vague concept, and it does not require critics to take into account the many different readers of texts and their localized interests (Scholes, 1989:129–48; Eagleton, 1991:167–69, 202). Because they finally locate meaning within an individual's imagination or within an amorphous reading community, reader-response critics in general have been criticized widely for their refusal to give some kind of moral justification for their reading practices (Eagleton, 1983:73; Leitch, 1988:218–19; Pratt, 1986:32–34; Tompkins, 1980:x). To give moral justifications for their reading practices would require reader-response critics to take ideological criticism seriously as a constant corrective to their current apolitical approaches (cf. Hogan, 1990a; Mailloux, 1989:chaps. 2–4). In biblical reader-response criticism several consequences would follow from an ideological analysis of reading practices.

Such an analysis would entail, first of all, an analysis of the constraints over the production of readings. Meaning could still be understood as an "event" of reading, but an understanding of the sociopolitical location of its production would become a paramount concern. Once reading conventions are acknowledged as the site of meaning production for both the text and for the reader-critic, then the formation of those conventions and the interests involved in their maintenance or change must be considered primary factors in the reading process. Pratt points out correctly that the ideological deficiency of the communication model that undergirds reader-response theories such as Iser's is "its tendency to view the message simply as a reflex of a preexisting, all-encompassing, uniform code *to which all participants stand in the same relation*" (1986:33, emphasis ours). The general communication model implies the existence of a textual object that invites an egalitarian response from everyone at the time of its production and in each subsequent reception so that one can return to the world of the text through one's imagination.

Although an egalitarian approach to the production and reception of texts seems to give equal access to everyone, it entails an ideology which obscures the fact that textual power is political power (Scholes, 1985:x–xi, 58–73). Reader-response critics, like many humanistic scholars, have ruthlessly avoided the question of politics and power by promoting the adjudication of different readings through dialogue and consensus (Leitch, 1988:226, 230; cf. Hogan, 1990a:22). The egalitarian communication model, favored primarily by Iser, and the dialogical-consensual model, favored more by Fish, both efface the insights offered by ideological critics that every reading is a contextualized reading, and that different readers of biblical texts (whether they be male or female, white, black, Latino, Asian, and so on) stand in asymmetrical relationships concerning power and in their ability to speak about the text *even within the same general interpretive community* (Pratt, 1987:54–55). Ideological criticism permits a way of thinking about interpretive communities in a way that Fish's model does not (Scholes, 1985:154–55). Fish's notion of interpretive communities certainly acts as a corrective to Iser's view of the individual reader's imagination, but without a corresponding acknowledgement of the coercive power of consensual community standards. Fish's view "can chill the spines of readers whose experience of the community is less happily benign than Fish assumes" (Freund, 110–11).

Reader-response analysis is incomplete without a discursive analysis of the asymmetrical aspects of the readers' subject positions in terms of both the production and reception of readings. Discourse analysis, however, is precisely the kind of scrutiny that reader-response critics avoid since it unmasks everyone's discourse for what it is: "a necessary contest of discursive positioning" (Burnett, 1990b:70). Reader-response critics have concentrated solely on the *hermeneutical* power struggle between text and reader, but if any point has been made in the last decade about the politics of reading, it is that hermeneutical power is political power.[23] Edward Said succinctly summarizes the point we are emphasizing:

> Criticism in short is always situated; it is skeptical, secular, reflectively open to its own failings. This is by no means to say that it is value-free. Quite to the contrary, for the inevitable trajectory of critical consciousness is to arrive at some acute sense of what political, social, and human values are entailed in the reading, production, and transmission of every text. To stand between culture and system is therefore to stand *close to* . . . a concrete reality about which political, moral, and social judgments have to be made and, if not only made, then exposed and demystified. If, as we have recently been told by Stanley Fish, every act of interpretation is made possible and given force by an interpretive community, then we must go a great deal further in showing what situation, what historical and social configuration, what political interests are concretely entailed by the very existence of interpretive communities. This is an especially important task when the communities have evolved camouflaging jargons. (1983:26; cf. 1991; Freund, 154)

In other words, if critics accept a model like Fish's view of interpretive communities without enacting a corresponding ideological critique, then for them there will be only "a large number of individual communities unable to argue with one another" (Culler, 1982:68). As Said implies, "camouflaging jargons" enable different reading communities to appropriate theories uncritically. If there is no analysis of the ends of their community's praxis, then no ideological critique is deemed necessary by a particular group of critics. In hermeneutical situations where critics refuse to do an ideological analysis of how they appropriate a theory, each critical community can just dig in, continue to produce readings encoded in the jargon that it has decided is true for itself, and ignore the sociopolitical worlds of other readers who are reading the same texts.

One crucial concept of ideological analysis that has survived critical assault is that if any theory (such as Iser's) is adopted uncritically, then the theory will serve primarily to reinforce the existing ideological ends of that community's reading strategies (Pratt, 1986:28–29, 39–45; cf. Althusser, 1969; Eagleton, 1991:148–49, 152–56; G. Elliott, 186–244; O'Neill, 1–42). As the appropriation of Iser's theory by biblical critics continues unabated, especially in North America, the role that ideological analysis could

---

[23] See, e.g., Bal, 1988a:chap. 1; Foucault, 1977b; Fraser, 1–34; Phillips, 1990a:1–5; Peter Rabinowitz, 1987; Rosen, 87–141; Spivak, 1990; Weber.

play in the process goes unheeded. Tompkins's critique of reader-response criticism in general is fully applicable to biblical reader-response criticism: *"Virtually nothing has changed as a result of what seems, from close up, the cataclysmic shift in the locus of meaning from the text to the reader. Professors and students alike practice criticism as usual; only the vocabulary with which they perform their analyses has altered"* (225, emphasis ours; cf. Pratt, 1986:28; Spencer, 241). We are not arguing that biblical interpretation will be or should be totally replaced by a more complete appropriation of reader-response criticism. We are arguing, rather, that if biblical critics want to unmask the ideological ends and the material effects of their readings, as many indeed do, then they must become more self-reflexive about their ideological appropriation of the theories of reader-response criticism. For although their methods have changed, biblical critics, like many other close readers, keep reading their texts with the same ideological goals that they have used for years.

To state the obvious, there is an increasing number of readers of biblical texts who demand to be heard and who are already engaging the public domain. These readers offer a promising prospectus for biblical reader-response criticism. We cannot be exhaustive, of course, but the following voices and strategies from within the field of biblical scholarship have already presented a forceful challenge. Given our spatial constraints, it is unfortunate (since it goes against the grain of our thesis about the need to elucidate the specificity of each reader's sociopolitical location) but necessary for us to categorize in a simplistic way many voices in biblical studies that are neither homogeneous nor harmonious. Each of these examples, however, refers to active voices within biblical scholarship which agree that reading is an agonistic affair between text, reader, and different reading conventions reflecting different social, economic, and political locations and emerging out of various cultural and identity formations. Each example, in its own way, embodies a form of resistance against the hegemonic impulses of texts and their traditional receptions.

One powerful set of reading strategies emerges from feminism's recognition that biblical texts are primarily androcentric texts which presuppose an asymmetrical reading praxis for men and women (e.g., Janice Capel Anderson, 1983; Tolbert, 116–17). Unlike those who employ Iser's model, in which neither the reader nor the text dominates, feminist readers attentive to the influence of gender on the activity of reading call both the text and reading conventions into question. For example, if a text was produced within an androcentric set of discursive practices, the implied reader would not be an "it," as for Iser. The implied reader would be a "he," and an implied "she" would stand in an asymmetrical relation to him. Analogously, the implied reader occupies the position of dominance; hence, the implied she is really the implied "other" and might include subordinate men as well as women. If a predominantly androcentric text were read with Iser's model, one's only option would be to comply with the androcentric gender roles that this text proffers because Iser's gender-neutral reading model cannot elucidate them. A feminist reading model, in contrast, would allow for a reader's resistance to the implied reader's role by elucidating what relationships the role would entail (Fetterley, 1978:xxii; Pardes; cf. Paul Julian Smith, 1990; 1992). Schweickart's remark is directly relevant to our point: "Reader-response critics cannot take refuge in the objectivity of the text, or even in the idea that a gender-neutral criticism is possible. Today they can continue to ignore the implications of feminist criticism only at the cost of incoherence or intellectual dishonesty" (1986:35; cf. Flynn, 1991; Kauffman; McLaughlin; Joan W. Scott, 1988; Showalter, 1989). Since the early 1980s, reader-response critics in general have not ignored the gender implications of feminist criticism (Leitch, 1988:234). Whatever may be the case in general, though, biblical reader-response critics have yet to experience the full force of feminist criticisms, particularly on the issue of the engendering of the implied reader.

While feminism has persistently raised the critical question of gender, it continues to struggle to transform itself into a politics and mode of reading capable of engaging questions of race, class, and cultural difference. At the same time, critical voices of women of color have emerged—sometimes as part of the conversation taking place within feminism, sometimes in direct conflict with feminism, sometimes fully autonomous from feminism—as a compelling challenge to the hegemonic power of texts and their interpretation (Anzaldúa; Cannon, 1988; Cannon and Schüssler Fiorenza; Childers and hooks; Christian; Patricia Hill Collins; Clarice Martin; Wall; Weems, among others). These voices are by no means unified nor homogeneous. Some bring a vigorous skepticism to reigning concepts like tradition and theory, some eschew them altogether. Some attempt to resist the reifying impulses of such terms and to transform them into terms whose adequacy must be measured by the extent to which they account for the experiences and readings of those traditionally left out of the realm of interpretation; in so doing, they resist a tendency to make of women of color the "concrete examples" for (white) theory (Homan), a tendency which leaves theory a tidily uninterrogated and unchanged term. Whether in feminist, womanist, *mujerista,* or other formulations, these strategies for reading texts in general and the Bible in particular derive from the insistence that resistance to the dominance of the text and its traditional modes of interpretation must take into account the range and complexity of institutional, social, economic, and political hegemony. (See further chap. 6.) The challenges raised by the reading strategies of such critics are decisive, their importance manifest in the equal measures of anxiety and resistance by which they are often met with in both feminism and biblical studies.

Whereas feminist and womanist strategies of reading emphasize resistance to political and social hierarchies, to textual and interpretive domination, deconstruction can provide a critical strategy for resisting the epistemological processes that allow hierarchies to be constructed and to become embedded. A typical reaction of biblical critics to deconstruction, bolstered by the ignorance of the popular press, is that deconstruction is the archenemy of Western civilization and that it has nothing to contribute to narrative and reader-response criticisms (cf. Powell, 1990b:68–69; also Morgan and Barton, 269; see Klein, Bromberg, and Hubbard, 441; Jacobs, 191; Jeanrond). Ill-informed pronouncements about Derrida and deconstruction amount to little more than sloganeering. O'Leary summarizes the caricature this way: "Derrida is acclaimed as a nihilist, abolishing the extra-linguistic referent of language, and an anarchist, replacing meaning with the pure randomness of the freeplay of signifiers without signification, signifiers whose meaning is merely their absolute negative reference to other signifiers. He is thought to be suffering from despair and anxiety, or to be full of Dionysian joy, and he digs the grave of logocentrism and sets loose the utterly arbitrary process of rewriting the texts of the past in light of their now manifest meaninglessness" (22). There is a huge gap between what is said about Derrida and deconstruction and what Derrida in fact does and says he does (e.g., Derrida, 1988b:146,n.1; 157,n.9.) One could easily argue, however, that deconstruction is integral to reader-response criticism. All of the critics who have pointed to the collapse of the reader-text (subject-object) dichotomy in reader-response criticism have done nothing other than point out what deconstructionist readers have also shown to be the case in a wider context.

Freund, for example, contends that Culler's turn from structural poetics to deconstruction occurred precisely over the question that reader-response criticism could not solve, namely, the question of "how much control is exercised by the reader and how much by the text" (Freund, 87; cf. Culler, 1982:82). For Culler, all that reader-response criticism at present seems to be capable of doing is presenting a narrative construction, a story of reading, which usually follows the plot of a happy ending (1982:78–79). Culler goes so far as to say that deconstruction can help reader-response critics become more self-reflexive about their reading practices because it has shown that an alternative plot of unreadability is inherent to the reading process itself (1982:81). There is "no single role that the reader is called upon to play," and therefore "an interpretation of a work thus comes to be an account of what happens to the reader: how various conventions and expectations are brought into play, where particular connections or hypotheses are posited, how expectations are defeated or confirmed. *To speak of the meaning of the work is to tell a story of reading*" (1982:35, emphasis ours). In other words, all that "is accessible is a *narrative* of what readers do" (Freund, 87). For Culler, then, deconstruction is "the culmination of recent work on reading," because it "explores the problematic situation to which stories of reading have led us" (1982:83; cf. Freund, 85, 88).

Another way to say this is that deconstruction has intensified our understanding of textuality. Deconstruction has shown that textuality is a disordering force, even within biblical texts that appear to be referentially stable, that precludes reading only for coherence and closure. Reading for any systematic totality is excluded by the notion of textuality since as soon as one possibility is realized by a reader, other possibilities by necessity disappear unless they are deliberately held in abeyance by a second reading that is recognized as equally plausible and legitimate (cf. Harvey, 1987:142, 145; cf. Derrida, 1976:158; 1988b:141 and the critique of "commentary"). In other words, the category of the "given" itself—the textual object, the implied reader, and so forth—is already a "text" that is always subject to further reading, thus disrupting the drive for coherence (Freund, 149, 151; cf. Burnett, 1992b; Phillips, 1990a:28–30).

It is not just so-called deconstructionists who see deconstruction's view of textuality as an integral part of reader-response criticism. In their anthology Suleiman and Crosman include Paul de Man, J. Hillis Miller, Roland Barthes, and Jacques Derrida within the broader reader-response movement (1980:6–7). Similarly, Tompkins calls deconstruction a close relative of reader-response criticism, because of the former's fascination with the process of reading (1980:224–25; cf. Leitch, 1988:270). For Tompkins, as we have seen, reader-response criticisms deconstruct their own subject-object dichotomy so that both of their given notions (the text and the reader) are disrupted by their own textuality—that is, the concepts of *text* and *reader* themselves become texts to be read interminably (1980:x). Even though it has not actually changed his general theoretical position, Iser himself has incorporated terminology whose semantic provenance is that of deconstruction—terms like *play, supplement, difference, the split signifier*, a *negativity* that is "continually subverting presence," and so on (1989:249–61). In light of the often symbiotic relation of reader-response criticism to deconstruction, it is strange that biblical reader-response critics continue to ignore the latter.

It is important to add that deconstruction as a reading strategy does not negate the practice of historical criticism nor eliminate the notion of history. On the contrary, deconstructive reading relies necessarily on traditional historical criticism as "an indispensable guardrail" or "safeguard" [Derrida, 1988b:141] for reading. If it were not so, Derrida cautions, "one could say just anything at all" (1988b:144–5; see chap. 3 below). As for the history that deconstruction finds problematic, it is the *"metaphysical* concept of history . . . the concept of history as *the history of meaning"* (1981b:56, emphasis ours). Deconstruction, by contrast, seeks a new conception of history—"monumental history" he calls it—that is concerned with "the-real-history-of-the-world" (1988b:252). It argues for a subtler understanding of the ways texts refer, represent, and bring about a new opening onto the world; it seeks a subtler understanding of the relations of speech, thought, and reality; it seeks a subtler, more "originary" understanding of the relation between text, context, and critical commentary. There is finally no one way to practice deconstructionist reading, and it does not necessarily entail trying to tumble the discipline "at a single, apocalyptic stroke" (Norris, 1985:222). Deconstructionist reading practices can uncover many problematic issues within the interpretive community's discourse without losing sight of the unique concerns of that discipline (Norris, 1985:11). And deconstruction can provide openings within historical-critical discourse so that oppressed voices can speak and, if heard, transform the discourse of the discipline.

A third group of reading strategies that work without the subject-object dichotomy issues from black African theological movements. Black African theologies have long emphasized orality at the core of their identities, so that it is an important sign of their difference. Given the fact that the biblical texts were first transmitted orally, biblical reader-response criticism is an area that exegetes in Africa and the African diaspora, as well as black American and European exegetes, could continue to enrich. With traditional emphases on written texts that talk and speak with one another in an intertextual vernacular performance (see esp. Blount; Gates, 1988:chaps. 5–6; cf. Julian; Okpewho), a cogent argument can be made that black African exegetes have a chance to understand better than perhaps any other group of scholars could the role that orality might have played for the implied (original) readers of biblical texts. In addition, since many black African and non-African scholars are keenly aware of the contextualization of all scholarship, yet also emphasize the need for historical criticism, their work could play a central role in enabling all biblical critics to take ethical and political responsibility for the contextualization of their readings (Costen; Swann; Felder, 1989a:156–57, 1989b:5–21; Gates, 1988:xix–xx; Mbiti:chap. 3; Wimbush, 1989a).

Moore has pointed out that the emphasis of reader-response critics upon the reader-in-the-text "transfers the psychocultural assumptions of a typographic (i.e., print-centered) culture back into the ancient oral and scribal context" (1989b:84; cf. 84–88; Robert Fowler, 1991:48–52). Since it is the case that written biblical texts were read aloud at or near the time of their production, and that writing and orality overlapped in ways that scholars are only beginning to understand, biblical reader-response critics might wish to take orality fully into account—and, consequently, black African theologies—if they are trying to read as implied (original) readers.[24]

One final general pattern of reading that must be mentioned, though it could embrace the three groups of reading strategies already discussed, is the *liberationist*. There are at least three points to highlight for biblical reader-response critics from this general category. First, most forms of liberation readings have little concern for the historical circumstances of the text's production (Frick, 231). The stories of biblical literature have an immediate presence and applicability as stories about the oppressed and the poor as the object of God's present concern and activity (Cormie, 186; Ela, chap.3). Biblical reader-response criticism, which is steeped in the Enlightenment tradition of historical criticism, may have no relevance for a great portion of the world's readers whose focus is not upon the past but upon present audience (Brown, 1984:21–23; Croatto, 1987:37). It is a pressing ethical

[24] Further on orality, see Ernest Abel, 1971; Gerhardsson; Harris; Kelber, 1983; Ong, 1982; Vansina.

concern for biblical reader-response critics to hear voices of the poor and the oppressed, so that the latter can show more clearly who controls the power of meaning production, who adjudicates acceptable readings, who controls the majority of theological educational institutions, and, most important, how the present production of biblical readings supports their oppression or liberation. If, as historical-critics seem to agree, the message of much of the Bible is indeed the story of the liberation of the poor and of the oppressed (Brown, 1984:158), then the stories of reading that biblical reader-response critics have produced so far have little relation to the liberation of the contemporary poor and oppressed (Cormie, 176–78; Holub, 1984:105–6; Jobling, 1990:94–97; Wuellner, 1989c:49). To paraphrase Mieke Bal, it is not enough to say with her and other women that the Bible kills; traditional ways of reading the Bible are equally deadly (1987:131–32). If her observation is correct, and we believe that it is, then it raises quite forcefully the question of how scholarly readings that "kill" could be historically, hermeneutically, or ethically correct (Cormie, 192–93; Miller, 1987a; 1989).

A second concern for biblical reader-response critics posed by liberationist readers is the question of the transformation and freedom of "the reader." Exactly what has been meant by these concepts? If biblical reader-response critics take liberationist voices seriously, then it would require both a theoretical and a personal commitment to the transformation of the real reader's situation (Mosala, 1989; 1991:269–70; 1992). The ethical and political questions can be focused thus: when should real readers decide to read against the conventions of the text or of the interpretive community, and how is that resistance to be enacted?

How the question about resistance is answered will depend upon how one answers the question about the meaning of *transformation*. Is transformation simply learning to read better, as for Fish (e.g., 1971:311), or does it mean gaining new insights about one's private life (cognitively? intellectually? aesthetically?) through the reading process, as for Iser (1974:41, 55–56)? What happens to the insights gained after the reading process has ended? Does the reader's individual transformation lead to the transformation of larger reading conventions, and then of society itself? If so, how? These are pressing questions for any reader-response critic (see Fetterley, 1978; Suleiman, 1976, 1990), but they are especially urgent ones for biblical critics in light of liberationists' critiques. The reader's struggle takes on quite different meanings in liberationist contexts, and it does not always issue in the happy ending of first world exegetes (Frick, 232–33, 237; Brown, 1984:13–14).

A third and final consequence of engaging liberationist exegesis is that biblical reader-response critics would have to engage "popular" readings. Given the fact that biblical reader-response critics are fixated on the implied (original) reader, little concern has been given to how nonacademic real readers from many different locations actually read. There has been little concern to do a systematic pedagogical study of their students' responses, even though a great deal of practical work has been done in this area by nonbiblical reader-response critics (Bleich, 1978, 1988; Chew; Flynn, 1991; Holland, 1975a, 1975b; Wilcox). Some feminist academicians are engaging popular readings by women in order to understand better how women read (Berg, 296). There also are many good analyses of popular readers from other academic areas—theology, religion in America, and so on—which biblical critics could utilize. It would seem that biblical reader-response critics—especially given the imperatives we surveyed above about the politics of reading—would want to engage the different kinds of biblical readers in order to clarify the nature of "the reader" for the specific contexts of the text's reception. Such an effort would obviously entail engaging readings other than the classics of biblical scholarship, and it would have to consider the influence of television and popular literature on the reading and reception of biblical texts (cf. Polan). If biblical reader-response critics do engage the responses of biblical readers from popular culture, then surely they would find that the text versus reader dichotomy that scholars use is not the operative one in the larger world (cf. Robert Fowler, 1989a).

If the major concern of biblical reader-response critics continues to be the hermeneutical one of reproducing the implied (original) reader for their dominant constituencies, then that concern may never be broadened to include constituencies such as black exegetes, feminist and womanist exegetes, liberationist exegetes, and readers in popular culture. In point of fact, whether or not biblical critics are aware of it, they are already involved politically with these constituencies. And until they admit candidly that the "reader" in biblical reader-response criticism is still primarily the white North American critic, the excluded "others" cannot accomplish their rightful roles in the reconstruction of biblical scholarship (Mosala, 1991:267–68).

RECOMMENDED FURTHER READING

Bleich, David. 1978. *Subjective Criticism*. Baltimore: Johns Hopkins University Press. A coherent theory that utilizes work from psychology and linguistics to show that readers' responses produce knowledge. A challenge to text-centered literary theories and pedagogical practices that focuses on the affective dimension of the reading process by studying the responses of student readers.

Booth, Wayne C. 1983. *The Rhetoric of Fiction.* Chicago: University of Chicago Press, 2d ed. Argues that the rhetoric of narrative necessitates the reader's active and affective involvement. Shows that the "implied author" of a narrative constantly requires the reader to reevaluate his or her beliefs and values. Comprehensive annotated bibliography.

Fetterley, Judith. 1978. *The Resisting Reader: A Feminist Approach to American Fiction.* Bloomington: Indiana University Press. A masterful argument that the traditional canon of American literature is androcentric. Unless women readers resist the roles offered to them by androcentric texts, they will be forced to read against their own experiences as women.

Fish, Stanley E. 1980. *Is There a Text in This Class? The Authority of Interpretive Communities.* Cambridge: Harvard University Press. A collection of essays that traces Fish's theoretical development from formalism to his view that interpretive communities write both texts and readers. This is the basic book for understanding Fish's general theoretical position.

Fowler, Robert M. 1991. *Let the Reader Understand: Reader Response Criticism and the Gospel of Mark.* Minneapolis: Augsburg/Fortress. Elucidates how the narrative rhetoric of Mark's Gospel impacts upon the experiences of its readers. To date, the most comprehensive monograph on any biblical narrative employing reader-response theory.

Freund, Elizabeth. 1987. *The Return of the Reader: Reader-Response Criticism.* New York: Methuen. A penetrating and lucid survey of reader-response criticism. Assesses key issues of reader-response criticism in light of poststructuralist literary theory.

Holland, Norman N. 1973. *Poems in Persons: An Introduction to the Psychoanalysis of Literature.* New York: W. W. Norton. Argues that real readers' responses to texts are based upon their "identity themes." A basic book for understanding Holland's development of his psychoanalytic approach to reader-response criticism.

Iser, Wolfgang. 1974. *The Implied Reader: Patterns of Communication in Prose Fiction from Bunyan to Beckett.* Baltimore: Johns Hopkins University Press. Argues that real readers actualize a text's proffered roles through an interactive and imaginative process of coherence building. A vital book for understanding Iser's view of the implied reader. Examples are drawn from novels spanning the seventeenth through the twentieth centuries.

—————. 1978. *The Act of Reading: A Theory of Aesthetic Response.* Baltimore: Johns Hopkins University Press. A theoretical account of Iser's view of the interaction between text and reader. Together with his *The Implied Reader* the fundamental works needed to understand Iser's theory of the reading process.

Jauss, Hans Robert. 1982. *Towards an Aesthetic of Reception.* Trans. Timothy Bahti. Theory and History of Literature 2. Minneapolis: University of Minnesota Press. A collection of five essays, including his seminal essay "Literary History as a Challenge to Literary Theory." Crucial for understanding Reception Theory and the larger philosophical context for Iser's form of reader-response criticism. Introduction by Paul de Man.

Mailloux, Stephen. 1982. *Interpretive Conventions: The Reader in the Study of American Fiction.* Ithaca: Cornell University Press. An excellent survey and critique of reader-response criticism that utilizes examples from American fiction. Appendix deals with reader-response criticism and teaching composition. Includes a partially annotated bibliography.

Moore, Stephen D. 1989. *Literary Criticism and the Gospels: The Theoretical Challenge.* New Haven: Yale University Press. The most comprehensive survey and analysis of Gospel narrative criticism and the development of biblical reader-response criticism. Includes a comprehensive bibliography.

Rabinowitz, Peter J. 1987. *Before Reading: Narrative Conventions and the Politics of Interpretation.* Ithaca: Cornell University Press. Argues that in order to understand the reading process, both textual features and readers' shared interpretive strategies must be elucidated. Contends that all interpretive acts are political acts.

Rosenblatt, Louise. 1978. *The Reader, the Text, the Poem: The Transactional Theory of the Literary Work.* Carbondale: Southern Illinois University Press. Explains her transactional theory of the interaction of the reader with the text and its implications for both pedagogy and literary criticism.

Suleiman, Susan R., and Inge Crosman. 1980. *The Reader in the Text: Essays on Audience and Interpretation.* Princeton: Princeton University Press. A judicious selection of sixteen essays that covers all of the major approaches to reader-response and audience-oriented criticisms. Includes a helpful introductory essay and annotated bibliography.

Tompkins, Jane P., ed. 1980. *Reader-Response Criticism: From Formalism to Post-Structuralism.* Baltimore: Johns Hopkins University Press. An anthology of eleven seminal essays. Includes an essay by Tompkins that gives an incisive theoretical assessment of reader-response criticism. Includes detailed annotated bibliography.

2 | Structuralist and Narratological Criticism

Along with reader-response criticism, structuralist and narratological criticism has offered biblical interpreters a crucial entryway into literary theory and the reading of the Bible. The theoretical models and language associated with structuralism and narratology, however, are quite distinct. Readers unfamiliar with these approaches may find the technical terminology complex and confusing. For this reason we concentrate our discussion on five key terms: *structuralism, formalism, semiotics, narratology,* and *poetics*. Their interrelations will be dealt with along the way. Suffice it to say here, by way of explaining the chapter title, that formalism and semiotics will be taken up in relation to structuralism, and that narratology encompasses poetics (which most often appears as the preferred term in Hebrew Bible studies for what New Testament critics call narratology). Of the two dominant terms, *narratology* gives the appearance of a random restriction of scope to the narrative parts of the Bible. But in fact all the methods considered here have been applied overwhelmingly more to the narrative than to other parts of the Bible. In defining our scope, structuralism has the priority over narratology; narratology is our concern to the extent that it grows in some way out of the structuralist impulse.

In its most basic definition, *structuralism* is a general theory of the intelligibility of the products of mind based on the view that what makes things intelligible is their perceived relatedness, rather than their qualities as separate items (cf. below). Literary structuralists posit general rules for the creation and interpretation of literature and affirm the priority of deductive over inductive method. Excluded in principle from the scope of this chapter is any work that does not, in some way, relate itself to a model or models (1) drawn from outside biblical studies, and (2) in some recognizable branch of formalism, structuralism, or semiotics.

We begin with two readings of biblical texts which employ the two forms of structuralist narratology that until now have had the greatest impact on biblical studies. One model is the linguistically based structuralism drawing its main impulse from the work of Ferdinand de Saussure; the other is a narratology with more diffuse origins, the most significant of which is the work of Gérard Genette. Our overall concern in this chapter is to engage critical questions rather than to provide a comprehensive methodological survey. To that end, in the third section we assess the extensive critique that has been made of structuralism against a backdrop of postmodern interests and consider structuralism's potential to survive and be reformed by this critique. In the last section we consider the ongoing potential for biblical structuralism in the light of this critical debate.

READINGS OF BIBLICAL NARRATIVES

Structuralist Approaches to 1 Kings 17–18 The text of 1 Kings 17–18 can be read as a *quest* story, specifically a quest for a lost or stolen object. King Ahab of Israel undertakes a quest to recover the rain that the prophet Elijah, representing the God Yahweh, has taken away. This quest is successful; at the end of the story, the needed rain falls.

Quests for lost or stolen objects figure largely among the tales that Vladimir Propp analyzed in his classic study *Morphology of the Folktale*. Propp (25–65) reduced one hundred Russian tales to thirty-one plot-elements or "functions" (e.g., "the hero is pursued," "the villain is exposed") and found that, though no tale included all these functions, those which a tale did include were always in the same order (22–23). Propp's functions fall into the following subgroups:

1. The "villainy" or "lack," that is, the disturbance of the *status quo* which sets the story in motion (functions I–VIII in Propp's numeration).

2. The finding, persuasion, equipping, and so on of the hero, and the hero's movement to the place of combat (IX–XIV).
3. The combat, in which the hero defeats the villain or overcomes the lack (XV–XIX).
4. The hero's return home, recognition, marriage, and so on (XX–XXXI).

Read as a quest story, 1 Kings 17–18 fits this pattern. 1: There is a *lack* of rain (in fact, of moisture in general), due to the *villain* (whether Elijah or Yahweh). 2: As *hero*, Ahab initiates the quest for moisture, and undertakes a journey to this end. 3: Ahab confronts Elijah *(combat)*, and the result of this confrontation is rainfall. 4: Ahab *returns home*. But such an analysis is likely to perplex the reader. It certainly covers the main action of the story but seems to turn the story on its head. Ahab is no hero, nor is Elijah (and still less Yahweh) a villain! Adopting Propp's categories works well at a formal level but leads to paradoxical conclusions. We shall return to this in a moment.

A second structuralist approach to the story reads it as the carrying out of the intention ("narrative program") of the God Yahweh to restore to himself the allegiance of the people Israel, which they have transferred to the God Baal (see 16:29–34). Such programs can be mapped onto the *actantial model* proposed by A. J. Greimas (see Patte, 1976b:42): a "sender" transfers (or intends to transfer) an "object" to a "receiver," by the agency of a "subject," who is helped or opposed by a "helper" or an "opponent." Each of these positions Greimas refers to as an *actant:*

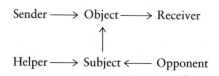

The model is of great generality. We could use it to account for "Little Red Riding Hood":

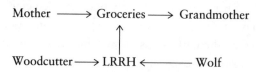

This story happens to provide six different actants for the six roles; but roles may be left empty, or the same actant may take more than one role. For example, "The Billy Goats Gruff":

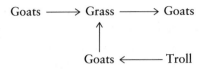

An actantial model for 1 Kings 17–18 might have as its top line or "axis":

Yahweh ──────→ Israel's allegiance ──────→ Yahweh

But it is not obvious how the positions in the lower line or axis, especially that of subject, are to be represented. One might intuitively suppose Elijah to be the subject. An analysis has, however, been proposed (Jobling, 1986a:66–88), which contrasts the whole story with a substory enclosed within it—18:21–44, the account of the combat on Mt. Carmel—and suggests the following actantial schemes. For the whole of 1 Kings 17–18:

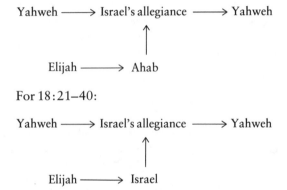

For 18:21–40:

Yahweh ──────→ Israel's allegiance ──────→ Yahweh

Elijah ──────→ Israel

(For comparison purposes, the opponent role is ignored; obviously in 18:21–40 it is taken by the prophets of Baal.) In Jobling's analysis, the first program fails, while the second succeeds, so that Ahab's inability to bring about the people's repentance, when confronted with a clear choice, is directly contrasted to the ability of the people themselves to repent when *they* are confronted with a clear choice. Such a reading reveals the point of the paradoxical Proppian analysis proposed above. The commonsense assumption that the prophet will play the central hero role misses the possibility that the king is to be presented precisely as a *failed* hero. If kings cannot lead in the right direction, and if people can move in the right direction without (or even in spite of) royal leadership, then the whole point of kingship is questioned. Elijah's role is to facilitate the drawing of the contrast.

A third and final approach illuminates the specifics of the story by reference to the myth-analysis of Claude Lévi-Strauss. Rain is a form of water, and not the only form of water mentioned in the story. In the combat scene, Elijah takes water to douse the offering and the wood (18:33–35). In Lévi-Strauss's analyses of myths, water typically has fire as its opposite term, and this opposition is one of the commonest features of myths (1970:passim). It is easy to see why so many myths deal with water and fire. They are basic to human life, which cannot be maintained without them; but they are ambiguous in that they exist in destructive as well as beneficial forms. It is equally easy to see why they are mythic opposites, for either, in a sufficient amount, will destroy the other. Read in these terms, the competition staged by Elijah is to test the gods' ability to produce enough fire (18:24, 38) to overcome the water in which he has doused the offerings.

But such a reading renders problematic the intuitive and common assumption that the story is about a rain-making competition. The goal of the narrative action is not to remove the lack directly, by bringing rain. Rather, the goal is epistemological, to show which god is capable of destroying moisture, and hence of causing the drought the people are experiencing. The people's acknowledgment of Yahweh is the precondition for the drought to end.

A Narratological Reading of Genesis 38   Narratives do not always present events in the chronological order of their occurrence. For example, they use the "flashback" to tell later something that took place earlier. Gérard Genette (1980:33–85) works out a system for nonsequential telling (*anachrony*) and proposes terminology for a great variety of particular cases (we introduce here only the terms relevant to the present analysis). The flashback he calls *analepsis*. Analepsis may be either *internal* or *external*. Internal analepsis is a flashback to a time within that of the whole narrative, external analepsis to a time before the narrative events began (a mixed case is possible when the flashback begins before but ends after the beginning of the time of the narrative). Analepsis may also be *homodiegetic* or *heterodiegetic*. This further pair of terms is necessary since narratives can have multiple story-lines overlapping in time in complex ways. Analepsis is homodiegetic when the flashback is to an earlier part of the same story-line, heterodiegetic when it is to a different story-line.

The events introduced in internal homodiegetic analepsis might in principle have been introduced in their chronological place in the story-line (and the critic will need to consider why they were not). Two cases have to be considered. There may be an actual temporal gap at an earlier point in the story-line, which the analepsis fills in; such a gap Genette calls an *ellipsis*. Or there may be no such temporal gap, but only the omission from the earlier narrative of some detail that the analepsis supplies. Genette (52) calls this sort of omission *paralipsis*. Apparently discontent, however, that the one term *analepsis* should correspond to two different terms—sometimes to ellipsis, sometimes to paralipsis—he introduces another term to correspond to the latter, *paralepsis*, "giving information that should be left aside" (195). But he does so in a different part of his book, not as part of his analysis of narrative temporality.

In her reading of Genesis 38, Mieke Bal (1987:91–95) both uses and problematizes Genette's terminology. This chapter breaks the narrative sequence in which it appears. The preceding chapter and the following ones tell the story of Joseph—the account of how he and his family came to Egypt— in chronological sequence. Chapter 38 has nothing to do with this story. It has in common with the Joseph story only one main character—Judah— and, far from referring to his going to Egypt, it assumes his remaining in Canaan for an extended period. Our instinct as readers of narrative is to look for some kind of anachrony; taking the Joseph story as the main narrative, we try to read chapter 38 as related to it by analepsis or prolepsis, but neither will work. (Analepsis is ruled out by the implausibility of Judah's returning to his father's house—to participate in chapter 37—after having established himself as a patriarch, as well as by 38:1, "at that time." Prolepsis is no more plausible, requiring all the events of chapter 38 to happen before Judah goes to Egypt with the rest of Jacob's family in chapter 46, and to be made to fit with various appearances of Judah in chapters 42–45.)

Genesis 38 relates to its context as paralepsis, "giving information that should be left aside," information incompatible, by accepted rules of narration, with the context. Bal relates this disturbing conclusion to Genette's failure to include paralepsis within his account of temporality in narrative. Paralepsis is not a temporal figure; rather, it is a figure that calls in question our internalized sense of narrative temporality. This sense has been formed in the framework of "the psychoanalytic nuclear family, which excludes any rival of the same generation" (1987:93). Genesis 38 marks the moment when the family story of Genesis changes character. From Abraham to Jacob, the story has run from father to one chosen son (with other sons being included only in stories of their exclusion). But Jacob has twelve sons, and a mode of narration determined by generational succession cannot cope with this. "It is easy to imagine a story where, from paralepsis to paralepsis, chronology disappears in favor of a movement of enlargement; rather than from father to son, the fabula would develop from brother to brother (as in Genesis 37–38–39), or sister to cousin, to second cousin, and so forth: what a nightmare!" (94). Judah's story is just as good as Joseph's; why should it not be told? But so is Reuben's, or Levi's, or Issachar's. Genesis 38 is a fragment of a nightmare, the nightmare of a story that cannot move forward because there are no limits on its moving sideways, a nightmare for the urgent sequentiality of biblical narrative, but also for the whole Western view of narration.

SURVEYING THE FIELD

The two foregoing readings are inspired, respectively, by what Robert Scholes (1974:157) calls "high" and "low" structuralism. *High structuralism,* which he sees exemplified in Lévi-Strauss, concentrates on "deep" structures (the static logical relationships among elements), while *low structuralism,* exemplified in Genette's narratology, is more concerned with the modalities of "surface" structures. A second important difference is that narratology has mostly been a native growth within the ongoing practice of literary criticism, whereas high structuralism has been more of an interdisciplinary invasion of the literary realm. Although the distinction is not perfect, we adopt it for working purposes here.

Daniel Patte and High Biblical Structuralism Structuralism originates with the linguistics of Ferdinand de Saussure, which is built on a number of axioms. First, the distinction between *parole* and *langue* (1959:14–15, the French words are retained in the English discussion). Parole is any particular piece of language, typically the sentence; langue is the system of relationships that constitute the language and that makes possible any parole. The langue is an abstraction posited through the study of those paroles that the linguistic community accepts as well formed; the members of the community typically have little conscious awareness of the system, but their ability to judge and to create acceptable sentences implies that they have internalized it. Second, the distinction between *synchronic* and *diachronic* method (79–100). Saussure stresses the synchronic study of the langue at a given point in time at the expense of diachronic study of its development over time. This represents a further level of abstraction, since we cannot stop the constant flux of language in order to examine its structure at a given

moment. Third, the tenet that the elements of language do not have meaning in themselves, but only through their systemic relations to all the other
elements of langue (111–20). (A classic example is the noncorrespondence
of color terms in different languages; the spectral range that a majority of
French-speakers call "bleu" does not correspond exactly to the range that
a majority of English-speakers call "blue." The "meaning" of "blue" is that
range which a majority of English-speakers do not call some other color!
Greimas, 1983a:27.) Fourth, the distinction between two sorts of relation
in which linguistic elements stand to each other: the *syntagmatic* relations
between the ordered elements that make up a sentence, and the *paradigmatic* relations between a given element and all the elements that could be
substituted for it in the same sentence (Saussure, 1959:122–27).

Saussure works at the level of the sentence. The possibility of a structural study of narrative depends on the hypothesis that analogous constraints
work on the story. A given story corresponds to Saussure's parole, and the
hypothesis is that narrative has its langue, an internalized system which
the narrative community unconsciously applies in determining whether a
given story is well formed. The findings of Propp, referred to in our first
exegetical example, immediately lend plausibility to such a hypothesis. The
invariable order in which the narrative functions occur in Russian folktales
seems to imply a constraint analogous to word order in sentences; the narrative community is admitting only well-ordered stories (ones that observe the
operative system of constraints) in just the way that the linguistic community
admits only well-ordered sentences.

The possibility of a narrative syntax, opened up by Propp, was pursued
by Greimas. But before turning to him, we must look at Lévi-Strauss's generalization of Saussure's linguistics, through which structuralism was established as an interdisciplinary method (its wide extension to other fields can
be seen by reference to the anthologies of de George and de George, Ehrmann, and Lane). An anthropologist, Lévi-Strauss suggested that social sub-
systems of primitive societies could be seen as analogous to language and
analyzed under the assumptions of Saussurean linguistics. In a kinship system, for example, permissible and impermissible marriages are analogous to
syntactical and asyntactical sentences, and marriage is organized according
to a system that the society has internalized without necessarily being aware
of the logic underlying it (in fact, Lévi-Strauss claims, there are only a very
few possible "logics" of kinship, and all manifest kinship systems represent
quite simple transformations of these; see 1969).

Lévi-Strauss's most extensive work is on myth (Lévi-Strauss, 1963b) and it provides a brief programmatic statement, but for real insight into his approach it is essential to consult his four-volume magnum opus on Amerindian mythology (1970, 1973, 1978, 1981). Myths, like Propp's folktales, are a form of language, so that a structural approach can be thought of as an extension of Saussure's linguistics. But Lévi-Strauss downplays Propp's *syntagmatic* approach, based on establishing a sequence of categories, in favor of a *paradigmatic* approach, which insists on the importance of the particular terms that are substituted for each other in myth. (Lévi-Strauss early recognized the importance of Propp but insisted that an adequate structural approach must deal with the possible meanings of terms and functions, not just their sequence; see his "Structure and Form" [1977:115–45].)

Lévi-Strauss's approach is to reduce a given myth to a complex "sentence," and then to relate it to other myth-sentences from which it differs only in a certain number of terms. For example, he analyzes several South American myths of the origin of tobacco as having one or the other of the following structures:

> A *husband* has a *jaguar wife* [*affine* relative], *destructive* through the *mouth* of a *husband* who has climbed a tree looking for *animal* food that the *wife ought not* to eat (but *does*); disjunction through the agency of the *husband*, the *mother* killed by *affine* relatives.
>
> A *mother* has a *snake son* [*blood* relative] *protective* through the *vagina* of a *son* who has climbed a tree looking for *vegetable* food that the *mother ought* to eat (but *does not*); disjunction through the agency of the *mother*, the *son* killed by *blood* relatives. (Adapted from 1970:104)

By this means, the many myths of a culture can be displayed as a complex set of "transformations" of each other, transformations that, at the most abstract level, are based on *binary oppositions*. Humanity is confronted by a world of oppositions (life and death, male and female, nature and culture, and so on), which it needs to explain to itself in such a way as to make the world livable. This is the work of myth. Myths organize the oppositions, and thus make the world comprehensible. But it must do more than this; it must *mediate,* render controllable, the most intolerable of the oppositions. For example, a myth may mediate the opposition between life and death by substituting the more tolerable opposition between farming and war (1963b:224). Lévi-Strauss suggests there is an innate human necessity to deal with the world in this sort of way.

Greimas takes from Propp the possibility of a narrative syntax. But as he attempts to define the elementary units of narrative and to frame rules governing their acceptable combination, he finds Propp's functions to be far from an adequate level of abstraction. Functions that Propp differentiates have, according to Greimas, an identical logical structure (1983a:222–35). In his early work, Greimas thus produces highly abstract and general models for narrative syntax, of which the actantial model is the most important and best known. But, like Lévi-Strauss, he is not content with a syntactics of semantically empty categories (even the actantial roles, though they can be filled in an endless variety of ways, are subject to constraints at the level of meaning). Thus Greimas intends from the outset a structural approach to narrative that will bring together syntagmatic and paradigmatic structural approaches, and his later work is an attempt to refine such a model.

Daniel Patte has applied Greimas's approach to biblical studies, while at the same time continuing to be one of Greimas's main collaborators in its theoretical development. His first attempt to develop a method (Patte, 1976b) consists (after an opening discussion, still well worth reading, of the relation in exegesis between structural and historical methods) of chapters on Saussure's linguistic model, on narrative structures (Greimas), and on mythical structures (Lévi-Strauss). Under "narrative structures," Patte presents a method whereby the action of any text can be syntactically represented as a set of sequences, each of which is itself represented by Greimas's actantial model. But at the end of this account, he admits that such analysis "yields very limited results" without subsequent "analysis in terms of the mythical structure" (1976b:52). Under "mythical structures," he then applies some basic Lévi-Straussian moves to New Testament texts, but his mythic analysis is felt by most readers to be less successful than the Greimasian narrative analysis and poorly integrated with it. So this first book does not fulfill the urgent need for a way of bringing the two together, but the later work of Patte is devoted to this need. It consists of two major forms of a theoretical proposal (Patte and Patte, 1978, Patte, 1990a), two attempts to show how such theory can undergird a much less technical and more widely accessible interpretation of biblical books (1983, 1987), and a second attempt to present structuralism at the level of "Guides to Biblical Scholarship," consisting mostly of step-by-step exegetical exercises (1990c). This work of a dozen years is not all of a piece because Patte has continued to incorporate the developing thinking of the Greimas circle.

Patte and Patte (1978) represents a major step forward in at least two respects. First, it defines a precise goal for structural work on the Bible, namely, to identify the system of "convictions" and "values" that generates a text (1–10). Second, it lays out and demonstrates a complete method for moving from a narrative to the mythic structure, or value system, that generates it. The major new tool (vis-à-vis Patte, 1976b) is the *semiotic square* (Patte and Patte, 19; the square is derived from Aristotle's logic, cf., for example, Güttgemanns, 32–33):

(1) A ⟷ B

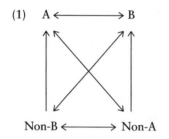

Non-B ⟷ Non-A

(2) Life ⟷ Death

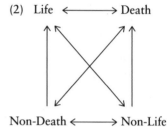

Non-Death ⟷ Non-Life

In (1) above, A and B are represented as contrary semantic categories, typically the categories of human experience that function as binary oppositions in Lévi-Strauss's view of myth, for example "life" and "death" in (2). But A and B are not absolute opposites, contradictories; logically, the contradictory to A must be non-A, everything that is not A. But this non-A opens up a whole range of possibilities, any one of which might be substituted for B, and Lévi-Strauss's work on myth can be understood precisely as this work of substitution.

Patte and Patte read a text first of all for its contradictions, narrative units that directly negate each other. In terms of Greimas's actantial model, the same object is transferred to opposed receivers, or opposed objects are transferred to the same receiver, or the same object is transferred and not transferred to the same receiver (Patte and Patte, 27). For example, in Mark 15:17 and 46 opposed objects—purple cloak and shroud—are transferred to one receiver—Jesus (53). Second, by reading these contradictory units in narrative sequence, they are able to create relations of contrariety between the terms of consecutive contradictories and thus build up a linked system of semiotic squares. From this system, eventually, the deep values of the whole text can be read off.

Patte's most recent theoretical statement (1990a) considerably refines the 1978 proposal, particularly in laying out the stages and levels of a narrative analysis in the form of a "generative trajectory." But his prescriptions for analyzing actual biblical texts (as laid out in Patte, 1990c), though they are expressed rather more simply, do not differ fundamentally from Patte and Patte. In Patte's books on Paul (1983) and Matthew (1987), virtually all the technical detail is absent, but Patte assures the reader that the complete theory is still operating behind the scenes in reaching exegetical conclusions. Throughout all these works, the steps involved are basically (1) the identification of *explicit oppositions* in the text, (2) using these to identify the author's *"faith"* or *"convictions,"* and (3) exhibiting the author's *way of persuading* the reader of these convictions.

Although Patte's work is dominant in the English-language development of this tradition of biblical structuralism, a good deal of other work needs to be mentioned.[1] First, his oeuvre needs to be seen in the context of French biblical structuralism, particularly the work of the Centre pour l'Analyse du Discours Religieux (CADIR), which is dedicated to the application of semiotic theory in general—and the structural semiotics of Greimas in particular—to the exegesis of the Bible (in fact, the development of the Greimasian system as a whole owes a great deal to CADIR). This work is distinguished by its appeal to both scholarly and nonscholarly readers of the Bible and by its commitment to pedagogical as well as theoretical concerns. The main organ for the work of CADIR is the journal *Sémiotique et bible* (1975–). (Cf. also Almeida; Calloud [1976]; Delorme [1973]; Panier [1973, 1984, 1991].) The collaborative and cross-disciplinary practice of CADIR has stimulated the production of numerous co-authored and multi-authored works (Calloud and Genuyt, 1982, 1987, 1989; Groupe d'Entrevernes, 1978, 1979; Giroud and Panier; Chené) and has led to institutional affiliations with universities in North America (e.g., Vanderbilt University). There has been relatively little translation into English of structural analysis of the Bible in French; the most important exceptions are Barthes et al. (including Roland Barthes's own celebrated reading of Gen. 32:23–33 [1974a], for which cf. chap. 3 on poststructuralism), Barthes (1988c), Calloud (1976), Genuyt, Groupe d'Entrevernes (1978), and Marin (who takes a notably interdisciplinary approach).[2] Another European journal owing its origin to the same

---

[1] For the most comprehensive survey to date of semiotics, in particular Greimasian semiotics, in relation to biblical studies, see Delorme, 1992.

[2] Indeed, the translation of Greimas's work was slow in coming; but see now Greimas, 1983a, 1987, 1988, 1990, and, perhaps most important, the dictionary of Greimas and Courtés.

impulse, and roughly contemporaneous with *Sémiotique et bible*, is Erhardt Güttgemanns's *Linguistica Biblica*. Again, there has been little translation of Güttgemanns's work to date (but see 1976).

During the 1970s, there was a good deal of experimentation by North American biblical scholars with approaches developed out of the work of Saussure, Lévi-Strauss, Propp, Greimas, and Roland Barthes (e.g., Crossan, 1973, 1975; Funk, 1982; Patte, 1976a [the papers of the important 1973 Vanderbilt Conference]); Polzin, 1977; Via; Hugh White, 1979). It was in the context of this movement that the journal *Semeia* was generated, and a number of its early issues were devoted to such work (1, 2 [1974], 6 [1976], 18 [1980], 26 [1983]). During this time, the Structuralism and Exegesis Group in the Society of Biblical Literature became established under Patte's leadership. Of particular interest among the structural work emerging from this group is *Semeia* 18, a large collection of alternative structural exegeses of a single text (Genesis 2–3), with a variety of critical responses (cf. also *Semeia* 26).

Since 1980, aside from Patte, there has been a decline in North American work along these lines. We may mention Elizabeth Struthers Malbon (1986b), whose work on the "geographical code" in Mark remains close to Lévi-Strauss; Hendrickus Boers, who uses the developed Greimasian theory; David Jobling, who in his work on the Hebrew Bible (1986a, b, 1991a, 1992) pursues a line more loosely adapted from both Lévi-Strauss and Greimas and tending toward deconstructive and ideological analysis; Robert Culley, who provides interesting readings with a rather slight theoretical base in structural folklore studies (1976; cf. the Proppian approach of Culley, 1992); and Terry Prewitt, who takes a Lévi-Straussian anthropological approach. The structuralist impulse, particularly from Lévi-Strauss, has had other important impacts on biblical studies outside of any specific literary theory, and they should be briefly noted here. Structural understandings of kinship have been applied to the Bible by Leach (esp. 1969:25–83), Leach and Aycock, and Mara Donaldson (as well as Prewitt). Indeed, Leach's was the first direct application of structural analysis to the Bible (1969:7–23, orig. 1961), and it has important implications for literary study. But Leach treats the Bible as a cluster of Lévi-Straussian mythic fragments, without regard for sequential narrative. Of at least as great importance, but further from our concerns, is Mary Douglas's application of structural anthropology to the Levitical prohibitions. In a quite different direction, Eugene Nida and his associates have developed the semantic aspects of structural linguistics, particularly for translation purposes (Nida, Nida et al., Louw).

The Narratological Tradition Although Scholes (1974:157–67) uses Gérard Genette to exemplify low structuralism, and although Genette is often included in the early surveys of literary structuralism (e.g., Culler, 1975b), further development along the lines he staked out has almost never used the term *structuralism* of itself, and *narratology* has become the term of choice. Narratology has drawn upon a great variety of literary streams, as can be seen from typical handbooks (Rimmon-Kenan, who mentions "Anglo-American New Criticism, French Structuralism, the Tel-Aviv School of Poetics and the Phenomenology of Reading" [5]; Bal, 1985; Toolan, 1988) or from the recent double issue of *Poetics Today* (11/2 and 4, 1990), "Narratology Revisited." But to the extent that it has maintained the urge to a comprehensive theory of narrative, the "isolating, characterizing, and classifying . . . of features distinctive of or pertinent to narrative" (adapted from Prince, 1990:271), it falls within the area of our concern in this chapter.

Genette's *Narrative Discourse* (1980, a translation of "Discours du récit," a self-contained unit within Genette, 1972) is an elegant dialectic of theoretical and descriptive poetics, in which description gives rise to inductive theory and theory enables further description. This dialectic is built on a firm refusal to give ultimate priority to either theory or description. In contrast to high structuralist predecessors who opted for less challenging primary material (e.g., myths or folktales), Genette adopts Marcel Proust's *A la recherche du temps perdu* as his primary text.

His initial move (1980:25–32) is to distinguish three levels that may be posited of any narrative. First there is that which is given, the *narrative* (*récit*), the text itself, from which can be reconstructed on the one hand the story (*histoire*), or signified content (the events that are the object of the narrative), and on the other hand the *narrating* (*narration*), the act of narrating with its spatial and temporal context. Once this tripartite distinction has been established, Genette's theoretical and descriptive activity takes the form of positing and categorizing the many possible relations between the three levels. *Tense* designates the temporal relation between story and narrative—the chronological sequence of events, for example, as opposed to a rearranged textual sequence (cf. our second biblical example, above). *Mood* designates the other, nontemporal modalities of story's realization as narrative—the narrator's filtering and coloring of the story content (e.g., Luke 3:23: "Jesus, when he began his ministry, was about thirty years of age, being the son, as was supposed, of Joseph"). *Voice*, finally, designates the shifting relation of the narrating to the story, on the one hand, and to the addressee(s), on the other (e.g., Luke 1:1–4).

Although Genette may be regarded as the most important founding figure (his is the name easily the most often cited in two recent dictionaries of narratology; cf. Coste, 407), his work represents only a beginning; when Proust is distilled from its pages it consists, as Dorrit Cohn has remarked, of "a slim, highly condensed, not always explicitly connected theoretical text" (1981:158). The work of Seymour Chatman is, in comparison, highly systematized (as is a third notable theory of narrative, that of Franz Stanzel; see 1984). Impelled by the example of Genette, as well as Barthes, Claude Brémond, Tzvetan Todorov, and other French narratologists, Chatman took up the challenge of a comprehensive theory of narrative in his *Story and Discourse* (1978), building on the dualistic distinction between the *what* of narrative (its content) and the *how* of narrative (the way in which that content is expressed): "We may ask, as does the linguist about language: What are the necessary components—and only those—of a narrative? Structuralist theory argues that each narrative has two parts: a story (*histoire*), the content or chain of events (actions, happenings), plus what may be called the existents (characters, items of setting); and a discourse (*discours*), that is, the expression, the means by which the content is communicated" (19). Genette had already begun a critical assimilation of Anglo-American work on point of view into the French tradition, and in Chatman this assimilation becomes synthesis; French narratology in the mode of Barthes, Genette, and Todorov merges with Anglo-American literary theory in the modes of Wayne C. Booth, Ronald Crane, and Northrop Frye. Chatman's synthetic project has been further extended by others, notably Rimmon-Kenan (1983).

Biblical developments along these lines were slow starting. Given the vigorous application of French structuralist theory to biblical texts in North America through the 1970s, it is surprising that biblical scholars did not then begin to draw upon the narratological tradition. It was only in the 1980s, with the decline of high biblical structuralism in North America, that narratological approaches became the preferred way of appropriating literary and cognate studies for biblical research. These developments have been eclectic, drawing on the low structuralist narratology of Genette and Chatman, on the influential Anglo-American development of narrative theory concerned especially with *point of view* (a term that at its most comprehensive encompasses everything the author does to impose a story-world upon an audience; Wayne C. Booth, 1961, is generally regarded its classic expression), on studies of readers and reading (Iser 1974, 1978; cf. our chap. 1), and on other impulses to be noted. Our criteria for inclusion here are the seriousness of the commitment to identifying formal features, and the nature and quality of ongoing dialogue between particular biblical studies and general narratology.

NARRATIVE CRITICISM OF THE GOSPELS In New Testament studies, it is mainly in work on the Gospels that narratological exegesis has assumed the unified aspect of a movement, under the name *narrative criticism* (see Malbon, 1992; Powell, however, notes that "secular literary scholarship knows no such movement as narrative criticism" [1990a:19]). This movement-like character of New Testament narrative criticism derives in part from its origins: it began in the 1970s in the Markan Seminar of the Society of Biblical Literature. The seminar was chaired first by Norman Perrin and then by Werner Kelber. Its members included Robert Fowler, Norman Petersen, David Rhoads, Robert Tannehill, and Mary Ann Tolbert, all of whom would make influential contributions to the new literary study of the Gospels. (In the 1980s and into the 1990s, work on narrative criticism has continued in the Literary Aspects of the Gospels and Acts Group.)

In 1980, the tenth and final year of the Markan Seminar, David Rhoads presented a paper "Narrative Criticism and the Gospel of Mark" (Rhoads, 1982), which surveyed the 1970s literary work on Mark and for the first time programmatically labeled the new approach *narrative criticism* (Petersen, 1978a and others had already used the term, but not in Rhoads's consistent and definitive way). For Rhoads, it denotes a broad area of inquiry whose principal foci are "plot, conflict, character, setting, narrator, point of view, standards of judgment, the implied author, ideal reader, style, and rhetorical techniques" (412).

He sees the shift to narrative criticism as a shift from "fragmentation" to "wholeness": "We know how to take the text apart to analyze it; adding narrative criticism to our study is an opportunity to reaffirm the original achievement of Mark in creating a unified story" (413). Mark's story-world has "autonomous integrity" for Rhoads, an internal consistency and validity that is quite independent of its resemblance or nonresemblance to the actual world of Jesus or Mark. Indeed, Rhoads would define narrative criticism precisely in terms of this idea:

> Narrative criticism works with the text as "world-in-itself." Other approaches tend to fragment, in part because their purpose is to put elements of the text into contexts outside the text; so, for example, biblical scholars may identify the feeding of the five thousand as an historical event in Jesus' time or as an oral story emerging from the early church or as a vehicle for a theological truth . . . or as a story which reveals the author's intentions, or as instructions to Mark's community. Narrative criticism brackets these historical questions and looks at the closed universe of the story-world. (Of course, knowledge of the history and culture of the first century is a crucial aid to understanding Mark's story-world, but that is a different matter from using elements of the text to reconstruct historical events.) (413; cf. Powell, 1990a:7–8)

Rhoads's conceptions of the text and of the critical task have marked affinities with those of the New Criticism, which was the dominant mode of Anglo-American literary criticism from the late 1930s through the 1950s (cf. Wellek, 144–292). Rejecting all "extrinsic" approaches to literature—biographical, historical, sociological, philosophical—the New Critics reconceived the literary work of art (epitomized by the poem) as an autonomous, internally unified organism. Rhoads makes a comparable claim for the Markan text. In fact, this holistic conception of the literary text, which is very basic for gospel narrative criticism, derives much less from the narratological tradition than from New Criticism.

A basic New Critical tenet was that form and content were inseparable. Form was no longer to be seen merely as instrumental, the vehicle for an ideational or propositional content or a cultural or historical reality, separable from the literary organism and independent of it. Instead the meaning of the text was said to be indissolubly bonded with its form. Compare Rhoads: having indicated how traditional scholarship might interpret the feeding of the five thousand in Mark (historically or theologically, i.e., in terms of some historical or theological content), he offers a formalist interpretation of the same event: "The feeding of the five thousand is a dramatic episode *in the continuum of Mark's story*." Within that continuum, each element has its place: "Jesus, Herod, the centurion—dramatic characters. The exorcisms, the healings, the journeys, the trial and crucifixion—vivid elements in the world of Mark's story, each element important and integral" (413–14, his emphasis; cf. Powell, 1990a:8; for the inseparability of form and content in Mark, cf. also Rhoads and Michie, 4, 62; and Beardslee, 1970:2: "Participation in the form is itself an essential part of the reading of a literary work").

Nowhere in "Narrative Criticism and the Gospel of Mark," or in his subsequent *Mark as Story* (with Donald Michie), does Rhoads acknowledge the similarity of his views with those of the New Critics. Indeed, it is not clear whether or to what extent he is even aware of this resemblance. And he is not alone. His insistence that participation in the narrative form of a gospel is essential for its adequate interpretation is widely echoed by other narrative critics as well (e.g., Culpepper, 4–5; Kingsbury, 1988a:2; Tannehill, 1986:8).

Norman Petersen's article " 'Point of View' in Mark's Narrative" (1978b) was the first published study of a New Testament text to focus on point of view. Drawing on Boris Uspensky, Petersen attempts a schematic analysis of the narrator's role in Mark. He analyzes the narrator's point of view in terms of its ideological, phraseological, spatio-temporal, and psychological dimensions. Ideologically, for example, he finds that everything in Mark is evaluated from one point of view, that which the narrator and Jesus share. Indeed, in Mark only two ideological viewpoints are possible: the divine or the human. This opposition receives explicit expression in Mark 8:33 when Jesus accuses Peter of thinking in human terms. Even demons and other opponents (e.g., 1:24; 14:61) are made vehicles for the narrator's ideology; it permeates every facet of the narrative.

Rhoads and Michie's *Mark as Story: An Introduction to the Narrative of a Gospel* (1982) takes its lead from Chatman's *Story and Discourse*. Rhoads and Michie's opening move is to distinguish between the content of a narrative, its *story,* and the form of a narrative, its *rhetoric.* Here they depart from Chatman's terminology, though not from his understanding of how narrative functions: "The story refers to 'what' a narrative is about—the basic elements of the narrative world—events, characters, and settings. Rhetoric refers to 'how' that story is told in a given narrative in order to achieve certain effects upon the reader. Thus we can distinguish between " 'what' the story is about and 'how' the story is told" (Rhoads and Michie, 1982:4). The authors hasten to assure us, however, that as content and form, the "what" and the "how" are nonetheless inseparable. "Only for purposes of analysis" are they separated, and even then the "fragmentary analysis" (of character or style, for example) is redressed by interpreting each feature in the context of the entire narrative. The organization of *Mark as Story* follows on from the separation of the "what" and the "how," story and rhetoric. Its first substantive chapter ("The Rhetoric") examines how the story is presented, that is, the role of the narrator, point of view, standards of judgment, style, narrative patterns, and so forth. The succeeding chapters ("The Settings," "The Plot," "Characters") examine the story, or the narrative "what."

In 1983 Alan Culpepper's influential *Anatomy of the Fourth Gospel* appeared. Culpepper's book, too (like a number of similar studies, e.g., Kingsbury, 1988, 1989, 1991), is heavily dependent on Chatman, though for different reasons than *Mark as Story*. Both books were faced with the same problem: what should a comprehensive narrative analysis of a gospel treat, and how should it be organized? Rhoads and Michie's solution was shaped, as we have seen, by Chatman's two-tiered model of story and discourse. Culpepper's solution is shaped more by Chatman's narrative communication model (Chatman, 1978:151):

Narrative Text

Real Author - - > | Implied Author → (Narrator) → (Narratee) → Implied Reader | - - > Real Reader

Chatman's diagram has had a profound impact on the way that New Testament narrative critics conceive of the gospel text (cf. Powell, 1990a:27). The communication from the real (actual, historical) author to the real reader is conducted instrumentally through the narrative personae within the box. Distinct from the flesh-and-blood author is the *implied author* (cf. Wayne C. Booth, 1961:70–76, 151). This term denotes the complex, shifting image of the real author that the reader infers as he or she reads—a selecting, structuring, presiding intelligence, indirectly discerned in the text, rather like God in his or her creation. The *narrator* is also said to be immanent in the text as the voice that tells the story, a voice which may or may not be that of one of the characters (John of Revelation and the "we"-narrator of Luke-Acts are biblical examples of narrators who participate in the story as characters). The *narratee* is defined as the narrator's immediate addressee (e.g., Theophilus in Luke-Acts), and the *implied reader* as the persona presupposed or produced by the text as (in some theories) its ideal interpreter.

Having set himself the task of "understanding the gospel as a narrative text, what it is, and how it works," Culpepper presents an elaborated version of Chatman's communications diagram. The main difference between Culpepper's version of the diagram and that reproduced above is that *story* is put in the space between narrator and narratee as the content of the narrative communication. Such a model will enable a fresh understanding of "what the gospel is and how it achieves its effects" (3), and Culpepper goes on to show how his book will be organized around it. Chapter 2, the first substantive chapter, "is devoted to a discussion of . . . the narrator," along with a look at the real and implied author. "Chapters 3 through 6 are devoted to various components of the story, its time, its plot, its characters, and the implicit commentary [e.g., irony and symbolism] which makes it so intriguing." Finally, chapter 7 is an analysis of the gospel's audience, as implied and circumscribed by the text.

THE POETICS OF THE HEBREW BIBLE Developments in Hebrew Bible studies have been different, though related (some of the gospel developments just considered were in fact anticipated in James Muilenberg's 1969 manifesto "Form Criticism and Beyond," which was similarly colored by Anglo-American formalism; e.g., "The literary unit is . . . an indissoluble whole, an artistic and creative unity, a unique formulation" [369]). The term *poetics* is often preferred to *narratology* or *narrative criticism;* this is the result of the influence (esp. through Meir Sternberg) of the Tel Aviv school of poetics (narratology is properly "a subdivision of poetics" [Berlin, 15], but "poetics" in the discussion usually means narrative poetics). In contrast to the focus in New Testament studies on the differences between the Gospels, there are few suggestions that different portions of Hebrew Bible narrative have special features (Polzin, 1980, 1989, on the Deuteronomic history is perhaps an exception), but there is a strong concern for a poetics special to the narrative of the Hebrew Bible as a whole. This often leads to a reluctance to explore the nonbiblical origins of methods in use.

Thus Shimon Bar-Efrat (1989) organizes biblical "narrative art" under the categories of narrator, characters, plot, time and space, and style but pays no attention to what these terms mean outside the Bible. Robert Alter, a highly prominent literary critic outside of biblical studies, likewise, in his highly sophisticated treatment (1981), applies to the Bible categories current in the wider debate (dialogue, repetition, etc.), while being very sparing in his references to that debate (though in Alter, 1989, he does bring some comments on biblical narrative into the context of a general literary discussion). The ideal of a special biblical poetics is affirmed by Adele Berlin: "The type of poetics that I am advocating is less foreign to biblical studies because it is derived from and restricted to the Bible. I do not seek a theory that can be applied to all narrative, but only a theory of biblical narrative. Before we can understand general poetics we must understand specific poetics" (19). Despite such statements, Berlin does, in fact, relate her poetics to general narrative theory (making, for example, systematic use of models proposed by Uspensky and William Labov); her insistence on a special poetics is meant to rule out structuralist approaches, which are abstract, and which aspire to reduce the Bible to some lowest common denominator with all other literature (19; cf. Rosenberg's rejection of synchronic approaches [104–6]).

But there are a number of writers on Hebrew Bible narrative who adopt a variety of more interesting stances toward structuralisms and formalisms. Jan Fokkelman (cf. somewhat similarly Eslinger, 1985), in his close analyses of Genesis (1991) and Samuel (1986), invokes a large range of formalist and structuralist figures (the following list is culled from Fokkelman, 1986: Jonathan Culler, Greimas, Eugene Nida, Genette, Bal, Michael Riffaterre, Propp, Roman Jakobson, Frank Kermode). But even he does not in a sustained way bring the Bible into relationship with any particular theory. His thoroughly inductive approach (in which he stands as far as possible from the deductive attitude essential to any structuralism) implies that no attempt at a comprehensive hypothesis will be appropriate until "some 2000 pages" of particular analyses have been completed (1986:1).

The most massive single contribution to the poetics of Hebrew Bible narrative is that of Meir Sternberg, who, as a prominent member of the Tel Aviv school of poetics, is very much a participant in the larger narratology debate in literary criticism (cf., among many contributions, 1978, 1990a—in relation to the latter, note that *Poetics Today* is published in Tel Aviv). The Tel Aviv school is generally formalist in orientation, with particular affinities to Russian formalism (Mintz, 216). Mintz discusses the founder of the school, Hrushovski, pointing to his scientific rather than aesthetic stance and his anti-hermeneutical concern for what literature is (cf. particularly Hrushovski's schematic diagram [Mintz, 221] whereby he wants to fix the role of every aspect of literary endeavor in relation to a total view of which poetics is the arbiter). Mintz contends (217) that the Tel Aviv school is not pluralistic in outlook and that it tends toward a near-contemptuous critique of the shallowness of most literary criticism (219). But its distinctive contribution to general narratology, particularly to our understanding of "textual energy and movement," is acknowledged, for example, by Pavel (350; cf. Coste, 405); and a book like David Bordwell's (e.g., 55–58), on film theory, makes clear how broad Sternberg's influence has been.

But the uninformed reader of *The Poetics of Biblical Narrative* (1985), where most of Sternberg's biblical work is found (but cf. 1986, 1990b, 1991), would guess at little of this theoretical background. The readings of biblical texts in this book do indeed bring to the foreground theoretical issues of great importance (point of view, repetition, and the like). But these issues are treated as inner-biblical; there is little sustained dialogue with narratological theory. And this is only somewhat less true of the three more directly theoretical chapters with which the book begins; the spasmodic references to figures like Booth, Culler, Iser, and Kermode do not establish dialogue. What Sternberg decidedly does bear out, however, is Mintz's remarks about contempt for other critics (cf. Sternberg's remarks on David Robertson [1985:4–7] or his reference to reading "in bad faith" [50]; cf. also Bal's remarks about his "insults" [1991:62]).

A North American critic whose work is closely related to Sternberg's is Robert Polzin. After some early work in the high structuralist mode (1977), Polzin turned in *Moses and the Deuteronomist* (1980) to a method drawing on the Russian formalists, especially the school of Mikhail Bakhtin. Bakhtin's method is to analyze the interplay of voices in the text, those of the narrator and the characters, especially under the categories of "monologue" and "dialogue," and to correlate different treatments of the voices with different narrative "ideologies" (1980:16–24, with reference to Bakhtin, Voloshinov [= Bakhtin], and Uspensky). Applying this to Deuteronomy, Joshua, and Judges, Polzin finds each of these books to differ in the way it understands divine initiative and human response, divine speech and human interpretation, so that a given book becomes an answer, or a corrective, to earlier ones. This work is of great interest, analyzing the role of the narrator with a depth and complexity rarely found in narratological work on the Bible.

Mieke Bal, even more than Sternberg, is a prominent participant in literary-critical debates over narratology and has written a handbook on the subject (1985). Most of her work on the Bible is found in a trilogy of books which, appearing in the late 1980s, have begun to have a profound impact on biblical studies (1987, 1988a, 1988b; cf. Jobling, 1991b, Boyarin, 1990b).

Bal's work developed first under the influence of Genette, and her name is particularly associated with the development of his concept of *focalization*. But her attitude toward the structuralist origins of her work is a critical one;

while continuing to acknowledge that "going through the early structuralist texts has been decisive for my thinking," especially by instilling the necessity of the "pursuit of rigor" (1991:5), she now claims that "narratology is at an impasse," having "not succeeded in . . . putting itself in the service of any critical practice" (1991:27). Bal's demand for a critical narratology in the service of a general cultural critique is even more important to us than the following particulars of her biblical readings, and we shall return to it below.

Bal's biblical writings draw on a variety of structuralist proposals. Although she is a sharp critic of Greimas's approach, she invokes his use of the semiotic square to present the theological and literary codes of the Book of Judges (1988b:41, 44, 77). In our second exegetical example, above, she critically adapts Genette's treatment of narrative temporality in relation to Genesis 38. But her most far-reaching and usable proposal (again a development of Genette) is for an analysis of texts according to their rendering of *narrative subjectivity.* At the simplest level, she asks of the text "who speaks? . . . who sees? . . . who acts?" How, that is, does the text distribute among the narrator and the characters the functions of direct speech, narrative action, and focalization (providing the eyes through which the events of the text are at a given moment being perceived)? Even a mere quantitative analysis (who speaks, who speaks most, who speaks not at all) is revealing, but the analysis needs to be much more subtle (who speaks first, who speaks with power, who gets to focalize the final result of the narrative events, and so on).

This scheme is capable of fruitful application to biblical texts, and Bal claims that it underlies all her biblical work. But she does not make it sufficiently clear, especially to the reader of her English biblical trilogy, how it is being applied. The scheme is summarized in a chart at the end of *Death and Dissymmetry* (1988a:248–49), and the theory is presented discursively, with useful examples from Judges, in the introductory theoretical chapter (34–38, cf. 234). But the analyses of which the central chapters of the book consist are only spasmodically related to the scheme, and, in fact, it is best to precede a reading of the biblical trilogy by reading the full statement of the theory in chapter 6 of Bal, 1991 (esp. 159–68).[3]

---

[3] The problem is that this chapter was part of the material omitted when *Femmes imaginaires* (1986b) was partially translated into English as *Lethal Love* (1987). In the original, the chapter was immediately preceded by one on the story of David and Bathsheba (translated as 1987:10–36), which is why it contains a number of illustrations from that story.

In *Narration and Discourse in the Book of Genesis* (1991), Hugh White draws on theoreticians not otherwise used by biblical scholars, the semiotic philosophy of Edmund Ortigues, the linguistics of Eugenio Coseriu, and the literary theory of Angel Medina. On more familiar ground, he employs a discourse analysis grounded in Bakhtin (and related to that used by Polzin, 1980), the Genettian narratological tradition, and speech-act theory. All this he is able to weave into a convincing whole which breaks new ground in biblical narratology. Before turning to the Genesis narrative, he devotes fully a third of the book to narratological theory, a procedure that other biblical narratologists would do well to copy.

For White, the human subject is created only in *intersubjectivity* as it relates linguistically with other subjects. The child's entry into language is traumatic, as the identity of consciousness and world is disrupted and the immediacy of the image gives way to the distance of the sign. But the trauma is also an entry into open possibility. The child is not merely subjected to an alien system of signs; it becomes, as it develops subjecthood through its intersubjective use of language, a co-creator of the system. The function of literature is to reenact and make the subject reflect on this fundamental process. According to White, the creation of narrative character "replicates . . . the trauma by which language was originally established in consciousness" (1991:45). Using the Russian formalist category of *defamiliarization,* he looks at literature in terms of its "effect upon the subject" (18).

He uses a typology of narrative based on the different modes in which the discourse of the narrator can be related to that of the characters. The typology correlates these modes with three "functions" of literature in general (cf. diagram, 58):

	Function		
Mode	Expressive	Representative	Symbolic
Passive	x	(x)	(x)
Indirect		x	(x)
Active			x

In this diagram, "x" indicates the dominant mode, "(x)" a subordinate mode used by a narrative function.

In simple terms, the representative function corresponds to the "she or he" of the narrator, and the expressive function to the "I" of the character.

In representative narrative, the narrator dominates, exercising control over the characters from a withdrawn, neutral perspective, claiming objective knowledge of the consciousness of the characters. The characters in such narratives generally play out conflicts over desired objects, rather than confronting open possibilities (the image dominates over the sign). Relevant for our purpose, White notes that this is Barthes's "readerly" text (Barthes, 1974b:4), which, according to Barthes (1974b:204), provides the material for structural analysis of the Propp-Greimas type. In extreme contrast is expressive narrative, which, in pure form, is very rare (White alludes to Ivy Compton-Burnett's novels as coming close). Here the characters break free of narratorial control, existing almost exclusively in dialogue with each other. In one sense, this constitutes the epitome of intersubjectivity; the subject is "wholly dependent on the other even for its own presence to itself" (Hugh White, 1991:71). But White sees this intersubjectivity in negative terms; the narrator's abdication looses the characters from the world of real subjects, and the plot can be driven only by "imaginary" conflicts of the characters' own devising; there is thus "an intersection of the dynamics of both the sign and the image."

It is through the symbolic function that this opposition is mediated. The barrier between narrator and character is lowered through the narrative production of an "impersonal consciousness" that belongs to neither narrator nor characters (76), but to which both "belong." The characters are in "inner dialogue within the author" (77). White finds a classic case in the work of Dostoyevsky, where the narrator is "dialogized" through the characters' inner dialogue with a "dominant idea" that transcends both author and characters. The writing that emerges is not fully under control, it is "unfinalizable" (88), in the process of coming to be. The act of writing becomes "a central force in the structure of the plot." There are no unequivocally good or bad personages and no normal resolution in the ending. The sign fully dominates the image.

In biblical narrative, specifically in Genesis, the "mediating language event" that breaks the barrier between narrator and characters and enables symbolic narrative, is, according to White, the divine voice. Formally, God is a character in the narrative. But the divine voice belongs neither to the given, stable world of representative narrative, nor to the relativistic world of expressive narrative. The narrator speaks as one who stands in the same relationship to the divine voice as the characters do; a single cause "impelled his characters to action and him to write about them" (Hugh White, 1991:102).

What constitutes characterhood in the Bible is being addressed by the divine voice, and White organizes his readings around the "micro-dialogues" between this voice and the character. Such characters are "free," but not in a "totally relativistic individualism." The micro-dialogue central to White's reading of Genesis is 12:1–3, a passage providing little referentiality or concrete context and no motivation for Abram's journey except the promise of "a positive relationship to the divine" (111). The time of the promise is, in part, future in relation to the narration, putting the author in the same relation to it as the characters.

But Gen. 12:1–3 requires a context, and it is provided especially by the Eden story in chapters 2–3. This narrative has a double task; to provide a foil for the intersubjective creation of Abram by telling of an earlier objective creation of human character, but to do so in such as way as to leave open the *possibility* of intersubjectivity. The Eden story seems like representative narration based on prohibition, villainy, the object of desire, and so on, and it concludes with objective bounds being set to human possibility and a hierarchical relationship between God and humans. Yet, within this framework, the symbolic perspective is kept open in a remarkable way. The desired object, knowledge of good and evil, lacks any specific content, and there is no human villain—rather, a hero-villain dynamic is set up *within* the humans; what humans lose is open communication with God, which is a source of unlimited possibility; and it is this that 12:1–3 restores.

A CRITIQUE OF STRUCTURALISM

Under the title *Structuralism and Semiotics,* Terence Hawkes tells a story of the development of the cluster of methods dealt with here. It is instructive to summarize this story, since it raises questions of scope and terminology that have bedeviled the entire structuralist debate.

The early chapters of Hawkes's book cover high structuralism, moving from Saussure, Propp, and Lévi-Strauss (Hawkes includes also Roman Jakobson) to the French literary structuralists of the 1960s (along with Greimas and Barthes, Hawkes includes Todorov). But this story does not directly lead anywhere; rather, after dealing with Greimas, Todorov, and

Barthes, Hawkes turns from structuralism to semiotics (chap. 4, "A Science of Signs"), first backtracking to C. S. Peirce, who predates any kind of structuralism, then revisiting Saussure and Barthes, but now from a semiotic angle, and concluding with a consideration of Jacques Derrida. It is not our intention to single out Hawkes's story of structuralism for special critique—its interest lies precisely in its similarity to those of many other commentators—but rather to probe the significance of some features of this typical account. (For purposes of comparison with Hawkes, the reader may refer to Scholes, 1974, and Culler, 1975b.)

First, Hawkes (despite some brief generalizing comments in his introduction) implies a quite narrow view of the scope of the structuralist impulse. Others (Lane, de George and de George, Piaget, Harland) cast the structuralist net wide, to include fields like mathematics, economics, and psychology. Hawkes's primary concern is literature. But who is responsible for the structuralist impact on literature? What, for example, of Marx and Freud? On the one hand, they have both had a profound effect on the recent study of literature. On the other hand, Lévi-Strauss, in a famous passage (1975:55–59), includes them as key influences in his development toward structuralism, and one anthology (de George and de George) opens with chapters on them (ahead of Saussure!). Are they not, then, part of the story of structuralism in literature?

Second, Hawkes deals poorly with the multiple lines of structuralist and related development in literary criticism in the 1960s and 1970s. Through his concentration on Greimas, Todorov, and Barthes he is complicit in the division between what we have called high and low structuralism. He mentions Genette only to suppress him without explanation: "Untreated in the present volume, Genette is an important figure in literary structuralism" (174). He has nothing about developments inspired by Mikhail Bakhtin, very different but related to the structuralist impulse (cf. Todorov, 1984). Like Genesis 38, this story has trouble handling a shift from "vertical" (generation to generation) narrative to a "horizontal" set of parallel and equal developments![4]

Third, Hawkes fails adequately to insert the French literary structuralism of the 1960s into its general intellectual context. All the vast developments associated with such figures as Derrida, Lacan, Althusser, Foucault, Deleuze

[4] Cf. Bal's reference to "the limitation of structuralism to a very narrow body of theory, that represented mainly by Greimas and Bremond in the wake of Propp" (1991:10).

and Guattari, Spivak, Kristeva, and Irigaray have close ties to structuralism. But none of these figure gets substantial treatment under "structuralism." Hawkes seems to assume a distinction between structuralism and *poststructuralism* (perhaps it was imposed on him under the terms of the series of which his book is a part). But the effect is to help establish this distinction, to indicate a story in which structuralism either is passé or has been absorbed into a vastly more comprehensive poststructuralism. However, most of the poststructuralist figures just listed haunt the book, at least through brief references, calling the sharp distinction between structuralism and poststructuralism into question.

Some of them are dealt with more at length, but in the chapter on semiotics (the later Barthes, Kristeva, and, oddly, Derrida), Hawkes seems to suggest that structuralism, as it comes to the end of its story, becomes absorbed in a more general semiotics. He suggests, first, that semiotics has a much longer history than structuralism (not only Peirce, but much further back in medieval sign-theory), and, second, that semiotics is necessary for an understanding of structuralism (semiotic aspects of Saussure must be suppressed in order to make him simply the precursor of structuralism; Barthes's early structuralism needs to be comprehended within his later semiotics). This would make structuralism just one direction within a semiotics that precedes it and comprehends it, and the recent move beyond structuralism could be interpreted as a move toward a much broader and more flexible semiotics.

Hawkes, then, provides an early instance of an account that has since become the prevalent one, an account in which structuralism has been overtaken by poststructuralism and general semiotics. Those who could handle this change ceased to be (or denied having been) structuralists and became leaders in the new developments (esp. Barthes; also Foucault as rendered, for example, by Harland, 101–20, 155–66). Those who could not adapt, notably Greimas, went the way of the dinosaurs. At best, structuralism has now become absorbed in wider currents, which it had indeed a role in initiating but which it was not capable of comprehending. Parts of its impulse can still be profitably developed, but preferably under other names. At the same time, however, Hawkes's book raises doubts as to the adequacy of this account. For example, if structuralism is an instance of semiotics, would he not have done better to set it within the story of semiotics, avoiding the flashback from the 1960s to Peirce? The reader may suspect that part of the reason for the placement of Hawkes's semiotics chapter is to enable him to deal with certain figures involved in the 1960s ferment not as part of structuralism but still in relation to it. But there is a cost; for example it is surely less plausible to associate Derrida with semiotics than with structuralism.

What, specifically, are the perceived problems in structuralism that have led to such reactions? In order to monitor the recent views of scholars who have been part of the development of narratology from its structuralist beginnings, we refer the following inventory of problems, where possible, to the 1990 double issue of *Poetics Today*, "Narratology Revisited."

First, structuralists have often claimed a global, objective validity for their models, assuming that the degree of scientific exactness supposedly achieved by structural linguistics will be achieved when the linguistic model is transferred to other fields. This, in the view of many critics, has proved a vain hope. Structuralism has tried to pattern itself on the model of an objective natural science; theoretically, any reader using its techniques will discover the same structure. In practice this is not found to be the case. Thus Brooke-Rose refers to "the scientific dream" of "a universal system" of literature (1990:287–88) and "that unfulfilled dream of objectivity" (289). It is in the context of such scientific pretensions that an offensive degree of jargon gets developed, and the study of literature gets bogged down in taxonomy and technical definition.

Structuralism methodologically brackets the role of subjectivity in both the production and the reading of the text. The individual work becomes merely one example of general laws. The contribution of the reader to the production of meaning is neglected (cf. chap. 1), and the attempt is made to withdraw the text from the hermeneutic circle. Structuralist procedures thus have to be reductive. Systems can be created out of the rich variety of real texts only by the programmatic exclusion of certain kinds of text, certain features of texts, certain aspects of the interpretive process, on so on. In particular, it is often noted that early structuralist systems were developed from the reading of relatively simple or homogeneous forms of literature (myths, folktales, popular fiction; cf. Brooke-Rose, 1990:285–86). It is in this light that we should see recent demands on behalf of the free play of semiosis and intertextuality, in counterpoint to the perceived semiotic narrowing involved in structuralist approaches to literature (e.g. Connerty, 398; Bal, 1990:728).

Structuralism is accused of ahistoricality, positing structures that are changeless over time and hence neglecting the embeddedness of the text in a particular history. Related is the accusation of anti-referentiality, the insistence that human productions must be seen as internal networks of meaning before being referred to anything outside themselves (e.g., Ronen, 825–26, discussing, among others, Propp and Greimas). Narratology is perceived to have concentrated on works of fiction, to the neglect of works of historiography (two essays in "Narratology Revisited," Cohn, 1990, and Genette, 1990, are devoted to this issue, and Sternberg, 1990a, touches on the same problem). The "formalist consensus," according to Pavel (350), has dealt poorly with the whole matter of temporality *within* the text. And there has been blindness on the part of structuralist practitioners to the historicity of structuralism itself. These accusations, different as they are, belong to a single impulse to convict structuralism of an unconcern for historicity (cf. Coste's reference to "narrow-minded structuralism . . . and an uncommitted, ahistorical vision of narratology" [407]).

Structuralism is often directly equated with formalism (cf. Pavel, 351), the notion that the structures perceived in human productions can be reduced to abstract mental categories (this is sometimes expressed in mentalist hypotheses like those of Noam Chomsky, who argues, from the homologous quality of the structures humans produce, for the existence of a structure of the mind itself, perhaps with some neurophysiological base; see Caws, 198). This suggests that structuralism is not only ahistorical but also anti-materialist, unconcerned with the real material world out of which the human productions spring and of which they partake.

Finally, summing up all the foregoing, structuralism is accused of being fundamentally positivistic, holding out the promise of *the* right answer to problems, claiming a point of reference that gives it mastery over texts (Brooke-Rose, 1990:289). Structuralist theories characteristically claim greater comprehensiveness than rival theories, claim to be able to "contain" the rivals; this is a characteristic error of all positivisms, namely, that they miss the point that no system can include itself in the critique it proposes (cf. Jameson, 1987:xv–xvi). Such structuralisms tend to avoid the ferment of a general cultural critique, to remain politically uncommitted (cf. Coste, 407), and eventually to serve conservative ends.

But Peter Caws, in *Structuralism: The Art of the Intelligible*, argues that the retreat from structuralism has more to do with the volatility of academic fashion than with a mature assessment of its achievement and potential. He does not disregard the criticisms just enumerated—indeed, he adds his own weight to some of them—but he considers that they can be answered and that many of them signal a failure to understand what structuralism is.

Structuralism's claim, according to Caws, is nothing less than to offer the most adequate account of the intelligibility to the mind of the "human" world (the world of the social sciences and the humanities, as opposed to the natural sciences).[5] He sees structuralism as a major philosophical option which "according to the calendar of philosophy . . . has only just arrived" (xiii). He regards as absurd the notion that we could possibly be in a position to close the books on it when it has been with us for so short a time.

To be human is to try to make experience intelligible (36–37), to seek for "congruence" among its "apparently unrelated features" (7). Structuralism implies a particular view of the way humans undertake this search; it is through *the matching of structured systems,* which *is experienced by us as primordially meaningful* (112; emphasis his). What mind experiences is not isolated particulars but systems of relations among things; hence "structure is fundamental to intelligibility, not merely one aspect of it" (114); it is both a necessary and a sufficient condition for intelligibility (181; Caws sees no philosophic interest in the "weak" kind of structural analysis which fails to make this claim, although cf. Bannet, esp. 228–65, on the relation of "weak structuralism" to poststructuralist thought).

Caws maintains a tight connection between signification and "mattering"—the structures that mind posits as significant are those that touch human existence most closely (at least in the first instance; at more developed stages, structure may be valued for its own sake [184]). "Structuralism . . . aims on the philosophical level not so much to explain facts as to explain why they make sense or matter to us" (170). In the paragraph following this statement, Caws quotes a celebrated remark of Lévi-Strauss, that structuralism might well lead to "the restoration of a sort of popular materialism" (1963a:652). The play on "matter," as noun ("the material") and verb ("to be of concern"), is a leitmotif of Caws's whole book; what matters is precisely what enables humans to live in their given world of matter, and it is particularly in relation to structuralism in anthropology that he orients his discussion. This radical material embeddedness implies that the brain's activity of structuring experience begins with what is at hand, what is local, "relative to us" (38); "we have at our disposal only the present moment and things in the world as they are, . . . our task is to make sense of these from

---

[5] Caws does not see structuralism as dependent on hypotheses about the nature of mind (though it is not incompatible with them). He prefers to define mind precisely *as* the structures it produces—language, myth, etc.—rather than as "some ineffable reality which lies behind them and from which they are separable" (28; page references in this section are to Caws).

a standpoint within the world" (169). The task of structuralism is "to show that the objects it studies have [the] dual character of systematic interrelation and of adequacy to the appropriate features of the world" (121).

One of the reproaches that Caws brings against most structuralisms, even ones of which he generally approves, is their attempt to get rid of the individual human subject as the locus of the perception of structure and to put in its place "the historical collective" (209). Against this, he insists on the irreducibility of the human subject, the "*radical* particularity . . . of mental functioning" (210). The only locus of intelligibility is individual consciousness (126–27, 154–55, 213–14).[6] However, part of the materiality of the human condition is life in particular communities. Caws describes structures as existing "distributively" in the minds of the multiplicity of individuals in these communities. This means that the structure exists nowhere, because no mind "intends" (borrowing a term from phenomenology) the whole of it, and no two minds intend it identically (220–21; language is an obvious example, see 195–96). The myth of a collective subject arises because the individual experiences structures that exist distributively in her community as objective and necessary, rather than as existing only in subjects like herself.

Caws's concept of structuralism implies answers to—or at least problematizes—the criticisms of structuralism reviewed above. Referring to "the apparently megalomaniac pretensions of some structuralists,"[7] he comes out vehemently for a local as against a global view of the intelligibility available to structuralist investigation and commends the local thrust of the work especially of Barthes and Foucault.[8] Structuralism should claim to be systematic not in the sense of discerning the complete system, but of seeking

[6] Knowledge stored in books and the like is only potential knowledge, which needs to be activated by individual consciousnesses.

[7] Page 153, cf. 159. Elsewhere he calls on structuralists to give up "hegemonic claims" (xiii). General theories of meaning are impossible beyond a very minimal level even in linguistics (78) and are quite out of the question in art (33–34). As to the scientific pretensions of structuralism, Caws excludes the natural sciences from its scope: "Structuralism emerged when it was realized that the intelligible world did not have to be constituted in imitation of the material world" (162, cf. 146–48).

[8] Barthes's local investigations reclaim "for intellect a territory that we had all but abandoned to the Absurd" (38), whereas Foucault's "linked series of micro- (or local) structures . . . seems more faithful to the facts of the matter than the schematic simplicities of early structuralism" (153–54).

the potential of everything for systematic connection (197–98). The quest for global, totalizing meaning diverts attention from local significances.[9]

Structuralist efforts to get rid of the subject must come to grief because they are still efforts by subjects (239). The presence of the subject undoes all claims to objectivity. Drawing on Lacan, Caws asserts that "The subject is an activity, not a thing" (31), and that *"The subject cannot be the object of a science because it is its subject"* (32, emphasis his). It can never be part of its own intelligible world—as Wittgenstein says, "The subject does not belong to the world: rather, it is the limit of the world" (1961:117, quoted by Caws, 237)—and hence prevents any systemic completion; the only world available to me is one that needs me as its complement or supplement (238–41).

Caws insists on a distinction between structuralism and formalism on the basis of structuralism's "material embodiment" (25). He admits that structural analysis may from time to time use techniques akin to those of formalism, but these should not be mistaken as defining its philosophical position. The conditions for a real formalism are hardly ever fulfilled in structuralism (106).[10] He speaks also to the supposed ahistoricality of structuralism, especially in his discussion of *synchronicity* (256–57). This term has not only the weak meaning of "the structural principles [that] remain unchanged over time" (256), but a stronger one, that everything available to thought exists *now,* including accounts of the past, so that "diachronic structures . . . are

---

[9] For Caws the central intellectual trauma of our civilization is that we no longer believe in universal meaning but cannot be content with meaning that is anything less than universal. As Western civilization has developed (and Caws would agree with Derrida about the need to retrace the steps involved) what has come to matter most is universal significance. We have come to need, or think we need, access to "the Answer" to "Life, the Universe, and Everything" (this way of putting it comes, of course, from Douglas Adams [113]). Caws shows convincingly why things like "life" can't have "meaning," since meaning develops only *within* the framework of life (183). But the chimera of universal significance makes people discontent with the local significance, which is all that is available. Humans must find contentment in local meaning, and a structuralism that has given up its global pretensions can be of great help in this (183–86 for the foregoing).

[10] Although Caws's point here seems correct, he perhaps undervalues the use of formal models in structuralism, and his conditions for "a nonspurious formalism" are too stringent. He sets two conditions: what such a formalism "deals with must be specifiable in formal language," and its use "must make possible formulations and operations *that would not be possible in ordinary language*" (106). The second of these conditions begs all the famous questions about "ordinary language" and denies the experience of those who handle complexity better through diagrams and formulae than through words.

just synchronic structures among others" (257). But this is not to say that the structures are ahistorical. On the contrary, all human structures include the element of temporality and work to render this element, like any other, intelligible.[11]

Caws refuses any sharp distinction between structuralism and poststructuralism. "The indispensable context of deconstruction is structuralism. . . . Deconstruction is one of its moments, one of its truths" (162; cf. Bannet, 4–11). The essential human "activity of seeking out and matching . . . *is* structuralist activity, even if the internal fitting is arrived at deconstructively or the external via critical theory (258)."[12] "A radically decentered view of [the] world . . . is still . . . compatible with everything that is valuable in structuralism" (159); Derrida's work is "in the best sense structuralist, . . . it exploits . . . the multiple layers of matched structure" (161). Conversely, structuralism cannot be itself without being critical in the fullest postmodern sense. Why, Caws asks (6), has no better term been found for what is supposed to have superseded structuralism than the compound *poststructuralism?* Does not this term imply a continuation of the working out of structuralism's own agenda?

Caws argues this theoretically, out of his understanding of intelligibility itself. What mind usually perceives is not a completed structure but a partial one looking for completion, and there will be a multiplicity of "potentially intelligible" ways of completing it.[13] But it is not mainly for such theoretical reasons that he insists on the deconstructive moment in structuralism. He aims to foster out of structuralism a cultural hermeneutic of suspicion. "The need for deconstruction arises when the externalization of knowledge [makes people] acquire ready-made structures . . . uncritically" (214). Past perceptions of the structuredness of the human world become ossified; "we inherit structures that if left undeconstructed will mislead, oppress, or entrap us" (164).

---

11 The only place Caws develops this in any detail is in his appreciation of Foucault's view of the synchronicity of history, as a fragmented network that one can traverse in any order rather than a grand scheme that imposes its own rules (153–54).

12 It should be explained that "internal" and "external" here refer to Caws's basic distinction (13) between structure as the "fitting together" of a single object and as the single object's "fitting into" a larger complex.

13 Page 206; he uses the example of different ways of completing incomplete drawings. Postmodernism represents an "unwillingness to rule out . . . any kind of . . . juxtaposition," however bizarre it seems, which yields something intelligible (213).

Closing his book, Caws quotes with approval David Lodge's suggestion that we learn "how to work with structuralism, not only in the sense of applying it when it seems useful to do so, but also in the sense of working *alongside* it, recognizing its existence as a fact of intellectual life *without being totally dominated by it*" (Lodge, 7, quoted in Caws, 254; emphasis ours). Caws sees in structuralism a defense against relativism and pragmatism, and hence fundamentalism and superstition. But it is not to be thought of as itself a foundation (one might dwell here on the etymological link between "fundamentalism" and "foundation"), rather as offering "stabilizers, gyroscopes, . . . *local* orientation, *limited* structural connections" (255). We should accommodate to structuralism as a philosophical option and a practical tool of the utmost importance, while disregarding its grandiose pretensions.

It is certainly not hard to discern in the classical development of structuralism impulses that, far from being conservative or positivist, are powerfully critical (Jobling, 1979). The enigmatic anagrams of Saussure (1971) indicate, according to Derrida (1976:329), "another text" hidden under Saussure's attempt (1959) at a closed linguistic system; Caws comments on the anagrams that "there is an unlimited number of potentially intelligible relationships among things in the world, and hence of coherent structures, so that . . . no paradigm of coherence can constrain novelty, and . . . no empirical inquiry is immune from it" (82). The best examples of the critical impulse in early structuralism are to be drawn from Lévi-Strauss. He analyzes myths primarily in terms of the category of *contradiction* in all human systems, contradiction that can never be resolved but only displaced (the appropriateness of his claiming Marx and Freud as precursors [1975:55–59] is clear). In his monumental treatment of Amerindian mythology (1970, 1973, 1978, 1981) he makes no attempt to impose on his texts a priori models; rather, he invents as he goes along the structural models that seem best able to account for the texts (cf. the remarks of Jameson, 1981:esp. 77–80). In his initial response to Propp (1977:15–45, orig. 1960), he differentiates clearly between structuralism and formalism.

Again, Genette's reading of Proust, whereby he chose to work out his structural narratology, is calculated more to unsettle than to reassure. As Genette reads it, this celebrated work, "which seems so massively committed to representing a world and a character's experience of it" (1980:12), is fraught with repeated violations, both flagrant and subtle, of the conventions of representation to which it ostensibly subscribes. The traditional, humanistic, comfortable view of the *Recherche* is repeatedly ruptured by Genette's disclosures of anomalies, impossible combinations, and internal contradictions. Moreover, Genette will not claim for his own book what he denies to Proust's: "readers will not find here [in *Narrative Discourse*] a final 'synthesis' in which all the characteristic features of Proustian narrative noted in the course of this study will meet and justify themselves to each other" (266).

A strong claim can be made on behalf of structuralism, particularly of the Lévi-Straussian type, that it lies behind the insistent interdisciplinarity of current intellectual life. Just as in structural anthropology the various productions of a society have to be studied together, because their structures are transformations of each other, so must we in dealing with our own culture keep its sectors in relation to each other.[14] The early structuralist impulse, however one assesses it now, certainly made itself felt throughout the social and human sciences and has arguably been uniquely productive of the whole current intellectual climate, even if that productivity has been by way of provoking anti-structuralist reaction that has led in new directions.

This history is reproduced in the personal experience of many individuals, even if they now distance themselves from structuralism. Thus Brooke-Rose, though she sees a need to jettison much of early narratology (1990:287), speaks of how she was "considerably strengthened by the rigor learned from linguistics" and "benefited immensely from understanding in every tiny detail how a narrative text functions" (290). Bal likewise acknowledges the decisive contribution of structuralism in instilling in her the critical habit of rigor in the early stages of her career, and refers to "structuralism, already passé for many, internalized by others (including me)" (1991:197–98, cf. 1–24). In an early work, Derrida attests with eloquence to the impact of structuralism: "If it recedes one day . . . the structuralist invasion might become a question for the historian of ideas, or perhaps even an object. But the historian would be deceived if he came to this pass; by the very act of considering the structuralist invasion as an object he would forget its meaning and would forget that what is at stake, first of all, is an adventure of vision, a conversion of the way of putting questions to any object posed before us" (1978b:3).

14 For the theory of *homology* between the structures of a society see Caws (26; cf. 18), and for a classic myth analysis along these lines, Lévi-Strauss, "The Story of Asdiwal" (1977:146–97). It is interesting to set this structuralist impulse to interdisciplinarity alongside the claim (presented, for example, by Bal, 1988b:135–38) that interdisciplinarity is integral to feminist method. The two impulses need not be in competition, and certainly are not in Bal.

Complaining of politically conservative tendencies in some narratologists, Coste claims that "narratology has a vocation to develop tools for strategies of peace and progress" (410). It is rare to find such a political claim so baldly stated, but grounds for agreement with it can be easily found in political programs, or programs with powerful political implications, relating themselves in very direct ways to the structuralist impulse. We may even begin with Derrida, despite the fierce debate over his political commitment. The starting point for his deconstruction is the structuralist category of *binary opposition* and, specifically, the identification of oppositions fundamental to culture (culture-nature, male-female, presence-absence, and so on); deconstructive critique exposes how culture is constituted by the systematic valuation of one term of the opposition over the other, and this takes us directly into the realm of the political (see Jobling, 1990:83–86).

Fredric Jameson's more clearly political Marxist analysis of texts (1981) is directly informed by structuralism, particularly by Lévi-Strauss and Greimas. In his introduction (1987) to the English translation of Greimas's *Du Sens,* Jameson powerfully reclaims and rehabilitates Greimas. Jameson insists (vi–viii) on his right to "bricolate" Greimas's system, that is, to accept only the parts he finds useful. But he sees in Greimas a tremendous technical advance over any earlier semiotic criticism (xii) and especially commends the dialectic treatment of the cognitive and the narrative as "a ceaseless two-way mediation between two types of language" (xiii). He sees Greimas's development of the semiotic square as a "supreme achievement" (xiv) and concludes his introduction with a lengthy demonstration of how the square can be used in ideological criticism (xvii–xxii, on Hayden White's *Metahistory*).

Jameson (esp. 1981) insists on the historical embeddedness of the text, but not on a facile correspondence between the text and some "history" thought of as independent of the text. The correlation between the world created by the text and the real social formation that generated it is at the point of contradiction. The text's contradictions, the points where it fails to close its structured system of meaning, are to be correlated with the contradictions inherent in the social formation, the points where it fails to close its structured systems of exchange (of goods, power, beliefs, and so on). Texts need, in this sense, to be historicized; but "objective" history needs equally to be "textualized," deconstructed (see chap. 3).

Mieke Bal, with whose biblical work we have dealt at length, is the active participant in the narratology debate who most insistently presses the issue of the relation of structuralism to current critical discourse. It is a "self-critical narratology . . . which alone can save a discipline grown sterile, by placing it in the service of a general critical theory" (1991:208–9, cf. 226). Her contribution to "Narratology Revisited" (1990) develops this critical narratology in several of the specific directions that our reading of Caws has indicated, keeping a balance between structuralism's critical potential and the need to critique existing structuralisms. Noting that "binarism itself is an ideologeme," she insists that theories based on binarism, like that of Greimas, "must be stripped of the positivistic truth claims often attached to them" before they can be critically useful (1990:740). She pursues the issue of subjectivity, drawing on Evelyn Fox Keller's demonstration, through a reading of scientists' accounts of their work, of how decisive is the presence of the subject in "objective" research (737–43). Against structuralism's ahistoricism, Bal argues that a rigorous "analysis of narrative structure," by countering "interpretations based on prejudice, convention, or ideology," actually "helps to position the object within history" (750). Bal's most far-reaching point is that if narratological discourse is to be truly critical, there can be nothing like a one-one fit between narrative as object and narratology as method. "The very discipline that tends to rigidify its own traditional object is able to de-rigidify other objects" (730). Narratology, in other words, can find new life in being applied to other fields, as Bal herself demonstrates by applying its methods to anthropology, visual art, and natural sciences. But conversely, narratology cannot be a privileged approach to narrative, which must open itself up to critical methods derived from elsewhere (750). Neither the object nor the method can serve a useful critical purpose outside of a radically interdisciplinary framework.

In view of the existence of such critical political impulses throughout the history of structuralism, it seems fair to suggest that the view of structuralism now accepted in much poststructuralist discussion does not correspond to anything that ever was, but is in fact a retrojection by means of which the various poststructuralisms want to indicate what they are not. This "structuralism" is created by, for example, taking at face value the claim that there is an early (structuralist) and a late (poststructuralist) Roland Barthes, a claim that finds little basis in Barthes's own work,[15] or again by accepting

---

[15] We actually use Barthes's reading of Genesis 32 (1974a), which by any reckoning must be ascribed to his structuralist phase, as one of our biblical examples in our poststructuralism chapter. An even more celebrated early work of Barthes, *S/Z* (1974b), likewise points the way to poststructuralist trajectory within structuralism.

Michel Foucault's protestation that he was not a structuralist (1970:xiv), when it is perfectly clear, for example, that his historical *epistemes* are best understood as structural transformations of each other (Caws, 152–53). Such a straw-man structuralism can be posited only by taking a very limited view of structuralist phenomena. It is simply not possible to do justice to the history of structuralism without coming to terms with all the recent critical currents in the social and human sciences.

We noted earlier that one of the directions in which the critics of structuralism seek to move beyond it is toward a more general and open semiotics (under the influence of such semioticians as Umberto Eco and Julia Kristeva). Basic to such a move is a turn from the semiotics of Saussure, long dominant in Europe and later in North America, to the very different approach of C. S. Peirce. Peircian semiotics has now established itself as a potent conceptual force in semiotic circles in both the United States (Sebeok, 1977) and Europe. Thomas Sebeok's renowned semiotics program at the University of Indiana at Bloomington has been the vanguard of Peircian semiotic scholarship in North America for well over a decade. Key Peircian terminology was first introduced into the French critical scene by Jakobson (1960) and Barthes (1969). The concepts of index, icon, and symbol (for which Peirce is perhaps best known; Charles W. Morris, 1964; 1971) enjoy a wide currency in anthropology and mythic studies.

Full comparative treatments of Saussure and Peirce are not widely available in English (cf. Deledalle, 1979:29–49). Saussure's concept of the sign is dyadic—the sign is made up of the two parts, signifier and signified (1959:65–70; see Culler, 1986:105–51). Peirce advanced a *triadic* structure of the sign—*representamen, object, and interpretant* (or Firstness, Secondness, and Thirdness). The "representamen" is more or less equivalent to Saussure's "signifier," but the latter's "signified" corresponds to two elements in Peirce's scheme, the "object," or referent, and the "interpretant" (Peirce, 1.339), which is a certain idea of the object to which the sign gives rise. This idea necessarily takes the form of another sign; further, each sign element or the relation between elements can function as a sign or complex of signs in relation to some other sign. Thus semiosis is for Peirce an indefatigable relational process in which a sign serves as an element within or for another sign by virtue of the structural and functional relation that it holds with elements of another sign: representamen, object, and interpretant or a combination of these elements in one sign can in whole or in part serve reciprocally as a representamen, object, or interpretant in another sign; and each of these elements may in turn function as a different sign with its own triadic elements for another sign, and so forth, ad infinitum (Peirce, 2.292; see Almeida; Phillips, 1982).

The contrast between Peirce and Saussure has prompted a vigorous debate over a number of issues. First, Peirce's controversial notion of interpretant, the category of Thirdness which mediates between representamen and object, has brought to the fore the issue of the limited or unlimited nature of semiosis (Derrida, 1976:49; Kristeva, 1969:206; although see Deledalle, 1979:198 and Calvet, 1975:75). Second, the representamen (Firstness) introduces the pragmatics of reference directly into the structure of the sign itself and is perceived by some as opening up the possibility of a pragmatics of the sign that is absent from Saussure's linguistic semiology altogether. Derrida remarks that the "property of the *representamen* is to be itself and another, to be produced as a structure of reference, to be separated from itself" (1976:49–50).

Thirdly, some commentators compare Peirce favorably to Saussure in respect of the social character of the sign (Amacker, 37). Saussure's psychological and idealist conception of the linguistic system—"a system of signs in which the only essential thing is the union of meanings and acoustic images" (Amacker, 15)—has led to a robust critique in which Saussurean semiology appears "as a persistent occultation of social and political facts, namely those facts of meaning which have a real sociological depth" (Calvet, 1973:84). Eco notes the social determination of the interpretant: "Interpretants are the testable and describable correspondents associated *by public agreement* to another sign" (Eco, 1976:71, our emphasis; cf. Peirce, 2.418). But this kind of claim seems double-edged. Saussure's linguistic model guarantees a social basis for his scheme, since language is a paradigm of the socially produced system ("the role of the interpretant in Saussurean linguistics is played by the *linguistic community*" [Caws, 76, emphasis his]). In contrast to the sociopsychological foundation of Saussure's linguistic semiology, Peirce's system is grounded upon a logico-mathematical base (Deledalle, 198; in this respect, Peirce has much in common with Greimas).

There is no doubt that the movement toward semiotics in general, and Peirce in particular, enriches and sharpens debate over structural and narratological approaches (cf. William Rogers on Peirce and Ricoeur). But a word of caution and clarification, again drawn from Caws, is in order. Caws calls the semiotic turn "a regressive shift" (21). He asserts the priority of structuralism over semiotics, because it claims to answer the fundamental question of how anything becomes significant; "we will not explain the structure in terms of the significance," but vice versa (111, cf. 112–16). He suggests that the structuring activity of the brain is separate from, prior to, and the ground for, the creation of sign systems. He even calls in question the tightness of the relation between structuralism and semiotics in their historical development. Although Saussure was a key figure in the development of both, "there is no essential connection between the Saussurean doctrine of system that led . . . to structuralism, and the other Saussurean doctrine of the sign" (44). The doctrines of system and of sign are quite different (for example, language would still be a system of differences even if signs were nonarbitrary; 79). Caws's argument here seems to be overdrawn; he fails to note the convergence between recent developments in semiotics and his own desire for a critical structuralism. Nonetheless, his caution reminds us again of the need to clarify our terms in the complex and controverted debate over structuralism and, further, that philosophy and epistemology are necessary partners in the debate.

LOOKING TO THE FUTURE

The impulse most basic to the writing of this book is that the practices of biblical criticism need to be brought into the fullest possible mutual critique with the practices of current literary criticism (as these have transcended their traditional bounds in the direction of a general cultural critique; cf. Eagleton, 1983: 194–217, esp. 204). We here ask the question, how are biblical structuralism and narratology related to this general critical impulse, both actually and potentially?

Mieke Bal entitles a review essay (including work of Alter and Sternberg) "The Bible as Literature: A Critical Escape" (1991:59–72). Much of the work on biblical narrative that we have reviewed in this chapter falls under this harsh stricture, as representing an avoidance of radical biblical criticism and an attempt to maintain for the interpretation of the Bible a privileged and protected place. This conservative impulse can enter into various sorts of alliance with tendencies in structuralism. A synchronic view of the text has appealed not only to those rightly concerned to subvert the dominance of the historical-critical paradigm, but also to those who want to avoid historical questions altogether (Polzin, 1989:225). Methodological escapism can reach such an extreme as the following, from the introduction to *The Literary Guide to the Bible:* "Critical approaches mainly interested in the origins of a text in ideology or social structure are not represented here; nor is Marxist criticism . . . or psychoanalytic criticism. . . . We have not included critics who use the text as a springboard for cultural or metaphysical ruminations, nor those like the Deconstructionists and some feminist critics who seek to demonstrate that the text is necessarily divided against itself" (Alter and Kermode, 5–6). This excludes, from what is intended as an authoritative literary work on the Bible, most of what is being done in current literary criticism, and specifically the methods taken up in the remaining chapters of this book. (The quote smacks more of Alter than of Kermode; contrast Alter's fulminations against theory in Alter, 1989 with Kermode's interesting readings of the Bible in Kermode, 1979 and 1986. Cf. also reviews of Alter and Kermode by Bal, 1989, and of Alter, 1989, by Beck, 1991.)

Gospel narrative critics have shown little interest in theory as such; rather, they have borrowed bits of theory to explicate texts. In particular, they have used narratology to produce sustained interpretations of complete Gospels (e.g., Rhoads and Michie; Culpepper; Kingsbury, 1988a, 1989, 1991; Tannehill, 1986, cf. 1990), interpretations that offer a comforting sense of unity; after the long history of fragmentation and exposure of internal contradictions, it is once again possible, using the methods of literary criticism, to see that the Gospel narratives do after all possess wholeness and internal consistency. But in the nonbiblical development of narratology, it is rare for a theoretical proposal to be developed on the basis of a single text, and, as we have seen, even an exceptional case like Genette's use of Proust's *Recherche* as a specimen text (*Narrative Discourse*) does not produce a comfortable sense of unity (this is a side of Genette not taken up by the Gospel narrative critics who make extensive use of him, e.g., Culpepper, 53–75; Powell, 1990a:36–40; cf. Funk, 1988:187–206).[16] As narrative criticism's influence continues to grow in biblical studies, the impression being fostered among biblical scholars and their students is that secular literary criticism is a discipline preoccupied with the unity of texts and the autonomy of story-worlds—an impression well wide of the mark.

Another favorite assumption of the Gospel narrative critics that needs examination is the contrast of *story* and *discourse*. "Story" denotes "the narrative events, abstracted from their disposition in the text" (Rimmon-Kenan,

---

[16] Another of the best-known instances of a theoretical proposal built on the interpretation of a single text—Barthes's *S/Z* (1974b)—contrasts even more strongly with the holistic agenda of narrative criticism.

3; cf. Chatman, 1978:19), while "discourse" denotes the active presentation of the story through the manipulation of point of view, temporal deformations, and so forth. This suggests the neo-Platonic notion of a story-in-itself, existing prior to and independently of things people do with it and gives the comforting illusion that there is after all such a thing as "the gospel story." It avoids the radical understanding of "discourse" of a Foucault (cf., e.g., 1967:189), who sees only shifting and unstable discourses interacting with other discourses without any stable terms (cf. our discussion of poststructuralism in chap. 3). The Gospel critics are here seen drawing on the most conservative tendencies in general narratology.

Turning to the poetics of the Hebrew Bible, there is a fine line between the legitimate project of a special biblical poetics and the acritical assumption (which can come in highly sophisticated forms), that *the Bible interprets itself*. In other words, that it contains within its own structures the means to its adequate understanding, rather than needing to be brought into relation with what is outside itself (the structures of comparative literature, of comparative religion, of individual or group psychology, of social formations). Is not the nub of the structuralist/narratological challenge precisely this, to force confrontation between the Bible and theory developed outside it? Is the Bible to be truly "at risk from a critical narratology," [17] or does it dictate the terms of interpretation?

In a few cases, narratological approaches are overtly complicit in undergirding the authority of the Bible, particularly by establishing on quasi-literary grounds a special kind of authority for the narrator. Writing on 1 Samuel, Lyle Eslinger refers to "the omniscient narrator, the author and finisher of our reading" (1985:75). The allusion is, of course, to "Jesus the author and finisher of our faith" (Heb. 12:2), with a subliminal appeal to (for some) final religious authority. The most extreme and the most influential case is Sternberg (cf. the critiques by Bal, 1991:59–72, Long, and Mintz). The upshot of Sternberg's investigations into the structure of the relationship between speaker and addressee in biblical narrative is a kind of reader-response criticism at the extreme conservative end of the spectrum (cf. chap. 1 above). The reader has to submit to being entirely the implied reader, the creation of the biblical narrator. In this "drama of reading," the

---

[17] Mieke Bal's first French language book on the Bible (of which *Lethal Love* is a partial translation) has as its subtitle *L'ancien testament au risque d'une narratologie critique* (Bal, 1986a).

reader is in one sense called upon to make all the decisions; but the ideological omnipotence of the narrator is such that these decisions have to be the right ones. The only difference between readers is their different levels of competence; but the biblical narrator has allowed even for this, delivering the message in so foolproof a way that the less competent "underreader" cannot get it really wrong, only less fully (1985:50).[18]

By this procedure, Sternberg can make a commitment to a certain view of biblical ideology masquerade as a theoretical literary judgment about the essential nature of the biblical literature. (It is striking that even when he is not writing directly about the Bible, the literary judgments he arrives at—for example, his impassioned defense of "chronological telling" [1990a]—are such as to favor biblical over other kinds of narrative.) At the beginning of his book, he announces his intention to show "how far the relationship between literary theory and biblical analysis is from the one-way traffic called 'application'" (1985:xiii). But what he is really doing is trying to set up a one-way traffic in the other direction. "Scripture," he says, "emerges as the most interesting as well as the greatest work in the narrative tradition" (1985:518), and he plainly believes that it has much more to teach general literary criticism than it has to learn. In his account, the Bible demands from the critic something perilously like religious commitment.

The terms of the debate over the critical status of high biblical structuralism are different, but the conclusions are not altogether dissimilar; this approach is also complicit in conservative tendencies. We concentrate on the Greimasian project of Daniel Patte. The brand of structuralism that Patte represents is most often accused of making global claims about how all narrative works, and correspondingly adopting reductive strategies in the reading of particular narratives. In fact, Patte works hard to avoid this—he does not make new findings fit old models but tries to propose models more adequate to the new findings (an excellent example is his review of Bal's *Murder and Difference* [Patte, 1990b]). He struggles here with a paradox that structuralism always finds hard to avoid: the search for more adequate models is a necessary part of the structuralist quest for intelligibility, but

---

[18] Similarly, if less extremely, Polzin's second volume on the Deuteronomic history (1989) represents a regression from the first (1980, referred to above); under the influence of Sternberg, Polzin becomes overly concerned with establishing the narrator's ideological control over the text. Consequently, the reader's role is diminished, except, of course, the reader Polzin as critic, who can "construct" the reality of the text.

the quest for *the* adequate model is doomed to failure. The Greimas-Patte system does not ignore other proposed systems but tries to contain them; a rhetoric of welcoming a variety of structural approaches is always accompanied (see, e.g., Patte 1990c:3–5) by the claim that the one approach is capable of comprehending all others. There is no recognition that any system is a system of exclusions, defined precisely by what it excludes (relevant here is White's suggestion that structural analysis in this tradition has confined itself to only one of several modes of narrative but has universalized this mode as if it comprehended all narrative; Hugh White, 1991:69–70).

In some instances, Patte does strike a distinctly conservative note. He and Aline Patte separate themselves from Roland Barthes' view that "the primary role of literature is iconoclastic with respect to the power of language" by insisting that "literature can also have the role of establishing and reinforcing semantic universes"; and they claim that since religious texts, including the Bible, give the establishing of values priority over the unsettling of values, structural analysis should observe the same priority (Patte and Patte, 9, with reference to Barthes, 1974a, 1982; these remarks give, however, the impression of walking a tightrope and should be read in conjunction with their earlier suggestion [5] that the political project of Foucault and Barthes, while representing indeed a departure from structuralism, "describes the ultimate object of Claude Lévi-Strauss's and A. J. Greimas's structuralist research"). It is arguable that Patte never, in any of his work, takes the iconoclastic side seriously (although in a recent piece with Gary Phillips on pedagogy of teaching the Bible, the iconoclastic function is underscored [Patte and Phillips]). Very instructive is the way he deals with the category of contradiction. The discernment of narrative contradictions is integral to his detailed method (based on the semiotic square). But in the fundamental structure of the faith generating a biblical text, no contradiction is allowed (in Patte's books on Paul and Matthew, "contradiction" is invariably qualified with "apparent"; e.g., 1983:46, 1987:11, 14 n. 3). The claim (fundamental to ideological or psychoanalytic approaches) that texts are at every level fragmented—sites of contradiction—is allowed no force. Patte's insistence on basing his method so much on explicit oppositions in the narrative is problematic in a similar way, as may be seen by contrast with Fredric Jameson's use of Greimas. In his ideological critique, Jameson suggests that texts, at the level of their "political unconscious," repress possibilities too much opposed to what is culturally acceptable (1981:168, 255); this means that what will be significantly missing in a text is precisely explicit oppositions.

Finally, though the Bible was obviously not involved in laying the foundation (from Saussure to Lévi-Strauss) of the Greimasian system, the large role it has played in the system's recent development may raise the question as to whether the Bible is not now providing the theoretical basis for its own interpretation (cf. our analogous critique of narratology and poetics). The current development of the Greimasian system is happening very little in dialogue with alternative semiotic proposals and very much in the biblical work of Patte and the CADIR group. Patte's working out of fundamental semantics in terms of faith gives a privileged position to religious texts (1990a:103–215, cf. Phillips's review, 1991a) and his working assumption that a self-consistent and noncontradictory belief system underlies each text potentially serves religious conservatism.

To point to such complicities, at various levels and in different degrees, of structuralist and structural-narratological approaches with conservative tendencies is not to deny their tremendous contribution to the revolution going on in biblical studies. They have had a major role to play (along with other new approaches) in decentering the historical-critical paradigm (Gottwald, 1985:6–34) and establishing the necessity of paying attention to the biblical text in its final form. These approaches have begun to generate major works of biblical scholarship.

Further, despite the conservative tendencies, structuralism has from the beginning been used in the service of methodologically and politically radical biblical writing. Perhaps the most important example is the extraordinary work of Fernando Belo, who as early as 1974 brought together Marxism with a Barthesian form of structuralism in the service of a revolutionary reading of the Gospel of Mark. In the heady early-structuralist days of the 1970s, creative, nondoctrinaire forms of structuralism were developed in biblical studies, issuing in the work of such scholars as Crossan, Funk, Jobling, and Hugh White. In the late 1980s, Mieke Bal demonstrated the immense critical potential, in biblical studies as elsewhere, of the Genettian narratological tradition. We have tried by our two exegetical examples to show such critical structuralisms at work; the Genesis 38 example in particular shows how the traffic between the narratological model and text is not one-way—the analysis called in question, even as it made use of, the model.

The direct influence on biblical studies of the turn to Peircian semiotics—with its raising both of issues related to the hermeneutics of texts and of broader philosophical questions concerning the nature of text and meaning—has up to now been very limited. Almeida (46–79) employs

Peirce's triadic sign structure to explain the structure of Markan narrative parables (*récits-paraboles*) and their hermeneutical effect; and Phillips extends Almeida's application to the parable cluster in Matthew 13 (1982; 1985:120–28), as well as to the intertextual relationship of parable to narrative text and to the pragmatics of parable-reader relationship in the Lucan parable of the good Samaritan (1986:1035–40; 1991b:86–89; cf. Voelz). Lategan and Vorster, even though they do not use Peircian categories directly, depend upon Eco's *semiotic triangle* a variation of Peirce's triadic sign, to account for the "real world reference" (83–84).

But the productivity of structuralism in biblical studies can by no means be fully measured by these palpable achievements. What remains untold is that the structuralist debate, and Daniel Patte himself, have to a unique degree provided the impulse, the context, and the organ for much of the experimental work now going on in biblical studies in North America, as a number of the collaborators on the present volume personally attest. *Semeia* (to which Patte returned in 1993 as general editor) has provided a unique opportunity and encouragement for developments that its structuralist founders could not have imagined; the range of topics that *Semeia* has taken up can fairly be read as an index of the productivity of the structuralist impulse. No less broad has been the variety of approaches taken up by the Structuralism and Exegesis (orig. Structuralism and Semiotics) Group in the Society of Biblical Literature under Patte's long leadership; he has encouraged and participated in the development of approaches not obviously related, or even antithetical, to his own work, including many of the ones developed in the remaining chapters of this book. This group continues, under the leadership of Gary Phillips, with the significant change of name to "Semiotics and Exegesis." Nor is it only in North America that structuralist-semiotic debate has been and continues to be a cradle for wide-ranging methodological experimentation. Likewise in France, CADIR anticipated the cross-disciplinary collaborative efforts of biblical exegetes who are currently engaged in feminist, poststructural, and ideological analysis of the Bible.

We return to the question with which we began this section: how are biblical structuralism and narratology related to the radical currents in literary criticism? Are these approaches part of the problem or part of the solution? Our survey has suggested both. The general tendency has been for the approaches we have dealt with here to avoid radical critique of the Bible, to fall into Bal's "critical escapism" and encourage conservative programs, whether with obvious ideological enthusiasm (Sternberg), through the inherent conservatism of New Testament studies (the Gospel narratologists), or, in Patte's case, perhaps *malgré lui*. The Bible's status as a foundational document in both religious and secular institutions puts a powerful pressure on all the methods applied to its interpretation, of course, to confirm it in its privileged position. But are such foundational tendencies inherent also in structuralism as such?

This is a question that divides even those of us who have collaborated on this book. Some of us perceive structuralism as indeed locked into positivist paradigms, as needing to be, along with other positivisms, the *object* of the radical critique we intend. Others of us, perceiving radical tendencies in the development of structuralism and in our own experience of it, would suggest that the structuralist turn was *the* turn in recent critical consciousness, and that the structuralist impulse not only can, but to be true to itself must, be developed into critical paradigms, be the *subject* as well as the object of critique. From this point of view, the prospect for biblical structuralism is precisely the rest of this book.

RECOMMENDED FURTHER READING

Bal, Mieke. 1988. *Death and Dissymmetry: The Politics of Coherence in the Book of Judges.* Chicago: University of Chicago Press. The most extended application to a biblical text of Bal's narratological method. Based originally on Genette, this method ranges far beyond Genette into feminist, psychoanalytic, and ideological issues.

Caws, Peter. 1988. *Structuralism: The Art of the Intelligible.* Atlantic Highlands, N.J.: Humanities Press International. In a probing examination of structuralism, Caws concludes that it constitutes a major philosophical option whose potential has hardly begun to be realized. He critiques existing structuralisms for failing to live up to the original radical vision of their method.

Chatman, Seymour. 1978. *Story and Discourse: Narrative Structure in Fiction and Film.* Ithaca: Cornell University Press. Perhaps the best and most influential introduction to North American narratology. Draws heavily on the formalist ("poetics") movement.

Eco, Umberto. 1976. *A Theory of Semiotics.* Bloomington: Indiana University Press. Represents a vein of structuralism which incorporates Peircian semiotics and linguistic philosophy. In his "unlimited semeiosis," Eco moves into a radically poststructuralist semiotics.

Genette, Gérard. 1980. *Narrative Discourse: An Essay in Method.* Trans. Jane E. Lewin. Ithaca: Cornell University Press. (Partial trans. of Gérard Genette, *Figures III.* Paris: Seuil, 1972.). Genette's work remains the most important statement of classical narratology. Contains what is still the best discussion of narrative temporality.

Greimas, A. J., and J. Courtés. 1982 [1979]. *Semiotics and Language: An Analytic Dictio-*

nary. Trans. Larry Crist et al. Bloomington: Indiana University Press. An enormously useful encyclopedic resource of all aspects of language and semiotic theory in its application to literary studies.

Jobling, David. 1986. *The Sense of Biblical Narrative: Structural Analyses in the Hebrew Bible.* 2 vols. Sheffield: JSOT. Using an eclectic method based on Lévi-Strauss and Greimas, these essays stress the potential of structuralism for practical biblical exegesis.

Lévi-Strauss, Claude. 1963 [1955]. "The Structural Study of Myth." Pp. 206–31 in *Structural Anthropology.* New York: Basic Books. A foundational statement which paves the way for the expansion of structural methodology to include larger narrative structures. It is very schematic, and needs to be augmented by Lévi-Strauss's extended myth analyses, e.g., *The Raw and the Cooked* (New York: Harper and Row, 1970).

Moore, Stephen D. 1989. *Literary Criticism and the Gospels: The Theoretical Challenge.* New Haven: Yale University Press. A comprehensive assessment of narratological and reader-response theories in New Testament studies.

Patte, Daniel. 1990a. *The Religious Dimensions of Biblical Texts: Greimas's Structural Semiotics and Biblical Exegesis.* Semeia Studies 19. Atlanta: Scholars. The most influential advocate of structuralism in North American biblical studies, presenting the work of another important transitional figure in the development and expansion of that methodology.

Propp, Vladimir. 1968. *Morphology of the Folktale.* 2d ed. Trans. Laurence Scott. Austin: University of Texas Press. Classic statement from a founder of the formalist movement and the first to apply a structural analysis to narrative, treating it as a sequence of interchangeable, irreducible units.

Saussure, Ferdinand de. 1959. *Course in General Linguistics.* Ed. Charles Bally et al. Trans. Wade Baskin. New York: McGraw-Hill. Although in some ways now surpassed, the views of the Swiss "founder" of structuralism have continued to influence later structuralists as well as poststructuralist thinkers such as Derrida and de Man.

White, Hugh. 1991. *Narration and Discourse in the Book of Genesis.* Cambridge: Cambridge University Press. Moving beyond the Saussurean linguistic model, White develops a highly sophisticated semiotic narratology, which he applies to Genesis in a series of original readings.

3 | Poststructuralist Criticism

DECONSTRUCTION AND DERRIDA

Structuralism, poststructuralism, deconstruction—these three terms are tightly knotted.[1] Derrida himself has fumbled with the knot on more than one occasion. "When I chose this word [deconstruction]," he explains, "or when it imposed itself upon me—I think it was in *Of Grammatology* [1967]—I little thought it would be credited with such a central role" (1988a:1; cf. Derrida, 1985a:85–86, 142).

> At that time structuralism was dominant. "Deconstruction" seemed to be going in the same direction since the word signified a certain attention to structures. . . . To deconstruct was also a structuralist gesture. . . . But it was also an antistructuralist gesture, and its fortune rests in part on this ambiguity. Structures were to be undone, decomposed, desedimented (all types of structures, linguistic . . . —struc-

---

[1] If poststructuralism is the genus, then deconstruction is its best-known species. Thus, while all deconstruction is poststructuralist, not all poststructuralism is deconstructionist. Derridean deconstruction has been the most influential form of poststructuralism, at any rate, in the English-speaking world. As such, it receives the lion's share of attention in the present chapter, although Foucault and Barthes also feature prominently. Lacan is discussed at length in chap. 5.

turalism being especially at that time dominated by linguistic models and by a so-called structural linguistics that was also called Saussurian—socio-institutional, political, cultural, and above all and from the start philosophical). This is why, especially in the United States, the motif of deconstruction has been associated with "poststructuralism" (a word unknown in France until its "return" from the United States). (1988a:2–3)

Derrida is careful to add: "But the undoing, decomposing, and desedimenting of structures . . . was not a negative operation" (3; cf. Derrida, 1985a:85–87). Deconstruction was not destruction, in other words. Rather it was a dismantling of structures (philosophical, cultural, political, institutional, and above all and from the start textual) that was designed to show how they were put together in the first place.

Every system is a construction, something that has been assembled, and construction entails exclusion. Every system excludes—is, in fact, a system of exclusions. Deconstruction seeks out those points within a system where it disguises the fact of its incompleteness, its failure to cohere as a self-contained whole. By locating these points and applying a kind of leverage to them, one deconstructs the system. This amounts neither to destroying nor dismantling the system in toto, but rather demonstrating how the (w)hole, through the masking of its logical and rhetorical contradictions, maintains the illusion of its completeness.

In contrast to the source criticism of the Bible, then, the construction that deconstruction disassembles is not the history of the text's assembly. Rather it is the grammar or logic of the text's linguistic organization (its structure) and the rhetoric of its expression that is dismantled. To deconstruct is to identify points of failure in a system, points at which it is able to feign coherence only by excluding and forgetting that which it cannot assimilate, that which is "other" to it. Derrida asks: "what if what cannot be assimilated, the absolute indigestible, played a fundamental role in the system, an abyssal role rather?" (Derrida, 1986b:151a).

Poststructuralists tend to distrust systems of every sort; one thinks in particular of Derrida, Foucault, Lacan, and the later Barthes. Indeed, Lacan's distrust of systems antedates French structuralism itself. "This kind of teaching is a refusal of any system," said Lacan in 1953, introducing his famous seminar. "It uncovers a thought in motion" (1988a:1; cf. Lacan, 1977c:xv). Twenty years later he would still be protesting: "they suppose me to have an ontology, or, what amounts to the same thing, a system" (1982b:142). Barbara Johnson has phrased the issue of exclusion especially sharply: " 'What's the bottom line?' What deconstruction does is to teach you to ask: 'What does the construction of the bottom line leave out? What does it repress? . . . What does it put in the margins?' " (1987:164).

Deconstruction's fascination with the marginal, the secondary, the repressed, and the borderline (cf. Derrida, 1988b:44) clearly offers opportunities for various forms of political criticism. Deconstruction's influence on feminist literary criticism has been especially pronounced in recent years, and it is beginning to make tentative inroads in feminist biblical criticism as well (e.g., Craig and Kristjansson; Susan Lochrie Graham; cf. Jobling, 1990:97–98). Derrida has not hesitated to tackle overt political issues on occasion, the most notable example to date being his essay on apartheid, "Racism's Last Word" (1985b). Nevertheless, there are marked differences between Derrida and other "thinkers of marginality," such as Foucault. Allan Megill observes: "In his opposition to the domineering tendencies of Western reason, Foucault has concentrated on the oppression (in his terms, the production) of the sick, the insane, criminals, and sexual 'deviants.' Derrida's concern with alterity, on the other hand, has been much less concrete in character, much less a matter of identifiable social groups being oppressed (or produced). His concern is much more clearly focused on the exclusion of deviant modes of thought" (276).

According to Megill, however, there is one striking exception to Derrida's relative lack of interest in social groups: "he has shown a persistent fascination with Judaism and with the problem of its relation to a predominantly Greek and Christian culture" (ibid.). More precisely, he has shown a persistent fascination with writing, and with Judaism's own fascination with writing (Judaism "elects writing which elects the Jew" [Derrida, 1978b:65]) and with the problem of writing's relation to speech in Greco-Christian metaphysics.

Reviewing Derrida's *Of Grammatology,* Paul de Man notes that it "tells a story." "Throughout, Derrida uses Heidegger's and Nietzsche's fiction of metaphysics as a *period* in Western thought in order to dramatize, to give tension and suspense to the argument. . . . Neither is Derrida taken in by the theatricality of his gesture or the fiction of his narrative," cautions de Man (1983:137). Picking up the fallen mantle of Heidegger, Derrida has, over the last thirty years, been engaged in a critique of Western metaphysics. (The term *deconstruction* itself, he tells us, goes back to two Heideggerian terms, *Destruktion* and *Abbau* [1985a:86–87; 1988a:1].) A report on that thirty-year war follows, at any rate of its opening skirmishes. Admittedly the report is a fiction. Absent are the elaborate maneuvers, the strategic retreats, and the ironic self-subversions that characterize the playful if frustrating style of Derrida's battle-plan.

Western thought has always based itself on binary oppositions, in Derrida's view: transcendent-immanent, intelligible-sensible, spirit (mind, soul)-body, necessary-contingent, primary-secondary, simple-complex, nature-culture, male-female, white-black (brown, red, yellow), inside-outside, object-representation, history-fiction, conscious-unconscious, literal-meta-phorical, content-form, text-interpretation, speech-writing, presence-absence, and so on. Such oppositions are founded on repression, the relation between the two terms being one of hierarchical violence rather than equal partnership. The first term in each pair has been forcibly elevated over the second.

The career of the speech-writing opposition, in which writing has been assigned a scapegoat role akin to that of the wandering Jew, has been of special interest to Derrida (himself of Algerian-Jewish extraction). Throughout the intellectual history of the West, speech has almost always been privileged over writing. Derrida singles out Plato, Rousseau, Hegel, Saussure, and Husserl as exemplars of this unease with the written, "specific nuclei in a process and a system" (1982a:94).[2]

But what could be more natural than to privilege speech? As I speak, my words appear to be one with my thoughts. My meaning seems to be fully present both to me and to my hearer, provided I am speaking effectively, affectively. At such moments, the voice, the breath, appear to be consciousness itself, presence itself.

Voice, presence, truth. In the West, speech has always been the paradigm not only for every form of presence but also for every form of truth.[3] All the names used to designate theological or philosophical fundamentals have always designated the constant of a presence: God, being, essence, existence, substance, subject, object, consciousness—the list is very long. Derrida's term for this litany of names and all it entails is *the metaphysics of presence.* He also uses the term *logocentrism* to denote the imbrication of the *logos*

---

[2] For Derrida's most sustained reading of Plato in this regard, see 1981a:61–171; for Rousseau (discussed with Lévi-Strauss), see 1976:97–316; for Hegel, see 1981a:1–59; 1982a:69–108, and 1986b; for Saussure, see 1976:27–73, and cf. 1981b:17–36; and for Husserl, see 1978a and 1973.

[3] "This experience of the effacement of the signifier in the voice is not merely one illusion among many—since it is the condition of the very idea of truth" (Derrida, 1976:20).

(speech, logic, reason, Word of God) and the notion of presence in Western thought. "Logocentrism is an ethnocentric metaphysics. It is related to the history of the West" (Derrida, 1976:79).

As lifeless written marks in place of present living speech, writing has often seemed to be an inferior, if necessary, substitute for speech. Cut off from the *pneuma,* the breath, severed at its source from the authorizing presence of a speaker, writing has often been thought to threaten truth with distortion and mischief. An orphan, no sooner born than set adrift, cut loose from the author who gives birth to it, writing seems fated endlessly to circulate from reader to reader, the best of whom can never be sure that he or she has fully grasped what the author intended to say. For authors have a way of being absent, even dead, and their intended meaning can no longer be directly intuited or double-checked through question and answer, as in the face-to-face situation of speech. Writing defaces speech.

Derrida deconstructs this opposition of speech and writing. "The crack between the two is nothing. The crack is what one must occupy" (Derrida, 1986b:207b). But to deconstruct a hierarchical opposition is not simply to argue that the term ordinarily repressed is in reality the superior term. Rather than stand the opposition on its head, thereby inverting it but leaving it intact, deconstruction attempts to show how each term in the opposition is joined to its companion by an intricate network of arteries. In consequence, the line ordinarily drawn between the two terms is shown to be a political and not a natural reality. "Like Czechoslovakia and Poland, [they] resemble each other, regard each other, separated nonetheless by a frontier all the more mysterious . . . because it is abstract, legal, ideal" (1986b:189b). As such it can always be redrawn. Derrida approaches the border between speech and writing by asking: What if the illegal alien, the parasite, were already within? What if speech were already the host of writing? What if the apparent immediacy of speech, the sensation of presence that it evokes, were but a mirage?

Crucial to Derrida's philosophical project is a strategic drawing on linguistics. Ferdinand de Saussure's *Course in General Linguistics* (1907– 11)—suitably boosted, of course—is an important part of the Derridean can(n)on. Indeed, Saussure's general significance for French structuralism and poststructuralism alike can hardly be overstated. Barthes, for example, recalls the beginning of his structuralist adventure in the 1950s: "it was then that I first read Saussure; and having read Saussure, I was dazzled by this hope: to give my denunciation of the self-proclaimed petit-bourgeois myths the means of developing scientifically" (1988a:5). Saussure was a no less dazzling discovery for other structuralists and poststructuralists, such as Lévi-Strauss, Lacan, and Kristeva.

Saussure's sign theory can be summarized as follows. The linguistic sign is composed of a *signifier* and a *signified*. The signifier is the material (acoustic) component of the sign (e.g., the sound "tree"), whereas the signified is its conceptual component (the concept "tree"). That to which the sign points is its *referent* (the object "tree"). But the relation between the signifier and its referent is arbitrary: different sounds designate the same object depending on the language being used (*tree, arbre, Baum, dendron, 'ets*). What is not arbitrary, however, but indispensable in order that the signifier have meaning, are the differences that distinguish a given signifier from all the other signifiers in the system. The sound "tree" is intelligible to a speaker of English not because of what it is, strictly speaking, since there is no resemblance between the sound (or its appearance when written) and the large leafy object we call a "tree." Rather, the sound is intelligible precisely because of what it *is not,* which is to say "three," "thee," "the," "tee," and every other sound in language. This prompts Saussure to state: "in language there are only differences. Even more important: a difference generally implies positive terms between which the difference is set up; but in language there are only differences *without positive terms*" (1983:118, emphasis his).

Derridean deconstruction can be understood in part as an emphatic affirmation of Saussure's dictum that language is a network of differences joined to a still more emphatic rejection of Saussure's order of signifieds. The signified for Derrida can neither orient nor stabilize the sign. Like the signifier, the signified can be grasped only differentially and relationally, through its difference from other signifieds, other concepts. Indeed, the very distinction between signifier and signified is itself an arbitrary and conventional one, for "the signified always already functions as a signifier" (Derrida, 1976:7). The history of Western thought for Derrida (Saussure's thought included) amounts to the "powerful, systematic, and irrepressible desire" for a *transcendental signified*—an order of meaning that would be originary, self-identical, and self-evident and that would "place a reassuring end to the reference from sign to sign" (49). But this would require a signified capable of being grasped in itself, nondifferentially.

What the play of differences prevents is any single element in language being simply present in and of itself. Each element means what it does only because of its relation to something that it is not, from which it differs. No element can be simply present; rather, each element is an effect of the traces within it of all the other elements in the system. Nothing is ever simply present or absent. The present is divided from itself (prevented from simply being itself) by the trace within it of what it is not (Derrida, 1982a:13; 1981b:26). And with it is divided everything that has been thought of as a species of presence: God, being, essence, identity, consciousness, self, intentionality.[4] This uncontrollable spillage Derrida terms *writing* (*l'écriture*), not writing as ordinarily conceived, which is to say as a substitute or storage container for speech, but writing writ large or generalized. "Discontinuity, delay, heterogeneity, and alterity already were working upon the voice, producing it from its first breath as a system of differential traces, that is as writing before the letter" (Derrida, 1982a:291).[5] The disseminating flow of this general writing swirls and eddies through the spoken word with unsensed and unsuspected force, eroding the apparently simple, intuitive self-identity of even the most immediate-seeming speech event.

BIBLICAL POSTSTRUCTURALISM

Regina Schwartz has depicted the Hebrew Bible as engaged in a process of loss and recovery, forgetting and remembering, one that militates against origins or teleology and that is explicitly depicted in the biblical "scenes of writing":

> Deuteronomy tells the story of the exodus, with a second Moses repeatedly enjoining his hearers to remember and retell the story themselves. But the injunctions of Deuteronomy are forgotten. The text is lost. Even the reminder to remember is forgotten. During a religious reform that included the restoration of the Temple, the lost book is found amid debris, according to the account in II Kings, and with the recovery of the book, the contents—to remember and what to remember—are remembered. This lost-and-found phenomenon recurs for another text: the scroll of Jeremiah. After reading the first twenty-five chapters of Jeremiah, we are told how they came to be, and not to be, and to be again. As each page is read

---

[4] ". . . presence of the thing to the sight as *eidos,* presence as substance/essence/existence (*ousia*), temporal presence as point (*stigmē*) of the now or of the moment (*nun*), the self-presence of the cogito, consciousness, subjectivity, the co-presence of the other and of the self" (Derrida, 1976:12).

[5] "Then one realizes that what was chased off limits, the wandering outcast . . . has indeed never ceased to haunt language as its primary and most intimate possibility" (Derrida, 1976:44).

to the king, it is torn off and burned in the fire in his winter apartments. Despite this destruction, Jeremiah and his scribe begin all over again. The text persists. Another book suffers the same fate: the Torah. When Moses receives the tablets of the law, before he even begins to promulgate it, he dashes the tablets to pieces. The Torah is rewritten; thus, all we have from the beginning is a copy, one that proliferates further copies. Silencing the narrative, forgetting the past, obliterating any account of it: memory is the Hebrew Bible's way of coping with this ever-pressing crisis of discontinuity. The Book itself is imperiled, lost over and over. And so it must be remembered, recovered, rewritten, and rediscovered over and over. (1990b:46)

This crisis of survival is also dramatized in the Joseph story where it is accompanied by an injunction for moral responsibility. Joseph's brothers abandon him, and they later claim to the powerful Egyptian vizier (Joseph incognito) that they once had a brother who "is no more." They only find Joseph, as it were, when they refuse to abandon their other favored brother, Benjamin. Their new-found responsibility prompts Joseph's memory of his painful past, but that memory ensures the continued survival of the lineage: "Do not be grieved or angry with yourselves for selling me here; for God has sent me before you to preserve life" (Gen. 45:5). Throughout the Hebrew Bible, Schwartz argues, remembering is persistently linked to survival. But she adds the caution, "when we say that remembering is the condition of survival in the Bible, we cannot mean it in any naive sense [for there is no original to be recalled]. With no such thing as accurate memory possible, dependence on such memory would enable no future at all" (53). Rather it is interpretation, re-construction, re-membering, re-writing, or simply writing (in the Derridean sense) that enables continuity.

Writing and scripture also intermingle in two early essays by Derrida on the Jewish poet Edmond Jabès (Derrida, 1978b:64–78, 294–300). Derrida and Jabès merge in these essays; it is frequently impossible to tell where one ends and the other begins. For Derrida and Jabès both, the "situation of the Jew" is "exemplary" of writing (65), because writing is always a matter of exile. " 'The fatherland of the Jews' is a 'sacred text surrounded by commentaries'. The necessity of commentary . . . is the very form of exiled speech. In the beginning is hermeneutics" (67, quoting Jabès, 109). In Jabès's haunting poetry, Derrida discovers a "confluence in which is recalled, conjoined, and condensed the suffering, the millennial reflection of a people . . . 'whose past and continuity coincide with those of writing,' the destiny that sum-

mons the Jew, placing him between the voice and the cipher; and he weeps
for the lost voice with tears as black as the trace of ink" (73, quoting Jabès,
41). The lost voice is first of all that of God: "God no longer speaks to us;
he has interrupted himself: we must take words upon ourselves. We must
entrust ourselves to traces . . . because we have ceased hearing the voice from
within the immediate proximity of the garden. . . . The *difference* between
speech and writing is sin, the anger of God emerging from itself, work outside the garden" (68, Derrida's emphasis). But to be thrust from the garden
is to be forced into the desert, a boundless semiotic "book . . . made of sand"
(ibid.). "The garden is speech, the desert writing. In each grain of sand a
sign surprises" (Jabès, 169, quoted in Derrida, ibid.).

According to a rabbinic tradition, the Torah existed with God before the
creation of the world: "He [the Holy One] looked into the Torah and created the world" (*Bereshit Rabbah* 1:1; cf. Handelman, 1982:37–38, 168).
Compare "Reb Derissa" (as Derrida jokingly signs himself—300; cf. 78),
as he exegetes Jabès's elaboration of this remarkable tradition: "everything
that is exterior in relation to the book . . . is produced within the book."
Every attempt to exit the book only leads back into it. "One emerges from
the book only within the book, because, for Jabès, the book is not in the
world, but the world is in the book" (76, Derrida's emphasis; cf. Derrida,
1976:158). Furthermore, "If God is, it is because He is in the book" (Jabès,
32, quoted in Derrida, 76). Besides the book there is only that which threatens it: "nothing, non-Being, nonmeaning" (76).

Is Derridean "writing" merely a synonym for Jabès's semiotic "sand-
book," then, the "desert" that establishes the horizon of all human reflection, the sum of all that is sayable? Or does writing somehow exceed the
book and the mirages of presence that it gives rise to (cf. Derrida, 1976:6–
26)? One suspects that it does. Derrida's concept of écriture is still under
(de)construction in this first essay on Jabès, which dates from 1964. But by
the closing pages of the essay, Derrida has begun to write (of) an "original
illegibility" (77), which he will later designate with such terms as *archē-
writing* (1982a:13), and which, for him, is uncontainable in any book, even
a "desert-book" as capacious and treacherous as that of Jabès. (Jabès says
of that book: "At noon, he found himself once more facing infinity, the
white page. Every trace of footsteps had disappeared. Buried" [56, quoted in
Derrida, 69–70].) Although Derrida will not "impugn Jabès for not having
pronounced these questions" (78), he is anticipating the tortuous "detours"

that lie ahead—detours that "will resemble those of negative theology, occa-sionally even to the point of being indistinguishable from negative theology" (1982a:6; though cf. 1978b:297; 1989:7ff.).

Poststructuralist writing has been marked by "a resurgence of interest in allegory" (Ulmer, 1985:88). In his two essays on Jabès, Derrida engages in a neo-allegorical reading of scripture. Whether he looks in the direction of Eden or at Israel's wilderness wanderings, Derrida sees only writing. He has also ventured an allegorical reading of another biblical narrative, the story of Babel:

> the narrative or the myth of the tower of Babel . . . does not constitute just one figure among others. Telling at least of the inadequation of one tongue to another, of one place in the encyclopedia to another, of language to itself and to meaning, and so forth, it also tells of the need for figuration, for myth, for tropes, for twists and turns. . . . In this sense it would be the myth of the origin of myth, the meta-phor of metaphor, the narrative of narrative, the translation of translation, and so on.
>
> The "tower of Babel" does not merely figure the irreducible multiplicity of tongues; it exhibits an incompletion, the impossibility of finishing, of totalizing, of saturating, of completing something on the order of edification. . . . What the multiplicity of idioms actually limits is not only a "true" translation, a trans-parent and adequate interexpression, it is also a structural order, a coherence of construct. There is then (let us translate) something like an internal limit to for-malization, an incompleteness of the constructure. It would be easy and up to a certain point justified to see there the translation of a system in deconstruction. (1985c:165–66)

Indeed, it would be easy to see there, yet again, a Derridean "scene of writ-ing."

Deconstruction has profound implications for translation, a topic that in turn has important theological dimensions. For Judaism and Christianity, the question of scripture—its nature, meaning, and authority—is insepa-rable from that of translation. (This is also true for Islam, which refuses to consider translations of the Quran as holy.) Readers of all sorts tend to regard an original work—whether holy scripture or secular writing—as superior to and more authoritative than any of its translated versions. How-ever, as we saw, the Hebrew Bible itself includes the myth that the original is lost. Moreover, that the Bible as an "original" is "not purely canonical is clear from the fact that it demands translation; it cannot be definitive since it can be translated" (de Man, 1986:82). The original is always "in the situation of demand, that is, of a lack or exile. The original is indebted a priori to the translation. Its survival is a demand and a desire for translation, somewhat like the Babelian demand: Translate me" (Derrida, 1985c:152). Every reading is a translation, a commentary on and supplement to the original text. Every reader is a translator, someone who takes things from their proper place and moves them somewhere else.[6] In this sense, all reading is intertextual,[7] an endless juxtaposition and interchange of texts, a kind of translation.[8]

Deconstruction is suspicious of any view that there is a natural fit between language, world, and meaning. A Babelian intervention, it challenges the erection of any concept of reality unscathed by interpretation, by translation, whether it take the form of a historical reconstruction, a literary reading, a scientific hypothesis, or a philosophical system. To this extent, deconstruction represents a series of critical positions taken against totalizing schemes. But as a reading activity, deconstruction is not reducible to a single concept, method, or technique. Because deconstruction is resolutely nonsystematic, there is no straightforward, universally accepted way of "doing" it. Indeed, one could well question whether there is any one thing to do. According to de Man, deconstruction merely makes explicit what occurs in any reading: "to read is to understand, to question, to know, to forget, to erase, to deface, to repeat. . . . No degree of knowledge can ever stop this madness, for it is the madness of words" (1979b:68). Nevertheless, attention to the inability of philosophers, literary critics, historians, theologians, and exegetes (along with politicians, lawyers, clergy, and so on) to establish fully coherent arguments or systems is one of the features that distinguishes deconstructive reading from other forms of critical activity.

Deconstruction is text-centered. Yet for deconstruction, there is no cen-

6 *Translatus* is the past participle of *transferre*, to transfer.

7 For more on the appropriation of the concept of intertextuality in biblical studies see Fewell whose volume of thirteen essays centers on Hebrew Scripture texts; Phillips, 1992; Aichele and Phillips, a forthcoming volume of *Semeia* featuring exegetical and theoretical pieces; Boyarin, 1990a, 1990b; also cf. Plett, 1991.

8 Further on the intersection of translation, theology, and deconstruction, see Aichele, 1991; 1992.

ter to the text. *Text* is not limited to written language. The self is a text; experience is a text; any instance of signification is a text, and as Barthes said, "everything signifies" (1978:63). Text is the product of signifying difference. Text and its related terms (such as *writing* and *reading*) are, for deconstruction, complex, fluid, and powerful metaphors. Whatever a text is, it is not a stable, self-identical, enduring object but a place of intersection in a network of signification. *Intertextuality*—a term introduced by Julia Kristeva—suggests that each text is situated for each reader in an ever-changing web composed of innumerable texts. There is no extratextual reality to which texts refer or which gives texts their meaning; meaning or reference are possible only in relation to this network, as functions of intertextuality.

Deconstructive interpretation for the most part consists of very close readings of specific texts (but only rarely, so far, of biblical texts).[9] These readings have been highly unorthodox as they have rejected certain well-established and central values: the univocity of meaning, the privileging of the author's intention (or any other point of origin), the location of meaning "in" the text, the separability of the text's "inside" from its "outside" (text from reader, text from context), the objective reality of history, and so forth. Deconstruction rejects the notion that the origin (*archē*), whatever its form (the author, God, the signified), should be given any sort of priority; it denies that there is an origin in any substantial sense. (The signified is always another signifier; the author is the product of his or her texts; every writing is a rereading; every reading a rewriting, and so forth.)

As a practice of reading, deconstruction makes explicit what is hidden, repressed, or denied in any ordinary reading. Every reading is blinded by a set of presuppositions about the nature of texts and of reality, and yet without some such assumptions no reading would be possible. Deconstructionists such as Derrida and de Man readily admit that these strictures apply as well to their own readings—that is, that their readings also need to be deconstructed. No neutral or objective reading is ever possible; reading is always interested. Deconstruction rejects all "container" theories of meaning. Meaning is not in the text but is brought to it and imposed upon it. The

[9] Assorted examples include Aichele, 1985; Barthes, 1988b, 1988c; Burnett, 1992a, 1992b; Clines, 1990a; Crossan, 1980; Derrida, 1982b, 1985c; Fewell and Gunn; Susan Lochrie Graham; Greenstein; Gunn and Fewell; Jobling, 1986b, 1990; Miscall; Moore, 1989b, 1992, 1994; Phillips, 1985, 1994a, 1994b; Schwartz, 1990b.

understanding of the author or of the original audience is not decisive; it is merely one reading among many. Texts may lend themselves more to some readings than to others, but the results of any reading have more to do with the reader's interests than with the text itself. Interpretation is an expression of power, the result of violence exercised upon the text in the act of reading, which is always an act of appropriation, a taking possession.

Against this hermeneutic of violence, deconstruction offers another metaphor to describe the reading process: *play,* with its connotations of free experimentation and endless alternatives. This becomes erotic play, *jouissance,* for a writer such as Barthes. If the written text be subject to the interests and desires of its readers, it is also by its very nature disseminated at large in the world, free of the restrictive control of an author or any authoritative body. The goal of a deconstructive reading is not some sort of decisive conclusion or valid interpretation. Deconstructive readings tend to circle about the textual object, playing with it and teasing it, seeking out the marks and folds that reveal the logic of its construction, the exclusions and deceptions that make it what it is. Although they are often quite respectful, these readings are never reverential.

At points such as this, the distinction between deconstructive criticism and reader-response criticism is important (see chap. 1 above). Although communities of interpretation play crucial roles in determining any actual reader's interpretation of a text, and although some communities may claim exclusive ownership of the true meaning of certain texts (sacred texts, especially), the text is never fully in the possession of any reader, nor is the reader ever fully in the possession of any text. For deconstruction, the text retains the power to elude and overturn every reading—while the reader retains the power endlessly to rewrite the text.

As an illustration of this struggle between reader and text, let us turn to Roland Barthes as he wrestles with an episode from the book of Genesis. Barthes is an important figure in twentieth-century criticism because of his role both as an advocate of structuralist criticism in France in the 1960s and as an outspoken voice of poststructuralist criticism in the later years of his life. Barthes's work underscores the historical and philosophical relation between poststructuralism and the structural analysis of language and culture practiced by Saussure and Lévi-Strauss, among others. Although Barthes is not usually thought of as a deconstructionist (as Derrida and de Man are), his later writings, especially his close and careful readings of texts, offer fine examples of deconstructive criticism.

For Barthes, the question of the text is ultimately a question of scripture, that is, a theological one. Taking his cue from Derrida, Barthes declares:

> To describe systems of meaning by postulating a final signified is to side against the very nature of meaning. . . . Scripture [*l'Ecriture*] is a privileged domain for this problem, because, on the one hand, theologically, it is certain that a final signified is postulated: the metaphysical definition or the semantic definition of theology is to postulate the Last Signified; and because, on the other hand, the very notion of Scripture, the fact that the Bible is called Scripture, Writing [*l'Ecriture*], would orient us toward a more ambiguous comprehension of the problems, as if effectively, and theologically too, the base, the *princeps,* were still a Writing, and always a Writing. (Barthes, 1988c:242, emphasis his)

As we have seen, this view of text as writing poses a serious challenge to a critical desire to "capture meaning," to fix language's function and arrive at the definitive truth of the text. And yet, a traditional metaphysical understanding of theology would posit just such truth.

Barthes opens his essay "Wrestling With the Angel: Textual Analysis of Genesis 32:23–33" by distinguishing between historical criticism ("where the text comes from"), structural analysis ("how [the text] is made"), and textual analysis ("how [the text] is unmade, how it explodes, disseminates" in that "*open* network, which is the very infinity of language") (1988d:247). Barthes states that his goal as critic is not to reduce the text to a signified (historical, theological, or otherwise), "but to keep its signifying power open" (260). For this reason he pays little attention to the results of traditional textual criticism, except for cursory acknowledgment of the documentary hypothesis concerning the composition and redaction of the Torah. Still, methodological distinctions notwithstanding, Barthes's textual analysis finds itself caught up between the structuralist approach of his earlier writings, with its characteristic desire for objective, scientific neutrality, and the poststructuralist interest in the indeterminacy of meaning, the role of ideology in the production and dissemination of the text, and the influence of the reader upon the text, themes that became increasingly prominent in Barthes's later writings.[10] This two-sidedness suggests that the complex relation between poststructuralism and structuralism is not adequately explained as an evolutionary development of the former out of the latter.

---

[10] This essay was first published in 1972. Its characteristic ambivalence is also a feature of Barthes's other biblical excursion, "The Structural Analysis of Narrative: Apropos of Acts 10–11" (Barthes, 1988c:217–45 [first published in 1969]).

The influence of structural analysis is especially pronounced in Barthes's organization of the narrative plot.[11] In his analysis of Genesis 32, Barthes locates three sequences: the Crossing (of the Jabbok River, vv. 23–25),[12] the Combat (vv. 25–30), and the Namings (vv. 28–33). Each sequence contains a critical ambiguity. In the first sequence, it is unclear whether Jacob has already crossed over the river when the wrestling occurs (v. 23) or whether he has remained behind on the far (foreign) side (vv. 24–25); however, the side of the river that Jacob is on is crucial for determining the nature of the wrestling match and the identity of his opponent. Barthes argues that this ambiguity creates "two different pressures of readability." On the one hand, if Jacob has not yet crossed the river, then a folkloristic reading would interpret the wrestling as mythic trial by combat: once victorious, Jacob can cross the river, achieve his goal. On the other hand, if Jacob has already crossed the river and his household has gone on ahead, the reading is less clearly determined. It would appear that Jacob struggles "to *mark himself* by solitude (this is the familiar *setting apart* of the chosen of God)" (250, Barthes's emphases).

Barthes has located a point where the reader reaches an impasse and must decide whether the story belongs to one of two genres: the archaic or mythic story, on the one hand, or the realistic or geographic story, on the other. However, the text does not offer an unambiguous resolution of this difficulty, and this will in turn have important bearing upon the last (Naming) sequence. A chain reaction has begun with the first ambiguous sequence, a ripple of uncertainty that runs throughout the entire episode.

In the second narrative sequence indeterminacy proliferates in an abundance of male pronouns: "he touched the hollow of his thigh . . . then he said . . . and he said to him," and so on. The syntax both conceals and reveals the victory of the weaker over the stronger. Jacob's victory reads as an inversion of narrative logic, for the decisive wrestling hold fails and

---

[11] Barthes contrasts his analysis with the classic structuralist approaches of A. J. Greimas and Vladimir Propp, whose actantial and functional analyses, respectively, have been influential for structural exegesis of the Bible (see chap. 2). Reading in terms of actantial roles, Barthes encounters the paradox and "scandal" that Jacob is simultaneously Subject and Helper and—what is even more ambiguous—that God is both Sender and Opponent, as a result of which he is defeated. Equally, the story's ambiguity fits Propp's functional description of the fairy tale, in which God stands as the Enemy and neither his motivations nor those of Jacob are explained (1988d:256–59).

[12] Barthes's verse numbers follow the Jerusalem Bible.

Jacob triumphs by enduring until daybreak. A symbolic displacement corresponds to this reversal of reader expectation; with the giving of the mark, names change. Out of the anonymity of the pronoun comes both a new name and the refusal of a name, which turns out to be a blessing. The "smallest difference" of the signifier becomes significant:

> God . . . is the substitute of the oldest Brother, who is once again defeated by the youngest: the conflict with Esau is *displaced*. . . . The Old Testament seems to be the world less of the Fathers than of the Enemy Brothers: the elder are ousted in favor of the younger. Freud has pointed out in the myth of the Enemy Brothers the narcissistic theme of *the smallest difference:* the blow on the hip, on that thin tendon—is this not just such a *smallest difference?* Whatever the case, in this universe, God marks the youngest, he acts as a counter-nature: his (structural) function is to constitute a *counter-marker*. (254–55, Barthes's emphases)

The final sequence manifests ambiguity in the form of transgression, both within the narrative and between the narrative and the reader. This story refers in a self-reflexive way both to the narrative requirement of meaning (closure) and to its resistance to closure (indeterminacy). These multiple traces of ambiguity are marked in Jacob's body, the food taboo, his new name, divine recognition of his patriarchal significance, and the naming of the place. Each of these transgressions involves a change in meaning, and yet even more, a change in the very rules of meaning. According to Barthes, language itself transgresses and is transgressed in this story (256).

The narrative indeterminacies adumbrated by Barthes's analysis generate what he calls a "metonymic montage" or "symbolic explosion of the text" (260). The content of Genesis 32:23–33 is about "crossing over," and at the same time its form crosses over the boundaries of reader expectation. Its transgressive representation of transgression exposes the fundamental irrationality of language and leaves the reader with the difficult and finally impossible task of arriving at a conclusive meaning for the text. This Scriptural text is undecidable. "The theologian would no doubt be distressed by this indecision; the exegete would acknowledge it, hoping that some element, factual or argumentative, would allow him to bring it to an end; [but] the textual analyst . . . will savor this sort of *friction* between two intelligibilities" (251, emphasis his).

In summary, Barthes's poststructuralist reading explores questions of linguistic form, narrative logic, and semantic productivity in Genesis 32. He examines the text's use of pronouns and names, the repetitive narrative structure, and the semantic irresolution facing the reader by the text's end. Barthes's style of analysis features the search for multiple rather than singular meanings, an open rather than closed narrative structure, textual tensions and ambiguities as an alternative to resolution and clarity. For Barthes, the reader takes an aggressive role in creating meaning. This implies that there are no neutral, innocent readings; every reading is an ethical and ultimately political act.

SCRIPTURAL A/THEOLOGY

Although deconstruction is more strategy than system, more tactic than theory, it has important implications for theology. What deconstruction implies is not a metaphysics of absence, as many have said; rather, deconstruction confuses and undercuts the binarism of absence and presence. Insofar as one can continue to speak of reality—much less Reality—within this postmodern framework, one's language will necessarily be undecidable, nonidentical with itself. But to say that reality is in some sense nothing but text, that writing is in some sense prior to speech, is to make substantial theological claims.

Deconstruction poses a serious challenge to traditional notions of meaning and truth. Other contemporary literary and philosophical theories, while they abandon univocity and tolerate polysemy, retain a nostalgia for meaning. Deconstruction deflects this desire with a renewed "allegorizing" of the text—not the classical allegory of a truth hidden beneath the folds of the text's literal surface, but a "ludic allegory" (Crossan, 1980:97) of surfaces that play upon one another, of intertextual juxtapositioning. For this sort of allegory, there are only surfaces. The text is a weave or trace that endlessly unravels itself. And the interpreter is caught up in the dynamism of the text, rather than searching for some extratextual reality.

For claims such as these, deconstruction is often charged with nihilism. Because it refuses to acknowledge any extratextual signified—much less an eternal Transcendental Signified, Barthes's "Last Signified"—deconstruction appears atheistic and anarchistic to many. Others have noted a mystical tendency in deconstruction and have argued that deconstruction is amenable to mysticism and negative theology in Jewish-Christian thought. De Man himself maintained that "however negative it may sound, deconstruction implies the possibility of a rebuilding" (1983:140). But does a move toward reconstruction risk returning to logocentrism and resubmitting to the metaphysics of presence, thereby foreclosing deconstruction's radically subversive potential? The reconstructed structure will have to be deconstructed in its turn.

Deconstructive theology is especially associated with the writings of Mark C. Taylor (1982, 1984, 1987, 1990b). Deconstruction, for Taylor, "is postmodernism raised to method" (1982:xx); it is "the hermeneutic of the death of God" (xix; cf. Mark C. Taylor, 1984:6). Modernity (the Enlightenment and its progeny) posits the singular self-identity of the real and the binarism of truth and falsehood that makes knowledge possible in the form of referential language. Postmodernism centers upon the nonidentity and self-referentiality of language that makes any absolute truth-claims impossible. Modernity is characterized by atheism, belief in the nonexistence of God; postmodernism is characterized by what Taylor calls *a/theology*.[13] The slash mark opens theology to the letter of negation, forming a fractured word, neither a seamless whole nor a binary disjunction.

Taylor argues that belief in the nonexistence of God enabled modern belief in the autonomy of the self, whereas the death of God actually requires the postmodern death of the self. In postulating the death of the self or the subject, Taylor is embroidering a theme that has been especially associated with French structuralism and poststructuralism, one that has elicited frequent charges of anti-humanism. Foucault expresses this theme succinctly: "As the archaeology of our thought easily shows, man is an invention of recent date. And one perhaps nearing its end" (1970:387). In Taylor's post-Christian account, the "death of the subject" is restaged on Golgotha: "Unable to accept loss and anxious about death, the partial nihilism of the modern humanistic atheist is a sign of weakness. For the writer who suffers the crucifixion of selfhood, nihilism is the mark of the cross. On Golgotha, not only God dies; the self also disappears" (1984:33). The theological fiction of the self must undergo a/theological crucifixion.

Earlier we noted Derrida's unease with the concept of the "book." For Taylor, the postmodern is marked by the closing of the book of logocentrism. "The book . . . constitutes a systematic totality or totalistic system," he writes (1987:226), echoing Hegel and his French discontents: Bataille, Blanchot, Derrida. The book is "an organic totality of signifiers closed in and upon itself" (1984:78). "Like God, self, and history," therefore, "the notion of the book is, in an important sense, theological" (76). But the theo-

---

[13] A term he borrows from Georges Bataille (see Mark C. Taylor, 1987:136).

logical book is also teleological; every good book must form "a complete whole, with a clear beginning, middle, and end" (79). The Good Book, then, would be the book of books, for it begins "In the beginning" and ends in Apocalypse. The Bible is a t(h)e(le)ological enclosure, as its very name signifies. "The Greek *biblos* refers to the inner bark of the papyrus and designates a paper, roll, scroll, or book. The circularity of the tree trunk and scroll are carried over in the Latin word *volumen,* which means coil, wreath, or roll" (77).

What would be the effects of a French revolution in the field of the Book itself, in biblical studies? Stretches of Taylor's *Erring* (1984:103–20, 170–82) supply graphic sketches of that spectacle. Taylor undertakes an a/ theological redrafting of Derrida's redraft of Saussure. As we saw, Derrida elaborated Saussure's dictum that linguistic systems are irreducibly relational. The linguistic sign can signify solely by its relation to other signs; it has no innate significance. Neither does it possess presence: "the movement of signification is possible only if each so-called 'present' element . . . is related to something other than itself, thereby . . . constituting . . . the present by means of this very relation to what it is not. . . . But this interval that constitutes it as present must, by the same token, divide the present in and of itself, thereby also dividing, along with the present, everything that is thought on the basis of the present" (Derrida, 1982a:13). To that which deconstructs presence in the same movement with which it constructs it, Derrida gives the name *writing* (l'écriture).

Following Derrida's thread, Taylor stitches Derridean écriture to scripture (cf. Derrida, 1978b:64–78). "In the liminal time-space of scripture," writes Taylor, "hard-and-fast oppositions are shattered and every seemingly stable either-or is perpetually dislocated." Scripture is a "divine milieu" that "is neither fully present nor absent. . . . It neither is nor is not." This paradoxical divine milieu "is not thinkable within the terms of classical logic" (1984:117, quoting Derrida, 1981a:153). Linguistic signs are commonly believed to designate concepts, or actual objects in the world, but insofar as signs are unintelligible apart from other signs, "the sign is a sign of a sign" (Mark C. Taylor, 1984:105). Words, writing, scripture are not so much *about* something as they *are* that something itself. "To interpret God as word is to understand the divine as scripture or writing." But scripture thus reinscribed no longer affirms the transcendent; rather it subverts it, giving birth to a thoroughly incarnational christology: "the divine is *forever* embodied." Incarnation thus reconceived "is not a once-and-for-all event, restricted to a specific time and place" (104). Writing is bodily or incarnate. In scriptural a/theology, materiality precludes transcendence: "word is made flesh and flesh is made word" (106). What becomes of God, then? Here Derrida steps in with an uncharacteristically forthright remark: "Language has started without us, in us and before us. This is what theology calls God" (1989:29).

Traditionally, theology has been concerned with revelation. It has sought the uncovering (*apokalypsis*) of truth. Deconstructive a/theology would be an/apocalyptic, however, an "apocalypse without apocalypse" (Derrida, 1982b:94) for which the text does not reveal but is revealed—as text, writing, scripture. A deconstructive a/theology would unveil its own non-presence in the dispersed materiality and violence of textual inscription, in a dissemination beyond the metaphysics of historical univocity or structural polysemy, in a fundamental undecidability. This theology would uncover the "not-itself" which lies unnamed at its own center, its nonidentity with itself which it forever excludes. It would necessarily be fragmentary, a collection of remains, the debris of theologies that have been and the portent of theologies to come.

FOUCAULT AND HISTORY

To date, deconstruction in biblical studies and in theology has lacked an overt political framework. Indeed, poststructuralism in general is charged with having little interest in historical or ethical matters. The dazzling needlework of a Taylor, for example, would seem to offer little to a reader whose primary concern is with issues of social justice. Arguably, however, readings such as Taylor's have helped to create a climate of greater interpretive freedom in the academy. That feminist or materialist readings even get a foot in the door owes much to the deconstructive insistence that "marginal" readings are not only to be tolerated, but welcomed (cf. Jobling, 1990:97).

The aim of a text such as Taylor's *Erring* might be said to be that of "show[ing] people that a lot of things that are part of their landscape—that people think are universal—are the result of some very precise historical changes." This quotation is not from Taylor, however, but from Michel Foucault. Foucault continues: "All my analyses are against the idea of universal necessities in human existence. They show the arbitrariness of institutions and show what space of freedom we can still enjoy and how many changes can still be made" (1988:11). This approximates the suggestion that readings such as Taylor's have a de-constricting effect on tight institutional structures. In other respects, however, Taylor and Foucault are worlds apart.

From the publication of his first book, *Madness and Civilization*, in 1961 until his death in 1984, Michel Foucault combined an approach to historiography that was uniquely philosophical with an approach to philosophy that was resolutely historical. Historiography and philosophy conspired in his writing to keep each other perpetually off-balance. Whether Foucault's ostensible object of study was the history of madness (1961), the emergence of modern medicine (1963), the emergence of the human sciences (1966), the birth of the modern prison (1975), the birth of the author (1977c), or the history of sexuality (1976; 1984a; 1984b), there was a more fundamental issue that always preoccupied him, one that might be formulated thus: discourses of knowledge conspire to produce that which they purport to describe.

Foucault's 1966 book, *Les mots et les choses* [Eng. trans. *The Order of Things,* 1970] investigated the birth of the modern human subject and issued a challenge to students of the human sciences to rethink their topic, "man." Foucault attempts to show that the instruments that have been developed to study "man" have in fact invented him. "If those arrangements [of knowledge] were to disappear as they appeared," he writes, "if some event of which we can at the moment do no more than sense the possibility— without knowing either what its form will be or what it promises—were to cause them to crumble, . . . then one can certainly wager that man would be erased, like a face drawn in sand at the edge of the sea" (1970:387).

Foucault's critique of the Enlightenment *epistēmē*—his term for the total set of relations that enable and delimit knowledge in any given period (1972a:191)—has important consequences for what is still the dominant force in biblical studies, namely, the historical-critical method(s), which emerged as a result of the Enlightenment's disruption of earlier forms of exegesis. Foucault's work demands a rethinking of the history of biblical studies as a disciplinary practice (Castelli, 1991a:40). No longer would biblical scholars approach their field as historians such as W. G. Kümmel have done, showing how the gradual refinement of methods enabled a progressive and inexorable matching of scholarly description to historical fact— facts anterior to discourse, awaiting discovery. Foucault joins Derrida when it comes to facts: "There is nothing absolutely primary to be interpreted, since fundamentally everything is already interpretation; every sign is . . .

but the interpretation of other signs" (Foucault, 1967:188).[14] A Foucauldian "archaeology" of biblical scholarship would approach it as a discourse of knowledge. It would ask when and how a new field of objects for investigation—authorial intentionality, originality, sources, influences, *Sitzen im Leben,* and so on—came to be constituted (cf. Foucault, 1977c). It would ask when and how a new class of experts—"biblical critics"—came to be legitimized. It would ask questions concerning the construction, circulation, and regulation of a new kind of knowledge. It would examine one more cog, an important one, in "the prodigious machinery of the will to truth" (1972b:220).

For Foucault, the will to truth and the will to power always work hand in glove. In his later work, Foucault increasingly addressed himself to the question of power (e.g., 1977a:26ff.; 1977b; 1978:92–97; 1980; 1982a; 1989a). Under Nietzsche's tutelage, he shifted from "archaeologies" of knowledge, centered on language and discourse, to "genealogies" centered on power and bodies. He abandoned the quest for deep structures (always a covert quest, in his case) that animated his earlier work and moved into a phase that is generally labeled *poststructuralist* (cf. Dreyfus and Rabinow, xii; Harland, 155ff.; Megill, 220ff.).

"Power" came to assume an ineffability in Foucault's thought that evoked the role accorded to "language" in earlier works such as *The Order of Things*—which is to say that it all but eluded definition. Arising from nowhere, power is present everywhere: "Power's condition of possibility . . . must not be sought in the primary existence of a central point, in a unique source of sovereignty . . . ; it is the moving substrate of force relations which, by virtue of their inequality, constantly engender states of power, but the latter are always local and unstable. The omnipresence of power: not because it has the privilege of consolidating everything under its invincible unity, but because it is produced from one moment to the next, at every point" (1978:93). Power circulates everywhere within the social body. Indeed, it is coextensive with the social itself.

Foucault's reformulation of power should give pause to any political or liberation theology constructed around a vision of eventual freedom from power. Specifically, Foucault challenges as utopian any notion that social transformation has to do with liberation from power (Castelli, 1991a:44–

---

[14] Foucault's stance is a Nietzschean one, as he would have been the first to admit.

45). For Foucault, power is both pervasive and invasive. Even when it engenders counter-discourses, power tends to colonize them. And it always gives rise to such discourses. "Where there is power, there is resistance, and yet, or rather consequently, this resistance is never in a position of exteriority in relation to power. Should it be said that one is always 'inside' power, there is no 'escaping' it, there is no absolute outside where it is concerned" (1978:95). Insofar as Foucault advocates a response to power, he seems to suggest that it should be as fluid and differentiated as power itself, endlessly dissolving and reconfiguring itself. For example, when asked what might replace the present system, he can only reply: "I think that to imagine another system is to extend our participation in the present system" (1977b:230)— implying that any new system must produce new oppressions or reproduce old oppressions. (The same suspicion of systems, accompanied by insistence on constant movement, characterized Derrida's critique of logocentrism, as we saw earlier.) Does such a vision of resistance, resolutely nonvisionary, necessarily lead to political paralysis? Or could it also lead to a new kind of empowerment (to use a term that has lost its innocence with Foucault)?

Foucault's reformulation of power also impels a reconsideration of the Bible. Many of the New Testament texts, for example, deal with problems of social formation and social order. They are concerned with establishing the boundaries of the group, as in Acts 15, and with maintaining order within the group, as in the Pastoral Epistles. They are concerned with disciplining the body, as in 1 Corinthians 7, and with questions of authority, as in 2 Corinthians 10 (Castelli, 1991b). And although particular technologies of power are located by Foucault in modern centralized societies, these technologies are based on claims to self-evidence and truth, just as the discourses intended to regulate power relations in the early Christian communities legitimized themselves by claims and appeals to truth (Castelli, 1991a:46).

Because of early Christianity's marginal status, discursive strategies for constructing and regulating power relations seem to have been all important, as other forms of power (military, political, economic) were largely unattainable. The efficacy of such strategies resided not so much in threats of physical force, but in equally coercive threats pertaining to the individual's access to salvation. Foucault has argued that the emergence of Christianity was marked less by a radical change in the ethical code than by the creation and dissemination of new power relations. He has termed this new form of power *pastoral power* and offers the following definition of it:

1) [Pastoral power] is a form of power whose ultimate aim is to assure individual salvation in the next world.
2) Pastoral power is not merely a form of power which commands; it must also be prepared to sacrifice itself for the life and salvation of the flock. Therefore, it is different from royal power, which demands a sacrifice from its subjects to save the throne.
3) It is a form of power which does not look after just the whole community, but each individual in particular, during its entire life.
4) Finally, this form of power cannot be exercised without knowing the inside of people's minds, without exploring their souls, without making them reveal their innermost secrets. It implies a knowledge of the conscience and an ability to direct it.

This form of power is salvation oriented (as opposed to political power). It is oblative (as opposed to the principle of sovereignty); it is individualizing (as opposed to legal power); it is coextensive and continuous with life; it is linked with a production of truth—the truth of the individual himself. (1982a:214)

In the New Testament, pastoral power manifests itself in the competing soteriologies of the evangelists and letter writers. It also manifests itself in the conception, inherited from Judaism, of martyrdom both as witness and as victory—an inversion of conventional power relations, suppression becoming exaltation (Castelli, 1991a:47). And it manifests itself in the claim of God on the life of the individual: the insistence on personal faith and repentance.

Power circulates within social networks but passes through structures where it is concentrated, defined, and deployed; these structures are social institutions. Foucault has studied institutions such as hospitals and prisons, but for the study of the New Testament the pertinent institution is the *ekklesia,* the church (Castelli, 1991a:48). Although it appears that no unified institution bearing that name existed in the period with which we are concerned, the image of a unified institution is present nonetheless as a nascent ideal in certain New Testament texts (notably, the Pastoral Epistles).

Foucault's analytic of power is especially focused on the minutiae of its workings (Deleuze, 1988:25ff)—its micro-technologies—whether in the hospital, the prison, the confessional, or the bedroom. He insists that power is exercised more often than not in quotidian, mundane ways; that bodies and populations are regulated less through the exercise of brute force than through micro-shifts in the production of truth; that power flows both ways between subject and sovereign, prisoner and jailer, patient and physician, defining each of them. This is not to deny the reality of physical coercion, but rather to suggest that the exercise of power is not limited to nor coextensive with the concept of repression (Foucault, 1977a:219–20; 1977b:215). A Foucauldian analysis of early Christianity would focus on the minutiae of its discourses, practices, and institutions, on its policing of bodies and relationships, on the accidents through which those discourses came to assume universal dimensions—dimensions of naturalness, internalized by entire populations—producing a unique regime of knowledge, truth, and power (Castelli, 1991a:48–49).

An important facet of this development concerns the question of who was invested with the authority to speak and who was deprived of it, a question that is linked in turn to the issue of deviance. This is an issue that always fascinated Foucault. Throughout his career, he struggled to show how the "deviant" in all its diverse guises (insane, infirm, criminal, perverse) is created and exists specifically so that the norm (rational, healthy, moral, normal) can be defined. The naming of the "other" is what enables the manufacture of identity, and that naming is always violent. Foucault writes of "the prodigious machinery of the will to truth, with its vocation of exclusion" (1972b:220).

This same scapegoating process can be observed in the texts of the New Testament—and in the history of their interpretation. Take the Pauline letters, for example. To what extent have the echoes of other voices in these letters been drowned out simply by being labeled *the opponents,* the biblical scholar's equivalent of the term *other?* To what extent does the term *opponents* connote the normativity of Paul's own discourse? And to what extent does such Pauline commentary become an extension of Paul's own discourse, a testament to its cooptive power, and a repetition of its gesture of exclusion? A Foucauldian reading would attempt a different rendering of the multiple voices echoing within the Pauline corpus. It would attempt to rearticulate competing interpretations of truth in terms other than those of norm and aberration (Castelli, 1991b).

In the larger scheme of things, canon formation, whether Jewish or Christian, represents a drastic solution to the problem posed by the existence of alternative forms of knowledge. Impelled by such archaeological finds as the Dead Sea Scrolls at Qumran and the Gnostic library at Nag Hammadi, biblical scholars have labored to restore long-suppressed voices. But for the most part, such scholarship has yet to come to terms with the elaborate system of exclusions and inclusions that *its* discourse establishes. It has simply reenacted, on another level, the exclusions whose effects it aims to redress.[15]

The complicity of any analytic of power with power itself helps to explain a facet of Foucault's work that is frequently overlooked. Allan Megill writes: "Foucault's 'analytic' [of power] ought to be read in ironic rather than in literalistic terms. It may certainly suggest to conventional historians, sociologists, and anthropologists ideas capable of animating their researches. But it is not itself worthy of our literal belief, for the whole question of its representational truth is not so much left in abeyance . . . as ordered off the stage forever" (248). Hayden White would concur: "[Foucault's] own discourse stands as an abuse of everything for which 'normal' or 'proper' discourse stands" (1979:93). In other words, its preferred subject matter is not only deviance; it is itself a deviant discourse. "It *looks* like history, like philosophy, like criticism, but it stands over against these discourses as ironic antithesis" (ibid.).

Foucault himself would go even further. As early as 1967, referring to *The Order of Things,* he announced: "My book is a pure and simple 'fiction': it's a novel" (1989b:20). Every author, even a historian, "constitutes that of which he speaks" (ibid.). Like all good fiction, however, Foucault's books are capable of unsettling the reader. The realization that they are fictions may be especially discomfiting for historians, as Vincent Descombes notes, "and difficult for them to admit insofar as their own work presents the same external features as that of Foucault: a seductive construct whose play of erudite cross-reference lends it an air of verisimilitude" (117). Foucault short-circuits the inevitable pretensions to truth of his own discourse by building into it an implicit acknowledgment that any configuration of the data is necessarily contingent; it could always have been configured otherwise. It is here that Foucault comes closest to Derrida: the bottom line is always bottomless, for both of them, and as such can always be redrawn. And so "the work of the intellect is to show that what is, does not have to be, what it is" (Foucault, 1989c:252).

---

15 For an exception see King, which includes feminist perspectives on Gnostic texts.

READING THE FUTURE

Does it follow that the "bottomless bottom line" means the denial of all meaning, the loss of history, the negation of the subject, the rejection of value, the absence of ethics, the impoverishment of spirit? Are the impulses that propel poststructuralism forward but the dark underside of other "positive" postmodern impulses that, by contrast, seem to quicken rhetorical, feminist, and ideological criticisms and empower readers to speak affirmatively to and about the world in which they live? Does poststructuralism simply drain away certainty and understanding, leaving us in that peculiar position of affirming only the negative? These are not altogether ridiculous concerns especially for readers of the Bible.

If we are to believe its harshest critics (e.g., Hirsch; but cf. Harrison, 19–70), poststructuralism is coterminous with nihilism, namely, the denial of all truth, of meaning, of authorial intent, of reference, of reality, and more. All too often, however, these critiques amount to little more than popularized (if not caricatured) reports three or four times removed from any primary source (although Harrison is a major exception). The great irony here, of course, is that it is Derrida, Foucault, Barthes, and others who are so frequently charged with ignoring the letter of the text, meaning, and history by readers who themselves do not wrestle with their writings and the history of ideas within which poststructuralism stands. Simplistic sloganeering is an inadequate response to the complex theoretical issues poststructuralism raises. But before succumbing to apocalyptic woes, we would do well to recall how disturbing the emergence of positivist historico-critical criticism was for the literate readers of the Bible in the eighteenth century (cf. Frei).

It is true that in one sense poststructural criticisms signals an end— not the end of meaning but the end of privileged and protected notions of text, meaning, truth, reader, and more; but in another way the critical gestures of Barthes, Foucault, Lacan, and Derrida could hardly be more traditional. Firmly indebted to the Western philosophical and literary traditions, their writing draws energy from these very same classical resources even as they question its standards of meaning. Against the backdrop of a tragic century that has seen two great world wars and the Holocaust, and now a "New World (dis)Order," poststructuralism may be regarded as a not-surprising theoretical response to a world fraught with indeterminacy, a world where the Enlightenment's humanizing project is suspect to some degree. In the terms of one of poststructuralism's most perceptive critics, the search for "real presence," which has characterized the Western intellectual and spiritual experience, is in great jeopardy, and the great traditions and texts—like the Bible—which instanciated purpose and meaning, no longer have the same currency. Just how are we to read the Bible the same way after Auschwitz and Buchenwald (Levinas, 1990a)?

If poststructuralist methods mirror in some appropriate ways the brokenness of Western culture today—the bankruptcy of the academy, the demise of the renaissance intellectual, the abandonment of tradition, the turning away from historicism—is that *all* that poststructuralism does? Or does it indeed make a contribution in concrete ways to the social fabric of "lived relations" (Althusser)? It may well be that biblical critics will find by means of engagement with poststructuralist theories the incentive to reexamine the question of history and historical criticism. Already the critical effort identified as "New Historicism" suggests that "a poetics of culture" (Veeser) is indeed possible as a direct result of the need to pull "historical consideration to the center stage of literary analysis" (Veeser, xi). The work of Foucault and, to a lesser extent, Derrida is playing an important role in this effort.

The significance of New Historicism for a biblical scholarship that has cast its lot methodologically and ideologically with positivist history and science may be far-reaching. The force of New Historicism, in part, is in placing historical inquiry in direct contact with literary and cultural theories. The result is a different type of critical encounter with theory than the naive (and often shallow) appropriation of literary theory characteristic of biblical critics who poured the new wine of reader-response or narratological categories into the old wineskin of redaction criticism. A reexamination of the relation of the text, its reading, and its reader through the lens of poststructuralist theory may serve as a bridge which enables traditional critics to see that traditional historical criticism may yet be salvageable, but not before an ideological critique of scholarship and of culture occurs.

A second area where poststructuralist discourse may prove important for biblical studies is on the question of ethics. We have mentioned the way Derrida and deconstruction has been roundly condemned for demoting the question of ethics (and also history). For a biblical scholarship whose critical work is tied institutionally either to the church or the academy, the poststructural critique of meaning offers an important resource when raising questions about the status of its reading and writing. What is at stake is a contrast and conflict between competing understandings of "ethics." The ethical question doesn't necessarily disappear in poststructuralism; rather its content and practice is assessed on different grounds. Its primary aim now is "the dissolution of the form of ethics associated with repression and violence" (Siebers, 32). In the words of Julia Kristeva: "Ethics used to be a coercive, customary manner of ensuring the cohesiveness of a particular group through the repetition of a code. . . . Now, however, the issue of ethics crops up wherever a code (mores, social contract) must be shattered in order to give way to the free play of negativity, desire, pleasure, and jouissance, *before being put together again*" (1980a:23; cited in Siebers, 32).

Derrida's own effort to rethink the foundations of ethics through a different kind of acutely self-critical engagement with method and literature (see 1988b:11–154; 1992a:1–29) that searches for a more originary understanding of the relation of text, context, and commentary returns not only the issues of epistemology and metaphysics but ethics to the circle of concerns that biblical scholarship has not thought sufficiently about since Bultmann. Levinas promises to become an important figure in this regard (see Critchley). Biblical scholarship might discover in the combined energies and critiques arising from feminist, womanist, and ideological criticisms in conversation with poststructuralist interests the opening for a Bultmann-style effort to place historical, theological, literary, and metaphysical discourses in a different conversation with one another again. In contrast to Bultmann, however, the desire for a global synthesis for the modern world has given way to a more regional and local concern to make the Bible speak to particular postmodern worlds. The extent to which biblical scholarship will find in poststructuralism resources for historical and ethical reflection will depend also upon how willing it is to undertake the self-critique demanded of its own historical methods and ethical practices.

RECOMMENDED FURTHER READING

Barthes, Roland. 1974b. *S/Z*. Trans. Richard Miller. New York: Hill & Wang. A close, textual analysis of Honoré de Balzac's novella *Sarrasine*. More than any other, this book bridges the gap between classical structuralism and poststructuralism.

Castelli, Elizabeth A. 1991a. *Imitating Paul: A Discourse of Power*. Louisville, Ky.: Westminster/John Knox Press. A Foucauldian reading of selected Pauline texts combined with a feminist critical perspective.

De Man, Paul. 1979a. *Allegories of Reading: Figural Language in Rousseau, Nietzsche, Rilke, and Proust*. New Haven: Yale University Press. A series of intricate, deconstructive readings, frequently imitated but seldom surpassed. De Man's most important book.

Derrida, Jacques. 1976. *Of Grammatology*. Trans. Gayatri Chakravorty Spivak. Baltimore:

Johns Hopkins University Press. Derrida's most influential work. The detailed translator's preface offers one of the best overall introductions to Derrida's thought.

———. 1981a. *Dissemination*. Trans. Barbara Johnson. Chicago: University of Chicago Press. Three lengthy essays, including an important deconstructive reading of Plato's "Phaedrus" and reflection on the writing of the literary work.

Foucault, Michel. 1977a. *Discipline and Punish: The Birth of the Prison*. Trans. Alan Sheridan. New York: Pantheon. Examines the emergence of the "disciplinary technologies" that shape and "rule" modern life. Perhaps Foucault's most accessible book and, in the opinion of many commentators and Foucault himself, his most successful.

———. 1978. *The History of Sexuality: An Introduction*. Trans. Robert Hurley. New York: Pantheon. Argues that sexuality was "invented" in nineteenth-century Europe. A book that has become central to the new academic field of gender studies.

Harari, Josué V., trans. and ed. 1979. *Textual Strategies: Perspectives in Post-Structuralist Criticism*. Ithaca: Cornell University Press. Includes important essays by Barthes, de Man, Derrida, Foucault, and others on a broad range of theoretical topics.

Harland, Richard. 1987. *Superstructuralism: The Philosophy of Structuralism and Post-Structuralism*. New York: Methuen. An excellent introduction to a wide range of structuralist and poststructuralist thinkers that addresses the epistemological foundation common to both.

Jobling, David, and Stephen D. Moore, eds. 1991. "Poststructuralism as Exegesis." *Semeia* 54. Atlanta: Scholars. Ten poststructuralist readings of texts drawn from the Hebrew Bible and New Testament.

Kamuf, Peggy, ed. 1990. *A Derrida Reader: Between the Blinds*. New York: Columbia University Press. Twenty-two selections from Derrida, each introduced by Kamuf, along with a helpful general introduction.

Moore, Stephen D. 1992. *Mark and Luke in Poststructuralist Perspectives: Jesus Begins to Write*. New Haven: Yale University Press. One of the first book-length treatments of Gospel narrative from a poststructuralist perspective. Mark and Luke in intertextual dialogue with Derrida, Lacan, and Foucault.

Phillips, Gary A., ed. 1990. "Poststructural Criticism and the Bible: Text/History/Discourse." *Semeia* 51. Atlanta: Scholars. Ten essays that address theoretical and exegetical topics emerging from poststructural critique of history and discourse.

Rabinow, Paul, ed. 1984. *The Foucault Reader*. New York: Pantheon. Twenty-two essays, book-excerpts, and interviews, with a general introduction by Rabinow.

Sturrock, John, ed. 1979. *Structuralism and Since: From Lévi-Strauss to Derrida*. New York: Oxford University Press. One of the best set of short introductions to Barthes, Foucault, Lacan, and Derrida in print.

Taylor, Mark C. 1984. *Erring: A Postmodern A/theology*. Chicago: University of Chicago Press. A book that explores deconstruction's contribution to theology. A major work with implications for other religious studies subfields.

4 | Rhetorical Criticism

Come now, let us reason together, says the Lord.
—Isaiah 1:18

Only through rhetoric does science become a social
factor in our lives.
—Hans Georg Gadamer (1988:279)

Over the past twenty-five years we have witnessed an explosion of publications on the rhetoric of biblical texts. The rich legacy of Western rhetoric, which has been neglected by scholars for several centuries, is now being reclaimed. As a result, rhetoric is no longer being reduced to a study of the biblical writer's style. Rhetoric as the use by biblical writers of commonly accepted rules and techniques for persuading their audiences of certain viewpoints, or for reaffirming them, is now being recovered. The revival of rhetorical criticism, conceived as a set of rules and techniques sanctioned by the scholarly guild, should enhance the interpreter's approach to specific texts, to the Bible as a whole, and to the process of interpretation. Our goal in this chapter is not only to survey the fields of classical and contemporary rhetorical theory, but also to situate rhetoric explicitly within a postmodern framework.

This chapter is divided into seven parts. First, we will illustrate rhetorical criticism by applying to a Pauline text, 1 Cor. 9:1–10:13, an outline put forward by George A. Kennedy, which has brought important issues concerning the reading of texts to the attention of biblical scholars. In the next section we will take a critical look at the historical and cultural contexts for the current revival of interest in rhetorical criticism and at how rhetoric came to be understood in terms of poetics, so that finally it became indistinguishable from literary criticism. This is followed by a critical examination of the theories that inform the various practices of rhetorical criticism, with a focus on the need for rhetorical analysis not only of texts but also of the practices of reading texts. Then we will consider briefly the liaison between rhetoric and religion, as well as some views of the nature and purpose of the rhetoric of religion. Next we will discuss the emergence of the new biblical rhetorical criticism and subject it to a theoretical critique, followed by a second, postmodern rhetorical reading of 1 Cor. 9:1–10:13 to test the force of this critique. In the final section we will ask: Where do we go from here? and suggest that rhetorical criticism should now function as cultural criticism in a postmodern context.

READING 1 CORINTHIANS

In 1 Cor. 9:1–10:13 there appears to be a jarring digression from the argument in chapter 8, resumed in 10:14–22, about socially divisive behavior in connection with Christians using, or not using, meat sacrificed to idols. Rhetorical critics would challenge the widely shared position of Pauline scholars who resort to source criticism to account for this abrupt transition. To illustrate how a rhetorical critic might approach this text, we will use Kennedy's steps (1984:33–38), with the crucial modifications made by Wuellner (1979; 1986; 1987) and Lausberg.

1. The first task is to identify the *rhetorical unit(s)* in the text. Rhetorical units are not the same as *literary units* (whether these be the smaller form-critical or the larger redaction-critical units). The difference lies in the emphasis on the context. By "context" the rhetorical critic means the overall argumentative and persuasive strategy that is designed to move the audience or reader to agree with the speaker or writer.

Several large rhetorical units can be identified within 1 Cor. 9:1–10:13.

One is the "apology" (9:3–27), with its constitutive parts of the accusation and the defense. In this passage the two parts appear in reverse order, the defense (9:3–12) coming before the accusation (9:13–27; cf. Willis, 1985a). As we shall see in step 3, however, this paradoxical reversal is consonant with Paul's argument that he is obligated to reverse cultural norms in light of eschatological ones. Each of the two parts contains a smaller rhetorical unit, a syllogism (*enthymeme;* 9:8–12a, 19–23).

The whole passage, 9:1–10:13, as a digression within Paul's argument, constitutes a rhetorical unit on a larger scale. It consists of the apology proper (9:3–27), followed by an exhortation (*parenesis;* 10:1–11), and finally by a brief conclusion or peroration (10:12–13). But 9:1–10:13 as a whole also functions as part of progressively larger units. The passage 8:1–10:22 is concerned with the issue of idol meat and the table fellowship of Jews and Gentiles, and this in turn is part of 6:12–11:1, which is identified as a unit by its beginning and ending with "all things are lawful" (6:12; 10:23). Every rhetorical unit is always more than the sum total of its constitutive parts, and, in turn, it is always part of still larger units. We may regard as rhetorical units in an extended sense 1 Corinthians as a whole, Paul's entire Corinthian correspondence, the Pauline corpus, and the whole canon of Scripture. Context, then, though central to rhetorical criticism, is not capable of exact definition; we shall return to this issue.

2. Once rhetorical units have been identified, the rhetorical critic's next task is to account for the *rhetorical situation* that generated the text, and the specific *rhetorical problem* facing the speaker-writer in this situation. This task is perhaps the most crucial, because it is here that one comes face-to-face with the intention in the texts to move readers to action. The rhetorical units identified in step 1 are more than just stylistic or literary devices. They aim at persuading the audience to agree, to commit themselves to the argument. All the speaker-writer's "invention" (in the sense of inventiveness) is called upon to find the right devices to achieve this. It is the rhetorical situation that determines what rhetorical options are the optimal ones to use in persuading the audience (Wuellner, 1987:455–56).

In 1 Cor. 9:1–10:13, Paul is confronted with actually or potentially divisive social practices associated with the use of "meat sacrificed to idols" (cf. 8:1, 13). His rhetorical situation is a mixed one because he partly supports existing social behavior in Corinth but seeks even more to challenge it and promote changed behavior. It is this mixed rhetorical situation that generates both Paul's argument in chapter 8 and the digression in chapter 9.

On this basis a rhetorical critic would deny that there is any need to resort to source-critical theories to explain the digression.

3. This leads directly to the next step, which is the choice of a *rhetorical genre*. If rhetorical situation corresponds to the familiar *Sitz im Leben* in form-criticism, this new step corresponds to the determination of the literary form (*Gattung*, genre). But, from the point of view of rhetorical criticism, form-criticism has erred by reducing the life-setting to generic historical contexts, to typical social conventions, and by treating the text as an aesthetic object, as a stock literary device available for use in such typical situations. The preeminent concern for rhetorical critics is the relation of the choice of a rhetorical genre to the specific rhetorical situation, to the basic issue (status or *stasis*) of the argument. The chosen genre, in its specificity rather than its typicality, becomes part of the rhetorical situation and must be a major factor in the delineation of that situation.

Such a mixed rhetorical situation as Paul finds himself in calls for a mixed rhetorical genre. Paul calls his argument an *apology* (*apologia*, 9:3), that is, a defense of his position and behavior (cf. Lausberg, 61, 88, 92, 105). But in using this term, Paul sets an ironic mood; his readers are led to anticipate a legal defense before some kind of a jury, though there is nothing in the rhetorical situation to indicate that he is under any actual legal indictment about his rights as an apostle (9:1–2). The speech functions as a parody of an apology; it plays in the argument of 1 Corinthians a role analogous to that of the "fool's speech" in 2 Cor. 10–13 (Sampley). The result is a strange but effective hybrid, a mix of apology and demonstration, a speech that assigns praise and blame in the guise of offering a judicial defense. In another surprising move, Paul forgoes rights and privileges that would be entirely appropriate to his defense (9:12, 15) and ends up apologetically praising what was offensive to some of the Corinthians in the first place—refusing to charge for his teaching and assuming the demeanor of a slave (9:16–19, 22). He has chosen from a number of possible mixed genres, or perhaps created ad hoc, the strategy that seems best to fit his rhetorical situation. Chapter 9 serves as an amplifying and ironic digression within the rhetorical situation underlying chapter 8.

The tone of the argument is set in 9:4–7 with the questionable, even enigmatic, status of the case before the jury. Paul's main argument begins and ends (9:4–6, 11–12a) with rhetorical questions that imply his (and Barnabas's) right to receive material support from the Corinthians. He appeals to typical cases (soldiers, vineyard workers, those who tend flocks). In a syllogism (9:8–12a), he lays out the premise that there is an established cultural norm, an ideology, that author and readers share. He appeals to a "universal audience" (Crosswhite); his appeal is like an "ideal speech situation" (Gripp, 46–55) in which speaker and hearers can agree on the basic premise: workers have a right to some rewards from their labor.

Paul then particularizes the argument to his rhetorical situation. If the general case be conceded, the particular right of an apostle to receive support becomes plausible. And within the frame of *any* apostle's right to support, the particular right of Paul and Barnabas to receive support for their apostolic work among the Corinthians should also be clear (vv. 11–12a). Paul's linkage of the universal and the particular (cf. Perelman, 1974:810) depends on the rhetorical genre he chooses.

The syllogism does not, however, appeal only to agreed cultural norms. It is based also upon the authority of God and of Christ (9:2, 5). And it goes beyond immediate cultural norms in appealing to the law of Moses (9:8–9). Here again Paul argues from the general (the "law of Moses") to the particular (9:10: "for our sake"). These appeals to God, to Christ, and to the law of Moses prepare Paul's readers for the next stage (9:12b–15), which is the heart of his argument.

By refusing payment for his teaching, Paul is challenging the validity of, even reversing, the universal cultural norm. This reversal is plausible, however, since Christian communities claim to be living by eschatological norms that encompass cultural ones—surely a group destined to be an eschatological jury, to judge the world and angels (6:2–3), can understand the eschatological norms to which Paul appeals. The self-exemplary argument is developed as an illustration, or amplification, of what on the mythic level is Christ-exemplary (as in 4:16–17 and 11:1), and ultimately God-exemplary (as in 1:25; 3:7, 23). What the argument is intended to accomplish is to increase the intensity of the readers' adherence to this culturally implausible and new social value. Both author and readers live under God's norms.

Yet even in his particularizing Paul seeks to create agreement among a new sort of universal audience (Perelman, 1979:31–35; 1982:17–18). What he says applies not only to the Corinthians, but to "believers everywhere" (this is already implicit in Paul's rhetorical situation, e.g., 7:17b; 11:2b; 12:13, 27). In the course of the argument, a universal situation has been particularized, and the particular then universalized in a different way. (This kind of universalizing tendency becomes even clearer in the Deutero-Pauline letters, especially Ephesians.)

In a powerfully executed argument, Paul now introduces a second syllogism (9:19–23), based on the familiar Hellenistic theme of the enslaved leader, the leader who laudably serves everyone as benefactor (cf. the designation of the Pope as "the servant of the servants of God"). This theme is based on the complementary notions of unselfish and distinguished service by the leader and acknowledgment of his generous service by the recipients; the fundamental idea is reciprocity (see Danker, 1982). Paul makes this "universal," the Hellenistic patronage system, fundamental to his appeal. His choice to become "a slave to all" (9:19) is based upon his acknowledgment of how God and Christ have acted toward him (1:1; 3:10; 4:1–2; cf. 2 Cor. 8:9). Paul acknowledges the beneficence of God and Christ toward him by enslaving himself to the Corinthians. Cannot the Corinthians, in turn, properly interpret his leadership role as that of a benefactor and respond with gratitude (see Danker, 1991:266–67)? This hierarchical reciprocity system enhances the significance of 9:24–27. Both Paul's and the Corinthians' "running" for the "prize" assumes the hierarchy God-Christ-Paul-Corinthians. Praise and reward come from God rather than from any societal source.

It is Paul's response to God and to Christ, then, that requires him to reverse social and cultural norms by relinquishing his right to material support. And the Corinthians' eschatological vindication by God (the prize of their running) is at stake in how they will respond to Paul's defense. This point Paul amplifies rhetorically in a form of argumentation recognizable as Jewish midrash (10:1–11).

Following rhetorical convention, Paul concludes the whole digression with a brief peroration (10:12–13). The overall aim of 9:1–10:11 has been to convince readers of the need in part to reaffirm, in part to change, their disposition and behavior. The passage 10:12–13 provides a rhetorical climax as Paul tries to move his readers to the kind of reciprocal action proposed in 8:13—action for the sake of "the other." Action on behalf of others is now revealed as the main rhetorical point of 9:1–10:13. Paul's refusal of support from the Corinthians has been part of his service to others. His digression is thus rhetorically linked to his main argument about food offered to idols, which he now resumes in 10:14.

4. The next step is to identify features of *rhetorical style*. At this stage of analysis the critic examines how the rhetorical choices made (the *invention*) create a particular organization (*disposition*) of the argument, and how this organization generates specific stylistic techniques. Rhetorical critics resist reducing rhetorical style to mere stylistics (cf. Wayne C. Booth,

1983a; Genette, 1982a). If stylistic techniques are seen only as artistic devices or ornamentation (so Bünker, 48–72), then their main function as argumentation will be diminished or discounted altogether. Wuellner calls for "the liberation from Babylonian captivity of rhetoric reduced to stylistics" (1987:457).

An outstanding example of one particular technique is the use in 1 Corinthians 9 (more than in any other chapter of the New Testament) of *rhetorical questions* (Wuellner, 1986). Yet Paul uses these questions in a paradoxical way, in line with the paradoxical quality of his whole argument. His form of argumentation (particularly through the theme of the enslaved leader) is by dissociation. Alongside the more familiar argumentation by association, dissociation is (according to Perelman and Olbrechts-Tyteca, 411–59; Perelman, 1982:126–37) the other major technique used in all argumentation. Dissociative techniques aim at a disjuncture between a "reality," which is to be valued as a result of the argument, and a given "appearance" which is to be devalued or decentered. Dissociation of ideas "results in a depreciation of what had until then been the accepted value . . . and in the replacement of this accepted norm by another conception to which is accorded the original value" (Perelman, 1979:24). Rhetorical questions would seem naturally to belong to associative reasoning, anticipating answers that conform to existing norms; but Paul's rhetorical questions anticipate answers that reverse existing norms.

5. The last task for the rhetorical critic is to analyze the overall *rhetorical strategy* that is designed to move the audience or reader to agree with the speaker or writer. The creativity of the speaker or writer has been seen at each analytical step, but now that inventiveness must be given its full due so that the whole argument is appreciated as something greater than its rhetorical parts. Nor does the critic just stand back and look at the text as an artifact whose beauty and wholeness has been revealed through objective analysis. "Criticism too," like composition, "can be a creative act" (Kennedy, 1984:38; cf. Wuellner, 1987:458).

In the case of 1 Cor. 9:1–10:13, the effectiveness of Paul's strategy can be measured by how it conforms to the rhetorical intention of the entire book. The introduction (1:1–9) leads to the statement of the central thesis (1:10): the unity (oneness or solidarity; *koinonia* or *agapē*) that Christians have experienced is to be maintained and strengthened in the face of ever-threatening distractions, distortions, or perversions. The overall rhetorical situation in 1 Corinthians is focused on praise of unity and shame of the neglect of unity. This assessment is vindicated by the recapitulation of the main thesis, now expressed in terms of love, at the end of Paul's argument (chap. 16, esp. vv. 13–14, 22, 24).

The characteristics that our analysis has discovered in 9:1–10:13 are found throughout 1 Corinthians. Paul ascribes praise and blame for the purpose of subverting some values and strengthening others. Such "epideictic" rhetoric, according to Perelman and Olbrechts-Tyteca, should be viewed not merely as laudatory or polemical, but as essentially educational in nature (47–54; cf. Aune; Duffy; Mark D. Jordan; Rosenfield). Rhetorical analysis suggests that education is the earmark of Paul's rhetoric in 1 Corinthians (and perhaps in his other epistles as well; Wuellner, 1987:460).[1]

THE EMERGENCE OF THE NEW RHETORIC

Classical rhetoric, the rhetorical rules developed in Greece and Rome and their codification in rhetorical handbooks, maintained a place of centrality in the Western intellectual tradition through about 1500 C.E. During the sixteenth and seventeenth centuries, however, there set in a period of decline of interest in rhetoric that culminated in its near demise, a situation that lasted well into the first quarter of the twentieth century. Since then we have witnessed a renaissance of rhetorical criticism, which aims at restoring "rhetoric to all its ancient rights" (Bakhtin, 1981:267; for treatments of this demise and spectacular rebirth see Conley; Horner; Vickers, 1988). The so-called *new rhetoric* is in large measure a modern rediscovery of ancient Western rhetoric. It brings with it, however, many issues that were never fully addressed in traditional rhetoric and which anticipate postmodern theoretical concerns. In what follows we will review critical factors in both the decline and the renaissance of rhetoric.

A first cause of the decline of rhetoric was "the idea of the unicity of truth" (Perelman, 1979:12) in the Western philosophical tradition. One fateful moment was the educational reform advocated by Peter Ramus in the sixteenth century, whose effect was the institutionalization of a separation of the study of thought or content from the study of form or feeling. Particularly from the time of Kant, the struggle on the one hand to relate ways

---

[1] This view that Paul's letters have a prevalent epideictic character is contested by the majority of scholars, even those committed to rhetorical criticism (Hans Dieter Betz, Margaret Mitchell, Bruce Johanson, Elisabeth Schüssler Fiorenza, and others).

of expressing feelings, and on the other to deal with the demand that word and object have a dependable and straightforward correlation, issued in the ascendancy of poetry for the former and of scientific discourse for the latter. Poetry generally became the discourse of the human spirit, scientific discourse the mode of demonstration and proof of the truth (see Reiss; with respect to the Bible, see Frei, 3–19). Rhetoric was consequently relegated to a second-class status in relation to both discourses and was viewed suspiciously as mere ornamentation. Modern scientific "analytico-referential" discourse (Reiss's term), with its univocal understanding of truth, played a major role in classical rhetoric's demise. Barilli refers to an "unfortunate 'dissociation of sensibility' that separates thinking from feeling and disdains all the intermediate pathways, which traditionally were implemented by rhetoric" (112, cf. 89–101).

A second cause was the growing identification of rhetoric with poetics, stylistics, hermeneutics, or, in general, the study of literature. Kennedy notes that during the Renaissance there was already "the tendency of rhetoric to shift its focus from persuasion to narration, from civic to personal contexts, and from discourse to literature, including poetry" (1980:5; cf. Vickers, 1987). The *Clavis Scripturae* of Matthias Flacius (1567), a hermeneutical textbook which has been called "the real beginning of scholarly hermeneutics" in Western culture, treated rhetoric and hermeneutics as indistinguishable (Wuellner, 1989a:11–12), and since this time rhetorical criticism has tended to become absorbed into the general hermeneutical task.[2] Kennedy's "shift . . . from persuasion to narration," and the subsequent bifurcation into what he calls "primary" and "secondary" rhetoric, is still operative in distinctions between " 'rhetoric' as a *kind* of text and 'rhetoric' as a *function* of texts of any kind" (Chatman, 1990:193; cf. 184–203). The term *rhetorical criticism* is still taken as a synonym for literary criticism, stylistics, discourse analysis, text linguistics, speech-act theory, reader-response criticism, and so forth. Some would go so far as to say that rhetoric, which before the rise of modernity used to be concerned with the whole of human discursive experience, has now become so fragmented that an analytic, formalistic, and scientific "philosophy of antirhetoric" has been produced (Barilli, 119).

A third cause of classical rhetoric's loss of authority was the emerging awareness of alternative theories and practices of rhetoric. There were two

---

[2] On the relation between rhetoric and hermeneutic, see Hyde and Smith; Mailloux, 1985, 1989; Mosdt; Rickman; Schrag (chap. 9); Todorov, 1975.

sources of this awareness. On the one hand, the vernacular movements of the late Middle Ages led to the study of rhetorics indigenous to European cultures (what Schanze calls the "new rhetoric" emerging around 1500 C.E.). On the other hand, conflict was experienced between Western rhetorics as a whole (whether classical or vernacular) and non-Western rhetorics, primarily in refined critical appreciation of Jewish rhetoric (Isaac Rabinowitz and see our section on new rhetorical criticism below) and in the clash with the conquering Muslim culture (Vickers, 1988:473, n. 44). The classical tradition was exposed as enshrining an undifferentiated, universalized notion of rhetoric that ignored cultural difference.

According to Eagleton (1983:205–6), we are now experiencing a reinvention of rhetoric. But the scope of rhetoric has expanded, as witness the great variety of definitions and practices of rhetorical criticism (Bashford; Brock and Scott; Plett, 1975a, 1975b; Reid; Sillars). Rhetoric has shifted from its traditional focus on oral rhetoric or letter writing to include all texts as "signs" through which text-sign producers and their products interact with text-sign receivers and validators. Modern rhetorical criticism, then, is the study of "the means by which a text establishes and manages its relationship to its audience in order to achieve a particular effect" (Patrick and Scult, 12). Rhetoric is recognized as inherent in all language usage, whether it is written or spoken, poetic or ordinary. Indeed, rhetoric is inherent in all use of signs as forms and functions of discourse. Rhetorical criticism aspires to a "full-bodied encounter with the . . . text" (Patrick and Scult, 18; cf. Josipovici).

Part of the impulse for this renaissance has been, paradoxically, the encounters with nonclassical rhetorics. In response to the new rhetoric, an opposition was set up between classical and popular culture (and entrenched in scholarship's categorical distinction between *Hochliteratur* and *Kleinliteratur* [high and low literature]), whereby popular literature was acknowledged to have expressive or stylistic features but was judged to be rhetorically deficient. But the "microrhetoric" of folk or popular culture became the focus of interest in, for example, Freud (Todorov, 1982:246–54), or the structuralists (Barilli, 106–10), who paved the way for the current revival by their minute analyses of popular discourse on jokes, dreams, fairy tales, and so on. Again, despite the initial Western response to global cultural confrontations—the imposition of Western rhetorics on non-Western cultures through colonial and missionary expansion—these encounters have proven a profuse if not subversive source of alternative perspectives on rhetorical theory and practice (for example, the diverse traditions of Asian rhetoric, on which cf. Garrett; Jensen).

Encounters with alternative rhetorics have also contributed to new ways of thinking about the classical tradition itself. Recognizing that cultural values cannot be separated from specific functions, Kennedy has emphasized that classical rhetoric and its legacy consisted of a wide diversity of theories and practices, each of which is "more or less defined by . . . values and functions of culture" (1984:8). Rhetoric's critical practices and theories reflect the wider social and cultural situations in which they were cultivated. Despite Western rhetorical handbooks that promoted the notion of rhetoric as a closed, self-perpetuating system, there never was a monolithic tradition of rhetoric or of rhetorical criticism (Bowman; Conley).

Recent rhetoric attempts to retrieve and utilize all of the emphases of classical rhetoric, to unshackle rhetoric from its modern critical constraints. Classical rhetoric originated as the art of persuasive communication (Perelman, 1986). Under the hegemony of the Western philosophical idea of the unicity of truth, it was reduced to an instrument for transmitting philosophical, theological, and cultural truths, so that between the seventeenth and the nineteenth century, rhetoric finally became a faint and distorted version of the classical tradition. In contrast, the "new" rhetoric seeks to retrieve the fullness of what had been taught by the ancients.[3]

The five crucial components of ancient rhetoric that the new rhetoric has retrieved can be briefly summarized. First, rhetoric as *verbal expression*. This traditional emphasis, what some call artifactual or operational rhetoric, has been revived in modern linguistics and discourse analysis, and the practical scope of traditional literary rhetoric in this respect is usually outlined in contemporary rhetorical handbooks (e.g., Lanham, 1968; Lausberg). The key theoretical issue, however, of the relation between rhetoric and language, particularly between the conscious art in rhetoric and the unconscious art in colloquial language, is often neglected.

A second component of traditional rhetoric, perhaps its primary one, is its view of the nature of truth as something to be discovered, to be *invented*.

---

[3] The "new" rhetoric is so called by Perelman, Burke, and others and is not to be confused with the post-1500 C.E new rhetoric just mentioned. It is not always noted that the New Critics took a deep interest in rhetoric. Barilli (114) goes so far as to contend that "the whole movement of the New Critics and of their associates [such as Richards, 1936] can be seen as trying to propose a global philosophy of rhetoric."

Rhetoric as the art of invention (McKeon), the art of dialectical persuasive reasoning (Perelman, 1979), even in narrative (W. R. Fisher), has given rise to theoretical discussions of this central aspect of rhetoric. Invention is the creative recasting of a given subject into discursive rules and topics appropriate for both the subject and the particular audience. Invention, then, relates to rhetorical disposition and elocution much as deep structure does to surface structure in generative transformational linguistics, as *parole* does to *langue* in structural linguistics (see chap. 2), or as the unconscious relates to consciousness in analytical psychology.

This emphasis in rhetoric leads on to a third: the concern with the creation of meaning and the domain of *hermeneutics*. The relation between rhetoric and hermeneutic, rooted in classical rhetoric, is to be maintained, though the tendency referred to above—to subsume rhetoric under hermeneutics—needs to be avoided. According to Perelman, rhetoric, as a theory of persuasive discourse, is "sometimes called hermeneutics . . . [because] the idea of looking for meaning is done now through the rhetorical method" (1986:11).

A fourth feature that distinguishes modern rhetorical criticism (grounded in traditional rhetoric's emphasis on social imagination and epitomized in this chapter's epigraph from Gadamer) is its emphasis on rhetoric as *a factor in social discourse and societal formation*. It highlights the social grounds of knowledge in the processes of argumentation and the interpersonal, interactive functions of language. Because rhetorical practices and theories arise in response to cultural, political, or social conditions, they will always have implications for the respective institutions.[4] This concern can be expressed in terms of the text's rhetorical situation (see above), that is, its intentionality or exigency. Critics focus on the practical intentions, or practical forces, for motivating action as a constitutive component of rhetorical discourse. Burke (1950), for example, sees personal transformation as the primary motive of all rhetoric, whereas Perelman, in a similar way, understands rhetoric in the context of public education and of commitment. The point is that for

[4] On rhetoric as the social grounds of knowledge, see Willard. On rhetoric as social imagination, see Dillon; on rhetoric as the logic of the behavioral sciences, see Loreau; on rhetoric in scholastic and public affairs, see Cahn, 1989/1990; Conley, 20–23; Eagleton, 1983:194–217; 1990b; Nelso, et al.; Perelman, 1984. On the connection between rhetoric and sixteenth-century reform, see Boyle. Cheney's work is relevant for discussion of rhetoric and the social both in modern society and societies in the Hellenistic age.

the rhetorical critic, texts or rhetorical discourses should be approached as having arisen, and as continuously arising, in response to a practical problem, that is, a problem about what to do (Cushman and Tompkins, 52–53). One of the main tasks of rhetorical critics, then, is to elucidate the practical intention of the rhetoric of texts.

Fifth, rhetoric has always *linked thinking and emotions* and emphasized that reason must be accompanied by an appeal to emotion if any audience is to be persuaded. In classical rhetorical theory, the appeal to the emotions (*pathos*) is the prime motivating force for action;[5] rhetorical figures as argumentative techniques are defined by how they affect the audience's imagination and volition. From this background comes modern rhetoric's recognition of the "rationality" of the emotions, a rationality different from that of logical demonstration. It is by virtue of this rationality that an appeal to the emotions of an audience can facilitate their understanding of what is at stake and enable them to examine "the best ends and the most efficient means for achieving them" (Cushman and Tompkins, 53–54). This distinction between rhetorical rationality and logical demonstration is a major characteristic of the new rhetoric (cf. Perelman and Olbrechts-Tyteca, 193–260).

But the new rhetoric is more than the sum total of these five emphases. In the history of rhetoric they have often been isolated from each other. The result has been understandings of rhetoric that, while not illegitimate, have been reductive, constraining the totality of rhetoric to one aspect or to an idiosyncratic hybrid. In spite of its contribution to the retrieval of an ample classical rhetoric, the new rhetoric continues in its own way to make similar reductive gestures. It reduces rhetoric to poetics, stylistics, and literary criticism generally (cf. above), to communication studies or social studies, or to text linguistics or discourse analysis (Johanson). Another way to restrain rhetorical criticism is to reduce it to social description or to historical reconstruction, as Mack (1989) tends to do when he stresses the promise of rhetorical criticism for the analysis of social formation. Rhetoric does indeed overlap with other sciences, but "the realm of rhetoric" (Perelman, 1982) has its own integrity and its own constraints.

---

[5] Auerbach, 1953:54–63; Bailey; Brinton, 1988; Craemer-Ruegenberg; De Sousa; Dockhorn, 1964; Fenner:90–104; Gelzer; Gordon; Marselaa; Plett, 1975b; Solomon.

A CRITICAL VIEW OF THE NEW RHETORIC

Even though a rhetoric conscious of its classical roots has reemerged, all is not well with rhetorical criticism today as critics—including postmodern critics—confront the formidable task of redefining the realm of rhetoric. As a method with ancient roots (unlike the other methods taken up in this book), it finds itself now in an unfamiliar landscape, both theoretical and political. So far, the new rhetorical criticism has paid little attention to these challenges. But it is not without its own characteristic resources for establishing a place for itself. The rhetorical tradition that we have outlined in the previous section has many features very much attuned to postmodern perspectives, and what we are calling for is not the imposition of entirely alien categories on traditional rhetoric.

The current theoretical scene in literary criticism, as we present it throughout this book, is highly conflicted and often appears anarchic; more and more theory is produced, there is "ceaseless discursive warfare" about theory, the "war of all against all" (Jameson, 1991:397; cf. Eagleton, 1990a:77). A paradoxical situation has developed in which we hear at one and the same time of the "almost universal triumph of theory" and the equally widespread "resistance to theory [as] an intrinsic, perennial aspect of theory itself" (J. Hillis Miller, 1987a:286). What is above all incumbent on theorists in this situation is the production of discourse that is self-reflexive and self-critical, and one that is intrinsic to theory itself. Theory must recognize and scrutinize its own specific ideological effects (Jameson, 391–99). This is one of the contributions postmodern criticism has to make to the new rhetoric.

Conley expresses the challenge to current rhetorical criticism when he notes that, while the rhetorics of previous generations were designed to preserve the existing social and cultural structures, "the goals of the rhetorics of the present century . . . involve education in rhetoric as a means, rather, of transforming society" (304). Up to the watershed of 1500 C.E., truth and persuasion were hardly separated. What the ancients had made persuasive through their rhetorical skill was accepted as abiding truth, and the scholarly task was to reaffirm that truth in new situations by studying and emulating the ancients' rhetorical techniques. The study of the ancients' powers of persuasion took place in a context that dogmatically accepted their persuasions. The decline of rhetoric coincided with a decline of that kind of authority; what now counted as true was the rational, and this was supposed to have no need of rhetorical techniques. The new rhetoric needs to resist the separation of truth and persuasion, showing how abstract rationality atrophies what counts as true for human beings in real contexts.

Rhetorical criticism is by its very nature exposed to the demand for self-reflection (McKeon). According to Barilli (126), every form of criticism "is a perfect case of rhetorical discourse." This is a critical insight of great importance, enabling the critic to perceive, for example, that the authority of the rational is just as much a rhetorical authority, based on (unacknowledged) techniques of persuasion, as any other. Indeed, the current theoretical warfare is, from the perspective of the critical rhetorician, a rhetorical war, in which techniques of persuasion inhabit all the expressions of theoretical alternatives. But the self-reflexive moment comes only when rhetorical critics recognize their own work as "a perfect case of rhetorical discourse." Rhetorical criticism has to theorize its own relation to truth and persuasion.

Our discussion at this point overlaps with our earlier discussion of reader-response criticism (chap. 1). Most current rhetorical criticism functions as a kind of conservative reader-response criticism, perceiving the reader as necessary to activate the text's rhetorical power. What is usually lacking is the recognition and critical evaluation of the interactive part played by readers in the creation of meaning. Kennedy provides a striking example. At the end of our reading of 1 Corinthians, we referred to his inclusion of the critic's work as part of the text's rhetorical situation. His actual words are these: "Rhetorical and literary composition are creative acts. . . . Criticism too can be a creative act, not only bringing the text into clearer focus, but looking beyond it to an awareness of the human condition, of the economy and beauty of discourse, and to religious or philosophical truth" (1984:38). At first sight, this does seem to make the critic, as much as the text, into an object of rhetorical criticism. But the rest of his book does not suggest that Kennedy is really ready to take this self-reflexive step. And even his words here invite a suspicious reading. Why "can"—does this suggest that composition *is* (always) creative, while criticism merely *can be?* Expressions like "clearer focus," "economy and beauty," and especially "truth," are really quite vacuous. Kennedy, along with most of the new rhetorical critics, limits the role of the critic to releasing the rhetorical power of the ancient text (in this case the Bible), rather than engaging it in creative rhetorical debate.

What is missing is awareness that the power of the text includes the reader as part of the text. When the reader reconstructs the text's rhetorical situation, its interests and contextualization, she does so out of a rhetorical situation of her own, her own interests and contextualization. The new rhetorical criticism emphasizes that rhetorical power is present in a text not just once, when it is first uttered or written, but also for future readers in their own rhetorical situations. The encounter with the text is a "dialogic relation [requiring] two consciousnesses and two subjects" (Bakhtin, 1986:125). Since rhetoric has always been concerned with persuasion, there is an intimate relation between the text's rhetorical strategies and the reader's response to them. This inescapable rhetorical dimension, what J. Hillis Miller (1987a, 1987b; cf. Brent) calls the task of rhetorical reading, means that the task of rhetorical criticism cannot be complete until the critic's own rhetoricity and rules of discourse have been laid bare. A self-reflexive rhetorical criticism, then, must account at the very least for two sets of constraints involved in the act of reading: constraints posed by the text and those posed by the reader.

The complexity of the interaction between text and reader has become a commonplace observation in literary theory. Alter notes the complexity of "the interaction of different elements in the literary text" and "the multiple interaction with the text of different readers and their sundry contexts" (1989:222). The readers' contexts are not inscribed in the textual object, but they are part of the rhetoricity involved in the act of reading the text. The involvement of the readers' contexts with the text is so intricate that "the permutations of perception of the selfsame text [by different readers] become virtually infinite" (1989:216). When the reader's agenda is itself seen as another text to be read, however, then the picture becomes "still more complicated" (1989:216), so much so that the interaction of text and reader lead to "seemingly limitless paths of overstanding" (Wayne C. Booth, 1979:335).

But current rhetorical criticism continues to be concerned almost exclusively with textual constraints. This "rhetorical analysis of the most vigilant and patient sort" (J. Hillis Miller, 1989:81) is indeed indispensable, but such textually oriented rhetorical theory has led to the belief that vigilance and patience with the text will enable the critic to distinguish clearly between text and context, to contemplate the textual object in terms of its original purity and then be transformed by its power. This problem can be expressed as an over-stressing of the first of the five components of rhetoric that we dealt with in the last section, the art of verbal expression, at the expense of the others. Full weight must be given to the other four components.

The term *multiple readings* is by itself inadequate to describe the situation that critics now experience in literary criticism. We need terms like *decentering* and *indeterminacy* (*contra* Alter's chapter on "Multiple Readings and the Bog of Indeterminacy" [1989:206–38]). The dialectic of clarity and obscurity, founded in Western antiquity and characteristic of the Western tradition, needs to become a dialectic of clarity and indeterminacy (Du Plessis; Eden; Fuhrmann, 1966, 1987; see Mainberger, 1988 for related but distinctive traditions; cf. Handelman, 1985). When the critic becomes aware of the complexity of the interaction between the reader, with all of his or her own contextual components, and the text, as it functions in "new contexts with new force" of signification (Culler, 1982:135), the apparently easy task of isolating textual from contextual elements seems increasingly impossible. One is reminded here of Derrida's often misunderstood observation that outside of texts there is nothing. The notion of permanently fixed boundaries separating text from reader from context has to be destabilized. It is this critical operation of destabilizing or decentering that opens the exegetical experience to multiple possibilities, and especially to the recognition that the multiplicity of readings is not controllable.

Decentering should not be an alien concept to rhetorical critics. Even our analysis of 1 Corinthians, an example of relatively conservative rhetorical criticism, raised several issues that if pursued lead inevitably to the experience of indeterminacy and decentering. If rhetorical units can be defined at any level from the paragraph to the entire canon of scripture, there is no way of determining *the* rhetorical unit, and considering each new level decenters the findings at earlier levels. The rhetorical oscillation in Paul's argument between the universal and the particular cannot be stopped—each decenters the other. Argumentation by dissociation is intended to decenter the audience's perceptions. We shall return to these issues below, in a rereading of 1 Corinthians.

Rhetorical critics continue to use theories primarily as techniques to be applied to textual objects and need to engage the ideological implications of theory. In a postmodern view, the analysis of rhetorical strategy in texts is theory dependent; for example, a rhetorical structure only appears to the reader who has the theoretical eyes to behold it. And theory is not merely a theoretical issue; practical—in other words, political—consequences flow from choices about how to do rhetorical criticism. As Eagleton warns, theory cannot flourish when it is separated from its "lively cultural dimension," for "theory cannot itself legislate [the cultural context] into being" (1990a:86). Like theory generally, all rhetorical theory is always inextricably bound up with politics. When attention to the rhetoricity of interpretation causes the interpreter to be more aware of both textual and contextual constraints, then we begin to see "the implications of a rhetorical study of literature for our political and ethical life" (J. Hillis Miller, 1989:84; cf. Wayne C. Booth, 1988a). A new rhetorical theory needs to emphasize the inescapable social, political, religious, and ideological constraints that are operative before, during, and after reading. Ideology in this context may be thought of as the rhetoric of basic communication, of what counts as true or goes without saying. These new readings may then be able to take place within discursive constraints that previously could not be exposed as restrictive because they were operative simply as "truth."

A rhetorical criticism that is not radically self-reflexive can too easily be harnessed to an ideologically conservative program of reaffirming classical texts and values. What happens when a modern scholar, through a skilled practice of rhetorical criticism, demonstrates the persuasiveness of an ancient text? Where does he stand, where does he place his students, in relation to the truth of that text? The rhetorical effect—intended or not—may be to establish the truth of the classics. When Alter, for example, speaks of "the powerful capacity of the literary work to refer its readers to a complex order of moral, emotional, and psychological realities" (1989:76), he not merely accepts, but consolidates this order. If the work can "refer" to it, it must exist. Consider what a different impression would be created if, in Alter's sentence, one were to put "conjure up for its readers" in place of "refer its readers to," and "possibilities" in place of "realities." Such considerations are of particular importance for the Bible, which carries enormous cultural (i.e., rhetorical) authority.

Against the backdrop of postmodernism the "new" rhetorical critic needs to study "discursive practices" and try to understand them "as forms of power and performance" or "as forms of *activity* inseparable from the wider social relations between writers and readers" (Eagleton, 1983:205–206). Such a critic not only studies the social history and social aspects of texts, but also sees the rhetoric of the texts themselves as a significant component of the texts' social context and ongoing formation. This provides a basis for relating the new rhetoric to political, social, and ideological criticisms.

The text's power, including any scientific demonstration of its power by rhetorical critics, is subject to critique to expose how it is used in the service of sexism, racism, social injustice, or pedagogical and physical abuses in society's betrayal of the child, and so forth. "New" radically self-reflexive rhetorical critics, then, will practice rhetorical criticism in a practical way as cultural criticism. They will expose, but also employ rhetorical power instead of perpetuating cultural norms in the name of some allegedly objective and neutral hermeneutical or rhetorical science (Lachmann; Lentricchia; Loubser; Robbins, 1993; Wuellner, 1978b; see our chap. 2). In doing so, the new rhetorical critics will be participating in resistance from below to the prevailing norms of society.

One further aspect of postmodern approach to the rhetorical tradition needs to be included, namely, a critique of rationality. We referred in the last section to "conscious art in rhetoric" and to the rhetor's appeal to the "rationality of the emotions." But rationality and the conscious are never fully in charge in any human interaction, and the meaning that happens in any rhetorical situation is generated largely by processes unconscious to speaker or hearer. The power released by effective speech not only affects the hearers in ways the speaker could not anticipate; it also makes the speaker say things he never anticipated saying (the phenomenon of "getting carried away by one's own rhetoric"). "Deep calls to deep" (Psalm 42:7)—any rhetorical event is a transaction between unconsciousnesses as well as rationalities, and this excess of power and meaning always returns to decenter any particular interpretation.

Finally, rhetorical performance takes place within many interpretive communities, each with its own institutional investments. Whatever discursive communities may be involved—religious, educational, political, economic, and so forth—or whatever the persuasive situation entails—for example, ethnic communities struggling for justice and freedom—rhetorical power is at work (Burke, 1950). There needs to be a high degree of critical self-reflection about these rhetorical communities, but nowhere more so than in the academic community. The postmodern era uniquely makes possible, and demands, critical reflection on the rhetoric of scholarship. Scholars, seeking to be persuasive, have generally adopted the rhetorical strategy of sharing their findings primarily with other like-minded scholars (in institutions like the learned society). But under the influence of poststructuralism, the rhetoric of shared critical inquiry is seen to be different from the logic of shared scholarly work (cf. Wayne C. Booth, 1979; Fiske and Shweder; Scult; Tracy; Wuellner, 1989c). Gadamer notes "the specific ability of rhetoric to communicate the provisionality of our knowledge," a provisionality that both illuminates and keeps open our self-understanding (1992:351). The recognition of such provisionality and indeterminacy as necessary to the interpretive task, and the cognizance by the interpreter of his or her own rhetorical performance, counter the logic of shared scholarship that has been characteristic of scientific modernism.

The emphasis on the relation of rhetoric to practice (cf. Wayne C. Booth, 1983b:44), insisted on by recent critics dedicated to feminist, womanist, and other forms of political or ideological criticisms (see chaps. 6 and 7), sharpens the focus on community, including academic community, as the locus of rhetorical performance. Scholars committed to such concerns have become increasingly aware of the rhetoric of scholarship and of the politics of interpretation involved in that rhetoric because they have read against the grain of scholarship's traditionally coherent rhetoric (Bach; Schüssler Fiorenza, 1988; J. Hillis Miller, 1989; Moi; Wall). The coherent rhetoric that has supported the dominant logic of criticism is confronted with "violators," interpreters who work "counter-hegemonically" in order to expose the logical-ideological constraints within which scholarship operates (Lentricchia, 148). For these groups, interpretation must be reconceived as rhetorico-political activity (145–63).

RHETORIC AND RELIGION

As a prelude to considering the new rhetorical criticism of the Bible, it is useful to explore the close relation that has always existed between rhetoric and religion in general. Rhetorical criticism is a much more ancient method than the others we are considering in this book, going back to a time when the modernist separation of religion from other aspects of reality was unknown. The application to biblical texts of the methods of classical rhetoric is by no means an application of secular methods to sacred texts, for classical rhetoric was developed in a setting in which the ethical, the philosophical, the political, and the religious belonged together.[6]

Up to about 1500 C.E., attention to classical rhetorical criticism was a

---

[6] Shuger (11) draws attention to specifically religious aspects of classical rhetoric that would eventually converge into a coherent concept of a sacred rhetoric in Renaissance Europe: (1) the "numinous and sacral cast" of certain categories of Hellenistic rhetoric; (2) the emphasis on the importance of "the connection between emotions and . . . stylistic features" in sacred texts; and (3) the pivotal role of the imagination, what the Greeks called *phantasia*, in generating emotions and thought, i.e., love and knowledge of God (Ijsseling, 75–83). For an example of how the canons of ancient religious literary style (see Norden's pioneering work, 1956 [Orig. 1913]) were rhetorically used by biblical authors, see Thielman, 169–83.

treasured part of both Christian and Jewish exegetical theories and practices (Kennedy, 1980). In the period of "the decline of rhetoric" (see above),
when univocal scientific discourse was privileged, the close relation of religion with rhetoric worked to the detriment of both. Ever since Ramus, the
West has been preoccupied with theology at the expense of religion. Villmar's polemic (1864) against "the theology of rhetoric" on behalf of "the
theology of truth" in mid-nineteenth-century Germany testifies to rhetoric's
marginal status in theology. This trend clearly affected the development of
scientific biblical scholarship from the seventeenth century (Scholder) on
into the twentieth (Meerhoff). We noted above, beginning with Matthias
Flacius, the absorption of rhetorical criticism of the Bible into the general
hermeneutical task.[7] One specific development was the abandonment of the
traditional religious concern with the rhetorical power of the Bible as a
whole in favor (already by the late eighteenth century) of the scientific study
of distinctive features of individual books or authors.[8] The Bible, and other
literature developed by both Jews and Christians out of their specific religio-
rhetorical practices, was assigned to *Kleinliteratur,* just as the rhetorics of
indigenous religions, as these were encountered in Western global expansion,
were suppressed by the imposition of Western "high" culture.

Despite this history, however, modern rhetorical theory gives every in-
dication of a recovered awareness of the traditional close relation between
rhetoric and religion. Religion is by nature persuasive, and the study of the
rhetoric of religion is a study of the persuasive motives that seem to be indigenous to religion (Burke, 1945; 1961; Cunningham; Ray Hart; Webb).
This includes the motive to "save sacred truth" (Bloom). All of God's (or
the sacred's) actions in history or in nature can be said to have virtuous intentions or a rhetorical purpose (Ledbetter). In this sense all religions are
purposeful, and Kennedy is correct to say that "all religious systems are
rhetorical."

Rhetorical theory is becoming recognized again as a necessary aid for the
interpreter of sacred texts. It is indispensable in the attempt to identify the
ingredients of religious texts as a unique mixture of "theological, ethical,

[7] On the relation between rhetoric and hermeneutic in biblical studies, see Scult; Wuellner;
1989a; Francis Young, 184–88.

[8] It is worth noting that for most of Western history, despite the intensive use of rhetoric
in interpreting the Bible, even the best-qualified rhetoricians, like Augustine or Melanchthon,
did not produce rhetorical analyses of specific works (Classen, 16; Shuger, 251).

psychological, and other cultural material," and to account for vividness, drama, passion, and expressive figures and tropes as the principal features of sacred literature (Shuger, 251–53). To put it succinctly, rhetorical theory enables the exegete to account for the power of religious texts. The appeal of rhetorical criticism to readers of the Bible (as of other religious literature) is due to the fact that it seems to explain better what they want explained: "not its sources, but its power" (Kennedy, 1984:158; cf. Fisch; Shuger).

In the view of some, rhetoric as such functions to open the realm of the sacred and the sublime (De Bolla). The essence of rhetoric, like that of poetry, is not communication but the creation of new states of being, what Perelman and Olbrechts-Tyteca call states of communion. The power of persuasion alludes to the mystery of meaning that comes through language, what Ong (1967) called "The Presence of the Word," and hence to the process by which all humans engage in making decisions about their living together (Mack, 1989:19–20). Burke (1950) uses the quasi-religious term *perfection* for the transformation that he sees as the primary motive of all rhetoric. The rhetoric of any persuasive text needs to be apprehended, notes Conley (following Burke), in the "context of the 'goadings of mystery'" (276). Rhetoric aspires—though such a thing can never be captured—to a "total" approach to human existence, embracing social life, communication, decision making, even the mysteries of life and death.

Kennedy argues that "there is a distinctive rhetoric of religion" that is characterized by authoritarian proclamation which lacks any rational efforts to persuade. It is a "pure sacred language" through which the speaker-writer conveys divine revelation, and it is designed to induce positive responses to the will of God (1984:6). This suggests an increased attention to myths and to the persuasive use of the arts in religion, which have "a rhetoric of their own to move the mind or the emotions" (1984:158), and raises again acutely the issue of the unconscious in rhetoric (the probable etymological link between "sublime" and "subliminal" is suggestive). For Burke (1950:291–333), there is a relation between the rhetoric of theology and the meta-rhetoric of "pure persuasion"; his "rhetorical radiance of the 'divine'" is concerned with the same issues that have engaged Jewish and Christian theologians in the pursuit of understanding "the passion, sublimity, and grandeur of sacred discourse" (Shuger, 7).[9] A coming to terms

---

[9] Burke, though, draws a distinction between "pure persuasion" and religious persuasion, a distinction which Kennedy does not make. For Burke it is an oxymoron to speak either of

with the rhetoric of religion, with the element of the ineffable and the sublime in rhetoric, would seem, then, obligatory for biblical exegetes. Regardless of the particular path chosen by the exegete,[10] the contribution of contemporary rhetorical theory to biblical rhetorical criticism includes the call to interpret it as religious literature.

A rhetorical theory that elucidates the relation of rhetoric and religion offers a better basis for guiding biblical interpretation than does one which relies exclusively on secular literary paradigms. Much recent work, in fact, is proceeding in the opposite direction, showing how sacred rhetoric and interpretation theory are fundamentally a part of the history of criticism and identifying their traces in the recent development of literary theory.[11] This complex connectedness of the domains of the rhetorical and the religious forms a necessary backdrop for the following survey and discussion of the new biblical rhetorical criticism.

THE NEW RHETORICAL CRITICISM OF THE BIBLE

Rhetorical criticism as an exegetical method surfaced again mainly in the United States as part of the New Criticism's influence on biblical exegesis (though most biblical scholars overlooked, in their initial appropriation of the New Critics, the latter's interest in rhetoric). The key moment was James Muilenberg's 1968 presidential address to the Society of Biblical Literature (Muilenberg, 1969). A Muilenberg school of rhetorical criticism emerged almost immediately in studies of the Hebrew Bible (Bernhard W. Anderson). A comparable development in New Testament studies took a little longer, though it had an important precursor in the work of Amos Wilder, which influenced New Testament scholarship for nearly half a century (1956; 1964; 1991). Six years after Muilenberg's address, Hans Dieter Betz delivered a

---

literary mysticism or of religious writing that claims to express, plausibly and persuasively, what is by nature ineffable (1950:324–28).

10 Other promising paths are opened by the approaches of Perelman, Lundeen (based on Whitehead's theory of language), or Patte (based on Greimas's structural semiotics; cf. chap. 2). See also the works of Kopperschmidt and Mainberger.

11 Schwartz (1991:12, 14). The work of the British scholars Stephen Prickett (1991) and David Jasper (1989, 1993) reminds biblical scholars of the biblical origins of some of the paradigms that they borrow from secular criticism. Burke's (1945; 1950) theoretical reflections on the grammar and rhetoric of religious motives offer one viable way for exegetes to proceed in studying the power of biblical rhetoric.

lecture to the Studiorum Novi Testamenti Societas on Paul's rhetoric in Galatians (Betz, 1975), and in the same year Wilhelm Wuellner presented a paper
to the Pauline Seminar of the Society of Biblical Literature on Paul's rhetoric
in Romans (Wuellner, 1976). Both papers fuelled a growing interest in rhetorical criticism as a method in New Testament studies. In both testaments,
there has been a proliferation of work developed out of these beginnings.[12]

Yet the new rhetorical criticism is only beginning to make its way in biblical studies. The field of biblical exegesis in general remains preoccupied
either with linguistic, literary, or social structures, or with theological and
ethical content. The history of "rhetoric restrained" (Genette, 1982a:103–
26), of the reduction in the last several centuries of rhetoric to poetics,
continues. Exegetes fail, for the most part, to take adequate account of
the affective semantics of biblical literature, of the power of the Bible to
move. It has to be said that much of the biblical work that has appeared
under the rubric of "rhetorical criticism" fails to develop the potential of the
method. What is often elaborated under such rubrics as "rhetorical structure, disposition, devices," is still the text's reconstructed literary or stylistic
coherence rather than its intentionality to move the reader precisely by its
heterogeneity. This is particularly the case with the kind of rhetorical criticism inspired by Muilenberg, which is justly criticized for falling short "of
bringing the interpreter into a full-bodied encounter with the Biblical text"
(Patrick and Scult, 13–19).[13] Even now, what Hebrew Bible scholars mean
by rhetorical criticism is much the same as what elsewhere we have called
"poetics" (see chap. 2), the intrinsic study of literary technique.

In New Testament, the initial impulse was to draw on classical rhetoric
(see esp. Kennedy, 1984), to see to what extent the categories of the highly

---

[12] The following are some examples classified according to genre. For didactic discourse in
the Hebrew Bible, see e.g., Gitay; Lundbom and many others. For the New Testament epistles,
see Betz, 1975, 1979; Classen; Hester; Johanson; Watson; Wire; Wuellner, 1978a and many
others. For biblical narrative and poetry, see Alter, 1981, 1985; Bar-Efrat; Eskhult; Fisch; Funk,
1988; Kugel; Robbins, 1991; Michael Roberts; Sternberg, 1985; Wilder, 1964, 1991. Unlike
the Hebrew Bible, with its full-length poetic texts, the New Testament has poetic texts embedded only in narrative and didactic discourse (Berger, 239–47). Subsequent transformations
of narrative and didactic biblical texts into poetry, familiar to Judaism and Christianity alike,
invite a rhetorical criticism all its own (see Michael Roberts).

[13] Similar misgivings arise when rhetorical criticism is brought into conjunction with text
linguistics or discourse analysis; cf. Johanson; Snyman, 1991.

developed and well-studied Hellenistic and Roman systems could illuminate New Testament literature. Tending to assume that any evidence of rhetorical sophistication must be explained by the all-pervasive influence of Greco-Roman rhetoric, some scholars saw the latter as the primary matrix for early Christian rhetoric.[14] But others questioned whether early Christians would be in close touch with the professional practices of Hellenistic rhetoricians; indeed, Kennedy was one of those who insisted that cultural values could not be so easily loosened from their specific functions (a point too often overlooked by exegetes who use his method).

An obvious influence upon early Christian rhetoric was Judaism, though it is often neglected. Part of the reason why scholars neglect this influence is that Judaism did not produce rhetorical textbooks and theories. It is now being recognized, however, that the Jewish world, like any other, had its distinctive rhetorical practices (Alexander; Katz; Isaac Rabinowitz; Wuellner, 1994). One commonality between Jewish and early Christian rhetoric, as Auerbach saw, is a resistance to the rigid hierarchies of Greco-Roman rhetorical theory and practice (cf. Droge; Fischel). The rhetoric of Jewish and early Christian literature constituted a challenge to the dominant discursive norms of Hellenistic and Roman societies. Rhetoric in Hellenistic-Roman culture usually depended on "a common value set as criteria for selecting . . . [the] means for resolving common problems" confronting society (Cushman and Tompkins, 51). This "common value set" was challenged by the cultural conflict between Athens and Jerusalem. The conflict for Jews and early Christians centered on resisting the homogenizing forces of cultural, political, racial, or gender ideologies in Hellenistic-Roman culture; and their rhetoric aimed "to recreate [for a culture in crisis] a sense of God as a familiar and as an intimate, as a God who still addresses [the reader] between the lines of Scripture" (Stern, 1981; 1985a; 1985b). The rhetoric of biblical literature is not that of those trained in the art of persuasion, who consciously employed language as an art, but neither is it rhetoric that is without eloquence and a conscious attempt to persuade its audience. The rhetoric of biblical literature is of the essence of language itself, as it was for Nietzsche (Blair; Gilman et al.), for it participates fully in the inviolable rhetorical rules for social intercourse, communication, critique, and persuasion. The "new"

---

[14] Kennedy, 1980; Kinneavy; Norden, 1971. For similar assumptions about the rhetoric of Patristic theologians, see Neuschäfer; Quacquarelli; Schlieben; Spira; Francis Young.

rhetoric of Jews and Christians, then, may be seen as an example of what classical rhetoric called invention, but one that was turned against classical culture itself as a subversive rhetoric of resistance to prevailing norms.

The new rhetorical criticism is beginning to offer a means of mending the separation and of renegotiating the relation between the textual world inside the Bible and its extra-textual social history, *text* and *context*. The power of the text does not inhere in it as an autonomous object, as words on a page, and cannot be adequately released by literary methods. Nor is the power supplied from outside by context, in the sense of social and cultural codes which can be reified and then "applied" to the text. Rhetorical criticism recasts the problem of reference by "its reliance on community, convention, and persuasion" (J. Hillis Miller, 1990:114). The operative word is "persuasion." "The turn toward rhetoric as argumentation is the single most important feature of this new rhetorical criticism" (Mack, 1989:21). The term that rhetorical criticism posits between text and context is *rhetorical situation* (Brinton, 1981), the particular situation in which someone attempts to persuade someone else.

As we pointed out in our exegetical example, the rhetorical critic is not satisfied with the procedures of traditional form-criticism. The form-critic's approach to text is to define each *Gattung* (literary form) by its typical features. For the rhetorical critic, such formal features are still crucial, but only as they serve the persuasion involved in the rhetorical situation. The persuasive intentionality has its own integrity and coherence and imposes its own textual constraints. Rhetorical units are to be defined by connections at the affective, persuasive level (Kennedy, 1984:34); they are built progressively. Intentionalities built up in one part of the argument are changed or deepened as the rhetorical strategy requires (Perelman and Olbrechts-Tyteca, 492). The form-critic's approach to context is to determine the *Sitz im Leben* (life-setting) of particular forms; but from the rhetorical critic's point of view such work has been marked methodologically by generalization of the settings, missing the particularity of the rhetorical situation. Every culture has established conventions, known as genres, for rhetorical disposition (*taxis*) or arrangement (*oikonomia;* Berger; cf. Wuellner, 1991b), but the rhetorical critic believes that this ordered arrangement can be identified only by a theory of argumentation, not by a method based on a claimed conformity either to the organic form of the text or correspondence to its historical situation. In other words, the rhetorical arrangement must be conceptualized as an "adaptive order" that focuses at all times on "the needs of adaptation to the audience" (Perelman and Olbrechts-Tyteca, 490–508).

Another strength, at least potentially, of the new rhetorical criticism lies in its attention to the canonical character of the Bible. As we saw in our reading of 1 Corinthians 9–10, the question of persuasion and the *persuasive unit* leads beyond the immediate literary context of a given text, and literary contexts can continue to be defined up to the level of the canon as a whole. That readers are concerned with the question of whether the Bible functions as a single persuasive unit, whether it possesses some rhetorical unity comprehending its immense variety, belongs to the Bible's functioning as a religious text. For the Bible is surely (within Western culture) the "archetypal example of how power [is] constituted by discourse" (Patrick and Scult, 27), and the great appeal that rhetorical criticism has begun to have for some exegetes stems from the fact that, perhaps more than all other critical approaches, it focuses on the power of the biblical text (Kennedy, 1984). Thus there are signs that the paradigm shift that once transformed exegesis from the traditional theological-spiritual commentary of the *via antiqua* to the academic exegesis of the *via moderna* (G. R. Evans) is now being followed by another shift, this time from scientific-hermeneutical readings to rhetorical ones. Despite its slowness to make headway, the achievements of the new rhetorical criticism of the Bible already deserve to be celebrated.

If rhetorical criticism in biblical studies has made slow progress, the development of self-reflection has been still slower. This also has much to do with the Bible's status as a central religious text. As we have noted in other chapters, and especially in the chapter on reader-response criticism, it is mostly in their most conservative and least self-reflexive forms that literary methods first become influential in biblical studies. We have seen how so authoritative a work as Alter and Kermode (1987) deliberately excludes any kind of self-reflexive literary theory. Hence serious exploration of the rhetorical power of criticism itself has been slow to develop in biblical work, even (or especially) under the rubric of rhetorical criticism of the Bible.[15]

Recently, though, there is a growing dissatisfaction among exegetes with

[15] Perhaps Bultmann's existentialist hermeneutic, which swept the mid-twentieth-century exegetical scene, was the last major effort at attending to a theory that would account for the rhetorical practices *in* the text, as well as those of the exegete *with* the text. Wuellner as rhetorical critic understands himself as a reconstructed Bultmannian.

the dominant practice of reducing theory to methods that can be taught as simple exegetical tools and techniques. It is beginning to be accepted that the encounter with general literary theory requires that rhetorical criticism attend both to the rhetoric of biblical texts and to the rhetoric of biblical scholarship within specific institutional discourses. In scholarly biblical societies like the Society of Biblical Literature, the coherent rhetoric of the "logic of shared scholarship" is being challenged by "violators," who wish both to expose the rhetorical constraints within which biblical scholarship has been practiced and to establish a new "rhetoric of shared critical inquiry." This book is a product of this impulse, not only in the stances we take, but also and especially in the method of collaborative authorship we have adopted.

We have noted how Jewish and Christian rhetorics share a history of subversion, that is, the subversion of dominant rhetorics. Critics like Mack (1989:17) hold out the promise that a new rhetorical criticism will elucidate the social and political exchanges reflected in biblical texts and rhetoric's own role in those exchanges. But it needs to be acknowledged that the social and political exchanges extend into readings of the biblical text—both past and present—and that it is only through a rhetorical examination of these exchanges that we can read the text at all. Schwartz (1990a:6) discusses the historical relations of Jewish and Christian biblical commentary and notes how "political and polemical impulses [which] informed Judaic scriptural exegesis no less than Christian" led each side to defend itself against, but nonetheless to become defined by, the "ideological cross-currents" with which each of the two parties presented the other. (Similar polemical impulses can also be traced, of course, within either religion, directed at groups and movements within its own ranks; e.g., Bauer.) These rhetorical ways and means of exclusion are only beginning to be elucidated. And they are not merely a thing of the past; rhetorical efforts continue to be made in the current scene to exclude "wrong" readings or "misreadings" (Alter, 1989:223; cf. Wayne C. Booth, 1979:277–339). But when the text's capacity to stimulate many readings is accepted, on what basis can one exclude certain readings? The ways and means of "the exclusion of error" deserve to be made more explicit in the new rhetorical situation of postmodern biblical exegesis.

In a surprising turn of events, "theology . . . is returning [to biblical studies] in the guise of theory"; this is "because questions of faith are matters of theory" (Schwartz, 1990a:12, 14). During the era of objectivist scholarship, issues of theology and faith have been banned from critical biblical studies (even within theological schools). This exclusion—by which alone objectivist scholarship could establish itself—avoids the fact that the Bible itself, through its rhetorical power as sacred text, has been a factor, perhaps the most powerful one, in shaping the history of its own reception, interpretation, and use (cf. Kort, 119–30; Wuellner, 1989b; 1989c). The individuals who engage in biblical scholarship and the institutions where they can do so have been formed by the biblical interpretation and practice of earlier generations. Recent literary theory has highlighted such historical-literary processes, and if biblical scholarship takes such theory seriously, it will no longer be able to see the Bible primarily merely as an object of investigation (whether historical-critical or otherwise). Exegetes can no longer only comment on the text, but they need to enact, through their performance of the text, its impact on the very scene—and we can expand this scene to take in the whole of Western culture—in which it gets interpreted. The interpretation of biblical texts can no longer be an activity with one subject, the exegete, and one object, the text, but it must be conceived as an activity with many participants, all of them simultaneously subject and object of interpretation (cf. Cheney on "managing multiple identities" in institutional settings, e.g., learned societies).

This "return of theology" requires, of course, constant critical examination. Literary approaches to the Bible have proved very attractive to conservative biblical scholarship because they enable avoidance of hard historical questions; it is even very possible for a quite uncritical theology to return in the guise of a most sophisticated literary theory (cf. Bal, 1991:59–72). The critical power of theory-theology in biblical studies will turn reactionary if the theory-theology itself is exempt from self-criticism. Some, not wanting to forget "the long night of superstition and the sacred" (Jameson, 1991:393), will feel suspicious about the possibility of a new religious or biblical triumphalism. But in the current changing climate, the new rhetorical criticism, as long as it is not subordinated to theology and ethics, has implications for doing theology and ethics, as well as exegesis, in new ways and provides the possibility for each discipline to be self-reflexive about its own actual and possible modes of discourse and their material effects.[16]

---

[16] In addition to such works in biblical studies as Classen; Kennedy, 1984; Lambrecht; Patrick and Scult; Warner, 1989b; cf., e.g., the rhetorical approach to Reformation theology in Schneider; Stamps; Warner, 1989b; cf. Boyle.

REREADING 1 CORINTHIANS

We return now to our opening example of rhetorical criticism (1 Cor. 9:1–10:13) to consider the impact of some of the critical issues we have been raising. We will pay particular attention to the work of Antoinette Clark Wire, who deals at length with this passage and explicitly in the framework of rhetorical criticism. Wire's aim is to reconstruct from the whole of 1 Corinthians a picture of women prophets in Corinth and to problematize rhetorical criticism in ways that anticipate our efforts. Within the rhetoric of current biblical studies, she expressly takes an engaged position, namely, a feminist one (5–6); and methodologically she attempts a rhetorical criticism that reads Paul's argument for traces of a voice which that very argument is organized to suppress.

Step 1 in our example from 1 Cor. 9:1–10:13 showed an instability in the delineation of the unit chosen for analysis. On the one hand it was made up of smaller units, while on the other it was a small unit in an expanding series of larger units, up to the level of the whole book. In which of these many units, from smallest to largest, can the structure of the argument best be analyzed; which is the persuasive unit? There is no right answer because one's sense of the argumentative unit and one's sense of what is being argued are interdependent; one has a hermeneutical circle. Nor should we underestimate the impact on our decisions of the Bible's canonical form—such things as chapter divisions—which represent an earlier generation's sense of the shape of the argument.[17] The sense one has of the argument of a unit like 1 Cor. 9:1–10:13 is decentered when other readers choose to divide the text into different units. Wire's delineation of the rhetorical units is fairly close to ours, but she has no sense of anything ending at 10:13; she sees 10:7–10, 14, 19–22 as a connected subargument (Wire, 26–27).

At the upper end of the scale, one's sense of the persuasive unit extends to the level of the whole book and beyond. The persuasive power of a piece of Pauline literature—particularly considered as religious literature—derives in large measure from its belonging to a collection of letters and finally to a canon of scripture. Such students of the Bible as literature as Northrop Frye (1982; 1990) make large claims for the coherence of the canon of scripture as a whole. Others, like Schneidau, see it as characteristic of the Bible's rhetoric to generate "a constant movement between granting certainty and

---

[17] Jobling (1993a) has shown how enormously the canonical book divisions in the Deuteronomic History influence scholarly understanding.

subverting it." Paul himself, as his frequent citations of the Hebrew Bible attest, wants to establish rhetorical coherence between his argument and "scripture" as a whole. A reader's sense of Paul's argument will be deeply dependent on her commitment to the coherence (or not) of the Pauline corpus, the New Testament, the entire Christian Bible.

But even such far-reaching textual considerations do not yet bring us to a postmodern understanding of "context." This can only happen when we take into account language's "ability to function in new contexts with new force" (Culler, 1982:135; cf. 32–33). All readings of the Pauline passage, including our rhetorical analysis, are part of its rhetorical situation. So are the settings—whether in scholarly guilds or elsewhere—where such readings are done. Self-reflexive rhetorical critics will analyze their discourse upon Paul's discourse, to try and determine what ideologies and values are at stake in their own rhetorical situations and how they relate to what was at stake in the first century. Only in this way can rhetorical criticism function as cultural criticism. We have noted how Wire, for example, seeks linkages between current feminist praxis and the role of women prophets in the early church and acknowledges her own intention to *persuade*.

Rhetorical criticism, as we have already emphasized, insists that the use of stylistic devices must be "explained by the requirements of argumentation" (Perelman and Olbrechts-Tyteca, 168), rather than reduced to general considerations. This insistence has yet to be clearly heard in biblical scholarship; for example, more attention is still being focused on the general characteristics of "master tropes," such as metaphor and irony, than on their argumentative function in particular situations (Camp and Fontaine; Good; Jasper, 1987:27–42; Macky; Dale Martin; Plank; Soskice; Tinsley). In the following assessment of some of Paul's argumentative devices, we keep in mind our expanded understanding of the rhetorical situation of the text.

We saw in 1 Corinthians 9:1–10:13 a great concentration of "rhetorical questions." The rhetorical question is usually understood as a particularly convincing way of arguing, suggesting that any answer other than the obviously implied one is absurd. A postmodern reading, though, will suggest that the absurdity of the alternative views is *produced* precisely by the rhetorical question. Such a reading will insist (in the manner of Derrida) that the rhetorical question itself includes the "trace" of other answers than the one implied, and hence subverts its own intended persuasion. Wire at one point suggests that a rhetorical question (10:22) disguises a decisive shift in Paul's argument (100).

The passage 1 Cor. 8:1–11:1 is particularly marked also by an *argument by dissociation,* in which community benefit is opposed to self-benefit (Wire, 18). Such argument, as we have seen, seeks to devalue an appearance that has been valued in favor of a reality which is what ought to be valued. In this case, the "spiritual" Corinthians are to be persuaded that what has appeared to them to be of value to the community, namely, their exercise of Christian freedom, is in reality a danger to the community, to its "weak" members. Dissociative argument, we may suggest, is particularly conducive to a postmodern outlook. Deconstruction often proceeds by suggesting that an appearance of unity (for example in a philosophical system) cloaks the reality of complexity and inner contradiction. But is Paul's dissociative argument dissociative enough? A critical reading might ask about Paul's own benefit and how it is to be dissociated from that of the weak *or* the spiritual. Wire pays special attention to this question of Paul's self-interest.[18]

Wire discerns a significant shift in the ground of Paul's argument in 1 Corinthians. The ostensible basis for the whole letter is "self-limitation for the common good" (100), for the good of the weak members of the community. But, claims Wire, "at the heart of Paul's argument the ultimate danger is not the other person's weakness but one's own strength" (100). For Paul, "Christ means some restriction, some act of self-discipline" (112). As his argument about the eating of idol food develops, such eating becomes less an offense against the weak and more an offense against *God* (1 Corinthians 10), with even a veiled threat of the death penalty (10:8, cf. 11:30, on which Wire, 101–2).

This line of thought requires reconsideration of Paul's appeal to the Hellenistic topic of the enslaved leader. Paul is able to present himself effectively as one who limits his own power, to become a servant to those he might dominate; and he commends this self-limitation to the spiritual in Corinth. Wire tries to reconstruct the point of view of the spiritual, and particularly of one group of them—the women prophets. They are not self-indulgent but "demonstrate in their eating and drinking the authority of free people" (Wire, 112). This exercise of a—particularly for women—new-found free-

---

[18] She notes (24–35) what a wide variety of argumentation Paul uses to press the issue of apostles' rights: a quasi-logical appeal to justice that similar cases should be similarly dealt with (9:5–6); appeal to scripture (9:8–10); and appeal to the Lord's command (9:13–15a). She comments on Paul's frequent use of the appeal to justice in gender matters and also on the fact that the burden of feeding the apostles would fall more heavily on women.

dom will have been seen by them as their contribution to the community, to the strengthening of its weaker members. To one of these, Paul's advice would strike at "the core of her identity in Christ" (111).

The topic of enslaved leader is serviceable to someone of established power, not to those now first tasting it. One might suggest that it serves, in fact, further to establish Paul's power—his rhetoric of self-limitation contributes to the success of his persuasion. Whether or not he won the immediate contest, he has been successful in the eyes of history; his is the voice that now gets heard, and the voice of his opponents must be laboriously and uncertainly reconstructed. (In the light of our earlier remarks on the unconscious in rhetoric,[19] one might further suggest that Paul is projecting on others an unresolved inner struggle with power. It is startling that in 9:15 self-limitation is a "ground for boasting." No less startling is 9:24, because it makes no sense to cajole all the Corinthians to seek a prize that only one can win. Perhaps what is really on Paul's mind is his own individual winning.)

For Paul to use the topic of the enslaved leader against women in particular (not to mention how it must have affected slaves in the Corinthian community) invokes for us a whole tradition of men as the "slaves" of women, from courtly love to the henpecked husband. The leader as benefactor has fatefully influenced cultural perceptions not only of women, but of the power status of public leaders in politics and religion. The intertextual force of such tropes is only now coming to be recognized and to be critically evaluated in authoritative texts like the Bible (see chaps. 6 and 7).

A traditional distinction of rhetorical critics, that between the *convincing* and the *persuasive* dimensions of texts (Perelman and Olbrechts-Tyteca, 26–31) may be brought into the discussion here. Convincing argumentation appeals to cultural norms presumed to be shared by the whole audience, while persuasive argumentation appeals only to hearers or readers who are in a special rhetorical situation. Paul makes tactical use of convincing argumentation, for example, 1 Cor. 9:7—everyone will agree that workers expect to be paid. But his overall aim is persuasive, for believers only; for example, the new eschatological values he puts forward in 1 Corinthians. Indeed, Paul's rhetorical strategy is to create a community of believers consisting exactly of those ready to be persuaded by his argument. The power of this strategy, in

[19] It can plausibly be claimed that the rising interest in psychological criticism of the Bible is ultimately rooted in modern psychology's indebtedness to rhetorical theory's linking of action with reason, motives, and emotions (Dockhorn, 1968:46–95; see our chap. 5).

both ancient and modern rhetorical situations, is not to be underestimated. Paul is interested only in hearers who are prepared to agree, and 1 Corinthians as a (biblical) text invites only readers who are prepared to agree. But just as Paul (according to Wire) encountered hearers who were *not* prepared to agree, so there has been a shift recently in the Bible's "convinceable" audience—even among those (like Wire) within the religious community.

The potential for rhetorical criticism to be in the service of a conservative agenda is even greater for the Bible than for other classic texts. To exhibit the rhetorical strategies of the Bible easily passes over into demonstrating the success of the strategies, and hence finding yet another way to prove that the Bible is true. What is not taken into account is the rhetorical strategy of the critic who performs such an operation and the program of persuasion to which such a critic may be committed. An excellent example is the poetics of Meir Sternberg. In his chapter "The Art of Persuasion" (1985:441–81), he attempts to show that the storytelling in Genesis 34 (the rape of Dinah) works to direct the reader's sympathy onto Jacob's sons and away from the Shechemites. Most readers of the story take the opposite view, that Simeon and Levi behave like scoundrels while the Shechemites do the best they can in a bad situation created by their prince. The rhetorical situation in this piece of interpretation is complex and even contradictory. Sternberg puts forth his formidable powers of persuasion to persuade us (Sternberg's readers) that the biblical narrator is a skillful persuader who puts forth his own formidable powers to persuade us (readers of Genesis) to side with the sons. But if the narrator is so rhetorically powerful, why are there so many readers he has failed to persuade? There is at least the suspicion that the one who wants to persuade readers of Genesis 34 to take a certain view is not the biblical narrator, but Sternberg himself. But such a question is excluded by Sternberg's own rhetoric, which forces us to concentrate only on text and narrator and not on questions of the location and agenda of different interpreters.

The adjudication of alternative rhetorical readings is itself a contest at the level of rhetoric. Kennedy provides an instructive example of this in his treatment of Betz's commentary on Galatians (1979). Betz reads Galatians as judicial rhetoric, whereas Kennedy (1984:144–51) pleads for the deliberative genre. Kennedy (20) defines these two genres, respectively, as "the question of truth or justice" and "the question of self-interest and future benefits." A self-reflexive criticism would note that Kennedy's rejection of Betz is judicial rhetoric, asking only the question of truth (cf. the very notion

of adjudicating readings), and might ask what a critique in the deliberative mode would look like, asking the questions of self-interest and benefit:
what is at stake ideologically and politically with each reading; what material effects might each have on their producers and on readers? Rhetorical
criticism doubtless plays a role in ruling out absurd readings; no one has
so far tried to persuade us that Galatians is imaginative fiction. But what
rhetorical criticism cannot rule out is that critics working on the same text
and even within the same sets of interpretive procedures may produce, because of their different hidden agendas, different interpretations of that text's
intentionality or rhetorical genre (Classen, 29–31, critiques both Betz and
Kennedy).

THE FUTURE OF RHETORICAL CRITICISM

Muilenberg and Kennedy, different in many ways, were both gifted teachers who inadvertently generated a school of rhetorical criticism in twentieth-
century North American biblical exegesis. Two other gifted teachers—
Walter Jens in Germany and Chaim Perelman in Belgium—while equally
effective in generating schools of their own, failed to have any impact on
European biblical exegetes. This discrepancy indicates that rhetoric cannot
be turned into a method that can be transmitted with a controlled outcome
(cf. J. Hillis Miller, 1989:100). Rhetorical criticism, like everything else in a
postmodern world, "is not something we can settle once and for all and then
use with a clear conscience. The concept, if there is one, has to come at the
end, and not at the beginning, of our discussion of it" (Jameson, 1991:xxii).

Jameson's appeal to literary critics to keep the production of theoretical
discourse from "lapsing back into habits or procedures" has been neither
heard nor heeded by most biblical exegetes (397, cf. 391–99). Biblical exegetes, especially North American ones, continue to turn rhetorical criticism
and other methods into reified commodities for use by the dominant systems
of interpretation. Models and methods of rhetorical analysis and interpretation continue to roll off the assembly line, and exegetes appear all too ready
to appropriate them for biblical studies, often without the benefit of any
literary or rhetorical theory. The job of exegetes being to produce interpretations of texts (cf. J. Hillis Miller, 1987a), there is much resistance to and
deliberate exclusion of a theoretical discussion that makes the process less
smooth and problematizes business as usual. Little good is to be expected
as long as rhetoric is partially appropriated, reified, and "commodified." If

exegetes need another warning against turning rhetorical criticism into a commodity of techniques to be transmitted to pupils and applied to texts, let the words of Medhurst suffice: "the possibilities of coming to know such a complex work of rhetorical and literary artistry as the Bible are infinite, resisting all systems, paradigms, models, or theories. Just when we think we understand, TL (shorthand for 'The Lord' in Burke's logological universe), appears to remind us: 'It's more complicated than that'" (225).

A veteran rhetorical critic who summed up his study a generation ago—in a book which "dethroned neo-Aristotelian criticism" (Leff and Procario, 15)—must be reaffirmed: "We have not evolved any *system* of rhetorical criticism, but only, at best, an orientation to it. . . . We simply do not know enough yet about rhetorical discourse to place our faith in *systems*, and it is only through imaginative criticism that we are likely to learn more" (Black, 1965:177; emphasis ours). More recently, another respected rhetorical critic put it this way: "no one to my knowledge has ever developed a fully articulated rhetorical criticism adequate to the 'structures of appeal' in works like [the Bible]" (Wayne C. Booth, 1979:307). Even if rhetorical theory were to succeed in developing rhetorical criticism as a method, it would still be the case that "no critical principles can prevent misreading" (277). In the final analysis, as yet another rhetorical critic has observed, the usefulness of rhetorical theory for biblical criticism depends on the critical discernment of the interpreter and on her or his relationship to an interpretive community. That is to say, the value of rhetorical criticism for biblical exegesis will ultimately depend on the interpreter's knowledge, experience, taste, and sensitivity in his or her given rhetorical situation (Classen, 33). The jury is still out, therefore, on just how successful and profitable the application of rhetorical theory has become in the rebirth of rhetorical criticism in biblical interpretation.

Many biblical exegetes have, though, begun to join other critical scholars in combating all forms of absolutism and religious superiority. The oppositions are indeed numerous: "dualism of reason and imagination, of knowledge and opinion, of irrefutable self-evidence and deceptive will, of a universally accepted objectivity and an incommunicable subjectivity, of a reality binding on everybody and values that are purely individual" (Perelman and Olbrechts-Tyteca, 510). One could add that the absolutism of modern science and technology has contributed to, if not generated, its own oppositional rhetoric: a world community, politically and ecologically, that is characterized at once by conflict and interdependence. Here is the chal-

lenge of the new rhetoric: by definition of its proper domain, it must subvert
the familiar Western distinctions between content and form, between theory
and practice, or, in hermeneutical terms, between interpretation and application. Contemporary rhetorical criticism needs to become a sustained
effort to subvert every tendency to solidify exegesis into some encompassing
and imperialistic system. In materialist terms, rhetorical criticism opposes
the tendency of powerful institutional structures—the "literary-industrial
complex"—to reify and commodify exegesis. A new rhetoric and a new rhetorical criticism have now begun to emerge in the world of oppositional
rhetoric. These need to be cultivated in biblical studies if readers of sacred
scriptures are going to accomplish their rhetorical work of cultural criticism,
of "transforming society" (Conley, 304) by decentering the oppositions and
revealing the indeterminacies that an oppositional and hegemonic rhetoric
tries to obscure.

Patrick and Scult make effective use of a proposal borrowed from Ronald
Dworkin: "Interpret the text as the best text it can be" (21; cf. 21–23 and
passim). This seems at first sight to be a problematic Pollyanna formulation.
They make clear, however, that " 'the best text' is not an objective claim,"
but rather "a rhetorical claim about the text's appeal" which "must be argued rhetorically" (22). In these terms, we argue in this book, as persuasively
as we are able, that the best text the Bible can be in the future development
of Western culture will be "the postmodern Bible."

RECOMMENDED FURTHER READING

Booth, Wayne C. 1983a. *The Rhetoric of Fiction*. 2d ed. Chicago: University of Chicago Press.
Widely used reference and resource for the analysis and interpretation of narrative rhetoric.
Comprehensive annotated bibliography.

Burke, Kenneth. 1950. *A Rhetoric of Motives*. Berkeley: University of California Press. Assessment of the most influential twentieth-century rhetorical critics in the United States.

Conley, Thomas. 1990. *Rhetoric in the European Tradition*. White Plains, N.Y.: Longman.
Critical overview of the cultural conditions in the developments of Euro-American rhetoric since its Greek origins. Needs to be supplemented by studies in the contributions of
non-Western rhetorical traditions (e.g., Jewish, Arabic, Asian).

Fish, Stanley E. 1989. *Doing What Comes Naturally: Change, Rhetoric, and the Practice of
Theory in Literary and Legal Studies*. Post-Contemporary Interventions. Durham, N.C.:
Duke University Press. Collection of essays highlighting the implications of rhetoric for
critical interpretations of literature and law.

Horner, Winifred Bryan, ed. 1990. *The Present State of Scholarship in Historical and Contem-*

porary Rhetoric. Foreword by Walter Ong. Columbia: University of Missouri Press. Critical overview of past and present rhetorical practices and theories.

Jasper, David. 1993. *Rhetoric, Power and Community: An Exercise in Reserve.* Louisville, Ky.: Westminster/John Knox. A critical, postmodern, impassioned defense of the power of rhetoric.

Kennedy, George A. 1984. *New Testament Interpretation through Rhetorical Criticism.* Chapel Hill: University of North Carolina Press. Historical and theoretical introductions to the place of rhetoric in New Testament exegesis and subsequent Christian history.

Lanham, Richard A. 1968. *A Handlist of Rhetorical Terms: A Guide for Students of English Literature.* Berkeley: University of California Press. Widely used reference work for technical terms familiar to the Western traditions of rhetorical theory and practice.

Mack, Burton L. 1989. *Rhetoric and the New Testament.* Guides to Biblical Scholarship. Minneapolis: Augsburg/Fortress. Introduction to the theories and applications of rhetorical criticism to select New Testament texts.

Nelson, John S., Allan Megill, and Donald N. McCloskey, eds. 1987. *The Rhetoric of the Human Sciences: Language and Argument in Scholastic and Public Affairs.* Madison: University of Wisconsin Press. Representative critical reflections on the rhetorical nature of scientific argumentation and its institutional sanctions, applicable to modern scientific biblical exegesis.

Perelman, Chaim, and L. Olbrechts-Tyteca. 1969. *The New Rhetoric: A Treatise on Argumentation.* Trans. J. Wilkinson and P. Weaver. Notre Dame: University of Notre Dame Press. Reconceptualization of the nature and function of rhetoric as central to cultural interaction.

Vickers, Brian. 1988. *In Defense of Rhetoric.* Oxford: Clarendon. Comprehensive overview of rhetorical traditions, ancient and modern, Western and non-Western.

Warner, Martin, ed. 1989b. *The Bible as Rhetoric: Studies in Biblical Persuasion and Credibility.* Warwick Studies in Philosophy and Literature. New York: Routledge. Critical studies of select aspects of the rhetoric of biblical literature and of the rhetoric of the Bible.

Wire, Antoinette Clark. 1990. *The Corinthian Women Prophets: A Reconstruction through Paul's Rhetoric.* Minneapolis: Augsburg/Fortress. A reading of the rhetorical impact of 1 Corinthians shaped by a feminist critique that anticipates postmodern concerns.

5 | Psychoanalytic Criticism

Quite by the way, why did none of the devout create psychoanalysis?
—Sigmund Freud (Meng and Freud, 63)

. . . one man, a discoverer, Freud, said, *There is the country where I shall take my people.*
—Jacques Lacan (1977b:33)

FREUD AS RELIGIONIST AND BIBLICAL SCHOLAR

By the time Sigmund Freud published *The Interpretation of Dreams* (1900), the principles of psychoanalysis were in place. What were they? Laplanche and Pontalis's scrupulous definition of psychoanalysis begins: "a method of investigation which consists essentially in bringing out the unconscious meanings of the words, the actions and the products of the imagination . . . of a particular subject" (367; cf. Freud, 1923b:235). This discovery or institution of the unconscious, that dark realm that governs us but which we cannot govern, whose contents express themselves obliquely—not transparently—in displacements, sublimations, condensations, and substitutions, was to be defining for psychoanalysis. It has also come to ally psychoanalysis to the displacements that mark postmodern thinking (cf. Krupnik, 6–8).

The empire Freud envisioned far exceeded the boundaries of medicine. For him, "the relevance of psychoanalysis, whether carried on behind the couch or at the desk, was universal." Thus he "was not embarrassed or apologetic about invading the domains of art or politics or prehistory, psychoanalytic instruments in hand" (Gay, 1988:524). Besides, for Freud, literary and religious texts qualified eminently as "products of the imagination," hence as grist for his mill. In 1925 Freud wrote: "My interest, after making a lifelong detour through the natural sciences, medicine and psychotherapy, returned to the cultural problems which had fascinated me long before, when I was a youth" (1925:72). Foremost among these problems, as Freud goes on to imply, was that of religion. That preoccupation surfaces explicitly in "Obsessive Acts and Religious Practices" (1907) and *Totem and Taboo* (1913) and begins to blossom into one of the main subjects that will haunt the final phase of his career with *The Future of an Illusion* (1927), *Civilization and Its Discontents* (1930), and his last great work, *Moses and Monotheism* (1939). A remark in Freud's autobiographical study sets the stage for this absorption: "My deep engrossment in the Bible story (almost as soon as I had learnt the art of reading), had, as I recognized much later, an enduring effect on the direction of my interest" (Freud, 1925:8). As dream interpreter, Freud saw himself as Joseph (Friedan, 47–58; Schwartz, 1990b); as the leader of a new movement, he saw himself as Moses, taking his people out of the bondage of ignorance (Rice; Yerushalmi); and as a son who renounced the authority of his Jewish father(s), he saw himself as a slayer of Moses (Handelman, 1982:129–52). Others have discerned Freud's debt to the Bible on another level, seeing it not so much as a source of plot as of theory, a theory of repression. To the extent that the Hebrew Bible offers a theory of resistance and recovery, a narrative working out of the theory of the return of the repressed, Freud is, for all of his efforts to slay his Hebraic fathers, its direct heir.

If Freud's relation to the New Testament is less direct than the Hebrew Bible, it is no less suggestive. Freudian psychoanalysis has frequently been adduced to illuminate Paul's conversion (see, most recently, Segal, 285–300).[1] Of more interest to Freud himself was the transition from Judaism

---

[1] Indeed, the psychoanalytic literature on all aspects of Paul's life and letters has been ample, ranging from the pioneering studies of Freud's friend Oskar Pfister (see esp. Pfister) to such recent landmarks as Richard Rubenstein's *My Brother Paul* (1972) and Gerd Theissen's *Psychological Aspects of Pauline Theology* (1987).

to Christianity in general and the attendant phenomenon of anti-semitism. Crucial to that transition, for Freud, was Paul's sacrificial interpretation of Jesus' crucifixion. Ultimately, for Freud, psychoanalysis came to concern "the question of two testaments, two religions . . . , and eventually Christian and New Testament anti-Semitism" (Jobling, 1994:452).

Despite Freud's indebtedness to the Bible—conscious and unconscious— his first forays into religion were derisive. He saw religion as essentially a mass neurosis, its rituals as obsessional, its adherents as infantile. Freud had remarked to Jung in 1910 that "the ultimate basis of man's need for religion is infantile helplessness" (McGuire, 283–84). And in his study of Leonardo da Vinci, published the same year, he states: "Psycho-analysis has made us familiar with the intimate connection between the father-complex and belief in God; it has shown us that a personal God is, psychologically, nothing other than an exalted father" (Freud, 1910:123). *The Future of an Illusion* picks up these threads. The believer's cultivated helplessness be-fore the Almighty is said to have "an infantile prototype" (Freud, 1927:17), namely, the infant's relationship to its father. We labor under a stubborn delusion that God is the omnipotent father who can protect us even as we fear him. Religion is "born from man's need to make his helplessness toler-able and built up from the material of memories of the helplessness of his own childhood and the childhood of the human race" (18). And so we de-velop an appropriate store of ideas, such as that of a providential design: "Everything that happens in this world is an expression of the intentions of an intelligence superior to us, which in the end, though its ways and byways are difficult to follow, orders everything for the best" (19).

Joachim Scharfenberg has described *The Future of an Illusion* as "prob-ably the harshest polemic against every form of religion to have appeared since Ludwig Feuerbach" (8), an apt comparison since Freud's critique of religion as projection seems indebted to Feuerbach's. Freud's cynicism and scathing derision are again evident in his account of the notion of afterlife as a projection of our deepest wishes: "The same moral laws which our civili-zations have set up govern the whole universe as well, except that they are maintained by a supreme court of justice with incomparably more power and consistency. In the end all good is rewarded and all evil punished, if not actually in this form of life then in the later existences that begin after death. In this way all the terrors, the sufferings, and the hardships of life are destined to be obliterated" (1927:19). "It would be very nice if there were a God who created the world and was a benevolent Providence, and if there were a moral order in the universe and an afterlife," he remarks later, "but it is a striking fact that all this is exactly as we are bound to wish it to be" (33). And that, for Freud, is the source of religion's power over us. Religious ideas "are not precipitates of experience or end results of our thinking" but "illusions, fulfillments of the oldest, strongest and most urgent wishes of mankind. The secret of their strength lies in the strength of those wishes" (30). Religion, then, is a kind of cultural neurosis (cf. Freud, 1933:168): a survival of infantile dependence into adult life, a fixation at a stage of unproblematic wish fulfillment to the exclusion of the reality principle and its demands, "an illusion hovering perilously close to delusional madness" (Gay, 1987:40).

The Future of an Illusion was not to be Freud's definitive word on religion. Later he came to condemn his theory that religion is the infantile projection of omnipotence onto a divine father as "childish" and "feeble analytically." In 1935 he commented: "In *The Future of an Illusion* I expressed an essentially negative valuation of religion. Later, I found a formula which did better justice to it" ("Postscript" to Freud, 1925:72). That formula finds expression in *Moses and Monotheism*, a work with which Freud struggled throughout the 1930s and the last years of his life. The conception of God as Father still fascinates him, but now he seeks its psychogenetic roots, no longer simply in the childhood of the believer, but in his story of the Jewish people, and beyond that in human prehistory. "The pious solution contains the truth—but the *historical* truth and not the *material* truth" (Freud, 1939:129, emphasis his; cf. Freud, 1925:72). Despite his earlier contempt, in *Moses and Monotheism*—the last work he was to complete—Freud shows a respect for religion that is so deep that religion becomes the new organizing principle of the psyche. Religion attains this stature because he sees it as founded on repression, and, as he claimed, "the theory of repression is the cornerstone on which the whole structure of psychoanalysis rests" (1914b:16). Although he spent most of his career elaborating the mechanisms of repression of the individual psyche, he came to be more and more fascinated with the notion of collective repression. In *Totem and Taboo* and *Moses and Monotheism*, Freud turns the Oedipal drama into a collective cultural inheritance, one that instituted not only the incest taboo but also monotheism. "Freud does not psychoanalyze the Bible in *Moses and Monotheism*; he rewrites it, complete with myths of origin, history, and prescriptions of ritual" (Schwartz, forthcoming).

According to *Moses and Monotheism*, Israelite religion does not go back

to the patriarch Abraham (most biblical historians would concur) but originated much later in Egypt with Moses. Moses was not a Hebrew, however,
but an Egyptian. He was deeply influenced by the pharaoh Akhenaton, who
had abolished the idolatrous polytheistic religion of his forebears and replaced it with a monotheistic religion.[2] Oddly enough, Freud fails to cite
Exod. 2:19, the one verse he might have adduced as evidence for his assertion (cf. Rice, 136). Moses adopted the Hebrew people, became their
leader, and made Egyptian monotheism—"the religion which Egypt had
disdained" (Freud, 1939:28)—the new basis of their religious identity. An
obscure hypothesis of the biblical historian Ernst Sellin provides a scholarly
alibi for the next, crucial step in Freud's reconstruction: after the exodus,
in the course of the wilderness wandering, the Israelites rebel against Moses
and slay him.

Freud's narrative resumes some time later at Kadesh, where the Egyptian Israelites—worshipers of Aton—meet another group of Israelites—
worshipers of Yahweh—who had never been to Egypt. This group was
led by a Midianite priest, who as it so happened was also called Moses.
The two groups unite and their religions combine. The Egyptian contingent
brings with it ethical monotheism, while the Midianites bring the worship
of Yahweh, whom Freud characterizes as "a coarse, narrow-minded, local
god, violent and bloodthirsty. . . . The Egyptian Moses had given to one
portion of the people a more highly spiritualized notion of god, the idea of
a single deity embracing the whole world, who was not less all-loving than
all-powerful, who was adverse to all ceremonial and magic and who set before men as their highest aim a life in truth and justice" (50). According
to Freud, however, the ethical monotheism of the Egyptian Moses was to
become submerged in Yahwism, and it would not reemerge until the time of
the great Israelite prophets centuries later.

Whether monotheism "laid open to view the father who had all along
been hidden behind every divine figure as its nucleus" (Freud, 1927:19), or
whether it merged with ethics upon the slaying of Moses and the guilty response to the murder, it is fraught with ambivalence. The infant's attitude

---

[2] Here Freud is drawing his inspiration from the Egyptologist J. H. Breasted. Freud had a
rather quixotic view of Egyptian religion. Today most scholars would want to label the religion
of Akhenaton and that of Israel in the pre-exilic period as either monolatry or henotheism,
neither of which deny existence to secondary deities. Freud does not concern himself with such
fastidious distinctions (cf. Rice, 139–40).

toward its real father is normally one of ambivalence—"it fears him no less than it longs for and admires him" (23)—and that ambivalence is explicit in Christianity which, for Freud, "reveals the essence of all religion with particular clarity: on the one hand, an infinite trust in the heavenly Father is regressively renewed, and on the other, the punishing Father emerges with archaic strictness and kills *the Son* vicariously for all sons" (Theissen, 19, his emphasis). This ambivalence also goes a long way toward explaining why Freud himself invested so deeply in the figure of Moses, the prophet-leader-father who is murdered by his ungrateful sons but whose memory is also held dear as the instigator of a new order.

In publishing *Moses and Monotheism* when he did, Freud risked ending up like his Moses. "In a time of terrible travail," writes Peter Gay, "with the Nazi persecution of the Jews in Germany and Austria intensifying beyond the bounds of the most vicious czarist pogroms, Freud had dared to call Moses an Egyptian and to claim that the Jews had murdered him" (1987:149). The result was an avalanche of angry reviews and abusive letters. Yet Freud would seem to have written *Moses and Monotheism* out of a sense of deep, if divided, identification with Judaism. In his preface to the Hebrew translation of *Totem and Taboo*, Freud had described himself as one "who is completely estranged from the religion of his fathers—as well as from every other religion— . . . but who has yet never repudiated his people, who feels that he is in his essential nature a Jew and who has no desire to alter that nature" (Freud, 1913:xv). If *The Future of an Illusion* was a stern critique of religion in general and Christianity in particular, *Moses and Monotheism* was a lightly veiled defense of the cultural and ethical value of Judaism. Frequently in his later writings, Freud alludes to "the renunciations on which the existence of civilization depends" (Freud, 1927:8; cf. Freud, 1930), and it is in relation to these renunciations that the Mosaic religion acquires its true significance: "to worship a God whom one cannot see . . . meant that a sensory perception was given second place to what may be called an abstract idea—a triumph of intellectuality over sensuality or, strictly speaking, an instinctual renunciation" (Freud, 1939:113). Judith Van Herik elaborates: "Followers of the Mosaic tradition do not passively submit to a comfortable dependence, which restricts their intellectual level; instead, they follow the masculine path of Oedipal renunciation of instinct under the law of the father, and they achieve its economic correlates: advance in intellectuality, culture, and morality" (178). Michelangelo's great sculpture of Moses symbolized these values for Freud: "For three lonely September weeks in 1913 I stood every day . . . in front of the statue, studied it, measured it, sketched it" (in Jones, 2:367). He concluded that "the giant frame with its tremendous physical power becomes only a concrete expression of the highest mental achievement that is possible in a man, that of struggling successfully against an inward passion for the sake of a cause to which he had devoted himself" (Freud, 1914b:233). In *Moses and Monotheism*, the Moses of Michelangelo with which Freud had so long been fascinated finally comes to life. *Moses and Monotheism* is a book about a giant, who happens to be father to his people; but behind that patriarchal giant is yet another father, or several, and if they are renounced or slain, it is only to return in the guise of civilization.

The speculative audacity of *Moses and Monotheism* is not confined to an intuitive reconstruction of Israelite origins. Freud takes the opportunity to resurrect a hypothesis first broached in *Totem and Taboo* (1913), one that he would subsequently describe as a "scientific myth" (Freud, 1921:135). The myth, in its barest essentials, concerns the father of a "primal horde," Freud's Darwinian conception of the earliest stage of human society. This father is a jealous and violent figure who keeps his sons at bay and all the females for himself. One day the sons band together and kill and devour their father. A deep sense of guilt succeeds the crime; hence the dead father becomes even more powerful than the living one had been. "What had up to then been prevented by his actual existence was thence forward prohibited by the sons themselves" (Freud, 1913:132). But in internalizing the father's prohibitions they created the conditions in which civilization became possible.

Now we can better appreciate the significance of Freud's assertion that the Israelites murdered Moses. For Freud, it was an unconscious repetition of the murder of the primal father, so that the murder of Moses, too, was attended by the guilt and morality that institute culture. Moreover, this primal parricide also stands at the remote origins of Christianity. Freud reads Paul's preoccupation with sacrificial atonement as a distorted acknowledgment of the murder of the primal father: "With the original sin death came into the world. In fact this crime deserving death had been the murder of the primal father who was later deified. But the murder was not remembered: instead of it there was a fantasy of its atonement. . . . A son of God had allowed himself to be killed without guilt and had thus taken on himself the guilt of all men" (Freud, 1939:86–87). But if Christianity allowed a partial return of the repressed knowledge of the primal parricide, it also entailed a regression from the "instinctual renunciations" of Judaism: "God the Father fell back behind Christ; Christ, the Son, took his place, just as every son had hoped to do in primaeval times" (87). Paradoxically, even as it matured doctrinally, Christianity regressed into Oedipal fantasy.

Nevertheless, Freud firmly believed that the Judeo-Christian conception of God as Father concealed a historical truth. *Moses and Monotheism* locates that truth in the distant past, ultimately in human prehistory. Among "the much canvassed disasters of psychohistory, on which its detractors have fastened with a kind of unholy glee" (Gay, 1985:x), *Moses and Monotheism* has always occupied a place of honor, second only to *Totem and Taboo*. Even in 1939, the year of its publication, none but Freud's most uncritical admirers were persuaded by *Moses and Monotheism* in its entirety (cf. Gay, 1987:149–50). Over the years, however, interest in the book has increased rather than lessened. Of late, a number of attempts have been made to read it as Freud presents it, that is, as expressing a historical truth—not the truth of ancient Israelite history, however, but the truth of Freud's own history: his ambivalent relation to Judaism and to his own father, his passionate identification with the figure of Moses, and his own role as patriarch of the "Jewish science" (cf. Gay, 1988:604–48 passim; Handelman, 1982:132ff.; Rice; Robert; Yerushalmi). This often entails reading Freud's psychohistory as if it were psychobiography. He issued a blank check to such readers, remarking of the first draft of *Moses and Monotheism:* "Two themes run through these pages: the story of my life and the history of psychoanalysis. They are intimately interwoven" ("Postscript" to Freud, 1925:71). The same could be said of almost everything that Freud wrote.

What should we conclude about Freud's relation to the Bible? Is psychoanalysis a reenactment of the biblical drama? Or does Freud's myth of the slaying of Moses offer an alternative Bible, vastly rewritten to conform to his own private neurosis? What is the relationship of Freud's Moses to the biblical Moses? As the hero of *Moses and Monotheism* is marked by displacements and identifications, so too does the biblical Moses disappear and reappear. His origins are shrouded in uncertainty. He is a powerful leader, not only in leading the Israelites out of bondage, but also in instituting their law, morality, and culture—in short, a new religion like Freud's own psychoanalysis. Moses' followers, like Freud's, murmur against their leader in the wilderness, and he dies before he can reach the promised land. But is this Moses a father who hoards the women and provokes his sons' wrath? Moses' people resent his leadership but it is his father—his God—and not his sons, whose wrath blazes out against him, his father and not his sons who kills him. The biblical Moses is both strikingly like and un-like the Freudian Moses. Despised leader but not omnipotent father, the biblical Moses is an obedient son, who, each time he is tempted to usurp his father's power, is beaten back and who acquiesces to that subordination even in death. But even as Moses/Freud is slain, the order he institutes—monotheism-psychoanalysis—survives.

Early on in his career, Freud subjected himself to a pioneering self-analysis: "an elaborate, penetrating, and unceasing census of his fragmentary memories, his concealed wishes and emotions. From tantalizing bits and pieces, he reconstructed fragments of his buried early life, and with the aid of such highly personal reconstructions combined with his clinical experience, sought to sketch the outlines of human nature" (Gay, 1988:97). Freud's ongoing self-analysis eventually issued in something less private: the discipline, the institution, the science of psychoanalysis. That private-made-public phenomenon has fascinated numerous commentators, among them Jacques Derrida. He asks in some wonderment: "how can an autobiographical writing, in the abyss of an unterminated self-analysis, give to a worldwide institution *its* birth?" (1987:305). The unscientific excess in psychoanalytic science—its ineradicable autobiographical residue—is increasingly of interest the more it becomes apparent that no scientific or scholarly enterprise is exempt from it. "What is Freud's invention?" asks Gregory Ulmer, and answers: "It consists of the generalization of his peculiar, personal, familial story, mediated through a literary text (and myth) into an expert system of medical science" (1989:43). To that extent Freud's text is the specimen text of science and scholarship in general. Academic discourse, increasingly unable to disclaim its autobiographical, "interested" elements, must now find ways to work with them. "Part of Freud's importance for us is his demonstration"—however inadvertent—"of the interrelationship and equality among the different registers of discourse, producing texts in which are integrated personal, popular, and high culture documents," notes Ulmer (93). And although we have begun to see that "different registers of discourse"—personal and public, popular and scholarly, fictional and historical, poetic and scientific—might be interrelated, we have barely begun to consider the possibility that they might be equal and to begin to write accordingly. Perhaps we should take our clue from the ancients, for the Bible is engaged in just such cross-disciplinary discourse precisely because it was predisciplinary.

LACAN AS MIDRASHIST, BIBLICAL SCHOLAR, AND THEOLOGIAN

Freud's object of investigation rapidly expanded from medicine until it became human culture as such, including the phenomenon of religion. The same can be said of two of Freud's most influential followers, Carl Jung and Jacques Lacan. Over the years, Jung has received a good deal of attention from biblical scholars (e.g., Schuyler Brown, 1989, 1990; Cox; Diel; Edinger; McGann, 1985, 1988; Rollins; Theissen; Wink). Lacan, in contrast, is still an unknown quantity in biblical studies.

A 1987 bibliography of secondary literature on Lacan lists some forty-eight books in English alone (Nordquist). The stream continues to swell; the last five years in particular have seen an exponential increase of books on this thinker. Ironically, Lacan himself did not publish a book (other than his doctoral dissertation) until he was sixty-five.[3] His was an oral teaching centered on his famous seminar, which began in 1951 and ran for almost thirty years.[4]

Lacan once remarked: "That is the first title I lay claim to: I am the one who has read Freud" (quoted in Roudinesco, 416). Lacan read Freud as Freud taught him to read, that is to say, midrashically: "For this people who have the Book, midrash represents a primary mode of which modern historical criticism could only be the bastardization. For if it takes the Book perfectly literally, it is not in order to make it the bearer of more or less patent intentions, but . . . to draw another statement from the text: nay, to imply in the text what it itself neglected" (Lacan, quoted in Handelman, 1982:154).[5] Through bold paraphrase and embellishment, Freud's "canonical" texts[6] would now speak to a new generation of analysts and critics.

Lacan implicitly styled himself a Joshua to Freud's Moses. He was capable

[3] In 1966 Lacan's *Ecrits*, a massive collection of conference papers and other addresses, appeared.

[4] The seminar was a major event in French intellectual life. Barthes, Derrida, Foucault, Kristeva, and Ricoeur were among the many who attended. To date, six volumes of the seminar have been published in French from recordings; eighteen more are pending. Three of the six volumes have been translated into English (Lacan, 1977b, 1988a, 1988b), along with part of a fourth (1982b:138–61).

[5] Midrash was an ancient mode of Jewish scriptural commentary that frequently exceeded the literal sense of the text in order to reinterpret its meaning for the present (see further, Neusner, 1987b; Boyarin, 1990a).

[6] Lacan refers to *The Interpretation of Dreams, The Psychopathology of Everyday Life,* and *Jokes and their Relation to the Unconscious* (1977a:170).

of such statements as: "one man, a discoverer, Freud, said, *There is the country where I shall take my people*" (1977b:33). But although Freud glimpsed that country from afar, he could not fully enter it, according to Lacan, one reason being that he did not know Saussure.[7] In a 1957 paper entitled "The Agency of the Letter in the Unconscious or Reason since Freud" (1977a:146–78), Lacan presented the first installment of his Saussurian translation of Freud. Lacan reads Saussure by drawing from the latter's text what it itself "neglected," or hesitated, to say. For Saussure, the two components of the linguistic sign, which he termed the *signifier* and the *signified,* were capable of bonding together in a stable and symmetrical relation. Once signifier and signified enter Lacan's paper, however, that stable relation is disrupted. Lacan reduces the essence of Saussure's discovery to the following algorithm,

$$\frac{S}{s}$$

"which is read as: the signifier over the signified, 'over' corresponding to the bar separating the two stages" (Lacan, 1977a:149). The signified is in lower-case italic; it leans precariously, bowed under the excessive weight of the signifier. Malcolm Bowie offers the following interpretation of Lacan's algorithmic parable: "Anyone who goes in search of meaning at its source, or in its essential forms, has no choice but to travel the way of language, and at every moment on this journey variously connected signifiers extend to the horizon in all directions. When the signified seems finally to be within reach, it dissolves at the explorer's touch into yet more signifiers" (64). Or, as Lacan himself puts it, "We are forced . . . to accept the notion of an incessant sliding of the signified under the signifier" (1977a:154). To demonstrate this, Lacan takes Saussure's "classic, yet faulty illustration" of the relation between signifier and signified—

TREE

—and shows how easily the concept *tree* (the signified, represented by the sketch) "crosses the bar of the Saussurian algorithm" to lose itself in a forest

[7] On Saussure, see chap. 2 above.

of signifiers (150–51). *Arbre* (tree) is, after all, an anagram of *barre* (bar), Lacan notes, and as such is already intertwined with it. Moreover, "even broken down into the double spectre of its vowels and consonants, it can still call up with the robur and the plane tree the significations it takes on, in the context of our flora, of strength and majesty. Drawing on all the symbolic contexts suggested in the Hebrew of the Bible, it erects on a barren hill the shadow of the cross. Then reduces to the capital Y, the sign of dichotomy which, except for the illustration used by heraldry, would owe nothing to the tree however genealogical we may think it. Circulatory tree, tree of life of the cerebellum, tree of Saturn, tree of Diana . . ."—and so on for several more pages (154–56). In short, for Lacan in "The Agency of the Letter," as for Derrida a decade later, the signified is always already a signifier (Derrida, 1976:7). Or to put it a little differently, the bar that indivisibly united signifier and signified for Saussure, irreversibly divided them for Lacan. Saussure's bar had become a barrier. The Saussure whom Lacan conjured up in the 1950s was in some sense already a poststructuralist Saussure—even though Saussurean structuralism had yet to take French intellectual life by storm.

This brings us to Freud: "the S and the *s* of the Saussurian algorithm are not on the same level," explains Lacan, "and man only deludes himself when he believes his true place is at their axis, which is nowhere. *Was* nowhere, that is, until Freud discovered it; for if what Freud discovered isn't that, it isn't anything" (1977a:166). For Lacan's Freud, the "true place" of the subject can only ever be on the side of the signifier. Lacan notes that in Freud's writings "the proportion of analysis of language increas[es] to the extent that the unconscious is directly concerned." Thus in Freud's *Interpretation of Dreams*, for example, every page deals with what Lacan would call "the letter of the discourse, in its texture, its usage, its immanence in the matter in question. For it is with this work that the work of Freud begins to open the royal road to the unconscious" (1977a:159).[8] What the Lacanian Freud glimpsed, albeit from afar, was that "the unconscious is structured like a language" (Lacan, 1977b:20; cf. 149; Lacan, 1977a:147). Later Lacan will add, somewhat hesitantly: "It is curious to note, even if in this case it is not absolutely proven, that words are the only material of the unconscious"

---

[8] Cf. Lacan, 1972:60: "If what Freud discovered and rediscovers with a perpetually increasing sense of shock has a meaning, it is that the displacement of the signifier determines the subjects in their acts, in their destiny, in their refusals, in their blindnesses, in their end and in their fate."

(1970:187). Here Lacan has parted company from Freud, at any rate the Freud of such writings as "The Unconscious," who seems to view the unconscious as a domain of mute drives and wordless images (Freud, 1915:201–2; cf. Bowie, 49–53; Harland, 33–37).

If the unconscious is indeed structured like a language, as Lacan claims, then it follows that the decipherer of unconscious discourse will need to be a skilled interpreter of language, a trained exegete: "Hieroglyphics of hysteria, . . . enigmas of inhibition, oracles of anxiety . . . these are the hermetic elements that our exegesis resolves" (Lacan, 1977a:69–70). The theological exegete is likewise presented with a challenge—and an opportunity—in Lacan's linguistic reformulation of Freudian theory, as Edith Wyschogrod has recognized: "One difficulty in developing a psychoanalytic discourse appropriate to theological texts arises because unconscious content has largely been viewed nondiscursively, in terms of force fields, images, and archetypes, and so could not be read in the same way as theological language. It is just here that Lacan opens up the possibility of linking the unconscious to theological discourse. . . . Lacan attributes a linguistic and textual character to the unconscious itself. On this view theological texts and manifestations of the unconscious are homologous and open to common interpretive strategies" (1989a:97). How does Lacan interpret the unconscious? The same way that Freud did, in part, which is to say, once again, midrashically: "That which is central in the analytic discourse is always this—to that which the signifier expresses you give a reading other than what it means" (Lacan, 1975:37). You read not so much for the main point, in other words, the manifest meaning, the stated intentions, the conscious disclosures, as for what reveals itself unintentionally through slips of the tongue or pen, subtle evasions, audible silences, logical digressions and other such "accidents" of expression.

As Shoshana Felman has noted, however, the unconscious "is not simply *that which must be read* but also, and perhaps primarily, *that which reads*" (21–22, her emphasis). Lacan interpreted the unconscious not only by reading it but also by letting it read, giving it free rein in his own discourse. The resulting language was singularly unacademic; Lacan's own term for it is *lalangue*,[9] a strange and surreal tongue in which the elements of regular language undergo condensation and displacement in the unconscious

---

[9] This is a play on *la langue* (language), specifically Saussure's technical usage of that term. For Saussure, *langue* is the total system of language, the matrix from which individual utterances emerge.

to form bizarre or nonsensical-sounding neologisms (cf. Lemaire, 139–52).
Unconscious discourse teeters permanently on the brink of nonsense, and
so does Lacan's own discourse, especially in his later seminars. His later
style is frequently a tissue of puns and anagrams, aphorisms and cryptic
allusions, witticisms and fake etymologies, rhymes and slang.[10] In short, his
style mimics his subject matter, as many of his commentators have noted
(e.g., Muller and Richardson, 3; Bowie, 12–13, 199–200; Meltzer; Ulmer,
1985:200–205).

A Lacanian reading of the biblical texts, then, might involve a miming of
biblical styles—a profusion of parables, proverbs, and aphorisms, a deluge
of potent images. The plain, propositional style of standard biblical scholarship would give way to something much more colorful, much more literary.
Stephen Moore has recently attempted to take his lead from Lacan in this
regard.[11] In the example that follows, Moore takes an image from Lacan—
"When I speak to you of the unconscious . . . you may picture it to yourselves
as a *hoop net* . . . at the bottom of which the catch of fish will be found"
(Lacan, 1977b:143–44)—and uses it to read the episode of the miraculous
catch of fish in Luke 5:1–11:

> On Jesus' advice, Simon "put[s] out into the deep . . . and let[s] down [his] nets
> for a catch." The result is traumatic, dreamlike: "When they had done this, they
> caught so many fish that their nets were beginning to break. So they signaled their
> partners in the other boat to come and help them. And they came and filled both
> boats, so that they began to sink." Ordinarily the unconscious announces itself
> in the *lapsus*, the slip. So this slithering morass must have been all but scream-
> ing at Simon. But it is a silent scream, a written communiqué: it presents itself
> as something to be read ("when Simon Peter saw [*horaō*] it"). Faced with the
> subaqueous representatives of his own unconscious writ(h)ing grotesquely in the
> analytic net . . . , Simon yields his own soft underbelly to the analyst's knife, lets
> himself be cleaned like a fish, spills his guts at the analyst's feet ("he fell down at
> Jesus' knees saying, 'Go away from me, Lord, for I am a sinful man!'"). Filleted,

[10] Typical in this regard is the performance entitled "Television" (Lacan, 1990b). And typical of the style of this performance is the sentence with which it concludes: "De ce qui perdure
de perte pure à ce qui ne parle que du pere au pire"—which the translators desperately render
as: "between that which perdures through pure dross, and the hand that draws only from Dad
to worse" (46).

[11] Lacan's periodic forays into the Bible (e.g., 1981:323–26; 1986:201–9; 1988b:309–14;
1990a:90–95) are not especially good examples of his technique of mimicking unconscious
discourse. For the most part they predate the 1970s, Lacan's Dadaist period.

Simon is forced to acknowledge that he too is a split subject. But only that he might better serve as bait. "From now on you will be taking human beings alive [*anthrōpous esē zōgrōn*]," Jesus reassures him. (1992:123)

Lacan never tired of differentiating the subject as *speaking* from the subject as *spoken*. This distinction emerges most clearly in the lie. To take a New Testament example, when Peter says to the servant-girl, "I do not know this man you are talking about" (Mark 14:71), there is a clear discrepancy between the speaking subject, who did indeed know the Nazarene, and the subject as constituted by his speech. For Lacan, however, "the distinction between these two subjects, speaking and spoken, is no less valid when the claims of the speech are true. Put simply, the description of a thing, no matter how accurate, is never the thing itself" (Hogan, 1990b:15–16). To speak of something is to put words in place of it, and substitution inevitably entails distortion. "All I can do is tell the truth," says Lacan, immediately adding: "No, that isn't so—I have missed it. There is no truth that, in passing through awareness, does not lie. But one runs after it all the same" (1977b, vii; cf. 1990b:xviii, 3, 95). Indeed, the division of the subject of speech (whom Lacan terms the *I*) from the subject as spoken (the *ego*) is what brings the unconscious itself into being: the unconscious is the "place" from which the *I* speaks its desire.[12] What Freud discovered, according to Lacan, is that a fissure opens up between the signified (here, unconscious desire) and the signifier (the alienated expression of desire in everyday speech), a fissure capable of swallowing up every conception of a unified human subject. As so often in French poststructuralism, the seemingly innocuous gap between signifier and signified is used to engineer a seismic upheaval (cf. Berman, 182, 187, 198). And what is thus opened cannot easily be closed: "The radical heteronomy that Freud's discovery shows gaping within man can never again be covered over without whatever is used to hide it being profoundly dishonest" (Lacan, 1977a:172; cf. 165–66).

Lacan's reading of Exod. 3:14, God's enigmatic self-disclosure to Moses from the burning bush, builds on this reading of Freud and is also an interesting example of how Lacan harnesses a pun for intellectual work. From a Lacanian perspective, the striking thing about this scene is that it depicts the God of Moses as one who reveals himself through speech, in marked contrast, say, to the God of Aristotle. For Lacan, God's verbal self-disclosure to Moses can only be a disclosure of self-division. Lacan takes his lead, mi-

---

12 For more on this difficult notion, see Ragland-Sullivan, 1–67.

drashically, from the "letter" of God's announcement—a Francophone God, as it happens. In saying *Je suis celui qui suis* to Moses, God says two things at once: "I am who I am" and "I am he who follows" (taking *suivre* rather than *être* to be the verb of *Je suis*). The I (*je*), even when it is God's I, must necessarily lag behind its speech; its speech precedes it only to misrepresent it. For Lacan, a talking God demands a special kind of atheism: "The word atheism has another sense for us altogether than that which it could have in reference to the Aristotilean deity, for example, where it is a question of a relationship to a superior being, to the supreme being. Our particular atheism situates itself in another perspective—it is tied to that side which is always stealing away from the I of the other [*il est lié à ce côté toujours se dérobant du je de l'autre*]. An other who announces himself as *I am who I am*/*I am he who follows* [*Je suis celui qui suis*] is by definition a God be-yond, a hidden God, and a God who never, under any circumstances, unveils his face" (1981:324, our translation). The "true formula" of this uncom-mon atheism, as Lacan will later explain, "is not *God is dead*," but rather, "*God is unconscious*" (1977b:59, his emphasis). The Judeo-Christian God is a hidden God—and he is hidden first of all from himself. Moreover, he is not a God who *is*, strictly speaking, not a God of Being; for if the divine *je* is unconscious, it follows that it cannot really *be*. For Lacan, "the gap of the unconscious may be said to be *pre-ontological*," so that the unconscious "does not lend itself to ontology. Indeed, what became apparent at first to Freud, . . . and what still becomes apparent to anyone in analysis . . . , is that it is neither being, nor non-being, but the unrealized" (29–30, his em-phasis).[13] Still, the death of God is something that Lacan feels "much less sure about . . . than most contemporary intellectuals, which is in no sense a declaration of theism," he hastens to add (27; cf. Lacan, 1982b:140–41). What if the modern myth of God's death were "simply a shelter against the threat of castration" (1977b:27)?

Castration, for Lacan, is a linguistic affair; it is the process through which the human infant is gradually inserted into language and culture. The agent of castration is a de-biologized father, whom Lacan names "the symbolic Father," or "the Law of the Name-of-the-Father," or simply "the pater-nal metaphor"—whoever or whatever intervenes to teach the infant that

---

[13] Later Lacan speaks of "the need to disappear that seems to be in some sense inherent in [the unconscious]—everything that, for a moment appears in its slit seems to be destined, by a sort of pre-emption, to close up again upon itself, . . . to vanish, to disappear" (1977b:43).

its mother and itself are not one being but two.[14] Like his contemporary, Melanie Klein (another influential neo-Freudian), Lacan believed that the infant experiences initial symbiotic fusion with its mother. The infant achieves separation, individuation, primarily through the "mirror stage,"[15] but also through the acquisition of language. Through language, the infant begins to symbolize or represent its desire and experience. Hesitantly at first, but then with ever greater facility, it begins to move through the maze of linguistic substitutions. The word, and hence the world, becomes "a presence made of absence" (Lacan, 1977a:65).

Lacan's insistence that the human world is a creation of the symbolic Father begs comparison with the opening chapter of the book of Genesis, in which the created order similarly emerges from the inseminating word of the Father. God's word imparts structure to the formless female earth: "and the earth (*ha'arets*) was without form and void" (Gen. 1:2). More precisely, God's word erects the binary oppositions from which culture will derive its structure: light and darkness, day and night, human and animal, male and female.

Significantly, too, Lacan's neologism "the Name-of-the-Father" began as a semi-facetious allusion to the Christian liturgy (Bowie, 108; cf. Lacan, 1977a:199) and to "the Father from whom every family in heaven and on earth takes its name" (Eph. 3:14–15; cf. Matthew 28:19). Freud reversed the Pauline formula, suggesting that if God has traditionally been conceived as a Father, it is because the father has been a god in the home. For Lacan, as for Freud, the father's function is precisely that of laying down the law: "It is in the *name of the father* that we must recognize the support of the symbolic function which, from the dawn of history, has identified his person with the figure of the law" (Lacan, 1977a:67, his emphasis; cf. Lacan, 1990a:88).

The question inevitably arises: Is Lacanian theory utterly complicit with

---

[14] Lacan's conception of the "mother" is also nonbiological; any primary nurturer can fulfill that function (Ragland-Sullivan, 16).

[15] Lacan locates the mirror stage between the ages of six and eighteen months. Still in a state of motor incoordination, the infant sees its image in a "mirror" (not a literal mirror, necessarily—it could be the image it receives from its primary caretaker). Henceforth, the infant will attempt to assume the image, to mimic it, to model itself upon it because the image seems to possess the unity that the infant lacks. The import of the mirror stage, for Lacan, is that subjectivity is founded upon a fiction, a misrecognition, a division. Like the mirror-stage infant, the adult subject will only ever be able to relate to itself through self-images that come to it from outside itself. For Lacan's explanation of the mirror stage, see 1977a:1–7.

the patriarchal and phallocratic social order? Or does it function as an implicit critique of that order instead?[16] Lacan himself does not say. Nevertheless, his theory does seem to lend itself to explicit critiques of patriarchal structures. For example, Laura Mulvey has argued that a certain conception of woman is the linchpin of the patriarchal order: a conception of woman as "castrated," and as such "the lack that produces the phallus as a symbolic presence" (quoted in MacCannell, 133). Unquestionably, this idea of woman has carried over into Freudian theory. "Women have always been considered 'castrated' in psychoanalytic thinking," as Jane Gallop notes. For Lacan, however, as Gallop goes on to argue, castration "is not only sexual; more important, it is also linguistic: we are inevitably bereft of any masterful understanding of language, and can only signify ourselves in a symbolic system that we do not command, that, rather, commands us. For women, Lacan's message that everyone, regardless of his or her organs, is 'castrated,' represents not a loss but a gain. Only this realization, I believe, can save us from 'phallocentrism'" (1985:20).

For Lacan, no one, female *or* male, can possess the phallus—it is not the penis, he insists (1977a:285). Identified with the Father, language, and social order, the phallus is a mark of prohibition. Initially, "the phallus forbids the child the satisfaction of his or her own desire, which is the desire to be the exclusive desire of the mother" (1957–58:14). As such, the phallic signifier is what sets substitutive desire in motion; symbiotic fusion with the mother is exchanged for the "otherness" of the father, of language, and of culture. Therefore the phallus is also the signifier of a lack; it establishes substitutive desire "as a permanent ontological state and makes adult 'wanting' a shadow pantomime of the primordial drama . . . between mother and infant" (Ragland-Sullivan, 271). Finally, since the function of the phallus is to be permanently absent, permanently unavailable, it is "the signifier that has no signified" (Lacan, 1982b:152). Its purpose is to fade and to recede; thus

---

[16] According to Elizabeth Grosz, feminist relations to Lacan tend to "fall into two broad categories: those committed to Lacan's work, and ultimately, to his underlying framework, seeing it as a means of describing and explaining patriarchal power relations [she assigns Julia Kristeva to this group]; and those who reject it from a pre- or non-psychoanalytic position." Then there are those, such as Luce Irigaray and Jane Gallop, who fall into neither category; they take their bearings from Lacan's work "while maintaining a critical distance from it" (1990:141–42). See also *L'Anti-Oedipe* (Anti-Oedipus) by philosopher Gilles Deleuze and psychoanalyst Félix Guattari. Kristeva and Irigaray will be discussed below.

Lacan can say that "the phallus, even the real phallus, is a *ghost*" (1982a:50, his emphasis).

All of this leaves the Father in a peculiarly fraudulent position: "The Father must be the author of the law, yet he cannot vouch for it any more than anyone else can, because he, too, must submit to the bar, which makes him, insofar as he is the real father, a castrated father" (Lacan, 1982a:44; cf. Lacan, 1977a:311). And what of *the* Father, the biblical Father, he who calls Israel "my firstborn son" (Exod. 4:22) and Jesus "my beloved son" (Matt. 3:17)? Lacan won't say, but he does drop some tantalizing hints. In his "Introduction to the Names-of-the-Father Seminar," he notes that the Jewish and Christian traditions, unlike most Eastern religious traditions, turn not on God's "bliss" (*jouissance*) but on his desire (1990a:89–90). The *locus classicus* of this desire, for Lacan, appears to be the *Akedah,* the binding of Isaac (Gen. 22:1–19). Lacan sketches out the scene: "There is a boy, his head blocked out against a small stone altar. Take one of the two paintings of the scene by Caravaggio. The child is suffering, he grimaces, and Abraham's knife is raised above him. The angel, the angel is there, the presence of him whose name is not pronounced" (91). This primal tableau comprises a child, two fathers, a raised knife, and a missing mother.

And yet the Father who issues the commands is not himself omnipotent; "I could show you a thousand demonstrations of it in the Bible," boasts Lacan (92). The patriarchal God is "he who makes one wait, who makes a son to be awaited for up to ninety years, who makes one wait for many another thing more" (92)—but only in order to keep his own desire at a fever pitch. God's addiction to foreplay tries even the patience of Abraham. For evidence of this, Lacan turns to Rashi, the eleventh-century rabbinic commentator: "When Abraham learns from the angel that he is not there in order to immolate Isaac, Rashi has him say: 'What then? If that is what is going on, have I thus come here for nothing? I am at least going to give him a slight wound to make him shed a little blood. Would you like that?' " (93). By staying Abraham's hand, however, God has signaled his preference for the substitute, the stand-in, the displaced object of desire—in this case a ram "caught in a thicket by its horns." Abraham seizes the ram and offers it up "as a burnt offering instead of his son" (22:13).

Here the plot thickens. Lacan notes that according to other rabbinic traditions, the ram in question is both "the primeval ram" and Abraham's own ancestor, "the God of his race" (94). The significance of these details for

Lacan is far from clear. Possibly he means that Abraham, in slaying the prim(ev)al ram, "castrates" the Father himself,[17] separating him from the real object of his desire. Lacan remarks: "Here may be marked the knife blade separating God's bliss from what in that tradition is presented as his desire. . . . The Hebrew hates the metaphysico-sexual rites which unite in celebration the community to God's erotic bliss. He accords special value to the gap separating desire and fulfillment." And the custodian of that gap for Lacan is "the law of circumcision, which gives as a sign of the covenant between the people and the desire of he who has chosen them what?—that little piece of flesh sliced off" (94).

Of course, the little piece of flesh is also a substitute, a metonym, for the real desire of God, which can no more be assuaged by this "bloody scrap" (Lacan, 1977a:265) than by the flesh of Abraham's son. For Lacan, all desire is the desire for recognition, and that includes the desire of a God who says: "Do not lay your hand on the boy or do anything to him; for now I know that you fear God, since you have not withheld your son, your only son, from me" (Gen. 22:12; cf. vv. 16–18). God's desire is the desire not of an object, but of another's desire—which, for Lacan, is the distinctive mark of all human desire (cf. Lacan, 1977a:viii; Roudinesco, 140).

But desire is also the mark of an emptiness. As Lacan puts it, "Desire is a relation of being to lack. This lack is the lack of being properly speaking. It isn't the lack of this or that, but lack of being." As a result, desire "is the desire for nothing nameable" (1988b:223).[18] What is most peculiar about the biblical God, then, is his hole in being, his lack, or—as Lacan would say—his "want-to-be" (*manque-à-être;* cf. Wyschogrod, 1989b:ix). This brings us back to the burning bush, however, for to say that the biblical God is a subject of substitutive desire is to say that he is a God who speaks: "words, symbols, introduce a hollow, a hole [in the subject], thanks to which all manner of crossings are possible. Things become interchangeable" (Lacan, 1988a:271). From before the beginning of Genesis right up to the non-ending of Revelation ("Surely I am coming soon"—Rev. 22:20), the Jewish and Christian God is caught up in the unending circuit of desire, the realm of substitutions and deferrals. Lacan's term for this realm is the *sym-*

[17] Earlier he refers to "the ram's horn, which has been undeniably torn from him" (94).

[18] Lacan's conception of desire was strongly influenced by his reading of Hegel (see Roudinesco, 138–40). The Lacanian understanding of desire as a relation to lack is powerfully criticized by Deleuze and Guattari (e.g., 1983:38, 104, 116, 239, 329).

bolic order; it is the domain of language,[19] of Law, and of culture—that which "preexists" each subject "and in accordance with which he will have to structure himself" (Lacan, 1977a:234).[20]

In contrast to the biblical tradition, Lacan does not locate God in the symbolic order. He prefers to locate God on the side of the ineffable, or, as he himself would say, the *real:* "a God is something one encounters in the real, inaccessible" (1990a:90).[21] Along with the symbolic and the imaginary,[22] the real is one of Lacan's three "orders," the last to emerge in his thought and the one that most preoccupied him in later years. The Lacanian real is not to be confused with "reality"; reality can be represented, the real cannot. The real is "that which is—minus its representation, description, or interpretation" (Ragland-Sullivan, 188). The real cannot be accessed by language, because language emerges from lack. But "the lack of the lack is what makes the real, which emerges only there, as a cork" (Lacan, 1977b:ix). For Lacan, the real is unmasterable because it cannot be caught in the word. The function of Lacanian psychoanalysis, then, is an oddly "miss-tical" one—that of staging "an appointment to which we are always called with a real that eludes us" (53). This appointment "is essentially the missed encounter" (55).

This is not to imply that the subject is never touched by the real. On the contrary, the real is that which is always threatening to subvert the reality of the subject. It is "a noise in which everything can be heard"—or nothing in particular—a noise ever "ready to drown in its outbursts what the 'reality principle' constructs within it under the name 'external world'" (Lacan, 1966:388). Lacan was a psychoanalyst first and foremost, and it is precisely in its relation to the Freudian unconscious that his concept of the real acquires its distinctive edge. The real is the impossible, for Lacan—but only because it is impassible. To come up against the real is to collide with

---

[19] The symbols in question are Saussurian signifiers (Lacan, 1977a:ix).

[20] Insightful discussions of the symbolic order include Jameson, 1992; MacCannell (121–54); and Ragland-Sullivan (162–83). According to Deleuze and Guattari (e.g., 1983:176–186, 208–209, 243–44, 268), the meaningful signifier is always already a sociocultural construct, a coding of desire, and thus Lacan's "Law" necessarily reinforces the status quo.

[21] Cf. Lacan, 1977b:45: "those who have been listening to me for some time know that I use . . . the formula—*The gods belong to the field of the real.*"

[22] Allied with the mirror stage, the Lacanian *imaginary* has little to do with the imagination. Rather, it is a "specular" realm of identifications and projections, which produces the ego as its prime effect (see further Ragland-Sullivan, 138–62). A Lacanian critique of the biblical God could proceed from the imaginary just as easily as from the symbolic ("Let us make humankind in our image, according to our likeness").

reality—not "external reality" so much as a reality within discourse itself that results from its impasses. "When discourse runs up against something, falters, and can go no further . . . that's the real" (Jacques-Alain Miller, xxiii). The real is that "before which the imaginary falter[s], that over which the symbolic stumbles, that which is refractory, resistant" (Lacan, 1977a: x). But to stumble over the real is painful. "Lacan's real is always traumatic; it is a hole in discourse" (Jacques-Alain Miller, xxiii).[23] As a hole, moreover, the real can never be a whole. For Lacan, "there are only 'bits-of-real' " (xxiv).

William J. Richardson concludes an essay "Lacan and Theological Discourse" by posing a question that he claims he has no intention of answering: "If God and the economy of grace are to be found not in the Symbolic but only in the Real, how can there be any serious theological discourse about them at all?" (72). But perhaps serious theological discourse is not appropriate for a real God. Against "the good old God of all times," the serious theological gentleman who has provoked so much serious theological discourse, Lacan counterposes a resistant and subversive *jouissance* (bliss, ecstasy), which he locates in the real, and which he codes as feminine. This is a *jouissance* "beyond the phallus," the phallus being the linchpin of the symbolic order and the Law of the Name-of-the-Father. As real, this *jouissance* is itself inarticulable and unknowable: "It is clear that the essential testimony of the mystics is that they are experiencing it but know nothing about it" (Lacan, 1982b: 147).

The real, for Lacan, is also on the side of the body; he speaks of "the real of the body and the imaginary of its mental schema" (1977a: 302). Elsewhere he refers to the real as "the mystery of the speaking body" (1975: 118). But the body in question is not only that of the subject. As Catherine Clément has remarked, "the Lacanian concept of the Real . . . partakes both of the Id's disconcerting and unpredictable powers . . . and the terrifying archaic images associated with the Mother" (169).

To relocate the Jewish and Christian God in the real, then, would mean stripping him of several of his most familiar attributes: first of all, his speech, which has kept him a prisoner of the symbolic order; second, his Law, which has simply been an extension of his Word; third, his phallus, which has barred him from the real (for real *jouissance* is "beyond the phallus"); and fourth, his wholeness-holiness, which has also kept him un-real (if there are

---

[23] Lacan's own term was *trou-matique*, according to Jacques-Alain Miller. (*Trou* is French for "hole.")

only "bits-of-real," then there can only be "bits-of-God"). What would be left of the biblical God, however, would not necessarily be nothing. "I don't believe that I have talked of nothingness," says Lacan in another connection. "The sliding and the difficulty of seizing the never-here (it is here when I search there; it is there when I am here) is not nothing" (1970:196; cf. Lacan, 1990a:95).

Clément has dubbed Lacanianism "a negative psychoanalysis," on the analogy of negative theology (144). For Lacan was a real a/theologian, a theologian of the real and the *petit á,* his term for the elusive object of desire,[24] the quest for which keeps "the culture machine" ticking over (cf. MacCannell, 166–67). A Lacanian theology would be a miss-tical a/theology, one that would involve real risks. Like the mystic, the Lacanian analysand is one who takes risks with the real. For Lacanian analysis "does not provoke any triumph of self-awareness," as Roudinesco rightly points out. "It uncovers, on the contrary, a process of decentering, in which the subject delves . . . into the loss of his mastery. . . . But such therapy also resembles the experience of an organized variety of insanity . . . , since the subject delivers himself over to a real that may shift into madness" (255–56). In later years, Lacan's attempts to deliver himself over to the real resulted in verbal productions that bore many of the traits of madness (cf. Clément, 32–33).

If we began with a "Jewish" Lacan, the midrashic expositor of a Freudian canon, we end with a "Christian" Lacan, a covert theologian. For Lacanian theory is not only related to the marginalia of the Christian tradition, such as negative theology; other aspects of the theory bear an odd resemblance to more orthodox strands of Christian theology. Lacan himself abandoned orthodox religious belief at an early age; yet he did not altogether renounce the religious culture of his upbringing (Roudinesco, 103–4; cf. 123–24; Schneiderman, 14).[25] Lacan's "doctrine" (as it is commonly called) is strongly scored with quasi-Christian traits, particularly the doctrine of original sin. Gallop rightly observes that "Lacan's major statement of ethical purpose and therapeutic goal . . . is that one must accept one's castration" (1985:20; cf.

---

[24] The *petit á* stands for *l'autre* (the other), itself a fill-in for the "big" Other. All desire "is the desire of the Other" (1977a:312). The Other is an extremely fluid concept for Lacan; it can mean the (m)Other, the Father, the unconscious, and so on. In general, it "invokes the Real unmanageable alterity that bounds our existence" (Crownfield, 1989b:94).

[25] Roudinesco notes that Lacan's mother was a devout Roman Catholic "with an ardent streak of mysticism" (103).

Lemaire, 246; Crownfield, 1988a:164). Lacan himself was capable of uttering such statements as: "forever, by dint of a central fault, desire is separated from fulfillment" (1990a:86).

But the affinities between Lacanianism and Christianity—Roman Catholicism in particular—extend beyond this. Lacan's seminar drew a significant number of Roman Catholic clergy, who found his theories more congenial than those of Freud.[26] According to Roudinesco, "Lacan's doctrine . . . attracted Catholic intellectuals, and particularly the Jesuits, insofar as it allowed for an acceptable assumption of Freudian *doxa*. . . . In his concern to privilege a subject constituted by the desire of the other, in his references to the mystical tradition, in his manifold winks at the technique of directing consciences, and finally in his quest of a Trinitarian order [Imaginary, Symbolic, Real] . . . , Lacan translated Freudian discourse into a language familiar to Catholic tradition" (261–62). In Lacan's teaching, those "accustomed to theological debates were apt to rediscover the Rome of the Vatican or the spiritual exercises of Ignatius of Loyola. All that was easier to digest for them than Freud's apparent positivism, his excessively radical critique of religious illusions, the remains of his biologism, and finally his violent affirmation of the primacy of sexuality" (262).

Lacan himself was not unaware of the religious undercurrents of his teaching. In 1963 he raised the question of what it is in psychoanalysis itself "that is so reminiscent of religious practice" (1977b:4). Later on in the same seminar he ventures an answer: "within religion . . . —the separation and impotence of our reason, our finitude—it is this that is marked with oblivion. It is in as much as psycho-analysis . . . finds itself in some way struck by a similar oblivion, that it manages to rediscover itself, marked . . . with what I will call the same empty face" (265). Collecting himself, he sternly adds: "But psycho-analysis is not a religion. It proceeds from the same status as Science itself. It is engaged in the central lack in which the subject experiences himself as desire" (265). But here Lacan protests too much. It is surely a defining characteristic of Jewish and Christian traditions and not of "Science" to be preoccupied with the "central lack" in the human subject. Thus, whereas Lacan's conception of God is at odds with the biblical conception, his "anthropology" (in the theological sense of the term, that is, his "doctrine of man") is surprisingly biblical or, to be more specific, Pauline. For

[26] Lacanian analysts and Lacanian study groups are especially common in areas of the world that are predominantly Roman Catholic, such as Latin America and Italy (Schneiderman, 14).

it is a trait of Paul above all other biblical writers to be preoccupied with a central lack or fault in the religious subject—even if Paul's solution to that problem (in Lacanian terms, his identification of Jesus as the phallus, which the believer may now possess through faith) is altogether as un-Lacanian as Lacan's stern refusal of a solution is un-Pauline.

PSYCHOANALYSIS AND FEMINISM: KRISTEVA AND IRIGARAY

The history of psychoanalysis has frequently been read through the lens of psychoanalysis itself, and so the relationship between Freud and his "sons" (the next generation of male analysts), for example, comes to be read as an enactment of the Oedipal drama. For women in and around psychoanalysis and for the relationship of feminism to psychoanalysis, the language of seduction, hysteria, and lack is often invoked. Meanwhile, the debates within feminism on the pitfalls or potential usefulness of psychoanalysis have often mirrored the alternately enticing, enigmatic, and infuriating treatments of femininity and woman within psychoanalysis itself. Whereas some feminists have asserted that psychoanalysis provides an understanding of the formation of subjectivity and sexual difference that is crucial to feminism, others have pointedly critiqued the marginalization of women in psychoanalysis and Freud's own inability to comprehend women's experience, an inability seen to be articulated in his classic question, "What does woman want?"[27]

Generally speaking, the feminist defenders of psychoanalysis argue that Freud's and Lacan's accounts of the institution of sexual difference and gender identity *describe* how subjectivity is formed within an androcentric, patriarchal society. They are descriptive not prescriptive accounts, in other words, and they highlight the culturally forged character of sex and gender identities, in contrast to the long tradition that has argued, or simply assumed, that such identities are somehow natural or intrinsic. These feminists argue that the insistence of Freud and Lacan on the centrality of the unconscious to psychic reality contributes to the postmodern critique of the essentialized, self-identical, rational(ized) individual—a critique crucial to the feminist resistance to deterministic or essentialist accounts of gender. As Jacqueline Rose, one of the proponents of psychoanalytic feminism, has

---

[27] A number of books offer entry into this complex discussion; see, e.g., Adams and Cowie; Brennan; Elliot; Feldstein and Roof; Gallop, 1982; Grosz, 1989, 1990. The pioneering work that argues for the importance of psychoanalysis for feminism is Mitchell, 1974.

put it: "If psychoanalysis can give an account of how women experience the path to femininity, it also insists, through the concept of the unconscious, that femininity is neither simply achieved nor is it ever complete. The political case for psychoanalysis rests on these two insights together—otherwise it would be indistinguishable from a functionalist account of the internalisation of norms. In fact the argument from a biological pre-given and the argument from sociological role have in common the image of utter passivity they produce: the woman receives her natural destiny or else is marked over by an equally ineluctable social world" (1986:7).

While Rose and other feminist theorists have taken up a defense of Freudian and Lacanian psychoanalysis as their primary project (see also Rose, 1982; Mitchell, 1982; Gallop, 1985; Grosz, 1990), some other women and feminists working in and around psychoanalysis continue to interrogate—often in highly critical fashion—some of Freud's and Lacan's central assumptions or attempt to refocus the discussion by examining the marginality of women and the feminine in traditional psychoanalytic theory. On the one hand, there are arguments that the psychoanalytic narrative offers a liberating description of the production of sexual difference; on the other hand, arguments that psychoanalysis simply replicates the patriarchal intellectual structures within which it was conceived. Freud and Lacan see the Oedipus complex as the critical moment in the formation of gendered subjects. This is a position with which many psychoanalytic feminists would agree, but others would prefer to add their voices to the tradition that critiques the phallocentrism and androcentrism of the Oedipus complex, a tradition that stems ultimately from Karen Horney, Ernest Jones, and other dissident Freudians of the 1920s and 1930s.[28] In short, whereas some psychoanalytic feminists have remained more or less within the Freudian or Lacanian camps, others have called into question the adequacy of the theoretical framework that classical psychoanalysis offers. Exemplary of the latter group are Julia Kristeva and Luce Irigaray.[29] As it happens, both of them have also written on the Bible and the Judeo-Christian tradition.[30]

Lacan, following Freud, posits the formative moment of the subject in the

---

[28] For a survey of the early debates, see Mitchell, 1982:15–26. For a radically postmodern critique of oedipal phallocentrism, see Deleuze and Guattari, 1987.

[29] Book-length studies of both these thinkers have now appeared. On Kristeva, see Lechte, Fletcher and Benjamin, and Oliver; on Irigaray, see Whitford.

[30] On Kristeva and religion, see Crownfield, 1992; Taylor, 151–83; on Kristeva, Irigaray, and religion, see Kim, St. Ville, and Simonaitis.

resolution of the Oedipus complex. Kristeva does not deny the importance of the Oedipal drama, but in contrast to Freud and Lacan, her characteristic preoccupation is with the pre-Oedipal mother-infant relationship. Over the years, Kristeva has produced some memorable redescriptions of the pre-Oedipal domain. The earliest of these (Kristeva, 1974) has also been the most influential. It hinges on Kristeva's unique conception of the *semiotic*. Jane Gallop provides a useful explanation of this difficult concept:

> Starting from Lacan's notion of "the symbolic" as the order of language, the paternal order which locates each subject, Kristeva goes on to posit a more archaic dimension of language, pre-discursive, pre-verbal, which has to do with rhythm, tone, color, with all that which does not simply serve for representation. The semiotic is a more immediate expression of the drives and is linked to the bodily contact with the mother before the paternal order of language comes to separate subject from mother. Although it can be examined clearly in the sounds produced by pre-linguistic infants, the semiotic is always traversing language, always a bodily presence disruptive to the sublimated symbolic order. The semiotic is given freer play in works of "art": it is the poetic dimension of language. . . . The semiotic is the locus of force, revolution and art in Kristeva's work. (1982:124; cf. Kristeva, 1984:19–106)

For the male theorist, Lacan, the symbolic order is that which intervenes to disrupt the unproductive fusion of mother and infant; for Kristeva, in contrast, this fusion, far from being stagnant, is a powerful creative force able to subvert the symbolic order and its patriarchal underpinnings (cf. Gallop, 1982:124; Deleuze and Guattari, 1983).

For Kristeva, certain forms of artistic production are in close alliance with the semiotic. Throughout her work, she ascribes particular importance to modernist and postmodernist literature. "Let us say that postmodernism is that literature which writes itself with the more or less conscious intention of expanding the signifiable and thus human realm," she states (1980c:137). "Despite its phobias, [such] writing is nonetheless venturing into the darkest regions where fear, anguish, and a defiance of verbal clarity originate. Never before in the history of humanity has this exploration of the limits of meaning taken place in such an unprotected manner" (141). Elsewhere she elaborates more fully what is at stake in such literary experiments: "in a culture where the speaking subjects are conceived of masters of their speech, they have . . . a 'phallic' position. The fragmentation of language in a text calls into question the very posture of this mastery" (1980b:165). For Kristeva, "all of these modifications in the linguistic fabric are the sign of a force that has not been grasped by the linguistic or ideological system" (ibid.; cf. Kristeva, 1980c:138–41).

To this unassimilable force, which can never find expression in rational Western discourse, Kristeva gives the name *woman:* "In 'woman' I see something that cannot be represented" (1980d:137). "Woman" is what the dominant tradition has repressed. And the purpose of literature, for Kristeva, is to expedite the return of the repressed. In the prototypical literary utterance— Kristeva's example is Molly Bloom's soliloquy in *Ulysses*—"the writer approaches the hysterical body [*hystera:* womb] so that it might speak . . . of what eludes speech and turns out to be the hand to hand struggle of one woman with another, her mother of course, the absolute because primeval seat of the impossible—of the excluded, the outside-of-meaning" (1982b:22).[31]

True to her conviction that woman is that which cannot be represented, Kristeva is critical even of feminism as long as it claims identity for women. In a 1974 interview with the French feminist group Psych et Pol (Psychanalyse et Politique) she declared:

> Believing oneself "a woman" is almost as absurd and obscurantist as believing oneself "a man." I say almost because there are still things to be got for women: freedom of abortion and contraception, childcare facilities, recognition of work, etc. Therefore, "we are women" should still be kept as a slogan, for demands and publicity. But more fundamentally, women cannot *be:* the category woman is even that which does not fit in to *being.* From there, women's practice can only be negative, in opposition to that which exists, to say that "this is not it" and "it is not yet." What I mean by "woman" is that which is not represented, that which is unspoken, that which is left out of namings and ideologies. (1981a:166, emphasis hers)

Adding fuel to the fire, she goes on to claim that "there are certain 'men' who are familiar with this phenomenon; it is what some modern texts never

---

[31] Many feminists are skeptical of the claims Kristeva makes for the political efficacy of experimental writing, claims also associated with Hélène Cixous (see esp. Cixous, 1980a). "True, conventional narrative techniques, as well as grammar and syntax, imply the unified viewpoint and mastery of outer reality that men have claimed for themselves," admits Ann Rosalind Jones. "But literary modes and language itself cannot be the only targets for transformation" (373). Jones and others urge attention to the political, economic, and other material factors that prop up the patriarchal establishments (367–75; cf. Moi, 121–26, 147–48, 170–72; Spivak, 1988:134–53).

stop signifying: testing the limits of language and sociality"—she cites Joyce and Antonin Artaud as examples (ibid.). Such literature is closely related to madness, for Kristeva, since it threatens the very identity of the subject.

In addition to literature and madness, however, there is a third limit-discourse in which the semiotic can freely manifest itself; Kristeva evokes a subversive triad of "madness, holiness, and poetry" (quoted in Grosz, 1990:153). Since "holiness" occupies a privileged position in Kristeva's schema, it is not surprising that she has always been interested in religious discourse. She sees such discourse as pulling in two very different directions. On the one hand, it can occasionally manifest the subversive power of the semiotic, but, on the other hand, it can all too easily take the form of an institutionalized discourse, domesticating its own semiotic potential and becoming the obverse of poetry and art (cf. Deleuze and Guattari, 1983:133–34).

Domestication and disruption often go hand in hand in Kristeva's analyses of religious discourse. For example, in her exploration of the central notion of the maternal body and its relationship to the infant's first experiences of love, Kristeva turns to the image of the Virgin Mary (1980a; 1987:234–63). In contrast to many feminist treatments of motherhood, Kristeva's meditation on maternity is not grounded in women's experiences of pregnancy or motherhood so much as in the imagery or ideology of maternity.[32] In accordance with her belief that "woman" is that which cannot be represented, she refuses to confer subject status on the maternal body; for her, it remains split and fluid. "Pregnancy seems to be experienced as the radical ordeal of the splitting of the subject: redoubling up of the body, separation and coexistence of the self and of an another." As such, it is a "fundamental challenge to identity" (1981b:31). Elsewhere, the impossibility of female subjectivity in relation to maternity is articulated yet more strongly: "Within the body, growing as a graft, indomitable, there is an other. And no one is present, within that simultaneously dual and alien space, to signify what is going on. 'It happens but I'm not there.' Motherhood's impossible syllogism" (1980a:237).

In the Virgin Mary, Kristeva sees the symbolic embodiment of femininity

---

[32] It would almost certainly be a mistake to take Kristeva's "autobiographical" prose-poem on pregnancy in "Stabat Mater" at face value (1987:240ff.). Contrast the influential writings of Nancy Chodorow (1978; 1990), a psychoanalytic feminist who, like Kristeva, accords a special privilege to the mother-child relationship, but whose work is firmly rooted in the empirical tradition.

as maternity *and* a subversive supplement to monotheism. "The Mother and her attributes . . . become representatives of a 'return of the repressed' in monotheism" (1987:249–50). For Kristeva, the Virgin Mother occupies a "tremendous territory on this and that side of the parenthesis of language," "extending to the extralinguistic regions of the unnameable" (250). The Virgin is a subversive feminine supplement to the homogeneous masculine Trinity. Given the bond between the semiotic and the maternal body, it is no accident, for Kristeva, that the Virgin Mother is both "patron saint and privileged object of the arts" (ibid.).

Sociohistorical studies of women in the biblical world, coupled with literary critical studies of women in the biblical narratives, have proliferated in biblical studies in recent years.[33] The following blanket description of American feminist criticism is especially true of recent feminist criticism of the Bible: "American feminists are interested in going back, in resurrecting lost women, . . . in reconstructing a past—'herstory.' They are engaged in filling in cultural silences and holes in discourse. The assumption is that women have been present but invisible and that if they look they will find themselves" (Marks and de Courtivron, xi). (Elisabeth Schüssler Fiorenza's *In Memory of Her* would be a prime example of such study.) "American feminists tend also to be focused . . . on describing the material, social, psychological condition of women. . . . Their style of reasoning, with few exceptions, follows the Anglo-American empirical, inductive, anti-speculative tradition. They are often suspicious of theories and theorizing" (ibid.).[34]

This empirical approach contrasts strikingly with that of Kristeva. Over the years Kristeva has ventured a number of readings of the biblical texts (e.g., 1975; 1982a; 1987:83–100, 139–50; 1989:98–103). The most ambitious of these occurs in her book, *Powers of Horror: An Essay on Abjection* (1982b:56–132). For Kristeva, as we have seen, the formation of the human subject entails a catastrophic loss of unity with the maternal body. The *abject* is Kristeva's term for everything that the subject must renounce in order to *be* a subject. Thus, the abject, like the semiotic, is rooted in the subject's archaic relationship to the maternal body. For Kristeva, the abject has darker connotations than the semiotic. The abject is a source of dread; its encroach-

---

[33] See Janice Capel Anderson, 1991, for a survey of these developments.

[34] This statement dates from 1980. Since then a great many feminist literary critics in the United States have begun to engage with theory. Marks and Courtivron's description would now be more applicable to feminist biblical criticism.

ment menaces the fragile identity of the subject. Constituted initially by "a violent, clumsy breaking away" from the mother, the subject runs the "constant risk of falling back" (13). More generally, the abject is anything that "disturbs identity, system, order. What does not respect borders, positions, rules. The in-between, the ambiguous, the composite" (4).

Powers of Horror is no Texts of Terror (cf. Trible, 1984). In contrast to most feminist readings of the Bible, the repressed "woman" who is the subject of Powers of Horror is not an oppressed female individual, biblical or otherwise. Kristeva's hypothesis is that different religious systems correspond to different structurations of the subject against the danger and fascination of the abject. Kristeva reads nascent Judaism as a "tremendous forcing that consists in subordinating maternal power (whether historical or phantasmatic, natural or reproductive) to symbolic order," that is, to a paternal power here embodied as an intricate legal system (91). The sacred, an external force for other religious systems, penetrates deep into the interior life of the Jew through the Law. Each subject must now wage a life-or-death struggle "in order to become separate"—from contaminated objects, from the maternal object, from the abject (94). But it is only with Christianity that the contaminating danger is perceived no longer as external to the subject but as fully internal. Although classically expressed in the Pauline conception of flesh (sarx), Kristeva finds the interiorization of impurity in progress everywhere in the New Testament. "Evil, thus displaced into the subject, will not cease tormenting him from within, no longer as a polluting or defiling substance, but as the ineradicable repulsion of his henceforth divided and contradictory being" (116). " 'Kill, and eat,' says God to an astonished Peter at Joppa (Acts 10:9–16). But that permission, far from being a liberalization, will lead the subject who complies with it to seek no longer his defilement but the error within his own thoughts and speech" (117). The abject takes up residence within the subject, never more to depart. And to the extent that the abject is allied with the mother, Kristeva can describe the Christian conception of defilement as "a revenge of paganism, a reconciliation with the maternal principle" (116).

Luce Irigaray's stance on Freud and Lacan, as on Christianity, is more polemical than that of Kristeva. Irigaray is the controversially excommunicated member of Lacan's école freudienne, cast out for her doctoral dissertation, Speculum of the Other Woman, which mimicked psychoanalysis' marginalization of women by marginalizing Irigaray's mentor Lacan, to the extent that his name never once appears in the study (Irigaray, 1975; 1985b).[35] Freud does feature prominently in *Speculum*, but as the object of a scathing critique (11–129).

Irigaray's critique of psychoanalysis—and indeed of the entire Western intellectual tradition—centers on its repressions, its silences, its unspoken dimensions. For Irigaray, these omissions can be traced to a primary repression—that of sexual difference itself. Whereas some feminists argue that psychoanalysis offers a useful account of the creation of sexual difference, Irigaray argues that, insofar as psychoanalysis is steeped in the values of the dominant Western philosophical tradition, it is capable only of narrating the subject formation of men. Women, meanwhile, are relegated to a negative position relative to men's positive position; therefore, Irigaray suggests, the system is not really about difference at all, but rather about sameness and deviance from the same. Women's true difference, their specificity, is repressed. In the course of her critique of Freud, Irigaray writes:

> Thus Freud discovers—in a sort of blind reversal of repressions—certain variously disguised cards that are kept preserved or stored away and that lie beneath the hierarchy of values of the game, of all the games: the desire for the same, for the self-identical, the self (as) same, and again of the similar, the alter ego and, to put it in a nutshell, the desire for the auto . . . the homo . . . the male, dominates the representational economy. "Sexual difference" is a derivation of the problematics of sameness, it is, now and forever, determined within the project, the projection, the sphere of representation, of the same. The "differentiation" into two sexes derives from the a priori assumption of the same, since the little man that the little girl is, must become a man minus certain attributes whose paradigm is morphological—attributes capable of determining, or assuring, the reproduction-specularization of the same. A man minus the possibility of (re)presenting oneself as a man = a normal woman. (1985b:26–27)

In opposition to what she sees as the elevation of the One and the Same, Irigaray attempts to assert real sexual difference, the sexual specificity of woman as embodied in her sexual organs, "this sex which is not one" (1977; 1985c:23–33).[36] Arguing that subjectivity is inscribed in bodies and derives

[35] The dissertation was first published in France in 1974. Irigaray takes on Lacan explicitly in her essay, "Così Fan Tutti" (1985b:86–105).

[36] For Irigaray, the vagina is a concrete symbol of woman's heterogeneity: "her genitals are formed of two lips in continuous contact. Thus, within herself, she is already two—but divisible into one(s)—that caress each other" (1985c:24).

its particularity from corporeal morphology, Irigaray critiques phallocentrism by turning to the body of the mother and that of the female lover, bodies that cannot be reduced to phallic oneness (205–18). If female bodies, desires, and pleasures are the repressed, silenced, unspoken dimensions of psychoanalysis, and ultimately of the Western tradition as a whole, Irigaray is prepared to make a further assertion: that "born of woman, man devises religion, theory, and culture as an attempt to disavow this foundational, unspeakable debt" to "the positive fecundity and creativity of women" (Grosz, 1990:181).

Irigaray's treatment of religion grows out of this critique. Her discussions of religion, however, tend to be citational and situational. Consequently, it would be difficult to systematize her theology, and any attempt to find a sustained reading of a biblical text in her work would be doomed to failure. Nevertheless, it is clear that the category of the "divine" is of great importance to her thought, and she sees it as offering unique possibilities for women. At the same time, she sees that the divine is itself a projection of male desire, a limit toward which male subjectivity strives. Consequently, God has been conceived as a sexed (masculine) being: "Man can exist because God helps him to define his *genre* [his species, his gender], to be situated as finite in relation to the infinite. . . . Man found the avoidance of this finitude in a unique *masculine* God. The God, he created him from his *genre*. . . . Man does not allow himself to be defined by another gender [*genre*]: feminine. His unique God would correspond to humankind [*le genre humain*] which we know is never neutral from the point of view of sexual difference" (1985a:297–98). God, for Irigaray, is therefore neither neutral nor neutered: "Monotheistic religions speak to us of God the Father and God made man; nothing is said of God the Mother or of God made Woman" (1989:71). No theological argument, however subtle, "can succeed in erasing this one reality that determines identities, rights, symbols, and discourse" (ibid.). Woman, therefore, requires a God capable of offering her what she can never receive from the masculine God:

> How can a woman reserve for herself some margin of singularity, of non-determinism which allows her to become and to remain herself? This margin of liberty and of power which permits us to still grow up, to grow stronger and to expand each one of us and in community, only a God in the feminine can provide it for us and protect it for us. This is our other still to be actualized, our on-this-side and on-that-side of life, powers, imagination, creation, our possibility of a present and

a future. Isn't God the name and the place which allows us the appearance of a new epoch of history and which resists this event? (1985a:308)

In all of this, the figure of Jesus occupies a position that is "complex and contradictory" (1989:64), yet surprisingly important. Of one thing Irigaray is certain: Jesus' teachings cannot be reduced to a social gospel. Here she takes issue with Elisabeth Schüssler Fiorenza, claiming that the latter's position "comes close to such a socio-economic appraisal of the Gospels" (ibid.).[37] Irigaray finds Schüssler Fiorenza's "interpretation too reductive when it comes to the question of a possible theology of women's liberation" (ibid.). Economic equality for women would be the social outcome of what Irigaray, in neo-Gnostic fashion, sees as the essence of Christianity—"respect for the incarnation of all bodies (men's and women's) as potentially divine; nothing more nor less than each man and woman being virtually gods" (ibid.).

This brings us back to the theme of repression that so occupies Irigaray. Jesus' message, "especially as it concerns women, is most often veiled, obscured, covered over" (ibid.). For Irigaray, Christianity has always been intent on disincarnating Jesus, in peeling the flesh away from him, in defeminizing him. (Irigaray sees Jesus as "a kind of androgyne," hence her interest in him; if he "is seen as the totality of Mankind understood generically, then he is both man and woman" [62].) She contrasts the bodily Jesus of the Gospels with the ethereal Jesus of the pulpit: "Every stage in the life of Christ is noted and described in the Gospels as an event of the body: conception, birth, growth, fasting in the desert, immersion in the River Jordan, treks to the mountains or walks along the water's edge, meals, festivals, the laying-on of hands, the draining of physical strength after a healing, transfiguration, trials, suffering death, resurrection, ascension.... His life cannot be reduced to speeches given in closed, airless structures, or to repetitive rituals or disincarnation, ... or arguing fine distinctions in which the body is lost to lessons in tact" (65). And again: "Why invite the people to a celebration of the Eucharist on Christmas day if not to glorify the felt, the corporeal and fleshly advent of the divine, this coming, all the consequences of which theology seems very far from understanding" (67).[38]

---

[37] This essay—"Equal to Whom?"—is actually a review of Schüssler Fiorenza's *In Memory of Her.*

[38] Irigaray's heterodox understanding of Jesus and Christianity also finds expression in her *Marine Lover of Friedrich Nietzsche* 7(1991; see esp. 164–90).

When all is said and done, however, Irigaray, while positing the need for a "God in the feminine," appears hesitant to suggest concrete ways of finding her. Instead she offers critiques of male practices of religion as well as female cooptation into male spirituality. For example, in a reading of the work of René Girard on the sacrificial crisis he sees at the heart of culture, Irigaray asks about the gendered character of the sacrificial imperative, about rituals organized solely around male desire, and about the necessity of religious articulation through violent action and not merely through discourse: "Why was the word lacking? How was it wanting? Why kill, dismember, and eat as a sign of covenant? To abolish a certain violence? Which one? Where does it come from? And isn't it possible to analyze how the word was so unsuitable that the gesture was necessary? Isn't it, for example, because of the absence of harmony among words, gestures, bodies? Are cultures which ally or which allied gestures, words, microcosmic and macrocosmic nature, and the gods, sacrificial cultures? How then are systems of exchange and sexual difference articulated?" (1986:373–74). If the foundation of religion is built on the dismembered body of the father (as Freud suggests in *Totem and Taboo*), Irigaray pushes the discussion back further, asking what has happened to the body of the mother, the mother whose sons murder their father over their desire for the women the father has hoarded. Male religion, she argues, compensates for the absent mother, not the dead father.

Male religion, she also contends, cannot account for female desire except in a distorted, foreshortened way. In any case, male analysts would be unable to recognize female desire and pleasure as it is articulated in ecstatic religious experience. Irigaray mocks Lacan's famous comment on Bernini's statue of St. Teresa in ecstasy. Accusing Lacan of refusing to recognize that women are capable of articulating their own pleasure, she adds: "And to make sure this does not come up, the right to experience pleasure is awarded to a statue. 'Just go look at Bernini's statue in Rome, you'll see right away that St. Theresa is coming, there's no doubt about it.' In Rome? So far away? To look? At a statue? Of a saint? Sculpted by a man? What pleasure are we talking about? Whose pleasure? For where the pleasure of the Theresa in question is concerned, her own writings are perhaps more telling" (1985c:90–91; cf. Lacan, 1975:70–71). At the same time, Irigaray does not hold up hysteric mystics ("la mystérique") as models for women to embrace, even when she sees a limited power in their ability to mime and therefore mock patriarchal expectations of femininity (1985b:191–202). Irigaray seeks a still-uncreated religion where sexual specificity might find its full expression and where women might find an Other to whose horizon they might strive. Short of that, women are closed out of religious discourse, just as they have been closed out of philosophical and psychoanalytic discourse.

LOOKING TO THE FUTURE

This chapter has ranged widely over territory that not only includes psychoanalysis and the Bible, but also psychoanalysis and theology, and even psychoanalysis and religion. This was inevitable to the extent that psycho-analysis, for us, is not a tool or instrument that can simply be applied to the Bible so much as a para-religious discourse in its own right, deeply engaged in many of the same issues that pervade the biblical texts. As we have seen, these points of contact or overlap include a preoccupation with the ineffable (cf. Lacan and Kristeva in particular); with the father as God, God as Father, and God as (m)Other; with guilt and its deleterious consequences; with the prescription (and subversion) of human gender roles; with generational inheritance and conflict; and with remembering and reconfiguring the past.

It is this homologous relationship that makes psychoanalytic reading of the Bible at once so difficult and so promising—difficult because of the dan-ger (or fear?) of anachronism, the imposition of twentieth-century cultural codes onto an ancient document, that animates modern biblical scholar-ship; and promising because the striking similarities between biblical and psychoanalytic thought enable a cross-fertilization that could enrich biblical studies and psychoanalytic theory.

At first glance, psychoanalysis and religion may seem unlikely bedfellows given the explicit rejection of religion that is characteristic of so much secu-lar discourse. Nevertheless, as our account of Freud in particular has shown, psychoanalysis, despite its surface rhetoric, has more often coopted religious preoccupations than replaced them with strictly secular ones. Sacred con-cerns have frequently found a new life—a life after death?—in the discourse of psychoanalysis with, as we have seen, the uncanny supplementing or displacing the "ineffable."

The challenge that future psychoanalytic work on the Bible faces is to tread the line between a naive anachronistic imposition of psychoanalytic categories upon the biblical world, on the one hand, and a no less naive dismissal of psychoanalysis as irrelevant to the critical reading of literary and religious texts, on the other hand—most of all, texts that are deeply obsessed with such issues as generation, guilt, confession, and law.

RECOMMENDED FURTHER READING

Crownfield, David, ed. 1992. *Body/Text: Julia Kristeva and the Study of Psychoanalysis and Religion*. Albany: SUNY Press. A rare effort to examine the religious thought of one of the leading French feminist theoreticians.

Deleuze, Gilles, and Félix Guattari. 1983. *Anti-Oedipus: Capitalism and Schizophrenia*. Trans. Robert Hurley, Mark Seem, and Helen R. Lane. Minneapolis: University of Minnesota Press. An important book for feminist criticism, co-authored by a philosopher and psychoanalyst, whose materialist "schizoanalysis" inverts and critiques the Freudian/Lacanian priority of the oedipal "family scene." Argues for the always already sociocultural and, therefore, ideologically constructed character of the signifier.

————. *A Thousand Plateaus: Capitalism and Schizophrenia*. 1987. Trans. Brian Massumi. Minneapolis: University of Minnesota Press. Less a sequel to *Anti-Oedipus* and more a rewriting and elaboration within a more explicitly postmodern framework. Presents a nonlinear tracing of the nomadic and the rhizomatic as text (including biblical texts) and as history.

Freud, Sigmund. 1900. *The Interpretation of Dreams*. In *The Standard Edition of the Complete Psychological Works of Sigmund Freud*, vols. 4–5. Ed. and trans. James Strachey. London: Hogarth [1953–74]. Immensely readable and indispensable for an understanding of Freud's view of the unconscious.

————. 1933. *New Introductory Lectures*. In *The Standard Edition*, vol. 22. Freud conveniently summarizes much of his work on sexuality and the unconscious.

————. 1939. *Moses and Monotheism*. In *The Standard Edition*, vol. 23. Freud's later, and most explicit, engagement with the Bible.

Felman, Shoshana, ed. 1982. *Literature and Psychoanalysis. The Question of Reading: Otherwise*. Baltimore: Johns Hopkins University Press. A landmark collection of critical essays that explores the nexus of psychoanalysis, poststructuralism, and literary criticism. Includes important contributions by Lacan, Barbara Johnson, Peter Brooks, and Felman.

Gallop, Jane. 1985. *Reading Lacan*. Ithaca: Cornell University Press. A very accessible, personal, and insightful introduction to Lacan.

Gay, Peter. 1988. *Freud: A Life for Our Time*. New York: Norton. Today's standard biography of Freud with an excellent introduction to Freud's theories.

Irigaray, Luce. 1985c. *This Sex Which Is Not One*. Trans. Gillian C. Gill. Ithaca: Cornell University Press. This series of essays offers a subversive, alternative epistemology grounded in the female body.

Kristeva, Julia. 1982. *Powers of Horror: An Essay on Abjection*. Trans. Leon S. Roudiez. New York: Columbia University Press. A provocative exploration of the concept of pollution that deals extensively with biblical texts and subject matter.

Lacan, Jacques. 1977. *Ecrits: A Selection*. Trans. Alan Sheridan. New York: Norton. Lacan's most influential work. A series of papers in which he elaborates his radical rereading of Freud.

————. 1982. *Feminine Sexuality: Jacques Lacan and the école freudienne*. Ed. Juliet Mitchell and Jacqueline Rose. Trans. Jacqueline Rose. New York: Norton. Essays by Lacan and his school on sexuality and gender. Valuable for its lengthy illuminating introductions by Mitchell and Rose on psychoanalysis and the feminine.

Laplanche, Jean, and J.-B. Pontalis. 1973. *The Language of Psychoanalysis*. Trans. Donald Nicholson-Smith. London: Karnac Books and the Institute of Psycho-Analysis. The definitive dictionary of psychoanalytic terminology, both Freudian and post-Freudian.

Ragland-Sullivan, Ellie. 1986. *Jacques Lacan and the Philosophy of Psychoanalysis*. Chicago: University of Illinois Press. An impressive, detailed introduction to Lacanian theory with a helpful emphasis on his philosophy.

Whitford, Margaret. 1991. *Luce Irigaray: Philosophy in the Feminine*. New York: Routledge. The first book-length introduction to Irigaray's work.

Wright, Elizabeth. 1987. *Psychoanalytic Criticism: Theory and Practice*. 2d ed. New York: Methuen. Excellent brief introduction to psychoanalytic literary criticism, Freudian and post-Freudian.

6 | Feminist and Womanist Criticism

One of the distinctive features of *The Postmodern Bible* is its effort to expose the interestedness of both texts and their readings and to argue for theory's role in developing methods and strategies that lay these interests bare. This chapter focuses on issues of gender and power relations. It presents a range of feminist and womanist readings—readings that demonstrate how texts construct readers by imposing ideologies of gender and power and how readers can resist those constructions through a critical engagement with *feminism* and *womanism*.

We begin with several feminist and womanist readings of a single biblical text, Hosea 1–3. The strategy of presenting multiple readings has several goals. First of all, we are interested in decentering, by example, the notion of a singular interpretation by presenting several simultaneously compelling readings of the same text. That one can identify several viable womanist and feminist readings of the same text is not symptomatic of a problem requiring a solution (i.e., women can't make up their minds), but rather enacts what this entire volume seeks to explore and enable: a foundational shift in biblical criticism *away* from a hermeneutical project whose goal it is to find the correct key to unlock the unitary truth of the text and *toward* projects focused on multiplicities of meanings, interpretations examining layers of ideology

225

and shifting meanings—in short, toward cultural critique. Second, the presentation of multiple readings of a single text serves to highlight the varieties of feminisms at work in interpretation, feminisms variously shaped by historical circumstances, political and theological allegiances, social identities, institutional locations, and intellectual interests. Finally, these different readings provide an occasion to examine in a preliminary way the ongoing dialogue and debate between womanism and feminism (or, as some would put it, within feminism) as it has grown out of struggles in academic and activist settings. Our focus here will be fixed predominantly on the United States, though we will also engage to a limited extent interventions from other national settings.

These different readings are not set in simple opposition to each other but approach the text from a range of perspectives within the general framework of feminism and womanism. In each case, questions concerning power, sexuality, and the ideologies that construct them are raised. What distinguishes the different readings is the perspective of each interpreter, shaped variously by social location, institutional position, personal and collective history and identity, and so on. A womanist reading, for example, emerges out of African American women's encounters with the text and is shaped by a consciousness deriving from the particular struggles many African American women have faced, including struggles with (and sometimes against) forms of feminism that have elided or suppressed the differences that exist among women of various classes, races, ethnicities, and circumstances.

Each of the following interpretations will, in various ways, take up questions about the problematic of gendered, sexualized, and violent imagery in Hosea 1–3. What does it mean that the relation of humanity to the divine is figured in terms of a human relationship? If the relationship between the divine and the human represents the huge gulf between two types of quite different quality and power, how does the hierarchy and distance implied in that relationship echo in the relationship of marriage to which it is analogized? How does gender figure in the relationship? What does it mean that God is analogous to a powerful husband, that humanity is likened to a loose woman? What happens to human relationships in this economy?

EXEMPLARY BIBLICAL READINGS

To the extent that religious language and metaphors are not bankrupt as some tend to suppose, that at least in some settings they continue to inspire, mobilize, convict, instruct, challenge, and transform, then the question of the insights and limitations of biblical metaphors should be a priority for all theological enterprises devoted to liberation, especially those who propose to speak for the alienated. Biblical metaphors are not simply examples of grandiloquence, not just instances of literary embellishment where the prophet rather naively or in a moment of inspiration expressed somewhat overdramatically what could have been stated more directly. Instead, they are explicitly what all human language is implicitly, analogical, and therefore limited. Although already doomed to failure, religious language represents human beings' desperate attempts to comprehend and articulate what is in fact beyond comprehension and articulation, the Divine and our experience of it. Biblical metaphors simply heighten our defeat. Biblical metaphors such as one which depends on sexual violence to make its point simply highlight our defeat. (Weems, 1989:101)

With these lines, Renita Weems draws to a close her reading of Hosea 1–3, in which the turbulent relationship between Yahweh and Israel is evoked through the metaphor of a human marriage between the prophet and an *'eset zenûmîm,* an "unfaithful woman."[1] Central to Weems's reading is the conviction that one may not simply explain away elements of biblical literature that modern sensibilities might find problematic or objectionable in order to produce a more congenial reading. Language must be taken seriously for the meanings it produces. At the same time, Weems does not reify language but asserts its contingent status, no less than its strategic potential. One committed to liberation can marvel at the ingenuity of a metaphor to represent a complex and volatile referent, but one must extend one's engagement with the metaphor to look also at the consequences of its use, its potential effects (89–90).

Weems situates her own engaged mode of interpretation within two specific realms, feminist biblical scholarship on the one hand, and black and womanist biblical scholarship on the other (90, n. 10). Her reading weaves together literary and historical questions with liberationist concerns, so that what results from the convergence of these approaches to interpretation is a complex matrix. One cannot read her essay as conventional biblical scholarship merely glossed by literary theory, feminism, and black womanism—a

---

[1] This is Weems's translation (see Weems, 1989:90 n. 11 for an explanation and examples of various commentators' translations). Other interpreters have highlighted the sexual connotations of the Hebrew. See Setel, esp. 89–91, where Setel translates the term *wife of harlotry* in order to emphasize the sexual and gendered specificity of the term. For other discussion of the Hebrew root *zonah,* see Bird and, in a different textual context, Bal, 1988a:80–93.

foundation on which thin layers of additives have been applied. Rather her reading presents itself as a subtle imbrication—a layering or interweaving—a braiding together of constitutive elements each of which contributes to the pattern of the whole in a substantial way.

Weems's reading of the imagery in Hosea 2 is unmistakeably theological; that is, the problem of the text emerges for her out of the conflict between two competing values. She describes divine retribution as based on "the presumably sound theological notion that the deity has the right to punish the people," a notion that is problematized when it is figured literarily by "the image of a husband physically retaliating against his wife" where "his right to do so [becomes] unquestionable" (87). Threats of violence to the unfaithful wife do not simply punctuate the text ornamentally, but rather lend structure and contour to the poem in 2:4–25 (95). Given the foundational nature of the imagery, Weems cannot simply excise the troubling elements and reclaim a purer and more congenial text; she rather must engage head-on the conflict between the sound theological notion and the politically problematic imagery of violence in which it is embedded. She does so by reflecting on the nature of metaphor.

The marriage metaphor, she argues, is particularly versatile for describing the relationship between the divine and the human, highlighting the emotive dimensions of that relationship in ways that other metaphors cannot (99). At the same time, the metaphor presents profound difficulties by associating God with sexual violence (100). Here Weems turns to the work of theologian Sallie McFague who articulates the necessity of maintaining a vibrant tension between the similarities and dissimilarities of the two elements compared within a metaphor. That is, McFague argues that there is a risk in any successful metaphor, any metaphor that collapses the distance between signification and referent (McFague). As Weems puts it, "a risky metaphor gives rise to a risky deduction. . . . It is the risk of oversimplification and rigid correspondence" (100). She urges, then, a reading of the metaphor as partially useful and argues along with McFague for a diversity of metaphors and resistance to the privileging of a few (100–101).

Weems's reading of the Hosea passage occurs within a specific interpretive frame, its interests rendered more clearly visible by their immediate textual context.[2] The essay under discussion appears in a 1989 issue of *Semeia*, a

---

[2] This line of analysis is suggested by Gallop's work on feminist literary theory anthologies produced in the late 1970s and early 1980s; see Gallop, 1992.

journal bearing the subtitle, "an experimental journal for biblical criticism." The issue is organized around the theme "Interpretation for Liberation." *Semeia* has, since its inception in 1974, situated itself in explicit contrast to the dominant modes of interpretation within the biblical studies scene (Wilder, 1974:1–16). Both ironically and appropriately, therefore, Elisabeth Schüssler Fiorenza, co-editor of "Interpretation for Liberation," introduces the essays by Weems and others with the statement, "The essays in this issue of *Semeia* are *different*" (Schüssler Fiorenza 1989a:1, emphasis ours): "They do not focus either on the discussion of a new literary critical method, nor on the introduction of sociological or anthropological theories, nor on the exploration of a certain biblical book or theological topic. Neither Bultmann nor Albright, Troeltsch nor Geertz, Derrida nor Foucault are their exegetical or theoretical 'Godfathers.' Rather they speak from social contexts, hermeneutical points of view, and theological interests quite different from those of Euro-American Christian biblical scholarship" (1).

The founders of *Semeia* understood themselves to be creating a new and experimental journal; by issue number 47, just fifteen years later, what was "new" and "experimental" has, according to Schüssler Fiorenza, been folded into the mix of "Euro-American Christian biblical scholarship," a mix whose sameness is to be distinguished from the "difference" both of the essays included in the volume and of their authors whom Schüssler Fiorenza describes as "the quintessential Other in the dominant white male academy" (1). Although Schüssler Fiorenza's construction of the center and the margins here might well be greeted with a certain amount of contention—there is ample debate about the character of marginality in much cultural criticism these days (Russell Ferguson et al.)—more striking is the implicit deconstructive move of the essays in the volume. That is, by laying bare precisely those questions rendered unanswerable by traditional biblical scholarship, by doing so in the journal most widely known for its experimental edge and thereby calling its previous forty-six issues into question, this particular issue of *Semeia* performs a postmodern act even when it does so while separating itself from postmodern theory. (It should be noted, of course, that the critique of theory here is itself a theoretical move.) Weems's reading of Hosea is framed by this gesture and participates in it.

The tension of sameness-difference in the volume is augmented by a tension concerning theological interestedness, recognizable in Schüssler Fiorenza's phrase, "Euro-American *Christian* biblical scholarship" (emphasis ours). Weems's essay emerges out of both political and theological concerns,

concerns that have often been linked historically and of necessity in the experience of African Americans.[3] As a consequence of the particular history of many African Americans' relationship to the Bible, Schüssler Fiorenza notes, Weems is reticent to lend support to a hermeneutical critique of biblical authority, a critique Schüssler Fiorenza has argued elsewhere is essential to feminist hermeneutics of liberation (Schüssler Fiorenza, 1989a:4; 1984). This difference between white feminist hermeneutics and black womanist interpretations points to but one of the areas where feminism and womanism may follow divergent, and perhaps even contradictory, paths; it will be explored further below in the discussion of the hermeneutics of recuperation and the hermeneutics of survival.

Weems's reading, then, is a strategic and engaged one. It does not reify linguistic formulations, nor does it excuse them. It is a reading located within an ethical frame, one willing to assert that "some metaphors . . . tend to create more problems than they solve" (101). At the same time, it is a reading caught up in multiple tensions, a reading at once critical and faithful, one attempting to speak from a complex of political, theological, and ethical allegiances. As Weems puts it early on in her essay: "In short, as a feminist biblical scholar, this writer is concerned about motifs and texts which rely upon the physical and sexual abuse of a *woman* to develop its larger, presumably congenial, theological point about divine love and retribution. As a black and womanist biblical scholar this writer is concerned about motifs and texts which rely upon the physical and sexual exploitation of *anyone* to develop its larger, presumably congenial theological point" (Weems 1989:90, n. 10). Weems's treatment of the text reflects these multiple affiliations, identities, and commitments; the tensions in her reading between critique and recuperation are grounded in the intricate relations produced in one who is simultaneously feminist and black and womanist and a biblical scholar.

The theological conflict Weems encounters in her reading of Hosea is diagnosed bluntly by Tikva Frymer-Kensky in her chapter "The Wanton Wife of God": "From the point of view of modern society, this is a pathological relationship: God has married a promiscuous wife and Israel has entered a punitive relationship with a dominant husband" (146). Frymer-Kensky

---

[3] This connection has been discussed and emphasized most recently by Gilkes, 1989; Wimbush, 1989a, 1989b, 1991; and for African American women in particular, see Weems, 1991.

is less concerned to engage this problem from a contemporary standpoint, that is, to assess how the metaphor might enable contemporary "pathological relationships." Rather, she is interested in seeing how this metaphor fits into the monotheistic innovation of ancient Israel, as well as to situate it historically in reference to ancient Israelite society.

Frymer-Kensky argues that the marriage metaphor found in Hosea and other biblical writings to symbolize the relationship between God and Israel is made possible by Israel's gender system "which combines the social inequality of the sexes with an ideological construction of the essential sameness of men and women" (144). Furthermore, the hierarchical nature of Israelite marriage makes the metaphor possible, at the same time as the metaphor is also slippery and not referential to the lived social reality in ancient Israelite society (insofar as it does not correspond to the legal norms of marriage in that society).

Frymer-Kensky sees the metaphor as particularly evocative, however, precisely because it resonates with powerful concerns within ancient Israelite society. That is, to use the image of unconfined female sexuality as a figure for religious apostasy, sexual infidelity for religious infidelity, taps into a source of enormous anxiety for the society that produces the text. This is not to argue that the text is descriptive of women's lives in ancient Israel, but rather to suggest that the metaphor functions as a projection of male fears about women's sexual autonomy. Like Weems, Frymer-Kensky sees in this metaphor multiple evocations which for her are also theologically powerful: "The closeness and intensity of the bond can be as terrible as they can be wonderful. The marital metaphor reveals the dramatic inner core of monotheism: the awesome solo mastery of God brings humans into direct unadulterated contact with supreme power" (152).

Once again, the immediate context of an argument can offer some insight into its meanings. Frymer-Kensky's reading of Hosea is situated within a book that traces the movement from pagan polytheism toward biblical monotheism. Throughout the book, Frymer-Kensky describes what she sees to be a central paradox within ancient Israelite ideology: that human beings occupy a socially hierarchical relationship with respect to gender while remaining equal ontologically. Viewing this paradox as an innovation of the Israelite tradition over its cultural neighbors, Frymer-Kensky reads the dominant metaphor of the passage as a strikingly appropriate *and* disturbing one for the relationship between the human and the divine. Unlike Weems, she does not call into question the adequacy of the metaphor for making its theological point; rather, she suggests that the very tension embodied in the marriage metaphor is itself peculiarly evocative.

A rather different interpretive stance is taken by Mary Joan Winn Leith in what might be termed an anthropological rendering of the Hosea text (Leith). Leith argues that the text may be read as a mythic articulation of the creation of Israel, a creation myth in which Israel journeys through three movements (accusation, punishment, restoration), which mirror the pattern of typical rites of passage with their own tripartite transformative structure (separation, transition, incorporation). This process of mythic retelling serves the prophet's interests in critiquing the historical experience of Israel. As Leith puts it, "Hosea takes advantage of the mythic and cultural symbols at his command to mark off the distinction between the Israel he sees and the Israel Israel thinks it is" (98). "Woman" is used here absolutely metaphorically, in no way standing for historically constituted women but as a theoretical or literary device. The text does not describe anything about women, but rather uses available gender imagery to make a point about something else; the author, in other words, is "using gender to think with." [4]

One can see the effects of this process most clearly in the disjuncture between the image and the reality, that is, in the recognition that Hosea's prophecies are addressed to the elite men of Israel, not to Israelite women. By using the image of the wicked woman, Hosea deploys a literary technique of reversal; by calling Israelite men "women," he conveys that things are not as they should be (98). Oddly enough for this reading, the woman is not transformed back into a man through the process of reconciliation; rather, Israel remains at the end of the text metaphorically a woman, though by now the image has been recuperated. Leith's reading, most removed from theological concerns, experiences the least tension or conflict over the violence described in the text; its careful demarcation of the text as mythic creates a certain crucial distance between what is narrated in the text and lived experience.

Leith's essay, in contrast to the two preceding ones, does not address the text from a theologically interested perspective. As Peggy Day suggests in the introduction to the volume in which it appears, *Gender and Difference in Ancient Israel* published in 1989, "the contributors to this volume are

---

[4] This felicitous formulation belongs to Karen King, personal communication, May 1991. See also Joan W. Scott, 1988 and, in relation to ancient religious texts, Michael A. Williams.

not united by a shared theological stance vis-à-vis the value, or indeed the relevance, of the biblical texts in the modern world" (Day, 1989a:1). Yet, as she also points out, theological questions are but one set of questions that feminist perspectives can help to answer (2–3). Interestingly, Leith's reading focuses more on questions of gender than on the possible living referents for the metaphors of husband and wife in the text.

None of the readings summarized here, nor all of them collectively, exhausts the range of interpretations one might present of the text in question. Each interpreter situates herself rather differently in relation to the text and therefore asks different questions. The intersection of politics and theology, for example, in Renita Weems's article highlights the problem of power in the text. Tikva Frymer-Kensky's historical and theological concerns cause her to emphasize both the disjunctures between the imagery and life in ancient Israel and the ideological evocativeness of the marriage metaphor. Seeing the text more as artifact than living scripture has created a space for Mary Leith to analyze the operations of gender within the mythic plane of the text.

Each reading reflects a renegotiation of the early stage of feminist interventions into biblical and other literary texts, what one might call the "images of women" stage. As feminist and womanist scholarship has developed, a sophistication in dealing with images and the broader problem of representation emerges. "Images of women" approaches have been supplanted by more focus on discourse and ideology. The task is no longer simply rediscovering the "lost" women of the Bible or isolating a transhistorical image of "woman" to be translated in a simple or unproblematized fashion into other cultural idioms. These first attempts to understand women in the Bible were naively focused on the image, perceived to be in some measure a distortion of reality, and one obvious corrective lay in the attempt to reconstruct that reality historically. Such a move may rely on essentialist presuppositions concerning woman and her reality, though it need not, especially if it is radically historicized. One may then use that reconstructed reality to reflect upon the ideological or rhetorical effect of a distorting discourse: in other words, if an image explicitly does *not* reflect reality, what exactly is it saying about reality? How does it serve to shape or transform reality?

In the three readings under discussion here, one can see different strategies for coping with this perceived disjuncture between image and reality, language and experience. Weems argues that it is in the nature of language itself to fall short of representing adequately theological reality. Frymer-

Kensky discerns a relation between the metaphor and the reality but shifts the focus of reality, suggesting that the metaphor reflects not women's reality but men's psychological reality projected onto women's bodies. Leith finds in the metaphor a reflection of reality-off-center or reality-turned-upside-down: Israel figured as a woman demonstrates that all is not right with the world. In each case, the interpreter finds her starting point at the recognition that the text presents a problem; each in some measure understands her reading to provide (at least) a (partial) solution. Each sees the problem residing in the capacity of language to reflect, shape, or underwrite relationships of power across time and cultures in short, in the ideological force of discourse. Each also believes in the redemptive power of interpretation, the transformative prerogative of reading.

What feminism and womanism have brought to the interpretive scene is a carefully differentiated focus on the problem of "woman" in the text, the ideological uses of language to authorize and sustain certain relationships of domination, and the way that gender has often been used across historical periods and cultural contexts to signify and support domination. As this work has been done, we have moved away from approaches grounded in the notion that texts simply mirror or distort reality and toward theorizing founded in the view that texts are constructors of and interactive partners with experience, a category helpfully problematized and deconstructed in recent years by numerous theorists.[5] It is to this matrix of politics and theory that we now turn.

FEMINISM, WOMANISM, AND THE
POLITICS OF INTERPRETATION

The phrase "as a woman" is the Trojan horse of feminist ethnocentrism.
—Elizabeth V. Spelman (13)

What has come to be called "feminist interpretation of the Bible" is not parallel to the other interpretive strategies explored in this volume insofar as *feminism* is itself not a method of reading, but rather both a set of political positions and strategies and a contested intellectual terrain. The political

---

[5] On the question of "women's experience," see in particular Chandra Mohanty, 1988; Judith Grant; Joan W. Scott, 1992a.

impulse of feminist critique grows out of some women's encounters with institutions (be they religious, social, or academic) and their interpretations of those encounters. When the intellectual categories of received traditions were found to be inadequate for thinking about the meanings of such encounters, feminism provided some new conceptual vocabulary organized around such notions as "women's experience," "androcentrism," "patriarchy," and so on. Many of these notions now seem naive, quaint, or imprecise and are used now only hesitantly, framed by quotation marks to signal the difficulty; still, they functioned (for a time and for some) as helpful ideas for refocusing some aspects of discussions of culture.

Feminist and womanist critiques of the Bible are situated within this intellectual trajectory and are not simply a gloss upon the historical-critical paradigm in which most "legitimate" biblical scholarship is grounded. It is not without significance that the historical-critical paradigm springs from the Enlightenment, the same intellectual current that put "man" at the center of understanding. Central to feminist critique is a critique of the humanist gesture that positioned "man" at the center of subjectivity, discourse, and epistemology, a self-identical and ahistorical agent who occupies not merely a particular space, but the normative and universal position whose perspective is privileged and subsumes all others. Womanist interpretation carries the critique a step further by observing that the unmarked category "man" is not coterminous with "all men," but rather stands for men of particular racial and class privileges. Womanism has gone on to point out that "woman," for all her specificity, has tended with remarkable regularity in feminist discourse to mirror the universalizing moves of "man." Still, both feminist and womanist approaches call into question the possibility of a universal knowledge and a scientific objectivity possessed by a supposedly positionless "man." Feminist and womanist theory assert that the unmarked category "man" is an abstraction masking the contingent and power-steeped positionality of all historical agents. Both call for a suspicion of methods that claim universalism and objectivity as part of their own production, of which the historical-critical paradigm within biblical studies certainly counts as one.

Feminist and womanist interpretations have both functioned in counterpoint to these universalist and objective claims, attempting instead to assert forms of counter-knowledge or what Foucault called "subjugated knowledges." In so doing, womanism in particular has challenged not only the abstraction "man" but also the abstraction "woman," pointing out the ways in which feminism has been at various moments complicitous with dominant modes of thought, merely inverting them rather than transforming them.

This is perhaps nowhere clearer than in the arena of feminist interpretation of the Bible, a major strand of whose history in North America leads back to the controversial nineteenth-century work of suffragist and women's rights activist Elizabeth Cady Stanton, *The Woman's Bible*. The devastating white supremacy that characterized Stanton's work for the enfranchisement of white propertied women (often through explicitly racist rhetoric which elevated white women's claims to a privileged position over against those of people [men] of color) situates her as a extraordinarily troubling emblem for white feminism, no less than for feminist biblical interpretation.[6] We are caught in the tension of, on the one hand, the commitment to repudiate the racism of her work (and of the broader expressions of feminism for which her work stands as synecdoche) and therefore the concomitant desire to distance ourselves from this feminism and, on the other hand, the recognition that we must also be in some way accountable for this history and may not simply erase it as discomforting.

Therefore, this theoretical overview does not begin with Stanton's work, but rather examines the debates about multiple identities and the differences they make within feminist investigation. *Feminist* will need to be read as a problematized term throughout this discussion because it does not represent a singular monolithic position. Rather, there are various feminisms, modulations that generally express rather different and perhaps incompatible political positions: liberal feminism, radical feminism, Marxist or socialist feminism.[7] Each of these categories points to the overlap of feminisms with other theoretical constructs that contribute to a distinctive approach to the analysis of gender. Each also possesses a particular epistemological stance, with liberal feminism aligning itself with a universalist understanding of human nature (the essential sameness of human beings); radical feminism finding its most congenial categories within a kind of essentialism (the radical difference of men and women qua men and women); and Marxist or

---

[6] The history of the distancing and eventual severance of women's suffrage from the cause of black suffrage and the racist ideology and discourse that underwrote this split is analyzed by Davis, Giddings, and, more recently, Caraway, 117–67. This history's continued presence as a stumbling block for coalitions between black and white women is noted by many authors, but see especially Delores S. Williams, 45–47.

[7] One could add various other categories, such as psychoanalytic feminism, postmodern feminism, liberationist feminism; although not explicitly political positions, they have their own particular formulations of feminism. For an overview of such positions, see Eisenstein; Tong.

socialist feminism understanding gender differences to be socially produced and constructed.

Feminism's contributions to the theory and practice of interpretation include certain conceptual innovations that offer new ways of looking at culture and history. The first of these is the notion of gender as a crucial and foundational category for the analysis of culture (history, literature, social relations, and political arrangements). Gender in this view is not merely the meanings that accrue to the biological "facts" of sexual difference, but also a way of signifying power (Joan W. Scott, 1988:42). An unmarked feminism might argue that gender is *the* crucial analytic category, as some have tried to assert that sexual difference and male dominance is the historically prior model for all other oppressions (see Lerner).[8] Others, like Sheila Briggs, for example, would argue that the notion of gender itself must be historicized and particularized with respect to culture; as Briggs puts it rather provocatively, "Twentieth-century women are not the gender to which the New Testament household codes admonished obedience to their husbands" (Briggs, 1990:285). Gender is not only a historically varied and discontinuous category, it also does not affect all women in the same way nor any woman in the same way all the time. Attending to these distinctions will be crucial to a more nuanced understanding of gender's workings.

Whatever version of feminism one might embrace, there remains an important and trenchant critique of the very notion of feminism among women who have been uncomfortable with the assumptions underlying much U.S. feminist discourse—particularly, that there is a self-evident commonality among women because they are women and that feminism itself is a self-evident politics for women because they are women.[9] *Womanist* has become a name taken over by many women of color, especially black women, who have critiqued the feminist movement for being, at heart, a white (middle-class) movement.[10] Womanist criticism has produced some important inter-

---

[8] Some forms of ecofeminism make such an argument by locating the possibility for the domination of nature in a two-stage process: first, the domination of women by men and, second, the symbolic linkage of women and nature in patriarchal fantasy.

[9] Mohanty calls this the "feminist osmosis theory": "Feminism is not defined as a highly contested political terrain; it is the mere effect of being female. . . . Females are feminists by association and identification with the experiences which constitute us as female" (1988:32).

[10] *Womanist* is a neologism coined by Alice Walker (xi):

1. From *womanish*. (Opp. of "girlish," i.e., frivolous, irresponsible, not serious.) A black feminist or feminist of color. From the black folk expression of mothers to female children, "You acting womanish," i.e., like a woman. Usually referring to outrageous, audacious, courageous

pretations of biblical texts, perhaps most importantly challenging feminist criticism by calling into question the traditional feminist view that the foundational unequal power relation is that of men to women. Womanist critics have pointed out that not all men have access to the same kinds of power nor have all women historically embraced each other as sisters, but rather some have been responsible for the oppression of others. Race and class concerns generally are more clearly confronted and articulated in womanist critique than in most feminist interpretation, though there are some changes on that front.

As seen in Renita Weems's terminology cited above, *feminism* and *womanism* were differential (if not oppositional) terms; and clearly the category of "womanism" has been crucial for work in the study of religion.[11] At the same time, other thinkers have urged that "feminism" as a category not be left to its historically limited definition but rather must be claimed and expanded. As bell hooks has put it in a recent dialogue concerning race and class within the framework of feminism:

> We foster an illusion that white people own this particular discourse in a way that people of color do not. . . . Reconstructing categories and allowing for race

---

or *willful* behavior. Wanting to know more and in greater depth than is considered "good" for one. Interested in grown-up doings. Acting grown up. Being grown up. Interchangeable with another black folk expression: "You trying to be grown." Responsible. In charge. *Serious.* 2. *Also:* A woman who loves other women, sexually and/or nonsexually. Appreciates and prefers women's culture, women's emotional flexibility (values tears as a natural counterbalance of laughter), and women's strength. Sometimes loves individual men, sexually and/or nonsexually. Committed to survival and wholeness of entire people, male *and* female. Not a separatist, except periodically, for health. Traditionally universalist, as in: "Mama, why are we brown, pink, and yellow, and our cousins are white, beige, and black?" Ans.: "Well, you know the colored race is just like a flower garden, with every color flower represented." Traditionally capable, as in: "Mama, I'm walking to Canada and I'm taking you and a bunch of other slaves with me. Reply: "It wouldn't be the first time." 3. Loves music. Loves dance. Loves the moon. *Loves* the Spirit. Loves love and food and roundness. Loves struggles. *Loves* the Folk. Loves herself. *Regardless.* 4. Womanist is to feminist as purple is to lavender.

See also Ogunyemi for an early definition of womanism.

[11] The work in this arena is diverse and ever-growing. As examples, see Jacquelyn Grant; Cannon, 1988; Sanders, et al.; Clarice Martin, 1990, 1991. For further literature, see Kelly Brown (cited in Clarice Martin, 1990:41 n. 1). It was only very recently, at the 1990 annual meeting, that the American Academy of Religion included a consultation titled "Womanist Approaches to Religion and Society" that systematically brings together historical, ethical, scriptural, and theological presentations organized around the experiences of African American women.

and class have to include challenging that notion of white authority and origin, which is so crucial to the history of white supremacy and intellectual hegemonic domination. . . . [A] lot of black women would say . . . [that] feminism belongs to white women, they originated it, it is a form of analysis that only takes into account their experience. Therefore we shouldn't be involved with it; we should come up with our own terms, like womanist, that allow us to name specifically what we are doing. I would argue that it makes more sense to expand categories. (Childers and hooks, 66)

It would, moreover, be an error to suggest that while white Euro-American women of a certain class (because of particular ties to the intellectual products of the Enlightenment) were first to call themselves feminists, they were necessarily the first or only women involved in "gender activism,"[12] that is, some kind of public activity on behalf of women. On the contrary, as recent historical work on the public lives of many African American women has shown, womanism is no late addition to the scene, but rather has deep roots in the intellectual and political work of the nineteenth century, roots that in some cases reach more deeply into the past than those of white feminism (Barkley; Caraway, 117–67; Carby). Our usage of these terms here will try to attend to these important differences, which make it crucial not to universalize "feminism" nor to leave it as an unmarked category.

This characterization of unmarked feminism as being concerned, really, with white, middle-class, heterosexual, U.S. women as the norm is not a recent phenomenon; nor have some white feminists been completely unaware of the problem. The theoretical problem for feminism becomes double-edged —how to speak oppositionally about "women in general" as a counter-discourse to the hegemonic patriarchal discourse which uses "man" as the unmarked norm, at the same time as to remark upon the significant differences among women in terms of class, race, ethnicity, religious identity, sexual orientation, national allegiance, and so on. Further, feminism risks making colonizing gestures the more inclusive it tries to become, insofar as "feminist" remains at the center of the discourse and remains the lens

---

12 This term, *gender activism* is one coined by Margot Badran to denote activism on behalf of women even when the activists themselves do not call themselves feminists and, indeed, may well reject the term. Although her phrase emerged out of her work on feminism and Islamic fundamentalism in Egypt, it seems more broadly useful in contexts where one seeks to discern whether they may not be points of common political ground. Badran introduces the term in a discussion of feminist and Islamist developments in contemporary Egyptian society, linking gender activism more broadly to questions of identity politics (see esp. Badran, 211–21).

through which one examines the issues.[13] For example, in a rather early attempt in the recent wave of feminist critique to take some of these issues into account, Phyllis Trible defines feminism in this way: "By feminism I do not mean a narrow focus upon women, but rather a critique of culture in light of misogyny. This critique affects the issues of race and class, psychology, ecology, and human sexuality" (Trible, 1978:7). True enough, and yet the practice of making those effects felt becomes a more difficult process. This is not to undercut the important critiques that feminist theories have brought nor to blame Trible (or other critics) for not getting it right, but rather to continue to raise the problematic of the partiality of theory and the difficulties its applications, even when accompanied by legitimate and serious good intentions, present.

Additionally, it is particularly important within feminist biblical criticism to analyze differences among women on the basis of religious identity, a set of differences usually only briefly acknowledged and too easily elided by Christian feminists who dominate the field of feminist biblical criticism. Such elision can be discerned in the language of Carolyn Gifford who writes in a historical essay on American women's relation to the Bible: "For over three and one-half centuries the Christian faith and its sacred book, the Bible, have been a shaping influence in the lives of American women," (11) where the implication is that "Christian" and "American" are coterminous; Jewish American women—who presumably have some relation to the "sacred book, the Bible"—are erased. Again, the point here is not to single out Gifford's linguistic slip but to suggest that examples of the conceptual conflation the slip represents are numerous and may be encountered with a remarkable regularity in the writings of Christian feminist biblical scholars.[14]

Womanism is both a critique of white Western feminism insofar as it has privileged gender as a unique source of oppression and category of analysis, as well as an articulation of women's historical experiences lived out

---

[13] Delores S. Williams warns against the universalizing potential of some white feminist discourse and the relative usefulness of certain feminist concepts, such as patriarchy, putting her argument bluntly in this way: "The implication of all the preceding discussion is that black women, *in their relation to white-controlled American institutions,* do not experience patriarchy" (51).

[14] One could carry the critique further, as both Canadian and Latin American feminists have on numerous occasions, and note that the term *American* being used to refer to women in the United States erases all the other nationalities within the Americas or subsumes them under the United States.

within multiple (sometimes competing) identities. Feminism ought to provide such a framework for analysis; its failure to do so has produced both the debates around race, class, ethnicity, religious identity, sexual orientation, among others, and new frameworks such as womanism to try to redress the deficiency. Some have raised the question of the value in trying to redeem feminism—in whose interests is such a redemption sought? One strategy might be, in fact, to abandon feminism because of its considerable Enlightenment failures; however, feminism, as bell hooks and others affirm, exceeds its conceptual and practical shortcomings and need not be left to be defined only by those shortcomings. Indeed, as Elizabeth Weed argues, the challenge is "to keep 'women' in a citational mode . . . to keep at bay truths too easily produced by cultural and political formations" (Weed, 1989:xxxi). Perhaps the question should be reframed: not, in whose interests is the redemption of feminism sought, but rather, in whose interests is the abandonment of feminism pursued?

Still, it is precisely these conceptual complexities that make the phrase "as a woman" so problematic at this juncture in the history of feminist thought. Not only, as Denise Riley has argued so persuasively, is the category of "woman" itself remarkably unstable (precisely because of its level of abstraction), but also "woman" does not exhaust the identities of "women" (see Riley; Butler, 1990). As Sheila Briggs has put it: "Our different identities impose different loyalties upon us. Thus women of color experience ambivalence in the women's movement not, I would argue, because it is a white women's movement, since there is and there has long been autonomous feminisms of color. To be a black woman is to embody two identities which call for disparate analyses and political commitments. To live with differently stigmatized identities, with a combination of stigmatized and privileged identities makes it hard sometimes to find one's face in the mirror" (Briggs, 1990:284). The problem of identity is linked to the problem of essentialism, as many theorists have pointed out. Patricia Hill Collins articulates the tension as one between essentialism and idealism in the context of discussing who can be a black feminist and what constitutes black feminist thought. Embracing an ideological definition and eschewing racialist biological definitions that presume a particular consciousness simply because one shares African descent (just as being a woman does not necessarily mean one is a feminist), Collins puts the point in this way:

> A definition of Black feminist thought is needed that avoids the materialist position that being Black and/or female generates certain experiences that automati-

cally determine variants of a Black and/or feminist consciousness. Claims that Black feminist thought is the exclusive province of African American women, regardless of the experiences and worldview of such women, typify this position. But a definition of Black feminist thought must also avoid the idealist position that ideas can be evaluated in isolation from the groups that create them. Definitions claiming that anyone can produce and develop Black feminist thought risk obscuring the special angle of vision that Black women bring to the knowledge production process. (Patricia Hill Collins, 21)

Another side to the essentialist problematic is a kind of political essentialism, the conflation of an ideology of authenticity with that of identity, that is, the unexamined notion of a true core of identity. In her essay "Not You/ Like You: Post-Colonial Women and the Interlocking Questions of Identity and Difference," filmmaker and theorist Trinh T. Minh-Ha writes:

> Identity as understood in the context of a certain ideology of dominance has long been a notion that relies on the concept of an essential, authentic core that remains hidden to one's consciousness and that requires the elimination of all that is considered foreign or not true to the self, that is to say, not-I, other. In such a concept the other is almost unavoidably either opposed to the self or submitted to the self's dominance. It is always condemned to remain its shadow while attempting at being its equal. Identity, thus understood, supposes that a clear dividing line can be made between I and not-I, he and she; between depth and surface, or vertical and horizonal identity; between us here and them over there. The further one moves from the core the less likely one is thought to be capable of fulfilling one's role as the real self, the real Black, Indian or Asian, the real woman. The search for an identity is, therefore, usually a search for that lost, pure, true, real, genuine, original, authentic self, often situated within a process of elimination of all that is considered other, superfluous, fake, corrupted or Westernized. (1988:71)

That politics are not inherent in identities is a conceptual complexity, but it is also a positive political opening that can enable transformation. That is, if "women" and "feminism" were exclusively and absolutely coterminous, then "feminism" would by definition lie outside of the category "men." It would be definitionally impossible for men to intersect with feminism. However, Beverly Guy-Sheftall, for example, can name Frederick Douglass and William E. B. Du Bois as black feminists precisely because of this nonidentity between politics and identity (54–57, cited in Patricia Hill Collins, 19). And this slippage between politics and identity can enable acts of solidarity within "imagined communities," to use Benedict Anderson's notion. As Chandra Mohanty puts it:

The idea of imagined community is useful because it leads us away from essential-ist notions of third world feminist struggles, suggesting political rather than bio-logical or cultural bases for alliance. Thus, it is not color or sex which constructs the ground for these struggles. Rather, it is the *way* we think about race, class, and gender—the political links we choose to make among and between struggles. Thus, potentially, women of all colors (including white women) can align them-selves with and participate in these imagined communities. However, clearly our relation to and centrality in particular struggles depend on our different, often conflictual, locations and histories. (Mohanty, 1991:4)

Françoise Lionnet, a Mauritanian literary critic, has produced an experi-mental theoretical model for reading these multiplicities within and slip-pages of identities, working with the concept of *métissage* that was intro-duced into cultural poetics by Martinican writer Edouard Glissant.[15] Lionnet argues that *métissage*, the braiding together of cultural forms, can open up a space where histories that have been occluded can find expression and where essentialisms can be replaced by diversity and movement. She writes:

Within the conceptual apparatuses that have governed our labeling of ourselves and others, a space is thus opened where multiplicity and diversity are affirmed. This space is not a territory staked out by exclusionary practices. Rather, it func-tions as a sheltering site, one that can nurture our differences without encouraging us to withdraw into new dead ends, without enclosing us within facile opposi-tional practices or sterile denunciations and disavowals. For it is only by imagining nonhierarchical modes of relation among cultures that we can address the crucial issues of indeterminacy and solidarity. . . . We can be united against hegemonic power only by refusing to engage that power on its own terms, since to do so would mean becoming ourselves a term within that system of power. We have to articulate new visions of ourselves, new concepts that allow us to think *otherwise*, to bypass the ancient symmetries and dichotomies that have governed the ground and the very condition of possibility of thought, of "clarity," in all of Western philosophy. *Métissage* is such a concept and a practice: it is the site of undecid-ability and indeterminacy, where solidarity becomes the fundamental principle of political action against hegemonic languages. (Lionnet, 5–6)

---

[15] Lionnet, who cites Glissant (1981; 1989). This line of theoretical work came to our at-tention through a paper by Laura Donaldson, presented at the 1990 American Academy of Religion panel "Womanist Approaches to the Study of Religion." Donaldson's essay has not yet been published, but she has kindly made a manuscript available to us and given permission for us to cite her work (see Laura E. Donaldson, 1990).

Lionnet's vision of a new liberatory cultural politics collapses the facile opposition between theory and practice, refuses reduction to a cog in the reigning machineries of power, and insists upon multiplicity as a radically new ground for thought. Rather than merely calling for the inversion of hegemonic power relations, her cultural politics of *métissage* demand a reformulation of the terms of debate and relation, a dispersion of power and identity into multiple locations simultaneously. As we move through an analysis of the work done by feminists and womanists on foundational textual traditions, we will hear some echoes of Lionnet's insistence on multiplicity and her challenge to rethink the contours of theory and practice.

HISTORY AND PRACTICE OF FEMINIST
AND WOMANIST READINGS

> Despite our desperate, eternal attempt to separate, contain, and mend, categories always leak.
> —Trinh T. Minh-Ha (1989:94)

Writing a history of an interpretive movement in its still-formative stages presents certain difficulties. Without a certain amount of distance, one's perspective may be skewed. Following out multiple trajectories of thought that overlap one another at certain points while contradicting each other at others can be frustrating. Many of these pathways are still being formed; therefore, this history is very much, in Foucault's sense, a history of the present.

The taxonomy by which this section is organized should not be understood in a thoroughly rigid way, for, as Trinh Minh-Ha points out, categories always leak. We have tried to group together works and approaches whose effects are similar; at the same time, we continue to be struck by the overlap of some of our categories and by the resistance or irony present in the categories. We have read all feminist and womanist readings of biblical texts as in some measure shaped by institutional constraints, constraints producing resisting readings. In so doing, we have been conscious that different readers face distinct institutional pressures in varying degrees. For some, the religious institution in which they work, think, and live shapes the contours of their constraint and their resistance. For others, the academic institution— be it a particular educational institution (college, university, seminary) or a discipline (like that of biblical studies itself)—provides the framework against which resistance is cast. For still others, social institutions—the family, marriage, or sexuality—constrain and confine, and the practice of reading against the grain becomes a resisting practice in that context. It is our position that feminist and womanist readings are always, in some measure, acts of resistance against some form of institutional constraint. Therefore, the outline that follows should not be read as an evolutionary model, pointing toward a utopian, pure form of feminist and womanist interpretation, anything short of which should be understood as false consciousness. Instead, we might remember Françoise Lionnet's appropriation of the concept of *métissage,* a "sheltering site" (5) allowing for solidarity across differences, a blending together, a weaving, a "crossover politics" of solidarity (Caraway, 171–203).

The Hermeneutics of Recuperation   In the various first-wave attempts to restore "women" to the biblical text, we locate a *hermeneutics of recuperation.* Often, such attempts were organized around images of women in the Bible, reclaiming the individual stories about specific women in the Bible (the matriarchs of the Pentateuch, the women around Jesus, and so on). The purpose was to redeem the tradition through the retrieval of strong foremothers, role models, characters with whom contemporary women located within religious communities and institutions might identify. Such works enact the rhetorical gesture embodied in the title of an important book for the reclamation of American women's history written in the mid-1970s: *"We Were There."*

The feminist hermeneutics of recuperation operates within a framework presupposing the naive identification between women across traditions, cultures, and historical periods; implicitly it claims that there exists a foundational and essential sameness among women, regardless of their circumstances, social location, historical context, and so on. Furthermore, often the recuperative move underwrites a particular form of personalism and avoids systemic analysis of the conditions of inequality or power asymmetry by focussing instead on individual exemplars whose complex implication within a matrix of social relations (constituted by the workings of power, gender ideology, racial and ethnic differences, class, and so on) is minimized or elided altogether. An interpretation emerging from this perspective seems capable of producing only the most individualized and decontextualized ethical reading, not an ethical critique of the social framework that enabled or rendered impossible particular narrative turns.

The hermeneutics of recuperation is driven by a clear theological impulse—the redemption of traditions which seem to many to be utterly incompatible with feminist interests. Biblical feminism argues, by contrast, that when interpreted properly, the Bible offers a feminist vision. Interpretation here is understood as an activity whose correct execution produces an authentic and unchanging biblical truth, while incorrect interpretation results in patriarchal distortions. Unlike other more critically oriented feminist interpretive strategies, the hermeneutics of recuperation remains thoroughly invested in the economy of truth and offers no critique of the philosophical grounds of the Bible's truth claims.

At the same time, it should be noted that the hermeneutics of recuperation also performs an important political function, insofar as it makes use of the tradition itself to rationalize change and justice both within society and in religious institutions. Some of the most important examples of this recuperative move may be found in the writings of nineteenth-century Protestant women seeking to justify their calls to religious leadership. In the *Memoirs of the Life, Religious Experience, Ministerial Travels and Labours of Mrs. Zilpha Elaw, an American Female of Colour; Together with Some Account of the Great Religious Revivals in America [Written by Herself]* originally published in 1846, the Methodist missionary articulated her own biblical hermeneutics of recuperation: "It is true, that in the ordinary course of Church arrangement and order, the Apostle Paul laid it down as a rule, that females should not speak in the church, nor be suffered to teach; but the Scriptures make it evident that this rule was not intended to limit the extraordinary directions of the Holy Ghost, in reference to female Evangelists, or oracular sisters; nor to be rigidly observed in peculiar circumstances" (Andrews, 124).

She goes on to cite important women in the early church, among them: Phoebe, the recipient of 2 John, Tryphena and Tryphosa, the sisters of Nereus, the mother of Rufus, the daughters of Philip, and "many other Christian females who promoted the cause of Jesus." In a similar fashion, the autobiographical *Life and Religious Experience of Jarena Lee*, which appeared for the first time in 1836, made use of the biblical assertion that women were the first to know and tell of the resurrection to justify women's claim to the authority to preach (Andrews, 36). And in a marvelous precursor to the historical-critical penchant to return to the primitive circumstances which produced the biblical text, Jarena Lee argues: "But some will say, that Mary did not expound the Scripture, therefore, she did not preach, in the proper sense of the term. To this I reply, it may be that the term *preach*, in those primitive times, did not mean exactly what it is now *made* to mean; perhaps it was a great deal more simple then, than it is now: if it were not, the unlearned fishermen could not have preached the gospel at all, as they had no learning" (Andrews, 36–37).

Such recuperative gestures toward the biblical text have several effects: they underwrite claims to authority by those who make them, even as they reauthorize the biblical text itself. Furthermore, they function to challenge the status quo of religious leadership, but only for a few individuals and only for the extraordinary. The hermeneutics of recuperation enacted by these nineteenth-century religious women were not initiated in a conscious attempt to promote a liberating agenda per se, although clearly they functioned in this way for a few special women. This hermeneutics opened the door for religious leadership for some women, though never through any direct challenge to or critique of biblical authority.[16]

This may be one occasion on which our categories leak. Although it is certainly the case that the hermeneutics of recuperation never calls for any kind of challenge to biblical authority, it is not clear that the refusal to challenge biblical authority necessarily implies a recuperative agenda. For example, Vincent Wimbush diagnoses a kind of internalization of white biblicism in some black churches' appropriation of biblical scholarship (Wimbush, 1989a), which is different language for the same phenomenon of recuperation. At the same time, others argue that "those without power and authority cannot afford to relinquish lightly any authorizing resource and heritage in the struggle for survival, freedom and dignity" (Schüssler Fiorenza, 1989a:4, citing Cannon, 1985). It is here, perhaps, that the hermeneutics of recuperation overlaps in significant ways with the third category in our taxonomy: the hermeneutics of survival.

The Hermeneutics of Suspicion The *hermeneutics of suspicion* is most immediately identified with the interpretive strategies promoted by Elisabeth

[16] A similar recuperative gesture may be found in the work of a nineteenth-century Sephardic Jewish woman, Grace Aguilar (1816–1847), whose two-volume work *The Women of Israel*, first published around 1831, appeared in at least three editions and was reprinted regularly until 1913. The subtitle of the work gives a sense of the sweep, hermeneutical focus, and strategy of reading employed in the volumes: or *Characters and sketches from the Holy Scriptures and Jewish History. Illustrative of the past history, present duties, and future destiny of the Hebrew females, as based on the Word of God.* Like the African American women's works under discussion, Aguilar's predates Elizabeth Cady Stanton's famous *Woman's Bible* by several decades. We thank Daniel Boyarin for bringing Aguilar's work to our attention.

Schüssler Fiorenza in her work appearing in the early 1980s, although they are enacted more broadly by a variety of feminists working in biblical interpretation. In contrast to feminist hermeneutics of recuperation, the hermeneutics of suspicion, in Schüssler Fiorenza's words, "does not presuppose the feminist authority and truth of the Bible, but takes as its starting point the assumption that biblical texts and their interpretations are androcentric and serve patriarchal functions" (Schüssler Fiorenza, 1984:15). The hermeneutics of suspicion goes further to argue that the evaluative key for the adequacy of biblical texts lies not within the text, but outside it in the social and political experience of liberation. Schüssler Fiorenza argues that "*the* litmus test for invoking Scripture as the Word of God must be whether or not biblical texts and traditions seek to end relations of domination and exploitation" (xiii). Such an argument shifts the location of an interpretation's authority to values external to the text. As Sheila Briggs puts it: "The liberation of oppressed groups and peoples is held to be the critical principle by which one judges between competing social positions and their knowledges/ interpretive strategies. One has moved from the authority of the text to the authority of social practices, from orthodoxy to orthopraxis.... A transmutation and transvaluation of hermeneutical categories has taken place which places normative value in the kind of social practices which aim at liberation of the oppressed" (Briggs, 1990: 277).

Locating interpretive authority outside the text in social practices causes the hermeneutics of suspicion to embrace and revalorize lived experience as a ground for both interpretation and ethics. Therefore, the retrieval of past experience (history) through strategies of reconstruction becomes a privileged part of the hermeneutics of suspicion (Brooten, 1985a; 1986; Hackett; Meyers; Moxnes; Schüssler Fiorenza, 1983; Wire). Indeed, the hermeneutics of suspicion is, to a degree, a thoroughly historical project, while it maintains its force in the present through its ethical and theological investments. That is, the hermeneutics of suspicion does not embody a simple and uncritical historicism. Rather, in varying degrees of explicitness, it poses questions concerning the uses of history in contemporary settings and concerning the very interestedness of history-writing itself. Furthermore, it asks what constitutes history and what theology, critically asserting that what has at times masqueraded as history is often a veiled theological agenda. Moreover, the hermeneutics of suspicion demands a reformation of the very structures of investigation, most often by arguing that as a corrective to androcentric perspectives, one must rather place women at the center of investigation. In calling for this kind of change in perspective, Bernadette Brooten argues that the entire terrain of historical interpretation will be altered:

> One who takes up the task of early Christian women's history discovers that the present framework of study is not suited to that task. . . . Placing women at the center of the study . . . will result in a different view of the relationship between religion and culture and between theology and society. If women are no longer relegated to the cultural background or the societal context, but are recognized as central for understanding early Christianity and its theology, a rethinking of the whole will be required. This will not mean a harmonious complementarity of women's history and men's history, simply adding the two together, thereby leaving the structures of male history and theology intact. Rather, early Christian women's history . . . demonstrates the fragmentary and perspectival nature of what has passed as early Christian history. (Brooten, 1985a:91)

In this sense, the hermeneutics of suspicion promotes a kind of deconstructive agenda, insofar as it lays bare the partialities, the lacunae, the aporias in what has passed as early Christian history in its entirety. At the same time, however, the hermeneutics of suspicion maintains a strong theological agenda, aimed not simply at restoring women to the center of history but to "the theological center or revelation" (Brooten, 1985a:66).

This strategy differs from the hermeneutics of recuperation in a number of ways. While sharing a historical interest, the hermeneutics of suspicion seeks less to retrieve individual women who might serve as objects of feminist identification for contemporary women than to restore a collective tradition. Even when traveling under the provocative and individualized title, *Discovering Eve,* Carol Meyers's book attempts to situate ancient Israelite women in their historical and social context rather than to recover the historical woman Eve from mythic construct in which her story is embedded. Indeed, the hermeneutics of suspicion is rather more willing to read Eve's story mythically, whereas the hermeneutics of recuperation might well desire to peel away the mythic chaff in order to expose the truth at the core. However, at the same time, the hermeneutics of suspicion remains very much a hermeneutics, that is, a mode of knowing that employs an ontology of discovery, assuming that there is some order in the world that stands on its own and that can be discovered or at least approached by human knowing. Truth is something discovered by employing a hermeneutics of suspicion, wherein one is suspicious of the various disguises that can cover up and distort reality. Interpretation values attunement with the discovered truth for its liberating potential: "Ye shall know the truth, and the truth shall set you free" (Kathy E. Ferguson, 326). Nevertheless, the hermeneutics of suspicion also maintains its critical investment and its resistant stance, largely through a focus on questions of method, as the work of scholars like Sheila Briggs, Elisabeth Schüssler Fiorenza, and Bernadette Brooten amply demonstrates.

The hermeneutics of suspicion is not limited to historical reconstruction, as central as this rewriting of the historical record is. Others situated within the hermeneutics of suspicion focus more on what one might broadly describe as literary questions, using rhetorical and literary methods to rethink the theological difficulties raised in the encounter between feminist values and androcentric religious literature. The work of Phyllis Trible is probably most emblematic of this strategy of reading, a critical strategy suspicious and recuperative at once. As Trible describes it, feminism functions theologically for her readings: "As a critique of culture and faith in light of misogyny, feminism is a prophetic movement, examining the status quo, pronouncing judgment, and calling for repentance" (Trible, 1984:3). Furthermore, her interpretations are interested readings, readings of texts "on behalf of their female victims," and readings aimed at "recover[ing] a neglected history, . . . remember[ing] a past that the present embodies, and . . . pray[ing] that these terrors shall not come to pass again" (3). The redemptive force of feminism in Trible's work is clear: "a feminist hermeneutic," she writes, "seeks to redeem the time" (3). In situating her feminist hermeneutic in this way, Trible joins with others who bring to their readings a focus on women's experience as a central ground for analysis and an ethic derived from an external set of claims regarding justice.

It is useful to note that the resistance enacted by most practitioners of the hermeneutics of suspicion takes place within liberal academic institutions linked to theological education—universities or seminaries.[17] In contrast to those feminists working in contexts where the Bible is authorized continuously, feminists taking up a hermeneutics of suspicion are not caught in the same kinds of recuperative positions and therefore are able, as Schüssler Fiorenza and others are, to call into question biblical authority while acting under another kind of authority, one linked to the commitment to liberation.

The contributions of the feminist hermeneutics of suspicion have been

---

[17] The university as a site of resistance and struggle has been discussed widely in recent literature. For a cogent discussion of the university as a site of feminist struggle, see Bannerji et al.; and as a site for the work of African American resistance, see hooks and West.

and continue to be substantial. Yet, recently they have been supplemented by another kind of hermeneutics, one also dedicated to liberatory ends but shaped by a rather different set of historical circumstances and constraints. Representing a diverse set of experiences of oppression from racist institutions in the United States to colonial domination across the globe the hermeneutics of survival articulate another layer in the *métissage* of feminism and womanism, the braiding together of multiple interests, forms of resistance, and responses to constraint.

The Hermeneutics of Survival Feminist and womanist biblical critique is not limited to the critique of biblical texts and of the methods by which one might read those texts but extends to a critique of social and political institutions, forces, and processes of domination. One begins to hear important resonances of such critiques in the hermeneutics of suspicion with its rejection of internal authority and its turn toward an authority grounded in an ethical commitment to liberation. However, a full-bodied critique of domination can be heard in the *hermeneutics of survival* (Delores Williams's term) articulated in various institutional and social locations, especially among African American theologians (men and women) and among interpreters from Latin America, Africa, and Asia.

For feminists outside of these communities, for feminists whose readings are shaped in large measure by different kinds of institutional constraints, the hermeneutics of survival present a special challenge. As Renita Weems puts it:

> An on-going challenge for scholars committed to a liberation perspective on the Bible is explaining how and why modern readers from marginalized communities continue to regard the Bible as a meaningful resource for shaping modern existence. . . . For example, feminist biblical scholars have made the helpful insights that the androcentric milieu of the ancient world pervades biblical texts, and they have convincingly demonstrated that specific texts are unalterably hostile to the dignity and welfare of women; because of these and other similar findings, these scholars are hard pressed to explain why large numbers of religious women (including feminists) still identify with many of the ideals and characters found in the Bible. (Weems, 1991:57)

Making use of literary theories that seek to account for the relation of the reader to the text, Weems argues that African American women's particular relation to the Bible is negotiated not simply through opposition but also through connection. As she puts it, "the Bible is in many ways alien and antagonistic to modern women's identity; yet, in other ways, it inspires and compels that identity" (Weems, 1991:59). Furthermore, she describes this hermeneutic of resistance not in terms primarily of an autonomous theory or articulated methodological stance, but rather in terms of a practice: the reading habits of African American women. Weems's reading of the relationship to African American women to biblical literature is an example of Lionnet's *métissage*, a theoretical practice that resists a singular form(ul)ation of identity while calling into question oppositional thinking, including the grounding opposition: theory-practice. Like much feminist and womanist critique in general, the hermeneutics of survival is linked inexorably to ethics.

As Weems understands it, "it has equally and more precisely to do with examining the *values* of those [African American women] readers and the corroboration of those values by the text; it has to do with how the text arouses, manipulates, and harnesses African American women's deepest yearnings" (Weems, 1991:59; emphasis hers). Like the hermeneutics of suspicion, which also demands an ethical commitment on the part of the interpreter (Schüssler Fiorenza, 1988), the hermeneutics of survival sets the relation between value and meaning in high relief. The difference between the two may be one of nuance rather than substance and may have once again to do with social and institutional location and the pressures and possibilities inhering in such contexts. That is, many practitioners of the hermeneutics of suspicion find themselves located in institutional contexts in which they claim multiple identities, identities shaped by both privilege and marginality. For white feminists in the academy, for example, who adhere to a program of hermeneutical suspicion, racial advantages *and* the absence of entitlements on the basis of gender lend a particular contour to their ethical stance. Their positions, if they are to be in solidarity with all other women and with men who do not have access to hegemonic power, must be shaped only partially self-interestedly. They must use the personal pronoun, "we," with special care when the predicate involves a statement concerning oppression and liberation. By contrast, at least at this juncture in the unfolding of liberatory hermeneutics, for the voices of the hermeneutics of survival, the "we" requires less hesitation or graduation. One can write, as Kwok Pui Lan does directly: "The Bible offers us insights for our survival" (Kwok, 38).

The hermeneutics of survival possesses a complex relation to both authority and truth claims. On the one hand, the hermeneutics of survival intensifies the self-authorization also visible in the hermeneutics of suspicion and may even call into question the monolithic character of truth, aligning this hermeneutics with some other postmodernist interpretive strategies. On the other hand, the hermeneutics of survival on other occasions makes rather straightforward claims to authority and truth. Rather than reading this multivalent relation to authority and truth as contradictory, it might be more useful to understand it as a strategic use of both authority and truth.

The hermeneutics of survival as a theologically invested interpretation has not as its goal simply to *understand* the world and therefore it is not grounded simply in what Kathy Ferguson calls the "ontology of discovery," (326) but rather is part of what Chung Hyun Kyung calls "a revolutionary praxis" geared toward *changing* the world (Chung, 113). Therefore, the act of interpretation that makes certain claims to biblical authority in this context may not be identical to the claims to biblical authority found in biblical feminism, or what we have called the hermeneutics of recuperation. Rather than beginning with biblical authority, the hermeneutics of survival starts at the point of struggle and may use biblical authority toward its own justice-oriented ends. This is a strategy different from arguing for an inherent meaning resident in an inspired text. It is a hermeneutics that distinguishes between a message of liberation hidden in a text and waiting for retrieval and a liberating reading performed by people engaged in a struggle against injustice. As Sheila Briggs sees it, it is "a hermeneutics which can probe beyond the structures of oppression, embedded in a text, to the possibilities of liberation *not given by the text but claimed from it by the oppressed*" (Briggs, 1989:151; emphasis ours).

Likewise, the hermeneutics of survival straddles two competing positions with respect to truth claims, calling into question the dominant Western tradition's monolithic system of truth while at the same time arguing that *truths* may be discerned from a whole range of cultural traditions, the Bible among them. In proposing a dialogical model of reading biblical texts, Kwok Pui Lan concludes: "In the end, we must liberate ourselves from a hierarchical model of truth which assumes there is one truth above many. This biased belief leads to the coercion of others into sameness, oneness, and homogeneity which excludes multiplicity and plurality" (Kwok, 38). She goes on to argue that the dialogical hermeneutics of survival must include "an open invitation" to other, perhaps competing truths. Here one hears echoes of Lionnet's *métissage*, the insistence on heterogeneity as a key to the resistance of domination.

Because many of the practitioners of a hermeneutics of survival possess identities shaped by multiple forces, constraints, and possibilities, it is often the case that they are particularly adept at locating with sharpness and clarity the resident tensions and contradictions of texts and interpretive traditions. One distinctive example of this kind of reading can be found in Clarice Martin's recent essay on the household codes in African American interpretation, where she poses the difficult question:

> Why is the African American interpretive tradition marked by a forceful critique and rejection of a literalist interpretation of the slave regulations in the *Haustafeln*, but not marked by an equally passionate critique and rejection of a literalist interpretation regarding the subordination of women to men in the *Haustafeln*? . . . If liberating biblical traditions regarding the kinship of humankind under God have comprised a treasury of antislavery apologia in the struggle for African American emancipation in the eighteenth and nineteenth centuries, why have we not witnessed the creation of a treasury of pro-women apologia to insure the full empowerment of African American women in the religious and socio-political spheres of African American culture and American national history? (Clarice Martin, 1991:225)

Martin suggests in this essay that the dominant hermeneutical presuppositions within African American interpretation have privileged "explicit" paradigms of liberation derived from biblical narratives, with the Exodus account occupying the position of greatest privilege. Given this hermeneutical orientation, much of African American biblical interpretation has been disabled from making the same kinds of justice claims for women as it has for enslaved peoples, insofar as biblical sources themselves contain no "equally explicit and *consistent* paradigm" critiquing androcentrism and women's suppression (226–27). In arguing for a womanist perspective as a corrective to the absence of explicit paradigms of justice for women, Martin participates in a hermeneutics of survival which calls into question the philosophical underpinnings of hegemonic culture. She sees womanist interpretation as a mode of resistance for the black church, a refusal to "be captive to elements in Western, post-Enlightenment culture that eliminate women as creators and shapers of theological discourse or of ecclesiastical policy and agendas" (231). The goal, as always, is ethically formulated. As Martin puts it: "The task is urgent. How, then will we live?" (231).

Postmodern Feminist Critique For all their significant differences, the previous three categories of interpretation share, to a degree at least, an institutional location within religious traditions. The work of postmodern feminist critique has, by contrast, been shaped less by theological constraint than by limitations imposed from within academic and intellectual disciplines.[18] Postmodern critique focuses its resistance, then, on disciplinary constraints and the theoretical foundations of those disciplines. Its resistance, while sharing political interests with the other hermeneutics, attempts to undercut philosophical hegemony through calling into question its terms of argument. Postmodern feminist critique is especially interested in the ideological effects of biblical texts and very little interested in any redemptive or recuperative gestures toward or aspects of the texts.

The work of narratologist and critic Mieke Bal is paradigmatic for postmodern biblical criticism. In introducing her reading of several biblical "love stories" (a designation provocatively ironic), Bal situates her work explicitly at the intersection of feminism and literary theory. Furthermore, she outlines her position in direct opposition to recuperative feminist work on the Bible: "I do not claim the Bible to be either a feminist resource or a sexist manifesto. That kind of assumption can be an issue only for those who attribute moral, religious, or political authority to these texts, which is precisely the opposite of what I am interested in. It is the cultural function of one of the most influential mythical and literary documents of our culture that I discuss, as a strong representative instance of what language and literature can do to a culture, specifically to its articulation of gender" (Bal, 1987:1). Bal, moreover, is not interested either in recovering original (and therefore more authentic) meanings of texts, nor in authorizing theory as a kind of postmodern replacement for divine authority. Instead, her goal is to bring together biblical and theoretical discourses into a dialogue (1).

This focus causes her to ask questions about the relation between politics and the text and to argue that the question, "Is there a relationship between ideological dominance and specific forms of representation?" (3) can only be answered affirmatively. Her procedure with her various texts—the stories of Ruth, Samson and Delilah, Bathsheba, Tamar, and Eve—is to borrow methodologically from a range of textual and reading practices in order to test the narratives themselves as well as the adequacy of the interpretive approaches. Whereas some interpreters might focus on the text, seeing theory as simply a tool for the production of a reading, Bal insists that what is at stake is rather the status of meaning itself; and her approach is to examine

[18] This opposition between theological and academic is, of course, tensive rather than absolute, given the institutional history of the rise of biblical criticism linked inexorably to theological interests.

the dense intersections of power, discourse, and ideology in the production of "meaning." As she argues in one of her two studies of the book of Judges,

> The critical feminist enterprise acts upon exegetical traditions in order to affect not only meanings, but also the status of meaning itself, its delusive stability. It will challenge every claim to semantic certainty by pointing out the motivations for the attribution of meaning, the force that guides it. One of the meanings it challenges is the status of the "original" text itself. . . . Meaning cannot be "pure," while the force that affects it cannot be grasped otherwise than *as* meaning.
>
> A feminist analysis has to bring to light the force that underlies, determines the constative illusion itself, that is, the illusion that meanings can be isolate, determined, and fixed—as well as the interests which motivate that illusion. . . . The only way out . . . is to rethink meaning, to reconsider meaning within its social functioning: to look at meaning *as* force. (Bal, 1988a:129–30)

The relation between ideological domination and representation— "meaning *as* force"—is locatable not only in the text submitting to exegesis but in the exegetical text itself. That is, Bal argues, interpretations that claim completeness and supremacy over all other readings are themselves enactments of domination. Therefore, her own readings are not an attempt to produce the one, true, overriding analysis of the biblical texts in question; rather, the very existence of her readings calls into question the claims of the dominant mode of exegesis: "The alternative readings I will propose should not be considered as yet another, superior interpretation that overthrows all the others. My goal is rather to show, by the sheer possibility of a different reading, that 'dominance' is, although present and in many ways obnoxious, not unproblematically established. It is the challenge rather than the winning that interests me. For it is not the sexist interpretation of the Bible as such that bothers me. It is the possibility of dominance itself, the attractiveness of coherence and authority in culture, that I see as the source, rather than the consequence, of sexism" (Bal, 1987:3).

The strength of Bal's reading strategy, its many remarkable insights aside, is that it simultaneously undermines the totalizing claims of texts and their interpretations. By reading strategically, making use of the contributions of narratology, semiotics, and psychoanalysis as it suits her, Bal effectively renders contingent the authorizing claims of any one of these theoretical approaches while at the same time destabilizing the truth claims (coherence and authority) of the biblical text itself. What is remarkable about this strategy is the effectiveness of its resistance to domination by both the ideology of the Bible and the ideology of theory. Postmodern feminist criticism has occupied a highly contested terrain, and a frequent critique of its practice is its connection to and apparent privileging of certain schools of theory.[19] Underlying such critiques is an assumption that theory is somehow foreign to women's experience, exists as an obstacle to an authentic feminist practice, and can only distort and divert the critical work of struggle for liberation. Yet, such critiques often uncritically embody an inverted form of the ontology of dominance Bal and other postmodern feminists interrogate, holding up the prospect of a coherent and authoritative women's vision as an unproblematic alternative to patriarchal domination. If Bal's approach works, then the strategic use of theory need not contribute to a diversion away from political change, but rather can underwrite it. As Daniel Boyarin has put it, "this is a most moving and beautiful exemplum of how to tear down the master's house without using the master's tools" (Boyarin, 1990b:41).

Another example of postmodern feminist and womanist biblical critique may be found in the polyvocal discussion of feminist translation of the New Testament published in 1990 in the *Journal of Feminist Studies in Religion*. Translation itself is a central theme in the postmodern context, as translation is a linguistic and interpretive process that lays bare the noncongruity of systems of reference.[20] In the context of feminist and womanist critique, the discussion of translation traces out multiple pathways. Elizabeth Castelli, for example, glosses some of the classic texts shaping the theory of translation in the West, offering a feminist deconstructive reading of the rhetoric of translation, a rhetoric that includes intensely gendered imagery, highly pitched claims concerning fidelity and betrayal, and resonances of colonialism (Castelli, 1990; also see Laura E. Donaldson, 1992). Clarice Martin's womanist intervention into the discussion on translation is an ideological reading of how translation can silence or elide experience; she narrates the shift in American translations of the Greek words *doulos* and *doulê* from

---

[19] This debate can be traced widely through a series of monographs and anthologies produced over the last decade or so. See, among them, Elizabeth Abel; Benstock; Flynn and Schweickart; Gates, 1986, 1990; Greene and Kahn; Meese, 1986, 1990; Nancy K. Miller; Moi; Ruthven; Showalter, 1985; Wall; Warhol and Herndl; Weedon. Gallop, 1992:21–38, provides a very brief and useful analysis of the underlying issues as they are enacted in Showalter, 1985. The debate, often critically couched in terms of race or elitism (see, for example, Christian's classic essay; Rich), has been complicated by works such as Wall; Gates, 1990; Trinh, 1989.

[20] For an introduction to the poststructuralist discussion of translation, see Derrida, 1985a, 1985c; Joseph F. Graham; Venuti. For a postcolonialist, poststructuralist reading of translation as contributing to colonial mastery, see Niranjana. See above chap. 3.

"slave" to "servant," a shift accompanying the rising resistance to slavery in the nineteenth-century South (Clarice Martin, 1990). The responses to these two essays, by Joanna Dewey, Peggy Hutaff, and Jane Schaberg, contribute to this postmodern polylogue, one shaped by a pronounced self-consciousness concerning institutional contexts, personal histories, and different theological relationships to the biblical text. Feminism, womanism, and postmodernism converge in these essays as they attend to the intricate relation of the rhetoric and ideology of texts and their (re)productions all framed in varying ways by social, political, and institutional constraints.

Feminist postmodernism finds an intriguing expression in Tina Pippin's analysis of the Apocalypse of John (1992). Here Pippin reads the rhetoric and the ideology of Revelation against a backdrop of feminism, ideology critique, and theories of the fantastic. She attempts to understand what it means that the cathartic effects of the Apocalypse reach their pinnacle in the violent death of a woman who stands (and falls) as a figure for political oppression. Her goal is not to redeem the text through a process of demythologization nor to turn away from the violence of the text. Rather, she argues for the crucial act of continuing to look at the painful landscapes of apocalypse, of "sustaining the gaze" as a necessary component of feminist transformation of our own apocalyptic times.

A final, rather more oblique, example of postmodern feminist critique may be found in some of the writings of Lacan-trained psychoanalyst Luce Irigaray, who was later expelled from the Lacanian school of psychoanalysis for her impertinent reading of the Freudian-Lacanian tradition (1974). In a series of articles published in the late 1980s in *Critique* (1985a; 1986; 1987), Irigaray reinscribed her view that women's exclusion from power in society is fundamentally linked to their exclusion from the symbolic realm. What is new in these essays is a direct link between women's exclusion from the symbolic realm in general and their exclusion from the realm of the transcendent or the divine in particular (Whitford, 140–47; see chap. 5).

Irigaray understands human subjectivity (identity) to be shaped by its relation to the symbolic, and this view leads her to see women's oppression primarily in ideological or cultural terms rather than in socio-economic terms (1989:64). Where her earlier work (1974; 1977) addressed the exclusion of female sexuality from the realm of masculine ideology, an exclusion upon which stable meanings are predicated, the later work opens up the discourse of religion as a discourse of the transcendent. Only when women have access to the symbolic force of the transcendent can meaning be transformed: "Monotheistic religions speak to us of God the Father and God made man; nothing is said of a God the Mother or of God made Woman, or even of God as a couple or couples. Not all the transcendental fancies, or ecstasies of every type, not all the quibbling over maternity and the neutrality (neuterness) of God, can succeed in erasing this one reality that determines identities, rights, symbols, and discourse" (1989:71).

Irigaray's style can be confounding because it is virtually always allusive and citational rather than clearly exegetical or interpretive. Yet at the same time she raises crucial questions for a feminist postmodern theology, even when one sometimes has the sense that she is playing fast and loose with her sources, as Morny Joy suggests she does in her reading of Schüssler Fiorenza's *In Memory of Her*. For example, she takes seriously the mythic complexities of the Christian idea of incarnation, reflecting on the circumstances and conditions of the figure of Mary in the tradition, in a fashion evocative of some modern feminist midrashic reconstructions of biblical traditions (1991:165–68). If woman is identified with the body and the earth, then Irigaray further suggests that a "sensible transcendence" would radically alter the philosophical ground of culture.

In this context, Irigaray flirts with accusations of essentialism—reinscribing "woman" with meanings imposed on her by man's identity. At the same time, she resembles certain post-Christian thinkers like Mary Daly, who argue that the biblical tradition cannot sustain a culture seriously focused on the preservation of women, materiality, and the earth; at one point she applauds Daly's concern with "the cosmic dimensions of culture" (1991:75). Later, in a statement resonating with both essentialism and some version of ecofeminism, Irigaray asserts: "I think that any sermon on the salvation of the soul, on love of the poor, any so-called Eucharistic ritual, any Evangelical discourse that doesn't concern itself with saving the earth and its natural resources, is perverted. How can certain men and women repeat the words 'This is my body, this is my blood' over the fruit of the earth without worrying about how long that earth will remain fruitful? What are these men and women talking about?" (75).

Moreover, Irigaray reads the institutional frame of Christian religion as symptomatic of an inability to sustain the connection of social and symbolic power in the form of Woman. Noting that Catholicism does not lack for symbols of female power while denying women access to institutional power (in the form of ordination), Irigaray points out that Protestantism can support women's religious leadership but only at the cost of women in the symbolic realm. Given this failure to accede both institutional and symbolic power to women—this failure to attribute subjectivity to women in culture altogether—Irigaray goes on to argue that women, then, cannot be written into the discourse of agency at all in these traditions. "Confronted with the reality of all this, what sense does it make to speak of a woman sinner? Isn't this a designation more appropriate to men, since by definition it is they who practice exclusion and sacrifice and are therefore sinners?" (1989:72). The difficulty and ingenuity of this argument is representative of Irigaray's method: a refusal of the patriarchal terms of definition and when that fails, a mimicry of their logic.

Postmodern feminism's contribution to the ongoing feminist critique of the Bible, literature, and religious ideology is characterized by its fundamental challenge to the interpretive frame conventionally placed around the text. Recognizing the constraints imposed by disciplinary systems, postmodern feminism argues for a valorization of the category of *difference* as a way to unseat or destabilize the reigning modes of interpretation. Whereas some have argued that postmodern feminism has avoided questions of power and therefore has removed itself from the fray of real political struggle, postmodern feminist critiques see power residing not only in the everyday relations of domination faced by so many, but in the ideological underpinnings that authorize and sustain those relations of domination (Butler and Scott; Laura E. Donaldson, 1992; Ebert, 1991; Nicholson).

If postmodern perspectives have, from our point of view, supplemented feminist scholarship on the Bible in significant and important ways, they have also inspired a significant level of suspicion and critique within feminism both inside and outside biblical studies. Although many have made feminist arguments against postmodernism and poststructuralism,[21] Elisabeth Schüssler Fiorenza's most recent book, *But She Said: Feminist Practices of Biblical Interpretation* (1992a), brings these arguments into feminist biblical studies in a sustained way even though many of her interests are shared by feminist postmodernists and postmodern feminists. Her critique of post-

---

[21] There is a large amount of literature here, reflecting a range of positions. See the recent nuanced arguments by Ebert, 1992–93, who argues for a form of "resistance postmodern feminism" against what she characterizes as "ludic postmodern feminism." See also many of the theoretical debates taking place in the *Journal of Women's History*, where the orthodox position opposes women's history (understood as political) to gender history (understood as apolitical).

modern versions of feminism falls into several general categories. First, she worries that the focus on linguistic constructions and the interpretation of the structures of gender in texts will simply reify these structures rather than dismantle them. Moreover, she believes that such modes of interpretation rob women of their history, a history she understands to be crucial to the project of liberation. She is also suspicious of feminism that situates itself within the institution of the academy, fearing that it loses its roots in the women's movement. Finally, she embraces the opposition familiar to the discussions of the relation of feminism to postmodernism, that of politics versus theory, and critiques postmodernism for its perceived disabling of political agency for change.

Schüssler Fiorenza promotes a critical feminist rhetorics of liberation, one which highlights the rhetorical maneuvers and contexts of biblical texts. Like all critics, she is engaged in a rhetorical project, as she acknowledges. One strategy of her rhetoric is to collapse a range of feminist literary strategies (formalist, reader-response, structuralist, narratological, deconstructionist); to applaud the recognition enabled by these positions that the biblical text is an ideological construct; but to characterize these approaches as ultimately beholden to a "deterministic conception of language" (41) and "positivist textualism" (42, 85–86). She goes on to argue that such strategies reinscribe unequal gender relations in spite of their good intentions to lay bare how texts embody and enable such relations:

> By tracing out the feminine/masculine binary structures of the biblical text, or by focusing on the "feminine" character constructs (e.g., mother, daughter, bride) of biblical narratives, structuralist and deconstructionist readings run the risk of re-inscribing rather than dislodging the dualistic gender politics of the text. Although feminist literary criticism seeks to foster a hermeneutics of resistance that deconstructs, debunks, and rejects the androcentric politics of the canonical text, by adopting linguistic determinism it cannot but reinscribe the totalizing dynamics of the androcentric text—a text which either marginalizes women and other non-persons or which eliminates them altogether from the literary record. (1992a:34–35; see also 42 and passim)

Interestingly, between the two sentences cited we move from readings that "run the risk of re-inscribing" gender dualism to approaches that "cannot but reinscribe the totalizing dynamics of the androcentric text;" that is, Schüssler Fiorenza moves from a provisional to a totalizing critique, one hinged on the concept of *linguistic determinism*, that goes undefined throughout the course of her discussion. By linguistic determinism, Schüssler Fiorenza may be referring to a view of language as the ubiquitous framework and mediator of experience, a view embraced by a diverse range of critics loosely grouped together as postmodernists. However, postmodern understandings of language do not necessarily include a belief that language is deterministic. Moreover, Schüssler Fiorenza's critique of the analysis of gender dynamics in texts—that such analysis reinscribes what it seeks to critique—echoes feminist rejection of other modes of interpretation, such as psychoanalysis. Here, the strategy is to imply (or, indeed, argue) that if an interpreter describes how something works, she or he is advocating for the maintenance of the practice. However, as feminist defenders of psychoanalysis (as one example) point out, to describe something is not to prescribe it.

Schüssler Fiorenza shares our recognition that the institutional location of feminism shapes the contours of its political critique of androcentrism and domination. Indeed, she dedicates an entire chapter of her book to the examination of feminist theological education and the constraints of its various institutional settings (168–94). In this chapter and elsewhere in the book, she argues that the institution of the academy, with its processes of socialization, professionalization, and dedication to scientific disciplines, is inimical to her feminist project (173–74). In a related discussion earlier in the book, she singles out for critique the volume edited by Peggy Day from which one of our initial interpretive examples was drawn as an example of feminist work that embodies "objectivist and depoliticized academic practices of biblical interpretation" (40) and thereby abandons its roots in the feminist movement. The rhetoric of Schüssler Fiorenza's critique is interesting for she begins by outlining Day's distinction between feminist theological interpretation, on the one hand, and feminist gender studies that draw on feminist critical approaches deriving from the humanities and social sciences, on the other. She then goes on to state: "If feminist theory and biblical interpretation no longer position themselves within the women's movement but orient themselves toward a 'scientific' male audience and primarily seek to win its respect, the 'critical energies of feminism' are in danger of being recuperated into the dominant ideology of biblical studies. The integration of biblical women studies [sic] into the academy will bring 'increased pressure' to accommodate itself and to make compromises, 'abandoning in the process the political priorities and the concerns for the personal that have made it so effective in the past'" (40–41). A curious opposition is constructed here between, on the one hand, feminist theological interpretation and feminist theory and interpretive practice grounded in the women's movement and, on the other hand, feminist gender studies and feminist theory and interpretive practice grounded in the academy. This opposition implies, of course, that there are good feminist (theological) interpreters who remain rooted in the women's movement and bad feminist (gender studies) interpreters who sell out to and seek affirmation from academic men in power. (This opposition is related to the *theory-politics dichotomy* discussed below.) But since all of us involved in this discussion make our livings, with varying levels of job security and prestige, in academic institutions and do our writing and interpreting within that context, it seems perhaps more honest to acknowledge (rather than gloss over) that fact, as Schüssler Fiorenza seems to be doing.

As a part of her anti-postmodern rhetoric, Schüssler Fiorenza adopts the opposition between theory and politics, an opposition constructed by opponents of postmodernism in such areas as feminist studies and invoked frequently by them. "As Chris Weedon succinctly observes: 'feminism is a politics, whereas postmodernism is not.' Instead, postmodernism remains politically ambivalent" (91). Schüssler Fiorenza does not provide a page reference for this quotation from Chris Weedon's *Feminist Practice and Poststructuralist Theory* (and we could not find the statement in a careful rereading of this book). Indeed, Schüssler Fiorenza's use of Weedon to make this point is curious, given that Weedon's book argues that feminism has contributed to the formulation of poststructuralism *and* that feminism can benefit from ongoing dialogue with poststructuralist theory. Weedon writes: "The task of this book is quite specific. It is to make a case for recent poststructuralist developments in the theory of language, subjectivity and power for knowledge production which will serve feminist interests. It does not claim that a poststructuralist perspective can answer every question which feminists wish to ask, but that poststructuralism offers a useful, productive framework for understanding the mechanisms of power in our society and the possibilities of change" (10). Furthermore, Schüssler Fiorenza's claim that "postmodernism is politically ambivalent" implies that feminism is not, a claim which can be called into question by the complex and contentious history of feminism. Two further illustrations of this political ambivalence on the part of feminism may be found in Susie Cunningham Stanley's recent biography of Alma White, a feminist and religious leader who was also a religious (anti-Catholic) bigot and a supporter of the Ku Klux Klan, and in Kathleen Blee's remarkable history of the Women of the Ku Klux Klan (WKKK), where discourses of women's rights were neatly interwoven with white supremacist and nativist discourses. These and other historical examples remind us that feminism is not immune to political ambivalence.

The theory-politics opposition has been discussed recently by historian Joan Scott, whose work brings the insights of poststructuralism to the project of historical writing. As Scott puts it:

> Feminists hostile to poststructuralism have generalized their critique as a denunciation of "theory" and they have labelled it as abstract, elitist, and masculinist. They have, in contrast, insisted that their position is concrete, practical, and feminist, and so politically correct. Whatever is theoretical about feminism is renamed as "politics" in this opposition because, (according to one recent account), its insights come "straight out of reflection on our own, that is, women's experience, out of the contradictions we felt between the different ways we were represented even to ourselves, out of the inequities we had long experienced in our situations." By casting the problem in terms of an intractable binary opposition, this formulation rules out the possibility of considering the usefulness of various theoretical approaches for feminist history and feminist politics, as well as the possibility of conceiving of theory and politics as inextricably linked.
>
> I think the opposition between "theory" and "politics" is a false one that seeks to silence debates we must have about *which* theory is most useful for feminism by making only one theory acceptable as "politics." (In the language of those who use this dichotomy "politics" really means good theory; "theory" means bad politics.) The "good" theory takes "women" and their "experience" as the self-evident facts that are the origin of collective identity and action. In effect, (in a move that is the inverse of history's reaction to women's history) those who use this opposition establish "politics" as the normative position, for some the ethical test of the validity of feminism and of women's history. And historians of women who reject "theory" in the name of "politics" are curiously allied with those traditional historians who find poststructuralism (and found women's history) antithetical to the tenets of their discipline. In both cases these historians are defending the concept of "experience" by refusing to problematize it; by opposing "theory" and "politics" they remove "experience" from critical scrutiny and protect it as the foundational and unproblematic ground of politics and historical explanation. (Joan W. Scott, 1992b:59) [22]

In the related critique that postmodernist feminism disables political agency, Scott's observations are again well taken: "The 'theory' versus 'politics' opposition also refers obliquely to the question of human agency, much

---

[22] For a general discussion of the intersections of poststructuralism and history, see also Attridge, Bennington, and Young.

insisted upon these days by historians. Poststructuralist theory doesn't deny that people act or that they have some control over their actions; rather it criticizes the liberal individual theory that assumes that individuals are fully autonomous, rational, self-creating actors. The issue is not agency *per se,* but the limits of the liberal theory of agency" (1992b:65–66, n. 40). More broadly, the contested relation between activism and critique to which the theory-politics opposition points invites further investigation, particularly when it may be endemic to feminism itself. As Teresa de Lauretis has argued, "The contradictory pressure toward affirmative political action . . . and toward the theoretical negation of patriarchal culture and social relations is glaring, unavoidable, and probably even constitutive of the specificity of feminist thought" (244).

Schüssler Fiorenza is also suspicious of some feminist critics who make use of male theorists' work and insights. Twice in the book, she characterizes male theologians and theorists as "godfathers." The use of this term is highly charged, of course, because a godfather is both a man who is responsible for the spiritual well-being of his godchild *and* a leader in clandestine criminal circles, a leader who demands absolute loyalty upon threat of death; the implication is that the goddaughters of such godfathers possess no autonomy. At one point, she characterizes the work of African American, Hispanic, and Asian American women scholars who do not fall under the shadow or spell of male thinkers. "Neither Jerome nor Thomas, Bultmann nor Albright, Troeltsch nor Geertz, Derrida nor Foucault are their exegetical or theoretical 'Godfathers' " (38; the capitalization of the term here suggests the criminal rather than the spiritual kind). Quite a bit later in the book, she critiques feminist theory inspired by French theorists of the feminine in this way: "Feminist essentialist theories or theologies of femininity, whether their godfathers be Goethe, Schleiermacher, Jung, Tillich, Lacan, Derrida, Teilhard de Chardin, or Pope John Paul II, have valorized Woman—body, sexuality, maternity, nature—as feminine archetype, essence, or divinity" (136). Weedon makes the following counterargument:

> The fact that most theory has been produced, until recently, by men has not been without its effects on the status of theoretical writing among feminists. It has helped fire the move to reject theory as inherently patriarchal. This tendency has been given impetus by the impenetrability of many important texts for women without privileged access to higher education and by the fact that most of the theorists who have produced poststructuralist texts are themselves unsympathetic to feminism. However it is important to distinguish between the political potential

and usefulness of a theory and the particular affiliations of its author. If Foucault's theory of discourse and power can produce in feminist hands an analysis of patriarchal power relations which enables the development of active strategies for change, then it is of little importance whether his own historical analyses fall short of this. (13)

It is perhaps significant that the one notable exception to the general critique of women scholars making use of the work of male theorists appears in the book when Schüssler Fiorenza discusses the important essay by Mae Gwendolyn Henderson "Speaking in Tongues: Dialogics, Dialectics, and the Black Woman Writer's Literary Tradition," an essay in which Henderson employs insights from both Gadamer and Bakhtin to create a model of discursive diversity or heteroglossia for reading black women's literary history (159ff.). Henderson's example clearly shows that hermeneutical and postmodern theories of discourse, irrespective of their paternity, can indeed provide a useful framework for feminist interpretation.

In spite of her strongly worded critiques of postmodern feminism, Schüssler Fiorenza's own rhetorical project in her book finds many resonances with postmodernism. For example, she praises feminist literary studies (in all their variety) for focusing on "the silences, contradictions, arguments, prescriptions, and projections of biblical texts, as well as the Bible's discourses on gender, race, class, or culture" in order "to show their ideological inscription of the patriarchal politics of otherness" (34). Such language is familiar to the postmodern and poststructuralist projects of concentrating on textual aporias and incongruities, on the marginal and the occluded. In addition, Schüssler Fiorenza describes her own project as one of "reading against the grain," (35) another practice familiar to practitioners of poststructuralism. Moreover, her critique of the "logic of identity," which she wishes to replace with a "logic of democracy" (139ff.), is quite akin to poststructuralist and postmodernist suspicion of the unified subject and their critiques of identity politics.

The point of this lengthy discussion is not to define postmodernism, poststructuralism, or any other cognate philosophical position or interpretive strategy as the hermeneutical panacea for feminism. Indeed, the intersection of poststructuralism and postmodernism, on the one hand, and feminism, on the other, is a contested and complex terrain, as the discussions throughout this volume have demonstrated and as feminist theorists like Joan W. Scott and Weedon are certainly willing to acknowledge (see Scott, 1992b:60; Weedon, passim; also see Butler and Scott; Cornell, 1991, 1992, 1993; Fraser and Bartky; Haraway). The point is not to valorize blindly the postmodern project, but to remain open to the contributions and insights it might contribute to the ongoing debates over which theories and which politics further the goals of social transformation and resistance to domination (see Ebert, 1992–93). Totalizing dismissals (or "displacements," in Schüssler Fiorenza's terms [40]) seem to be a less helpful response, particularly when we share political goals and, indeed, many interpretive strategies.

There is no easy rapprochement among these different interpretive positions and strategies of resistance, nor is it clear that one position or strategy possesses a totalizing force. Indeed, as Bal's argument would have it, any strategy posing as totalizing necessarily serves the interests of domination and therefore would not easily carry the name "feminist." These strategies are different from one another and at times at odds with one another. Yet taken together they offer an overlapping range of interpretive options, an imbricated structure of resistance to domination resembling Lionnet's *métissage*. Looking to the future, we can begin to imagine what other forms of feminist resistance might look like and how they contribute to this braiding together of strategic modes of reading.

THE FUTURE OF FEMINIST AND WOMANIST READINGS

A thread running through this chapter and, indeed, through this volume is the assertion that reading and interpretive strategies are socially, politically, and institutionally situated and that they draw their energy and force from the subject positions of readers and interpreters. Feminist and womanist interpretations additionally attempt to call attention to the ideological constraints implied by that situatedness and those subjectivities, to ask questions about what is rendered unspeakable when certain frameworks are in place and taken for granted, to ask why some questions are at best impertinent and at worst unaskable within different institutional contexts. Feminist and womanist interpretations challenge the uninterrogated separation imposed between academic discourse and the concerns of the world, a separation that "is tacitly permitted by a practice which historicizes the work in the producing culture but regards historical intervention in its reception as an inexcusable tampering with the truth of the work" (Pathak, 427). Given the ground that they have already traversed and given that feminism and womanism are still-emerging interpretive disciplines, what might their future practices look like, especially in relation to biblical studies?

Much feminist and womanist interpretation takes place in different institutional contexts which all, nevertheless, share in the work of teaching. Furthermore, as womanism and feminism both continually interrogate the relation between theory and practice, pedagogy remains a crucial arena: how does one use these interpretive strategies in relation to the Bible to teach others about processes of reading? Those of us who teach biblical literature are perhaps a step removed from the academic "canon wars" that have been raging in institutions of higher learning. We are not called upon to defend *what* we teach—the most canonical of Western literature—but the question of *how* we teach it has become a highly contentious one.

Zakia Pathak teaches undergraduate women at Miranda House, a women's college within Delhi University, and she teaches from a prescribed syllabus of Western classics. In her recently published article "A Pedagogy for Postcolonial Feminists," she explains from the beginning the engaged nature of her pedagogical practice, which "is directed at producing from the literary 'work' a 'text' which engages our concerns as Indians and women at the present time. While respecting the cultural specificity of the work in the producing culture, we are committed to 'making' a politics for it that will enable us to live our lives more critically" (426). In the course of her essay, she describes how she has used the Book of Job and Eliot's *Murder in the Cathedral* to discuss the contemporary controversy between Hindus and Muslims over the contested religious site in Uttar Pradesh. By highlighting what she calls the discourse of law and the discourse of religion in the Book of Job, Pathak demonstrates an affinity between the ideologies of the biblical text and those of certain political parties attempting to use the controversy over religious priority at a sacred site (claimed by both Hindus and Muslims) to secure political gain, ideologies both organized around nationalism (428–29). Although admitting that "the feminist concern was temporally subordinated" (430) because the reading was an immediate response to the political situation that included massive and bloody riots, Pathak points to the marginalized voice of Job's wife and the constraints faced by women in the institutional contexts of the various political parties in her contemporary setting. Pathak argues, in short, for a feminist pedagogy explicitly opposed to domination and unapologetically grounded in one's social location by using interpretation as a means for gaining understanding of the nature and dynamics of the present situation through the medium of a historical text. In this strategy Pathak differs very little from liberation theologians, although clearly her interests are other than theological.

Taking account of social location can involve the teaching and production of such readings of texts. However, another dimension of social location is the broader intellectual context in which the work is done, in particular the academy. The academy as an institution is a rather different place than it was in the 1970s when feminist work and women's studies began to make their presence felt. In the 1990s, feminist studies finds sometime allies in gender studies, gay and lesbian studies, men's studies, and studies of sexuality (Schor). At the same time, all of these studies, along with black studies, ethnic studies, and the like—in short, what has come to be called "multiculturalism"—have come under increasing attack by groups like the National Association of Scholars and government officials like former National Endowment for the Humanities chair Lynne Cheney. We need barely mention the likes of Robert Bly and Camille Paglia, who add their blustery versions of romanticized and essentialist sex differences to the mix. Feminist and womanist interpretation now takes place in this diffuse and often more highly contentious field of play, one in which the identity politics of previous seasons have been replaced by politics of difference, which present their own difficulties. Christina Crosby has articulated the problematic eloquently where she writes:

> The question remains of how to deal with difference and how to work for difference—how to think difference as a problem for theory and not a solution. These questions must be asked, especially now when the politicization of the academy is a given, the call to historicize is insistent, and diversity is on everyone's lips. "Differences" has passed into the realm of the slogan which makes it even harder to think, of course, since slogans are by their very nature self-evident: you are either for or against differences, for or against diversity. Thus in the academy we are confronted with a duopoly, a structure of "simultaneous opposition" which seems agonistic but is remarkably stable. What is foreclosed is the possibility of thinking differently about differences, yet that is precisely what is to be done. Otherwise differences will remain as self-evident as identity once was, and just as women's studies once saw woman everywhere, the academy will recognize differences everywhere, cheerfully acknowledging that since everyone is different, everyone is the same. Such is the beauty of pluralism. (139–40)

The urgency of thinking differences differently, of working for difference and against domination within a feminist and womanist framework is twofold. First of all, despite some small successes in unveiling phallocentrism and ethnocentrism in some quarters, feminism and womanism remain oppositional discourses at the margins of power institutionally. The ideological

force of the phallocentric metanarrative of female sexuality remains powerfully in place; it operates in the figure of Hosea's wanton wife and echoes
repetitively in contemporary American public life as the ongoing struggles
in public discourse around sexual harassment and rape remind us. Secondly,
if perhaps more hopefully, feminism and womanism, because of their double
focus on subjectivity and the production of knowledge, offer an ongoing,
dialogical, and critical process that maintains a kind of edginess and a refusal
to settle or to master. As Elizabeth Weed has put it: "The critical advantage of the feminist project has been that when one area of feminism has
settled on a truth, another has emerged to disrupt that truth, to keep at bay
truths too easily produced by cultural and political formations. . . . As long
as feminism remains a process of coming to terms but never arriving, always
interrogating the very terms it constitutes and never mastering them, it will
continue to be a challenging mode of inquiry" (1989:xxxi). It is perhaps
this refusal of mastery that is womanism's and feminism's most radical edge,
offering not a new system of domination but a continuous critique of all
such systems. This refusal creates the only real possibility for rethinking and
resignifying difference.

RECOMMENDED FURTHER READING

Anzaldúa, Gloria, ed. 1990. *Making Face, Making Soul/Haciendo Caras: Creative and Critical
Perspectives by Women of Color.* San Francisco: Aunt Lute. A rich anthology of theoretical,
political, and creative writings by women of color. Provides a range of feminist thinking
found on the American scene.

Bal, Mieke. 1987. *Lethal Love: Feminist Literary Readings of Biblical Love Stories.* Bloomington: Indiana University Press. A collection of readings showcasing Bal's narratological
reading of biblical texts. Demonstrates the relation between ideological dominance and
forms of representation.

Briggs, Sheila. 1990. " 'Buried with Christ': The Politics of Identity and the Poverty of Interpretation." Pp. 276–303 in *The Book and the Text: The Bible and Literary Theory.* Ed. Regina
Schwartz. New York: Blackwell. An important essay that analyzes intersection of hermeneutical practices with social relationships of domination. Calls for a form of interpretation
that begins to address structures of oppression and the limits of identity politics.

Butler, Judith, and Joan W. Scott, eds. 1992. *Feminists Theorize the Political.* New York: Routledge. A crucial anthology of feminist discussion of theory and politics. Examines highly
charged concepts of "identity," "agency," "experience," and "difference."

Cannon, Katie Geneva, and Elisabeth Schüssler Fiorenza, eds. 1989. "Interpretation for Liberation." *Semeia* 47. Atlanta: Scholars. Collection of essays that challenge and supplement Euro-American biblical criticism. Featuring Katie Geneva Cannon, Kwok Pui Lan,

Vincent L. Wimbush, Cheryl Townsend Gilkes, Renita Weems, Clarice J. Martin, and Sheila Briggs.

Collins, Adela Yarbro, ed. 1985. *Feminist Perspectives in Biblical Scholarship.* Chico, Calif.: Scholars. A collection of essays by Gifford, Setel, Schüssler Fiorenza, Brooten, Osiek, Furman, and Fuchs featuring a range of methodological discussions as well as different feminist readings of specific biblical texts.

Day, Peggy. 1989b. *Gender and Difference in Ancient Israel.* Minneapolis: Augsburg/Fortress Press. Anthology featuring the interdisciplinary interests of women's studies in the Hebrew Bible using a range of methodologies drawn from sociology, psychology, anthropology, folklore, literary criticism, and history.

James, Stanlie M., and Abena P. A. Bousia, eds. 1993. *Theorizing Black Feminisms: The Visionary Pragmatism of Black Women.* New York: Routledge. Essays from the first Black Feminist Seminar, sponsored by the Afro-American Studies Department at the University of Wisconsin-Madison, May 10–12, 1992.

Martin, Clarice J. 1991. "The *Haustafeln* (Household Codes) in African American Biblical Interpretation: 'Free Slaves' and 'Subordinate Women.'" Pp. 206–31 in *Stony the Road We Trod: African American Biblical Interpretation.* Ed. Cain Hope Felder. Minneapolis: Augsburg/Fortress Press. An important essay on New Testament household codes that reads for gender and race. Demonstrates the fruitfulness as well as limitations of blending perspectives.

Schüssler Fiorenza, Elisabeth. 1992. *But She Said: Feminist Practices of Biblical Interpretation.* Boston: Beacon. Continues Schüssler Fiorenza's important effort to bring a sustained, critical feminist perspective to New Testament interpretation. Develops a rhetorical approach that attempts to bridge the gap between historical and literary interpretations.

Schüssler Fiorenza, Elisabeth, ed. 1993. *Searching the Scriptures: A Feminist Introduction.* New York: Crossroad. A collection of methodological essays on feminist biblical interpretation.

Warhol, Robyn R., and Diane Price Herndl, eds. 1991. *Feminisms: An Anthology of Literary Theory and Criticism.* New Brunswick, N.J.: Rutgers University Press. Anthology that brings together the most important articles in the field of feminist literary theory over the past twenty years. Thematically arranged with helpful, innovative index.

Weed, Elizabeth, ed. 1989. *Coming to Terms: Feminism/Theory/Politics.* New York: Routledge. Anthology of the classic essays in poststructuralist feminist theory, deriving from an ongoing seminar, "Cultural Constructions of Gender," at the Pembroke Center at Brown University. An excellent introduction to the debate.

Weedon, Chris. 1987. *Feminist Practice and Poststructuralist Theory.* Oxford: Blackwell. Demonstrates the usefulness of poststructuralism for understanding structures of power and modes of change, enabling use of those tools in service of feminist interests.

Weems, Renita. 1991. "Reading *Her Way* through the Struggle: African American Women and the Bible." Pp. 57–77 in *Stony the Road We Trod: African American Biblical Interpretation.* Ed. Cain Hope Felder. Minneapolis: Augsburg/Fortress Press. Provides important historical examples of the use African American women have put the Bible. Examines reading strategies in the face of multiple structures of oppression.

7 | Ideological Criticism

The Bible, of all books, is the most dangerous one, the one
that has been endowed with the power to kill.
—Mieke Bal (1991:14)

DEFINING IDEOLOGY AND IDEOLOGICAL CRITICISM

The most complex problem in this chapter is also the most basic: defining
ideology and *ideological criticism*. Definitions of ideology abound, and they
differ widely on what is of central or marginal importance. Such definitions
are, of course, never neutral; they are vested with sociopolitical significance
in their own right, that is they are as "ideological" as ideological criticism
itself.

Michèle Barrett provides us with a place to begin: "Ideology is a generic term for the processes by which meaning is produced, challenged,
reproduced, transformed" (1980:97). Ideological criticism, it follows, is
concerned with theorizing and critiquing those processes of meaning production as social and political realities. Found in various theoretical quarters
and in different forms, ideological criticism's interests overlap, for example,
with different forms of liberation hermeneutics, cultural criticism, rhetori-

cal criticism (see chap. 4), sociological criticism, Marxist literary criticism, reader-response criticism (see chap. 1), and ethical critique. For its part ideological criticism exposes three dimensions of the struggle present in the production of meaning: it reveals the tensive relation between the production of meaning and language; it highlights the multiple discourses operating within the text; and it lays bare the complex nature of power relations that produce texts, construct the institutional contexts of texts and their reception, and affect readers of those texts in their particular social locations.

Contemporary literary critics engaged in ideological criticism, including a growing number of biblical interpreters, draw heavily on the writings of the Marxist theorists Fredric Jameson and Terry Eagleton (see *Semeia* 59).[1] Both Jameson and Eagleton operate with a definition of ideology derived from Louis Althusser, for whom ideology is to be understood as the system of representations located in the everyday practices (especially the rituals) of a society. Eagleton speaks metaphorically of this system of representation as a "text" of the power relations of a society (1991:1; 1983:14–15). One of the tasks of ideological criticism, then, is to "read" this text. This entails paying special attention to the role of interpretation and interpreters within the system and to the various ways the text's system of representation operates to instanciate and empower particular notions of truth—whether individual, corporate, or transcendental truth—and particular values and actions.

Ideology lies at the very heart of the signification process. Employing Saussurean semiotics, Eagleton exposes ideology as a language-based phenomenon that bears in a special way on the literature of a society. "Ideology," Eagleton claims, "pre-exists the text; but the *ideology of the text* defines, operates and constitutes that ideology in ways unpremeditated, so to speak, by ideology itself" (1978:80). Ideology relates not just to the production of literary texts, but to the historical production of each and every signifier and signified within a society. This enables Eagleton to say about history that it serves as "the *ultimate* signifier of literature, as it is the ultimate signified. For what else in the end could be the source and object of any signifying practice but the real social formation which provides its material matrix?" (1978:72, emphasis his).

Also for Eagleton, ideology is to be explained in relation to discourse and power. Ideology is encountered in the discourse of every text—in both what

---

[1] Jameson might accurately be described as a poststructuralist Marxist theorist.

a text says and what it does not say (cf. 1978:89). Literature in particular expresses and reproduces ideologies in overt and covert fashion, namely, through the conscious or unconscious appropriation of signs. Ideology, however, is not to be equated with a specific sign or a particular author's intended use of signs. It resides in the link that a society forges between discourse and power that empowers signification (e.g., in the reading and writing of literary texts) at its most basic level. "Indeed," Eagleton says, " 'ideology' can be taken to indicate no more than this connection—the link or nexus between discourses and power" (1983:210). Therefore, it is not surprising that ideological criticism has come to be closely identified with the politics of reading or that the overtly political discourses of a society provide a rich treasure trove for ideological analysis. For Eagleton, politics (that is political discourse and action) and literature find themselves inextricably—in other words, ideologically—linked.

Central to most discussions of ideology and ideological criticism at present are issues of power and power relations (understood in personal, corporate, as well as societal terms). J. B. Thompson has said of ideology that it is "meaning in the service of power" (1990:7 and 20; cf. Eagleton, 1991:5).[2] Power must be associated here not just with issues of class dominance and what Marx calls "the economics of untruth" but with a host of other material relations as well, including sexuality, race, ethnicity, and gender (see Barrett, 1991:134–41; cf. J. Hillis Miller, 1988). From this point of view ideological criticism has as its primary purpose the task of exposing and charting the structure and dynamics of these power relations as they come to expression in language, in the conflicting ideologies operating in discourse, and in flesh and blood readers of texts in their concrete social locations and relationships.

Historically, literature enjoys a special relationship to power: "I mean more particularly those modes of feeling, valuing, perceiving and believing which have some kind of relation to the maintenance and reproduction of social power" (Eagleton, 1983:15). In the same way that people are implicated in the working of social order, literature plays an important role in the ideological operations of a culture, whether it be for just or unjust (or some combination of both) reasons. However, the ideological character of a society is tied to and reflected in not only literary texts but also its aesthetic productions which are regarded as "texts"—its art, architecture,

---

[2] Thompson maintains that to study ideology "is to study the ways in which the multifarious uses of language intersect with power, nourishing it, sustaining it, enacting it" (1984:2).

music, dance, and more. In post-Enlightenment Western culture in particular a special bond exists between the production of ideology and aesthetics. About this relation Eagleton says: "the text itself" is not to be thought of as "the production" as opposed to the "reflection of an ideological 'solution'" (1978:88–89). Eagleton here relies on a Marxist conception of art that regards art not simply as the reflection of the social order and its ideology but as a *producer* of ideology in its own right (cf. Macherey). Texts are implicated in both the representation and reproduction of ideology.

To say that all readings of a text are ideological is to insist that the act of reading is fundamentally ethical (cf. Siebers; J. Hillis Miller, 1987b; Levinas, 1994). This ethical force is present in Althusser's conception of ideology as a "material practice" (see esp. 1972:155–59)—that is, "the 'lived' relation between [people] and their world" (Althusser and Balibar, 1979:314; see Eagleton, 1991:18–23); the ethical question, therefore, belongs at the heart of the ideological discussion. Althusser's emphasis on the "lived relation" between people is meant to expose and underscore the differences and conflicts of these human relations as systemic and corporate realities, that is, something more than the individual person's actions and desires. As signifying *practice*, the ideology of a text is tied structurally to the ethical push and pull of interpretation. Ideological criticism, we might conclude, at root has to do with the ethical character of and response to the text and to those lived relations that are represented and reproduced in the act of reading. When it comes to reading biblical texts in particular and making sense of the ideological discourse, struggles and conflicts of the Bible, the reader is faced with the challenge of and responsibility for ethical questioning and action (Levinas, 1994).

Ideological reading, as we define it, is a deliberate effort to read against the grain—of texts, of disciplinary norms, of traditions, of cultures. It is a disturbing way to read because ideological criticism demands a high level of self-consciousness and makes an explicit, unabashed appeal to justice. As an ethically grounded act, ideological reading intends to raise critical consciousness about what is just and unjust about those lived relations that Althusser describes, and to change those power relationships for the better. It challenges readers to accept political responsibility for themselves and for the world in which they live.

By way of summary, Catherine Belsey gathers together a number of the key defining elements this way. As a signifying practice (and as part of the "language games" people play), ideology is "the sum of the ways in which people both live and represent to themselves their relationship to the conditions of their existence. Ideology is *inscribed in signifying practices*—in discourses, myths, presentations and re-presentations of the way 'things' are—and to this extent it is inscribed in language. . . . While ideology cannot be reduced to language and, more important, language certainly cannot be reduced to ideology, the signifying system can have an important role in naturalizing the way things are" (1980:42, emphasis hers).

For Belsey, the experience of reality is fundamentally discursive: discourse shapes and gives expression to our common sense (1980:5–7) and to the real power relationships that exist among people. Appealing to Roland Barthes (1972a), Belsey contends that the way people ordinarily talk, tell stories, and relate those stories to their lives is one of the central means by which ideology is represented and reproduced. To learn what is ideologically important about a community or a culture, we need only listen carefully to the stories it tells and how it tells them. In Western culture, the stories most influential in shaping and producing its ideology are found in the Bible.

As a political and literary concept, then, ideology has enjoyed a long and complex history, and in the course of its career, the reception and use of this term has often been negative. In the index to *The Bible and Liberation*, for example, Norman Gottwald compiles references to ideology under two broad categories: "used non-pejoratively" and "used pejoratively" (539). Owing to Marxist influence, ideology has been narrowly defined in a negative way as idealistic political thinking grounded in a certain type of false consciousness about the fundamental historical realities of the world. In its broader, popularized use, ideology has come to be equated with the imposition of leftist politics, whether it has to do with forms of social activism or the narrow interpretation of values in texts. For example, the adjective *ideological* is commonly associated with "bias." In fact, in light of these associations the term has become so highly charged and diluted that some theorists have argued for the adoption of a different terminology altogether in order to refocus and preserve the heart of ideological critique: "we [need language that can] point with more accuracy to an instance that might previously be labelled ideological: a partial truth, a naturalized understanding or a universalistic discourse, for example" (Barrett, 1991:168; we will return to the issue of the "ideological" nature of ideology below). Reflecting the movement away from a concentration on the classic notion of class struggle and the negative identification of ideology with the mystification of truth that comes from the dominant state power, ideological criticism has in recent years taken a decided textual or literary turn, as Eagleton's efforts underscore. In raising the question about ideological criticism of the Bible we are concerned, therefore, not only with texts, the ideology of texts, and the subjects of texts, but with the ethical demand to respond through critique to the material conditions of the lives of people past and present who have a stake in those texts. And as Erich Auerbach (1953) has so convincingly demonstrated, the narrative text central to Western culture's self-definition and understanding of the world is the Bible.

Hence, ideological criticism of the Bible entails the twin effort (1) to read the ancient biblical stories for their ideological content and mode of production and (2) to grasp the ideological character of contemporary reading strategies (see Schüssler Fiorenza, 1988). This is far from the disinterested objective exercise prescribed within certain positivist circles. In today's highly charged theoretical atmosphere, and against the backdrop of a postmodern condition where aesthetic, epistemic, and political norms are rapidly being transformed, ideological criticism is to be seen as a resistant act, a positive, ethical response. It is a critical action designed to expose cultural systems of power that shape the lived relations not only of readers of the Bible but of the vast majority of the world's peoples who in varying ways have suffered real poverty, oppression, and violence. Not all ideological-critical readings are transformative: some are resistant readings that work to alter present conditions for the better, while others strive to reinforce the present lived relations, the status quo. How are we to distinguish one kind of ideological reading from another? How can ideological reading itself become coopted? Who is to decide? How can biblical critics read the Bible ideologically without being coopted? What are the implications for today's postmodern culture of reading the Bible against the grain? What possible practical difference does ideological critique make in readers' individual and corporate lives? These are some of the theoretical and practical concerns ideological criticism brings to the foreground when reading the Bible.

IDEOLOGICAL CRITICISM AND THE BIBLE:
CRACKING THE SINGULAR VOICE

Ideological commitment is not first and foremost a matter of moral choice but of the taking of sides in a struggle between embattled groups.
—Fredric Jameson, (1991:290).

Today it is commonplace for literary critics of the Bible to charge historical critical exegesis with refusing to give sufficient attention to its own ideological character. The simplistic (and ideological) appeal to objectivity, as opposed to subjectivity, no longer works as an adequate response to the need to disclose self-interest and value (Bernstein, 1983, 1992); the invoking of positive knowledge and the appeal to objective historical reality are elements of the value-laden gesture of modern scientific discourse (Aronowitz, 1988:3–34; Reiss). Echoing historical criticism, ideological criticism insists that each and every biblical reader comes to the text with expectations and preconceptions, with hope and imagination (Bultmann 1960). But going beyond historical criticism ideological criticism insists that every engagement with the text is conflictual: it produces some degree of struggle and rupture in what would appear to be the natural expectations readers bring to their reading of texts (cf. Wink; Clevenot). Totalizing universal and essentialist claims about the text are rightly regarded with suspicion: ideological criticism problematizes, undermines, and ultimately subverts such claims. Biblical scholars would be wise to follow the lead of feminist hermeneutics in this regard. Elisabeth Schüssler Fiorenza in *The Anchor Bible Dictionary* observes: "feminist inquiry . . . deliberately articulates its theoretical perspective without pretending to be value-free, positivistic, universal knowledge" (1992b: vol. 2b:783).[3] When readers of the Bible dispute the meaning of the Bible, critical approaches—whether traditional historical-critical or feminist—expose their ideological interests. To employ a martial metaphor, today the biblical text is an interpretive battlefield in which power is sought by all and truth is claimed by everyone.

Even ideological criticism cannot exempt itself from the ideological struggle that takes place in and over texts. The postmodern condition sets the stage for a reading against the grain not only of those historical approaches that would bracket or deny ideology, but also of those literary and cultural critical approaches that would posit a singular, unitary reading of the Bible (ideological or otherwise). For example, Meir Sternberg argues that the Bible is an ideological text written in didactic style but with a single, unifying, nonconflictual ideological theme. Sternberg regards the Bible as "ideologically singular" in its values and ideas (1985:36–37). He summarizes his position: "Most significant, even where or so far as the ideological

---

[3] In a recent book on criticism edited by McKenzie and Haynes, the title of Danna Nolan Fewell's chapter is "Reading the Bible Ideologically: Feminist Criticism." Several questions emerge: Of all the criticisms discussed in this book, is feminist criticism the only ideological reading? Does an ideological reading imply or require a feminist reading? Isn't every criticism ideological? Is any criticism more or less ideological than any other?

and the aesthetic functions (or viewpoints) part company, the Bible recognizes no conflict between them, such that whatever is not all for the heavenly cause must be against it" (1985:156). The ideologically singular character of the Bible is expressed through its rhetoric (in its canonical form), which constantly teaches this one ideology. Sternberg's forceful narratological approach leads him to all but ignore the political side of ideology by imposing his own agenda—the need to chart a single ideology for the text. As a result, ideological conflict is ruled out for Sternberg because as omniscient narrator he imagines himself completely in control of his own reading (see esp. his chap. 3, "Ideology of Narration and Narration of Ideology," 84–128). Since the Bible has an ideology and because it is written in such an indoctrinating style, Sternberg remains confident that the interpreter is in a position to recognize both easily. But the cost of Sternberg's univocal reading is high: it is insufficiently self-reflexive, and, most important, it can not allow for conflict and differences among readers and readings.

This reading is not entirely surprising given Sternberg's fuzzy understanding of ideology. Ideology sounds vaguely like faith in a "flexible hierarchy" (composed of the trinity of history, aesthetics, and ideology; 1985:156). Whereas other ideologically sensitive readers, like Norman Gottwald, for example, refuse to privilege history over ideology or aesthetics, Sternberg wants both an interplay and a separation of these functions. He asserts, "literary theory has not yet fashioned the tools for making *poetic* sense of ideas and ideology" (1985:36). Here is an instance where the fear of Marxist theory, especially Marxist literary theory, leads to a one-sided statement. Sternberg's ideological criticism of the Bible is not ample enough to take into account historical (in particular, Marxist) and literary critical aspects of ideology at once.

Sternberg's position on the singular "truth claim" for the Bible raises a number of important questions about ideological criticism: Do texts have one ideology or several ideologies? Is ideology a hermeneutical construct that resides outside of the text, and if so where precisely is it? Does every text have its own ideology(ies)? Is there such a thing as a corporate ideology to be located in the canon of sacred scripture? What happens ideologically when reader-hearer-audience and text meet and converge? Is there an "ideology of meeting"? And the question that constantly hounds ideological criticism: How do these criticisms connect specifically with issues of social justice, ethical action, and transformation? Recalling Catherine Belsey, "it is the role of ideology to *construct people as subjects*" (1980:58). The important question that ideological criticism raises in this culture of criticism is how does criticism—narrative, feminist, poststructuralist, rhetorical, and so on—make a difference in the texture of lived relations in a postmodern world today? How does criticism aid in affirming difference and encountering the Other as valued human being, as subject? Recognizing the constructive role ideology plays in cultural and literary criticism is of vital importance.

The notion of ideological singularity raises multiple problems for a postmodern reading that would be tempted to detach itself from history. To argue against the Bible having a singular ideology is not necessarily to insist on the claim that the Bible has multiple ideologies, that the Bible has an ideology at all, or even that ideology is buried in the subtext or deep structures of the text. Ideological readings do tend to focus on the texts that support their political agendas. But the ideological use of ideological criticism per se is a matter of extreme concern. It is incumbent on ideological critics to subject their approaches to critical self-appraisal to expose their own agendas, knowing all the while that it is impossible to expose everything completely. As is true with any reading strategy—but especially so for ideological criticism—the ideological rationalization of appropriating biblical texts raises the issue of the ethics of reading and the status of the many, often-conflicting voices that claim the authority of the Bible in their lives.

Like the ideology of a text, ideological criticism is not one thing, one way of reading; it is legion. It comes in many voices, speaks many languages, and resides in many different disciplines and critical approaches, including psychoanalytic theory, cultural criticism, sociolinguistics, subaltern studies, feminist theory, and deconstruction, to name a few. For this reason, the discussion of ideological criticism can serve as an important bridge between literary criticism and cultural criticism. In this respect it has some of the characteristics of a "criticism encompassing criticism." For many of today's critical readers of the Bible, ideological criticism is helping to forge alliances among discourses that are, in Bakhtin's terms, a *heteroglossia* or *polyglossia* but have shared commitment to transformation of society. In the postmodern context, ideological criticism of the Bible is one place where critical forces are converging with common purpose.

THE IDEOLOGICAL STANCES OF LIBERATION HERMENEUTICS

In critical biblical studies today, one important place where ideological criticism plays a central role is in liberation theologies and materialist readings of the Bible. The focus of our discussion henceforth will be on liberation

theology as a form of ideological criticism. Some of the better-known liberation theologies include: Latin American, Asian (Minjung in South Korea),
Mujerista, African American, South African,[4] feminist,[5] and gay and lesbian
theologies. Reflecting a perspective concerned with issues like class, gender,
sex, race, and ethnicity, these "readings from below" attempt to interpret
the Bible out of their own concrete political, economic, and social circumstances. This makes for great diversity—and a certain level of conflict and
tension—among liberationist readings. Every liberationist reading is potentially different because, it seems, each marginalized or oppressed group can
produce a liberation theology out of its unique historical context. The aim
of this part of the chapter is to examine select readings of the Bible that
openly claim to be ideological, some of which define themselves explicitly
in liberation theological terms.

Whether Marxist or not, liberation readings find themselves constantly
pushing against the boundaries of the text, asking questions that challenge
the given social order by questioning its dominant myths, values (in particular, of the colonizer, of patriarchy), and practices. Liberation readings
tend to state their political purpose and stance up front. We want to say
again that those critics who prescind from talking subjectively about their
approach are equally engaged in making an ideological statement—as Eagleton notes about nontheoretical readers who operate with their theory (see
our Introduction)—for by not admitting their ideological stance they effectively reinstate, by default, the normative criticism. Liberationist forms of
ideological criticism are important because they expressly declare the value-
laden character of biblical texts and readings, which is a necessary first step
toward bringing about transformation.

In the language of liberation, ideological readers are engaged in a hermeneutic of suspicion and a hermeneutic of survival.[6] Ideological criticism

---

[4] Some key texts in liberatory biblical studies include Sugirtharajah; Mosala; Ela; Ateek;
Moon; Tamez; Pixley; Pixley and Boff; Felder, 1989b; Copher; and Weems, 1988.

[5] See Daniel Boyarin's statement in his review of Mieke Bal's *Lethal Love:* "Feminist
readings, then, can model the ways that other suppressed subjects can 'creep in, and rewrite
themselves back into the history of ideology' [*Love* 132], including gays, blacks, and Jews into
European culture and women and Palestinians into Jewish/Israeli culture. To me, this is a most
moving and beautiful exemplum of how to tear down the master's house without using the
master's tools" (1990b:41).

[6] Schüssler Fiorenza offers that "a critical feminist interpretation insists on a *hermeneutics
of suspicion* that can unmask the ideological functions of androcentric text and commentary"
(1992b:785). See also chap. 6.

from this perspective is inherently suspicious, but not in the sense that the reader is cautious about taking risks. Reading and dealing with texts (especially the Bible) is always a risky business whether it be by the privileged or the powerless, risky for the knowledgeable critic or the ordinary reader. A text and reading that is liberating for one person or group may well be oppressive to another. Ideological criticism, to repeat, must ever be concerned with exposing the discourse-power relations wherever they may be found, especially those at work in their own readings.

Two biblical texts central to liberation theology are the Exodus-Conquest and the Cross-Resurrection narratives. By examining conflicting readings of these narratives, we will draw attention to the issues of inclusiveness-exclusiveness and the ethics of reading; in this way we will discover something about the ideology operating behind ideological criticism.

DECOLONIZING EXODUS AND CONQUEST: READINGS IN TENSION

> The peoples heard, they trembled;
> pangs seized the inhabitants of Philistia.
> Then the chiefs of Edom were dismayed;
> trembling seized the leaders of Moab;
> all the inhabitants of Canaan melted away.
> —Exodus 15:14–15

The stories of the Exodus and Conquest have been central to liberation readings of the Bible from its inception: Gustavo Gutierrez was one of the first theologians to apply the Exodus to the oppressive political situation in Peru (1973); in the early days of the American Civil Rights movement, Martin Luther King, Jr., employed Exodus imagery to reflect the freeing of African Americans from the hands of the white oppressor; James Cone (1969, 1984, 1990) compared the liberating event of the Exodus to the African American response to white oppression and privilege; black South Africans relied on this biblical story in their ultimately successful struggle to bring an end to government-imposed Apartheid; Moon Hee-Suk Cyris (1985) cites the need to preserve the Exodus memory among South Koreans held as political prisoners. Thus, Moses' words to Pharaoh, "let my people go," have a resonance for oppressed and marginalized communities throughout the world. The Exodus narrative speaks to the common experience of suffering and the aspirations for life and freedom in all kinds of contexts.

The Spanish theologian Alfredo Fierro suggests that the Exodus event is paradigmatic for Christians acting in historical situations of oppression. He summarizes the Exodus theology this way: "It becomes an image and a standard accompanying one's revolutionary understanding of the time. In the case of theology, the Exodus is a symbol of throwing off the yoke, breaking away from established institutions, and evincing the ability of a people to fashion or refashion a life for themselves. They throw off the suffocating convenience of their age-old situation, lured on by the enticements of a new promised land. The Exodus symbolizes a theological grasp of history as the possibility for change and discontinuity, as malleable material in human hands, as a line of action based on the awareness that one has been liberated by God" (144–45).

A typical element of liberationist readings is the narrative identification of the context of ancient Israel with the contemporary context of the reader. But is the identification of the oppressed reader with the Israelites the only narrative possibility? Ideological critique raises a suspicious question about this dominant reading of Exodus and of the tendency to read these foundational narratives in just such a singular way. South African scholar Itumeleng Mosala warns that the liberatory text must be read suspiciously because those readings justified in terms of being the Word of God can become a dominant reading that excludes others. "The insistence on the Bible as the Word of God must be seen for what it is: an ideological maneuver whereby ruling-class interests evident in the Bible are converted into a faith that transcends social, political, racial, sexual, and economic divisions. In this way the Bible becomes an ahistorical, interclassist document" (1989:18). "There is no cultural document that is not at the same time a record of barbarism," says Walter Benjamin (1979:359), who reminds us of the risk of making any particular reading of the Bible dominant.

In the case of liberation readings of the Exodus and Conquest narratives, ideological criticism insists that we recognize the Bible as a conflictual site of multiple readings, investments, and historical experiences and that every reading has the potential of becoming dominant and of suppressing other readings. Ideological criticism, then, raises very pragmatic questions about reading the Bible: what are the lived relationships of the different conflicting readers of this text, and how can theory help us understand these different contexts? In the words of liberation theology: whose side are we on, God's or Pharaoh's? And which side is God on? Are there even sides at all? As readers battling for our readings how do we keep the question of interests open and keep from silencing the text? Cheryl Exum offers this explanation: "The relation of reading to truth involves the issue of interests, and our interests determine the questions we ask of a text" (46, after Bal). Ideological criticism helps to keep our interests and concerns in front of us as we read. Or to put it another way, ideological criticism keeps reading from becoming sedimented and naturalized, even liberationist readings.

The effort to "decolonize" the Exodus and Conquest narrative is consistent with ideological criticism's aim to recognize the manifold voices and conflicting interests that must enter the exegetical fray. To decolonize is, on the one hand, to identify oppressive sociopolitical presence in the text and in the history of its interpretation in the dominant ideology and, on the other hand, to identify the liberating message of the text and the history of interpretations of the text by oppressed readers. As a bridge between the social and the literary worlds of the Bible, ideological criticism has the potential of leading toward a different hearing of the Bible's liberatory message by insisting we include indigenous readings that are not typical or natural.

At its best, ideological criticism brings out those voices that have been subject to suppression, marginalization, even exclusion and violence. Those familiar with liberation theology and its readings from below have perhaps identified with the ancient Israelites in the story, but what about the other indigenous voices that are there to be heard in this story? A Native American reading of the Exodus and Conquest offers a very different kind of identification and reading from below, an indigenous reading from a very different context that makes other sense of these biblical texts.

Native American Reading: Robert Allen Warrior Latin American liberation theologians by and large make a connection in these stories between the class struggle of the poor against the rich and the indigenous against the imperialist powers. The journey to the promised land serves as a source of hope and inspiration in a revolutionary situation, whether it be nonviolent revolution (King) or the violent overthrow of a dictatorship (the Nicaraguan Sandinistas). The cathartic effect or emotional release from the status quo of oppressed people in liberation theology is directly tied to the promise that "all the inhabitants of Canaan have melted away" (Exod. 15:15) and that God has prepared the land for the oppressed. At the heart of the liberation reading of the Exodus story is the opposition of the freedom of the Israelites to the suppression of the Canaanites.

In "Canaanites, Cowboys, and Indians: Deliverance, Conquest, and Liberation Theology Today," Robert Allen Warrior offers a different ideological reading. Warrior asks, We are very familiar with who the Israelites are, but who are the Canaanites? His answer: They are the indigenous people of the land of Canaan who were eventually conquered and subjugated by the Israelites.[7] As an Osage Indian, Warrior provides a Native American liberation reading that is grounded in a very different experience than the normative liberationist readings of the Exodus narrative. He relates, "The obvious characters in the story for Native Americans to identify with are the Canaanites, the people who already lived in the promised land" (262). The Canaanites and the Canaanite side of the story have not been told. Not only were the Canaanites destroyed in the biblical text; they have been erased from the reconstruction of these biblical stories altogether. Warrior's concern here is to raise the question about the presentation-representation of the Canaanites in the narrative (262) and their role within the stories of the Exodus and Conquest.

This liberatory text is therefore not nearly as hospitable to the Canaanites as to the Israelites. Warrior centers attention on the biblical passages that emphasize the deliverer-warrior Yahweh who will destroy the Canaanites and all other indigenous people (Deut. 7:1–2). The language, culture, religion, and heritage of the Canaanites are seen as the negative "other," foreign and thus dangerous and to be avoided at all costs. Warrior sees this "interreligious praxis" as deadly to the Canaanites because the God of the Israelites is the destroyer of the Canaanites: "They were assimilated into another people's identity and the history of their ancestors came to be regarded as suspect and a danger to the safety of Israel. In short, they were betrayed" (264).

Warrior makes the hermeneutical and historical point that the myth of the chosen people and the Exodus and Conquest narratives provided the Puritans and other European settlers in North America with a biblical text whose particular ideological reading justified the destruction of indigenous peoples. Warrior concludes, "As long as people believe in the Yahweh of deliverance, the world will not be safe from Yahweh the conqueror" (265). The god of the oppressor is not to be trusted. The dominant reading of the

---

[7] Edward Said also reads from a Canaanite perspective in his review of Michael Walzer's *Exodus and Revolution*. This reading has been adopted by Rob Nixon to interpret the apartheid story in South Africa: "The Exodus narrative and its New Testament analogues have a hold on the imaginings of Afrikaans and African nationalism alike" (1991:48).

text by the oppressed in this case proves to be dangerous—oppressive—for indigenous peoples. Warrior's Native American liberation reading serves as a critique of the normative character of liberationist readings of Exodus by suspiciously searching out his own specific culture and experiences for an understanding of liberation that is suppressed by the dominant reading strategy.

Warrior's reading shows that the ideology of one liberation reading has paradoxically become the dominant ideology against which another liberation reading reacts. The oppressed have reversed roles and become the oppressors. Warrior's reading also reveals the "strategies of containment" (Jameson) used in liberation readings that make it possible to ignore and even erase the voices and history of the Canaanites. The Exodus and Conquest narratives, therefore, serve up more than historical and archaeological contradictions. They expose the interpretive contradictions and tensions inherent within liberation exegesis and the dangers of an ideological reading that does not recognize in itself multiple and heterogeneous reading (Derrida's *différance*, see our chap. 3)—even reading against its own grain—as an essential feature of the construction of meaning. Multiple, conflicting stories are exposed through an open ideological reading, and Warrior's linking of Native Americans with the indigenous Canaanites is one way to distill yet another voice and experience.

To use Belsey's poststructuralist terms, ideological critique serves as an important critical tool for *decentering* the reading subject and the subject matter being read. This means first recognizing the privileged identification made between the reader's interest and the narrative and then deliberately shifting that identification to allow for the text to be a text "for" another reader and reading experience. Here we see the ethical character of ideological reading of the Bible emerge. It is tied to efforts to expose the structures of power and containment that operate not just for their reading, but for all readings, including liberationist ones. This way the endless cycle of revolution and the binary oppositions or dualisms that ever-link oppressed and oppressor are exposed, revealed, and, we hope, transformed in accordance with the central message of liberation the text transmits. At the same time, an ideological reading may force readers to face up to another aspect of the text, in this case its holy war ideology. However liberatory the Bible may be, it is also, as the feminist critic Mieke Bal says, a text that kills (1991). Warrior's reading of the Exodus narrative leaves us wondering whether in the ideology of Exodus Israelites can be free only if the Canaanites "melt away."

A Sociopolitical Reading of the Exodus: Norman Gottwald A Native American reading of the Exodus and Conquest stories serves as a critique and ideological counterpoint to traditional liberationist readings. A reading like Warrior's, which begins from another place, calls the dominant readings into question and forces into the open the question of accountability. Focusing on the Canaanites as a people displaced from the land (and narrative) by the Israelites by means of a holy war ideology demonstrates that an absolute privileging of the Israelites, while understandable, is to be resisted. The ideological character of the flight of the slaves from their Egyptian oppressors and the conquering of the land of Canaan and the setting up of a new nation of Israel, which are elements in the fiction of revolution, now begs reexamination. What is hidden and suppressed here? Can we identify the ideology(ies) of ancient Israel? Are those investments written into the biblical narrative, and if so at whose cost?

The biblical narrative preserves an ideology that invites identification with the Israelites. An important reader in search of this ideology is Norman Gottwald. He sets out to describe this ideology without placing a value judgment on whether it is true or false. Gottwald's interest lies in showing how ancient Israelites understood their existence and the ways they organized themselves in light of their perception and memory of certain social and class conflicts.

Gottwald proposes a peasant-revolt model that attempts to factor into account both the hermeneutics of liberation theology and the Marxist analysis of class and class struggle. The elements of Gottwald's critical framework are drawn from sociology, cultural anthropology, literary criticism, and a Marxist analysis of history. Within the model that he develops the Exodus narrative serves a double function as both *event* and *process:* Exodus as event designates the flight from Egypt through the settlement in Canaan; Exodus as process marks the movement "from a collective life determined by others to a collective life that is self-determined" through "social and political revolution" (1989:253). Gottwald calls for the acknowledgment of the "nonhistoriographic nature of the traditions" of the Exodus that derive from exilic and postexilic times (253–54). All that can be said historically about the Exodus is summarized by Gottwald this way: "Whatever happened in Egypt, Israel sprang to birth in Canaan in the approximate sociohistorical manner attested in the exodus traditions: by resistance to state oppression and by a bold bid for self-determination" (254). The Exodus is "a divine-human collaboration in social revolution" (259). The broad categories of class consciousness and struggle developed here are consistent with the popular liberation readings of the Exodus and with liberation hermeneutic, but his analysis differs in the extent to which it pays careful attention to the competing sociohistorical realities that are reflected in the biblical narratives.

Gottwald delineates four "horizons" or "moments" expressed in the biblical stories: "Horizon no. 1 is that of the hypothetical participants in the events reports" (254); "Horizon no. 2 is that of the Israelite social revolutionaries and religious confederates in the highlands of Canaan in the twelfth and eleventh centuries" (255); "Horizon no. 3 is that of Israelite traditionists in monarchic times who conceive Israel of the exodus experience as an essentially national entity in transit toward its secure establishment as a state of Canaan" (256–7). "Horizon no. 4 is that of the late exilic and postexilic restorers of Judah as a religious and cultural community that had lost its political independence" (257). By assessing the Exodus in terms of these four horizons or moments, the textual levels and contradictions come to the surface. The bottom line is also exposed, namely, that God liberated the Israelites and had special plans and a special place for them. The authority of God in the Exodus is central, whether or not Israel was armed against the Egyptians or whether Jericho was a walled city in the twelfth century B.C.E.

Accordingly, Gottwald's peasant-revolt model centers on an ideology of class consciousness and revolt. Gottwald posits a peasant farming situation comparable to serfdom, with Canaanite overlords and Egyptian pharaohs overseeing the overlords. Peasant Israelites and Canaanites joined forces to revolt against the feudal system. The 'apiru were mercenary rebels who added to the class warfare. It is Israel's response to the cultural systems of Egypt and Canaan, therefore, that serves as the basis for the ideology of the biblical narratives.

In Gottwald's model ideology means "the consensual constitutive concepts and attitudes of early Israel" (1979:65). These attitudes include the religious beliefs and theology of ancient Israel in the realm of its larger social world and the interrelationships of Israel with other cultural systems. For Gottwald, the ideology of ancient Israel is "the consensual religious ideas which were structurally embedded in and functionally correlated to other social phenomena within the larger social system . . . and also to define and energize the Israelite social system oppositionally or polemically over against other social systems" (1979:66). What Gottwald shows so persuasively is that the ideology of holy war *and* liberation are woven together into the fabric of the Exodus and Conquest narratives. For Gottwald the ideological function of these narratives in the life of ancient Israel is multiple—not singular—and in their complexity they are integral parts of the overall religious system.

It is important to note that Gottwald enlarges the common definition of ideology that operates within much liberation theology to include elements of Marxist theory. For many liberationists, ideology is synonymous with "theology" (see Hardegree, 99). In reaction, Juan Luis Segundo returns to the Greek root of the word *ideology* to find *idea*. For Segundo, "Ideology, then, would be the systematization of my perception of the real" (16). Gottwald borrows this positive definition for his work. Ideology is one feature of the theological discourse, but not co-terminus with it. As Henri Mottu puts it, the discourse of ideology in the Bible is "cultural formation" and "cultural production" to be distinguished from theology (241). Ideology develops out of relationships formed in and from a particular culture.

The Exodus and Conquest stories are deeply embedded narratives in the historical memory, imagination, and social experience of the ancient Israelites. The subject who is addressed by the ideology of the Exodus and Conquest—both the individual and corporate subject—is shaped by these narratives and their ideology. Belsey argues (in agreement with Althusser): "The destination of all ideology is the subject (the individual in society) and it is the role of ideology to *construct people as subjects*" (1980:58; see Eagleton, 1990a:87). Ideology and the aesthetic are directed to the subject who is supposed to "know" and understand the inner workings and messages of the text. To translate these theoretical terms into biblical ones, the Exodus reader is confronted with an imagined group of Hebrew slaves who escaped or fought their way to freedom from the oppressive Egyptian Pharaohs. They were led by the stronger warrior god Yahweh and Yahweh's servant Moses into the wilderness and later into Canaan. Victorious, they were blessed when obedient and struck down when disobedient. On the whole, this ideology shapes and gives supports to a "centered subject" who is "reassuringly pliable." The traditional reading of the history of ancient Israel inscribes an ideology that supports a certain group of male warriors who are faithful to Yahweh. One of the ways Gottwald speaks of this imagining is in terms of the "ideological impulse" of the so-called Deuteronomic Historian. But we must remember that the ideology of Exodus is a system, which is complex and permits multiple responses. The inequities of this ideological system we have already discussed in our treatment of Robert Warrior, who imagines an alternative ideological response to the Canaanite presence (or better, absence) in the text.

Gottwald's interdisciplinary approach makes an important appeal and contribution to ideological criticism grounded in sociological methodology. His particular combination of liberationist and materialist concerns reflects upon the complex ideological character of the biblical narrative and of the need for an ideological criticism that is subtle and flexible. What Gottwald has not concentrated on in his analysis, however, is the determinant of race. Turning to African American biblical hermeneutics we will see how the combination of liberation and race set the stage for a different ideological reading.

African American Biblical Hermeneutics Another example of liberation reading of the Exodus narrative is found in the writings and preaching of African American theologians. The Exodus is a central motif in the recent collection of the writings of African American biblical scholars entitled *Stony the Road We Trod: African American Biblical Interpretation*. Clarice Martin explains: "In light of the socially restricting and often brutalizing forces to which African Americans have been subjected psychologically, socially, economically, and politically, it is not at all surprising that they could identify with the struggles and the victory of the Israelites" (1991:226; see also, Wimbush, 1991:91). The basic thrust of this volume is to recover the African-centered parts and players of the biblical text. A *politics of omission* (Martin's term) has operated in the dominant readings of the Exodus story; like Native Americans, Africans (and Africa) have been read out of the text, but for different reasons.

Charles Copher seeks to recover the African presence in the Exodus narrative (1991:155). Of the main characters—Moses, Zipporah, Aaron, and Miriam—Copher argues that "the issue was hardly one of black color, for all of them were black" (156). He bases his argument on several factors: "the three definitions of black/Negro; scholarly opinion that views Moses' family as of Nubian origin; and the existence of Cushites in Asia as well as in Africa" (1991:156, n. 23). The implications of his reading are far-reaching, for it forces into the foreground consideration of the ideological character of white Eurocentric (and sometimes white supremist) exegesis against which it stands in stark contrast.

For the most part, issues of power and control, rather than those of inclusivity and liberation, dominate reading within the academy today. The politics of omission that characterizes much of academia takes many forms: from maps that omit North Africa and the Sudan and Ethiopia to a passing over of race and ethnicity when reading biblical characters who come from Africa. African American biblical hermeneutics makes the omission of race and ethnicity a central concern as it rereads and reconstructs the biblical narratives and its racist interpretive history.

Some womanist biblical scholars also engage in reconstructive work on the biblical text in the effort to recover the lives and voices of African women in the narrative. With respect to the Exodus, the focus is on the female characters: the Hebrew midwives, Shiprah and Puah (Exod. 1:8–22); the daughter of Pharaoh, Bithiah; the mother of Moses, Miriam; the women who danced (Exod. 15:20–21); and Zipporah. In Renita Weems's womanist ideological reading entitled "The Hebrew Women Are Not Like the Egyptian Women: The Ideology of Race, Gender, and Sexual Reproduction in Exodus 1," she locates conflict between masters and slaves in the story of the Hebrew midwives who confront Pharaoh. From her perspective, "biblical texts take sides in ideological debates, debates which usually center around issues of power where literature becomes a form of public discourse seeking either to challenge or defend the way in which people are socially constituted" (1992:25). The way women and slaves were treated—how race, gender and power interconnect in the reading of Exodus—is both a past and present concern for African American biblical hermeneutics.

Weems reads Exodus with an Eagletonian-Althusserian understanding of ideology as material production. Her goal is to identify the codes of race and gender embedded in the text and rooted in the matrices of social and political production. A power struggle is taking place in the text: "the story pivots around the threat that Israel's religious heritage (e.g., 'be fruitful and multiply') presents to Egyptian hegemony. Here, obedience to the Hebrew god stands in sharp opposition to obedience to Egyptian power" (29). And the women stand in opposition to male power. Weems notes that the concept of difference is at the heart of the Exodus 1 narrative—difference of gender, race, and social class. The ideology and rhetoric of the text are linked for Weems (as for Sternberg) in that the text exhorts and pushes the reader-audience to act. She calls for careful consideration in applying the gender ideology of the Exodus to women in particular, since women do not benefit in terms of rank as a result of liberation from slavery. Weems's reading demonstrates the weakness of an ideological criticism that ignores or isolates issues of gender, race, ethnicity, or class from one another. To do so would be to deny the complex nature of social identity and relationships both with respect to the persons in the narrative and the readers of the biblical narrative.

Contemporary Jewish Biblical Hermeneutics Almost by default liberation theology is regarded as a Christian interpretive issue. Contemporary Jewish voices, in particular, are virtually absent from the discussion of the Exodus as a liberating paradigm. Why that is so is an interesting interpretive issue. One important exception is Michael Walzer, who is involved in the hermeneutics of Exodus: "The study of the Bible leads to a view of political action as a kind of communal performance: what happened in Egypt and at Sinai provides a precedent for early modern (and present-day) efforts to mobilize men and women for a politics without precedent in their own experience" (1985:90). In his political study of the Exodus, Walzer holds these presuppositions: (1) that wherever you live, it is probably Egypt; (2) that there is a better place, a world more attractive, a promised land; and (3) that "the way to the land is through the wilderness." There is no way to get from here to there except by joining together and marching (149). In short, the Exodus event is about revolution. And any serious consideration of the story, any committed retelling is also about revolution and positive social change.

Walzer's reading brings us to ask, who and where are contemporary Jews in the discussion about Exodus theology? Bringing the text to the present day, Conservative Jewish theologian Marc Ellis notes this gap in the conversation and also the great irony in the Israeli government's failure to draw on its ancient memory, texts, and responsibility to do the right thing in relation to the "Palestinian problem." For Ellis, the modern Canaanites are the Palestinians, especially those living in the Occupied Territories in the land of Israel. And Ellis claims that the Israeli government (not the Jewish people) has become, paradoxically, the modern equivalent of Egypt. Jewish theology of liberation is grounded on the stories of the Exodus and Conquest, along with the prophetic exhortations. But what does remembering and acting on these stories entail? Ellis summarizes: "A new Jewish theology speaks of a renaissance of Jewish life as well as its cost: Israel as an occupying power, expropriator of land, torturer of prisoners, and arms exporter. The return to Israel may be our ideology; a new Jewish theology faces the fact that 75 percent of the Jewish people do not and will not live in Israel and that now more Israelis leave Israel each year than emigrate to it" (1989:379).

According to Ellis, the narrative roles have been reversed: the oppressed have become the oppressor. The ideology of the Exodus means for Ellis and others freedom for all the ancient Israelites but at the same time the destruction of the Canaanites who dwell in the promised land. This ideology and its implications over the last thirty years have been deadly, literally, to the Palestinians. The recent peace accord signed between Israel and the Palestine Liberation Organization, however, suggests that neither ideology or the ideology of a text may be enough to stand in the way of peace. The ideological voices of the biblical text must be allowed to speak their liberating message. At the same time it must be remembered that this message may not be liberating for everyone.

MARK AND MATERIALISM: READINGS IN TENSION

When it was noon, darkness came over the whole land until three in the afternoon. At three o'clock Jesus cried out with a loud voice, "Eloi, Eloi, lema sabachtani?" which means, "My God, my God, why have you forsaken me?" . . . Then Jesus gave a loud cry and breathed his last.
—Mark 15:33–37

Like the Exodus and Conquest texts, the narratives of the death and resurrection of Jesus of Nazareth also function as central stories for liberation theology and for other ideological readings of the New Testament. And like Exodus, the death and resurrection stories raise a number of questions: What is the sociopolitical significance of Jesus's transforming life and ignominious death? What was Jesus's political stance? Was Jesus a radical, a Zealot who advocated the violent overthrow of the Roman imperial government? Was he made a scapegoat for teaching against the dominant ideology? Or was Jesus an advocate of nonviolence toward the imperial power and others along the lines of Gandhi's *satyagraha*, truth or soul force? What is the ideology of Jesus as presented in the Gospels? And how has the story of Jesus's crucifixion been a dominant force in the institutional church and the lives of believers? In liberation theology, in particular, has the story of the cross and resurrection ever been oppressive?

A number of liberation theologians identify a fundamental class conflict in the gospel narratives about Jesus: Jesus is the one who heals and teaches the poor and is always clearly in tension with Jewish and Roman authorities. It is the dichotomy of poor and nonpoor that is brought to the surface in the teaching of Jesus. In addressing the role of ideology in the pedagogy of the poor and the nonpoor, the Brazilian educator Paulo Freire says: "Education involves power. . . . And there is the question of ideology, the ideology of power which seeks to reproduce and emphasize the interests of the dominant class, as well as ideology understood as a possible confrontation with the dominant interests" (221). Political readings of the Jesus of the New Testament that lift up the indigenous voices of the poor and oppressed (for example, the community at Solentiname [Cardinal]) find in the stories and life of Jesus and in the theology of the cross a symbol of hope for the revolutionary overthrow of the dominant powers (economical, political, cultural). Liberationist (and we can also say *materialist*) readings are intentionally in conflict with the interests of the dominant class, sex, and race.

The rallying cry for a materialist reading of the Jesus's narratives is offered by Kuno Füssel: "A materialist reading of the Bible means: to awaken the sense of the text as the liberating praxis of life" (1987:27). This statement echoes quite deliberately the apocalyptic call of Jesus in Mark's Gospel when he says to the disciples: "And what I say to you I say to all: Keep awake" (13:37). Ideological criticism of Mark's Gospel reissues Jesus's wake-up call, although this time directed to today's readership. Notwithstanding the identification with Jesus's apocalyptic call, we must remember that the textual ideology is not singular but multiple: there is not an exclusive reading of the text, nor a single, definitive portrait of Jesus (as the Old and New Quests for the so-called historical Jesus have demonstrated; see Crossan, 1991). The ideology of the myth resists all monological readings.

The Political Hermeneutic of Ched Myers In a very focused and compelling way, Ched Myers utilizes contemporary social and political theory for a reading of the Markan narrative. Myers's interests arise from his work with the American Friends Service Committee and his commitment to peace and justice issues. He is one of several North American white male Christians attempting to translate liberation theology for first world readers in a first world context. Daniel Berrigan, Robert McAfee Brown, and Frederick Herzog are Myers's predecessors in this effort to use the privilege and position of their social location to promote the causes of the oppressed. Myers quite explicitly applies his own political interests to the reading of Mark. He admits up front the nature of his own personal, invested reading and the specific ideological agenda he wishes to pursue. It is an agenda that seeks to uncover the effect the Markan text and our critical readings of the Gospel have on the lives of the poor.

Myers's ideological method is grounded in a Marxist reading of the problem of class struggle. For Myers, class distinctions in the Gospel of Mark are political (Roman occupation of Palestine), social (class conflict), economic (conflict over ownership of the land between the rich and the poor), and religious (the authorities and the disciples). Myers is not particularly concerned with gender oppression, although he finds models for women's leadership in Mark and even goes so far as to note that "Mark has offered critiques of three systems of power: political domination, patriarchy, and the family system" (280). Myers's main concern, however, is not to expose Mark's ambiguous portrayal of women (especially at the tomb), but to immerse himself in a political reading of the Gospel that reveals the Markan Gospel to be a radical political writing, which subverted and continues to subvert the dominant ideology, whether of the first or the latest Markan readers.

The line of ideological criticism Myers follows is one filtered through Marxist definitions, one he also shares with Eagleton, Jameson, and Gottwald. Myers locates himself squarely on the side of semiotic and materialist definitions of ideology, which allows him to speak of his preference for an eclectic approach he calls a "literary sociology" (26ff.): "I . . . am content to adopt definition 3a in *Webster's Third International Dictionary*: ideology is 'a systematic scheme or coordinated body of ideas or concepts about human life or culture.' I also hasten to affirm, with the Marxist tradition, that the study of ideology is for purposes of determining not only how symbolic discourse functions socially, but also on *whose behalf*" (18). Although his take on ideology is a broad one, Myers's aim is quite specific: to shake up North American churches by means of a revolutionary reading of Mark.

Myers's preference for the mainline dictionary definition of ideology is telling because the critique of his ideological reading is provided by other parts of the definition. Webster's *Third* also defines ideology as "visionary speculation: idle theorizing; often an impractical theory or system of theories"; "an extremist sociopolitical program or philosophy constructed wholly or in part on factitious or hypothetical ideational bases." The negative assessment reflects the negative reaction to early Marxist philosophy and stems from the view that ideology is idealistic, nonpragmatic, that is, the very opposite of common sense.

One of the most frequent criticisms of liberation readings encountered is that they are merely giving voice to utopian desires for a society that we know can never be implemented. Common sense tells us we must be realists: we know what human nature is all about—the poor will always be with us, as Jesus himself said. By this view ideology is something reserved for political extremists on the right or left, not ordinary people who find themselves outside the realms of power. It is this very commonsense view of the poor that Myers criticizes and exposes. He maintains the focus of his ideological reading on the ideology of the poor (and how the nonpoor are to respond) over against the ideology of the ruling class.

Myers's subversive reading of Mark corresponds to Mark's own ideology: here is a case where the ideology of the text and the ideology of the critical reader overlap. His reading of Mark is influenced by the need for a nonviolent but revolutionary Jesus who ironically suffered a violent death on the cross. Myers sees in first-century Palestine a situation of social unrest and tension, and Mark's ideological response is delivered by way of a story about Jesus that labors to unmask class relations and the ideology of the oppressive systems of domination that rule the lives of the vast majority of people in the Mediterranean world. By Myers's reading, the Jesus of Mark made oppression of people the central concern of his teaching and ministry. The logical hermeneutical implication is that contemporary readers should also make the poor their central concern. As to why readers are either so antagonistic or disinterested in the Gospel's poor, Myers would likely have to agree with James Kavanagh who suggests that "the depoliticization of the social subject is one of the major political effects that the work of American ideology as a whole helps to reinforce" (313). There is no better place to see this gesture of depoliticization than in the ways mainstream biblical scholarship and Protestant theology do their business. The Gospel of Mark, however, aggressively pushes a very different ideology.

However, Myers is not uncritical of materialist and Marxist hermeneutics in their appropriation of the cross event. Myers observes, "Here is where problems arise for the otherwise most promising advances in political hermeneutics: the disconcerting tendency shared by virtually all Marxist-oriented reading strategies to avoid or suppress the ideological and narrative fulcrum of Mark's Jesus story: his 'strategy' of the cross" (469). Ideological critics must be very careful to attend to the narrative and ideological strategy of the Markan text lest their own agenda—which wants to celebrate and is tied to an "imperial ideology of triumph"—dominate the text. Against the imperial ideology of triumph found in a number of traditional readings of the Markan cross event, Myers counters, "Mark . . . has given us narrative clues that identify all the apocalyptic moments with the one event of the cross" (391). The Markan ideology of the cross can be summarized in this way: "the world order has been overthrown, the powers have fallen (13:24ff.)" (392). Jesus's crucifixion is the central metaphor for a political hermeneutic of nonviolence—both past and present.

The Materialist Method of Fernando Belo Materialist readings of the Bible on the whole focus on the social class distinctions created by economic and political forces. For Portuguese scholar Fernando Belo (and Michel Clevenot in his summary book), a materialist reading of Mark is the type of subversive reading needed to uncover the social class conflict in the Gospel and to reveal Mark's Gospel as a politically subversive text. Belo's pathbreaking reading of Mark underscores the class struggle through an examination of Palestine in the first century C.E. The realities of slavery and social and economic inequities then and now influence, indeed dominate, his materialist reading of the text.

Belo's materialist reading is an amalgam of several methods combined for ideological purpose: semiotics, structuralism, sociological exegesis, and Marxist political philosophy. Relying on the structuralist Barthes, Belo rereads Mark for its various codes (hermeneutic, cultural, proairetic, semic, referential, symbolic; see Barthes, 1974b), which structure the message of the text (91). These codes shape the political identity of the text with its powerless classes pitted against the elite and the Roman government. Jesus is the messianic liberator of the poor and oppressed masses. Mark tips off the reader at the very beginning about the messianic identity of Jesus: "The beginning of the good news of Jesus Christ, the son of God" (Mk. 1:1). Mark associates Jesus with the early church (*ekklēsia*) and against the dominant state ideology of Rome.

Concerning the crucifixion of Jesus, in Belo's analysis the scene of Jesus' murder is central to the formation of Markan theology. Jesus' murder becomes a *death* in the Markan presentation; the cross is a predestined event that Jesus must go through with in order to fulfill the will of God and bring on salvation for the believers (277ff.). Jesus' scream from the cross (Mk. 15:37), which is frequently represented in Latin American art, signifies the oppression of the Roman system on the body.

Mark's theological discourse takes place on the political site of the *ekklē-*

sia. For Belo, the priesthood replaces the apostles in the second generation of Christianity, creating an *episcopal* site (282–83) in the powerless Roman church. Belo calls for the return to the kerygma, the message that is present in the text before the layers of institutionalized Christianity covered it over (288). Yet even this Markan kerygma is already tainted by issues such as predestination and messianism. In this way Belo shows that the Markan text is already from the beginning the result of conflicting readings and inter-pretations about the death and resurrection of Jesus. The effort to deal with these conflicts produced a softening of the radical praxis of Jesus' message and altered it to fit institutional needs.

For Belo the resurrection of Jesus is also subversive. "The resurrection can only be the fruit of insurrection. . . . It is when we accept the supremely ma-terialist site of the daily violence exercised against the bodies of the poor, that we cannot fail to posit the affirmation-question of the resurrection" (295). The resurrection of Jesus provides subversive hope for the reader in the face of political oppression. In other words, the hope of resurrection lies in the practice of insurrection, namely, political involvement directed against op-pressive state power.[8] This action is not a utopian dream, but a concrete act that links the believer to the realm of God and God's promise to the believers through Jesus. "The resurrection," Myers proposes, "represents the apoca-lyptic hope that the blood of the martyrs will be vindicated and the pain of the world healed, and conforms the call to historical insomnia" (408).

Although there are a number of places of overlapping interests and cri-tique of Mark, Myers criticizes Belo on the issue of determining layers of theological discourse in the Cross-Resurrection narratives.[9] He accuses Belo of "avoiding the cross" by focusing instead upon the "theological over-lay" of the narratives. Myers argues that this emphasis drains away the power of the martyrdom of Jesus on the cross. Once again, for Myers the heart of the Jesus story remains the cross event, which needs to remain central and connected to the whole Jesus story.

Myers also differs with Belo on methodological grounds. Myers is very suspicious of structuralism and deconstruction because he wants to posit a

---

[8] David Batstone also states this concern for the results of positive social change in reading the Cross-Resurrection narrative: "Though liberationists believe that the redemption effected by Jesus Christ has these transcendent and universal dimensions, they emphasize that these truths must nonetheless be mediated and rendered visible in concrete acts of salvation" (122).

[9] Compare the critique of materialist readings by Kuno Füssel (1984).

specific sociohistorical context to the Markan narrative. In relying on both the earlier and the later Barthes, Belo is viewed as being overly concerned with the sequence of codes in the text at the expense of the sociohistorical context. In spite of those differences, Myers and Belo are both convinced that they have discovered Mark's political ideology. Both methods offer sociohistorical-socioliterary approaches to reading. And both Myers and Belo are subject to their own ideological interests in promoting a nonviolent ethic (in Myers's case, Gandhian *satyagraha*).

Myers and Belo also identify ideological criticism with the theological task. It is a proper theological task to identify the ideological point of view of the text (plot, author, characters, narrator) and of the readers (see Uspensky; Moore 1989b:56–57) using a political hermeneutic, a materialist-structuralist methodology or some other critical strategy.[10] Myers states that "the proper vocation of theology is the practice of 'ideological literacy,' the critical discipline of political hermeneutics" (21). In Myers's liberation reading, Mark is "a manifesto for radical discipleship" (11) and an ideological narrative that leads to a new socioeconomic and political order brought about by nonviolence. For his part, Belo is keen to demythologize Mark's "theological discourse" in order to examine issues of class struggle and economic and political deprivation. Both readers incorporate what we could call a political christology (one shared with the El Salvadoran theologian Jon Sobrino) in their work, which attempts to arrive at the political implications of Jesus' death and resurrection for the first and the twentieth centuries.

Political christology is an aspect of a liberation reading of the life and teachings of Jesus and of the centuries of theological-ideological baggage brought forward with the institutionalized forms of Christianity. Political christology, central to most liberation theologies, has liberative power as the base communities of Latin America can attest. The suffering of Jesus on the cross represents the suffering that brings liberation from oppression. The messianic power of Jesus is revealed in the cross and resurrection, giving hope to the oppressed. While liberation readings of these narratives vary in terms of having a greater (Latin American) or lesser (Minjung) interest in Marxism and class struggle per se, liberation readings as a rule are united

---

10 Boris Uspensky (8) defines the ideological plane of point of view as follows: "whose point of view does the author assume when he evaluates and perceives ideologically the world which he describes." Point of view belongs to the narrator, author, or characters in the story.

in their regard for the cross as a political event that is repeated in different ages and in different oppressive contexts.

Feminist Rereadings of the Cross Feminist liberation readings provide a different approach to the christological issue. With the tools of feminist theory, Rita Brock and others move the critical focus away from the class to the gender implications associated with the death and resurrection of Jesus. They find in traditional sacrificial christology a glorification of suffering, which has served as the theological-christological basis for abuse of women. When Brock reads Mark, she sees "erotic power;" that is, the lifeforce (from Audre Lorde) that acknowledges and affirms all life forms. Brock's feminist ideological critique leads to a call for a "Christa community" (52–53), one that breaks with the patriarchal-hierarchical family-religious institution of mainstream Christianity as a way to create space where women are treated as equals. In the traditional Trinitarian understanding, which the majority of liberation readings adopt, the Father grieves over the death of the Son and through the cross knows the suffering of humanity (see Moltmann; Sobrino). Nonetheless, Jesus is a liberator because the realm of God about which he preaches is ultimately inclusive and empowering of women.

In the Gospel of Mark Brock finds the presence of people of "heart" and stories of "brokenheartedness." The miracles enacted by Jesus are described in this way: "Actions to heal brokenheartedness shatter old orientations to self and power and open fissures that birth erotic power" (74). Here we see a feminist christology at work, one that is ideologically self-focused on erotic power that will lead believers to heal the brokenheartedness of the world. The passion narrative in Mark does not tell women to be self-sacrificing like Jesus in order to be saved. Rather, Brock understands the cross to be saying: "The brokenheartedness revealed in his death is created by the political systems of patriarchal society and was neither inevitable nor necessary" (93–94). The death of Jesus on the cross is a tragic event that should not continue to be visited on the lives of women.

Still, suffering in the Markan Gospel has been read as redemptive, even with the political overtones given to the theology of suffering by certain liberation theologians who find the complete love of God in the cross event. Not every political christology glorifies suffering; in the death and resurrection of Jesus hope is seen for the future liberation from suffering (see Sobrino). But feminist scholars have pushed the issue further to examine the effects of the sacrificial theology of the cross on the lives of women. Joanne

Brown and Rebecca Parker represent one of the more radical approaches to the notion of atonement. They hold that if one accepts the view that the cross was part of the divine plan of God, then God is a sadistic deity. They conclude: "Christianity is an abusive theology that glorifies suffering. Is it any wonder that there is so much abuse in modern society when the predominant image or theology of culture is of 'divine child abuse'—God the Father demanding and carrying out the suffering and death of his own son? If Christianity is to be liberating for the oppressed it must itself be liberated from this theology." We do not need to be saved by Jesus' death from some original sin. We need to be liberated from the oppression of racism, classism, and sexism, that is, from patriarchy (26–27). The attention paid to Jesus' death diverts attention from that oppression.

In their analysis Brown and Parker move away from both traditional theories of the atonement (and the concept of atonement as viable) and specific gospel understandings of the death and resurrection of Jesus. They make a much longer hermeneutical leap than most liberation readings. The reason in part is that they do not find much that is liberating for women in mainstream liberation readings marked so heavily as they are by a Trinitarian understanding of the cross and its privileged Father-Son relationship. Oppression in patriarchal societies is to be measured in terms of the multiple systems of race, class, and gender. Although it may be true that the resurrection represents hope against death, unless gender considerations enter into the ideological fray in a direct and forceful way, the resurrection and the liberation readings of the Gospels will not speak to *all* oppressed within an unjust system. What we learn from the feminist contribution to ideological criticism through the critique of liberation theology is the central importance of gender and the need for a hermeneutics of suspicion that challenges and resists the gendered nature of past and present-day liberation and ideological readings. Like Native Americans and African Americans women ask whether the biblical text is not conflicted and at war with itself on this question of freedom from oppression. If reading is multiple, then the text can make possible a reading that omits, suppresses, even kills.

THE DISCOURSES OF RESISTANCE

Ideological criticism situates itself in the context of interpreting the Bible from points of view shaped by many different cultures and social and political locations. If it is anything, ideological criticism is an affirmation of difference as a principle that precludes univocal, singular readings of texts, cultures, interests, and ideologies.[11] In the contemporary context, ideological criticism is oppositional reading that calls into question, exposes, undermines, and transforms the strategies of power of mainstream white male Western readings of the Bible. One of feminist criticism's most important contributions to the debate over ideological criticism is its insistence that mainstream ideological criticism recognizes how it, too, can engage in a politics of omission—in this case, *gender* omission.

Ideological criticism is a critical mediation between text and reader which contends there can never be a pure, ideology-free, uninvested meeting between text and reader. There is always bias: on the part of readers, of critical approaches, of texts. This holds true for ideological critics and ideological criticism as well: the ideological character of ideological reading is as necessary to expose and guard against as any other reading. Reading, as we have argued, is an ethical act that involves an encounter between reader and text, an encounter that is always situated within individual lives and institutional systems. This means that some readings are "better" than others. Better ideological readings are those that support and encourage positive social change that affirms difference and inclusion. There are also ethically mixed readings, such as a reading that improves the conditions of one oppressed group—for example, the status and power of heterosexual women in the church through ordination—but which at the same time ignores the specific issues and conditions surrounding the ordination of lesbians. Ideological critique lifts up the internal conflicts and exposes systems of privilege.

Ideological criticism in all its many forms is resistance reading. Resistance reading means different readings that resist the oppressive use of power in discourse. Resistance readings demonstrate the fundamental openness of texts and how meaning cannot be determined absolutely (that is, meaning cannot be decontextualized) but is itself resistant to ultimate or final interpretation. This is but another way of stating Bultmann's dictum that there are no presuppositionless readings of the New Testament. Resistant readings are always shaped by political interests. Dominant readings, by contrast, typically do not—or will not—admit to having political interests.

---

[11] In terms of feminist critique, the concept of *difference* works in three ways: differences between men and women; differences within woman and between women; difference as "a recognition of diversity" among women (Barrett, 1989:44). See our discussion of womanist criticism in chap. 6.

Some of the broader questions raised by these political readings of the Exodus-Conquest and Cross-Resurrection narratives include: Does the text or a particular reading of the text liberate? Does the reading bring about positive social change? Does the reading expose injustices of race, class, neo-colonialism, gender, and sexuality? Who is represented? Who is excluded? In other words, who is not there? Who is silent or silenced? We have taken the position in this chapter and throughout our volume that because there is no nonideological reading of the Bible, there is no reading of the Bible that is not political or that does not have political consequences. The tendency to see the ideological effort in neat, binary oppositional categories too often gives confidence that the political or ethical reading is to be identified without remainder with the creation of contexts of justice and equality, and unethical readings are those that support structures of oppression. This binary reduction of issues has unfortunately led to the outright rejection of ideological critical readings as too dichotomized (e.g., between the oppressed and oppressor categories of liberation hermeneutics), or it has lead to a kind of "scripturephobia" (J. Michael Clark's term) on the part of some groups left marginalized by a well-intentioned but narrowly focused liberation reading.[12]

If ideological criticism teaches us anything it is that language, categories, concepts, and contexts are not simple and single but complex and multiple, not univocal but multivocal. This is one reason why ideological criticism finds a home today in the postmodern context, which, as Lyotard points out, is a time of "many language games," many micro-narratives (versus "large" metanarrative), many micro-politics. Take, for example, the concept of oppression, which is pivotal for liberation criticism. *Oppression* is a complex term, as are the categories of "oppressed" and "oppressor."

Philosopher Iris Young offers the type of detailed and nuanced thinking about the term that ideological critics in general must be prepared to pursue. Young identifies "five faces of oppression." First is exploitation, which involves class distinctions and dominance and the unequal distribution of wealth. The second is marginalization, which means "people the system

[12] Take for example the dichotomy of "readings from above" that protect the status quo or Barthes's "essential enemy (the bourgeois norm)" (1972a:9) and "readings from below," from individuals and groups who announce their oppression. Dichotomies like this ignore the fact that a reader and context could be dominant in some aspects and marginalized in others. See, e.g., the relationship of feminist and womanist discourse (chap. 6).

of labor cannot or will not use" in work or other social structures (53). The third face is powerlessness, which has to do with people who cannot change their social situation or change the unjust system in which they find themselves suffering. The fourth face is cultural imperialism, which implies dominant and subordinate cultures. For Young, "Cultural imperialism involves the paradox of experiencing oneself as invisible at the same time that one is marked out as different" (1990:60).[13] The fifth and last face is violence, mainly systemic violence, which members of oppressed groups experience. Young's nuanced definition is sensitive to the way oppression evokes a variety of different meanings given the context and application of use. Thinking through categories in this manner helps protect against a reductionist use of language.

Ideological critics must also be prepared to acknowledge that what makes their criticism ethical is itself a complex matter not open to simple reduction. Ideological criticism is interested in examining the content and context of these various faces of oppression and their ethical significance: from modes of production in ancient Israel (Norman Gottwald) to decolonizing readings of the messianism of Jesus (Richard Horsley; Marcus Borg—Jesus as subversive sage). The power and privilege of the exegete-interpreter in part determines the ethical boundaries of reading, but the ethical is not reducible to the reading method or approach. Like meaning, the ethical exceeds the particular desire of the reader, the text, the context (see Levinas, 1969; 1990a).

As we have seen, ideological criticism of the Bible is often tied to theories of ideology because of Marx and Althusser. Other more recent understandings of ideology and ideological critique have begun to move away from the totalizing systems (based on the class structure) that Marxism assumes. For example, studies that focus on the mode of production in ancient Israel or the New Testament world are being reexamined to include a broader focus on literary production in which poststructuralist methods, including deconstruction, promises to play a very energizing role.[14] In addition, class, race, and gender are no longer seen as totalizing categories or systems but are

---

[13] For a discursive analysis of cultural imperialism through media representations, see Tomlinson.

[14] See David Jobling, "Feminism and 'Mode of Production' in Ancient Israel: Search for a Method" (in Jobling, et al., 1991:239–51), where he calls for an interdisciplinary method of sociological, feminist, and literary theories.

themselves seen as representing more complex structures and matrices of relations.

Among biblical critics engaged in ideological criticism today, the relation to historical approaches remains a concern. Meir Sternberg and others who have succeeded in finding a singular cohesive "ideology of the text" link that to an authorial intent. To say that a text has been overlayed with ideology or that ideology is buried in the text (and that a dig into the deep structures will bring it to the surface) is to point to the presence of an author with an ideology. There is a strong temptation here to think about ideology in redaction critical terms and associate the ideology of the text with "the theology of the author," which many postmodern readings of the Bible have resisted. David Gunn and Danna Fewell warn about the dangers: "Reconstructing the ideology of a text is a delicate process due to the complicated relationship between text and reader. . . inevitably. . . readers not only bring their own ideologies to bear on the interpretations of texts, but they use texts to push their ideologies on to others" (193–94), including the text's author. It remains to be seen how biblical critics will be able to wed traditional historical interests with newly self-aware ideological concerns.

In engaging in ethical readings, the method of ideological criticism is contextual: whether history or History (Jameson's term) is intended or the play of signifiers is the central focus. As Paul de Man understands it, "literature is condemned to being the truly political mode of discourse" (1979a:157). In biblical studies ideological critics are paying more attention to issues emerging out of the postmodern debate over aesthetics, politics, epistemology, and critical strategy, especially the strategy of deconstruction. There is a concern for the margins—the margins of discourse, the marginal of society. The emphases are different, but the concern for the ethical and political is shared.

Deconstruction is an important means for critiquing ideology. Ideological criticism is confronted with postmodern concerns—of culture, of theory, of the mosaic of human existence—and all of these concerns appear to have potential ethical and political consequences. Although disputed by many, deconstructive criticism offers a different way to approach the problem of the subject of ethical discourse in ideological criticism.[15] For Marxist decon-

---

[15] We are incorporating the definition of discourse used by Foucault: "discourse can be both an instrument and an effect of power, but also a hindrance, a stumbling block, a point of resistance and a starting point for an opposing strategy" (1979:101). Discourses are unstable and are linked to the distribution of power relations.

structionist Michael Ryan, "Ideology is the political use of metaphysics in the domain of practice" (118).[16] Ryan demonstrates that ideological criticism can incorporate deconstructive concerns of the text over against itself and read "reality" against the grain. Among biblical critics, David Jobling has shown a way to bridge the interests of deconstruction, ideological critique, and feminist theory (1990).

Thus, in the final analysis, ideological criticism is a limited, reductionist term for a much larger context of cultural relations and processes. Ideological criticism is resisting, ruptured, incomplete, chaotic, yet imaginative. The interpretive conflicts that are inherent in reading biblical texts create the context for readings that can decolonize, liberate, and continually subvert. Of course, this view of the play of interpretive conflicts is an ideal one,[17] and the reality is most often turf battles and ego positioning. How does something viable happen out of conflict? The decentering of the subject that occurs with conflictual readings is never simply abstract or theoretical. For example, curriculum and pedagogy are both affected by changing the literary canon. The inescapable social location of every biblical reader does not remain static when readers are interacting and engaging with each other.

Perhaps using the term *engage* or *engagement* helps make it clearer what we mean by the transformative nature of these interpretive conflicts. As the structures of power (of theory and of institutions—in both positive and negative senses) are exposed, so too the theory of ideology or ideological critical reading is exposed. The goal of social transformation is not really a goal at all; there is no static teleology in a deconstructive ideological criticism. We are condemned and privileged to listen to the lives and voices of others, adding our own voice to the discourse, just as this book adds to the various criticism and assessments that make up today's discourse about the Bible, our discipline, and our culture. The implications of what it means not to have a telos or a universal ethic or a transcendent truth, however, have not been sufficiently worked through by biblical critics. Ideological criticism is

---

[16] Paul Armstrong relates: "Psychoanalysis, Marxism, phenomenology, structuralism—each has a different method of interpretation because each has a different metaphysics, a different set of convictions that makes up its point of departure and defines its position in the hermeneutic field" (4).

[17] See the comments by Paul Armstrong (150): "Unless openness to otherness includes the possibility that the encounter might change our mind, we are not really testing our beliefs but are merely disguising our dogmatic commitment to them. . . . We need to create structures that make it likely that our differences will productively confront each other and not just sit inertly side by side."

certainly one of the theoretical discourses that is playing a role as we attempt to sort through the variations, conflicts, contests, disputes, and antagonisms. Continued engagement with critical theory in literary and cultural critical circles by biblical exegetes is likely to be more not less disorienting. We have but begun to glimpse the fullness and complexity of the postmodern context, a context that frames our aspirations to understand the role of the Bible, the purposes of criticism, and the political and ethical challenges embedded within the practices of reflective and responsible reading.

RECOMMENDED FURTHER READING

Barrett, Michèle. 1991. *The Politics of Truth: From Marx to Foucault.* Stanford: Stanford University Press. Barrett employs the thought of Michel Foucault to critique traditional Marxist definitions of ideology. She calls for a post-Marxist critique of ideology by exposing the truth claims of traditional Marxist theories. Barrett incorporates literary studies, sociological theory, and psychoanalysis in examining the power claims of ideological criticism.

Belo, Fernando. 1981. *A Materialist Reading of the Gospel of Mark.* Maryknoll, N.Y.: Orbis. Belo utilizes a detailed structuralist approach to reading the Gospel of Mark. He formulates a "materialist ecclesiology" based on Latin American liberation theology.

Belsey, Catherine. 1980. *Critical Practice.* New York: Methuen. This book is a concise discussion of recent poststructuralist theories of reading. Beginning with Saussure, Belsey traces critical theories of reading for the "subject" or "the subject in ideology." For Belsey, ideological criticism is about discourses, ruptures, and representations of the subject in a text.

Coward, Rosalind, and John Ellis. 1977. *Language and Materialism: Developments in Semiology and the Theory of the Self.* Boston: Routledge. Coward and Ellis trace the development of semiological studies in its philosophical, literary, and psychoanalytic contexts. From their Marxist theoretical base, the authors discuss ideology as representative of the practical action of a subject.

Eagleton, Terry. 1976. *Criticism and Ideology.* London: New Left Books. This book is a summary of Marxist literary criticism drawing mainly from the works of Raymond Williams and theories on the literary mode of production or the social and economic production of literary texts. Eagleton connects the concepts of ideology and the aesthetic and moves beyond the Marxist theories of Louis Althusser and Pierre Macherey in his detailed evaluation of literary texts.

——. 1991. *Ideology: An Introduction.* London: Verso. Eagleton outlines the development of ideological criticism in Marxist thought from Marx to postmodern theories of ideology. He lists many definitions of ideology and then shows how ideological strategies work in text, discourse, and society.

Goldstein, Philip. 1990. *The Politics of Literary Theory: An Introduction to Marxist Criticism.* Tallahassee: Florida State University Press. A summary of the "politics of reading" from structuralist to poststructuralist Marxist literary critics. Different reading strategies (including feminist and deconstructionist) are included. Goldstein argues for a poststructuralist approach.

Jameson, Fredric. 1981. *The Political Unconscious: Narrative as a Socially Symbolic Act.* Ithaca: Cornell University Press. Jameson's Marxist theory of reading is a main resource for ideological criticism. Jameson traces the interpretive process from formalism to post-structuralism. Central to his reading strategy is a model of four levels (literal, allegorical, moral, anagogical), which are applicable to ancient and modern texts.

Jobling, David, and Tina Pippin, eds. 1992. "Ideological Criticism of Biblical Texts." *Semeia* 59. Atlanta: Scholars. This volume of essays comes out of a Society for Biblical Literature consultation on ideological criticism. Articles on both Hebrew Bible and New Testament texts are included, along with a conversation with Fredric Jameson and a bibliography.

Keohane, Nannerl O., Michelle Z. Rosaldo, and Barbara C. Gelpi, eds. 1983. *Feminist Theory: A Critique of Ideology.* Chicago: University of Chicago Press. In this collection of essays, ideology critique is read against the lived experiences of women and of different feminist theories. They point to the creation of new ideologies out of critiques of old ideologies and the need to be in a constant process of ideology critique.

Myers, Ched. 1988. *Binding the Strong Man: A Political Reading of Mark's Story of Jesus.* Maryknoll, N.Y.: Orbis. Myers uses liberation hermeneutics and Marxist theories to re-read Mark. Myers has certain liberal, church-political concerns in mind as he reads through Mark in commentary form. For Myers ideology is synonymous with theology.

Ryan, Michael. 1982. *Marxism and Deconstruction: A Critical Articulation.* Baltimore: Johns Hopkins University Press. In a move from Althusser to Derrida, Ryan relates Marxist and deconstructive theories. Ryan's move is also from metaphysics to practice, and he shows how ideology in a text both stabilizes and ruptures meanings.

Sternberg, Meir. 1985. *The Poetics of Biblical Narrative: Ideological Literature and the Drama of Reading.* Bloomington: Indiana University Press. Sternberg's literary analysis of the Hebrew Bible is based on narratological models of time, repetition, point of view, character-ization, and so on. His view of the Bible is that it is "ideologically singular." Poststructuralist approaches to the study of ideology (or narrative) are omitted.

Thompson, John B. 1984. *Studies in the Theory of Ideology.* Berkeley: University of California Press. Thompson uses history, philosophy, and sociology to examine theories of ideology. He includes discourse analysis and studies in hermeneutics (Ricoeur and Habermas) to reveal the function of ideology in narratives.

————. 1990. *Ideology and Modern Culture: Critical Social Theory in the Era of Mass Com-munication.* Stanford: Stanford University Press. Thompson explores theories of ideology through an analysis of mass communication. Mass communication is one of the "symbolic forms" of power relationships, and ideology is a part of the struggle for power. Thomp-son looks at modern culture and societies and how humans interact through structures and discourse.

Warrior, Robert Allen. 1989. "Canaanites, Cowboys, and Indians: Deliverance, Conquest, and Liberation Theology Today." *Christianity and Crisis* 49:261–65. Warrior offers a Native American reading of the Exodus and Conquest narratives and reveals that texts that are liberating for some groups can be oppressive narratives for others. Warrior critiques Gott-wald's liberation reading. For Native Americans the traditional reading of these texts for concepts of liberation, land, and God taking sides is problematic.

Postscript

The Postmodern Bible emerges in a world of competing discourses and global conflicts and connections. Readers of literary and cultural critical theory on the Bible will continue to face a multitude of methodologies and readings that give no promise of a coherent picture. When we first began to imagine writing this book, we thought we could provide a guide to the terrain of contemporary culture and criticism. What we now better understand is that the ideological gesture of providing such a map communicates the notion that somehow we know everything that is going on and can assess and communicate it meaningfully for someone else. The sense of distanciation and omniscience that the map metaphor suggests is the last thing we would want to communicate; it also is the farthest thing from the truth about what we are able to do. We do not have a totalizing vision of the field; it is changing so rapidly that we don't think anyone knows the where, when, why, who, and hows of its energizing forces. What we offer here is something much more modest and truthful, and we hope helpful: a text that reflects and reflects upon aspects of the world of biblical scholarship by ten women and men whose individual and now collective voices have entered into that cacophony (or heteroglossia) that is postmodern culture.

The voices of biblical scholarship in this book represent many possible entry points into the biblical text: structuralist, poststructuralist, psycho-analytic, reader-response, rhetorical, feminist, womanist, and ideological. Ideological criticism's enabling function, if it has one at all, is that it provides one place where these and other methodologies, epistemologies, and "lived relations" can stand in conflict as well as conversation. It also invites a resistance to easy assessments and cheap understanding.

Bibliography

Abel, Elizabeth, ed. 1982. *Writing and Sexual Difference*. Chicago: University of Chicago Press.

Abel, Ernest L. 1971. "The Psychology of Memory and Rumor Transmission and Their Bearing on Theories of Oral Transmission in Early Christianity." *Journal of Religion* 51:270–81.

Abrams, M. H. 1979. "How to Do Things With Texts." *Partisan Review* 46:566–88.

———. 1991. *Doing Things with Texts: Essays in Criticism and Critical Theory*. Ed. Michael Fisher. New York: Norton.

Achtemeier, Paul J. 1990. "*Omne verbum sonat:* The New Testament and the Oral Environment of Late Western Antiquity." *Journal of Biblical Literature* 109:3–27.

Adam, A. K. M. 1990. "The Sign of Jonah: A Fish-Eye View." *Semeia* 51:177–92.

Adams, Douglas. 1989. *The More Than Complete Hitchhiker's Guide*. New York: Wings.

Adams, Parveen, and Elizabeth Cowie, eds. 1990. *The Woman in Question*. Cambridge: MIT Press.

Aguilar, Grace. n.d. *The Women of Israel; or, Characters and sketches from the Holy Scriptures and Jewish History. Illustrative of the past history, present duties, and future destiny of the Hebrew females, as based on the Word of God*. London: Routledge.

Aichele, George, Jr. 1985. *The Limits of Story*. Atlanta: Scholars.

———. 1989. "On Postmodern Biblical Criticism and Exegesis." *Forum* 5:31–35.

———. 1991. "Translation, Narrative, and Theology." *Explorations* 9:61–80.

———. 1992. "Two Theories of Translation with Examples from the Gospel of Mark." *Journal for the Study of the New Testament* 47:95–116.

Aichele, George, and Gary Phillips, eds. "Intertextuality and Reading the Bible." *Semeia* 69.

Alexander, Philip S. 1990. "Quid Athenis et Hierosolymis? Rabbinic Midrash and Herme-neutics in the Greco-Roman World." Pp. 101–24 in *A Tribute to Geza Vermes: Essays on Jewish and Christian Literature and History*. Ed. P. R. Davies and R. T. White. Sheffield: Sheffield Academic Press.

Almeida, Ivan. 1978. *L'Opérativité sémantique des récits-paraboles: Sémiotique narrative et textuelle. Herméneutique du discours religieux*. Paris: Cerf.

Alter, Robert. 1981. *The Art of Biblical Narrative*. New York: Basic Books.

———. 1985. *The Art of Biblical Poetry*. New York: Basic Books.

———. 1989. *The Pleasures of Reading in an Ideological Age*. New York: Simon and Schuster.

———. 1992. *The World of Biblical Literature*. New York: Basic Books.

Alter, Robert, and Frank Kermode, eds. 1987. *The Literary Guide to the Bible*. Cambridge: Harvard University Press.

Althusser, Louis. 1969. *For Marx*. Trans. Ben Brewster. Harmondsworth: Penguin.

———. 1970. "From *Capital* to Marx's Philosophy." Pp. 11–39 in *Reading Capital*. By Louis Althusser and Etienne Balibar. Trans. Ben Brewster. New York: Verso.

———. 1972. *Lenin and Philosophy and Other Essays*. Trans. Ben Brewster. New York: Monthly Review.

———. 1977. "Ideology and Ideological State Apparatuses." Pp. 121–73 in *Lenin and Philosophy and Other Essays*. Trans. Ben Brewster. London: New Left Books.

Althusser, Louis, and Etienne Balibar. 1970. *Reading Capital*. Trans. Ben Brewster. London: Verso.

Amacker, René. 1975. *Linguistique saussurienne*. Langue et Cultures 6. Geneva: Droz.

Anchor, Robert. 1983. "Realism and Ideology: The Question of Order." *History and Theory* 22:107–19.

Anderson, Benedict. 1983. *Imagined Communities: Reflections on the Origin and Spread of Nationalism*. New York: Verso.

Anderson, Bernhard W. 1974. "The New Frontier of Rhetorical Criticism." Pp. ix–xviii in *Rhetorical Criticism*. Ed. J. J. Jackson and M. Kessler. Pittsburgh: Pickwick.

Anderson, Janice Capel. 1983. "Matthew: Gender and Reading." *Semeia* 28:3–27.

———. 1985a. "Double and Triple Stories, the Implied Reader, and Redundancy in Matthew." *Semeia* 31:71–90.

———. 1985b. "Over and Over and Over Again: Studies in Matthean Repetition." Ph.D. diss., University of Chicago.

———. 1991. "Mapping Feminist Biblical Criticism: The American Scene, 1983–1990." *Critical Review of Books in Religion* 4:21–44.

Andrews, William L., ed. 1986. *Sisters of the Spirit: Three Black Women's Autobiographies of the Nineteenth Century*. Bloomington: Indiana University Press.

Anzaldúa, Gloria, ed. 1990. *Making Face, Making Soul/Haciendo Caras: Creative and Critical Perspectives by Women of Color*. San Francisco: Aunt Lute.

Apter, David, ed. 1964. *Ideology and Discontent*. London: Glencoe Free Press.

Arac, Jonathan, ed. 1986. *Postmodernism and Politics*. Theory and History of Literature 28. Minneapolis: University of Minnesota Press.

Armstrong, Paul B. 1990. *Conflicting Readings: Variety and Validity in Interpretation*. Chapel Hill: University of North Carolina Press.

Arnheim, Rudolf. 1980. "A Plea for Visual Thinking." *Critical Inquiry* 6:489–98.

Aronowitz, Stanley. 1988. *Science as Power: Discourse and Ideology in Modern Science.* Minneapolis: University of Minnesota Press.

———. 1990. "On Intellectuals." Pp. 3–56 in *Intellectuals: Aesthetics, Politics, Academics.* Ed. Bruce Robbins. Cultural Politics 2. Minneapolis: University of Minnesota Press.

Arvon, Henri. 1973. *Marxist Aesthetics.* Trans. H. Lane. Ithaca: Cornell University Press.

Ateek, Naim Stifan. 1989. *Justice, and Only Justice: A Palestinian Theology of Liberation.* Maryknoll, N.Y.: Orbis.

Attridge, Derek, ed. 1992. *Acts of Literature.* New York: Routledge.

Attridge, Derek, Geoff Bennington, and Robert Young, eds. 1987. *Post-Structuralism and the Question of History.* New York: Cambridge University Press.

Auerbach, Erich. 1953. *Mimesis: The Representation of Reality in Western Literature.* Trans. Willard Trask. Princeton: Princeton University Press.

———. 1958. *Literatursprache und Publikum in der lateinischen Spätantike und im Mittelalter.* Bern: Francke.

Aune, David. 1991. "Romans as a Logos Protreptikos." Pp. 278–96 in *The Romans Debate.* Rev. and exp. ed. Ed. Karl P. Donfried. Peabody, Mass.: Hendrickson.

Austin, J. L. 1962. *How to Do Things with Words.* Oxford: Oxford University Press.

Bach, Alice. 1990. *The Pleasure of Her Text: Feminist Readings of Biblical and Historical Texts.* Philadelphia: Trinity Press International.

Badran, Margot. 1994. "Gender Activism: Feminists and Islamists in Egypt." Pp. 202–27 in *Identity Politics and Women: Cultural Reassertions and Feminisms in International Perspective.* Ed. Valentine M. Moghadam. Boulder, Colo.: Westview.

Bailey, Frederick G. 1983. *The Tactical Uses of Passion: An Essay on Power, Reason, and Reality.* Ithaca: Cornell University Press.

Baker, Houston A. 1984. *Blues, Ideology, and Afro-American Literature: A Vernacular Theory.* Chicago: University of Chicago Press.

Bakhtin, Mikhail. 1973. *Problems of Dostoevsky's Poetics.* Trans. R. W. Rotsel. Ann Arbor: Ardis.

———. 1981. *The Dialogic Imagination: Four Essays.* Ed. Michael Holquist. Trans. Caryl and Michael Holquist. University of Texas Press Slavic Series 1. Austin: University of Texas Press.

———. 1986. *Speech Genres and Other Late Essays.* Trans. Vern W. McGee. University of Texas Press Slavic Series 8. Austin: University of Texas Press.

Bal, Mieke. 1985. *Narratology: Introduction to the Theory of Narrative.* Toronto: University of Toronto Press.

———. 1986a. "The Bible as Literature: A Critical Escape." *Diacritics* 16:71–79.

———. 1986b. *Femmes imaginaires: L'ancien testament au risque d'une narratologie critique.* Utrecht: HES.

———. 1987. *Lethal Love: Feminist Literary Readings of Biblical Love Stories.* Bloomington: Indiana University Press.

———. 1988a. *Death and Dissymmetry: The Politics of Coherence in the Book of Judges.* Chicago: University of Chicago Press.

———. 1988b. *Murder and Difference: Gender, Genre, and Scholarship on Sisera's Death.* Bloomington: Indiana University Press.

———. 1989. "Literature and Its Insistent Other." *Journal of the American Academy of Religion* 57:373–83.

———. 1990. "The Point of Narratology." *Poetics Today* 11:727–53.

———. 1991. *On Story-Telling: Essays in Narratology.* Ed. David Jobling. Sonoma, Calif.: Polebridge.

Bal, Mieke, ed. 1989. *Anti-Covenant: Counter-Reading Women's Lives in the Hebrew Bible.* Sheffield: Almond.

Balbus, Isaac. 1988. "Disciplining Women: Michel Foucault and the Power of Feminist Discourse." Pp. 138–60 in *After Foucault: Humanistic Knowledge, Postmodern Challenges.* Ed. Jonathan Arac. New Brunswick, N.J.: Rutgers University Press.

Bannerji, Himani, Linda Carty, Kari Dehli, Susan Heald, and Kate McKenna. 1991. *Unsettling Relations: The University as a Site of Feminist Struggles.* Toronto: Women's Press.

Bannet, Eve Tavor. 1989. *Structuralism and the Logic of Dissent: Barthes, Derrida, Foucault, Lacan.* Chicago: University of Illinois Press.

Bar-Efrat, Shimon. 1989. *Narrative Art in the Bible.* Trans. Dorothea Shefer-Vanson. Sheffield: Almond.

Barilli, Renato. 1989. *Rhetoric.* Trans. Giuliana Menozzi. Theory and History of Literature 63. Minneapolis: University of Minnesota Press.

Barkley Brown, Elsa. 1989. "Womanist Consciousness: Maggie Lena Walker and the Independent Order of Saint Luke." *Signs* 14:610–33.

Barnet, Steve, and Martin G. Silverman. 1979. *Ideology and Everyday Life.* Ann Arbor: University of Michigan Press.

Barre, Lloyd M. 1988. *The Rhetoric of Political Persuasion: The Narrative Artistry and Political Intention of 2 Kings 9–11.* Catholic Biblical Quarterly Monograph Series 20. Washington, D.C.: Catholic Biblical Association of America.

Barrett, Michèle. 1985. "Ideology and the Cultural Production of Gender." Pp. 65–85 in *Feminist Criticism and Social Change.* Ed. Judith Newton and Deborah Rosenfelt. New York: Methuen.

———. 1988. *Women's Oppression Today: The Marxist/Feminist Encounter.* Rev. ed. New York: Verso.

———. 1989. "Some Different Meanings of the Concept of 'Difference': Feminist Theory and the Concept of Ideology." Pp. 37–48 in *The Difference Within: Feminism and Critical Theory.* Ed. Elizabeth Meese and Alice Parker. Philadelphia: John Benjamins.

———. 1991. *The Politics of Truth: From Marx to Foucault.* Stanford: Stanford University Press.

Barrett, Michèle, and Anne Phillips, eds. 1992. *Destabilizing Theory: Contemporary Feminist Debates.* Stanford: Stanford University Press.

Barth, Hans. 1976. *Truth and Ideology.* Trans. Frederic Lilge. Berkeley: University of California Press.

Barthes, Roland. 1969. *Elements of Semiology.* Trans. Annette Lavers and Colin Smith. London: Jonathan Cape.

———. 1972a. *Mythologies.* Trans. Annette Lavers. New York: Hill and Wang.

———. 1972b. "What is Criticism?" Pp. 255–60 in *Critical Essays*. Trans. Richard Howard. Evanston, Ill.: Northwestern University Press.

———. 1974a. "The Struggle with the Angel: Textual Analysis of Genesis 32:23–33." Pp. 21–33 in Barthes et al. *Structural Analysis and Biblical Exegesis: Interpretational Essays*. Trans. Alfred M. Johnson, Jr. Pittsburgh Theological Monograph Series 3. Pittsburgh: Pickwick.

———. 1974b. *S/Z*. Trans. Richard Miller. New York: Hill and Wang.

———. 1975. *The Pleasure of the Text*. Trans. Richard Miller. New York: Hill and Wang.

———. 1977a. "The Death of the Author." Pp. 142–48 in Barthes, *Image—Music—Text*. Trans. Stephen Heath. New York: Hill and Wang.

———. 1977b. *Image—Music—Text*. Trans. Stephen Heath. New York: Hill and Wang.

———. 1977c. *Roland Barthes by Roland Barthes*. Trans. Richard Howard. New York: Hill and Wang.

———. 1978. *A Lover's Discourse: Fragments*. Trans. Richard Howard. New York: Hill and Wang.

———. 1981a. *Camera Lucida: Reflections on Photography*. Trans. Richard Howard. New York: Hill and Wang.

———. 1981b. "Theory of the Text." Pp. 31–47 in *Untying the Text: A Post-Structuralist Reader*. Ed. Robert Young. Boston: Routledge.

———. 1982. "Inaugural Lecture." Trans. Richard Howard. Pp. 457–78 in *A Barthes Reader*. Ed. Susan Sontag. New York: Hill and Wang.

———. 1988a. "Introduction to the Structural Analysis of Narratives." Pp. 95–135 in Roland Barthes, *The Semiotic Challenge*. Trans. Richard Howard. New York: Hill and Wang. (Orig. 1966.)

———. 1988b. *The Semiotic Challenge*. Trans. Richard Howard. New York: Hill and Wang.

———. 1988c. "The Structural Analysis of Narrative: Apropos of Acts 10–11." Pp. 217–45 in Barthes, *The Semiotic Challenge*. Trans. Richard Howard. New York: Hill and Wang.

———. 1988d. "Wrestling with the Angel: Textual Analysis of Genesis 32:23–33." Pp. 246–60 in Roland Barthes, *The Semiotic Challenge*. Trans. Richard Howard. New York: Hill and Wang.

Barthes, Roland, F. Bovon, F.-J. Leenhardt, R. Martin-Achard, and J. Starobinski. 1974. *Structural Analysis and Biblical Exegesis: Interpretational Essays*. Trans. Alfred M. Johnson, Jr. Pittsburgh Theological Monograph Series 3. Pittsburgh: Pickwick.

Barton, John. 1984. *Reading the Old Testament: Method in Biblical Study*. Philadelphia: Westminster.

Bashford, Bruce. 1976. "The Rhetorical Method in Literary Criticism." *Philosophy & Rhetoric* 9:133–46.

Bassler, Jouette M. 1986. "The Parable of the Loaves." *Journal of Religion* 66:157–72.

Bastides, F. 1985. "Domaines actuelles de la recherche sémiotique." *Sémiotique et bible* 33:32–39.

Batstone, David. 1991. *From Conquest to Struggle: Jesus of Nazareth in Latin America*. Albany: SUNY Press.

Baudrillard, Jean. 1976. *The Mirror of Production*. Trans. Mark Poster. St. Louis: Telos.

———. 1981. *For a Critique of the Political Economy of the Sign*. Trans. Charles Levin. St. Louis: Telos.

———. 1984. "The Precession of Simulacra." Pp. 253–81 in *Art After Modernism: Rethinking Representation*. Ed. Brian Wallis. Boston: Godine.

Bauer, Walter. 1971. *Orthodoxy and Heresy in Earliest Christianity*. Ed. R. A. Kraft and G. Krodel. Trans. Philadelphia Seminar on Christian Origins. Philadelphia: Fortress.

Bauman, Zygmunt. 1988. "Is There a Postmodern Sociology?" *Theory, Culture and Society* 5:217–37.

———. 1989. *Modernity and the Holocaust*. Ithaca: Cornell University Press.

———. 1991. *Modernity and Ambivalence*. Ithaca: Cornell University Press.

———. 1992. *Intimations of Postmodernity*. London: Routledge.

———. 1993. *Postmodern Ethics*. Oxford: Blackwell.

Beardslee, William A. 1970. *Literary Criticism of the New Testament*. Guides to Biblical Scholarship. Philadelphia: Fortress.

———. 1989. "Recent Literary Criticism." Pp. 175–200 in *The New Testament and Its Modern Interpreters*. Ed. Eldon Jay Epp and George W. MacRae. Atlanta: Scholars.

———. 1993. "Poststructuralist Criticism." Pp. 221–36 in *To Each Its Own Meaning: An Introduction to Biblical Criticisms and Their Application*. Ed. Steven L. McKenvie and Stephen R. Haynes. Louisville, Ky: Westminster/John Knox.

Beavis, Mary Ann. 1987. "The Trial before the Sanhedrin (Mark 14:53–65): Reader Response and Greco-Roman Readers." *Catholic Biblical Quarterly* 49:581–96.

———. 1989. *Mark's Audience: The Literary and Social Setting of Mark 4:11–12*. Journal for the Society of New Testament Supplement Series 33. Sheffield: JSOT.

Beck, Jonathan. 1991. "Salvaging Literature, Salvaging Theory." *Diacritics* 21:76–90.

Bell, Daniel. 1976. *The Cultural Contradictions of Capitalism*. New York: Basic Books.

Belo, Fernando. 1981. *A Materialist Reading of the Gospel of Mark*. Trans. Matthew J. O'Connell. Maryknoll, N.Y.: Orbis.

Belsey, Catherine. 1980. *Critical Practice*. New Accents. New York: Methuen.

———. 1986. "The Romantic Construction of the Unconscious." Pp. 57–76 in *Literature, Politics and Theory: Papers from the Essex Conference 1976–84*. Ed. Francis Barker, et al. New Accents. New York: Methuen.

Benjamin, Walter. 1969. *Illuminations: Essays and Reflections*. New York: Schocken.

———. 1979. *One Way Street and Other Writings*. Trans. Edmund Jephcott and Kingsley Shorter. London: New Left Books.

Bennington, Geoffrey, and Jacques Derrida. 1993. *Jacques Derrida*. Trans. Geoffrey Bennington. Religion and Postmodernism. Chicago: University of Chicago Press.

Benstock, Shari, ed. 1987. *Feminist Issues in Literary Scholarship*. Bloomington: Indiana University Press.

Benveniste, Emile. 1970. "L'Appareil formel de l'énonciation." *Langages* 17:12–18.

Bercovitch, Sacvan, and Myra Jehlen, eds. 1986. *Ideology and Classic American Literature*. Cambridge Studies in American Literature and Culture. New York: Cambridge University Press.

Berg, Temma F. 1987. "Psychologies of Reading." Pp. 248–77 in *Tracing Literary Theory*. Ed. Joseph Natoli. Chicago: University of Illinois Press.

Berger, Klaus. 1984. *Formgeschichte des Neuen Testaments*. Heidelberg: Quelle & Meyer.

Berkenkotter, Carol. 1991. "Evolution of a Scholarly Forum *Reader*, 1977–1988." *Reader* 26:1–26.

Berlin, Adele. 1983. *Poetics and Interpretation of Biblical Narrative.* Sheffield: Almond.

Berman, Art. 1988. *From the New Criticism to Deconstruction: The Reception of Structuralism and Post-Structuralism.* Urbana: University of Illinois Press.

Bernasconi, Robert, and Simon Critchley, eds. 1991. *Re-Reading Levinas.* Studies in Continental Thought. Bloomington: Indiana University Press.

Bernstein, Richard J. 1983. *Beyond Objectivism and Relativism: Science, Hermeneutics, and Praxis.* Philadelphia: University of Pennsylvania Press.

———. 1992. *The New Constellation: The Ethico-Political Horizons of Modernity/Postmodernity.* Cambridge: MIT Press.

Berry, Alice Fiola. 1991. "'L'Isle Medamothi': Rabelais's Itineraries of Anxiety (*Quart livre* 2–4)." *PMLA* 106:1040–53.

Betz, Hans Dieter. 1975. *Paul's Apology: 2 Corinthians 10–13 and the Socratic Tradition.* Berkeley, Calif.: Center for Hermeneutical Studies.

———. 1979. *Galatians: A Commentary on Paul's Letter to the Churches in Galatia.* Hermeneia. Philadelphia: Fortress.

Bird, Phyllis. 1989. "'To Play the Harlot': An Inquiry into an Old Testament Metaphor." Pp. 75–94 in *Gender and Difference in Ancient Israel.* Ed. Peggy L. Day. Minneapolis: Augsburg/Fortress.

Bitzer, Lloyd F. 1968. "The Rhetorical Situation." *Philosophy and Rhetoric* 1:1–14.

———. 1978. "Rhetoric and Public Knowledge." Pp. 67–93 in *Rhetoric, Philosophy, and Literature: An Exploration.* Ed. Don M. Burks. West Lafayette, Ind.: Purdue University Press.

Black, C. Clifton. 1988. "Rhetorical Criticism and the New Testament." Pp. 77–92 in *Proceedings of the Eastern Great Lakes and Midwest Biblical Societies.* Vol. 8. Ed. Paul Redditt. Georgetown, Ky.: Georgetown College.

Black, Edwin. 1965. *Rhetorical Criticism: A Study in Method.* New York: Macmillan.

Blair, Carole. 1983. "Nietzsche's Lecture Notes on Rhetoric: a Translation." *Philosophy and Rhetoric* 16:94–129.

Blee, Kathleen. 1991. *Women of the Klan: Racism and Gender in the 1920s.* Berkeley: University of California Press.

Bleich, David. 1975a. *Readings and Feelings: An Introduction to Subjective Criticism.* Urbana, Ill.: National Council of Teachers of English.

———. 1975b. "The Subjective Character of Critical Interpretation." *College English* 36:739–55.

———. 1976a. "Pedagogical Directions in Subjective Criticism." *College English* 37:454–67.

———. 1976b. "The Subjective Paradigm in Science, Psychology, and Criticism." *New Literary History* 7:313–34.

———. 1978. *Subjective Criticism.* Baltimore: Johns Hopkins University Press.

———. 1988. *The Double Perspective: Language, Literacy, and Social Relations.* New York: Oxford University Press.

Blistine, Bernard. 1985. "A Conversation with Jean-François Lyotard." *Flash Art* 121:21–35.

Bloch, Ernst. 1972. *Atheism in Christianity: The Religion of the Exodus and the Kingdom.* New York: Herder and Herder.

Bloom, Harold. 1989. *Ruin the Sacred Truths: Poetry and Belief from the Bible to the Present.* Cambridge: Harvard University Press.

Bloom, Harold, Paul de Man, Jacques Derrida, Geoffrey Hartman, and J. Hillis Miller. 1979. *Deconstruction and Criticism.* New York: Seabury.

Blount, Marcellus. 1992. "The Preacherly Text: African American Poetry and Vernacular Performance." *PMLA* 107:582–93.

Boers, Hendrickus. 1988. *Neither on This Mountain Nor in Jerusalem: A Study of John 4.* Society of Biblical Literature Monograph Series 35. Atlanta: Scholars.

Boesak, Allan Aubrey. 1977. *Farewell to Innocence: A Socio-Ethical Study on Black Theology and Power.* Maryknoll, N.Y.: Orbis.

Bolter, Jay David. 1991. *Writing Space: The Computer, Hypertext, and the History of Writing.* Hillsdale, N.J.: Erlbaum.

Boomershine, Thomas E. 1987. "Biblical Megatrends: Towards a Paradigm for the Interpretation of the Bible in Electronic Media." Pp. 144–57 in *Society of Biblical Literature 1987 Seminar Papers.* Ed. Kent Harold Richards. Atlanta: Scholars.

Booth, Stephen. 1969a. *An Essay on Shakespeare's Sonnets.* New Haven: Yale University Press.

———. 1969b. "On the Value of Hamlet." Pp. 137–76 in *Reinterpretation of Elizabethan Drama.* Ed. Norman Rabkin. New York: Columbia University Press.

Booth, Wayne C. 1961. *The Rhetoric of Fiction.* Chicago: University of Chicago Press.

———. 1974. *A Rhetoric of Irony.* Chicago: University of Chicago Press.

———. 1977. " 'Preserving the Exemplar' or, How Not to Dig Our Own Graves." *Critical Inquiry* 3:407–23.

———. 1978. "The Pleasures and Pitfalls of Irony: Or, Why Don't You Say What You Mean?" Pp. 1–13 in *Rhetoric, Philosophy and Literature: An Exploration.* Ed. Don M. Burks. West Lafayette, Ind.: Purdue University Press.

———. 1979. *Critical Understanding: The Powers and Limits of Pluralism.* Chicago: University of Chicago Press.

———. 1982. "Freedom of Interpretation: Bakhtin and the Challenge of Feminist Criticism." *Critical Inquiry* 9:45–76.

———. 1983a. *The Rhetoric of Fiction.* 2d ed. Chicago: University of Chicago Press.

———. 1983b. "Rhetorical Critics Old and New." Pp. 123–41 in *Deconstructing Literature.* Ed. L. Lerner. Oxford: Blackwell.

———. 1988a. *The Company We Keep: An Ethics of Fiction.* Berkeley: University of California Press.

———. 1988b. *The Vocation of a Teacher: Rhetorical Occasions, 1967–1988.* Chicago: University of Chicago Press.

Booth, Wayne, and Wolfgang Iser. 1977. "In Defense of Authors and Readers." *Novel* 11:5–25.

Borch-Jacobsen, Mikkel. 1991. *Lacan: The Absolute Master.* Trans. Douglas Brick. Stanford: Stanford University Press.

Bordwell, David. 1985. *Narration in the Fiction Film.* Madison: University of Wisconsin Press.

Borg, Marcus J. 1984. *Jesus: A New Vision: Spirit, Culture, and the Life of Discipleship.* San Francisco: Harper.

Bouwsma, William J. 1987. *Calvinism as Theologia Rhetorica.* Ed. Wilhelm Wuellner. Protocol of the 54th Colloquy. Berkeley, Calif.: Center for Hermeneutical Studies.

Bové, Paul. 1986. "The Ineluctability of Difference: Scientific Pluralism and the Critical Intelligence." Pp. 3–25 in *Postmodernism and Politics*. Ed. Jonathan Arac. Theory and History of Literature 28. Minneapolis: University of Minnesota Press.

Bovon, François, and G. Rouiller, eds. 1975. *Exegesis: Problèmes de méthode et exercices de lecture (Gn 22 et Lc 15)*. Bibliothèque théologique. Paris: Delachaux et Niestlé.

Bowie, Malcolm. 1991. *Lacan*. Cambridge: Harvard University Press.

Bowman, Frank Paul. 1980. *Le Discours sur l'Eloquence sacrée à l'Epoque romantique: Rhétorique, apologétique, herméneutique (1777–1851)*. Geneva: Droz.

Boyarin, Daniel. 1985. "Rhetoric and Interpretation: The Case of the Nimshal." *Prooftexts* 5:269–76.

———. 1990a. *Intertextuality and the Reading of Midrash*. Indiana Studies in Biblical Literature. Bloomington: Indiana University Press.

———. 1990b. "The Politics of Biblical Narratology: Reading the Bible Like/As a Woman." *Diacritics* 20:31–42.

Boyle, Marjorie O'Rourke. 1983. *Rhetoric and Reform: Erasmus' Civil Dispute with Luther*. Cambridge: Harvard University Press.

Braet, Antoine C. 1987. "The Classical Doctrine of STATUS and the Rhetorical Theory of Argumentation." *Philosophy and Rhetoric* 20:79–93.

Branscomb, B. Harvie. 1937. *The Gospel of Mark*. The Moffatt New Testament Commentary. New York: Harper and Bros.

Bremond, Claude, ed. 1970. *Communications* 16.

Brennan, Teresa, ed. 1989. *Between Feminism and Psychoanalysis*. New York: Routledge.

Brent, Douglas Allan. 1989. "Toward A Rhetoric of Reading." Ph.D. diss., University of British Columbia.

Brettler, Marc Z. 1989. "Ideology, History, and Theology." *Vetus Testamentum* 39:268–82.

Briggs, Sheila. 1987. "Sexual Justice and the 'Righteousness of God.'" Pp. 251–77 in *Sex and God: Some Varieties of Women's Religious Experience*. Ed. Linda Hurcombe. New York: Routledge.

———. 1989. "Can an Enslaved God Liberate? Hermeneutical Reflections on Philippians 2:6–11." *Semeia* 47:137–53.

———. 1990. "'Buried with Christ': The Politics of Identity and the Poverty of Interpretation." Pp. 276–303 in *The Book and the Text: The Bible and Literary Theory*. Ed. Regina Schwartz. New York: Blackwell.

Brinker, Menachem. 1980. "Two Phenomenologies of Reading: Ingarden and Iser on Textual Indeterminacy." *Poetics Today* 1:203–12.

Brinton, Alan. 1981. "Situation in the Theory of Rhetoric." *Philosophy & Rhetoric* 14:234–48.

———. 1988. "Pathos and the Appeal to Emotion: An Aristotelian Analysis." *History of Philosophy Quarterly* 5:207–19.

Brock, B. L., and Robert L. Scott, eds. 1980. *Methods of Rhetorical Criticism: A Twentieth Century Perspective*. Rev. 2d ed. Detroit: Wayne State University Press.

Brock, Rita Nakashima. 1988. *Journeys by Heart: A Christology of Erotic Power*. New York: Crossroad.

Brooke-Rose, Christine. 1990. "Whatever Happened to Narratology?" *Poetics Today* 11:283–93.

———. 1992. "Palimpsest History." Pp. 125–38 in Umberto Eco, Richard Rorty, Jonathan Culler, and Christine Brooke-Rose. *Interpretation and Overinterpretation*. Ed. Stefan Collini. Cambridge: Cambridge University Press.

Brooks, Cleanth. 1983. "The Primacy of the Reader." *The Missouri Review* 6:189–201.

Brooten, Bernadette J. 1985a. "Early Christian Women and Their Cultural Context: Issues of Method in Historical Reconstruction." Pp. 65–91 in *Feminist Perspectives on Biblical Scholarship*. Ed. Adela Yarbro Collins. Chico, Calif.: Scholars.

———. 1985b. "Paul's Views on the Nature of Women and Female Homoeroticism." Pp. 61–87 in *Immaculate and Powerful: The Female in Sacred Image and Social Reality*. Ed. Clarissa W. Atkinson, Constance H. Buchanan, and Margaret R. Miles. Boston: Beacon.

———. 1986. "Jewish Women's History in the Roman Period: A Task for Christian Theology." *Harvard Theological Review* 79:22–30.

Brown, Joanne Carlson, and Carole R. Bohn, eds. 1989. *Christianity, Patriarchy, and Abuse: A Feminist Critique*. New York: Pilgrim.

Brown, Joanne Carlson, and Rebecca Parker. 1989. "For God So Loved the World?" Pp. 1–30 in *Christianity, Patriarchy, and Abuse: A Feminist Critique*. Ed. Joanne Carlson Brown and Carole R. Bohn. New York: Pilgrim.

Brown, Kelly D. 1989. "God Is as Christ Does: Toward a Womanist Theology." *Journal of Religious Thought* 46:7–16.

Brown, Robert McAfee. 1984. *Unexpected News: Reading the Bible with Third World Eyes*. Philadelphia: Westminster.

Brown, Schuyler. 1988. "Reader Response: Demythologizing the Text." *New Testament Studies* 34:232–37.

———. 1989. "John and the Resistant Reader: The Fourth Gospel after Nicea and the Holocaust." *Journal of Literary Studies* 5:252–61.

———. 1990. "The Beloved Disciple: A Jungian View." Pp. 366–77 in *The Conversation Continues: Studies in Paul and John in Honor of J. Louis Martyn*. Ed. Robert T. Fortna and Beverly R. Gaventa. Nashville: Abingdon.

Budick, Sanford, and Wolfgang Iser, eds. 1989. *Languages of the Unsayable: The Play of Negativity in Literature and Literary Theory*. Irvine Studies in the Humanities. New York: Columbia University Press.

Bühlmann, W., and K. Scherer. 1973. *Stilfiguren der Bibel: Ein kleines Nachschlagewerk*. Biblische Beiträge 10. Fribourg: Schweizerisches Katholisches Bibelwerk.

Buelow, George J. 1980. "Rhetoric and Music." Pp. 793–803 in *The New Grove: Dictionary of Music and Musicians*. Ed. Stanley Sadie. Vol. 15. London: Macmillan.

Bünker, M. 1984. *Briefformular und rhetorische Disposition im 1. Korintherbrief*. Göttingen theologische Arbeiten 28. Göttingen: Vandenhoeck & Ruprecht.

Burke, Kenneth. 1945. *A Grammar of Motives*. Berkeley: University of California Press.

———. 1950. *A Rhetoric of Motives*. Berkeley: University of California Press.

———. 1961. *The Rhetoric of Religion: Studies in Logology*. Berkeley: University of California Press.

Burnett, Fred. 1985. "Prolegomenon to Reading Matthew's Eschatological Discourse: Redundancy and the Education of the Reader in Matthew." *Semeia* 31:91–110.

———. 1987. "Characterization in Matthew: Reader Construction of the Disciple Peter." *McKendree Pastoral Review* 4:13–43.

———. 1990a. "Avatars of Greimassian Semiotics: A Post-structuralist Response to Daniel Patte's *The Religious Dimensions of Biblical Texts.*" Paper presented to the Semiotics and Exegesis Section at the annual meeting of the Society of Biblical Literature/American Academy of Religion, New Orleans, November 17–20.

———. 1990b. "Postmodern Biblical Exegesis: The Eve of Historical Criticism." *Semeia* 51:51–80.

———. 1992a. "Exposing the Implied Author in Matthew: The Characterization of God as Father." *Semeia* 55:155–91.

———. 1992b. "The Undecidability of the Proper Name 'Jesus' in Matthew." *Semeia* 54:123–44.

Butler, Judith. 1990. *Gender Trouble: Feminism and the Subversion of Identity.* New York: Routledge.

———. 1992. "Contingent Foundations: Feminism and the Question of 'Postmodernism.'" Pp. 3–21 in *Feminists Theorize the Political.* Ed. Judith Butler and Joan W. Scott. New York: Routledge.

Butler, Judith, and Joan W. Scott, eds. 1992. *Feminists Theorize the Political.* New York: Routledge.

Buttigieg, Joseph A. 1987. *Criticism without Boundaries: Directions and Crosscurrents in Postmodern Critical Theory.* Notre Dame, Ind.: University of Notre Dame Press.

Cahn, Michael. 1986. *Kunst der Überlistung. Studien zur Wissenschaftsgeschichte der Rhetorik.* Munich: Fink.

———. 1989–90. "L'Ideologia della Retorica." *Helikon* 29/30:25–42.

Cain, William E. 1978. "'Lycidas' and the Reader's Response." *Dalhousie Review* 58:72–84.

Calinescu, Matei. 1987. *Five Faces of Modernity: Modernism, Avant-Garde, Decadence, Kitsch, Postmodernism.* Urbana: University of Illinois Press.

Calloud, Jean. 1976. *Structural Analysis of Narrative.* Trans. Daniel Patte. Semeia Supplements. Philadelphia: Fortress.

Calloud, Jean and François Genuyt. 1982. *La première Epître de Pierre: Analyse sémiotique.* Lectio divina. Paris: Cerf.

———. 1987. *L'Evangile de Jean, II: Lecture sémiotique des chapitres 7 à 12.* Eveux-Lyons: Centre Thomas More-CADIR.

———. 1989. *L'Evangile de Jean, I: Lecture sémiotique des chapitres 1 à 6.* Eveux-Lyons: Centre Thomas More-CADIR.

Calvet, Louis-Jean. 1973. *Roland Barthes, un regard politique sur le signe.* Paris: Payot.

———. 1975. *Pour et contre Saussure: Vers une linguistique sociale.* Paris: Payot.

Camp, Claudia V., and Carole R. Fontaine, eds. 1992. "Metaphor and Society in the Bible and Its Interpretation." *Semeia* 56.

Canadian Feminist Ethics Theory Group. 1992. "Some Issues in the Ethics of Collaborative Work." Pp. 131–37 in *Explorations in Feminist Ethics.* Ed. Eve Browning Cole and Susan Coultrap-McQuin. Bloomington: Indiana University Press.

Cannon, Katie Geneva. 1985. "The Emergence of Black Feminist Consciousness." Pp. 30–40 in *Feminist Interpretation of the Bible.* Ed. Letty M. Russell. Philadelphia: Westminster.

———. 1988. *Black Womanist Ethics.* Atlanta: Scholars.

Cannon, Katie Geneva, and Elisabeth Schüssler Fiorenza, eds. 1989. "Interpretation for Liberation." *Semeia* 47.

Caputo, John. 1993. *Against Ethics: Contributions to a Poetic of Obligation with Constant Reference to Deconstruction.* Bloomington: Indiana University Press.

Caraway, Nancie. 1991. *Segregated Sisterhood: Racism and the Politics of American Feminism.* Knoxville: University of Tennessee Press.

Carby, Hazel V. 1987. *Reconstructing Womanhood: The Emergence of the Afro-American Woman Novelist.* New York: Oxford University Press.

Cardenal, Ernesto. 1979. *The Gospel in Solentiname.* 4 vols. Maryknoll, N.Y.: Orbis.

Cassel, Jay F. 1983. "The Reader in Mark: The Crucifixion." Ph.D. diss., University of Iowa.

Castelli, Elizabeth A. 1990. "Les belles infidèles/Fidelity or Feminism? The Meanings of Feminist Biblical Translation." *Journal of Feminist Studies in Religion* 6(2):25–39.

——. 1991a. *Imitating Paul: A Discourse of Power.* Literary Currents in Biblical Literature. Louisville, Ky.: Westminster/John Knox.

——. 1991b. "Interpretations of Power in 1 Corinthians." *Semeia* 54:197–222.

Caughie, Pamela L. 1988. "Women Reading/Reading Women: A Review of Some Recent Books on Gender and Reading." *Papers on Language and Literature* 24:317–35.

Caws, Peter. 1988. *Structuralism: The Art of the Intelligible.* Atlantic Highlands, N.J.: Humanities Press International.

Chabrol, Claude, and Louis Marin. 1974. *Le récit évangélique.* Bibliothèque de Sciences Religieuses. Paris: Cerf.

Chalier, Catherine. 1991. "Ethics and the Feminine." Pp. 119–29 in *Re-Reading Levinas.* Ed. Robert Bernasconi and Simon Critchley. Studies in Continental Thought. Bloomington: Indiana University Press.

Chaney, Marvin L. 1983. "Ancient Palestinian Peasant Movements and the Formation of Premonarchic Israel." Pp. 39–90 in *Palestine in Transition: The Emergence of Ancient Israel.* Ed. David N. Freedman and David F. Graf. Sheffield: Almond.

Chatman, Seymour. 1978. *Story and Discourse: Narrative Structure in Fiction and Film.* Ithaca: Cornell University Press.

——. 1989. "The 'Rhetoric' 'of' 'Fiction.' " Pp. 40–56 in *Reading Narrative: Form, Ethics, Ideology.* Ed. J. Phelan. Columbus: Ohio State University Press.

——. 1990. *Coming to Terms: The Rhetoric of Narrative in Fiction and Film.* Ithaca: Cornell University Press.

Chené, Adèle, et al. 1987. *De Jésus et des Femmes: lectures sémiotiques.* Recherches 14. Montreal: Bellarmin.

Cheney, George. 1991. *Rhetoric in an Organizational Society: Managing Multiple Identities.* Studies in Rhetoric/Communication. Columbia: University of South Carolina Press.

Chew, Charles. 1986. *Reader Response in the Classroom.* Liverpool, N.Y.: New York State English Council.

Childers, Mary, and bell hooks. 1990. "A Conversation about Race and Class." Pp. 60–81 in *Conflicts in Feminism.* Ed. Marianne Hirsch and Evelyn Fox Keller. New York: Routledge.

Chodorow, Nancy. 1978. *The Reproduction of Mothering: Psychoanalysis and the Sociology of Gender.* Berkeley: University of California Press.

——. 1990. *Feminism and Psychoanalytic Theory.* New Haven: Yale University Press.

Christian, Barbara. 1988. "The Race for Theory." *Feminist Studies* 14:67–80.

Chung, Hyun Kyung. 1990. *Struggle to Be the Sun Again: Introducing Asian Women's Theology.* Maryknoll, N.Y.: Orbis.

Cixous, Hélène. 1972. *The Exile of James Joyce or the Art of Replacement.* New York: David Lewis.

———. 1980a. "The Laugh of the Medusa." Pp. 245–64 in *New French Feminisms: An Anthology.* Ed. Elaine Marks and Isabelle de Courtivron. New York: Schocken.

———. 1980b. "Sorties." Pp. 90–98 in *New French Feminisms: An Anthology.* Ed. Elaine Marks and Isabelle de Courtivron. New York: Schocken.

Clark, Michael J. 1992. "Confessions of Scripture-phobia, or, Why I Don't Use the Bible in My Theology." Paper presented to the Ideological Criticism Group at the annual meeting of the Society of Biblical Literature/American Academy of Religion, San Francisco, November 21–24.

Classen, Carl Joachim. 1991. "Paulus und die antike Rhetorik." *Zeitschrift für die neutestamentliche Wissenschaft* 82:1–33.

Clayton, Jay, and Eric Rothstein. 1992. "Figures in the Corpus: Theories of Influence and Intertextuality." Pp. 3–36 in *Influence and Intertextuality in Literary History.* Ed. Jay Clayton and Eric Rothstein. Madison: University of Wisconsin Press.

Clément, Catherine. 1983. *The Lives and Legends of Jacques Lacan.* Trans. Arthur Goldhammer. New York: Columbia University Press.

Clevenot, Michel. 1985. *Materialist Approaches to the Bible.* Trans. William J. Nottingham. Maryknoll, N.Y.: Orbis.

Clines, David J. 1990a. "Deconstructing the Book of Job." Pp. 65–80 in *The Bible as Rhetoric: Studies in Biblical Persuasion and Credibility.* Warwick Studies in Philosophy and Literature. Ed. Martin Warner. New York: Routledge.

———. 1990b. *What Does Eve Do to Help? And Other Readerly Questions to the Old Testament.* Journal for the Society of Old Testament Supplement Series 94. Sheffield: JSOT.

Clines, D. J. A., D. M. Gunn, and A. J. Hauser, eds. 1982. *Art and Meaning: Rhetoric in Biblical Literature.* Journal for the Society of Old Testament Supplement Series 19. Sheffield: JSOT.

Cohen, Richard Eric. 1987. "Topic, Rhetoric, Logic: Analysis of a Syllogistic Passage in the Yerushalmi [on Ber. 8:2]." Pp. 87–125 in *Judaic and Christian Interpretation.* New Perspectives on Ancient Judaism 3. Ed. Jacob Neusner and E. Frerichs. Lanham, Md.: University Press of America.

Cohn, Dorrit. 1981. "The Encirclement of Narrative: On Franz Stanzel's *Theorie des Erzählens.*" *Poetics Today* 2:157–82.

———. 1990. "Signposts of Fictionality: A Narratological Perspective." *Poetics Today* 11:775–804.

Collins, Christopher. 1992. *Reading the Written Image: Verbal Play, Interpretation, and the Roots of Iconophobia.* University Park: Pennsylvania State University Press.

Collins, Patricia Hill. 1990. *Black Feminist Thought: Knowledge, Consciousness, and the Politics of Empowerment.* Boston: Unwin Hyman.

Commission on Theological Concerns of the Christian Conference of Asia, ed. 1981. *Minjung Theology: People as the Subjects of History.* Maryknoll, N.Y.: Orbis.

Cone, James. 1969. *Black Theology and Black Power.* San Francisco: Harper.

———. 1972. *The Spirituals and the Blues.* New York: Seabury.

———. 1984. *God of the Oppressed.* San Francisco: Harper.

———. 1990. *A Black Theology of Liberation Twentieth Anniversary with Critical Responses.* 20th Anniversary Edition. Maryknoll, N.Y.: Orbis.

Conley, Thomas. 1990. *Rhetoric in the European Tradition*. White Plains, N.Y.: Longman.

Connerty, J. P. 1990. "History's Many Cunning Passages: Paul Ricoeur's *Time and Narrative*." *Poetics Today* 11:383–403.

Connor, Steven. 1989. *Postmodernist Culture: An Introduction to Theories of the Contemporary*. Oxford: Blackwell.

Connors, Robert J. 1986. "Greek Rhetoric and the Transition from Orality." *Philosophy and Rhetoric* 19:38–65.

Cook, Albert. 1988. *History/Writing*. New York: Cambridge University Press.

Copher, Charles B. 1991. "The Black Presence in the Old Testament." Pp. 146–64 in *Stony the Road We Trod: African American Biblical Interpretation*. Ed. Cain Hope Felder. Minneapolis: Augsburg/Fortress.

Corbett, Edward P. 1971. *Classical Rhetoric for the Modern Student*. 2d ed. New York: Oxford University Press.

Cormack, Mike. 1992. *Ideology*. Ann Arbor: University of Michigan Press.

Cormie, Lee. 1991. "Revolutions in Reading the Bible." Pp. 173–94 in *The Bible and The Politics of Exegesis*. Ed. David Jobling, Peggy L. Day, and Gerald T. Sheppard. Cleveland: Pilgrim.

Cornell, Drucilla. 1991. *Beyond Accommodation: Ethical Feminism, Deconstruction, and the Law*. New York: Routledge.

———. 1992. *The Philosophy of the Limit*. New York: Routledge.

———. 1993. *Transformations: Recollective Imagination and Sexual Difference*. New York: Routledge.

Coseriu, Eugenio. 1974. *Synchronie, Diachronie und Geschichte*. Munich: Wilhelm Fink.

Coste, Didier. 1990. "A Tale of Two Dictionaries." *Poetics Today* 11:405–10.

Costen, Melva Wilson. 1986/1987. "African Roots of Afro-American Baptismal Practices." *Journal of the Interdenominational Theological Center* 14:23–42.

Coward, Rosalind, and John Ellis. 1977. *Language and Materialism: Developments in Semiology and the Theory of the Subject*. Boston: Routledge.

Cox, David. 1959. *Jung and St. Paul: A Study of the Doctrine of Justification by Faith and Its Relation to the Conception of Individuation*. New York: Association.

Craemer-Ruegenberg, Ingrid, ed. 1981. *Pathos, Affekt, Gefühl: Philosophische Beiträge*. Alber-Broschur Philosophie. Freiburg: Alber.

Craig, Kenneth M. 1993. *A Poetics of Jonah: Art in the Service of Ideology*. Columbia: University of South Carolina Press.

Craig, Kerry M., and Margret A. Kristjansson. 1990. "Women Reading as Men/Women Reading as Women: A Structural Analysis for the Historical Project." *Semeia* 51:119–36.

Craig, Randall. 1984. "Reader-Response Criticism and Literary Realism." *Essays in Literature* 11:113–26.

Critchley, Simon. 1992. *The Ethics of Deconstruction: Derrida and Levinas*. Cambridge, Mass.: Blackwell.

Croatto, J. Severino. 1981. *Exodus: A Hermeneutics of Freedom*. Trans. Salvator Atanasio. Maryknoll, N.Y.: Orbis.

———. 1987. *Biblical Hermeneutics: Toward a Theory of Reading as the Production of Meaning*. New York: Orbis.

Crosby, Christina. 1992. "Dealing with Differences." Pp. 130–43 in *Feminists Theorize the Political*. Ed. Judith Butler and Joan W. Scott. New York: Routledge.

Crosman, Inge. 1983. "Reference and the Reader." *Poetics Today* 4:89–97.

Crosman, Robert. 1977. "In Defense of Authors and Readers." *Novel* 1:15–25.

———. 1980. *Reading Paradise Lost*. Bloomington: Indiana University Press.

Crossan, John Dominic. 1973. *In Parables: The Challenge of the Historical Jesus*. New York: Harper and Row.

———. 1975. *The Dark Interval: Towards a Theology of Story*. Niles, Ill.: Argus.

———. 1976. *Raid on the Articulate: Comic Eschatology in Jesus and Borges*. New York. Harper and Row.

———. 1979. *Finding Is the First Act: Trove Folktales and Jesus' Treasure Parable*. Semeia Supplements. Philadelphia: Fortress.

———. 1980. *Cliffs of Fall: Paradox and Polyvalence in the Parables of Jesus*. New York: Seabury.

———. 1991. *The Historical Jesus: The Life of a Mediterranean Jewish Peasant*. San Francisco: Harper.

Crosswhite, James. 1989. "Universality in Rhetoric: Perelman's Universal Audience." *Philosophy and Rhetoric* 22:157–73.

Crownfield, David. 1989a. "Summaries." Pp. 35–38, 55–58, 73–75, 93–96, 115–18, 131–34, 157–60 in *Lacan and Theological Discourse*. Ed. Edith Wyschogrod, David Crownfield, and Carl A. Raschke. Albany: SUNY Press.

———. 1989b. "Extraduction." Pp. 161–69 in *Lacan and Theological Discourse*. Ed. Edith Wyschogrod, David Crownfield, and Carl A. Raschke. Albany: SUNY Press.

Crownfield, David, ed. 1992. *Body/Text: Julia Kristeva and the Study of Psychoanalysis and Religion*. Albany: SUNY Press.

Culler, Jonathan. 1975a. "Stanley Fish & the Righting of the Reader." *Diacritics* 5:26–31.

———. 1975b. *Structuralist Poetics: Structuralism, Linguistics and the Study of Literature*. London: Routledge.

———. 1981. *The Pursuit of Signs: Semiotics, Literature, Deconstruction*. Ithaca: Cornell University Press.

———. 1982. *On Deconstruction: Theory and Criticism after Structuralism*. Ithaca: Cornell University Press.

———. 1986. *Ferdinand de Saussure*. Rev. ed. Ithaca: Cornell University Press.

———. 1988. *Framing the Sign: Criticism and Its Institutions*. Norman: University of Oklahoma Press.

Culley, Robert. 1976. *Studies in the Structure of Hebrew Narrative*. Semeia Studies. Philadelphia: Fortress.

———. 1985. "Exploring New Directions." Pp. 167–200 in *The Hebrew Bible and Its Modern Interpreters*. Ed. Douglas A. Knight and Gene M. Tucker. Atlanta: Scholars.

———. 1992. *Themes and Variations: A Study of Action in Biblical Narrative*. Atlanta: Scholars.

Culpepper, R. Alan. 1983. *Anatomy of the Fourth Gospel: A Study in Literary Design*. Philadelphia: Fortress.

Cunningham, David S. 1992. *Faithful Persuasion: In Aid of a Rhetoric of Christian Theology*. South Bend, Ind.: University of Notre Dame Press.

Cushman, D. P., and P. K. Tompkins. 1980. "A Theory of Rhetoric for Contemporary Society." *Philosophy & Rhetoric* 13:43–67.

Cyris, Moon Hee-Suk. 1986. *A Korean Minjung Theology: An Old Testament Perspective.* Maryknoll, N.Y.: Orbis.

Dane, Joseph A. 1986. "The Defense of the Incomplete Reader." *Comparative Literature* 38:53–72.

Danker, Frederick W. 1982. *Benefactor: Epigraphic Study of a Graeco-Roman and New Testament Semantic Field.* St. Louis: Clayton.

———. 1991. "Paul's Debt to the *De Corona* of Demosthenes: A Study of Rhetorical Techniques in Second Corinthians." Pp. 262–80 in *Persuasive Artistry: Studies in New Testament Rhetoric in Honor of George A. Kennedy.* Journal for the Study of the New Testament Supplement Series 50. Ed. Duane F. Watson. Sheffield: JSOT.

Danto, Arthur C. 1985. *Narration and Knowledge.* New York: Columbia University Press.

Darr, John A. 1987. "Glorified in the Presence of Kings: A Literary-Critical Study of Herod the Tetrarch in Luke-Acts." Ph.D. diss., Vanderbilt University.

———. 1992. *On Character Building: The Reader and the Rhetoric of Characterization.* Literary Currents in Biblical Interpretation. Louisville, Ky.: Westminster/John Knox.

Davies, Margaret. 1990. "Literary Criticism." Pp. 402–5 in *A Dictionary of Biblical Interpretation.* Ed. R. J. Coggins and J. L. Houlden. Philadelphia: Trinity Press International.

Davies, Margaret, and E. P. Sanders. 1989. *Studying the Synoptic Gospels.* Philadelphia: Trinity Press International.

Davis, Angela. 1983. *Women, Race and Class.* New York: Vintage.

Davis, Lennard. 1987. *Resisting Novels: Ideology and Fiction.* New York: Methuen.

Davis, Walter A. 1984. "The Fisher King: *Wille zur Macht* in Baltimore." *Critical Inquiry* 10:668–94.

Dawsey, James M. 1986. *The Lukan Voice: Confusion and Irony in the Gospel of Luke.* Macon, Ga.: Mercer University Press.

Day, Peggy L. 1989a. "Introduction." Pp. 1–11 in *Gender and Difference in Ancient Israel.* Ed. Peggy L. Day. Minneapolis: Augsburg/Fortress.

———, ed. 1989b. *Gender and Difference in Ancient Israel.* Minneapolis: Augsburg/Fortress.

De Bolla, Peter. 1989. *The Discourse of the Sublime: Readings in History, Aesthetics, and the Subject.* Oxford: Blackwell.

De George, Richard T., and Fernande M. De George, eds. 1972. *The Structuralists: From Marx to Lévi-Strauss.* New York: Doubleday.

Deist, F. E. 1979. *Heuristics, Hermeneutics and Authority in the Study of Scripture.* Port Elizabeth, N.J.: University of Port Elizabeth.

———. 1979–1980. "Idealistic *Theologiegeschichte,* Ideology Critique and the Dating of Oracles of Salvation. Posing a Question Concerning the Monopoly of an Accepted Method." In *Studies in Isaiah.* Ou-Testamentiese Werkgemeenskap in Suider-Afrika 22 and 23: Old Testament Essays. Ed. W. C. van Wyk. Pretoria: NHW.

de Lauretis, Teresa. 1989. "The Violence of Rhetoric: Considerations on Representation and Gender." Pp. 239–58 in *The Violence of Representation: Literature and the History of Violence.* New York: Routledge.

Deledalle, Gérard. 1971. *Le pragmatisme.* Paris: Bordas.

———. 1979. *Théorie et pratique du signe: Introduction à la sémiotique de Charles S. Peirce.* Langages et Sociétés. Paris: Payot.

Deleuze, Gilles. 1988. *Foucault.* Ed. and trans. Seán Hand. Minneapolis: University of Minnesota Press.

Deleuze, Gilles, and Félix Guattari. 1983. *Anti-Oedipus: Capitalism and Schizophrenia.* Trans. Robert Hurley, Mark Seem, and Helen R. Lane. Minneapolis: University of Minnesota Press.

———. *A Thousand Plateaus: Capitalism and Schizophrenia.* 1987. Trans. Brian Massumi. Minneapolis: University of Minnesota Press.

Delorme, Jean. 1973. *Lecture de l'évangile selon saint Marc.* Cahiers évangile. Paris: Cerf.

———. 1992. "Sémiotique." Pp. 281–333 in *Dictionnaire de la Bible. Supplément.* Ed. L. Pirot, A. Robert, Jacques Briend and Edouard Cothenet. Vol. 12. Paris: Letouzey & Ané.

De Man, Paul. 1979a. *Allegories of Reading: Figural Language in Rousseau, Nietzsche, Rilke, and Proust.* New Haven: Yale University Press.

———. 1979b. "Shelley Disfigured." Pp. 39–74 in Harold Bloom et al., *Deconstruction and Criticism.* New York: Continuum.

———. 1982. "Introduction." Pp. vii–xxv in Hans Robert Jauss, *Toward an Aesthetic of Reception.* Theory and History of Literature 2. Trans. Timothy Bahti. Minneapolis: University of Minnesota Press.

———. 1983. *Blindness and Insight: Essays in the Rhetoric of Contemporary Criticism.* 2d ed. Ed. Wlad Godzich. Theory and History of Literature 7. Minneapolis: University of Minnesota Press.

———. 1986. *The Resistance to Theory.* Theory and History of Literature 33. Minneapolis: University of Minnesota Press.

———. 1989. "What Is Modern?" Pp. 137–44 in Paul de Man, *Critical Writings, 1953–1978.* Ed. Lindsay Waters. Minneapolis: University of Minnesota Press.

DeMaria, Robert, Jr. 1978. "The Ideal Reader: A Critical Fiction." *PMLA* 93:463–74.

———. 1979. "The Thinker as Reader: The Figure of the Reader in the Writings of Wallace Stevens." *Genre* 12:243–68.

Derrida, Jacques. 1964. "Violence at Métaphysique, essai sur la pensée d'Emmanuel Levinas." *Revue de Métaphysique et de Morale* 69:322–54, 425–73.

———. 1973. *Speech and Phenomena: And Other Essays on Husserl's Theory of Signs.* Trans. David B. Allison. Evanston, Ill.: Northwestern University Press.

———. 1976. *Of Grammatology.* Trans. Gayatri Chakravorty Spivak. Baltimore: Johns Hopkins University Press.

———. 1978a. *Edmund Husserl's "Origin of Geometry": An Introduction.* Trans. John P. Leavey, Jr. Stony Brook, N.Y.: Nicholas Hays.

———. 1978b. *Writing and Difference.* Trans. Alan Bass. Chicago: University of Chicago Press.

———. 1981a. *Dissemination.* Trans. Barbara Johnson. Chicago: University of Chicago Press.

———. 1981b. *Positions.* Trans. Alan Bass. Chicago: University of Chicago Press.

———. 1982a. *Margins of Philosophy.* Trans. Alan Bass. Chicago: University of Chicago Press.

———. 1982b. "Of an Apocalyptic Tone Recently Adopted in Philosophy." Trans. John P. Leavey, Jr. *Semeia* 23:63–97.

———. 1982c. "The Time of a Thesis: Punctuations." Pp. 34–50 in *Philosophy in France Today.* Ed. Alan Montefiore. Cambridge: Cambridge University Press.

———. 1985a. *The Ear of the Other: Otobiography, Transference, Translation.* Ed. Christie McDonald. Trans. Peggy Kamuf and Avital Ronell. Lincoln: University of Nebraska Press.

———. 1985b. "Racism's Last Word." Trans. Peggy Kamuf. Pp. 329–38 in *"Race," Writing and Difference.* Ed. Henry Louis Gates, Jr. Chicago: University of Chicago Press.

———. 1985c. "Des Tours de Babel." Trans. Joseph F. Graham. Pp. 165–248 in *Difference in Translation*. Ed. Joseph F. Graham. Ithaca: Cornell University Press.

———. 1986a. *Altéritiés*. Paris: Osiris.

———. 1986b. *Glas*. Trans. John P. Leavey, Jr., and Richard Rand. Lincoln: University of Nebraska Press.

———. 1987. *The Post Card: From Socrates to Freud and Beyond*. Trans. Alan Bass. Chicago: University of Chicago Press.

———. 1988a. "Letter to a Japanese Friend." Trans. David Wood and Andrew Benjamin. Pp. 1–5 in *Derrida and Differance*. Ed. David Wood and Robert Bernasconi. Evanston, Ill.: Northwestern University Press.

———. 1988b. *Limited Inc*. Ed. Gerald Graff. Trans. Samuel Weber and Jeffrey Mehlman. Evanston, Ill.: Northwestern University Press.

———. 1989. "How to Avoid Speaking: Denials." Trans. Ken Frieden. Pp. 3–70 in *Languages of the Unsayable: The Play of Negativity in Literature and Literary Theory*. Ed. Sanford Budick and Wolfgang Iser. New York: Columbia University Press.

———. 1992a. *Acts of Literature*. Ed. Derek Attridge. New York: Routledge.

———. 1992b. "At This Very Moment in This Work Here I Am." Pp. 11–50 in *Re-Reading Levinas*. Ed. Robert Bernasconi and Simon Critchley. Studies in Continental Thought. Bloomington: Indiana University Press.

Descombes, Vincent. 1980. *Modern French Philosophy*. Trans. L. Scott-Fox and J. M. Harding. Cambridge: Cambridge University Press.

De Sousa, Ronald. 1987. *The Rationality of Emotion*. Cambridge: MIT Press.

de Ste. Croix, G. E. M. 1981. *The Class Struggle in the Ancient Greek World: From the Archaic Age to the Arab Conquests*. Ithaca: Cornell University Press.

Detweiler, Robert, ed. 1985. "Reader Response Approaches to Biblical and Secular Texts." *Semeia* 31.

———. 1989. *Breaking the Fall: Religious Readings of Contemporary Fiction*. Studies in Literature and Religion. London: Macmillan.

de Vries, Hent. 1989. *Theologie im Pianissimo & Zwischen Rationalität und Dekonstruktion: Die Aktualität der Denkenfiguren Adornos und Levinas*. Studies in Philosophical Theology. Kampen, Neth.: J. H. Kok.

Dewey, Joanna. 1990. "Response." *Journal of Feminist Studies in Religion* 6(2):63–69.

Diamond, Irene, and Lee Quinby, eds. 1988. *Feminism and Foucault: Reflections on Resistance*. Boston: Northeastern University Press.

Diel, Paul. 1986. *Symbolism in the Bible: The Universality of Symbolic Language and Its Psychological Significance*. Trans. Nelly Marans. San Francisco: Harper and Row.

Dillon, George L. 1986. *Rhetoric as Social Imagination: Exploration in the Interpersonal Function of Language*. Bloomington: Indiana University Press.

Docherty, Thomas, ed. 1993. *Postmodernism: A Reader*. Ithaca: Cornell University Press.

Dockhorn, Klaus. 1964. " 'Memoria' in der Rhetorik." *Archiv für Begriffsgeschichte* 9:27–35.

———. 1968. *Macht und Wirkung der Rhetorik*. Respublica Literaria 2. Bad Homburg: Gehlen.

———. 1974. "Rhetorica movet: Protestantischer Humanismus und karolingische Renaissance." Pp. 17–42 in *Rhetorik: Beiträge zu ihrer Geschichte in Deutschland vom 16–20. Jahrhundert*. Ed. Helmut Schanze. Frankfurt: Fischer.

———. 1980. "Hans-Georg Gadamer's *Truth and Method.*" Trans. Marvin Brown. *Philosophy and Rhetoric* 13:160–80.

Doležel, Lubomír. 1980. "Eco and His Model Reader." *Poetics Today* 1:181–88.

Dollimore, Jonathan. 1984. *Radical Tragedy.* Brighton: Harvester.

Donaldson, Laura E. 1990. "From the Woman's Bible to the Womanist Bible: Sexual Difference and the Crisis of Feminist Hermeneutics." Paper presented at the Womanist Approaches to Religion and Society Consultation at the annual meeting of the Society of Biblical Literature/American Academy of Religion, New Orleans, November 17–20.

———. 1992. *Decolonizing Feminisms: Race, Gender and Empire Building.* Chapel Hill: University of North Carolina Press.

Donaldson, Mara E. 1981. "Kinship Theory in the Patriarchal Narratives." *Journal of the American Academy of Religion* 49:77–87.

Donoghue, Denis. 1981. "Making Room for the Reader." *Times Literary Supplement* 4075: 507–8.

Dorfman, A., and A. Mattelart. 1975. *How to Read Donald Duck: Imperialist Ideology in the Disney Comic.* New York: International General Editions.

Douglas, Mary. 1966. *Purity and Danger: An Analysis of Concepts of Pollution and Taboo.* London: Routledge.

Downing, David B., and Susan Bazargan, eds. 1991. *Image and Ideology in Modern/Postmodern Discourse.* Albany: SUNY Press.

Drasima, Sipke, ed. 1989. *Intertextuality in Biblical Writings: Essays in Honour of Bas van Iersel.* Kampden, Neth.: J. H. Kok.

Dreyfus, Hubert L., and Paul Rabinow. 1983. *Michel Foucault: Beyond Structuralism and Hermeneutics.* 2d ed. Chicago: University of Chicago Press.

Droge, Arthur. 1989. *Homer or Moses? Early Christian Interpretations of the History of Culture.* Hermeneutische Untersuchungen zur Theologie 26. Tübingen: Mohr.

Duffy, Bernard K. 1983. "The Platonic Functions of Epideictic Rhetoric." *Philosophy and Rhetoric* 16:79–93.

Duke, Paul D. 1985. *Irony in the Fourth Gospel.* Atlanta: John Knox.

Du Plessis, Johannes G. 1985. "Clarity and Obscurity: A Study in Textual Communication of the Relation between Sender, Parable and Receiver in the Synoptic Gospels." Th.D. diss., University of Stellenbosch, Stellenbosch, South Africa.

Eagleton, Terry. 1976. *Criticism and Ideology: A Study in Marxist Literary Theory.* London: Verso.

———. 1980. "Text, Ideology, Realism." Pp. 149–73 in *Literature and Society.* Ed. Edward W. Said. Baltimore: Johns Hopkins University Press.

———. 1982. "The Revolt of the Reader." *New Literary History* 13:449–52.

———. 1983. *Literary Theory: An Introduction.* Minneapolis: University of Minnesota Press.

———. 1985. "Capitalism, Modernism and Postmodernism." *New Left Review* 152:60–73.

———. 1986. *Against the Grain: Selected Essays.* London: Verso.

———. 1990a. *The Ideology of the Aesthetic.* Oxford: Blackwell.

———. 1990b. *The Significance of Theory.* Oxford: Blackwell.

———. 1991. *Ideology: An Introduction.* New York: Verso.

Ebeling, Gerhard. 1963. *Word and Faith.* Trans. James W. Leitch. Philadelphia: Fortress.

Ebert, Teresa L. 1991. "The 'Difference' of Postmodern Feminism." *College English* 53:886–904.

———. 1992–93. "Ludic Feminism, the Body, Performance, and Labor: Bringing *Materialism* Back into Feminist Cultural Studies." *Cultural Critique* 23:5–50.

Eco, Umberto. 1976. *A Theory of Semiotics*. Advances in Semiotics. Bloomington: Indiana University Press.

———. 1979. *The Role of the Reader: Explorations in the Semiotics of Texts*. Advances in Semiotics. Bloomington: Indiana University Press.

———. 1988. *The Open Work*. Trans. Anna Concogni. Cambridge: Harvard University Press.

———. 1990. *The Limits of Interpretation*. Advances in Semiotics. Bloomington: Indiana University Press.

Eco, Umberto, Richard Rorty, Jonathan Culler, and Christine Brooke-Rose. 1992. *Interpretation and Overinterpretation*. Ed. Stefan Collini. Cambridge: Cambridge University Press.

Edelson, Marshall. 1975. *Language and Interpretation in Psychoanalysis*. Chicago: University of Chicago Press.

Eden, Kathy. 1987. "Hermeneutics and the Ancient Rhetorical Tradition." *Rhetorica* 5:59–86.

Edinger, Edward F. 1986. *The Bible and the Psyche: Individuation Symbolism in the Old Testament*. Toronto: Inner City Books.

Edwards, Richard A. 1985. *Matthew's Story of Jesus*. Philadelphia: Fortress.

Ehninger, Douglas. 1972. *Contemporary Rhetoric: A Reader's Coursebook*. Glenview, Ill.: Scott, Foresman.

Ehrmann, Jacques, ed. 1970. *Structuralism*. New York: Doubleday.

Eisenstein, Hester. 1983. *Contemporary Feminist Thought*. Boston: G. K. Hall.

Ela, Jean-Marc. 1980. *African Cry*. Maryknoll, N.Y.: Orbis.

Elliot, Patricia. 1991. *From Mastery to Analysis: Theories of Gender in Psychoanalytic Feminism*. Ithaca: Cornell University Press.

Elliott, Gregory. 1987. *Althusser: The Detour of Theory*. New York: Verso.

Ellis, Marc H. 1987. *Toward a Jewish Theology of Liberation*. Maryknoll, N.Y.: Orbis.

———. 1989. "Critical Thought and Messianic Trust: Reflections on a Jewish Theology of Liberation." Pp. 375–89 in *The Future of Liberation Theology: Essays in Honor of Gustavo Gutierrez*. Ed. Marc H. Ellis and Otto Maduro. Maryknoll, N.Y.: Orbis.

Ellul, Jacques. 1988. *Jesus and Marx: From Gospel to Ideology*. Grand Rapids, Mich.: Eerdmans.

Eskhult, Mats. 1990. *Studies in Verbal Aspects and Narrative Technique in Biblical Hebrew Prose*. Acta Universitatis Upsaliensis. Studia Semitica Upsaliensis 12. Uppsala: Almquist & Wiksell.

Eslinger, Lyle. 1985. *Kingship of God in Crisis: A Close Reading of 1 Samuel 1–12*. Bible and Literature 10. Sheffield: Almond.

———. 1987. "The Wooing of the Woman at the Well: Jesus, the Reader and Reader-Response Criticism." *Journal of Literature & Theology* 1:167–83.

Evans, G. R. 1984. *The Language and Logic of the Bible: The Earlier Middle Ages*. Cambridge: Cambridge University Press.

Evans, J. Claude. 1991. *Strategies of Deconstruction: Derrida and the Myth of the Voice*. Minneapolis: University of Minnesota Press.

Everman, Welch. 1988. *Who Says This? The Authority of the Author, the Discourse, and the Reader.* Carbondale: Southern Illinois University Press.

Exum, Cheryl. 1990. "Murder They Wrote: Ideology and the Manipulation of Female Presence in Biblical Narrative." Pp. 45–67 in *The Pleasure of Her Text: Feminist Readings of Biblical and Historical Texts.* Ed. Alice Bach. Philadelphia: Trinity Press International.

Featherstone, M. 1988. "In Pursuit of the Postmodern." *Theory, Culture and Society* 5:195–215.

Felder, Cain Hope. 1989a. "The Bible, Re-Contextualization and the Black Religious Experience." Pp. 155–71 in *African American Religious Studies: An Interdisciplinary Anthology.* Ed. Gayraud Wilmore. Durham, N.C.: Duke University Press.

————. 1989b. *Troubling Biblical Waters: Race, Class, and Family.* Maryknoll, N.Y.: Orbis.

Felder, Cain Hope, ed. 1991. *Stony the Road We Trod: African American Biblical Interpretation.* Minneapolis: Augsburg/Fortress.

Feldstein, Richard, and Judith Roof, eds. 1989. *Feminism and Psychoanalysis.* Ithaca: Cornell University Press.

Felman, Shoshana. 1987. *Jacques Lacan and the Adventure of Insight: Psychoanalysis in Contemporary Culture.* Cambridge: Harvard University Press.

Felman, Shoshana, ed. 1992. *Literature and Psychoanalysis: The Question of Reading, Otherwise.* Baltimore: Johns Hopkins University Press.

Felperin, Howard. 1985. *Beyond Deconstruction: The Uses and Abuses of Theory.* Oxford: Clarendon.

Fenner, M. William. 1650. *A Treatise of the Affections, or, The Souls Pulse.* London: A. M. for J. Rothwell.

Ferguson, Kathy E. 1991. "Interpretation and Genealogy in Feminism." *Signs* 16:322–39.

Ferguson, Russell, Martha Gever, Trinh T. Minh-Ha, and Cornel West, eds. 1990. *Out There: Marginalization and Contemporary Cultures.* Cambridge: MIT Press.

Fetterley, Judith. 1978. *The Resisting Reader: A Feminist Approach to American Fiction.* Bloomington: Indiana University Press.

————. 1986. "Reading about Reading 'A Jury of Her Peers,' 'The Murders in the Rue Morgue,' and 'The Yellow Wallpaper.' " Pp. 147–64 in *Gender and Reading: Essays on Readers, Texts, and Contexts.* Ed. Elizabeth A. Flynn and Patrocinio P. Schweickart. Baltimore: Johns Hopkins University Press.

Feuer, Lewis. 1975. *Ideology and the Ideologists.* New York: Harper.

Fewell, Danna Nolan, ed. 1992. *Reading between Texts: Intertextuality and the Hebrew Bible.* Literary Currents in Biblical Interpretation. Louisville, Ky.: Westminster/John Knox.

Fewell, Danna Nolan, and David M. Gunn. 1993. *Gender, Power and Promise: The Subject of the Bible's First Story.* Nashville: Abingdon.

Fierro, Alfredo. 1977. *The Militant Gospel: A Critical Introduction to Political Theologies.* Maryknoll, N.Y.: Orbis.

Fisch, Harold. 1988. *Poetry with a Purpose: Biblical Poetics and Interpretation.* Indiana Studies in Biblical Literature. Bloomington: Indiana University Press.

Fischel, Henry A. 1977 (1969). "Story and History: Observations on Greco-Roman Rhetoric and Pharisaism." Pp. 443–72 in *Essays in Greco-Roman and Related Talmudic Literature.* New York: KTAV.

Fischer, Norman. 1987. "Modernism, Postmodernism, and Values." *Poetics Journal* 7:114–16.

Fish, Stanley E. 1970. "Literature in the Reader: Affective Stylistics." *New Literary History* 2:123–62.

———. 1971. *Surprised by Sin: The Reader in Paradise Lost.* 2d ed. Berkeley: University of California Press.

———. 1972. *Self-Consuming Artifacts: The Experience of Seventeenth-Century Literature.* Berkeley: University of California Press.

———. 1975. "Facts and Fiction: A Reply to Ralph Rader." *Critical Inquiry* 1:883–91.

———. 1976a. "Interpreting the *Variorum.*" *Critical Inquiry* 24:65–85.

———. 1976b. "How to Do Things with Austin and Searle: Speech-Act Theory and Literary Criticism." *Modern Language Notes* 91:983–1025.

———. 1978. *The Living Temple: George Herbert and Catechizing.* Berkeley: University of California Press.

———. 1980. *Is There a Text in This Class? The Authority of Interpretive Communities.* Cambridge: Harvard University Press.

———. 1981. "Why No One's Afraid of Wolfgang Iser." *Diacritics* 1:12–13.

———. 1983. "Short People Got No Reason to Live: Reading Irony." *Daedalus* 112:175–91.

———. 1984. "Fear of Fish: A Reply for Walter Davis." *Critical Inquiry* 10:695–705.

———. 1989. *Doing What Comes Naturally: Change, Rhetoric, and the Practice of Theory in Literary and Legal Studies.* Durham, N.C.: Duke University Press.

———. 1990. "Rhetoric." Pp. 203–24 in *Critical Terms for Literary Study.* Ed. Frank Lentricchia and Thomas McLaughlin. Chicago: University of Chicago Press.

Fisher, David H. 1990. "Self in Text, Text in Self." *Semeia* 51:137–54.

Fisher, Walter R. 1987. "Technical Logic, Rhetorical Logic, and Narrative Rationality." *Argumentation* 1:3–21.

Fiske, Donald W., and Richard A. Shweder, eds. 1986. *Metatheory in Social Science: Pluralisms and Subjectivities.* Chicago: University of Chicago Press.

Flax, Jane. 1987. "Postmodernism and Gender Relations in Feminist Theory." *Signs* 12:621–43.

———. 1990. *Thinking Fragments: Psychoanalysis, Feminism and Postmodernism in the Contemporary West.* Los Angeles: University of California Press.

Fleischer, Rudi. 1982. "Zeichen, Symbol und Transzendenz." Pp. 169–92 in *Zeichen: Semiotik in Theologie und Gottesdienst.* Ed. Rainer Volp. Munich: Kaiser.

Fletcher, John, and Andrew Benjamin, eds. 1990. *Abjection, Melancholia and Love: The Work of Julia Kristeva.* New York: Routledge.

Flynn, Elizabeth A. 1983. "Women as Reader-Response Critics." *New Orleans Review* 10:20–25.

———. 1986. "Gender and Reading." Pp. 267–88 in *Gender and Reading: Essays on Readers, Texts, and Contexts.* Ed. Elizabeth A. Flynn and Patrocinio P. Schweickart. Baltimore: Johns Hopkins University Press.

———. 1991. "Engendering the Teaching of Reading." *College Literature* 18:80–93.

Flynn, Elizabeth A., and Patrocinio P. Schweickart, eds. 1986. *Gender and Reading: Essays on Readers, Texts, and Contexts.* Baltimore: Johns Hopkins University Press.

Fokkelman, J. P. 1986. *Narrative Art and Poetry in the Books of Samuel: A Full Interpretation*

Based on Stylistic and Structural Analyses. Vol. 2, *The Crossing Fates (I Sam. 13–31 & II Sam. 1).* Studia Semitica Neerlandica. Aasen: Van Gorcum.

———. 1991. *Narrative Art in Genesis: Specimens of Stylistic and Structural Analysis.* 2d ed. Sheffield: JSOT.

Foss, Sonja K., Karen A. Fass, and Robert Trapp. 1991. *Contemporary Perspectives on Rhetoric.* 2d ed. Prospect Heights, Ill.: Waveland.

Foster, Hal. 1983. "Postmodernism: A Preface." Pp. ix–xvi in *The Anti-Aesthetic: Essays on Postmodern Culture.* Ed. Hal Foster. Port Townsend, Wash.: Bay.

———. 1985. *Postmodern Culture.* London: Pluto.

Foucault, Michel. 1961. *Folie et déraison: histoire de la folie à l'âge classique.* Paris: Plon.

———. 1963. *Naissance de la clinique: Une archéologie du regard médical.* Paris: Presses Universitaires de France.

———. 1966. *Les mots et les choses: une archéologie des sciences humaines.* Paris: Gallimard.

———. 1967. "Nietzsche, Freud, Marx." Pp. 183–200 in *Cahiers de Royaumont philosophie 6, Nietzsche.* Paris: Minuit.

———. 1970. *The Order of Things: An Archaeology of the Human Sciences.* World of Man. New York: Pantheon.

———. 1972a. *The Archaeology of Knowledge.* Trans. A. M. Sheridan Smith. New York: Pantheon.

———. 1972b. "The Discourse on Language." Pp. 215–37 in *The Archeology of Knowledge.* Trans. A. M. Sheridan Smith. New York: Pantheon.

———. 1975. *Surveiller et punir: Naissance de la prison.* Paris: Gallimard.

———. 1976. *Histoire de la sexualité.* Vol. 1, *La volonté de savoir.* Paris: Gallimard.

———. 1977a. *Discipline and Punish: The Birth of the Prison.* Trans. Alan Sheridan. New York: Vintage.

———. 1977b. "Intellectuals and Power." Pp. 205–17 in *Language, Counter-Memory, Practice: Selected Essays and Interviews.* Ed. Donald Bouchard. Trans. Donald Bouchard and Sherry Simon. Ithaca: Cornell University Press.

———. 1977c. "What Is an Author?" Pp. 113–38 in *Language, Counter-Memory, Practice.* Ed. Donald Bouchard. Trans. Donald Bouchard and Sherry Simon. Ithaca: Cornell University Press.

———. 1978. *The History of Sexuality.* Vol. 1, *Introduction.* Trans. Robert Hurley. New York: Vintage.

———. 1979. *Discipline and Punish: The Birth of the Prison.* Trans. Alan Sheridan. New York: Vintage.

———. 1980. *Power/Knowledge: Selected Interviews and Other Writings, 1972–1977.* Ed. Colin Gordon. Trans. Colin Gordon et al. New York: Pantheon.

———. 1982a. "The Subject and Power." Pp. 208–26 in *Michel Foucault: Beyond Structuralism and Hermeneutics.* Ed. Hubert L. Dreyfus and Paul Rabinow. 2d ed. Chicago: University of Chicago Press.

———. 1982b. *This Is Not a Pipe.* Berkeley: University of California Press.

———. 1983. "Structuralism and Post-Structuralism: An Interview." *Telos* 55:195–211.

———. 1984a. *Histoire de la sexualité.* Vol. 2, *L'usage des plaisirs.* Paris: Gallimard.

———. 1984b. *Histoire de la sexualité.* Vol. 3, *Le souci de soi.* Paris: Gallimard.

———. 1984c. "What is Enlightenment?" Pp. 32–50 In *The Foucault Reader*. Ed. Paul Rabinow. New York: Pantheon.

———. 1985. *The Use of Pleasure*. Trans. Robert Hurley. New York: Pantheon.

———. 1986. *The Care of the Self*. Trans. Robert Hurley. New York: Pantheon.

———. 1988. *Politics, Philosophy, Culture: Interviews and Other Writings, 1977–1984*. Ed. Lawrence D. Kritzman. Trans. Alan Sheridan et al. New York: Routledge.

———. 1989a. "Clarifications on the Question of Power." Pp. 179–92 in *Foucault Live (Interviews, 1966–84)*. Ed. Sylvère Lotringer. Trans. John Johnston. New York: Semiotext(e).

———. 1989b. "The Discourse of History." Pp. 11–34 in *Foucault Live (Interviews, 1966–84)*. Ed. Sylvère Lotringer. Trans. John Johnston. New York: Semiotext(e).

———. 1989c. "How Much Does It Cost for Reason to Tell the Truth?" Pp. 233–56 in *Foucault Live (Interviews, 1966–84)*. Ed. Sylvère Lotringer. Trans. John Johnston. New York: Semiotext(e).

Fowler, Robert M. 1981. *Loaves and Fishes: The Function of the Feeding Stories in the Gospel of Mark*. Society of Biblical Literature Dissertation Series 54. Chico, Calif.: Scholars.

———. 1985. "Who Is 'The Reader' in Reader Response Criticism?" *Semeia* 31:5–23.

———. 1986. "Reading Matthew Reading Mark: Observing the First Steps Toward Meaning-as-Reference in the Synoptic Gospels." Pp. 1–16 in *Society of Biblical Literature 1986 Seminar Papers*. Ed. Kent Harold Richards. Atlanta: Scholars.

———. 1989a. "Post-Modern Biblical Criticism: The Criticism of Pre-Modern Texts in a Post-Critical, Post-Modern, Post-Literate Era." *Forum* 5:3–30.

———. 1989b. "The Rhetoric of Direction and Indirection in the Gospel of Mark." *Semeia* 48:115–34.

———. 1991. *Let the Reader Understand: Reader-Response Criticism and the Gospel of Mark*. Minneapolis: Augsburg/Fortress.

———. 1992. "Reader-Response Criticism: Figuring the Reader." Pp. 50–83 in *Mark and Method: New Approaches in Biblical Studies*. Ed. Janice Capel Anderson and Stephen D. Moore. Minneapolis: Augsburg/Fortress.

———. 1993. "Is 'What Is?' Enough? A Review of Mark Powell's *What Is Narrative Criticism?*." Pp. 171–75 in *Proceedings of the Eastern Great Lakes and Midwest Biblical Societies*. Vol. 12. Ed. Benjamin Fiore. Buffalo, N.Y.: Canisius College.

———. 1994. "Mapping the Varieties of Reader-Response Criticism." *Biblical Interpretation* 1:1–28.

Fowler, Roger. 1986. *Linguistic Criticism*. Oxford: Oxford University Press.

Fraser, Nancy. 1989. *Unruly Practices: Power, Discourse and Gender in Contemporary Social Theory*. Minneapolis: University of Minnesota Press.

Freedman, David Noel, and David Frank Graf, eds. 1983. *Palestine in Translation: The Emergence of Ancient Israel*. Sheffield: Almond.

Frei, Hans. 1974. *The Eclipse of Biblical Narrative: A Study in Eighteenth and Nineteenth Century Hermeneutics*. New Haven: Yale University Press.

Freire, Paulo. 1987. "Conversations with Paulo Freire on Pedagogies for the Non-Poor." Pp. 219–31 in *Pedagogies for the Non-Poor*. Ed. Alice Frazer Evans, Robert A. Evans, and William Bean Kennedy. Maryknoll, N.Y.: Orbis.

Freud, Sigmund. 1900. *The Interpretation of Dreams. The Standard Edition of the Complete*

Psychological Works of Sigmund Freud, vols. 4–5. Ed. and trans. James Strachey. London: Hogarth.

————. 1907. "Obsessive Actions and Religious Practices." *Standard Edition*, vol. 9.

————. 1910. *Leonardo da Vinci and a Memory of His Childhood. Standard Edition*, vol. 9.

————. 1913. *Totem and Taboo. Standard Edition*, vol. 13.

————. 1914a. "On the History of the Psycho-Analytic Movement." *Standard Edition*, vol. 14.

————. 1914b. "The Moses of Michelangelo." *Standard Edition*, vol. 13.

————. 1915. "The Unconscious." *Standard Edition*, vol. 14.

————. 1921. *Group Psychology and the Analysis of the Ego. Standard Edition*, vol. 18.

————. 1923a. *The Ego and the Id. Standard Edition*, vol. 19.

————. 1923b. "Two Encyclopaedia Articles." *Standard Edition*, vol. 18.

————. 1925. *An Autobiographical Study. Standard Edition*, vol. 20.

————. 1927. *The Future of an Illusion. Standard Edition*, vol. 21.

————. 1930. *Civilization and Its Discontents. Standard Edition*, vol. 21.

————. 1933. *New Introductory Lectures on Psycho-Analysis. Standard Edition*, vol. 22.

————. 1939. *Moses and Monotheism. Standard Edition*, vol. 23.

Freund, Elizabeth. 1987. *The Return of the Reader: Reader-Response Criticism*. New Accents. New York: Methuen.

Frick, Frank S. 1991. "Sociological Criticism and Its Relation to Political and Social Hermeneutics with a Special Look at Biblical Hermeneutics in South African Liberation Theology." Pp. 225–38 in *The Bible and The Politics of Exegesis*. Ed. David Jobling, Peggy L. Day, and Gerald T. Shepphard. Cleveland: Pilgrim.

Friedan, Ken. 1990. *Freud's Dream of Interpretation*. Albany: SUNY Press.

Frow, John. 1986. *Marxism and Literary History*. Cambridge: Harvard University Press.

————. 1989. "Discourse and Power." Pp. 198–217 in *Ideological Representation and Power in Social Relations: Literary and Social Theory*. Ed. Mike Gane. New York: Routledge.

Frye, Northrop. 1982. *The Great Code: The Bible and Literature*. New York: Harcourt Brace Jovanovich.

————. 1990. *Words with Power: Being a Second Study of "The Bible and Literature"*. New York: Harcourt Brace Jovanovich.

Frymer-Kensky, Tikva. 1992. *In the Wake of the Goddesses: Women, Culture, and the Biblical Transformation of Pagan Myth*. New York: Free Press.

Fuchs, Ernst. 1964. *Studies of the Historical Jesus*. Studies in Biblical Theology 42. Naperville, Ill.: Alec R. Allenson.

Füssel, Kuno. 1981. *Sprache, Religion, Ideologie: Von einer sprachanalytischen zu einer materialistischen Theologie*. Frankfurt: Peter Lang.

————. 1984. "Materialist Readings of the Bible: Report on an Alternative Approach to Biblical Texts." Pp. 13–25 in *God of the Lowly: Socio-Historical Interpretations of the Bible*. Ed. Willy Schottroff and Wolfgang Stegemann. Trans. Matthew J. O'Connell. Maryknoll, N.Y.: Orbis.

————. 1985. "Materialistische Lekture der Bibel." *Theologische Berichte XIII: Methoden der Evangelien-Exegese*. Zurich: Benziger.

————. 1987. *Drei Tage mit Jesus im Tempel: Einfuhrung in die Lekture der Bibel für Religionsunterricht, Theologiestudium und Pastoral*. Munster: Edition Liberacion.

Fuhrmann, Manfred. 1966. "Das Problem der Dunkelheit in der rhetorischen und literatur-ästhetischen Theorie der Antike." Pp. 47–72 in *Immanente Ästhetik: Ästhetische Reflexion.* Ed. Wolfgang Iser. Poetik und Hermeneutik. Munich: Fink.

———. 1987. *Antike Rhetorik. Eine Einführung.* 2d ed. Munich: Artemis.

Funk, Robert W. 1966. *Language, Hermeneutic, and Word of God. The Problem of Language in the New Testament and Contemporary Theology.* New York: Harper and Row.

———. 1976. "The Watershed of the American Biblical Tradition: The Chicago School, First Phase, 1892–1920." *Journal of Biblical Literature* 95:4–22.

———. 1982. *Parables and Presence: Forms of the New Testament Tradition.* Philadelphia: Fortress.

———. 1988. *A Poetics of Biblical Narrative.* Sonoma, Calif.: Polebridge.

Fuss, Diana. 1989. "Reading Like a Feminist." *differences* 1:77–92.

Gabus, Jean-Paul. 1981. "Le Statut Symbolique du Langage Biblique et la Fonction Idéologique." Pp. 99–110 in *Theolinguistics.* Ed. J. P. van Noppen. Studiereeks Tijdscrift Vub Nieuwe Serie 8. Brussels: Vrije Universiteit Brussel.

Gadamer, Hans-Georg. 1975. *Truth and Method.* New York: Seabury.

———. 1988 (1967). "Rhetoric, Hermeneutics, and the Critique of Ideology: Metacritical Comments on *Truth and Method.*" Pp. 274–92 in *The Hermeneutics Reader: Texts of the German Tradition from the Enlightenment to the Present.* Ed. Kurt Mueller-Vollmer. New York: Continuum.

———. 1992. "The Expressive Power of Language: On the Function of Rhetoric for Knowledge." *PMLA* 107:345–52.

Gaggi, Silvio. 1989. *Modern/Postmodern: A Study in Twentieth Century Arts and Ideas.* Penn Studies in Contemporary American Fiction. Philadelphia: University of Pennsylvania Press.

Gallop, Jane. 1982. *The Daughter's Seduction: Feminism and Psychoanalysis.* Ithaca: Cornell University Press.

———. 1985. *Reading Lacan.* Ithaca: Cornell University Press.

———. 1992. *Around 1981: Academic Feminist Literary Theory.* New York: Routledge.

Garbini, Giovanni. 1988. *History and Ideology in Ancient Israel.* New York: Crossroad.

Gardiner, Michael. 1992. *The Dialogics of Critique: M. M. Bakhtin and the Theory of Ideology.* New York: Routledge.

Garrett, Mary. 1991. "Asian Challenge." Pp. 295–314 in *Contemporary Perspectives on Rhetoric.* Ed. S. K. Foss, K. A. Foss, and R. Trapp. 2d ed. Prospect Heights, Ill.: Waveland.

Gasché, Rodolphe. 1986. *The Tain of the Mirror: Derrida and the Philosophy of Reflection.* Cambridge: Harvard University Press.

Gates, Henry Louis, Jr. 1988. *The Signifying Monkey: A Theory of African-American Literary Criticism.* New York: Oxford University Press.

Gates, Henry Louis, Jr., ed. 1986. *"Race," Writing, and Difference.* Chicago: University of Chicago Press.

———. 1990. *Reading Black, Reading Feminist: A Critical Anthology.* New York: Meridian.

Gathercole, Peter. 1984. "Epilogue: A Consideration of Ideology." Pp. 149–54 in *Marxist Perspectives in Archeology.* Ed. Matthew Spriggs. Cambridge: Cambridge University Press.

Gay, Peter. 1985. *Freud for Historians.* New York: Oxford University Press.

——. 1987. *A Godless Jew: Freud, Atheism, and the Making of Psychoanalysis.* New Haven: Yale University Press.

——. 1988. *Freud: A Life for Our Time.* New York: Norton.

Geertz, Clifford. 1964. "Ideology as a Cultural System." Pp. 47–76 in *Ideology and Discontent.* Ed. D. E. Apter. London: Free Press of Glencoe.

Gelzer, Thomas. 1987. *How to Express Emotions of the Soul and Operations of the Mind in a Language That Has No Words for Them: Exemplified by Odysseus and Calypso.* (ODYSSEY v, 1–281). Ed. William. S. Anderson. Protocol of the 55th Colloquy. Berkeley, Calif.: Center for Hermeneutical Studies.

Genest, Olivette. 1978. *Le Christ de la Passion: Perspective structurale.* Recherches 21. Montreal: Bellarmin.

Genette, Gérard. 1972. *Figures III.* Paris: Seuil.

——. 1980. *Narrative Discourse: An Essay in Method.* Trans. Jane E. Lewin. Ithaca: Cornell University Press.

——. 1982a. *Figures of Literary Discourse.* New York: Columbia University Press.

——. 1982b. *Paimpsestes: La Littérature au second degré.* Collections Poétique. Paris: Seuil.

——. 1990. "Fictional Narrative, Factual Narrative." *Poetics Today* 11:755–74.

Gerhardsson, Birger. 1979. *The Origins of the Gospel Traditions.* Philadelphia: Fortress.

Gerhart, Gail M. 1979. *Black Power in South Africa: The Evolution of an Ideology.* Los Angeles: University of California Press.

Gibson, Walker. 1950. "Authors, Speakers, Readers, and Mock Readers." *College English* 11:265–69.

Giddings, Paula. 1984. *When and Where I Enter: The Impact of Black Women on Race and Sex in America.* New York: William Morrow.

Gifford, Carolyn De Swarte. 1985. "American Women and the Bible: The Nature of Woman as Hermeneutical Issue." Pp. 11–33 in *Feminist Perspectives on Biblical Scholarship.* Ed. Adela Yarbro Collins. Biblical Scholarship in North America 10. Chico, Calif.: Scholars.

Gilkes, Cheryl Townsend. 1989. " 'Mother to the Motherless, Father to the Fatherless:' Power, Gender, and Community in Afrocentric Biblical Tradition." *Semeia* 47:57–85.

Gilman, Sander L., Carol Blair, and David J. Parent, eds. 1989. *Friedrich Nietzsche on Rhetoric and Language.* New York: Oxford University Press.

Giroud, Jean-Claude and Louis Panier. 1987. "Sémiotique. Une pratique de lecture et d'analyse des textes bibliques." *Cahiers Evangile* 59.

Gitay, Yehoshua. 1981. *Prophecy and Persuasion: A Study of Isaiah 40–48.* Forum Theologiae Linguisticae 14. Bonn: Linguistica Biblica.

Gitlin, Todd. 1989. "Postmodernism Defined, at Last!" *Utne Reader* 34:52–61.

Glissant, Eduoard. 1981. *Le Discours antillais.* Paris: Seuil.

——. 1989. *Caribbean Discourse.* Trans. J. Michael Dash. Charlottesville: University of Virginia Press.

Goldmann, Lucien. 1964. *The Hidden God.* London: Routledge.

Goldstein, Philip. 1990. *The Politics of Literary Theory: An Introduction to Marxist Criticism.* Tallahassee: Florida State University Press.

Gombrich, E. H. 1956. *Art and Illusion: A Study in the Psychology of Pictorial Representation.* Bollingen Series 35. Princeton: Princeton University Press.

Good, Edwin M. 1981. *Irony in the Old Testament.* Bible and Literature Series 3. 2d ed. Sheffield: Almond.

Gordon, Robert M. 1987. *The Structure of Emotions: Investigations in Cognitive Philosophy.* New York: Cambridge University Press.

Gottwald, Norman K. 1979. *The Tribes of Yahweh: A Sociology of the Religion of Liberated Israel 1250–1050 B.C.E.* Maryknoll, N.Y.: Orbis.

———. 1985. *The Hebrew Bible: A Socio-Literary Introduction.* Philadelphia: Fortress.

———. 1989. "The Exodus as Event and Process: A Test Case in the Biblical Grounding of Liberation Theology." Pp. 250–60 in *The Future of Liberation Theology: Essays in Honor of Gustavo Gutierrez.* Ed. Marc H. Ellis and Otto Maduro. Maryknoll, N.Y.: Orbis.

———. 1992. "Social Class and Ideology in Isaiah 40–55: An Eagletonian Reading." *Semeia* 59:43–57.

Gottwald, Norman K., ed. 1983. *The Bible and Liberation: Political and Social Hermeneutics.* Maryknoll, N.Y.: Orbis.

Gould, Ezra A. 1896. *A Critical and Exegetical Commentary on the Gospel According to St. Mark.* International Critical Commentary. Edinburgh: T. & T. Clark.

Gouldner, Alvin. 1976. *The Dialectic of Ideology and Technology: The Origins, Grammar and Future of Ideology.* London: Macmillan.

Graff, Gerald. 1979. *Literature against Itself: Literary Ideas in Modern Society.* Chicago: University of Chicago Press.

Graham, Joseph F. 1985. *Difference in Translation.* Ithaca: Cornell University Press.

Graham, Susan Lochrie. 1991. "Silent Voices: Women in the Gospel of Mark." *Semeia* 54:145–58.

Grant, Jacquelyn. 1989. *White Women's Christ and Black Women's Jesus: Feminist Christology and Womanist Response.* Atlanta: Scholars.

Grant, Judith. 1987. "I Feel Therefore I Am: Experience as a Category for Feminist Epistemology." *Women and Politics* 7:99–114.

Grassi, Ernesto. 1980. *Rhetoric as Philosophy: The Humanist Tradition.* University Park: Pennsylvania State University Press.

Greene, Gayle, and Coppélia Kahn, eds. 1985. *Making a Difference: Feminist Literary Criticism.* New York: Methuen. Rpt. New York: Routledge, 1987.

Greenstein, Edward L. 1989. "Deconstruction and Biblical Narrative." *Prooftexts* 9:43–71.

Greimas, A. J. 1983a. *Structural Semantics: An Attempt at a Method.* Trans. Daniele McDowell, Ronald Schleifer, and Alan Velie. Lincoln: University of Nebraska Press.

———. 1983b. "La Traduction de la bible. Un Problème sémiotique (III)." *Sémiotique et bible* 29:1–12.

———. 1987. *On Meaning: Selected Writings in Semiotic Theory.* Trans. Paul J. Perron and Frank H. Collins. Theory and History of Literature 38. Minneapolis: University of Minnesota Press.

———. 1988. *Maupassant: The Semiotics of Text: Practical Exercises.* Trans. Paul J. Perron. Semiotic Crossroads Series 1. Philadelphia: John Benjamins.

———. 1990. *On Meaning: Selected Writings in Semiotic Theory.* Trans. Paul J. Perron and Frank H. Collins. Theory and History of Literature 38. Minneapolis: University of Minnesota Press.

Greimas, A. J., and J. Courtés. 1982. *Semiotics and Language: An Analytic Dictionary*. Trans. Larry Crist et al. Bloomington: Indiana University Press.

Griffin, David Ray, and Huston Smith. 1989. *Primordial Truth and Postmodern Theology*. SUNY Series in Constructive Postmodern Thought. Albany: SUNY Press.

Grimm, Gunter. 1977. *Rezeptionsgeschichte Grundlegung einer Theorie*. Munich: Wilhelm Fink.

Gripp, Helga. 1984. *Jürgen Habermas: Und es gibt sie doch—Zur kommunikationstheoretischen Begründung von Vernunft bei Jürgen Habermas*. Paderborn: Schöningh.

Groden, Michael and Martin Kreiswirth, eds. 1990. *The Johns Hopkins Guide to Literary Theory and Criticism*. Baltimore: Johns Hopkins University Press.

Groeben, Norbert. 1977. *Rezeptionsforschung als empirische Literaturwissenschaft: Paradigma durch Methodendiskussion an Untersuchungsbeispielen*. Kronberg: Athenaum.

Grosz, Elizabeth. 1989. *Sexual Subversions: Three French Feminists*. Sydney: Allen & Unwin.

———. 1990. *Jacques Lacan: A Feminist Introduction*. New York: Routledge.

Group μ. 1981. *A General Rhetoric*. Trans. J. B. Burrell and E. M. Slotkin. Baltimore: Johns Hopkins University Press.

Groupe d'Entrevernes. 1978. *Signs and Parables: Semiotics and Gospel Texts*. Trans. Gary A. Phillips. Pittsburgh Theological Monograph Series 23. Pittsburgh: Pickwick.

———. 1979. *Analyse sémiotique des textes: Introduction-Théorie-Pratique*. Lyons: Press Universitaire du Lyons.

Guelich, Robert A. 1989. *Word Biblical Commentary*. Vol. 34A, *Mark 1–8:26*. Dallas, Tex.: Word.

Gumpel, Liselotte. 1985. *Metaphor Reexamined: A Non-Aristotelian Perspective*. Bloomington: Indiana University Press.

Gunn, David M., and Danna Nolan Fewell. 1993. *Narrative in the Hebrew Bible*. New York: Oxford University Press.

Gunn, Giles. 1987. *The Culture of Criticism and the Criticism of Culture*. New York: Oxford University Press.

Gutierrez, Gustavo. 1973. *A Theology of Liberation: History, Politics and Salvation*. Trans. Caridad Inda and John Eagleson. Maryknoll, N.Y.: Orbis.

———. 1983. *The Power of the Poor in History*. Trans. Robert R. Barr. Maryknoll, N.Y.: Orbis.

Güttgemanns, Erhardt. 1976. "Generative Poetics." Trans. William G. Doty. *Semeia* 6.

Guy-Sheftall, Beverly. 1986. "Remembering Sojourner Truth: On Black Feminism." *Catalyst*: 54–57.

Habermas, Jürgen. 1976. *Legitimation Crisis*. Trans. Thomas McCarthy. London: Heinemann.

———. 1981. "Modernity versus Postmodernity." *New German Critique* 22:3–18.

———. 1983. "Modernity—An Incomplete Project." Trans. Seyla Benhabib. Pp. 3–15 in *The Anti-Aesthetic: Essays on Postmodern Culture*. Ed. Hal Foster. Port Townsend, Wash.: Bay.

———. 1985. "Questions and Counterquestions." Pp. 192–216 in *Habermas and Modernity*. Ed. Richard Bernstein. Cambridge: MIT Press.

———. 1987. *The Theory of Communicative Action*. Vol. 2, *Moral Consciousness and Communicative Action*. Boston: Beacon.

Hackett, Jo Ann. 1985. "In the Days of Jael: Reclaiming the History of Women in Ancient

Israel." Pp. 15–38 in *Immaculate and Powerful: The Female in Sacred Image and Social Reality*. Ed. Clarissa W. Atkinson, Constance H. Buchanan, and Margaret Miles. Boston: Beacon.

Hagner, D. A. 1991. "The New Testament, History, and the Historical-Critical Method." Pp. 73–100 in *New Testament Criticism and Interpretation*. Ed. David A. Black and David S. Dockery. Grand Rapids, Mich.: Zondervan.

Hallam, Paul. 1993. *The Book of Sodom*. New York: Verso.

Hamburger, Käte. 1973. *The Logic of Literature*. Trans. Marilynn J. Rose. Bloomington: Indiana University Press.

Handelman, Susan A. 1982. *The Slayers of Moses: The Emergence of Rabbinic Interpretation in Modern Literary Theory*. Albany: SUNY Press.

———. 1985. "Fragments of the Rock: Contemporary Literary Theory and the Study of Rabbinic Texts—A Response to David Stern." *Prooftexts* 5:75–95.

Handy, Bruce. 1989. "A Guide to Postmodern Everything." *Utne Reader* 34:53–69.

Harari, Josué V., trans. and ed. 1979. *Textual Strategies*. Ithaca: Cornell University Press.

Haraway, Donna J. 1991. *Simians, Cyborgs, and Women: The Reinvention of Nature*. New York: Routledge.

Hardegree, Joseph L., Jr. 1983. "Bible Study for Marxist Christians: The Book of Hosea." Pp. 94–107 in *The Bible and Liberation: Political and Social Hermeneutics*. Ed. Norman Gottwald. Maryknoll, N.Y.: Orbis.

Harland, Richard. 1987. *Superstructuralism: The Philosophy of Structuralism and Post-Structuralism*. New York: Methuen.

Harlow, Barbara. 1987. *Resistance Literature*. New York: Methuen.

Harris, William V. *Ancient Literacy*. Cambridge: Harvard University Press.

Harrison, Bernard. 1991. *Inconvenient Fictions: Literature and the Limits of Theory*. New Haven: Yale University Press.

Hart, Kevin. 1989. *The Trespass of the Sign: Deconstruction, Theology and Philosophy*. Cambridge: Cambridge University Press.

Hart, Ray. 1990 (1968). *Unfinished Man and the Imagination: Toward an Ontology and a Rhetoric of Revelation*. Atlanta: Scholars.

Hartsock, Nancy. 1990. "Foucault on Power: A Theory for Women?" Pp. 157–75 in *Feminism/Postmodernism*. Ed. Linda J. Nicholson. New York: Routledge.

Harvey, David. *The Condition of Postmodernity: An Enquiry into the Origins of Cultural Change*. Oxford: Blackwell.

Harvey, Irene. 1987. "The Wellsprings of Deconstruction." Pp. 127–48 in *Tracing Literary Theory*. Ed. Joseph Natoli. Chicago: University of Illinois Press.

Hassan, Ihab. 1971. *The Dismemberment of Orpheus: Toward a Postmodern Literature*. New York: Oxford University Press.

———. 1980. "The Question of Postmodernism." Pp. 117–26 in *Romanticism, Modernism, Postmodernism*. Ed. Harry R. Garvin. Lewisburg, Pa.: Bucknell University Press.

———. 1986. "Pluralism in Postmodern Perspective." *Critical Inquiry* 12:503–20.

———. 1987. *The Postmodern Turn: Essays in Postmodern Theory and Culture*. Columbus: Ohio State University Press.

Hauser, Gerard A. 1986. *Introduction to Rhetorical Theory.* Speech Communication Series. New York: Harper and Row.

Hawkes, Terence. 1977. *Structuralism & Semiotics.* New Accents. London: Methuen.

Heil, John Paul. 1987. *Paul's Letter to the Romans: A Reader-Response Commentary.* New York: Paulist.

———. 1990. "Mark 14:1–52: Narrative Structure and Reader-Response." *Biblica* 71:305–32.

———. 1991. *The Death and Resurrection of Jesus: A Narrative-Critical Reading of Matthew 26–28.* Minneapolis: Augsburg/Fortress.

———. 1992. *The Gospel of Mark as a Model for Action: A Reader-Response Commentary.* New York: Paulist.

Henderson, Mae Gwendolyn. 1989. "Speaking in Tongues: Dialogics, Dialectics, and the Black Woman Writer's Literary Tradition." Pp. 16–37 in *Changing Our Own Words: Essays on Criticism, Theory, and Writing by Black Women.* Ed. Cheryl A. Wall. New Brunswick, N.J.: Rutgers University Press. Rpt. pp. 144–66 in *Feminists Theorize the Political.* Ed. Judith Butler and Joan W. Scott. New York: Routledge, 1992.

Henkel, Jacqueline. 1988. "Speech-Act Theory Revisited: Rule Notions and Reader-Oriented Criticism." *Poetics* 17:505–30.

Hernadi, Paul. 1976. "Clio's Cousins: Historiography as Translation, Fiction and Criticism." *New Literary History* 7:247–57.

Hernadi, Paul, ed. 1989. *The Rhetoric of Interpretation and the Interpretation of Rhetoric.* Durham, N.C.: Duke University Press.

Hester, James. 1991. "Placing the Blame: The Presence of Epideictic in Galatians 1 and 2." Pp. 281–307 in *Persuasive Artistry: Studies in New Testament Rhetoric in Honor of George A. Kennedy.* Ed. Duane F. Watson. Journal for the Study of the New Testament Supplement Series 50. Sheffield: JSOT.

Higginbotham, Evelyn Brooks. 1992. "African-American Women's History and the Metalanguage of Race." *Signs* 17:251–74.

Hindess, Barry, and Paul Hirst. 1977. *Mode of Production and Social Formation.* London: Macmillan.

Hirsch, David H. 1991. *The Deconstruction of Literature: Criticism after Auschwitz.* Hanover, N.H.: University Press of New England.

Hirst, Paul. 1979. *On Law and Ideology.* London: Macmillan.

Hoesterey, Ingeborg, ed. 1991. *Zeitgeist in Babel: The Postmodernist Controversy.* Bloomington: Indiana University Press.

Hoetker, James. 1982. "A Theory of Talking about Theories of Reading." *College English* 44:179–81.

Hogan, Patrick Colm. 1990a. *The Politics of Interpretation.* New York: Oxford University Press.

———. 1990b. "Structure and Ambiguity in the Symbolic Order: Some Prolegomena to the Understanding and Criticism of Lacan." Pp. 3–38 in *Criticism and Lacan: Essays and Dialogue on Language, Structure, and the Unconscious.* Ed. Patrick Colm Hogan and Lalita Pandit. Athens: University of Georgia Press.

Hohendahl, Peter Uwe. 1977. "Introduction to Reception Aesthetics." *New German Critique* 10:29–63.

Holland, Norman N. 1968. *The Dynamics of Literary Response.* New York: Norton.

——. 1973. *Poems in Persons: An Introduction to the Psychoanalysis of Literature.* New York: Norton.

——. 1975a. *5 Readers Reading.* New Haven: Yale University Press.

——. 1975b. "Unity Identity Text Self." *PMLA* 90:813–22.

——. 1976a. "The New Paradigm: Subjective or Transactive?" *New Literary History* 23:35–46.

——. 1976b. "Transactive Criticism: Re-Creation through Identity." *Criticism* 18:334–52.

——. 1977. "Stanley Fish, Stanley Fish." *Genre* 10:433–41.

——. 1980. "Why Ellen Laughed." *Critical Inquiry* 7:345–71.

——. 1982. *Laughing: A Psychology of Humor.* Ithaca: Cornell University Press.

——. 1990. *Holland's Guide to Psychoanalytic Psychology and Literature-and-Psychology.* New York: Oxford University Press.

——. 1992. *The Critical I.* New York: Columbia University Press.

Holland, Norman N., and David Bleich. 1976. "Comment and Response." *College English* 38:298–301.

Holub, Robert C. 1984. *Reception Theory: A Critical Introduction.* New York: Methuen.

——. 1992. *Crossing Borders: Reception Theory, Poststructuralism, Deconstruction.* Madison: University of Wisconsin Press.

Homan, Margaret. 1994. " 'Women of Color' Writers and Feminist Theory." *New Literary History* 25:73–94.

hooks, bell, and Cornel West. 1991. *Breaking Bread: Insurgent Black Intellectual Life.* Boston: South End.

Horner, Winifred Bryan, ed. 1990. *The Present State of Scholarship in Historical and Contemporary Rhetoric.* Foreword by Walter Ong. Rev. ed. Columbia: University of Missouri Press.

Horsley, Richard. 1987. *Jesus and the Spiral of Violence: Popular Jewish Resistance in Roman Palestine.* San Francisco: Harper.

——. 1988. *Bandits, Prophets, and Messiahs: Popular Movements at the Time of Jesus.* New Voices in Biblical Studies. San Francisco: Harper.

Horton, Susan R. 1977. "The Experience of Stanley Fish's Prose or the Critic as Self-Creating, Self-Consuming Artificer." *Genre* 10:443–53.

——. 1980. *Interpreting Interpreting: Interpreting Dickens's Dombey.* Baltimore: Johns Hopkins University Press.

——. 1981. *The Reader in the Dickens World.* Style and Response. Pittsburgh: University of Pittsburgh Press.

Howell, David B. 1990. *Matthew's Inclusive Story.* Journal for the Study of the New Testament Supplement Series 42. Sheffield: JSOT.

Hoy, David Couzens. 1982. *The Critical Circle: Literature, History, and Philosophical Hermeneutics.* Berkeley: University of California Press.

Hurcombe, Linda, ed. 1987. *Sex and God: Some Varieties of Women's Religious Experience.* New York: Routledge.

Hutaff, Peggy. 1990. "Response." *Journal of Feminist Studies in Religion* 6(2):69–74.

Hutcheon, Linda. 1988a. *A Poetics of Postmodernism: History, Theory, Fiction.* New York: Routledge.

——. 1988b. "A Postmodern Problematics." Pp. 1–10 in *Ethics/Aesthetics: Post-Modern Positions.* Ed. Robert Merrill. PostModernPositions 1. Washington, D.C.: Maisonneuve.

——. 1989. *The Politics of Postmodernism.* New York: Routledge.

Huyssen, Andreas. 1986. *After the Great Divide: Modernism, Mass Culture, Postmoderism.* Bloomington: Indiana University Press.

Hyde, Michael J., and Craig R. Smith. 1979. "Hermeneutics and Rhetoric: A Seen but Unobserved Relationship." *Quarterly Journal of Speech* 65:347–63.

Ijsseling, Samuel. 1976. *Rhetoric and Philosophy in Conflict: An Historical Survey.* Trans. Paul Dunphy. The Hague: Nijhoff.

Irele, Abiole. 1990. *The African Experience in Literature and Ideology.* Bloomington: Indiana University Press.

Irigaray, Luce. 1974. *Speculum de l'autre femme.* Paris: Editions de Minuit.

——. 1977. *Ce Sexe qui n'en est pas un.* Paris: Editions de Minuit.

——. 1981. "La croyance même." Pp. 367–93 in *Les fins de l'homme: A partir du travail de Jacques Derrida.* Ed. Philippie Lacoue-Labarthe and Jean Luc Nancy. Paris: Galilée.

——. 1985a. "Les Femmes Divines." *Critique* 41:294–308.

——. 1985b. *Speculum of the Other Woman.* Trans. Gillian C. Gill. Ithaca: Cornell University Press.

——. 1985c. *This Sex Which Is Not One.* Trans. Catherine Porter. Ithaca: Cornell University Press.

——. 1986. "Les femmes, le sacré, l'argent." *Critique* 42:372–83.

——. 1987. "Egales à qui?" *Critique* 43:420–37.

——. 1989. "Equal to Whom?" Trans. Robert L. Mazzola. *differences* 1(2):59–76.

——. 1991. *Marine Lover of Friedrich Nietzsche.* Trans. Gillian C. Gill. New York: Columbia University Press.

——. Forthcoming. *Dieu Qui? Dieu Quoi? Le Divin conçu par nous.* Paris: Grasset.

Iser, Wolfgang. 1972. "The Reading Process: A Phenomenological Approach." *New Literary History* 3:279–99.

——. 1974. *The Implied Reader. Patterns of Communication in Prose Fiction from Bunyan to Beckett.* Baltimore: Johns Hopkins University Press.

——. 1975a. "The Pattern of Negativity in Beckett's Prose." *Georgia Review* 29:706–19.

——. 1975b. "The Reality of Fiction: A Functionalist Approach to Literature." *New Literary History* 7:7–38.

——. 1978. *The Act of Reading: A Theory of Aesthetic Response.* Baltimore: Johns Hopkins University Press.

——. 1979. "The Current Situation of Literary Theory: Key Concepts and the Imaginary." *New Literary History* 11:1–20.

——. 1980a. "Interview: Wolfgang Iser." *Diacritics* 10:57–74.

——. 1980b. *Spenser's Arcadia: The Interrelation of Fiction and History.* The Center for Hermeneutical Studies in Hellenistic and Modern Culture 38. Berkeley, Calif.: Center for Hermeneutical Studies.

——. 1980c. "Texts and Readers." *Discourse Processes* 3:327–43.

———. 1981. "Talk Like Whales: A Reply to Stanley Fish." *Diacritics* 11:82–87.

———. 1983. "The Dramatization of Double Meaning in Shakespeare's 'As You Like It.'" *Theatre Journal* 35:307–32.

———. 1989. *Prospecting: From Reader Response to Literary Anthropology*. Baltimore: Johns Hopkins University Press.

———. 1990a. "The Aesthetic and the Imaginary." Pp. 201–20 in *The States of "Theory": History, Art, and Critical Discourse*. New York: Columbia University Press.

———. 1990b. "Fictionalizing: The Anthropological Dimension of Literary Fictions." *New Literary History* 21:939–55.

———. 1991. "Concluding Remarks." *New Literary History* 22:231–39.

———. 1993. *The Fictive and the Imaginary: Charting Literary Anthropology*. Baltimore: Johns Hopkins University Press.

Jabès, Edmond. 1963. *Le Livre des questions*. Paris: Gallimard.

———. 1976. *The Book of Questions*. Trans. Rosmarie Waldrop. Middletown, Conn.: Wesleyan University Press.

Jacobs, Alan. 1991. "Deconstruction." Pp. 172–98 in *Contemporary Literary Theory: A Christian Appraisal*. Ed. Clarence Walhout and Leland Ryken. Grand Rapids, Mich.: Eerdmans.

Jakobson, Roman. 1960. "Linguistics and Poetics." Pp. 350–77 in *Style in Language*. Ed. Thomas A. Sebeok. Cambridge: MIT Press.

———. 1963. *Essais de linguistique générale: les fondations du langage*. Trans. Nicolas Ruwet. Paris: Editions de Minuit.

———. 1978. *Six Lectures on Sound and Meaning*. Trans. John Mepham. Cambridge: MIT Press.

James, Stanlie M., and Abena P. A. Busia, eds. 1993. *Theorizing Black Feminisms: The Visionary Pragmatism of Black Women*. New York: Routledge.

Jameson, Fredric. 1971. *Marxism and Form: Twentieth-Century Dialectical Theories of Literature*. Princeton: Princeton University Press.

———. 1972. *The Prison-House of Language: A Critical Account of Russian Formalism*. Princeton: Princeton University Press.

———. 1981. *The Political Unconscious: Narrative as a Socially Symbolic Act*. Ithaca: Cornell University Press.

———. 1982. "Imaginary and Symbolic in Lacan: Marxism, Psychoanalytic Criticism, and the Problem of the Subject." Pp. 338–95 in *Literature and Psychoanalysis: The Question of Reading, Otherwise*. Ed. Shoshana Felman. Baltimore: Johns Hopkins University Press.

———. 1984. "The Politics of Theory: Ideological Positions in the Postmodernism Debate." *New German Critique* 53:53–65.

———. 1985. "Postmodernism and Consumer Society." Pp. 111–25 in *Postmodern Culture*. Ed. Hal Foster. London: Pluto.

———. 1987. "Foreword." Pp. vi–xxii in Greimas, *On Meaning: Selected Writings in Semiotic Theory*. Trans. Paul J. Perron and Frank H. Collins. Theory and History of Literature 38. Minneapolis: University of Minnesota Press.

———. 1988. *The Ideologies of Theory: Essays 1971–1986*. 2 vols. Theory and History of Literature 48: *Situations of Theory*; and Theory and History of Literature 49: *The Syntax of History*. Minneapolis: University of Minnesota Press.

———. 1991. *Postmodernism, or the Cultural Logic of Late Capitalism*. Durham, N.C.: Duke University Press.

Japhet, Sara. 1989. *The Ideology of the Book of Chronicles and Its Place in Biblical Thought*. Trans. Anna Barber. New York: Peter Lang.

Jardine, Alice. 1985. *Gynesis: Configurations of Women and Modernity*. Ithaca: Cornell University Press.

Jasper, David. 1987. *The New Testament and the Literary Imagination*. Atlantic Highlands, N.J.: Humanities Press International.

———. 1989. *The Study of Literature and Religion: An Introduction*. Minneapolis: Augsburg/Fortress.

———. 1990. "'In the Sermon Which I Have Just Completed, Wherever I Said Aristotle, I Meant Saint Paul.'" Pp. 133–52 in *The Bible as Rhetoric: Studies in Biblical Persuasion and Credibility*. Ed. M. Warner. New York: Routledge.

———. 1993. *Rhetoric, Power and Community: An Exercise in Reserve*. Louisville, Ky.: Westminster/John Knox.

Jauss, Hans Robert. 1970. "Literary History as a Challenge to Literary Theory." *New Literary History* 2:7–37.

———. 1975. "The Idealist Embarrassment: Observations on Marxist Aesthetics." *New Literary History* 7:191–208.

———. 1982a. *The Aesthetic Experience and Literary Hermeneutics*. Trans. Michael Shaw. Theory and History of Literature 3. Minneapolis: University of Minnesota Press.

———. 1982b. "Job's Questions and Their Distant Reply: Goethe, Nietzsche, Heidegger." *Comparative Literature* 34:193–207.

———. 1982c. *Towards an Aesthetic of Reception*. Trans. Timothy Bahti. Theory and History of Literature 2. Minneapolis: University of Minnesota Press.

———. 1989. "The Communicative Role of the Fictive." Pp. 3–50 in *Question and Answer: Forms of Dialogic Understanding*. Ed. and trans. Michael Hays. Theory and History of Literature 68. Minneapolis: University of Minnesota Press.

Jay, Martin. 1984. *Marxism and Totality: The Adventures of a Concept from Lukács to Habermas*. Berkeley: University of California Press.

Jeanrond, Werner R. 1988. *Text and Interpretation as Categories of Theological Thinking*. Trans. Thomas J. Wilson. New York: Crossroad.

Jefferson, Ann, and David Robey, eds. 1982. *Modern Literary Theory: A Comparative Introduction*. Totowa, N.J.: Barnes and Noble.

Jegher-Bucher, Vreni. 1991. *Der Galaterbrief auf dem Hintergrund antiker Epistolographie und Rhetorik: Ein anderes Paulusbild*. Abhandlungen zur Theologie des Alten und Neuen Testaments 78. Zurich: Theologischer Verlag.

Jensen, Vernon J. 1987. "Rhetoric of East Asia—A Bibliography." *Rhetoric Society Quarterly* 17:213–31.

Jobling, David. 1979. "Structuralism, Hermeneutics, and Exegesis: Three Recent Contributions to the Debate." *Union Seminary Quarterly Review* 34:135–47.

———. 1986a. *The Sense of Biblical Narrative: Structural Analyses of the Old Testament*. Vol. 1, 2d ed. Journal for the Study of the Old Testament Supplement Series 7. Sheffield: JSOT. Rpt. *The Sense of Biblical Literature: Three Structural Analyses in the Hebrew Bible*. Journal for the Study of the Old Testament Supplement Series 7. Sheffield: JSOT, 1978.

——. 1986b. *The Sense of Biblical Narrative*. Vol. 2. Sheffield: JSOT.

——. 1990. "Writing the Wrongs of the World: The Deconstruction of the Biblical Text in the Context of Liberation Theologies." *Semeia* 51:81–118.

——. 1991a. " 'Forced Labor': 1 Kings 3–10 and the Question of Literary Representation," *Semeia* 54:57–76.

——. 1991b. "Mieke Bal on Biblical Narrative." *Religious Studies Review* 17:1–9.

——. 1992. "Deconstruction and the Political Analysis of Biblical Texts: A Jamesonian Reading of Psalm 72." *Semeia* 59:95–127.

——. 1993a. "What, If Anything, Is I Samuel?" *Scandinavian Journal of the Old Testament* 7:17–31.

——. 1993b. "Transference and Tact in Biblical Studies: A Psychological Approach to Gerd Theissen's *Psychological Aspects of Pauline Theology*." *Studies in Religion/Sciences Religieuses* 22/4:451–62.

Jobling, David, Peggy L. Day, and Gerald T. Sheppard, eds. 1991. *The Bible and the Politics of Exegesis*. Cleveland: Pilgrim.

Jobling, David, and Stephen Moore, eds. 1992. "Poststructuralism as Exegesis." *Semeia* 54.

Jobling, David, and Tina Pippin, eds. 1992. "Ideological Criticism of Biblical Texts." *Semeia* 59:1–248.

Johanson, Bruce C. 1987. *To All the Brethren: A Text-Linguistic and Rhetorical Approach to I Thessalonians*. Coniectanea biblica. New Testament Series 16. Lund: Almquist & Wiksell.

Johnson, Barbara. 1980. *The Critical Difference: Essays in the Contemporary Rhetoric of Reading*. Baltimore: Johns Hopkins University Press.

——. 1981. "Translator's Introduction." Pp. vii–xxxiii in Jacques Derrida, *Dissemination*. Chicago: University of Chicago Press.

——. 1987. "Barbara Johnson." Pp. 150–75 in *Criticism in Society: Interviews with Jacques Derrida, Northrop Frye, Harold Bloom, Geoffrey Hartman, Frank Kermode, Edward Said, Barbara Johnson, Frank Lentricchia, and J. Hillis Miller*. Ed. Imre Saluskinszky. New York: Methuen.

Johnston, John. 1990. "Ideology, Representation, Schizophrenia: Toward a Theory of the Postmodern Subject." Pp. 67–95 in *After the Future: Postmodern Times and Places*. Ed. Gary Shapiro. Albany: SUNY Press.

Jones, Ann Rosalind. 1985. "Writing the Body: Toward an Understanding of *l'Ecriture feminine*." Pp. 361–77 in *The New Feminist Criticism: Essays on Women, Literature, and Theory*. Ed. Elaine Showalter. New York: Pantheon.

Jones, Ernest. 1953–57. *The Life and Work of Sigmund Freud*. 3 vols. New York: Basic Books.

Jordan, Constance. 1991. "Introduction: Cluster on Reader-Response Criticism." *PMLA* 106:1037–39.

Jordan, Mark D. 1986. "Ancient Philosophic Protreptic and the Problem of Persuasive Genres." *Rhetorica* 4:309–33.

Joseph, John E., and Talbot J. Taylor, eds. 1990. *Ideologies of Language*. New York: Routledge.

Josipovici, Gabriel. 1988. *The Book of God: A Response to the Bible*. New Haven: Yale University Press.

Joy, Morny. 1990. "Equality or Divinity: A False Dichotomy?" *Journal of Feminist Studies in Religion* 6(1):9–24.

Julian, Eileen. 1992. *African Novels and the Question of Orality*. Bloomington: Indiana University Press.

Kaiser, Otto, and W. G. Kümmel. 1981. *Exegetical Method: A Student Handbook*. Rev. ed. Trans. E. V. M. Goetschius and M. J. O'Connell. New York: Seabury.

Kamuf, Peggy, ed. 1990. *A Derrida Reader: Between the Blinds*. New York: Columbia University Press.

Kaplan, E. Ann, ed. 1991. *Postmodernism and Its Discontents: Theories, Practices*. Haymarket Series. London: Verso.

Katz, Ronald C. 1977. *The Structure of Ancient Arguments: Rhetoric and Its Near Eastern Origin*. New York: Shapolsky/Steinmatzky.

Kaufer, David. 1977. "Irony and Rhetorical Strategy." *Philosophy and Rhetoric* 10:90–110.

Kaufer, David, and Gary Waller. 1985. "To Write Is to Read Is to Write, Right?" Pp. 66–92 in *Writing and Reading Differently: Deconstruction and the Teaching of Composition and Literature*. Ed. C. Douglas Atkins and Michael Johnson. Lawrence: University of Kansas Press.

Kauffman, Linda, ed. 1989. *Gender and Theory Dialogues on Feminist Criticism*. New York: Blackwell.

Kavanaugh, James. 1990. "Ideology." Pp. 306–20 in *Critical Terms for Literary Study*. Ed. Frank Lentricchia and Thomas McLaughlin. Chicago: University of Chicago Press.

Kearney, Richard. 1988. *The Postmodern Imagination: Toward a Postmodern Culture*. Minneapolis: University of Minnesota Press.

Keegan, Terence J. 1985. *Interpreting the Bible: A Popular Introduction to Biblical Hermeneutics*. New York: Paulist.

Kelber, Werner H. 1976. "The Hour of the Son of Man and the Temptation of the Disciples (Mark 14:32–42)." Pp. 41–60 in *The Passion in Mark*. Ed. Werner H. Kelber. Philadelphia: Fortress.

——— . 1979. *Mark's Story of Jesus*. Philadelphia: Fortress.

——— . 1983. *The Oral and the Written Gospel: The Hermeneutics of Speaking and Writing in the Synoptic Tradition, Mark, Paul, and Q*. Philadelphia: Fortress.

Kelley, Donald R. 1981. *The Beginning of Ideology: Consciousness and Society in the French Reformation*. New York: Cambridge University Press.

Kennard, Jean E. 1981a. "Personally Speaking: Feminist Critics and the Community of Readers." *College English* 43:140–45.

——— . 1981b. "Convention Coverage, or How to Read Your Own Life." *New Literary History* 13:69–88.

Kennedy, George A. 1980. *Classical Rhetoric and Its Christian and Secular Tradition from Ancient to Modern Times*. Chapel Hill: University of North Carolina Press.

——— . 1984. *New Testament Interpretation through Rhetorical Criticism*. Chapel Hill: University of North Carolina Press.

——— . 1990. " 'Truth' and 'Rhetoric' in the Pauline Epistles." Pp. 195–202 in *The Bible as Rhetoric: Studies in Biblical Persuasion and Credibility*. Warwick Studies in Philosophy and Literature. Ed. Martin Warner. New York: Routledge.

——— . 1991. *On Rhetoric: A Theory of Civil Discourse*. New York: Oxford University Press.

Keohane, Nannerl, Michelle Z. Rosaldo, and Barbara C. Gelpi, eds. 1983. *Feminist Theory: A Critique of Ideology*. Chicago: University of Chicago Press.

Kermode, Frank. 1975. "The Reader's Share." *Times Literary Supplement* 117:51–52.

———. 1979. *The Genesis of Secrecy.* Cambridge: Harvard University Press.

———. 1983. "The Common Reader." *Daedalus* 112:1–11.

———. 1986. "The Plain Sense of Things." Pp. 179–94 in *Midrash and Literature.* Ed. G. Hartman and S. Budick. New Haven: Yale University Press.

Kilpatrick, George D. 1990. *The Principles and Practice of New Testament Textual Criticism: Collected Essays of G. D. Kilpatrick.* Ed. J. K. Elliott. Bibliotheca ephemeridum theologicarum lovaniensium 96. Louvain: Louvain University Press.

Kim, C. W. Maggie, Susan St. Ville, and Susan Simonaitis, eds. 1993. *Transfigurations: Theology and the French Feminists.* Minneapolis: Augsburg/Fortress.

Kincaid, James R. 1977. "Coherent Readers, Incoherent Texts." *Critical Inquiry* 3:781–802.

King, Karen L., ed. 1988. *Images of the Feminine in Gnosticism.* Studies in Antiquity and Christianity. Philadelphia: Fortress.

Kingsbury, Jack Dean. 1988a. *Matthew as Story.* 2d ed. Philadelphia: Fortress.

———. 1988b. "Reflections on 'the Reader' of Matthew's Gospel." *New Testament Studies* 34:442–60.

———. 1989. *Conflict in Mark: Jesus, Authorities, Disciples.* Minneapolis: Augsburg/Fortress.

———. 1991. *Conflict in Luke.* Minneapolis: Augsburg/Fortress.

Kinneavy, James L. 1987. *Greek Rhetorical Origins of Christian Faith: An Inquiry.* New York: Oxford University Press.

Kintgen, Eugene R. 1974. "Effective Stylistics." *Centrum* 2:43–55.

———. 1983. *The Perception of Poetry.* Bloomington: Indiana University Press.

Kinukawa, Hisako. 1994. *Women and Jesus in Mark.* The Bible and Liberation Series. Maryknoll, N.Y.: Orbis.

Kirk, J. Andrew. 1979. *Liberation Theology: An Evangelical View from the Third World.* Atlanta: John Knox.

Klauck, Hans-Josef. 1982. "Die Erzählerische Rolle der Jünger im Markusevangelium: Eine narrative Analyse." *Novum Testamentum* 24:1–26.

Klein, William, Craig Bromberg, and Robert Hubbard. 1993. *Introduction to Biblical Interpretation.* Dallas, Tex.: Word.

Koelb, Clayton. 1984. *The Incredulous Reader: Literature and the Function of Disbelief.* Ithaca: Cornell University Press.

Kolb, David. 1987. *The Critique of Pure Modernity: Hegel, Heidegger, and After.* Chicago: University of Chicago Press.

———. 1990. *Postmodern Sophistications: Philosophy, Architecture, and Tradition.* Chicago: University of Chicago Press.

Kolodny, Annette. 1980. "A Map for Rereading: Or, Gender and the Interpretation of Literary Texts." *New Literary History* 11:451–67.

Kopperschmidt, Josef. 1985. *Rhetorika. Aufsätze zur Theorie, Geschichte und Praxis der Rhetorik.* Philosophische Texte und Studien 14. Hildesheim: Olms.

Kort, Wesley A. 1988. *Story, Text, and Scripture: Literary Interests in Biblical Narrative.* University Park: Pennsylvania State University Press.

Kotzé, P. P. A. 1985. "John and Reader's Response." *Neotestamentica* 19:50–63.

Kozicki, Henry, and Robert H. Canary, eds. 1978. *The Writing of History: Literary Form and Historical Understanding.* Madison: University of Wisconsin Press.

Krentz, Edgar. 1975. *The Historical-Critical Method*. Philadelphia: Fortress.

Kristeva, Julia. 1969. *Sémeiotiké: Recherches pour une sémanalyse*. Paris: Seuil.

——. 1974. *La révolution du langage poétique*. Paris: Seuil.

——. 1975. "A propos du 'discours biblique.'" Pp. 223–27 in *La Traversée des signes*. Ed. Julia Kristeva et al. Paris: Seuil.

——. 1980a. *Desire in Language: A Semiotic Approach to Literature and Art*. Ed. Leon S. Roudiez. Trans. Thomas Gora, Alice Jardine, and Leon S. Roudiez. New York: Columbia University Press.

——. 1980b. "Oscillation between Power and Denial." Trans. Marilyn A. August. Pp. 165–67 in *New French Feminisms: An Anthology*. Ed. Elaine Marks and Isabelle de Courtivron. New York: Schocken.

——. 1980c. "Postmodernism?" Pp. 136–41 in *Romanticism, Modernism, Postmodernism*. Ed. Harry R. Garvin. Lewisburg, Pa.: Bucknell University Press.

——. 1980d. "Woman Can Never Be Defined." Trans. Marilyn A. August. Pp. 137–41 in *New French Feminisms. An Anthology*. Ed. Elaine Marks and Isabelle de Courtivron. New York: Schocken.

——. 1981a. "Interview—1974." Trans. Claire Pajaczkowska. *m/f* 5/6:164–67.

——. 1981b. "Women's Time." Trans. Alice Jardine and Harry Blake. *Signs* 7:13–35.

——. 1982a. "Lire la Bible." *Esprit* 69:143–52.

——. 1982b. *Powers of Horror: An Essay on Abjection*. Trans. Leon S. Roudiez. New York: Columbia University Press.

——. 1984. *Revolution in Poetic Language*. Trans. Margaret Waller. New York: Columbia University Press.

——. 1987. *Tales of Love*. Trans. Leon S. Roudiez. New York: Columbia University Press.

——. 1989. *Language—The Unknown: An Initiation into Linguistics*. Trans. Anne M. Menke. New York: Columbia University Press.

Kroker, Arthur, and David Cook. 1986. *The Postmodern Scene: Excremental Culture and Hyperaesthetics*. New York: St. Martin's.

Krupnik, Mark, ed. 1983. *Displacement: Derrida and After*. Bloomington: Indiana University Press.

Kugel, James L. 1981. *The Idea of Biblical Poetry*. New Haven: Yale University Press.

Kümmel, Werner Georg. 1972. *The New Testament: The History of the Investigation of Its Problems*. Trans. S. MacLean Gilmour and Howard C. Kee. Nashville: Abingdon.

Kunneman, Harry and Hent de Vries, eds. *Enlightenments: Encounters Between Critical Theory and Contemporary French Thought*. Kampen, Neth.: Kok Pharos.

Kurz, William S. 1989. "The Beloved Disciple and Implied Readers." *Biblical Theological Bulletin* 19:100–107.

Kustas, George L. 1985. *Before Discourse*. Ed. Daniel F. Melia and Nancy M. Bradbury. Protocol of the 50th Colloquy. Berkeley, Calif.: Center for Hermeneutical Studies.

Kwok Pui Lan. 1989. "Discovering the Bible in the Non-Biblical World." *Semeia* 47:25–42.

Labov, William. 1972. *Language in the Inner City: Studies in the Black English Vernacular*. Philadelphia: University of Pennsylvania Press.

Lacan, Jacques. 1957–58. "Les formations de l'inconscient." *Bulletin de Psychologie* 2:1–15.

——. 1966. *Ecrits*. Paris: Seuil.

——. 1970. "Of Structure as an Inmixing of an Otherness: Prerequisite to Any Subject Whatever." Pp. 186–200 in *The Structuralist Controversy: The Languages of Criticism and the Sciences of Man.* Ed. Richard Macksey and Eugenio Donato. Baltimore: Johns Hopkins University Press.

———. 1972. "Seminar on 'The Purloined Letter.'" Trans. Jeffrey Mehlman. *Yale French Studies* 40:38–72.

———. 1975. *Le Séminaire, livre XX: Encore.* Ed. Jacques-Alain Miller. Paris: Seuil.

———. 1977a. *Ecrits: A Selection.* Trans. Alan Sheridan. New York: Norton.

———. 1977b. *The Four Fundamental Concepts of Psycho-Analysis.* Ed. Jacques-Alain Miller. Trans. Alan Sheridan. New York: Norton.

———. 1977c. "Preface." Pp. vii–xv in Anika Lemaire, *Jacques Lacan.* Trans. David Macey. New York: Routledge.

———. 1981. *Le Séminaire, livre III: Les Psychoses.* Ed. Jacques-Alain Miller. Paris: Seuil.

———. 1982a. "Desire and the Interpretation of Desire in *Hamlet.*" Ed. Jacques-Alain Miller. Trans. James Hulbert. Pp. 11–52 in *Literature and Psychoanalysis. The Question of Reading, Otherwise.* Ed. Shoshana Felman. Baltimore: Johns Hopkins University Press.

———. 1982b. *Feminine Sexuality: Jacques Lacan and the école freudienne.* Ed. Juliet Mitchell and Jacqueline Rose. Trans. Jacqueline Rose. New York: Norton.

———. 1986. *Le Séminaire, livre VII: L'Ethique de la psychanalyse.* Ed. Jacques-Alain Miller. Paris: Seuil.

———. 1988a. *The Seminar of Jacques Lacan. Book I: Freud's Papers on Technique 1953– 1954.* Ed. Jacques-Alain Miller. Trans. John Forrester. New York: Norton.

———. 1988b. *The Seminar of Jacques Lacan. Book II: The Ego in Freud's Theory and in the Technique of Psychoanalysis 1954–1955.* Ed. Jacques-Alain Miller. Trans. Sylvana Tomaselli. New York: Norton.

———. 1990a. "Introduction to the Names-of-the-Father Seminar." Ed. Jacques-Alain Miller. Pp. 81–95 in Jacques Lacan, *Television/A Challenge to the Psychoanalytic Establishment.* Ed. Joan Copjec. Trans. Denis Hollier et al. New York: Norton.

———. 1990b. "Television." Ed. Jacques-Alain Miller. Pp. 1–46 in *Television/A Challenge to the Psychoanalytic Establishment.* Ed. Joan Copjec. Trans. Denis Hollier et al. New York: Norton.

LaCapra, Dominick. 1983. *Rethinking Intellectual History: Texts, Contexts, Language.* Ithaca: Cornell University Press.

———. 1985. *History & Criticism.* Ithaca: Cornell University Press.

———. 1989a. "Culture and Ideology: From Geertz to Marx." Pp. 125–42 in *The Rhetoric of Interpretation and the Interpretation of Rhetoric.* Ed. Paul Hernadi. Durham, N.C.: Duke University Press.

———. 1989b. *Soundings in Critical Theory.* Ithaca: Cornell University Press.

Lachmann, Renate. 1978. "Rhetorik und Kulturmodell." Pp. 279–98 in *Slavistische Studien. Zum VIII. Internationalen Slavistenkongress in Zagreb 1978.* Cologne: Böhlau. Rpt. pp. 264–88 in *Rhetorik.* Vol. 1, *Rhetorik als Texttheorie.* Ed. J. Kopperschmidt. Darmstadt: Wissenschaftliche Buchgesellschaft, 1990.

Laclau, Ernesto. 1977. *Politics and Ideology in Marxist Theory: Capitalism, Fascism, Populism and Ideology in Marxist Theory.* London: New Left Books.

Lakoff, Robin Tolmach. 1990. *Talking Power: The Politics of Language.* New York: Basic Books.

Lambrecht, Jan. 1989. "Rhetorical Criticism and the New Testament." *Bijdragen* 2:39–53.

Landow, George P. 1992. *Hypertext: The Convergence of Contemporary Critical Theory and Technology*. Baltimore: Johns Hopkins University Press.

Landry, Donna, and Gerald MacLean. 1993. *Materialist Feminism*. Cambridge, Mass.: Blackwell.

Lane, Michael, ed. 1970. *Introduction to Structuralism*. New York: Basic Books.

Lanham, Richard A. 1968. *A Handlist of Rhetorical Terms: A Guide for Students of English Literature*. Berkeley: University of California Press.

———. 1993. *The Electronic Word: Democracy, Technology, and the Arts*. Chicago: University of Chicago Press.

Laplanche, Jean, and J.-B. Pontalis. 1973. *The Language of Psychoanalysis*. Trans. Donald Nicholson-Smith. London: Karnac Books and the Institute of Psycho-Analysis.

Larrain, Jorge. 1979. *The Concept of Ideology*. London: Hutchinson.

———. 1983. *Marxism and Ideology*. London: Macmillan.

Lasky, Melvin J. 1976. *Utopia and Revolution: On the Origins of Metaphor; or, Some Illustrations of the Problem of Political Temperament and Intellectual Climate and How Ideas, and Ideologies, Have Been Historically Related*. Chicago: University of Chicago Press.

Lategan, Bernard C., and Willem S. Vorster. 1985. *Text and Reality: Aspects of Reference in Biblical Texts*. Semeia Studies. Philadelphia: Fortress.

Lausberg, Heinrich. 1973. *Handbuch der Literarischen Rhetorik: Eine Grundlegung der Literaturwissenschaft*. 2d ed. Munich: Hueber.

Leach, Edmund. 1969. *Genesis as Myth and Other Essays*. London: Jonathan Cape.

Leach, Edmund, and D. Alan Aycock. 1983. *Structuralist Interpretations of Biblical Myth*. Cambridge: Cambridge University Press.

Leatt, J., T. Kneifel, and K. Nurnberger, eds. 1986. *Concerning Ideologies in South Africa*. Cape Town: David Philip.

Lechte, John. 1990. *Julia Kristeva*. New York: Routledge.

Ledbetter, Mark. 1989. *Virtuous Intentions: The Religious Dimension of Narrative*. Atlanta: Scholars.

Leff, Michael C., and Margret O. Procario. 1985. "Rhetorical Theory in Speech Communication." Pp. 3–27 in *Speech Communication in the 20th Century*. Ed. T. W. Benson. Carbondale: Southern Illinois University Press.

Leitch, Vincent B. 1983. *Deconstructive Criticism: An Advanced Introduction*. New York: Columbia University Press.

———. 1988. *American Literary Criticism from the Thirties to the Eighties*. New York: Columbia University Press.

Leith, Mary Joan Winn. 1989. "Verse and Reverse: The Transformation of the Woman, Israel, in Hosea 1–3." Pp. 95–108 in *Gender and Difference in Ancient Israel*. Ed. Peggy L. Day. Minneapolis: Augsburg/Fortress.

Lemaire, Anika. 1977. *Jacques Lacan*. Trans. David Macey. New York: Routledge.

Lentricchia, Frank. 1983. *Criticism and Social Change*. Chicago: University of Chicago Press.

Lerner, Gerda. 1986. *The Creation of Patriarchy*. New York: Oxford University Press.

Levenson, Jon D. 1985. "Is There a Counterpart in the Hebrew Bible to New Testament Anti-semitism?" *Journal of Ecumenical Studies* 22:242–60.

———. 1987a. "The Hebrew Bible, the Old Testament, and Historical Criticism." Pp. 19–59 in *The Future of Biblical Studies: The Hebrew Scriptures*. Ed. Richard Elliott Friedman and H. G. M. Williamson. Atlanta: Scholars.

———. 1987b. "Why Jews Are Not Interested in Biblical Theology." Pp. 281–307 in *Judaic Perspectives on Ancient Israel*. Ed. Jacob Neusner, Baruch A. Levine, and Ernest S. Frerichs. Philadelphia: Fortress.

Levinas, Emmanuel. 1969. *Totality and Infinity: An Essay on Exteriority*. Trans. Alphonso Lingis. Duquesne Studies Philosophical Series 24. Pittsburgh: Duquesnes University Press.

———. 1976. "Sécularisation et faim." Pp. 101–9 in *Hérmeneutique de la sécularisation*. Ed. E. Castelli. Paris: Aubier-Montaigne.

———. 1990a. *Difficult Freedom: Essays on Judaism*. Trans. Seán Hand. Baltimore: Johns Hopkins University Press.

———. 1990b. *Nine Talmudic Readings*. Trans. Annette Aronomicz. Bloomington: Indiana University Press.

———. 1994. "The Strings and the Wood: On the Jewish Reading of the Bible." Pp. 126–34 in *Outside the Subject*. Trans. Michael B. Smith. Meridian Crossing Aesthetics. Stanford: Stanford University Press.

Lévi-Strauss, Claude. 1963a. "Réponses à quelques questions." *Esprit* 31:628–53.

———. 1963b. "The Structural Study of Myth." Pp. 206–31 in *Structural Anthropology*. New York: Basic Books. (Orig. 1955.)

———. 1969. *The Elementary Structures of Kinship*. Rev. ed. Trans. James Harle Bell et al. Boston: Beacon.

———. 1970. *The Raw and the Cooked*. Trans. John and Doreen Weightman. New York: Harper and Row.

———. 1973. *From Honey to Ashes*. Trans. John and Doreen Weightman. New York: Harper and Row.

———. 1975. *Tristes tropiques*. Trans. John and Doreen Weightman. New York: Athenaeum.

———. 1977. *Structural Anthropology*. Vol. 2. Trans. Monique Layton. London: Allen Lane.

———. 1978. *The Origin of Table Manners*. Trans. John and Doreen Weightman. New York: Harper and Row.

———. 1981. *The Naked Man*. Trans. John and Doreen Weightman. New York: Harper and Row.

Lichtheim, George. 1967. *The Concept of Ideology and Other Essays*. New York: Random House.

Linguistica Biblica. 1970–. Bonn: Linguistica Biblica.

Link, Hannelore. 1976. *Rezeptionsforschung: Eine Einführung in Methoden und Probleme*. Stuttgart: Kohlhammer.

Lionnet, Françoise. 1989. *Autobiographical Voices: Race, Gender, Self-Portraiture*. Ithaca: Cornell University Press.

Lodge, David. 1981. *Working with Structuralism: Essays and Reviews on Nineteenth-and Twentieth-Century Literature*. London: Routledge.

Long, Burke. 1991. "The 'New' Biblical Poetics of Alter and Sternberg." *Journal for the Study of the Old Testament* 51:71–84.

Loreau, Max. 1965. "Rhetoric as the Logic of the Behavioral Sciences." *Quarterly Journal of Speech* 51:455–63.

Lorraine, Tamsin E. 1991. *Gender, Identity and the Production of Meaning*. Boulder: Westview.

Loubser, J. A. 1987. *The Apartheid Bible: A Critical Review of Racial Theology in South Africa*. Cape Town: Maskew Miller Longman.

Louw, P. J. 1982. *Semantics of New Testament Greek*. Philadelphia: Fortress.

Lundbom, Jack. 1975. *Jeremiah: A Study in Ancient Hebrew Rhetoric*. Society of Biblical Literature Dissertation Series 18. Missoula, Mont.: Scholars.

Lundeen, Lyman T. 1972. *Risk and Rhetoric in Religion: Whitehead's Theory of Language and the Discourse of Faith*. Philadelphia: Fortress.

Lyotard, Jean-François. 1984. *The Postmodern Condition*. Trans. Geoff Bennington and Brian Massumi. Theory and History of Literature 10. Minneapolis: University of Minnesota Press.

———. 1989a. "Defining the Postmodern." Pp. 7–10 in *Postmodernism: ICA Documents*. Ed. Lisa Appignanesi. London: Free Association Books.

———. 1989b. "An Interview." *Theory, Culture and Society*. 5:277–309.

Lyotard, Jean-François, and Jean-Loup Thébaud. 1985. *Just Gaming*. Trans. Wlad Godzich. Theory and History of Literature 20. Minneapolis: University of Minnesota Press.

Mabee, Charles. 1991. *Reading Sacred Texts through American Eyes: Biblical Interpretation as Cultural Critique*. Studies in American Biblical Hermeneutics 7. Macon, Ga.: Mercer University Press.

McCaffery, Larry, ed. 1986. *Postmodern Fiction: A Bio-Bibliography*. London: Greenwood.

MacCannell, Juliet Flower. 1986. *Figuring Lacan: Criticism and the Cultural Unconscious*. Lincoln: University of Nebraska Press.

McCarney, Joe. 1980. *The Real World of Ideology*. Brighton: Harvester.

McCarthy, Paul. 1990. "The Reductionary Complex and the World of Signifiers." *Theory, Culture and Society* 7:119–29.

McClellan, David. 1986. *Ideology*. Concepts in Social Thought. Minneapolis: University of Minnesota Press.

McCormick, Kathleen. 1985. "Psychological Realism: A New Epistemology for Reader-Response Criticism." *Reader* 14:40–53.

McCracken, Ellen. 1991. "Metaplagiarism and the Critic's Role as Detective: Ricardo Piglia's Reinvention of Roberto Arlt." *PMLA* 106:1071–82.

McFague, Sallie. 1982. *Metaphorical Theology*. Philadelphia: Fortress.

McGann, Diarmuid. 1985. *The Journeying Self: The Gospel of Mark through a Jungian Perspective*. New York: Paulist.

———. 1988. *Journeying within Transcendence: A Jungian Perspective on the Gospel of John*. New York: Paulist.

McGowan, John. 1991. *Postmodernism and Its Critics*. Ithaca: Cornell University Press.

McGuire, Michael. 1979. "The Ethics of Rhetoric: The Morality of Knowledge." *Southern Speech Communication Journal* 45:133–48.

McGuire, William, ed. 1974. *The Freud/Jung Letters: The Correspondence between Sigmund Freud and C. G. Jung*. Trans. Ralph Manheim and R. F. C. Hull. Princeton: Princeton University Press.

Macherey, Pierre. 1985. *A Theory of Literary Production*. Trans. Geoffrey Wall. New York: Routledge.

Machor, James L., ed. 1993. *Readers in History: Nineteenth-Century American Literature and the Contexts of Response*. Baltimore: Johns Hopkins University Press.

Mack, Burton L. 1987. "Anecdotes and Arguments: The Chreia in Antiquity and Early Christianity." *Occasional Papers of the Institute for Antiquity and Christianity* 10:15–41.

———. 1989. *Rhetoric and the New Testament*. Guides to Biblical Scholarship. Minneapolis: Augsburg/Fortress.

Mack, Burton L., and Vernon K. Robbins. 1988. *Patterns of Persuasion in the Gospels*. Sonoma, Calif.: Polebridge.

McKee, John B. 1974. *Literary Irony and the Literary Audience: Studies in the Victimization of the Reader in Augustan Fiction*. Amsterdam: Rodopi.

McKenna, Andrew. 1992. *Violence and Difference: Girard, Derrida, and Deconstruction*. Urbana: University of Illinois Press.

McKenzie, Steven L., and Stephen R. Haynes, eds. 1993. *To Each Its Own Meaning: An Introduction to Biblical Criticisms and Their Applications*. Louisville, Ky.: Westminster/John Knox.

McKeon, Richard. 1987. *Rhetoric: Essays in Invention and Discovery*. Ed. and Intro. Mary Backman. Woodbridge, Conn.: Ox Bow.

McKnight, Edgar V. 1985. *The Bible and the Reader: An Introduction to Literary Criticism*. Philadelphia: Fortress.

———. 1988. *Postmodern Use of the Bible: The Emergence of Reader-Oriented Criticism*. Nashville: Abingdon.

McKnight, Edgar V., ed. 1989. "Reader Perspectives on the New Testament." *Semeia* 48.

McKnight, Scot. 1988. *Interpreting the Synoptic Gospels*. Grand Rapids, Mich.: Baker.

Macky, Peter W. 1990. *The Centrality of Metaphors to Biblical Thought*. Studies in the Bible and Early Christianity 19. Lewiston, N.Y.: Edwin Mellen.

McLaughlin, Megan. 1991. "Gender Paradox and the Otherness of God." *Gender & History* 3:147–59.

Maclean, Ian. 1986. "Reading and Interpretation." Pp. 122–44 in *Modern Literary Theory: A Comparative Introduction*. Ed. Ann Jefferson and David Robey. 2d ed. Totowa, N.J.: Barnes and Noble.

Madison, G. B. 1988. *The Hermeneutics of Postmodernity: Figures and Themes*. Studies in Phenomenology and Existential Philosophy. Bloomington: Indiana University Press.

Magass, Walter. 1985. "Hermeneutik, Rhetorik und Semiotik. Studien zur Rezeptionsgeschichte der Bibel." Ph.D. diss., University of Constance.

Mai, Hans-Peter. 1991. "Bypassing Intertextuality: Hermeneutics, Textual Practice, Hypertext." Pp. 30–59 in *Intertextuality*. Ed. Henrich Plett. Untersuchungen zu Texttheorie 15. Berlin: Walter de Gruyter.

Maier, Gerhard. 1977. *The End of the Historical-Critical Method*. St. Louis: Concordia Publishing House.

Mailloux, Steven. 1976. "Evaluation and Reader-Response Criticism: Values Implicit in Affective Stylistics." *Style* 10:329–43.

———. 1977. "Reader-Response Criticism?" *Genre* 10:413–31.

———. 1979. "Learning to Read: Interpretation and Reader-Response Criticism." *Studies in the Literary Imagination* 12:93–108.

———. 1982. *Interpretive Conventions: The Reader in the Study of American Fiction*. Ithaca: Cornell University Press.

——— . 1985. "Rhetorical Hermeneutics." *Critical Inquiry* 11:620–41.

——— . 1989. *Rhetorical Power.* Ithaca: Cornell University Press.

——— . 1990. "The Turns of Reader-Response Criticism." Pp. 38–54 in *Conversations: Contemporary Critical Theory and the Teaching of Literature.* Ed. Charles Moran and Elizabeth F. Penfield. Urbana, Ill.: National Council of Teachers of English.

Mainberger, Gonsalv K. 1982. "Der Leib der Rhetorik." *Linguistica Biblica* 51:71–86.

——— . 1987. *Rhetorica, I: Reden mit Vernunft. Aristoteles, Cicero, Augustinus.* Problemata 116. Stuttgart-Bad Canstatt: Frommann-Holzboog.

——— . 1988. *Rhetorica, II: Spieglungen des Geistes. Sprachfiguren bei Vico und Lévi-Strauss.* Problemata 117. Stuttgart-Bad Canstatt: Frommann-Holzboog.

——— . 1990. "Jacques Derridas Rhetorik. Ein mimetischer Versuch." *Rhetorik* 9:23–37.

Makarushka, Irena. 1990. "Nietzsche's Critique of Modernity: The Emergence of Hermeneutical Consciousness." *Semeia* 51:193–214.

Malbon, Elizabeth Struthers. 1986a. "Disciples/Crowds/Whoever: Markan Characters and Readers." *Novum Testamentum* 28:104–30.

——— . 1986b. *Narrative Space and Mythic Meaning in Mark.* San Francisco: Harper.

——— . 1992. "Narrative Criticism: How Does the Story Mean?" Pp. 23–49 in *Mark and Method: New Approaches in Biblical Studies.* Ed. Janice Capel Anderson and Stephen D. Moore. Minneapolis: Augsburg/Fortress.

Malina, Bruce J. 1991. "Interpretation Reading, Abduction, Metaphor." Pp. 267–74 in *The Bible and The Politics of Exegesis: Essays in Honor of Norman K. Gottwald on his Sixty-fifth Birthday.* Ed. David Jobling, Peggy L. Day, and Gerald T. Shepard. Cleveland: Pilgrim.

Mander, Jerry. 1991. *In the Absence of the Sacred: The Failure of Technology and the Survival of the Indian Nations.* San Francisco: Sierra Club.

Mannheim, Karl. 1936. *Ideology and Utopia.* Trans. Louis Wirth and Edward Shils. New York: Harcourt Brace Jovanovich.

Margolis, Joseph. 1989. *The Persistence of Reality: Texts without Referents. Reconciling Science and Narrative.* New York: Blackwell.

Marin, Louis. 1980. *The Semiotics of the Passion Narrative: Topics and Figures.* Pittsburgh Theological Monograph Series 25. Pittsburgh: Pickwick.

Marks, Elaine, and Isabelle de Courtivron. 1980. "Why This Book?" Pp. ix–xiii in *New French Feminisms: An Anthology.* Ed. Elaine Marks and Isabelle de Courtivron. New York: Schocken.

Marselaa, Anthony J., Michael D. Murray, and Charles Golden. 1976. "Ethnic Variations in the Phenomenology of Emotions." Pp. 134–44 in *Intercultural Communication: A Reader.* Ed. Larry A. Samovar and Richard E. Porter. Belmont, Calif.: Wadsworth.

Marshall, Donald G. 1983. "Reading as Understanding: Hermeneutics and Reader-Response Criticism." *Christianity and Literature* 33:37–48.

Martin, Clarice J. 1989. "A Chamberlain's Journey and the Challenge of Interpretation for Liberation." *Semeia* 47:105–35.

——— . 1990. "Womanist Interpretations of the New Testament: The Quest for Holistic and Inclusive Translation and Interpretation." *Journal of Feminist Studies in Religion* 6(2): 41–61.

——— . 1991. "The *Haustafeln* (Household Codes) in African American Biblical Interpretation: 'Free Slaves' and 'Subordinate Women.'" Pp. 206–31 in *Stony the Road We Trod: African American Biblical Interpretation.* Ed. Cain Hope Felder. Minneapolis: Augsburg/ Fortress.

Martin, Dale B. 1990. *Slavery as Salvation: The Metaphor of Slavery in Pauline Christianity.* New Haven: Yale University Press.

Martin, Josef. 1974. *Antike Rhetorik: Technik und Methode.* Handbuch der Altertumswissenschaft 2, 3. Munich: Beck.

Martin, P. J., and J. H. Petzer, eds. 1991. *Text and Interpretation: New Approaches in the Criticism of the New Testament.* New Testament Tools and Studies 15. Leiden: E. J. Brill.

Marx, Karl, and Friedrich Engels. 1970. *The German Ideology.* New York: International Publications.

Massey, Marilyn C. 1983. *Christ Unmasked: The Meaning of* THE LIFE OF JESUS *in German Politics.* Chapel Hill: University of North Carolina Press.

Mbiti, John S. 1986. *Bible and Theology in African Christianity.* Paddock Lectures. Nairobi: Oxford University Press.

Medhurst, Martin J. 1991. "Rhetorical Dimensions in Biblical Criticism: Beyond Style and Genre." *Quarterly Journal of Speech* 72:214–26.

Medina, Angel. 1979. *Reflection, Time and the Novel: Toward a Communicative Theory of Literature.* London: Routledge.

Medvedev, P. N., and M. M. Bakhtin. 1978. *The Formal Method in Literary Scholarship: A Critical Introduction to Sociological Poetics.* Trans. Albert J. Wehrle. Baltimore: Johns Hopkins University Press.

Meerhoff, Kees. 1986. *Rhétorique et poétique au XVIe siècle en France. Du Bellay, Ramus, et les autres.* Studies in Medieval and Reformation Thought 36. Leiden: E. J. Brill.

Meese, Elizabeth A. 1986. *Crossing the Double-Cross: The Practice of Feminist Criticism.* Chapel Hill: University of North Carolina Press.

———. 1990. *(Ex)tensions: Re-Figuring Feminist Criticism.* Urbana: University of Illinois Press.

Megill, Allan. 1987. *Prophets of Extremity: Nietzsche, Heidegger, Foucault, Derrida.* Berkeley: University of California Press.

Mellencamp, Patricia. 1987. "Images of Language and Indiscrete Dialogue: 'The Man who Envied Women.'" *Screen* 28:87–102.

Meltzer, Françoise. 1988. "Eat Your *Dasein:* Lacan's Self-Consuming Puns." Pp. 156–63 in *On Puns: The Foundation of Letters.* Ed. Jonathan Culler. Oxford: Blackwell.

Meng, Heinrich, and Ernst L. Freud, eds. 1974. *Psycho-Analysis and Faith: The Letters of Sigmund Freud and Oskar Pfister.* Trans. Eric Mosbacher. London: Hogarth.

Merod, Jim. 1987. *The Political Responsibility of the Critic.* Ithaca: Cornell University Press.

Merrill, Robert, ed. 1988. *Ethics/Aesthetics: Post-Modern Positions.* PostModernPositions 1. Washington, D.C.: Maisonneuve.

Messmer, Michael. 1985. "Making Sense of/with Postmodernism." *Soundings* 68:404–26.

Meyer, Michel and Wolfgang Iser. 1987. "On 'Meaning and Reading': An Exchange." *Review of International Philosophy* 41:414–19.

Meyers, Carol. 1988. *Discovering Eve: Ancient Israelite Women in Context.* New York: Oxford University Press.

Miller, Jacques-Alain. 1990. "Microscopia: An Introduction to the Reading of *Television.*" Pp. xi–xxxi in *Television/A Challenge to the Psychoanalytic Establishment.* Ed. Joan Copjec. Trans. Denis Hollier et al. New York: Norton.

Miller, J. Hillis. 1987a. *The Ethics of Reading: Kant, de Man, Eliot, Trollope, James and Benjamin.* New York: Columbia University Press.

———. 1987b. "Presidential Address, 1986: 'The Triumph of Theory, the Resistance to Reading, and the Question of the Material Base.'" *PMLA* 102:281–91.

———. 1989. "Is There an Ethics of Reading?" Pp. 79–101 in *Reading Narrative: Form, Ethics, Ideology.* Ed. J. Phelan. Columbus: Ohio State University Press.

———. 1990. *Versions of Pygmalion.* Cambridge: Harvard University Press.

———. 1991. "Recent Trends in Different Disciplines: Literary Theory, Telecommunications, and the Making of History." Pp. 11–20 in *Scholarship and Technology in the Humanities.* Ed. May Katzen. London: Bowker/Saur.

Miller, Nancy K., ed. 1986. *The Poetics of Gender.* New York: Columbia University Press.

Miller, Patrick D., Jr. 1976. "Faith and Ideology in the Old Testament." Pp. 464–79 in *Magnalia Dei: The Mighty Acts of God: Essays on the Bible and Archeology in Memory of G. Ernest Wright.* Ed. Frank Moore Cross, Werner E. Lemke, and Patrick D. Miller, Jr. Garden City, N.Y.: Doubleday.

Mintz, Alan. 1984. "On the Tel Aviv School of Poetics." *Prooftexts* 4:215–35.

Miscall, Peter D. 1986. *1 Samuel: A Literary Reading.* Indiana Studies in Biblical Literature. Bloomington: Indiana University Press.

Mitchell, Juliet. 1974. *Psychoanalysis and Feminism.* New York: Vintage.

———. 1982. "Introduction—I." Pp. 1–26 in *Feminine Sexuality: Jacques Lacan and the école freudienne.* Ed. Juliet Mitchell and Jacqueline Rose. Trans. Jacqueline Rose. New York: Norton.

Mitchell, Margaret M. 1992. *Paul and the Rhetoric of Reconciliation: An Exegetical Investigation of the Language and Composition of 1 Corinthians.* Hermeneutische Untersuchungen zur Theologie 27. Tübingen: J. C. B. Mohr.

Mitchell, W. J. T., ed. 1983. *The Politics of Interpretation.* Chicago: University of Chicago Press.

———. 1986. *Iconology: Image, Text, Ideology.* Chicago: University of Chicago Press.

Mohanty, Chandra Talpade. 1988. "Feminist Encounters: Locating the Politics of Experience." *Copyright* 1:30–44.

———. 1989. "Us and Them: On the Philosophical Bases of Political Criticism." *Yale Journal of Criticism* 2:1–31.

———. 1991. "Cartographies of Struggle: Third World Women and the Politics of Feminism." Pp. 1–47 in *Third World Women and the Politics of Feminism.* Ed. Chandra Talpade Mohanty, Ann Russo, and Lourdes Torres. Bloomington: Indiana University Press.

Moi, Toril. 1985. *Sexual/Textual Politics: Feminist Literary Theory.* London: Methuen.

Moltmann, Jürgen. 1990. *The Crucified God: The Cross of Christ as the Foundation and Criticism of Christian Theology.* San Francisco: Harper.

Moon, Cyris H. S. 1985. *A Korean Minjung Theology: An Old Testament Perspective.* Maryknoll, N.Y.: Orbis.

Moore, Stephen D. 1986a. "Narrative Homiletics: Lucan Rhetoric and the Making of the Reader." Ph.D. diss., Trinity College, University of Dublin.

———. 1986b. "Negative Hermeneutics, Insubstantial Texts: Stanley Fish and the Biblical Interpreter." *Journal of the American Academy of Religion* 54:707–19.

———. 1988. "Stories of Reading: Doing Gospel Criticism as/with a Reader." Pp. 141–59 in *Society of Biblical Literature 1988 Seminar Papers.* Ed. David J. Lull. Atlanta: Scholars.

———. 1989a. "Doing Gospel Criticism as/with a Reader." *Biblical Theology Bulletin* 19:85–93.

———. 1989b. *Literary Criticism and the Gospels: The Theoretical Challenge.* New Haven: Yale University Press.

———. 1989c. "The 'Post-' Age Stamp: Does It Stick?" *JAAR* 57:543–59.

———. 1992. *Mark and Luke in Poststructuralist Perspectives: Jesus Begins to Write.* New Haven: Yale University Press.

———. 1994. *Poststructuralism and the New Testament: Derrida and Foucault at the Foot of the Cross.* Minneapolis: Augsburg/Fortress.

Moran, Charles, and Elizabeth F. Penfield, eds. 1990. *Conversations: Contemporary Critical Theory and the Teaching of Literature.* Urbana, Ill.: National Council of Teachers of English.

Morey, Ann-Janine. 1991. "Feminist Perspectives on Arts, Literature, and Religion." *Critical Review of Books in Religion* 4:45–61.

Morgan, Robert, with John Barton. 1989. *Biblical Interpretation.* New York: Oxford University Press.

Morris, Charles W. 1964. *Signification and Significance: A Study of the Relations of Signs and Values.* Cambridge: MIT Press.

———. 1971. "Foundation of the Theory of Signs." Pp. 28–54 in *Writings on the General Theory of Signs.* The Hague: Mouton.

Morris, Meaghan. 1988. *The Pirate's Fiancée: Feminism, Reading, Postmodernism.* New York: Verso.

Mosala, Itumeleng J. 1986. *The Unquestionable Right To Be Free: Black Theology from South Africa.* Maryknoll, N.Y.: Orbis.

———. 1989. *Biblical Hermeneutics and Black Theology in South Africa.* Grand Rapids, Mich.: Eerdmans.

———. 1991. "Bible and Liberation in South Africa in the 1980s: Toward an Antipopulist Reading of the Bible." Pp. 267–74 in *The Bible and The Politics of Exegesis.* Ed. David Jobling et al. Cleveland: Pilgrim.

———. 1992. *Biblical Hermeneutics and Black Theology in South Africa.* Grand Rapids, Mich.: Eerdmans.

Mosala, Itumeleng J., and Buti Tlhagale, eds. 1987. *Hammering Swords into Ploughshares: Essays in Honour of Archbishop Desmond Tutu.* Grand Rapids, Mich.: Eerdmans.

Mosdt, Glen W. 1984. "Rhetorik und Hermeneutik: Zur Konstitution der Neuzeitlichkeit." *Antike und Abendland* 30:62–79.

Mottu, Henri. 1983. "Jeremiah vs. Hananiah: Ideology and Truth in Old Testament Prophecy." Pp. 235–51 in *The Bible and Liberation: Political and Social Hermeneutics.* Ed. Norman Gottwald. Maryknoll, N.Y.: Orbis.

Moxnes, Halvor, ed. 1989. "Feminist Reconstruction of Early Christian History." *Studia Theologica* 43:1–163.

Muilenberg, James. 1969. "Form Criticism and Beyond." *Journal of Biblical Literature* 88:1–18.

Muller, John P., and William J. Richardson. 1982. *Lacan and Language: A Reader's Guide to Ecrits.* New York: International Universities Press.

Mulvey, Laura. 1976–1985. "Visual Pleasure and Narrative Cinema." Pp. 303–15 in *Movies and Methods, Volume II: An Anthology.* Ed. Bill Nichols. Berkeley: University of California Press.

Murfin, Ross C. 1989. "What Is Reader-Response Criticism?" Pp. 139–47 in *Heart of Darkness: A Case Study in Contemporary Criticism/ Joseph Conrad.* Ed. Ross C. Murfin. New York: St. Martin's.

Murphy, James J., ed. 1983. *A Synoptic History of Classical Rhetoric.* Davis, Calif.: Pergamon.

Myers, Ched. 1988. *Binding the Strong Man: A Political Reading of Mark's Story of Jesus.* Maryknoll, N.Y.: Orbis.

Neirynck, Frans. 1988. *Duality in Mark: Contributions to the Study of the Markan Redaction.* Rev. ed. Bibliotheca ephemeridum theologicarum lovaniensum 31. Louvain: Louvain University Press.

Nelso, John S., Allan Megill, and Donald N. McCloskey, eds. 1987. *The Rhetoric of the Human Sciences: Language and Argument in Scholastic and Public Affairs.* Madison: University of Wisconsin Press.

Nelson, Cary, and Lawrence Grossberg, eds. 1988. *Marxism and the Interpretation of Culture.* Urbana: University of Illinois Press.

Nelson, William. 1976–77. "From 'Listen, Lordings' to 'Dear Reader.'" *University of Toronto Quarterly* 46:110–24.

Neuschäfer, Bernard. 1987. *Origines als Philologe.* Schweizerische Beiträge zur Altertumswissenschaft 18. Basel: Reinhardt.

Neusner, Jacob. 1987a. *Understanding Seeking Faith: Essays on the Case of Judaism.* Vol. 2, *Literature, Religion and the Social Study of Judaism.* Atlanta: Scholars.

———. 1987b. *What Is Midrash?* Philadelphia: Fortress.

Newman, Charles. 1985. *The Post-Modern Aura: The Act of Fiction in an Age of Inflation.* Evanston, Ill.: Northwestern University Press.

Newton, Judith, and Deborah Rosenfelt, eds. 1985. *Feminist Criticism and Social Change: Sex, Class and Race in Literature and Culture.* New York: Methuen.

Nicholas, Marie H. 1963. *Rhetoric and Criticism.* Baton Rouge: Louisiana State University Press.

Nicholson, Linda, ed. 1990. *Feminism/Postmodernism.* New York: Routledge.

Nida, Eugene A. 1975. *Componential Analysis of Meaning: An Introduction to Semantic Structures.* The Hague: Mouton.

Nida, Eugene A., John P. Louw, Andries H. Snyman, and J. v. H. Cronje. 1983. *Style and Discourse with Special Reference to the Text of the Greek New Testament.* Cape Town: Bible Society.

Niranjana, Tejaswini. 1992. *Siting Translation: History, Post-Structuralism, and the Colonial Context.* Berkeley: University of California Press.

Nixon, Rob. 1991. "Mandela, Messianism, and the Media." *Transition* 51:42–55.

Noakes, Susan. 1988. *Timely Reading: Between Exegesis and Interpretation*. Ithaca: Cornell University Press.

Norden, Eduard. 1956. *Agnostos Theos: Untersuchungen zur Formgeschichte religiöser Rede*. Darmstadt: Wissenschaftliche Buchgesellschaft. (Orig. 1913.)

——. 1971. *Die antike Kunstprosa vom vi. Jahrhundert v.Chr. bis in die Zeit der Renaissance*. 2 vols. Darmstadt: Wissenschaftliche Buchgesellschaft. (Orig. 1918.)

Nordquist, Joan. 1987. *Jacques Lacan: A Bibliography*. Santa Cruz: Reference and Research Services.

Norris, Christopher. 1982. *Deconstruction: Theory and Practice*. New Accents. New York: Methuen.

——. 1983. *The Deconstructive Turn: Essays in the Rhetoric of Philosophy*. New York: Methuen.

——. 1985. *The Contest of Faculties: Philosophy and Theory after Deconstruction*. New York: Methuen.

——. 1988. *Paul De Man: Deconstruction and the Critique of Aesthetic Ideology*. New York: Routledge.

——. 1990. *What's Wrong with Postmodernism: Critical Theory and the Ends of Philosophy*. Baltimore: Johns Hopkins University Press.

——. 1991. *Spinoza & the Origins of Modern Critical Theory*. The Bucknell Lectures in Literary Theory. Oxford: Blackwell.

——. 1992. *Uncritical Theory: Postmodernism, Intellectuals, and the Gulf War*. Amherst, Mass.: University of Massachusetts Press.

O'Day, Gail. 1986. "Narrative Mode and Theological Claim: A Study in the Fourth Gospel." *Journal of Biblical Literature*. 105:657–68.

Ogunyemi, Chikwenye Okonjo. 1985. "Womanism: The Dynamics of the Contemporary Black Female Novel in English." *Signs* 11:63–80.

O'Hara, Daniel T. 1985. *The Romance of Interpretation: Visionary Criticism from Pater to de Man*. New York: Columbia University Press.

Okpewho, Isidore. 1992. *African Oral Literature: Backgrounds, Character, and Continuity*. Bloomington: Indiana University Press.

Olbricht, Thomas H., and Stanley E. Porter, eds. 1993. *Rhetoric and the New Testament: Essays from the 1992 Heidelberg Conference*. Journal of the Study of the New Testament Supplement Series 90. Sheffield: JSOT.

O'Leary, Joseph S. 1985. *Questioning Back: The Overcoming of Metaphysics in Christian Tradition*. Minneapolis: Winston.

Oliver, Kelly. 1993. *Reading Kristeva: Unraveling the Double-Bind*. Bloomington: Indiana University Press.

Olson, Alan. 1990. "Postmodernity and Faith" *Journal of the American Academy of Religion* 58:37–53.

O'Neill, John. 1982. *For Marx against Althusser, and Other Essays*. Current Continental Research 201. Washington, D.C.: Center for Advanced Research in Phenomenology and University Press of America.

Ong, Walter J. 1967. *The Presence of the Word*. New Haven: Yale University Press.

————. 1971. *Rhetoric, Romance, and Technology: Studies in the Interaction of Expression and Culture.* Ithaca: Cornell University Press.

————. 1975. "The Writer's Audience is Always a Fiction." *PMLA* 90:9–21.

————. 1977. "Beyond Objectivity: The Reader-Writer Transaction as an Altered State of Consciousness." *CEA Critic* 40:6–13.

————. 1982. *Orality and Literacy: The Technologizing of the Word.* London: Methuen.

Ortigues, Edmond. 1962. *Le discours et le symbole.* Paris: Aubier.

Owens, Craig. 1985. "The Discourse of Others: Feminists and Postmodernism." Pp. 57–82 in *The Anti-Aesthetic: Essays on Postmodern Culture.* Ed. Hal Foster. Port Townsend, Wash.: Bay.

Palinkas, Lawrence A. 1989. *Rhetoric and Religious Experience: The Discourse of Immigrant Chinese Churches.* Fairfax, Va.: George Mason University Press.

Palmer, Richard E. 1983. "Postmodern Hermeneutics and the Act of Reading." *Religion and Literature* 15:55–84.

Panier, Louis. 1973. *Ecriture, Foi, Révélation.* Lyon: Profac.

————. 1984. *Récits et commentaires de la Tentation de Jésus au désert.* Thèses. Paris: Cerf.

————. 1991. *La naissance du fils de Dieu: Sémiotique et théologie discursive. Lecture de Luc 1–2.* Cogitatio Fidei 164. Paris: Cerf.

Pardes, Ilana. 1992. *Countertraditions in the Bible: A Feminist Approach.* Cambridge: Harvard University Press.

Pathak, Zakia. 1992. "A Pedagogy for Postcolonial Feminists." Pp. 426–41 in *Feminists Theorize the Political.* Ed. Judith Butler and Joan W. Scott. New York: Routledge.

Patrick, Dale, and Allen Scult. 1990. *Rhetoric and Biblical Interpretation.* Bible and Literature Series 26. Sheffield: Almond.

Patte, Daniel, ed. 1976a. *Semiology and Parables: An Exploration of the Possibilities Offered by Structuralism for Exegesis.* Pittsburgh Theological Monograph Series 9. Pittsburgh: Pickwick.

————. 1976b. *What Is Structural Exegesis?* Philadelphia: Fortress.

————. 1983. *Paul's Faith and the Power of the Gospel: A Structural Introduction to the Pauline Letters.* Philadelphia: Fortress.

————. 1987. *The Gospel According to Matthew: A Structural Commentary on Matthew's Faith.* Philadelphia: Fortress.

————. 1990a. *The Religious Dimensions of Biblical Texts: Greimas's Structural Semiotics and Biblical Exegesis.* Semeia Studies 19. Atlanta: Scholars.

————. 1990b. Review of Bal, 1988b. Paper presented to the Structuralism and Exegesis section of the annual meeting of The Society of Biblical Literature/American Academy of Religion, Anaheim, Calif., November 18–21.

————. 1990c. *Structural Exegesis for New Testament Critics.* Minneapolis: Fortress.

Patte, Daniel, and Aline Patte. 1978. *Structural Exegesis: From Theory to Practice.* Philadelphia: Fortress.

Patte, Daniel, and Gary Phillips. 1991. "A Fundamental Condition for Ethical Accountability in the Teaching of the Bible by White Male Exegetes: Recovering and Claiming the Specificity of Our Perspective." *Scriptura: Issues in Contextual Hermeneutics.* 9:7–28.

Pavel, Thomas G. 1990. "Narrative Tectonics." *Poetics Today* 11:349–64.

Pêcheux, Michel. 1982. *Language, Semantics, and Ideology.* New York: St. Martin's.

Pecora, Vincent P. 1991. "Ethics, Politics, and the Middle Voice." *Yale French Studies* 79:203–30.

Pedrick, Victoria, and Nancy S. Rabinowitz, eds. 1986. "Audience-Oriented Criticism and the Classics." *Arethusa* 19.

Pefanis, Julian. 1991. *Heterology and the Postmodern: Bataille, Baudrillard, and Lyotard.* Post-Contemporary Interventions. Durham, N.C.: Duke University Press.

Peirce, Charles S. 1931–58. *Collected Papers.* Ed. Charles Hartshorne and Paul Weiss. 8 vols. Cambridge: Harvard University Press.

Perelman, Chaim. 1974. "Rhetoric in Philosophy: The New Rhetoric." Pp. 808–10 in *The New Encyclopedia Britannica.* Vol. 26. Chicago: Encyclopedia Britannica.

———. 1979. *The New Rhetoric and the Humanities: Essays on Rhetoric and Its Application.* Synthese Library 140. Dordrecht: Reidel.

———. 1982. *The Realm of Rhetoric.* Trans. William Kluback. Intro. by Carroll C. Arnold. Notre Dame, Ind.: University of Notre Dame Press.

———. 1984. "Rhetoric and Politics." *Philosophy and Rhetoric* 17:129–34.

———. 1986. "Old and New Rhetoric." Pp. 1–9 in *Practical Reasoning in Human Affairs: Studies in Honor of Chaim Perelman.* Ed. J. L. Golden and J. J. Pilotta. Dordrecht: Reidel.

Perelman, Chaim, and L. Olbrechts-Tyteca. 1969. *The New Rhetoric: A Treatise on Argumentation.* Trans. J. Wilkinson and P. Weaver. Notre Dame, Ind.: University of Notre Dame Press.

Perrin, Norman. 1972. "The Evangelist as Author: Reflections on Method in the Study and Interpretation of the Synoptic Gospels and Acts." *Biblical Research* 17:5–18.

Petersen, Norman R. 1978a. *Literary Criticism for New Testament Critics.* Philadelphia: Fortress.

———. 1978b. "'Point of View' in Mark's Narrative." *Semeia* 12:97–121.

———. 1980. "Literary Criticism in Biblical Studies." Pp. 25–50 in *Orientation by Disorientation: Studies in Literary Criticism and Biblical Literary Criticism Presented in Honor of William A. Beardslee.* Ed. Richard A. Spencer. Pittsburgh Theological Monograph Series 35. Pittsburgh: Pickwick.

———. 1984. "The Reader in the Gospel." *Neotestamentica* 18:38–51.

Pfister, Oskar. 1920. "Die Entwicklung des Apostels Paulus: Eine religionsgeschichtliche und psychologische Skizze." *Imago* 6:243–90.

Phelan, James, ed. 1988. *Reading Narrative: Form, Ethics, Ideology.* Columbus: Ohio State University Press.

———. 1989. *Reading People, Reading Plots: Character, Progression, and the Interpretation of Narrative.* Chicago: University of Chicago Press.

Phillips, Gary A. 1983. "'This Is a Hard Saying: Who Can be Listener to It': Creating a Reader in John 6." *Semeia* 26:32–56.

———. 1985. "History and Text: The Reader in Context in Matthew's Parables Discourse." *Semeia* 32:111–38.

———. 1986. "Text and Enunciation as Interpretant: A Peircian Contribution to Textual Semiotics." Pp. 1031–40 in *Exigences et Perspectives de la Sémiotique/Semiotics—Critical Process and New Perspectives: Récueil d'hommage pour Algirdas Julien Greimas.* Vol. 2. Ed. H. Parret and H.-G. Ruprecht. Brussels: John Benjamins.

———. 1990a. "Exegesis as Critical Practice: Reclaiming History and Text from a Postmodern Perspective." *Semeia* 51:7–49.

———. 1990b. "Rethinking the Place of Biblical Studies: Some Questions." Pp. 29–48 in *Rethinking the Place of Biblical Studies in the Academy*. Ed. Burke Long. Brunswick, Maine: Bowdoin College.

———. 1990c. "Toward a Philosophical Biblical Criticism: Cutting the Umbi(b)lical Cord: A Review of Stephen Moore's *Literary Criticism and the Gospels: The Theoretical Challenge*." Paper presented to the Literary Aspects of the Gospels and Acts Group, at the annual meeting of the Society of Biblical Literature/American Academy of Religion, New Orleans, November 17–20.

———. 1991a. Review of Daniel Patte's *The Religious Dimensions of Biblical Texts: Greimas' Structural Semiotics and Biblical Exegesis* and Stephen D. Moore's *Literary Criticism and the Gospels: The Theoretical Challenge*. *Union Seminary Quarterly Review* 44:341–51.

———. 1991b. "Sign/Text/Différance: The Contribution of Intertextual Theory to Biblical Criticism." Pp. 78–101 in *Intertextuality*. Ed. Henrich Plett. Untersuchungen zu Texttheorie 15. Berlin: Walter de Gruyter.

———. 1992. " 'What Is Written and How Do You Read?' The Gospel, Intertextuality and Doing Lukewise." Pp. 266–301 in *Society of Biblical Literature 1992 Seminar Papers*. Ed. Eugene H. Lovering. Atlanta: Scholars.

———. 1994a. "Drawing the Other: The Postmodern and Reading the Bible Imaginatively." Pp. 447–82 in *In Good Company: Essays in Honor of Robert Detweiler*. Ed. David Jasper and Mark Ledbetter. Atlanta: Scholars.

———. 1994b. "The Ethics of Reading Deconstructively, or Speaking Face-to-Face: The Samaritan Woman Meets Derrida at the Well." Pp. 283–325 in *The New Literary Criticism and The New Testament*. Ed. Elizabeth Struthers Malbon and Edgar McKnight. Sheffield: Sheffield University Press.

Phillips, Gary A., ed. 1990. "Poststructural Criticism and the Bible: Text/History/Discourse." *Semeia* 51.

Phillipson, Michael. 1989. *In Modernity's Wake: The Ameurunculus Letters*. London: Routledge.

Piaget, Jean. 1970. *Structuralism*. New York: Basic Books.

Pippin, Tina. 1992. *Death and Desire: The Rhetoric of Gender in the Apocalypse of John*. Literary Currents in Biblical Interpretation. Louisville, Ky.: Westminster.

Pixley, George V. 1987. *On Exodus: A Liberation Perspective*. Maryknoll, N.Y.: Orbis.

Pixley, George V., and Leonardo Boff. 1989. *The Bible, the Church, and the Poor*. Maryknoll, N.Y.: Orbis.

Plamenatz, John P. 1979. *Ideology*. London: Macmillan.

Plank, Karl A. 1987. *Paul and the Irony of Affliction*. Atlanta: Scholars.

Plaskow, Judith. 1990. *Standing Again at Sinai: Judaism from a Feminist Perspective*. San Francisco: Harper.

Plett, Heinrich. 1975a. *Einführung in die rhetorische Textanalyse*. 3d ed. Hamburg: Buske.

———. 1975b. *Rhetorik der Affekte: Englische Wirkungsästhetik im Zeitalter der Renaissance*. Studien zur Englischen Philologie, New Series 18. Tübingen: M. Niemeyer.

——. 1991. "Intertextualities." Pp. 3–29 in *Intertextuality*. Ed. Heinrich Plett. Untersuchungen zu Textheorie 15. Berlin: Walter de Gruyter.

Podlewski, Renate. 1982. *Rhetorik als Pragmatisches System*. Hildesheim: Olms.

Polan, Dana. 1990. "The Spectacle of Intellect in a Media Age: Cultural Representations and the David Abraham, Paul de Man, and Victor Farias Cases." Pp. 343–64 in *Intellectuals: Aesthetics, Politics, Academics*. Cultural Politics 2. Ed. Bruce Robbins. Minneapolis: University of Minnesota Press.

Poland, Lynn M. 1985. *Literary Criticism and Biblical Hermeneutics: A Critique of Formalist Approaches*. American Academy of Religion Academy Series 48. Chico, Calif.: Scholars.

Polzin, Robert. 1977. *Biblical Structuralism: Method and Subjectivity in the Study of Ancient Texts*. Semeia Supplements. Philadelphia: Fortress.

——. 1980. *Moses and the Deuteronomist: Part One: Deuteronomy, Joshua, Judges*. A Literary Study of the Deuteronomic History. New York: Seabury.

——. 1989. *Samuel and the Deuteronomist: Part Two: 1 Samuel*. A Literary Study of the Deuteronomic History. San Francisco: Harper.

POROI [The Project on Rhetoric of Inquiry]. 1988–. Iowa City: University of Iowa.

Porter, Stanley E. 1989. *Verbal Aspect in the Greek of the New Testament, with Reference to Tense and Mood*. Studies in Biblical Greek 1. New York: Lang.

——. 1990. "Why Hasn't Reader-Response Criticism Caught on in New Testament Studies?" *Journal of Literature & Theology* 4:278–92.

Poulakos, John. 1983. "Toward a Sophistic Definition of Rhetoric." *Philosophy and Rhetoric* 16:35–48.

Poulet, Georges. 1969–70. "Phenomenology of Reading." *New Literary History* 1:53–68.

Powell, Mark Allan. 1990a. *What Is Narrative Criticism?* Minneapolis: Augsburg/Fortress.

——. 1990b. "Types of Readers and Their Relevance for Biblical Hermeneutics." *Trinity Seminary Review* 12:67–76.

Pratt, Mary Louise. 1977. *Toward a Speech Act Theory of Literary Discourse*. Bloomington: Indiana University Press.

——. 1986. "Interpretive Strategies/Strategic Interpretations: On Anglo-American Reader-Response Criticism." Pp. 26–54 in *Postmodernism and Politics*. Theory and History of Literature 28. Ed. Jonathan Arac. Minneapolis: University of Minnesota Press.

——. 1987. "Linguistic Utopias." Pp. 48–66 in *The Linguistics of Writing: Arguments between Language and Literature*. Ed. Nigel Fabb et al. New York: Methuen.

Preminger, Alex, Leon Golden, O. B. Hardison, Jr., and Kevin Kerrane, eds. 1974. *Classical Literary Criticism: Translations and Interpretations*. New York: Frederick Ungar.

Prewitt, Terry J. 1990. *The Elusive Covenant: A Structural-Semiotic Reading of Genesis*. Advances in Semiotics. Bloomington: Indiana University Press.

Prickett, Stephen. 1986. *Words and the Word: Language, Poetics and Biblical Interpretation*. Cambridge: Cambridge University Press.

Prickett, Stephen, ed. 1991. *Reading the Text: Biblical Criticism and Literary Theory*. Oxford: Blackwell.

Prince, Gerald. 1971. "Notes Towards a Categorization of Fictional Narratees." *Genre* 4:100–105.

———. 1980. "Introduction to the Study of the Narratee." Pp. 7–25 in *Reader-Response Criticism: From Formalism to Post-Structuralism.* Ed. Jane P. Tompkins. Baltimore: Johns Hopkins University Press.

———. 1990. "On Narrative Studies and Narrative Genres." *Poetics Today* 11:271–82.

Propp, Vladimir. 1968. *Morphology of the Folktale.* 2d. ed. Trans. Laurence Scott. Publications of the American Folklore Society Bibliographical and Special Series 9. Austin: University of Texas Press.

Quacquarelli, Antonio. 1971. *Saggi Patristici: Retorica ed esegesi biblica.* Bari: Adriatica.

Rabinow, Paul, ed. 1984. *The Foucault Reader.* New York: Pantheon.

Rabinowitz, Isaac. 1985. "Pre-Modern Jewish Study of Rhetoric: An Introductory Bibliography." *Rhetorica* 3:137–44.

Rabinowitz, Nancy Sorkin. 1986. "Aphrodite and the Audience: Engendering the Reader." *Arethusa* 19:171–85.

Rabinowitz, Nancy, and Peter J. Rabinowitz. 1980. "The Critical Balance: Reader, Text, and Meaning." *College English* 41:924–32.

Rabinowitz, Peter J. 1977. "Truth in Fiction: A Reexamination of Audiences." *Critical Inquiry* 4:121–41.

———. 1981. "Assertion and Assumption: Fictional Patterns and the External Worlds." *PMLA* 96:408–19.

———. 1985. "The Turn of the Glass Key: Popular Fiction as Reading Strategy." *Critical Inquiry* 11:418–31.

———. 1986. "Shifting Stands, Shifting Standards: Reading, Interpretation, and Literary Judgment." *Arethusa* 19:115–34.

———. 1987. *Before Reading: Narrative Conventions and the Politics of Interpretation.* Ithaca: Cornell University Press.

———. 1989. "Whirl without End: Audience-Oriented Criticism." Pp. 81–100 in *Contemporary Literary Theory.* Ed. Douglas G. Atkins and Laura Morrow. Amherst: University of Massachusetts Press.

Radhakrishnan, R. 1983. "The Post-Modern Event and the End of Logocentrism." *Boundary 2* 13:33–60.

Radway, Janice. 1985. *Reading the Romance: Women, Patriarchy, and Popular Literature.* Chapel Hill: University of North Carolina Press.

Ragland-Sullivan, Ellie. 1986. *Jacques Lacan and the Philosophy of Psychoanalysis.* Urbana: University of Illinois Press.

Ragland-Sullivan, Ellie, and Mark Bracher, eds. 1991. *Lacan and the Subject of Language.* New York: Routledge.

Rajan, Rajeswari Sunder. 1993. *Real and Imagined Women: Gender, Culture and Postcolonialism.* New York: Routledge.

Rajan, Tilottama. 1992. "Intertextuality and the Subject of Reading/Writing." Pp. 61–74 in *Influence and Intertextuality in Literary History.* Ed. Jay Clayton and Eric Rothstein. Madison: University of Wisconsin Press.

Rajchman, John. 1987. "Postmodernism in a Nominalist Frame: The Emergence and Diffusion of a Cultural Category." *Flash Art* 137:49–51.

Ray, William. 1984. *Literary Meaning: From Phenomenology to Deconstruction*. New York: Blackwell.

Readings, Bill. 1991. *Introducing Lyotard: Art and Politics*. Critics of the Twentieth Century. London: Routledge.

Regis, Edward, Jr. 1976. "Literature by the Reader: The Affective Theory of Stanley Fish." *College English* 38:263–80.

Reid, Loren D. 1944. "The Perils of Rhetoric Criticism." *The Quarterly Journal of Speech* 30:416–22.

Reinhartz, Adele. 1989. "Great Expectations: A Reader-Oriented Approach to Johannine Christology and Eschatology." *Literature and Theology* 3:67–76.

Reiss, Timothy. 1982. *The Discourse of Modernism*. Ithaca: Cornell University Press.

Rendall, Steven F. 1982. "Fish versus Fish." *Diacritics* 12:49–57.

Resseguie, James. 1982. "Reader-Response and the Synoptic Gospels." *Journal of the American Academy of Religion* 52:307–24.

Rhoads, David. 1982. "Narrative Criticism and the Gospel of Mark." *Journal of the American Academy of Religion* 50:411–34.

Rhoads, David, and Donald Michie. 1982. *Mark as Story: An Introduction to the Narrative of a Gospel*. Philadelphia: Fortress.

Rice, Emanuel. 1990. *Freud and Moses: The Long Journey Home*. Albany: SUNY Press.

Rich, Adrienne. 1990. "Words Out of the Whirlwind: Review Essay." *Bridges: A Journal for Jewish Feminists and Our Friends* 1(2):111–20.

Richards, Ivor Armstrong. 1936. *The Philosophy of Rhetoric*. New York: Oxford University Press.

Richardson, William J. 1990. " 'Coufontaine, *adsum!*' Lacan and Theological Discourse." Pp. 60–73 in *Psychoanalysis and Religion*. Ed. Joseph H. Smith and Susan A. Handelman. Baltimore: Johns Hopkins University Press.

Richter, David H. 1989. "Reader-Response Criticism." Pp. 158–73 in *The Critical Tradition: Classic Texts and Contemporary Trends*. Ed. David H. Richter. New York: St. Martin's.

Rickman, H. P. 1981. "Rhetoric and Hermeneutic." *Philosophy and Rhetoric* 14:100–111.

Ricoeur, Paul. 1977. *The Rule of Metaphor: Multidisciplinary Studies of the Creation of Meaning in Language*. Trans. Robert Czerny et al. Toronto: University of Toronto Press.

———. 1981a. "The Hermeneutical Function of Distanciation." Pp. 131–44 in *Paul Ricoeur: Hermeneutics and the Human Sciences: Essays on Language, Action and Interpretation*. Ed. and trans. John B. Thompson. Cambridge: Cambridge University Press.

———. 1981b. *Hermeneutics and the Human Sciences: Essays on Language, Action and Interpretation*. Ed. and trans. John B. Thompson. Cambridge: Cambridge University Press.

———. 1986. *Lectures on Ideology and Utopia*. Ed. George H. Taylor. New York: Columbia University Press.

Riffaterre, Michael. 1959. "Criteria for Style Analysis." *Word* 15:154–74.

———. 1978. *The Semiotics of Poetry*. Bloomington: Indiana University Press.

———. 1979. "Sémiotique intertextuelle: l'interpretant." *Revue d'Esthétiques* 1:116–28.

Riley, Denise. 1988. *"Am I That Name?" Feminism and the Category of 'Women' in History*. Minneapolis: University of Minnesota Press.

Rimmon-Kenan, Shlomith. 1983. *Narrative Fiction: Contemporary Poetics.* New York: Methuen.

Robbins, Vernon K. 1991. "Writing as a Rhetorical Act in Plutarch and the Gospels." Pp. 142–68 in *Persuasive Artistry: Studies in New Testament Rhetoric in Honor of George A. Kennedy.* Ed. Duane F. Watson. Journal for the Study of the New Testament Supplement Series 50. Sheffield: Sheffield Academic Press.

———. 1993. "Rhetoric and Culture: Exploring Types of Cultural Rhetoric in a Text." Pp. 443–63 in *Rhetoric and the New Testament: Essays from the 1992 Heidelberg Conference.* Ed. Stanley E. Porter and Thomas H. Olbricht. Journal for the Study of the New Testament Supplement Series 90. Sheffield: Sheffield Academic Press.

Robbins, Vernon K., and John H. Patton. 1980. "Rhetorical and Biblical Criticism." *Quarterly Journal of Speech* 66:327–50.

Robert, Marthe. 1974. *From Oedipus to Moses: Freud's Jewish Identity.* Trans. Ralph Mannheim. New York: Doubleday.

Roberts, Michael. 1985. *Biblical Epic and Rhetorical Paraphrase in Late Antiquity.* Liverpool: Francis Cairns.

Rodino, Richard H. 1991. " 'Splendide Mendax': Authors, Characters, and Readers in *Gulliver's Travels.*" *PMLA* 106:1054–70.

Roemer, Marjorie Godlin. 1987. " 'Which Reader's Response?' " *College English* 49:911–21.

Rogers, Robert. 1982. "Amazing Reader in the Labyrinth of Literature." *Poetics Today* 3:31–46.

Rogers, William Elford. 1994. *Interpreting Interpretation. Textual Hermeneutics as an Ascetic Discipline.* University Park: Pennsylvania State University Press.

Rollins, Wayne G. 1983. *Jung and the Bible.* Atlanta: John Knox.

Ronen, Ruth. 1990. "Paradigm Shift in Plot Models: An Outline of the History of Narratology." *Poetics Today* 11:817–42.

Rooney, Ellen. 1986. "Who's Left Out? A Rose by Any Other Name Is Still Red; Or, The Politics of Pluralism." *Critical Inquiry* 12:550–63.

Rorty, Richard. 1984. "Deconstruction and Circumvention." *Critical Inquiry* 11:1–23.

Rose, Jacqueline. 1982. "Introduction—II." Pp. 27–57 in *Feminine Sexuality: Jacques Lacan and the école freudienne.* Ed. Juliet Mitchell and Jacqueline Rose. Trans. Jacqueline Rose. New York: Norton.

———. 1986. *Sexuality in the Field of Vision.* London: Verso.

Rosen, Stanley. 1987. *Hermeneutics as Politics.* New York: Oxford University Press.

Rosenberg, Joel. 1986. *King and Kin: Political Allegory in the Hebrew Bible.* Indiana Studies in Biblical Literature. Bloomington: Indiana University Press.

Rosenblatt, Louise. 1964. "The Poem as Event." *College English* 26:123–28.

———. 1969. "Towards a Transactional Theory of Reading." *Journal of Reading Behavior* 1:31–47.

———. 1976. *Literature as Exploration.* 3d ed. New York: Noble and Noble.

———. 1978. *The Reader, the Text, the Poem: The Transactional Theory of the Literary Work.* Carbondale: Southern Illinois University Press.

———. 1986. "The Literary Transaction." Pp. 66–85 in *The Creating Word: Papers from an*

International Conference on the Learning and Teaching of English in the 1980s. Ed. Patricia Demers. Edmonton: University of Alberta Press.

Rosenfield, L. W. 1980. "The Practical Celebration of Epideictic." Pp. 131–55 in *Rhetoric in Transition.* Ed. E. E. White. University Park: Pennsylvania State University Press.

Rosmarin, Adena. 1989. "Darkening the Reader: Reader-Response Criticism and Heart of Darkness." Pp. 148–69 in *Heart of Darkness: A Case Study in Contemporary Criticism/ Joseph Conrad.* Ed. Ross C. Murfin. New York: St. Martin's.

Ross, Andrew, ed. 1988. *Universal Abandon: The Politics of Postmodernism.* Minneapolis: University of Minneapolis Press.

Ross, James F. 1972. "On the Concept of Reading." *The Philosophical Forum* 6:93–141.

Roudinesco, Elisabeth. 1990. *Jacques Lacan & Co.: A History of Psychoanalysis in France, 1925–1985.* Trans. Jeffrey Mehlman. Chicago: University of Chicago Press.

Rubenstein, Richard. 1972. *My Brother Paul.* New York: Harper and Row.

Ruland, Vernon. 1978. "Understanding the Rhetoric of Theologians." 13:203–24.

Ruthrof, Horst. 1981. *The Reader's Construction of Narrative.* Boston: Routledge.

Ruthven, K. K. 1984. *Feminist Literary Studies: An Introduction.* Cambridge: Cambridge University Press.

Rutledge, David W. 1987. "Ludwig Wittgenstein: Don't Think, But Look!" *Furman Studies* 33:22–48.

Ryan, Michael. 1982. *Marxism and Deconstruction: A Critical Articulation.* Baltimore: Johns Hopkins University Press.

Ryken, Leland. 1991. "Afterword." Pp. 292–302 in *Contemporary Literary Theory: A Christian Appraisal.* Ed. Clarence Walhout and Leland Ryken. Grand Rapids, Mich.: Eerdmans.

Said, Edward. 1978. *Orientalism.* New York: Pantheon.

———. 1983. *The World, the Text, and the Critic.* Cambridge: Harvard University Press.

———. 1991. "The Politics of Knowledge." *Raritan* 11:17–31.

———. 1993. *Culture and Imperialism.* New York: Alfred A. Knopf.

Salvivar, Ramon. 1979. "Readings and Systems of Reading." *Studies in the Novel* 11:472–81.

Sampley, J. Paul. 1988. "Paul, His Opponents in 2 Corinthians 10–13, and the Rhetorical Handbooks." Pp. 162–77 in *The Social World of Formative Christianity and Judaism: Essays in Tribute to Howard Clark Kee.* Ed. J. Neusner, E. S. Frerichs, P. Borgen, and R. Horsley. Philadelphia: Fortress.

Sanders, Cheryl J., Katie G. Cannon, Emilie M. Townes, M. Shawn Copeland, bell hooks, and Cheryl Townsend Gilkes. 1989. "Christian Ethics and Theology in Womanist Perspective." *Journal of Feminist Studies in Religion* 5(2):83–112.

Sarup, Madan. 1989. *An Introductory Guide to Post-Structuralism and Postmodernism.* Athens: University of Georgia Press.

Saussure, Ferdinand de. 1959. *Course in General Linguistics.* Ed. Charles Bally et al. Trans. Wade Baskin. New York: McGraw-Hill.

———. 1983. *Course in General Linguistics.* Trans. Roy Harris. La Salle, Ill.: Open Court.

Sawicki, Jana. 1988. "Feminism and the Power of Foucauldian Discourse." Pp. 161–78 in *After Foucault: Humanistic Knowledge, Postmodern Challenges.* Ed. Jonathan Arac. New Brunswick, N.J.: Rutgers University Press.

Schaberg, Jane. 1990. "Response." *Journal of Feminist Studies in Religion* 6(2):74–85.

Schanze, Helmut ed. 1974. *Rhetorik: Beiträge zu ihrer Geschichte in Deutschland vom 16.–20. Jahrhundert.* Frankfurt: Fischer.

Scharfenberg, Joachim. 1988. *Sigmund Freud and His Critique of Religion.* Trans. O. C. Dean, Jr. Philadelphia: Fortress.

Schaub, Thomas. 1992. "Allusion and Intertext." Pp. 181–203 in *Influence and Intertext: Influence and Intertextuality in Literary History.* Ed. Jay Clayton and Eric Rothstein. Madison: University of Wisconsin Press.

Schlieben, Reinhard. 1974. *Christliche Theologie und Philologie in der Spätantike: Die schulwissenschaftlichen Methoden der Psalmenexegese Cassiodors.* Arbeiten zur Kirchengeschichte 46. Berlin: Walter de Gruyter, 1974.

Schmidt, Henry J. 1979. "Text-Adequate Concretizations and Real Readers: Reception Theory and Its Application." *New German Critique* 17:157–69.

———. 1981. "Reception Analysis Theory and Practice." *Papers in Comparative Studies* 1:112–25.

Schneidau, Herbert N. 1977. *Sacred Discontent: The Bible and Western Tradition.* Berkeley: University of California Press.

Schneider, John R. 1990. *Philip Melanchthon's Rhetorical Construal of Biblical Authority.* Oratio Sacra. Texts and Studies in Religion 51. Lewiston, Maine: Edwin Mellen.

Schneiderman, Stuart. 1983. *Jacques Lacan: The Death of an Intellectual Hero.* Cambridge: Harvard University Press.

Schneiders, Sandra M. 1985. "Church and Biblical Scholarship in Dialogue." *Theology Today* 42:353–58.

———. 1989a. "Does the Bible Have a Postmodern Message?" Pp. 56–73 in *Postmodern Theology: Christian Faith in a Pluralistic World.* Ed. Frederic Burnham. San Francisco: Harper.

———. 1989b. "Feminist Ideology Criticism." *Biblical Theology Bulletin* 19:3–10.

Schnider, Franz. 1977. "Das Gleichnis vom Verlorenen Schaf und seine Redaktoren: Ein Intertextueller Vergleich (Lk. 15:4–7, Mt. 18:12–14)." *Kairos* 19:146–54.

Scholder, Klaus. 1990. *The Birth of Modern Critical Theology: Origins and Problems of Biblical Criticism in the Seventeenth Century.* Philadelphia: Trinity Press International.

Scholem, Gershom. 1981. *Walter Benjamin: The Story of a Friendship.* Trans. Harry Zohn. New York: Schocken.

Scholes, Robert. 1974. *Structuralism in Literature: An Introduction.* New Haven: Yale University Press.

———. 1975. "Cognition and the Implied Reader." *Diacritics* 5:13–15.

———. 1985. *Textual Power: Literary Theory and the Teaching of English.* New Haven: Yale University Press.

———. 1989. *Protocols of Reading.* New Haven: Yale University Press.

Schor, Naomi A. 1992. "Feminist and Gender Studies." Pp. 262–87 in *Introduction to Scholarship in Modern Languages and Literatures.* 2d ed. Ed. Joseph Gibaldi. New York: Modern Language Association of America.

Schrag, C. O. 1986. *Communicative Praxis and the Space of Subjectivity.* Studies in Phenomenology and Existential Philosophy. Bloomington: Indiana University Press.

Schrift, Alan D. 1990. *Nietzsche and the Question of Interpretation: Between Hermeneutics and Deconstruction*. New York: Routledge.

Schüssler Fiorenza, Elisabeth. 1983. *In Memory of Her: A Feminist Theological Reconstruction of Christian Origins*. New York: Crossroad.

———. 1984. *Bread Not Stone: The Challenge of Feminist Biblical Interpretation*. Boston: Beacon.

———. 1985. "The Followers of the Lamb: Visionary Rhetoric and Social-Political Situation." Pp. 144–65 in *Discipleship in the New Testament*. Ed. Fernando Segovia. Philadelphia: Fortress.

———. 1986. "A Feminist Critical Interpretation for Liberation: Martha and Mary: Luke 10:38–42. *Religion and Intellectual Life* 3:21–35.

———. 1987. "Rhetorical Situation and Historical Reconstruction in 1 Corinthians." *New Testament Studies* 33:386–403.

———. 1988. "The Ethics of Biblical Interpretation: Decentering Biblical Scholarship." *Journal of Biblical Literature* 107:3–17.

———. 1989a. "Introduction." *Semeia* 47:1–8.

———. 1989b. "The Politics of Otherness: Biblical Interpretation as a Critical Praxis for Liberation." Pp. 312–25 in *The Future of Liberation Theology*. Essays in Honor of Gustavo Gutierrez. Ed. Marc H. Ellis and Otto Maduro. Maryknoll, N.Y.: Orbis.

———. 1992a. *But She Said: Feminist Practices of Biblical Interpretation*. Boston: Beacon.

———. 1992b. "Feminist Hermeneutics." Pp. 783–91 in *The Anchor Bible Dictionary*. Vol. 2. Ed. David Noel Freedman. New York: Doubleday.

Schüssler Fiorenza, Elizabeth, ed. 1993. *Searching the Scriptures: A Feminist Introduction*. New York: Crossroad.

Schwartz, Regina. 1990a. "Introduction: On Biblical Criticism." Pp. 1–15 in *The Book and the Text: The Bible and Literary Theory*. Ed. Regina Schwartz. Cambridge, Mass.: Blackwell.

———. 1990b. "Joseph's Bones and the Resurrection of the Text." Pp. 40–59 in *The Book and the Text: The Bible and Literary Theory*. Ed. Regina Schwartz. Cambridge, Mass.: Blackwell.

———. 1991. "Adultery in the House of David: The Metanarrative of Biblical Scholarship and the Narratives of the Bible." *Semeia* 54:35–55.

———. Forthcoming. "Freud's God." In *Post-Secular Theology*. Ed. Philip Blond. London: Routledge.

Schweickart, Patrocinio P. 1985. "Add Gender and Stir." *Reader* 13:1–9.

———. 1986. "Reading Ourselves: Toward a Feminist Theory of Reading." Pp. 31–62 in *Gender and Reading: Essays on Readers, Texts, and Contexts*. Ed. Elizabeth A. Flynn and Patrocinio P. Schweickart. Baltimore: Johns Hopkins University Press.

Scott, Bernard Brandon. 1983a. "How to Mismanage a Miracle: Reader-Response Criticism (Luke 12:16–20)." Pp. 439–49 in *Society of Biblical Literature 1983 Seminar Papers*. Ed. Kent Harold Richards. Chico, Calif.: Scholars.

———. 1983b. "A Master's Praise: Luke 16:1–8a." *Biblica* 64:173–88.

Scott, Charles E. 1990. *The Question of Ethics: Nietzsche, Foucault, Heidegger*. Studies in Continental Thought. Bloomington: Indiana University Press.

Scott, Joan Wallach. 1988. *Gender and the Politics of History.* New York: Columbia University Press.

———. 1992a. " 'Experience.' " Pp. 22–40 in *Feminists Theorize the Political.* Ed. Judith Butler and Joan W. Scott. New York: Routledge.

———. 1992b. "Women's History." Pp. 42–66 in *New Perspectives on Historical Writing.* Ed. Peter Burke. University Park: Pennsylvania State University Press.

Scott, Robert L. 1975. "A Synoptic View of Systems of Western Rhetoric." *The Quarterly Journal of Speech* 61:439–47.

———. 1980a. "Intentionality in the Rhetorical Process." Pp. 39–60 in *Rhetoric in Transition.* Ed. E. E. White. University Park: Pennsylvania State University Press.

———. 1980b. *Methods of Rhetorical Criticism: A Twentieth Century Perspective.* Rev. 2d ed. Detroit: Wayne State University Press.

Scult, Allen. 1983. "The Relationship between Rhetoric and Hermeneutics Reconsidered." *Central States Speech Journal* 34:221–28.

Searle, John R. 1969. *Speech Acts: An Essay in the Philosophy of Language.* Cambridge: Cambridge University Press.

Sebeok, Thomas, ed. 1977. *A Perfusion of Signs.* Bloomington: Indiana University Press.

Segal, Alan F. 1990. *Paul the Convert: The Apostolate and Apostasy of Paul the Pharisee.* New Haven: Yale University Press.

Segers, Rien T. 1975. "Readers, Text and Author: Some Implications of Rezeptionsästhetik." *Yearbook of Comparative and General Literature* 24:15–23.

———. 1978. *The Evaluation of Literary Texts: An Experimental Investigation into the Rationalization of Value Judgements with Reference to Semiotics and Esthetics of Reception.* Lisse: Peter de Ridder.

———. 1979. "An Interview with Hans Robert Jauss." *New Literary History* 11:83–95.

Segundo, Juan Luis. 1984. *Jesus of Nazareth Yesterday and Today.* Vol. 1, *Faith and Ideologies.* Trans. John Drury. Maryknoll, N.Y.: Orbis.

Selden, Raman. 1982. "The Reader and the Text." *Durham University Journal* 74:269–74.

Seliger, Martin. 1976. *Ideology and Politics.* London: George Allen & Unwin.

———. 1977. *The Marxist Conception of Ideology: A Critical Essay.* Cambridge: Cambridge University Press.

Semeia: An Experimental Journal for Biblical Criticism. 1974–. Atlanta: Scholars.

Sémiotique et bible. 1975–. Lyon: Centre pour l'Analyse du Discours Religieux.

Setel, T. Drorah. 1985. "Prophets and Pornography: Female Sexual Imagery in Hosea." Pp. 86–95 in *Feminist Interpretation of the Bible.* Ed. Letty M. Russell. Philadelphia: Westminster.

Showalter, Elaine, ed. 1985. *The New Feminist Criticism: Essays on Women, Literature, and Theory.* New York: Pantheon.

———. 1989. *Speaking of Gender.* New York: Routledge.

Shuger, Deborah K. 1988. *Sacred Rhetoric: The Christian Grand Style in the English Renaissance.* Princeton: Princeton University Press.

Siebers, Tobin. 1988. *The Ethics of Criticism.* Ithaca: Cornell University Press.

Siegert, Folker. 1991. *Drei hellenistisch-jüdische Predigten.* II. *Ps.Philon, "Über Jona," "Über Simson," und "Uber die Göttesbezeichnungen 'wohltatig verzehrendes Feuer.' "* Wissenschaftliche Untersuchungen zum Neuen Testament 61. Tübingen: J. C. B. Mohr.

Sigmund, Paul. 1984. "Christianity, Ideology, and Political Philosophy." Pp. 79–91 in *Essays on Christianity and Political Philosophy*. Ed. George W. Carey and James V. Schall. Lanham, Md.: University Press of America.

Sillars, M. O. 1976. "Persistent Problems in Rhetorical Criticism." Pp. 69–88 in *Rhetoric and Communication: Studies in the University of Illinois Tradition*. Ed. J. Blankenship and H. G. Stelzner. Urbana: University of Illinois Press.

Silverman, Hugh J. 1991. *Writing the Politics of Difference*. Albany: SUNY Press.

Silverman, Hugh, and Donn Welton, eds. 1988. *Postmodernism and Continental Philosophy*. Selected Studies in Phonomenological and Existential Philosophy 13. Albany: SUNY Press.

Simons, Herbert, ed. 1990. *The Rhetorical Turn: Invention and Persuasion in the Conduct of Inquiry*. Chicago: University of Chicago Press.

Simpson, David, ed. 1991. *Subject to History: Ideology, Class, Gender*. Ithaca: Cornell University Press.

Slatoff, Walter J. 1970. *With Respect to Readers: Dimensions of Literary Response*. Ithaca: Cornell University Press.

Slaughter, Cliff. 1980. *Marxism, Ideology and Literature*. Critical Social Studies. London: Macmillan.

Slawinski, J. 1988. "Reading and Reader in the Literary Historical Process." *New Literary History* 19:521–39.

Sloane, Thomas O. 1974. "Rhetoric in Literature." Pp. 803–8 in *The New Encyclopedia Britannica*. Vol. 26. Chicago: Encyclopedia Britannica.

Smart, Barry. 1984. *Foucault, Marxism and Critique*. London: Routledge.

——— . 1992. *Modern Conditions, Postmodern Controversies*. Routledge Social Futures Series. London: Routledge.

Smith, Barbara Herrnstein. 1978. *On the Margins of Discourse: The Relation of Literature to Language*. Chicago: University of Chicago Press.

——— . 1988. *Contingencies of Value: Alternative Perspectives for Critical Theory*. Cambridge: Harvard University Press.

Smith, Huston. 1990. "Postmodernism's Impact on the Study of Religion." *Journal of the American Academy of Religion* 58:653–70.

Smith, Paul Julian. 1990. *The Body Hispanic: Gender and Sexuality in Spanish and Spanish American Literature*. New York: Oxford University Press.

——— . 1992. *Representing the Other: "Race," Text, and Gender in Spanish and Spanish American Narrative*. New York: Oxford University Press.

Snyder, Joel. 1980. "Picturing Vision." *Critical Inquiry* 6:499–526.

Snyman, Andries H. 1988. "On Studying the Figures (schemata) in the New Testament." *Biblica* 69:93–107.

——— . 1991. "Discourse Analysis: A Semantic Discourse Analysis of the Letter to Philemon." Pp. 83–99 in *Text and Interpretation: New Approaches to the Criticism of the New Testament*. Ed. P. J. Martin and J. H. Petzer. New Testament Tools and Studies 15. Leiden: E. J. Brill.

Sobrino, Jon. 1978. *Christology at the Crossroads: A Latin American Approach*. Trans. John Drury. Maryknoll, N.Y.: Orbis.

Solomon, Robert C. 1989. *The Passions: The Myth and Nature of Human Emotions.* Notre Dame, Ind.: University of Notre Dame Press.

Soskice, Janet M. 1987. *Metaphor and Religious Language.* New York: Oxford University Press.

Spanos, William, ed. 1979. *Martin Heidegger and the Question of Literature: Toward a Postmodern Literary Hermeneutics.* Bloomington: Indiana University Press.

Spanos, William V., Paul A. Bové, and Daniel O'Hara, eds. 1982. *The Question of Textuality: Strategies of Reading in Contemporary American Criticism.* Bloomington: Indiana University Press.

Spelman, Elizabeth V. 1988. *Inessential Woman: Problems of Exclusion in Feminist Thought.* Boston: Beacon.

Spence, Donald P. 1982. *Narrative Truth and Historical Truth: Meaning and Interpretation in Psychoanalysis.* New York: Norton.

Spencer, A. B. 1991. "Literary Criticism." Pp. 227–54 in *New Testament Criticism and Interpretation.* Ed. David A. Black and David S. Dockery. Grand Rapids, Mich.: Zondervan.

Spira, Andreas. 1989. "The Impact of Christianity on Ancient Rhetoric." *Studia Patristica* 18(2):137–153.

Spivak, Gayatri Chakravorty. 1988. *In Other Worlds: Essays in Cultural Politics.* New York: Routledge.

———. 1990. "Criticism, Feminism, and the Institution." Pp. 153–72 in *Intellectuals: Aesthetics, Politics, Academics.* Cultural Politics 2. Ed. Bruce Robbins. Minneapolis: University of Minnesota Press.

Sprinker, Michael. 1987. *Imaginary Relations: Aesthetics and Ideology in the Theory of Historical Materialism.* London: Verso.

Staiger, Janet. 1989. "Reception Studies: The Death of the Reader." Pp. 353–67 in *The Cinematic Text: Methods and Approaches.* Ed. R. Barton Palmer. New York: AMS.

Staley, Jeffrey Lloyd. 1988. *The Print's First Kiss: A Rhetorical Investigation of the Implied Reader in the Fourth Gospel.* Society of Biblical Literature Dissertation Series 82. Atlanta: Scholars.

Stamps, Dennis L. 1992. "Rhetorical Criticism and Rhetoric of New Testament Criticism." *Literature and Theology* 6:268–79.

Standaert, Benoît. 1986. "La rhétorique ancienne dans saint Paul." Pp. 78–92 in *L'Apôtre Paul: Personalité Style et Conception du Ministère.* Ed. A. Vanhoye. Bibliotheca Ephemeridum Theologicarum Lovaniensum 73. Louvain: Louvain University Press.

Stanley, Susie Cunningham. 1993. *Feminist Pillar of Fire: The Life of Alma White.* Philadelphia: Pilgrim.

Stanton, Elizabeth Cady, and the Revising Committee. 1974. *The Woman's Bible.* Rpt. Seattle: Coalition Task Force on Women and Religion, 1985.

Stanzel, Franz K. 1984. *A Theory of Narrative.* Trans. Charlotte Goedsche. New York: Cambridge University Press.

Starobinski, Jean, ed. 1971. *Les Mots sous les mots: les anagrammes de Ferdinand de Saussure.* Le Chemin. Paris: Gallimard.

Steig, Michael. 1977. "The Intentional Phallus." *Journal of Aesthetics and Art Criticism* 36:51–61.

——. 1982. "Reading and Meaning." *College English* 44:182–89.

——. 1988. *Stories of Reading: Subjectivity and Literary Understanding.* Baltimore: Johns Hopkins University Press.

Stein, R. L. 1981. "Historical Fiction and the Implied Reader: Scott and Iser." *Novel* 14:213–21.

Steiner, George. 1979. " 'Critic'/'Reader.' " *New Literary History* 10:423–52.

——. 1989. *Real Presences.* Chicago: University of Chicago Press.

Steiner, Wendy. 1986. "Collage or Miracle Historicism in a Deconstructed World." Pp. 323–51 in *Reconstructing American Literary History.* Harvard English Studies 13. Ed. Sacvan Bercovitch. Cambridge: Harvard University Press.

Stern, David. 1981. "Rhetoric and Midrash: The Case of the Mashal." *Prooftexts* 1:261–91.

——. 1985a. "Literary Criticism or Literary Homilies? Susan Handelman and the Contemporary Study of Midrash." *Prooftexts* 5:96–103.

——. 1985b. " 'Response' to Boyarin's 'Rhetoric and Interpretation.' " *Prooftexts* 5:276–80.

——. 1991. *Parables in Midrash: Narrative and Exegesis in Biblical Literature.* Cambridge: Harvard University Press.

Sternberg, Meir. 1978. *Expositional Modes and Temporal Ordering in Fiction.* Baltimore: Johns Hopkins University Press.

——. 1983. "The Bible's Art of Persuasion: Ideology, Rhetoric and Poetics in Saul's Fall." *Hebrew Union College Annual* 54:45–82.

——. 1985. *The Poetics of Biblical Narrative: Ideological Literature and the Drama of Reading.* Indiana Literary Biblical Series. Bloomington: Indiana University Press.

——. 1986. "The World from the Addressee's Viewpoint: Reception as Representation, Dialogue as Monologue." *Style* 20:295–318.

——. 1990a. "Telling in Time (I): Chronology and Narrative Theory." *Poetics Today* 11:901–48.

——. 1990b. "Time and Space in Biblical (Hi)story Telling: The Grand Chronology." Pp. 81–145 in *The Book and the Text: The Bible and Literary Theory.* Ed. Regina Schwartz. Cambridge, Mass.: Blackwell.

——. 1991. "Double Cave, Double Talk: The Indirections of Biblical Dialogue." Pp. 28–57, 227–31 in *'Not in Heaven': Coherence and Complexity in Biblical Narrative.* Ed. Jason P. Rosenblatt and Joseph C. Sitterson. Bloomington: Indiana University Press.

Stoldt, Hans-Herbert. 1977. *Geschichte und Kritik der Markushypothese.* Göttingen: Vandenhoeck & Ruprecht.

Stonum, Gary Lee. 1977. "For a Cybernetics of Reading." *Modern Language Notes* 92:945–68.

Sturrock, John, ed. 1979. *Structuralism and Since: From Lévi-Strauss to Derrida.* New York: Oxford University Press.

Sugirtharajah, R. S. 1991. *Voices from the Margin: Interpreting the Bible in the Third World.* Maryknoll, N.Y.: Orbis.

Suleiman, Susan Rubin. 1976. "Ideological Dissent from Works of Fiction: Toward a Rhetoric of the *roman à thèse.*" *Neophilologus* 60:162–77.

——. 1980a. "Introduction: Varieties of Audience-Oriented Criticism." Pp. 3–45 in *The Reader in the Text: Essays on Audience and Interpretation.* Ed. Susan R. Suleiman and Inge Crosman. Princeton: Princeton University Press.

———. 1980b. "Redundancy and the 'Readable Text.'" *Poetics Today* 1:119–42.

———. 1981. "Of Readers and Narrators: The Experience of Pamela." *L'Esprit Créateur* 21:89–97.

———. 1983. *Authoritarian Fictions: The Ideological Novel as a Literary Genre.* New York: Columbia University Press.

———. 1990. *Subversive Intent: Gender, Politics, and the Avant-Garde.* Cambridge: Harvard University Press.

Suleiman, Susan R., and Inge Crosman, eds. 1980. *The Reader in the Text: Essays on Audience and Interpretation.* Princeton: Princeton University Press.

Sumner, Colin. 1979. *Reading Ideologies: An Investigation into the Marxist Theory of Ideology and Law.* London: Academic.

Surin, Kenneth. 1986. "Christology, Tragedy and Ideology." *Theology* 89:283–91.

Swann, Darius Leander. 1986/1987. "Black Aesthetics and Black Worship." *Journal of the Interdenominational Theological Center* 14:117–26.

Swearingen, C. Jan. 1991. *Rhetoric and Irony: Western Literacy and Western Lies.* New York: Oxford University Press.

Tamez, Elsa. 1982. *Bible of the Oppressed.* Maryknoll, N.Y.: Orbis.

Tannehill, Robert C. 1977. "The Disciples in Mark: The Function of a Narrative Role." *Journal of Religion* 57:386–405.

———. 1986. *The Narrative Unity of Luke-Acts: A Literary Interpretation.* Vol. 1, *The Gospel According to Luke.* Foundations and Facts. Philadelphia: Fortress.

———. 1990. *The Narrative Unity of Luke-Acts: A Literary Interpretation.* Vol. 2, *The Acts of the Apostles.* Foundations and Facts. Minneapolis: Augsburg/Fortress.

Taylor, Mark C. 1982. *Deconstructing Theology.* New York: Crossroad.

———. 1984. *Erring: A Postmodern A/theology.* Chicago: University of Chicago Press.

———. 1987. *Altarity.* Chicago: University of Chicago Press.

———. 1990a. "The Eventuality of Texts." *Semeia* 51:215–40.

———. 1990b. *Tears.* Albany: SUNY Press.

Taylor, Vincent. 1966. *The Gospel According to St. Mark.* 2d ed. New York: St. Martin's.

Theissen, Gerd. 1987. *Psychological Aspects of Pauline Theology.* Trans. John P. Galvin. Philadelphia: Fortress.

Therborn, Goran. 1980. *The Ideology of Power and the Power of Ideology.* London: New Left Books.

Thielman, Frank. 1991. "The Style of the Fourth Gospel and Ancient Literary Critical Concepts of Religious Discourse." Pp. 169–83 in *Persuasive Artistry: Studies in New Testament Rhetoric in Honor of George A. Kennedy.* Ed. Duane F. Watson. Journal for the Study of the New Testament Supplement Series 50. Sheffield: Sheffield Academic Press.

Thiselton, Anthony C. 1985. "Reader-Response Hermeneutics, Action Models, and the Parables of Jesus." Pp. 79–126 in *The Responsibility of Hermeneutics.* Ed. Roger Lundin, Anthony C. Thiselton, and Clarence Walhout. Grand Rapids, Mich.: Eerdmans.

———. 1992. *New Horizons in Hermeneutics: The Theory and Practice of Transforming Biblical Reading.* Grand Rapids, Mich.: Zondervan.

Thompson, David W., ed. 1983. *Performance of Literature in Historical Perspectives.* Lanham, Md.: University Press of America.

Thompson, John B. 1984. *Studies in the Theory of Ideology.* Berkeley: University of California Press.

———. 1990. *Ideology and Modern Culture: Critical Social Theory in the Era of Mass Communication.* Stanford: Stanford University Press.

Tilborg, Sjef van. 1986. *The Sermon on the Mount as an Ideological Intervention: A Reconstruction of Meaning.* Assen: Van Gorcum.

Tinsley, John. 1985. *Tragedy, Irony and Faith.* Bristol, Ind.: Wyndham Hall.

Todorov, Tzvetan. 1975. "Rhétorique et Herméneutique." *Poétique* 23:289–415.

———. 1982. *Theories of the Symbol.* Trans. Catherine Porter. Ithaca: Cornell University Press.

———. 1984. *Mikhail Bakhtin: The Dialogical Principle.* Trans. Wlad Godzich. Theory and History of Literature 13. Minneapolis: University of Minnesota Press.

Tolbert, Mary Ann. 1983. "Defining the Problem: The Bible and Feminist Hermeneutics." *Semeia* 28:113–26.

Tomlinson, John. 1991. *Cultural Imperialism.* Baltimore: Johns Hopkins University Press.

Tompkins, Jane P. 1978. "Review of *Subjective Criticism* by David Bleich." *Modern Language Notes* 93:1068–75.

———. 1985. *Sensational Designs: The Cultural Work of American Fiction 1790–1860.* New York: Oxford University Press.

Tompkins, Jane P., ed. 1980. *Reader-Response Criticism: From Formalism to Post-Structuralism.* Baltimore: Johns Hopkins University Press.

Tong, Rosemarie. 1989. *Feminist Thought: A Comprehensive Introduction.* Boulder: Westview.

Toolan, Michael J. 1984. "Stanley Fish and the Interpretive Communities of Responding Readers." *Dutch Quarterly Review of Anglo-American Letters* 14:62–73.

———. 1988. *Narrative: A Critical Linguistic Introduction.* London: Routledge.

Toulmin, Stephen. 1958. *The Uses of Argument.* Cambridge: Cambridge University Press.

———. 1986. "Die Verleumdung der Rhetorik." *Neue Hefte für Philosophie* 26:55–68.

Tracy, David. 1987. *Plurality and Ambiguity: Hermeneutics, Religion, Hope.* San Francisco: Harper.

Trible, Phyllis. 1978. *God and the Rhetoric of Sexuality.* Philadelphia: Fortress.

———. 1984. *Texts of Terror: Literary-Feminist Readings of Biblical Narrative.* Philadelphia: Fortress.

Trinh T. Minh-Ha. 1988. "Not You/Like You: Post-Colonial Women and the Interlocking Questions of Identity and Difference." *Inscriptions* 3:71–77.

———. 1989. *Woman Native Other: Writing Postcoloniality and Feminism.* Bloomington: Indiana University Press.

Trotsky, Leon. 1971. *Literature and Revolution.* Ann Arbor: University of Michican Press.

Trotter, David. 1984. *The Making of the Reader: Language and Subjectivity in Modern American, English, and Irish Poetry.* New York: St. Martin's.

Tuckett, Christopher. 1987. *Reading the New Testament: Methods of Interpretation.* Philadelphia: Fortress.

Tufte, Edward R. 1990. *Envisioning Information.* Cheshire, Conn.: Graphics.

Tyler, Stephen A. 1987. *The Unspeakable: Discourse, Dialogue, and Rhetoric in the Postmodern World.* Rhetoric of the Human Sciences. Madison: University of Wisconsin Press.

Ulmer, Gregory L. 1985. *Applied Grammatology: Post(e)-Pedagogy from Jacques Derrida to Joseph Beuys.* Baltimore: Johns Hopkins University Press.

————. 1989. *Teletheory: Grammatology in the Age of Video*. New York: Routledge.

Uspensky, Boris. 1973. *A Poetics of Composition: The Structure of the Artistic Text*. Trans. Valentin Zavarin and Susan Wittig. Berkeley: University of California Press.

Van Aarde, A. G. 1988. "Narrative Point of View: An Ideological Reading of Luke 12:35–48." *Neotestamentica* 22:235–55.

Vander Weele, Michael. 1991. "Reader-Response Theories." Pp. 125–48 in *Contemporary Literary Theory: A Christian Appraisal*. Ed. Clarence Walhout and Leland Ryken. Grand Rapids, Mich.: Eerdmans.

Van Eemeren, Frans H., Rob Grootendorst, and Tjark Kruiger. 1987. *Handbook of Argumentation Theory: A Critical Survey of Classical Backgrounds and Modern Studies*. Studies of Argumentation in Pragmatics and Discourse Analysis. Dordrecht: Foris.

Van Herik, Judith. 1982. *Freud on Femininity and Faith*. Berkeley: University of California Press.

van Iersel, Bas, et al. 1987. *Parabelverhalen in Lucas: Van semiotiek naar pragmatiek*. Theologische Faculteit Tilburg Studies 8. Tilburg: Tilburg University Press.

van Iersel, Bas, and Anton Weiler, eds. 1987. *Exodus: A Lasting Paradigm*. Concilium 189. Edinburgh: T. & T. Clark.

Vansina, Jan. 1965. *Oral Tradition: A Study in Historical Methodology*. Chicago: Aldine.

Van Straaten, Z., ed. 1987. *Ideological Beliefs in the Social Sciences*. Methodology. Research Report Series 5. Investigation into Research Methodology. Pretoria: Human Sciences Research Council.

Veeser, H. Aram, ed. *The New Historicism*. New York: Routledge.

Venuti, Lawrence, ed. 1992. *Rethinking Translation: Discourse, Subjectivity, Ideology*. New York: Routledge.

Via, Dan O., Jr. 1975. *Kerygma and Comedy in the New Testament: A Structuralist Approach to Hermeneutic*. Philadelphia: Fortress.

————. 1985. *The Ethics of Mark's Gospel—In the Middle of Time*. Philadelphia: Fortress.

Vickers, Brian. 1987. "Rhetoric and Poetics." Pp. 715–45 in *Cambridge History of Renaissance Philosophy*. Cambridge: Cambridge University Press.

————. 1988. *In Defense of Rhetoric*. Oxford: Clarendon.

Villmar, August F. C. 1864. *Die Theologie der Tatsachen wider die Theologie der Rhetorik*. 3d ed. Stuttgart: Liesching.

Voelz, James W. 1989. "Multiple Signs and Double Texts: Elements of Intertextuality." Pp. 2–34 in *Intertextuality in Biblical Writings: Essays in Honour of Bas van Iersel*. Ed. Sipke Draisma. Kampden, Neth.: J. H. Kok.

Vogels, Walter. 1986. *Reading and Preaching the Bible: A New Semiotic Approach*. Background Books 4. Wilmington, Del.: M. Glazier.

Voloshinov, V. N. 1973. *Marxism and the Philosophy of Language*. New York: Seminar.

Volp, Rainer, ed. 1982. *Zeichen: Semiotik in Theologie und Gottesdienst*. Munich: Kaiers.

Wakefield, Neville. 1990. *Postmodernism: The Twilight of the Real*. London: Pluto.

Walhout, Clarence, and Leland Ryken, eds. 1992. *Contemporary Literary Theory: A Christian Appraisal*. Grand Rapids, Mich.: Eerdmans.

Walker, Alice. 1983. *In Search of Our Mothers' Gardens*. New York: Harcourt, Brace, Jovanovich.

Wall, Cheryl A. 1989. *Changing Our Own Words: Essays on Criticism, Theory, and Writing by Black Women*. New Brunswick, N.J.: Rutgers University Press.

Wallace, Edwin R. 1985. *Historiography and Causation in Psychoanalysis: An Essay on Psychoanalytic and Historical Epistemology*. Hillsdale, N.J.: Analytic.

Walsh, David. 1990. *After Ideology: Recovering the Spiritual Foundations of Freedom*. New York: Harper Collins.

Walzer, Michael. 1985. *Exodus and Revolution*. New York: Basic Books.

Warhol, Robyn R., and Diane Price Herndl, eds. 1991. *Feminisms: An Anthology of Literary Theory and Criticism*. New Brunswick, N.J.: Rutgers University Press.

Warner, Martin. 1989a. *Philosophical Finesse: Studies in the Art of Rational Persuasion*. New York: Oxford University Press.

Warner, Martin, ed. 1989b. *The Bible as Rhetoric: Studies in Biblical Persuasion and Credibility*. Warwick Studies in Philosophy and Literature. New York: Routledge.

Warning, Rainer, ed. 1975. *Rezeptionsästhetik: Theorie und Praxis*. Munich: Wilhelm Fink.

Warrior, Robert. 1989. "Canaanites, Cowboys, and Indians: Deliverance, Conquest, and Liberation Theology Today." *Christianity and Crisis* 29:261–65.

Watson, Nigel. 1988. "Reception Theory and Biblical Exegesis." *Australian Biblical Review* 36:45–56.

Waxman, Chaim, ed. 1968. *The End of Ideology Debate*. New York: Simon and Schuster.

Webb, Stephen H. 1991. *Re-Figuring Theology: The Rhetoric of Karl Barth*. SUNY Series in Rhetoric and Theology. Albany: SUNY Press.

Weber, Samuel. 1987. *Institution and Interpretation*. Theory and History of Literature 31. Minneapolis: University of Minnesota Press.

Weed, Elizabeth, ed. 1989. *Coming to Terms: Feminism/Theory/Politics*. New York: Routledge.

Weedon, Chris. 1987. *Feminist Practice and Poststructuralist Theory*. Oxford: Blackwell.

Weems, Renita. 1988. *Just a Sister Away: A Womanist Vision of Women's Relationships in the Bible*. San Diego: Lura Media.

———. 1989. "Gomer: Victim of Violence or Victim of Metaphor?" *Semeia* 47:87–104.

———. 1991. "Reading *Her Way* through the Struggle: African American Women and the Bible." Pp. 57–77 in *Stony the Road We Trod: African American Biblical Interpretation*. Ed. Cain Hope Felder. Minneapolis: Augsburg/Fortress.

———. 1992. "The Hebrew Women Are Not Like the Egyptian Women: The Ideology of Race, Gender and Sexual Reproduction in Exodus 1." *Semeia* 59:29–34.

Weinfeld, Moshe. 1983. "Zion and Jerusalem as Religious and Political Capital: Ideology and Utopia." Pp. 75–115 in *The Poet and the Historian: Essays in Literary and Historical Biblical Criticism*. Ed. Richard Elliott Friedman. Harvard Semitic Studies 26. Cambridge: Harvard University Press.

Weinrich, Harald. 1971. *Literatur für Leser: Essays und Aufsätze zur Literaturwissenschaft*. Stuttgart: W. Kohlhammer.

Welch, Sharon. 1985. *Communities of Resistance and Solidarity: A Feminist Theology of Liberation*. Maryknoll, N.Y.: Orbis.

Wellek, René. 1986. *A History of Modern Criticism, 1750–1950*. Vol. 6, *American Criticism, 1900–1950*. New Haven: Yale University Press.

West, Cornel. 1982. *Prophesy Deliverance: An Afro-American Revolutionary Christianity.* Philadelphia: Westminster.

West, Gerald O. 1991. *Biblical Hermeneutics of Liberation: Modes of Reading the Bible in the South African Context.* Pietermaritzburg: Cluster Publications.

White, E. Frances. 1990. "Africa on My Mind: Gender, Counter Discourse, and African-American Nationalism." *Journal of Women's History* 2:73–97.

White, Eugene E. 1972. *Puritan Rhetoric: The Issue of Emotion in Religion.* Landmarks in Rhetoric and Public Address. Carbondale: Southern Illinois University Press.

White, Hayden. 1973. *Metahistory: The Historical Imagination in Nineteenth-Century Europe.* Baltimore: Johns Hopkins University Press.

———. 1978. *Tropics of Discourse: Essays in Cultural Criticism.* Baltimore: Johns Hopkins University Press.

———. 1979. "Michel Foucault." Pp. 81–115 in *Structuralism and Since: From Lévi-Strauss to Derrida.* Ed. John Sturrock. Oxford: Oxford University Press.

———. 1986. "Historical Pluralism." *Critical Inquiry* 12:480–93.

———. 1988. *The Content of the Form.* Baltimore: Johns Hopkins University Press.

White, Hugh. 1979. "Structural Analysis of the Old Testament Narrative." Pp. 45–66 in *Encounter with the Text: Form and History in the Hebrew Bible.* Ed. Martin J. Buss. Semeia Supplements. Philadelphia: Fortress.

———. 1991. *Narration and Discourse in the Book of Genesis.* Cambridge: Cambridge University Press.

Whitford, Margaret. 1991. *Luce Irigaray: Philosophy in the Feminine.* New York: Routledge.

Wicke, Jennifer. 1988. "Postmodernism: The Perfume of Information." *The Yale Journal of Criticism* 1:145–60.

Wilcox, Mary. 1979. *Developmental Journey: A Guide to the Development of Logical and Moral Reasoning and Social Perception.* Nashville: Abingdon.

Wilde, Alan. 1981. *Horizons of Assent: Modernism, Postmodernism, and the Ironic Imagination.* Baltimore: Johns Hopkins University Press.

Wilder, Amos N. 1956. "Scholars, Theologians, and Ancient Rhetoric." *Journal of Biblical Literature* 75:1–11.

———. 1964. *The Language of the Gospel: Early Christian Rhetoric.* New York: Harper and Row.

———. 1974. *"Semeia: An Experimental Journal for Biblical Criticism:* An Introduction." *Semeia* 1:1–16.

———. 1991. *The Bible and the Literary Critic.* Minneapolis: Augsburg/Fortress.

Willard, Charles Arthur. 1983. *Argumentation and the Social Grounds of Knowledge.* University: University of Alabama Press.

Williams, Delores S. 1986. "The Color of Feminism: Or Speaking the Black Woman's Tongue." *Journal of Religious Thought* 43:42–57.

Williams, Michael A. 1988. "Variety in Gnostic Perspectives on Gender." Pp. 2–22 in *Images of the Feminine in Gnosticism.* Ed. Karen L. King. Philadelphia: Fortress.

Williams, Raymond. 1977. *Marxism and Literature.* New York: Oxford University Press.

Willis, Wendell Lee. 1985a. "An Apostolic Apologia? The Form and Function of 1 Corinthians 9." *Journal for the Study of the New Testament* 24:33–48.

——. 1985b. *Idol Meat in Corinth: The Pauline Argument in 1 Corinthians 8 and 10*. Society of Biblical Literature Dissertation Series 68. Chico, Calif.: Scholars.

Wilson, W. Daniel. 1981. "Readers in Texts." *PMLA* 96:848–63.

Wimbush, Vincent L. 1989a. "Biblical-Historical Study as Liberation: Toward an Afro-Christian Hermeneutic." Pp. 140–54 in *African American Religious Studies: An Interdisciplinary Anthology*. Ed. Gayraud S. Wilmore. Durham, N.C.: Duke University Press.

——. 1989b. "Historical/Cultural Criticism as Liberation: A Proposal for an African American Biblical Hermeneutic." *Semeia* 47:43–55.

——. 1991. "The Bible and African Americans: An Outline of an Interpretive History." Pp. 81–97 in *Stony the Road We Trod: African American Biblical Interpretation*. Ed. Cain Hope Felder. Minneapolis: Augsburg/Fortress.

Wimmers, Inge Crosman. 1988. *Poetics of Reading: Approaches to the Novel*. Princeton: Princeton University Press.

Wimsatt, William K., Jr. 1954. *The Verbal Icon: Studies in the Meaning of Poetry*. Lexington: University of Kentucky Press.

Wink, Walter. 1973. *The Bible in Human Transformation: Toward a New Paradigm for Biblical Study*. Philadelphia: Fortress.

Wire, Antoinette Clark. 1990. *The Corinthian Women Prophets: A Reconstruction through Paul's Rhetoric*. Minneapolis: Augsburg/Fortress.

Wittgenstein, Ludwig. 1961. *Tractatus Logico-Philosophicus*. Trans. D. F. Pears and B. F. McGuinness. London: Routledge.

Woodmansee, Martha, and Peter Jaszi, eds. 1994. *The Construction of Authorship: Textual Appropriation in Law and Literature*. Durham, N.C.: Duke University Press.

Wright, Elizabeth. 1987. *Psychoanalytic Criticism: Theory and Practice*. 2d ed. New York: Methuen.

——. 1989. *Postmodern Brecht: A Re-Presentation*. Critics of the Twentieth Century 7. London: Routledge.

Wuellner, Wilhelm. 1976. "Paul's Rhetoric of Argumentation in Romans." *Catholic Biblical Quarterly* 38:330–51.

——. 1978a. "Der Jakobusbrief im Licht der Rhetorik und Textpragmatik." *Linguistica Biblica* 43:5–66.

——. 1978b. "Toposforschung und Torahinterpretation bei Paulus und Jesus." *New Testament Studies* 24:463–83.

——. 1979. "Greek Rhetoric and Pauline Argumentation." Pp. 177–88 in *Early Christian Literature and the Classical Intellectual Tradition: In Honorem Robert M. Grant*. Ed. William Schoedel and Robert L. Wilken. Théologie Historique 53. Paris: Beauchesne.

——. 1986. "Paul as Pastor: The Function of Rhetorical Questions in First Corinthians." Pp. 49–77 in *L'Apôtre Paul: Personalité, Style et Conception du Ministère*. Ed. A. Vanhoye. Bibliotheca Ephemeridum Theologicarum Lovaniensium 73. Louvain: Louvain University Press.

——. 1987. "Where Is Rhetorical Criticism Taking Us?" *Catholic Biblical Quarterly* 49: 448–63.

——. 1989a. *Hermeneutics and Rhetorics: From "Truth and Method" to "Truth and Power."* Scriptura 3. Stellenbosch: Centre for Hermeneutical Studies.

────. 1989b. "The Rhetorical Structure of Luke 12 in Its Wider Context." *Neotestamentica* 22:283–310.

────. 1989c. "Is There an Encoded Reader Fallacy?" *Semeia* 48:41–54.

────. 1990. "The Argumentative Structure of 1 Thessalonians as Paradoxical Encomium." Pp. 117–36 in *The Thessalonian Corrspondence*. Ed. R. F. Collins. Louvain: Louvain University Press.

────. 1991a. "Rhetorical Criticism and Its Theory in Culture-Critical Perspective: The Narrative Rhetoric of John 11." Pp. 171–85 in *Text and Interpretation: New Approaches to the Criticism of the New Testament*. Ed. P. J. Martin and J. H. Petzer. New Testament Tools and Studies 15. Leiden: E. J. Brill.

────. 1991b. "The Rhetorical Genre of Jesus's Sermon in Luke 12:1–13:9." Pp. 103–31 in *Persuasive Artistry: Studies in New Testament Rhetoric in Honor of George A. Kennedy*. Ed. Duane F. Watson. Sheffield: Sheffield Academic Press.

────. 1991c. "Putting Life Back into the Lazarus Story and Its Reading: The Narrative Rhetoric of John 11 as the Narration of Faith." *Semeia* 53:113–32.

────. 1993. "Biblical Exegesis in the Light of the History and Historicity of Rhetoric and the Nature of the Rhetoric of Religion." Pp. 492–513 in *Rhetoric and the New Testament: Essays from the 1992 Heidelberg Conference*. Ed. Thomas H. Olbricht and Stanley E. Porter. Journal for the Study of the New Testament Supplement Series 90. Sheffield: Sheffield Academic Press.

────. 1994. "Der Vorchristliche Paulus und die Rhetorik." In *Tempelkult und Tempelzerstörung (70 n.Chr.). FS Clemens Thoma*. Ed. Simon Lauer. Judaica et Christiana. Bern: Peter Lang.

Wuthnow, Robert. 1987. *Meaning and Moral Order: Explorations in Cultural Analysis*. Berkeley: University of California Press.

Wyschogrod, Edith. 1989a. "Recontextualizing the Ontological Argument: A Lacanian Analysis." Pp. 97–113 in *Lacan and Theological Discourse*. Ed. Edith Wyschogrod, David Crownfield, and Carl A. Raschke. Albany: SUNY Press.

────. 1989b. "Re-Marks." Pp. ix–xi in *Lacan and Theological Discourse*. Ed. Edith Wyschogrod, David Crownfield, and Carl A. Raschke. Albany: SUNY Press.

Yerushalmi, Yosef Hayim. 1991. *Freud's Moses: Judaism Terminable and Interminable*. New Haven: Yale University Press.

Young, Francis. 1989. "The Rhetorical Schools and Their Influence on Patristic Exegesis." Pp. 182–99 in *The Making of Orthodoxy: Essays in Honour of Henry Chadwick*. Ed. R. Williams. Cambridge: Cambridge University Press.

Young, Iris Marion. 1990. *Justice and the Politics of Difference*. Princeton: Princeton University Press.

Young, James E. 1988. *Writing and Rewriting the Holocaust: Narrative and the Consequences of Interpretation*. Bloomington: Indiana University Press.

Young, Robert, ed. 1981. *Untying the Text: A Post-Structuralist Reader*. London: Routledge.

Zavarzadeh, Mas'ud, and Donald Morton. 1992. *Theory, (Post)Modernity, Opposition: An Other "Introduction" to Literary and Cultural Theory*. Washington, D.C.: Maisonneuve.

Index

Diachronic, 76, 102. *See also* Synchronic
Diel, Paul, 196
Dillon, George L., 160n4
Dinah, 182
Dockhorn, Klaus, 161n5, 181n19
Donaldson, Laura E., 243n15, 257, 260
Donaldson, Mara E., 82
Dostoyevsky, Fyodor, 94
Douglas, Mary, 82
Douglass, Frederick, 242
Dreyfus, Hubert L., 140
Droge, Arthur, 173
Du Bois, William E. B., 242
Duffy, Bernard K., 156
Duke, Paul D., 33
Du Plessis, Johannes G., 165
Dworkin, Ronald, 185

Eagleton, Terry, 5; and ideology, 40, 57, 59, 110, 162, 165, 166, 273–75, 276, 281, 289, 291, 295, 307; and reader-response criticism, 25n3, 26; and rhetoric, 33, 158, 160n4
Ebeling, Gerhard, 47
Ebert, Teresa L., 260, 267
Eco, Umberto, 35n14, 108, 109, 116, 117
Edelson, Marshall, 50n21
Eden, Kathy, 165
Edinger, Edward F., 196
Edwards, Richard A., 39, 40
Ego psychology, 28
Ehrman, Jacques, 77
Eisenstein, Hester, 236n7
Ela, Jean-Marc, 65, 281n4
Elijah, 71–74
Eliot, T. S., 268
Elliott, Gregory, 59
Elliott, Patricia, 211n27
Ellis, John, 307
Ellis, Marc, 292–93
Ephesians, Letter to the, 153
Esau, 134
Eskhult, Mats, 172n12
Eslinger, Lyle, 90, 112

Evans, G. R., 175
Eve, 249, 255
Everman, Welch, 52
Exegesis. *See* Reading
Exodus, Book of, 201–2, 254, 282–93 passim
Exum, Cheryl, 284

Felder, Cain Hope, 65, 271, 281n4
Feldstein, Richard, 211n27
Felman, Shoshana, 199, 223
Feminism, 111; applied to Bible, 226–28, 258; and biblical translation, 257–58, and deconstruction, 121; defined, 234–35, 240; as hermeneutics of recuperation, 245–47; as hermeneutics of survival, 251–54; as hermeneutics of suspicion, 247–51, 281n6; and historical criticism, 235; and ideological criticism, 278, 300–301, 302; and master narratives, 14–15, 269–70; and pedagogy, 268; and postmodernism, 254–67; and poststructuralism, 263–67; and psychoanalysis, 203–5, 208, 211–22, 258, 262; and reader-response criticism, 36–38, 60–62, 67; and rhetorical criticism, 178–82; and structuralism, 105n14; and theology, 230–33, 248–49, 250, 258–59; varieties of, 236–37, 244–67; and womanism, 226, 230, 234–44. *See also* Gender; Womanism
Fenner, M. William, 161n5
Ferguson, Kathy E., 250, 253
Ferguson, Russell, 229
Fetterley, Judith, 27, 36–38, 61, 66, 68
Feuerbach, Ludwig, 189
Fewell, Danna Nolan, 129n7, 130n9, 278n3, 305
Fierro, Alfredo, 283
Fisch, Harold, 170, 172n12
Fischel, Henry A., 173
Fish, Stanley E., 68, 185; on interpretive communities, 55–59 passim, 66; and